A HISTORY OF AMERICAN POLITICAL THOUGHT

A. J. Beitzinger
University of Notre Dame

DODD, MEAD & COMPANY

New York   1972   Toronto

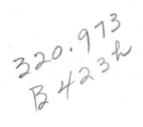

320.973
B423h

To my sons, Michael and Carl

Editor's Introduction

The history of American political thought reflects, in its sweep through about three and a half centuries of experience, almost every major theme known to the modern world. The earliest colonies in the new world were largely based upon religious principles, but they were, at the same time, parts of the world's greatest empire. Nurtured by distance, local self-determination—couched in liberal terms—eventually triumphed over royalist and imperial thinking. But since men and women came to the new world in search of a new life, and since a largely empty continent invited experiment on a tremendous scale, Americans pursued their objectives along many different ideological paths.

Professor Beitizinger seeks, in this book, to explore these different roads to political salvation. Recognizing the powerful influence of religion, particularly in the earlier years of American history, the author seeks to give religious thought the attention it must have if we are to understand the essential elements of the country's political thought. But this is not at the expense of those strands of political thought which jostled each other for breathing space since independence was achieved. Thus Professor Beitizinger does justice to Federalists and Anti-Federalists, Jeffersonians and Jacksonians, the pro-slavery and anti-slavery elements of the antebellum period, and to the great variety of political conceptions which flourished in the country after the Civil War. A review of contemporary thought brings this complex story down to our own times.

The author is not a partisan of any special point of view. He seeks, in a wholly objective way, to describe the main elements of all significant bodies of political thought which have appeared in the course of American history. His is also a scholarly treatment, though he has not permitted the book to be over-borne by needless impediments of formal scholarship. The objective has been to present an interesting, reliable, and well-written analysis of American political thought.

While this book was designed for use in college and university courses, it is by no means limited to such use. The general, nonacademic reader will find here a rich storehouse of information which will help him to understand the American political heritage.

DAVID FELLMAN

Spectemur Agendo.
Judge us by our deeds.
 —Motto of JOHN ADAMS taken from Ovid

Preface

This book was written in the conviction that American political thought is best studied and understood in terms of its historical development. It attempts a descriptive analysis and critical discussion of the origins, growth, and interrelationships of American political ideas—against the background of the foundations, birth, development, and crises of the republic—and of the major historical movements of thought. Main emphasis is on the idea of constitutionalism and the related conceptions of higher law, liberty, equality, democracy, and the balanced state, as well as underlying notions of human nature, motivation, and behavior.

Because American political thought has been, in good part, unsystematic and responsive to particular events and problems, this book is concerned with all serious and important reflections and observations regarding political man and government. Consequently it uses as basic sources state papers, public records and documents, published works, treatises, commentaries, essays, debates, polemical writings, private papers, and manuscripts, as well as the growing number of important interpretive studies. Similarly, because American political thought has been to a good degree derivative, European origins and continuing European influences are considered.

Generally speaking, the method used has been to present first the thought of the principal figures and historical periods and to follow this with critical analysis, comparison, and evaluation. In this connection it should be said that the writer's personal view is that there is an objective order of truth and morality which is discernible by man and, as such, both limits and guides him. In reference to the practice of politics the writer acknowledges that except for first principles, the cultivation of prudential judgment is paramount, a virtue which cannot be acquired apart from experience. Likewise, he believes, that in the study of politics, method and technique must conform to the subject matter in its manifold diversity and complexity.

The writer wishes to express deep gratitude to the following gentlemen for reading part or all of the manuscript and extending suggestions and comments: the late John T. Farrell, Marshall Smelser, Walter Nicgorski, Raymond Cour, C. S. C., Gerald Goodwin, Walter F. Murphy, Lane Davis, and, above all, David Fellman. For help in checking quotations and documentation, he thanks Robert McDonough, the late Joseph Sullivan, Regis Factor, Michael Melody, George Block, Patrick Geary,

Wilfred Dues, and, most particularly, Richard Linquanti. Finally, he is especially indebted to the ladies of the Steno Pool at the University of Notre Dame for their efficient and patient typing of the manuscript.

A. J. BEITZINGER

Contents

PART ONE

PHILOSOPHICAL AND JURISPRUDENTIAL BACKGROUND

Chapter 1

PHILOSOPHICAL AND LEGAL ROOTS OF AMERICAN POLITICAL THOUGHT

. . . The treasures of knowledge, acquired by the labours of Philosophers, Sages, and Legislators, through a long succession of years, are laid open for our use, and their collected wisdom may be happily applied in the Establishment of our forms of Government.

GEORGE WASHINGTON

Constitutionalism (limited government under fundamental law) has its religious roots in the idea of divine law, its philosophical roots in the idea of natural law, its specifically Anglo-Saxon legal roots in the common law tradition, and its institutional roots in the idea of the balanced state. In the eighteenth century the contemporary formulations of these ideas merged in America to provide the seedbed from which could spring, when nurtured by experience and practice, not only the moral justification of, and active participation in, revolution, but American constitutionalism. American constitutionalism stresses individual rights, consent of the governed, the rule of law equally applied, institutional forms, separation of powers, checks and balances upon passions and interests, and the conception of a written constitution as "higher law" to be interpreted ultimately not by natural or common reason but by those versed in "the artificial reason of the law." Because the root ideas greatly influenced the principal American colonial, revolutionary, and Founding Fathers and because they have played an abiding role in American political thought, it is necessary to examine the main historical traditions of natural law as well as the balanced state and the common law in relation to the "higher law."

3

Classic Natural Law

The concept of "natural right," which in its original sense is synonymous with "natural justice," the dictates of which are termed "natural
law," has had two main historical formulations, the classic and the
modern. Classic natural right was expounded by such thinkers as Plato,
Aristotle, Cicero, and Aquinas. It sprang from an attempt to overcome
both the relativism of the view that justice is purely customary and the
hedonistic identification of pleasure as the highest good for man. It
distinguished between nature as that which is originally given and
nature considered teleologically in terms of full realization of potentialities. Assuming the ability of the intellect to attain a knowledge of man's
essential developed nature, it stressed the need of man to fulfill his
natural inclinations in disciplined accord with the rule of right reason.
Because it was believed that men cannot fully develop outside politically
organized society, the state was considered prior in nature to individual
man. It followed as a dictate of natural right that the state exists not
merely to protect life, secure rights, or promote liberty, but primarily to
aid the development of virtuous men. Because men are unequal in the
possession of reason and in the degree of virtue and wisdom achieved,
democracy was deemed fundamentally unjust. Distinguishing between
absolute and relative justice, the classical thinkers saw as the dictate
of the former that the state should be ruled by the wise and virtuous.
They recognized, however, that because the conditions allowing for such
government were only quite remotely realizable and because the people-
at-large in their peculiar stage of development must be taken into account, the element of consent must be reckoned with. Thus they concluded that the best practicable polity was a balanced state combining
various principles under the rule of law.[1]*

Also important to an understanding of the classical view is the distinction drawn by Aristotle between theoretical science, practical science
and art. The theoretical intellect is directed to a knowledge of in-
variables and reveals to man knowledge of ends which are fixed in his
nature. While conceding a hierarchy of goods, Aristotle defined man's
ultimate end, happiness, as rational activity of the soul in accordance
with virtue in a complete life. The fixed ends and the natural institutions which men form serve as first principles, norms and limits for the
practical sciences—politics, economics, and ethics—which are concerned
with variables and directed to action. Of these, politics, since it is directed toward the broadest common good, is the master science. Consequently, political prudence ultimately is concerned with right reason in
acting for the common good in an order in which the whole presupposes
the continuing existence and realization of its component entities. Thus

* Footnotes appear at the end of each chapter.

classical thinkers concluded that to equate politics with art, defined as
the free and unlimited imposition of forms upon malleable materials, and
render it autonomous in a Machiavellian sense by divorcing it from
prudence, was immoral and unjust.[2]

The Stoic conception of natural law, which heavily influenced Roman
law and the Church Fathers, was best defined by Cicero.

> There is in fact a true law—namely right reason—which is in accordance
> with nature, applies to all men, and is unchangeable and eternal. By its com-
> mands this law summons men to the performance of their duties; by its
> prohibitions it restrains them from doing wrong. . . . To invalidate this law
> by human legislation is never morally right, nor is it permissible ever to restrict
> its operation, and to annul it wholly is impossible.[3]

Stoic pantheism, which identified God, nature, and reason, indicated a
moral order and pattern of justice in the cosmos to which man must
conform in order to fulfill his nature. Believing that, in principle, reason
is possessed by all men, the Stoic concluded that all must be considered
equal. Even though he postulated human equality not as a fact but as
a moral imperative, this was a distinct departure from previous natural
law thought.

The pagan stress upon the sufficiency of natural virtue and creative
politics in the realization of the good life was replaced in the thought of
the Christian Fathers by an insistence upon the necessity of divine grace
and the cultivation of the theological virtues of faith, hope, and charity.
In the Middle Ages Thomas Aquinas synthesized Aristotelian philosophy
and Christian theology on the principle that faith is the fulfillment of
reason and grace is the perfection of nature. He regarded natural law
as part of eternal law, which emanates from the Prime Intellect and
informs all creation. Divine law, or revelation, was seen as supplementary to natural law. Positive or human law was defined as the implementation of natural law or the treatment of matters indifferent thereto.
Nature was defined as reason written into things by the divine will,
which in animals is observable in the instincts. In man, a moral and
rational free agent, the basic principles of nature's dictates are intuitively grasped; conclusions therefrom form secondary principles
which, owing to the contingent nature of life, give rise to varied applications in practice. In Aquinas' view, which was expounded in England
by Richard Hooker, the architectonic structure of cosmic law is ultimately dependent upon a Prime Intellect and directed toward an
eternal common good. If that basic consideration is eliminated from
natural law thought, as was the case subsequently, nature becomes
autonomous, and a tendency emerges to render human reason the measure of all things.[4]

In sum, classic natural right and its dictate, natural law, assumed a hierarchical cosmic order issuing from and ruled by a divine rational principle; interpreted man and nature teleologically; preached an objective order of goods, ends, and norms; stressed the ability of man to reach a knowledge of his end; and concluded the primacy of obligation in the pursuit thereof. In this light the political order, an essential dictate of man's nature and the highest common good, is subject to the strictures and direction of the higher truth. Prudence, however, indicates that the varieties of human development and capacities demand a corresponding variety of forms of government calculated in each case to aid in the self-realization of the citizenry.

Modern Natural Law

Thomas Hobbes (1588–1679)

Hobbes stands as the most articulate and consistent exponent of modern natural right.[5] Proceeding from a mechanical metaphysic of matter-in-motion, a sensationist psychology,* and a nominalist epistemology,† he concluded that man, in a prepolitical state of nature, is radically egotistical and antisocial. In this condition man is prodded on by the ubiquitous passion of pride. Unlike the Christian Fathers, who taught the equality of men in terms of an immortal soul, Hobbes maintained that men are equal by nature, principally because of their equal ability to kill or harm each other and to acquire experience. The war of each against all which marks the state of nature produces a situation in which life is "solitary, poor, nasty, brutish and short."[6] Hobbes believed that in positing a warlike state of nature he was correcting what he regarded to be the fundamental error of classical political thought: the assumption that man is by nature a social and political animal.[7] The difficulty encountered by the political thinker who postulates a prepolitical state of nature, even if only as a logical construct, is to explain how and why men remove themselves into civil society. Because the Hobbesian natural man is no more than a predatory, conscienceless animal moved primarily by the powerful passion of pride, he can be brought to sober reflection only by the pull of an even more awesome passion. Hobbes found this in the fear of a violent death which, in the form of its counterpart, the desire for self-preservation, becomes the basis of his political thought. Overwhelming fear incites reason, which to Hobbes is mere reckoning or calculation, to produce rules of peace, or laws of nature, by which security can be obtained. Reason is thus placed in a position ancillary to the basic passion; there is no natural right

---

* Sensationism in psychology is the doctrine that ideas derive from and are reducible to sensations.

† Nominalism is the doctrine that universal concepts are mere words having no mental or extramental reality.

in the sense of natural justice; self-preservation (provision for one's existence) is *the* natural right underlying the rules of peace. Such rules have no justification except in the state. Hobbes taught that civil society, the instrument of security, comes into being by a mutual contract wherein each person submits to a common sovereign whose authority is limited only by the effectiveness of the power he can command at any given moment. Thus the sovereign state (the "mortal God") is made by human artifice, through the juridical instrument of contract. Because the laws of nature are deduced from the right of self-preservation, the desire to be replaces the Classic-Christian desire to be good as the formative principle. What the ancients regarded as merely one aspect of the common good—mutual security—was for Hobbes the whole of it. The restrictions in classical thought upon the lust for power were removed, except for those embodied in Hobbes' prescriptions for peace. Commodious living replaces excellence in virtue; the classical task of rulers—to make citizens good—is replaced by the need for them "to study, as much as by laws can be affected, to furnish the citizens abundantly with all good things . . . which are conducive to delectation."[8] Similarly, the sovereign, whether one, few, or many, possesses power because of the contract, not because of wisdom or virtue, and will replaces reason as the source and justification of law. Emphasis on duty is replaced by stress upon the absolute right of self preservation; the right to revolt is a right to act not against tyranny in the moral sense, but against weakness in the governance of the state. Revolutions are justified only if they are successful, and it is bootless to make distinctions between "good" and "bad" forms of government, simply because effectiveness, not morality, is the only feasible norm. Finally, the concept of common good is a fiction; there exist naught but particulars, and the state is a mere collection of individuals united in the person of the sovereign for the realization of safety, security, and material plenty.

John Locke (1632–1704)

Locke stands as the most important English philosopher influencing American political thought. Jefferson, Madison, and Samuel and John Adams were only a few of the Founding Fathers who drew upon his works. The Declaration of Independence, the revolutionary state constitutions, and the federal Constitution of 1787 embodied Lockian ideas. Similarly, the long tradition in American constitutional law stressing the primacy of vested property rights owes much to Locke. Thus there is ample reason why he should be called "America's philosopher" and studied closely.[9]

Although Locke admitted it possible that God endowed material substances with the power of thinking, unlike Hobbes he concluded that it is most probably true that man is a mental substance, as opposed to the physical objects in nature, including his body, which he called material substances.[10] Thus he turned away not only from materialism but from the medieval conception of man as a substantial union of body and soul predisposed to an end. Similarly, he rejected the organic, teleological conception of nature by treating nature as the sum total of material substances obeying the mechanical laws of physics.

Locke's notion of man had important implications for his religious and political thought. As mental substances devoid of innate ideas, men must be considered equal. Because the mental substance is simple and immaterial, it is equivalent to man's immortal soul. Religion must be regarded as a strictly private, introspective concern; its public manifestations in the formation of churches must be voluntary; and the principle of toleration of dissent must be recognized. Finally, because free and equal mental substances, as distinguished from material substances, have no necessary relation to each other in nature, political society cannot be considered a dictate of nature; instead, it is effected by artifice and rendered legitimate only if based, in its origin and continuing existence, upon individual consent.[11]

In his first *Letter Concerning Toleration* (1689), Locke maintained that the care of souls is outside the jurisdiction of the civil magistrate because: God has given no authority to any man to compel others to his religion; his power consists only in outward force; and even though the law may be vigorous enough to compel compliance, this could not further the salvation of souls. He concluded, however, that toleration is inapplicable to "opinions contrary to human society, or to those moral rules which are necessary to the preservation of civil society," as well as to atheists, who cannot be trusted in an oath, and to any church which is so constituted "that all those who enter into it, do thereby *ipso facto* deliver themselves up to the protection and service of another prince."[12]

In his *Essay Concerning Human Understanding* (1690), Locke argued that all human knowledge is derived from sensory experience and that innate ideas do not exist. Unlike Hobbes, he did not deny the mental reality of universal concepts, but because he regarded them as "the inventions and creatures of the understanding, made by it for its own use," and as concerning "only signs, whether words or ideas," knowledge of real (as opposed to nominal) essences, or of intelligible forms was precluded.[13] As a consequence, such concepts in Locke's political thought as civil society, public good, and natural rights exist merely as shorthand terms for discrete individuals and their particular and mutual interests. Similarly, because essential human nature could not be used as an explanation of man's existence in civil society, it was replaced by the device of contract, and the state was reduced to a legal arrangement between individuals for particular, limited purposes. Then, too, the link posited by Aristotle and Aquinas, for example, between the order of being and the moral order was removed.

Whereas Hobbes emphasized the political factor in life, Locke, in his *Two Treatises of Civil Government* (1689–1690), exalted the social at the expense of the political. Government entered into his consideration "as a kind of afterthought."[14] Postulating a prepolitical state of nature, he described it as a condition wherein men are free and equal and under the obligation to submit to the dictates of the law of nature. Thus it is a condition without political organization, but with a binding law. Locke denied the Hobbesian contention that the state of nature is necessarily a state of war, although he admitted it might so become.[15] In this prepolitical state each man has a right to that with which he mixes his labor. Thus there is a natural right to property, a term which Locke used in a generic sense to include life, liberty, and estate. The inconveniences of the state of nature—the lack of a settled, known law and a common superior to enforce it—led men to the formation by mutual consent of civil society and the establishment of political power, which Locke defined as "a right of making laws, with penalties of death, and consequently all less penalties for the regulating and preserving of property, and of employing the force of the community in the execution of such laws, and in the defence of the commonwealth from foreign injury, and all this only for the public good."[16] The centrality of coercion in the definition is quite evident. In fact, the equation of government with coercion leaves no doubt that to Locke and his followers, government is at best a necessary evil.

The contract whereby individuals freely agree to join in civil society involves the relinquishment of the right to enforce the law of nature. Individual natural rights to life, liberty, and property, however, can never be granted away, although they may be somewhat modified in their use. Thus government, which is set up on a fiduciary basis as the active organ of civil society, is limited to the protection and implementation of individual rights, a task which is descriptive of the Lockian conception of common good. As a consequence, the state is not conceived as a unity of order in which individuals are directed to an objective common good, as in the Aristotelian tradition, nor as a unity of simple composition in a mortal god, the absolute sovereign, as in the Hobbesian formulation, but as a facilitating instrument by which each individual can pursue his private good with minimal interference.

Once men are joined in civil society, Locke argued, "it is necessary [that] the body should move that way whither the greater force carries it, which is the consent of the majority." After having asserted that the majoritarian principle is a dictate of the law of nature and right reason, he retreated to the more plausible utilitarian argument that the only alternative is the unworkable principle of unanimity. It is to be noted that to Locke the majority is the vehicle by means of which society moves; because it antedates government, it is distinct therefrom. A majority of men in civil society decide the form of government.[17]

Locke laid down the following conditions which are imposed on government as dictates of the law of God and the law of nature: Government must proceed by established known laws and regularized procedures, equally applied to all; the laws must have no other end than the good of the people; taxes must not be levied on the property of the people without their personal or represented consent; and legislative power must not be redelegated by the entity to which the majority has delegated it. Finally, Locke asserted that "where the body of the people, or any single man, are deprived of their right, or are under the exercise of a power without right, having no appeal on earth they have a liberty to appeal to Heaven whenever they judge the cause of sufficient moment." Cognizant of his responsibility to give a moral justification of the right of revolution, Locke denied that an admission of its existence lays "a perpetual foundation for disorder," because revolution does not obtain until "the inconvenience is so great that the majority feel it, and are weary of it, and find necessity to have it amended." This identification of revolution with the movement of the majority can be interpreted as meaning either that active resistance is not moral until a majority agrees openly or tacitly to pursue it, in which case the so-called natural rights of man are subservient to the will of the majority, or that Locke believed that the majority would always be quick to react whenever fundamental rights are habitually violated. He was careful to add that "such revolutions happen not upon every little mismanagement in public affairs." Thus "a long train of abuses, prevarications and artifices," which make the unjust design of the government visible to the people, is the precondition for exercise of the "appeal to Heaven." Locke saw in the recognition of the right of the people to provide for their safety by turning out rulers who violate their trust, "the best fence against rebellion." The true rebels, he contended, are those who violate their trust and abuse their authority.[18]

Professor Leo Strauss has recently argued that Locke is Hobbes in sheep's clothing. He contends that Locke conceived of natural law not in terms of man's perfection, but in the more mundane, utilitarian terms of those conclusions which follow in implementation of the basic desire for self-preservation. The contract, political power, majority rule, the rights to life, liberty, and property, and the appeal to heaven, all of these are in implementation of the basic desire. Thus Locke differs from Hobbes not in the end sought, security, but in the way to get there. Whereas Hobbes thought it essential that absolute power be vested in the sovereign, Locke saw limited government as necessary.[19]

Strauss' interpretation appears essentially correct in view of Locke's repeated emphasis upon the preservation and protection of property as the end of government. Because property, as Aristotle acknowledged, is a necessary instrument of life, the establishment of its protection as the sole task of government, even when it is construed in the broad sense of life, liberty, and estate, is justifiable only if one considers the right to self-preservation the basic and controlling factor. Locke considered the acquisitive spirit to be the cause of labor, which in turn is the cause of wealth. Civil society, which can subsist only in plenty, is held together by the protection of private pursuits. The common good is realized by the individual pursuit of private good. Thus Locke stands as a philosophical father of *laissez-faire* classical liberalism.[20]

David Hume (1711–1776)

The works of David Hume, the great modern critic of natural law, have had a significant and much-overlooked influence in the development of early American political thought. They were read and quoted by John Adams, Hamilton, and Madison. Madison drew heavily upon important insights in Hume's essays in writing his famous tenth Federalist paper. Then, too, Hume was the foremost figure in the eighteenth-century Scottish school of moral science, which included men such as Francis Hutcheson, Adam Smith, and Adam Ferguson; his writings, along with theirs, were standard textbooks in the colleges of William and Mary, Princeton, King's (Columbia), Harvard, Pennsylvania, and Yale in the late colonial period.[21]

In his *Treatise of Human Nature* (1736), Hume essayed a new science of man, hoping to do for the moral sciences what Newton had done for the physical sciences. Using what he called the experimental approach, which was merely a logical extension of Locke's empiricism, he maintained that all we can know are perceptions, which are divided into two categories—impressions of sensation and of reflection—and ideas, which, to be valid, are reducible to impressions. Our understanding is limited by our imagination: we can conceive only what we can imagine and we can imagine only what we can experience. Parts of any complex experience can be imagined as having separate existences, and we can never perceive any real connection between distinct perceptions. Thus man can never know more than sense impressions and the ideas built upon them. Because on this basis the Lockian conception of man as a mental substance becomes indefensible, Hume had to provide a substitute. Since he precluded any cognitive basis for the concept of the self or mind, he could only conclude that the self is "nothing but a bundle or collection of different perceptions." He also undermined the rational basis of causality by denying any necessary connection between cause and effect. On his premises all that one can perceive is a succession of discrete sensations. We infer cause from effect, or vice versa, on the basis of the psychological principle of association of ideas, which because we habitually see event Y follow event X, brings us by custom to infer a necessary connection between them. Because the contrary of any matter of fact does not imply a contradiction, our factual knowledge is at best probable, in contrast to the pure comparison of ideas involved in mathematical reasoning or in logical analysis, wherein the conclusions are certain because their predicates are contained in their subjects. Thus did Hume eliminate reason and necessity from nature. He saved the appearances of commonsense convictions such as the existence of an extramental world, the self, and causality, by ascribing these to the non-cognitive but irresistible faculty of "belief."[22]

With nature reduced to apparent regularity in its material and efficient principles, and with man reduced to a bundle of sense impressions predisposed to no end, it was but logical that Hume should reduce ethics to feeling. Because Hume believed that ethical choices involve neither comparison of ideas nor causal inferences, he concluded that "Reason is, and ought only to be, the slave of the passions."[23] In posing a sharp disjunction between the *is* and the *ought* and delimiting valid knowledge to the nonnormative discovery of logical relations and matters of fact, Hume laid the grounds for modern logical positivism and the empirical, behavioral attitude of many modern American social scientists.

Hume's nominalism precluded natural law in any but a purely descriptive sense; on his premises there can be no objective, transcendent standard to which man must conform if he is to realize his nature. With moral choice relegated to the noncognitive level of feeling, Hume argued that the index of the moral quality of an action, quality, or character is the sentiment of approval or disapproval felt by the impartial spectator. Thus morality becomes, like aesthetics, a matter of taste. In determining the composition of the impartial spectator, the individual moral agent must be excluded because another person conceivably could disagree with his preference. Because Hume assumed a uniformity of human nature, a good case can be made for holding that, practically speaking, the approval or disapproval of most people was to him the crucial factor. As A. H. Basson, in speaking of Hume's view, puts it: "It is the democratic view of morals; what most people feel to be right is right."[24] But a good case can also be made for the thesis that Hume really intended that the cultivated (and, by implication, the propertied) be the ultimate judges, particularly on the more complex and less basic questions. Hume argued that although reason is not constitutive of ends or norms, it can aid the passions not only in their satisfactory implementation, but in laying bare the probable consequences of alternative courses of action. Hume called passions so aided by reason and directed toward the remote and not the immediate view, the "calm" passions. Those directed toward immediate gratification he called the "violent" passions. Because he believed that cultivated men are more apt to act in accordance with the "calm" than with the "violent" passions, an aristocratic theory of morals and politics can be inferred from his thought. In any case, the emphasis upon the impartial observer tended to subvert the individual conscience by projecting onto society, or a leading segment thereof, the role of normgiver. After this note was taken and developed by his student, Adam Smith, in his *Theory of the Moral Sentiments,* the stage was set for the later appearance of the "socialized conscience," and the "other-directed man" of contemporary life.[25]

Hume used the term law of nature in his political thought, but in the limited empirical sense of regularity of human behavior, or what is common to the species. He believed that because the elemental needs of men are everywhere the same, experience leads them to common conclusions concerning basic social norms. The key to his analysis is his emphasis on the primacy and ubiquity of self-interest. He contended that "whether the passion of self-interest be esteemed vicious or virtuous, 'tis all a case; since itself alone restrains it: so that if it be virtuous, men become social by their virtue; if vicious, their vice has the same effect."[26] What Hume had in mind is that men gradually learn the benefits of society from experience in the family, but that society is difficult to effect because the selfishness and confined generosity of men, combined with the natural scarcity of materials, leads to an "avidity . . . of acquiring goods and possessions," which is "insatiable, perpetual, universal." Because this avidity is rooted in the passion of self-interest, it cannot be overcome by reason; instead self-interest must redirect itself from the "violent" to the "calm" view, as men gradually perceive the defeat of their interests in a perilous situation devoid of rules of justice. Thus the original motive to justice is self-interest and the source of its moral approbation, which develops after its establishment, is a sentiment of sympathy with public interest. Society is instituted by convention upon the establishment of three laws of nature, or rules of justice—stability of possession, transference of possessions by consent, and the performance of promises. These define the content of justice and establish private property. After these conventions are set up, "there remains little or nothing to be done toward settling a perfect harmony and concord. All the other passions, beside this of interest, are either easily restrained or are not of such pernicious consequence, when indulged."[27]

It would seem that on this view, a natural harmony of interests is effected upon the establishment of a simple, unaffected society and the rules of justice. Hume went so far as to maintain that society, if small and uncultivated, can long exist without government. What makes government necessary is "an increase of riches and possessions," which brings men again to take the short or "violent" view of interest and results in insecurity and disorder. It is plain that Hume deemed it the purpose of government to ensure that the three rules of justice be enforced so that men might peacefully pursue their own interests. Thus was common good identified with the sum of particular goods within the framework of the impartial enforcement of rules derived from experience and designed for the acquisition, preservation, and protection of property: property, in a sense far more restricted than Locke's life, liberty, and estate.

Concerning the origin of government, Hume maintained that self-interest again corrects itself gradually until men realize the necessity for political rule. He believed that, historically, government probably arose out of war. It is not sustained, as Hobbes, Locke, and the Whigs asserted, on a promissory, contractual basis; instead it is rooted in custom and habit. The basic motive for its establishment is the natural sentiment of self-interest; the sense of individual obligation to obedience and moral approval develops after its establishment and consists in a feeling of sympathy with public interest and a regard for right.[28]

Hume's psychological approach, which brought him to dismiss as unhistorical and metaphysical such concepts as state of nature, contract, and law of nature in its transcendental sense, also served to explain the administration of justice within the state. Rulers and magistrates are analogous in political society to individual and group opinion in prepolitical society in the enforcement of the terms of justice. This is effected by making it their immediate interest to act impartially. Being indifferent to the greatest part of society, they "will decide . . . more equitably than every one would in his own case," and men will "acquire a security against each other's weakness and passion, as well as against their own."[29] But to bring this about, Hume, who believed that forms of government are more important than men in realizing public interest, maintained that government must be constructed on the Machiavellian principle that "every man must be supposed a knave," even though that is not the fact.[30] Thus he extolled a principle of balanced government, in which interest is made to check interest. Similarly, in treating of factions, or political parties, Hume defined two principal types, those arising from interest and those arising from principle. The former he considered to be "the most reasonable and excusable." The latter, which are based on "abstract speculative principle," he deemed dangerous, the source of irreconcilable divisions and of enthusiasm and fanaticism. Finally, Hume propounded against prevailing dogma the conception that a republican form of government built upon strong local government and a system of indirect elections can obtain in a large territory with more facility and freedom from tumult and faction that it can in a small territory. In words Madison would later fasten on, Hume maintained that "in a large government which is modelled with masterly skill, there is compass and room enough to refine the democracy, from the lower people . . . to the higher magistrates. . . . At the same time, the parts are so distant and remote that it is very difficult, either by intrigue, prejudice, or passion, to hurry them [the people] into any measures against the public interest."[31]

In sum, it can be said that in his rigorous analysis of man as a creature motivated principally by self-interest and ruled by habit, Hume arrived at the same basic conclusions concerning government as had Locke. It is true that he consigned the Lockian fictions of contract, state of nature, and law of nature to the metaphysical rubbish heap. But in doing this he was merely drawing out the logical implications not only of Locke's empiricism, but of Locke's conception of man as interested essentially in self-preservation. Property antedates the state in the thought of both men, as does justice, and the state serves the limited task of implementing what Locke called basic rights, but what Hume conceived of in terms of fundamental interest. Resistance to tyrannical rule was insisted upon by both men, with Locke again talking of it in terms of right, and Hume, more cautiously, in terms of interest. Both men exalted the free workings of man in society and reduced politics to an ancillary role.

Hume went beyond Locke by emphasizing fully the primacy of the passions and focusing on groups (factions, parties) as primary political forces. The idea of passion redirecting or checking itself in the realization of public good, the preachment that every man must be supposed a knave, the emphasis on balancing institutional forms above the character of the citizenry, all these along with the observation that in a republic of republics, in a large territory, passion might, on balance, redirect itself from the "violent" to the "calm" state, were destined to play important roles in American political thought.

The Theory of the Balanced State and English Classical Republicanism

The ancient conception of the balanced state historically has taken many forms. It has meant, variously, a sharing in power by different social classes; a balancing of estates; a balancing of qualities such as strength, wisdom, and goodness; institutional representation of the principles of the one, the few, and the many; and a rigid separation of the three basic functions of legislation, administration, and adjudication. It has been most commonly applied to republican forms of government, but it does not necessarily preclude an hereditary monarch, as the term mixed monarchy indicates. Similarly, it is amenable to a vertical division of power exemplified in the presence within the state of strong, autonomous local government.[32]

The notion originally proceeded from the Platonic-Aristotelian doctrine that the three "pure" forms, monarchy, aristocracy, and moderate democracy, tend to degenerate into the "corrupt" forms of tyranny, oligarchy, and ochlocracy (mob rule). To arrest the tendency and attain relative stability, Plato proposed in *The Laws* that the monarchical principle of wisdom be combined in the state with the democratic principle of freedom. Aristotle recommended as the best practicable state one which blends oligarchy and democracy on the basis of a strong middle class. The Greek historian Polybius attributed the success of the Roman Republic to the fact that its institutions represented monarchical, aristocratic, and democratic principles "accurately adjusted and in exact equilibrium."

In the Middle Ages, Aquinas propounded a theory of "mixed monarchy," wherein the rule of the monarch was qualified by subjecting him to the elective process, and by the establishment beneath him of an aristocratic body having governing powers. This conception was best illustrated in the English monarchy of the late medieval period. Sir John Fortescue, Chief Justice of the King's Bench under Henry IV (1422–1461), wrote of a *dominium regale* (royal rule) and a *dominium politicum et regale* (royal and political rule), using Aquinas as an authority to support the distinction. He defined *dominium regale* as a government in which the king "may rule his people by suche lawes as he makyth hymself," and a *dominium politicum et regale* as a regime wherein the king "may not rule his peple bi other laws than such as thai assenten unto." In the latter form, which Fortescue considered as legitimate, the king rules according to laws of the constitution which the corporate people have instituted. Like Plato and Aristotle, however, Aquinas and Fortescue did not believe that institutional forms solved the question of government. They never departed from an original stress upon the necessity for virtuous men as the foundation of sound political rule.[33]

Admiration for the thought and institutions of antiquity in the Renaissance period brought men like Machiavelli to extol the balanced states of the past. Machiavelli's writings, along with the examples of Sparta and Rome, but most particularly, sixteenth-century Venice, were relied upon heavily by the greatest of the English "classical republicans" of the seventeenth century, James Harrington (1611–1677). As expounded in his *Oceana* (1656), Harrington's thought bespeaks a strong reliance upon institutional forms and a distrust of men. Thus he proclaimed: "Give us good men and they will give us good Lawes, is the Maxime of a Demogogue. . . . But give us good orders, and they will

make us good men, is the Maxime of a Legislator, and the most infallible in the Politickes." To the proponents of aristocratic rule by the
few wise men, he pronounced: "The wisdom of the Few may be the light
of mankind . . . the interest of the Few is not the profit of Mankind
nor of a Commonwealth." As against "modern prudence," which he identified with the feudal "Gothick balance" of king and nobles, Harrington
posed the superiority of "ancient prudence," which indicated a republican mixed government. Accordingly, he proposed for Oceana an
aristocratic senate to act as the deliberative body and a larger popularly
elected body to accept or reject the proposals of the senate. Magistrates
elected by and answerable to the people were to serve in an executive
capacity. He justified separation of the advisory and decisional functions
on the basis of his acceptance of the Machiavellian maxim that every
man must be supposed a knave. He illustrated his point by giving an
example of two girls and an undivided cake. If the girl who cuts the
cake may also choose the part she wishes, an unequal division will result;
if, however, one girl cuts and the other chooses, justice will result in
an equal division. The moral was: establish governmental forms to make
it the interest of men to act in pursuit of the public good. Thus Harrington believed that the perfection of government lies in the establishment
of a balance which will preclude men from having either an interest or
a power to subvert it.[34]

Separation of powers, rotation in office, the rule of law, and the secret
ballot constitute, along with the "law agrarian," the principles of
Harrington's "equal commonwealth." The agrarian law, which was designed to maintain a fairly broad distribution of property, was a dictate
of his belief that the form of government follows the mode of land
distribution. Because property is power, a commonwealth (republic)
must ensure perpetuation of the distribution of land which originally
made it possible. Even though Harrington failed to grasp the importance
of other than landed forms of property, his realistic emphasis on the
influence of the economic factor upon government has had perhaps an
even more abiding influence upon the American mind than his republicanism, as evidenced in the thought of Madison, Hamilton, Calhoun, Webster, and Charles A. Beard.[35]

John Milton (1608–1674) stands as the second most important of the
English classical republicans. Widely read in colonial America, Milton's
political works were praised by Jonathan Mayhew as embodying "the
principles which, God be thanked, generally prevail in New England."
Subscribing to republicanism as a moral ideal justified in terms of natural
justice, Milton embraced a conception of natural law related more
closely to the earlier Classic-Christian notion than to the secularized
modern version. Ever the aristocrat, Milton believed that the justification
of authority lies in moral and intellectual superiority. Although he

originally championed mixed monarchy, as the Puritan Revolution moved on, his basic republicanism became manifest. Emphasizing rule by the "best men," he was convinced that freedom could best be guaranteed and the common good subserved in an elective aristocratic balanced republic.[36]

Milton stressed the need for an educated, virtuous electorate, and the ultimate dependence of good government upon men of sound character. To be truly virtuous and Christian, men must be recognized as moral free agents. This entailed recognition by the civil authority of the fact that religion is not its concern, and that freedom of expression, as eloquently defended against censorship in his *Areopagitica,* must be guaranteed. Milton, however, firmly believed that the Bible and reason indicate the path of virtue. Because of this, he stopped short of defining virtue in terms of subjective preference. Unlike Machiavelli, Hobbes, Harrington, and later Hume, Milton placed passion and interest in a position secondary to reason. Similarly, he regarded liberty not as an end in itself, as Locke and Montesquieu were to do, but as the necessary condition for the realization of virtue.[37]

The idea of a mechanical equilibrium of executive, legislative, and judicial powers institutionalized in separate branches was elaborated by the French theorist, Montesquieu (1689–1755) in his work *The Spirit of the Laws,* which was first published in 1748. Of all the early modern continental writers, Montesquieu exerted the most influence upon American political thought. His book was studied closely by the principal Founding Fathers. Madison was able to quote parts of it from memory and, in 1788, wrote that if Montesquieu was not the author of the separation of powers doctrine, "he has the merit of at least displaying and recommending it most effectively to the attention of mankind." Although Jefferson was later critical of the *Spirit of the Laws,* he copied passages from it to fill twenty pages in his *Commonplace Book.* Montesquieu's ideas were popularized and widely disseminated, particularly in the constitution-making period after the Declaration of Independence. It is probably true that the knowledge which many colonists possessed of the English Constitution came from Montesquieu's interpretation of it.[38]

Montesquieu attempted to show that the structure and operation of governments and systems of law were relative to the factors of geography, climate, the state of development of the arts, commerce and industry, moral and psychological temperaments, popular customs and habits, and the particular form of political constitution. Within the framework of this sociological relativism, he discussed four main types of government and their principles—democracy and virtue, aristocracy and moderation, monarchy and honor, and despotism and fear. But to find a government which had liberty as its motive force and end,

Montesquieu looked to England. As he saw it, liberty was effected in England because of a separation of governmental powers, which he erroneously attributed to the English Constitution, and to the sense of safety and security possessed by each citizen. In England, he believed, one could pursue one's passion for wealth and power with a minimum of constraint. As a result, commerce, industry, the arts, and philosophy flourish. In effect, Montesquieu was saying that the pursuit of self-interest, which the ancients would have called ignoble, within the framework of a separation of powers, wherein passion checks passion and power checks power, provides the condition for the realization of freedom of religion, of conscience, and of the mind.[39]

The benefits of the balanced state were trumpeted loudly by partisan and publicist alike after the settlement of 1689 in England. Even the Tories turned from Filmer to sing its praises. Bolingbroke, for example, declared: "It is by this mixture of monarchical, aristocratical, and democratical power, blended together in one system, and by these three estates balancing one another, that our free constitution of government hath been preserved so long inviolate."[40] Perhaps more important to us, because of the broad dissemination of their writings in colonial America, are those Whigs who called themselves Commonwealthmen and exalted, in Lockian tones, English liberties, which they tended to equate with natural rights, the right of resistance, the contract theory, public virtue, and the balanced constitution.[41] Two of these men, John Trenchard and Thomas Gordon, were the authors of *Cato's Letters,* which were so widely read in colonial America that a recent student of the times has concluded that they, rather than Locke's *Treatises on Civil Government,* were "the most popular, quotable, esteemed source of political ideas in the colonial period."[42]

Common Law and Higher Law

In 1759, John Adams, then a young lawyer, wrote:

It has been my amusement for many years past, as far as I have had leisure, to examine the systems of all the legislators, ancient and modern, fantastical and real . . . and the result . . . is a settled opinion that the liberty, the unalienable, indefeasible rights of man, the honor and dignity of human nature, the grandeur and glory of the public, and the universal happiness of individuals, were never so skillfully and successfuly consulted as in that most excellent monument of human art, the common law of England.[43]

The colonial charters contained stipulations that the laws to be established should not run contrary to the laws of England. But they did not provide for the introduction of any particular form of English law. The "laws of England" in the seventeenth century included mercantile

130 years later in 1608 when Sir Edward Coke, Chief Justice of the King's Bench, who like Fortescue, believed the law to be a mystery, told James I that no king possessed the power personally to administer justice in England because that was the duty of the established courts. When the king answered that "he thought the law was founded upon reason, and that he and others had reason, as well as the Judges," Coke replied:

True it was, that God has endowed his Majesty with excellent science, and great endowments of nature; but his Majesty was not learned in the laws of his realm of England, and causes which concern the life, or inheritance, or goods, or fortunes of his subjects, are not to be decided by natural reason, but by the artificial reason and judgment of the law, which law is an act which requires long study and experience, before that a man can attain to the cognizance of it . . .[48]

When the king replied that "then he should be under the law, which was treason to affirm," Coke answered by quoting Bracton's aforementioned maxim.

Even more important for the American constitutional tradition was Coke's later pronouncement in *Dr. Bonham's Case:*

And it appears in our books, that in many cases, the common law will control acts of parliament, and sometimes adjudge them to be utterly void: for when an act of parliament is against common right and reason, or repugnant, or impossible to be performed, the common law will controul it and adjudge such act to be void.[49]

"Common right reason" to Coke was higher law, but it was also the "artificial reason and judgment of the law." Thus the courts and the learned men of the robe were to Coke, as to Bracton and Fortescue, the proper interpreters of higher law. The dictum in Bonham's case, when considered apart from Coke's other ideas, became, in Corwin's words, "the most important single source of the notion of judicial review." Judicial review, based solely on "common right and reason," however, could have no viability. Coke gave some substance to this abstraction, in his *Institutes,* where he declared that judgments and statutes against *Magna Carta* are void and that its benefits, as indicated in the common law (use of the processes of the ordinary courts, indictment by grand jury, trial by "law of the land," *habeas corpus,* security against monopoly, taxation by consent of Parliament) and by the maxims, "a statute should have prospective, not retrospective operation," "no one should be twice punished for the same offense," "everyman's house is his own castle," and "delegated authority cannot legitimately be redelegated," were available to all. Missing from the necessary conditions of judicial review in Coke's formulation was the separation of powers principle.

Thus the dictum in *Bonham's Case* was addressed from one judicial body, the court, to another, the Parliament.[50]

It would be erroneous to conclude that Coke intended, in his dictum in *Bonham's Case,* to maintain that the courts possessed power to pronounce void, statutes in conflict with higher law, although Americans later so interpreted him. In the words of a recent commentator: "When he said that the common law would 'control' an act of parliament he meant that the courts would interpret it in such a way as not to conflict with those same accepted principles of reason and justice which . . . were presumed to underlie all law." When he spoke of adjudging an act void, "he did not mean that the court could declare it beyond the power of parliament to enact, but that the court would construe it strictly. . . ."[51]

The first generation of the American bar, which came to maturity around 1750, comprised men who were nurtured on Coke. Jefferson testified that "Coke's Lyttleton was the universal lawbook of students, and a sounder Whig never wrote, nor of profounder learning in the orthodox doctrine of the British Constitution, or in what was called British liberties."[52] In 1765 Sir William Blackstone's *Commentaries on the Law of England* was published, many copies of which were sold in America before the Revolution. It soon became the basic text in American legal education. A prominent clergyman wrote, in 1771, that the *Commentaries* made the study of law so "easy and agreeable . . . that numbers of young Gentlemen at the Universities chuse to study the Law instead of going into Orders."[53] In his speech, "Conciliation with the Colonies," in 1775, Edmund Burke remarked: "In no country perhaps in the world is the law so general a study. . . . I hear they have sold nearly as many of Blackstone's *Commentaries* in America as in England."[54] John Quincy Adams later summed up the attitude of the new crop of lawyers by contending that Coke's was a "very improper" work to put into the hands of a beginning student of law, but that Blackstone's was "an inestimable advantage."[55] To such sentiment, Jefferson took strong exception. Because the *Commentaries* contained a staunch defense of parliamentary sovereignty and were traditionalist and quite conservative in approach, he railed against the "young group of lawyers," who, seduced by the "honeyed Mansfieldism of Blackstone . . . began to slide into Toryism."[56]

Corwin describes Blackstone as "eloquent, suave, undismayed in the presence of the palpable contradictions in his pages, adept in insinuating new points of view without unnecessarily disturbing old ones, . . . the very model of legalistic and juridical obscurantism."[57] Like Fortescue and Coke before him, Blackstone believed the law to be a mystery, discernible only by those most advanced in its study. Daniel Boorstin has shown in his study of Blackstone how the English commentator ingeniously employed eighteenth-century ideas of science, religion, history, aesthetics, and philosophy to render the law at once a conservative and a mysterious science.[58]

Blackstone talked in terms of "laws of nature" and "natural rights," not to measure the common law and English Constitution by a rationalist standard, as did many Whigs and disciples of Locke, but to identify these terms with existing English laws and liberties. The end of the law in his eyes was civil liberty, which is no other than natural liberty "so far restrained by human laws (and no farther) as is necessary and expedient for the general advantage of the public." Thus civil society is a framework of conventional legal prescriptions to regularize and protect the natural rights to life, liberty, and property—the "absolute rights" of Englishmen. The common law as the dictate of reason, self-love, history, and nature, supplies the content of these prescriptions. The mixed English Constitution with its balancing of social classes and political powers assures political liberty. At the same time, "there . . . must be . . . a supreme, irresistible, absolute, uncontrollable authority." To Blackstone this was Parliament and as a consequence, he allowed a basis in law to neither judicial review of its acts nor the right of revolution.[59]

Blackstone's work had a profound and abiding influence upon American students of the law until the end of the nineteenth century. The legal historian Holdsworth tells us that it was largely due to the *Commentaries* that the English common law became the common law of the United States.[60] This statement seems somewhat overdrawn in view of the influence that the common law exerted in the colonies before Blackstone wrote, but it points up the fact that the text from which lawyers for the most part learned the common law in America was Blackstone's. He gave to it the clear and concise statement it needed. Chief Justice John Marshall reflected the influence of Blackstone in his landmark decisions favoring a strong central government and vested property rights, and in his tort and contract rulings. Then, too, the great nineteenth-century American commentators, James Kent, Joseph Story, and Thomas M. Cooley, were all influenced in the direction of conservatism by Blackstone.[61] Thus if the American legal mind has been traditionally conservative, it is owing in no small measure to the influence of a single great book.

The "Whig" Interpretation of History

Americans were greatly influenced by what has come to be known as the "Whig" version of English history which stressed the claims of Parliament against the royal prerogative. This view idealized Saxon government as free, democratic rule, and looked upon later feudalism as a yoke fastened on free Anglo-Saxons by the Norman invaders. It regarded *Magna Carta* as a step toward the restoration of original Saxon liberty.[62]

Although this conception of history was for the most part mythical, it was a convenient instrument to use against the Crown (and later Parliament), and begot in its adherents a psychology of a golden past. Most, if not all, of the major American revolutionary publicists and thinkers used it effectively; in fact, in its attribution of liberty and superiority to a Germanic source, it was propounded by prominent American historians of the late nineteenth and early twentieth centuries.

NOTES

1. For a discussion of classical natural law, see Leo Strauss, *Natural Right and History* (Chicago, 1953), pp. 81–165. I have relied considerably in the text upon Strauss's treatment of the question. For a discussion of the influence of classical thought on the early American, see Richard M. Gummere, *The American Colonial Mind and the Classical Tradition* (Cambridge, Mass., 1963). See also B. F. Wright, *American Interpretations of Natural Law* (Cambridge, Mass., 1931) and J. A. C. Grand, "The Natural Law Background of Due Process," *Columbia Law Review*, XXXI (Jan., 1931), 56–81.

2. Consult Aristotle's *Nicomachean Ethics* and his *Politics* in Richard McKeon (ed.), *The Basic Works of Aristotle* (New York, 1941), pp. 935–1324. See also C. N. R. McCoy, *The Structure of Political Thought* (New York, 1963), pp. 29–70.

3. Marcus Tullius Cicero, *The Republic*, III, 22. Translated by George Sabine and Stanley Smith (Columbus, 1929).

4. Aquinas' treatise on law is found in his *Summa Theologica*, I. II. pp. 90–108 (translation by the English Dominican Fathers, London, 1911–1912). Aquinas' political writings have been conveniently brought together by Alessandro D'Entreves (ed.), *Aquinas: Selected Political Writings* (Oxford, 1948).

5. For a general treatment of modern natural law see Strauss, *op. cit.*, pp. 165–202. See also C. B. MacPherson, *The Political Theory of Possessive Individualism: Hobbes to Locke* (New York, 1962); Hobbes' principal political work was *Leviathan*, first published in 1651. The best modern edition, which is used here, is by Michael Oakeshott, published at Oxford in 1957.

6. *Leviathan*, xiii, 82.

7. Strauss, in *Natural Right and History*, pp. 167–169, develops this point, concluding that Hobbes used the apolitical view for a political purpose and, by trying to instill the spirit of political idealism into the hedonistic tradition, became the creator of political hedonism.

8. *Leviathan*, xiii, 84; Hobbes, De Corpore, I, 6 (quoted in Strauss, *op cit.*, p. 189).

9. For Locke's influence on the American Revolution, see John C. Miller, *The Origins of the American Revolution* (Boston, 1943), pp. 170–172; Alice Baldwin, *The New England Clergy and the American Revolution* (Durham, N.C., 1968), pp. 7, 10; and Carl Becker, *The Declaration of Independence* (New York, 1922), pp. 27, 28, 53, 56, 57, 75. For Locke's later influence in America, see Merle Curti, "The Great Mr. Locke: America's Philosopher, 1783–1861," in Curti, *Probing Our Past* (Gloucester, Mass., 1955), pp. 60–119. See also Louis Hartz, *The Liberal Tradition in America* (New York, 1955) for an account of the abiding influence of Locke upon American life.

10. John Locke, *Essay Concerning Human Understanding*, Book IV, Chap. 3, Sect. 6: Book IV, Chap. 10, Sect. 9. (Gateway ed., Chicago, 1956), pp. 245–246, 302–303.

11. F. S. C. Northrop, *The Meeting of East and West* (New York, 1946), Chap.

3, "The Free Culture of the United States," pp. 66–165. Northrop propounds the thesis that Locke's political thought was a conclusion from his scientific thought.

12. John Locke, *A Letter Concerning Toleration, The Works of John Locke* (London, 1801), VI; See also his *The Reasonableness of Christianity, Works,* VII.

13. *Essay*, Book II, Chap. 1, Sect. 2, p. 17; Book III, Chap. 3, Sect. 11, p. 49.

14. Ewart Lewis, "The Contribution of Mediaeval Thought to the American Political Tradition," *American Political Science Review* (June, 1956), p. 468.

15. *Two Treatises of Civil Government*, Book II, Chap. 9, Sect. 123. (Everymans Library ed., London, 1924), pp. 179–180.

16. *Ibid.*, Book II, Chap. 1, Sect. 3, p. 118.

17. *Ibid.*, Book II, Chap. 8, Sect. 95–99, pp. 164–166. For a consideration of Locke's conception of majority rule, see Willmoore Kendall, *John Locke and the Doctrine of Majority Rule* (Urbana, Ill., 1941).

18. *Ibid.*, II, Chap. 9, Sect. 134–142; Chap. 14, Sect. 168; II, Chap. 19, Sect. 220–243, pp. 183–190, 203, 228–242.

19. Strauss, *op. cit.*, pp. 202–252. For a dissenting view see John W. Yolton, "Locke on the Law of Nature," *The Philosophical Review,* LXVII (1958), 477–498 and Martin Seliger, *The Liberal Politics of John Locke* (New York, 1968).

20. *Ibid.*, pp. 244, 245.

21. See Douglass Adair, "That Politics May Be Reduced To a Science: David Hume, James Madison and the Tenth *Federalist*," *Huntington Library Quarterly,* XX (Aug., 1957), 343–360. Adair discusses the Scottish influence on pp. 345, 346. See also on this point, Caroline Robbins, "When It Is That Colonies May Turn Independent," *William and Mary Quarterly,* XI (Apr., 1954), 214–251. Hamilton ended the concluding *Federalist* paper (No. 85) by quoting from Hume's essay, "The Rise of the Arts and Sciences."

22. For an elementary treatment of Hume's philosophy consult either A. H. Basson, *David Hume* (Pelican Books, London, 1958) or D. G. C. MacNabb, *David Hume: His Theory of Knowledge and Morality* (London, 1951). Hume's essential political writings can be conveniently found in Frederick Watkins (ed.), *Hume: Theory of Politics* (New York, 1951) or in Charles Hendel (ed.), *David Hume's Political Essays* (New York, 1953).

23. David Hume, *A Treatise of Human Nature,* Book II, Part III, Sect. 3 (Selby-Bigge ed., London, 1888, reprinted in 1967), p. 415.

24. Basson, *op. cit.*, p. 104.

25. A. J. Beitzinger, "Hume's Aristocratic Preference," *The Review of Politics,* 28 (Apr., 1966), 154–171. See also McCoy, *op. cit.*, pp. 236, 237 and Sheldon Wolin, *Politics and Vision* (Boston, 1960), pp. 344, 345.

26. *Treatise of Human Nature,* Book III, Part II, Sect. 2, p. 492.

27. Hume's conception of the origin of society, property, and justice can be found in essays in Book III, Part II of the *Treatise*, pp. 477–534.

28. Hume's essays on the origin of government and the nature of obligation can be found in Book III, Part II of the *Treatise*, pp. 534–567 and in David Hume, *Essays, Moral, Political and Literary* (Green and Grose ed., London, 1880), Part I, pp. 109–117 and Part II, pp. 443–460.

29. *Treatise*, Book III, Part II, Sect. 7, p. 538.

30. "Of the Independence of Parliament," *Essays*, Part I, p. 117.

31. "That Politics May be Reduced to A Science," and "Of Parties in General," *ibid.*, pp. 98–109, 127–133. The passage relevant to Madison is in "Idea of a Perfect Commonwealth," *ibid.*, p. 492.

32. On the antiquity of the mixed-state concept, see Zera Fink, *The Classical Republicans* (Evanston, 1945), Chap. 1, pp. 1–27. See also Stanley Pargelis, "The Theory of Balanced Government," in Conyers Read (ed.), *The Constitution Reconsidered* (New York, 1938), pp. 36–49.

33. McCoy, *op. cit.*, p. 143.

34. The best available edition of Harrington's *Oceana* is by S. B. Lilijgren (Heidelberg, 1924). For treatments of Harrington's political thought, see Fink, *op. cit.*,

Chap. 3, "Immortal Government: Oceana," pp. 52–89, and Charles Blitzer, *An Immortal Commonwealth* (New Haven, 1960).

35. On this point see Charles A. Beard, *Economic Basis of Politics* (New York, 1945). On Harrington's general influence upon American thought, see H. F. Russell Smith, *Harrington and his Oceana* (Cambridge, 1914), Chaps. 7 and 8, pp. 152–200.

36. Fink, *op cit.*, pp. 90–122.

37. William J. Grace, "Milton, Salmasius and the Natural Law," *Journal of the History of Ideas*, XXIV (July–Sept., 1963), 323ff.

38. Paul Spurlin, *Montesquieu in America* (Baton Rouge, 1940), is a thorough treatment of the subject. See also James Madison, *The Federalist* No. 47. Other continental writers of lesser significance were Samuel Pufendorf, whose *Jus Naturae et Gentium* (1672) was heavily relied upon by John Wise; and J. J. Burlamaqui, who in his *Principles of Natural and Politic Law* (1747), emphasized separation of powers and judicial review. See R. F. Harvey, *J. J. Burlamaqui: A Liberal Tradition in American Constitutionalism* (Chapel Hill, 1937).

39. The best one-volume English translation of *The Spirit of the Laws* is in the Hafner Library of Classics (New York, 1949).

40. Quoted in George Sabine, *A History of Political Theory* (New York, 1937), p. 560.

41. Consult Caroline Robbins, *The Eighteenth Century Commonwealthman* (Cambridge, Mass., 1961).

42. Clinton Rossiter, *Seedtime of the Republic* (New York, 1953), p. 141.

43. Quoted in Edward S. Corwin, *The "Higher Law" Background of American Constitutional Law* (Ithaca, 1955), p. 24. These essays first appeared in *Harvard Law Review*, XLII (1928–1929), 149, 365 and were reprinted in *Selected Essays in American Constitutional Law* (Chicago, 1938), I, 1–67.

44. George Lee Haskins, *Law and Authority in Early Massachusetts* (New York, 1960), pp. 4–6. For an earlier view, criticized in part by Haskins, see Richard B. Morris, *Studies in the History of American Law* (New York, 1930), pp. 9–67. See also Julius Goebel, "King's Law and Local Custom in Seventeenth Century New England," *Columbia Law Review*, XXXI (Mar., 1931), 417

45. John T. Farrell, "The Administration of Justice in Connecticut About the Middle of The Eighteenth Century" (unpublished Ph.D. dissertation, Yale University, 1937), pp. 212–214.

46. Corwin, *op. cit.*, pp. 27–30.

47. *Ibid.*, pp. 32, 35–38, 39. For an excellent discussion of *Magna Carta* see S. E. Thorne, *et al.*, *The Great Charter* (New York, 1966).

48. Corwin, *op. cit.*, pp. 38–39.

49. *Ibid.*, p. 44.

50. *Ibid.*, pp. 57, 47–55. For a divergent interpretation see S. E. Thorne, "The Constitution and the Courts," in Read, *op. cit.*, pp. 15–24. Thorne argues that Coke's argument was derived from the ordinary common-law rules of statutory interpretation.

51. J. W. Gough, *Fundamental Law in English Constitutional History* (Oxford, 1955), p. 35; See also S. E. Thorne, "The Constitution and the Courts," in Read, *op. cit.*, pp. 15–24, and S. E. Thorne, "Dr. Bonham's Case," *Law Quarterly Review*, 54 (1938), 545, 549, 551.

52. Corwin, *op. cit.*, pp. 41, 42.

53. David A. Lockmiller, *Sir William Blackstone* (Chapel Hill, 1938), p. 169.

54. *Ibid.*, p. 172.

55. *Ibid.*, p. 177.

56. Corwin, *op. cit.*, p. 85. Jefferson praised the *Commentaries* but regretted their perversion. In a letter to Judge Tyler in 1812, he wrote, "Though the most eloquent and best digested of our catalogues, [it] has been perverted more than all other to the degeneracy of our legal science. A student finds there a smattering of everything, and his indolence easily persuades him that if he understands that book he is master of the whole body of the law." Lockmiller, *op. cit.*, p. 178.

57. Corwin, *op. cit.*, p. 85.
58. Daniel Boorstin, *The Mysterious Science of the Law* (Boston, 1958).
59. Corwin, *op. cit.*, pp. 85, 86, 87.
60. Cited in Lewis C. Worden, *The Life of Blackstone* (Charlottesville, 1938), p. 320.
61. Worden, *op. cit.*, pp. 328, 329; Lockmiller, *op. cit.*, pp. 176, 177.
62. On Whig history see H. T. Colbourn, *The Lamp of Experience* (Chapel Hill, 1965), pp. 6–10. See also Herbert Butterfield, *The Englishman and His History* (Cambridge, 1957).

PART TWO

THEOLOGICAL AND RELIGIOUS BACKGROUND

Chapter 2

THE CITY ON A HILL: PURITAN POLITICAL THOUGHT

Let All Things be done decently and in right order.
ST. PAUL, 1 COR. xiv, 40

The Puritan fathers sailed to the New World in the conviction, as their distinguished first governor John Winthrop expressed it, that they were divinely commissioned to set up "a Citty upon a hill," an archetype for all of Christendom. The model city, approved "by a mutuall consent" and blest by "a special overruling providence" and "a more than an ordinary approbation of the Churches of Christ," was to be established under what Winthrop called "a due forme of Government both civill and ecclesiasticall."[1]

The Great Reformers: Luther and Calvin

Much of the early modern period of Western history can be viewed as a dialectical interplay between the original Protestant conception of Christian liberty and the demands of society. Believing in the doctrines of justification by faith alone and the priesthood of all believers, Martin Luther could abide no intermediaries between God and man except Christ and the Word of God in Scripture. Thus he declared: "Neither pope nor bishop nor any other man has the right to impose a single syllable of law upon a Christian man without his consent."[2] Similarly, Luther believed that if works are pursued as a means to sanctity and salvation, they negate both freedom and faith by putting men under necessity.

Ideally speaking, Luther had a theological doctrine but no conception of ecclesiastical polity. The true church was to him invisible, "an assembly of hearts in one faith" with no external organizational structure. As a recent commentator has put it, Luther's conception of spiritual power disavowed the coercive, conclusive character which such power entailed in the medieval church and took on what Thomas Hobbes would have called a "ghostly" form.[3]

Luther's nonpolitical conception of the church was also rooted in his acceptance of the idea of the depravity of man in the eyes of God as the result of original sin. Total depravity, in turn, along with Luther's desire to sweep away all influence of the pagan philosopher, Aristotle, as embodied in scholasticism, necessarily precluded the Catholic philosophical conception of cosmic order flowing from the divine reason and discernible, in terms of basic principles, by man in light of his reason. Filling this unstructured, orderless power vacuum was a heightened Lutheran emphasis upon secular authority—in essence, coercive power —no longer held in check by a viable institutionalized church polity. By accepting the order imposed by the secular authority upon church and society, Luther could with some justification be looked upon by enthusiasts such as the Anabaptists as having betrayed the Reformation.[4]

John Calvin also accepted the notion of total depravity. His somber insistence that original sin had effected the totality of man's being was accompanied by an unrelenting emphasis upon the sovereign power of an arbitrary, inscrutable God, whose will is just, simply because it is the source of justice. Whereas to the Catholic, reception of the sacraments and rectitude of life, informed by implicit faith in Christ and His Church, afforded moral if not metaphysical certainty of salvation, and whereas to the Lutheran an individual could hopefully strive for the faith which justifies, to the Calvinist salvation could come only as a free, unwarranted gift from God in the form of irresistible grace. This infusion of grace was afforded, under the doctrine of limited atonement, to but a few, the elect of Christ, while the rest of mankind was foredoomed to damnation.

Calvin, a lawyer gifted with the qualities of the statesman who recognizes the ubiquity of power, believed in the necessity of an articulated church organization independent of control by the state. His notion of order, civil and ecclesiastical, consisted in a "well regulated polity, which excludes all confusion, incivility, obstinacy, clamours and dissensions." In alluding to the visible church he remarked that "the external call without the internal efficacy of grace, which would be sufficient for their preservation, is a kind of medium between the rejection of all mankind and the election of the small number of believers." He thus admitted that the church as a social organization and the coercive state as its counterpart were compromises between the demands of social order and the ideal of Christian liberty. Theretofore tradition, right reason, and historical practice had served as important bases of ordered polity. It was not merely Calvin's theology but also the revolutionary character of his break with the past which brought him to put prime reliance upon the Bible as the source of fundamental law for both polities. Although the Calvinist church in Geneva formally disavowed a hierarchical conception of order, its doctrine of an elect and its practice of allowing its members power only to reject or ratify the actions of church officers show it to have been a mixed ecclesiastical polity combining democracy with aristocracy, but inclining heavily toward the latter.[5]

If Calvin had proceeded in a rigorously logical manner, his embrace of the doctrine of total depravity would have precluded any qualification of his conception that order in society is of necessity externally imposed and essentially repressive. Excluded from Calvin's system was the recognition of natural virtue as delineated, for example, in Aristotle's *Nicomachean Ethics*. In Calvin's view the virtue of the non-Christian was merely "political" and thus of no intrinsic worth. Calvin could see no spiritual midpoint between predestinate regeneration and corrupt desire. This being the case, the content of a natural moral law must remain unknown or at best incapable of being acted upon by those whose natures are depraved. Order cannot emanate from that which is radically disordered.

Confronted with this logical necessity, Calvin qualified his major premise. He proclaimed that man "is naturally a creature inclined to society" who "has also by nature an instinctive propensity to cherish and preserve that society." Thus there exist "in the minds of all men general impressions of civil probity and order." The constant consent of all nations and men to laws obtains "because the seed of them [laws] are innate in all mankind, without any instructor or legislator."[6]

To the degree that human reason is a source of truth, as Calvin's statement supposes, it cannot be totally corrupt. If Calvin's main emphasis in the *Institutes* had been placed on this point he would, in effect, have come close to affirming what he had previously denied—the Catholic conception that original sin effected a removal of supernatural and preternatural graces but left man's nature fundamentally intact. In any case, the main emphasis in Calvin was upon total depravity which left the light of man's reason so dim and his will so perverse that external aid in the form of the revealed word of God, as contained principally in the Decalogue and the Mosaic code, must serve as the basis of order, ecclesiastical and civil.

Man's nature and his corruption thus make requisite a political order. Calvin's civil polity, although distinct from the church, existed "to cherish and support the external worship of God, to preserve the pure doctrine of religion, to defend the constitution of the Church" as well as

to promote civic virtue and the common good. Both tables of the
Decalogue, that which lists offenses against God as well as that which
lists offenses against man, were to be enforced by the state. Thus Calvin
could proclaim that the state must ensure that "idolatry, sacrileges
against the name of God, blasphemies against his truth and other
offenses against religion, may not openly appear and be disseminated
among the people."[7]

Like his ecclesiastical polity, Calvin's civil polity was a mixed state,
the main principles being democratic and aristocratic, with decided
emphasis upon the latter. This is borne out in his treatment of the office
of the civil magistrate, whom he called a "vice-regent of God." The
magistrate, like the elected officers of the church, was not an agent of
the people but a servant of justice and the common good. However,
allegiance was due not to his person but to the office he filled. In pursuit of the Pauline injunction ("Let every soul be subject unto the higher
powers. Whosoever resisteth the power, resisteth the ordinance of God"),
Calvin emphasized passive obedience to civil authority. Although this
was the rule, he allowed exceptions where a tyranny existed and lower
constituted officers could act against it, or, more importantly, when a
political command was given to act against the law of God, in which
case passive resistance was incumbent upon all.[8]

A religious revolutionary, Calvin nevertheless manifested a basic conservatism, a passion for order, and a distrust of change. But changes,
particularly among his English auditors, there were to be; changes
designed to soften the rigors of his implacable doctrinal stand and to
take from it some of the deadening weight of its pessimism. Before
discussing these developments, we must first note the course of Calvinism in England where Puritanism evolved to take the form which
Winthrop and his doughty cobelievers embraced when they brought it to
New England on the *Arbella* in 1630.

The Reformation in England

Under Henry VIII papal authority was rejected in England and the
English church was nationalized, with the monarch assuming the role
of head. Under Edward VII and Elizabeth I, the episcopal form of
organization was maintained but doctrinal changes were effected which
made the official theology Protestant. The Erastian principle of civil
supremacy over the spiritual was affirmed in the Acts of Supremacy and
Uniformity which, in effect, established that the monarch in the interest
of society could judge all disputes, theological as well as eccesiastical.
This settlement was justified as preserving the unity of the state by the
greatest of Anglican ecclesiastical statesmen, Richard Hooker, the

author of the important work, *Of the Laws of Ecclesiastical Politie.*[9]

Puritanism in England generally indicated the objective of completing the Reformation by purging the church of all Catholic practices, doctrinal as well as ecclesiastical, in accordance with the Bible and Calvin's teachings so that the pristine purity and simplicity of primitive Christianity might be regained. Because doctrinal reforms had in good part been realized, the main thrust of Puritan energy was in the direction of substituting a Presbyterian form of organization for the Episcopal order which was considered a residue of Catholicism.[10]

The Presbyterian concept of ecclesiastical polity struck directly at the heart of the Anglican polity, not merely by disavowing the episcopacy, but by denying to the monarch the right to appoint church officers. Presbyterianism tended toward democracy by rendering all ministers equal in rank but departed from democracy insofar as the congregations were to be governed and controlled by a graded series of ministerial conferences and synods. Originally the plan involved election of the ministers by the people, but later it was determined that they be named by one of the conferences and merely approved by the congregations.[11]

When James I was importuned to establish the Presbyterian form, he drew on his Scottish experience to answer that Presbyterianism "as well agreeth with Monarchy, as God, and the Divell." He told the Anglican bishops: "If once you were out, and they in place, I knowe what would become of my *Supremacie. No Bishop, no King.*" To James any change in the ecclesiastical polity entailed a political revolution.[12]

James's judgment was correct for two reasons. First, his authority in ecclesiastical matters would be effectively nullified by a Presbyterian polity. As the Presbyterian saw it, although the prince should rule the church, he was bound to respect its basic constitution, which implied that the scope of his authority be decided by the ministers who would insist that he "doe nothing in these matters, but by the faithfull advice of them, that know [God's] will, and are bounde to teache it unto all men."[13] Second, on the purely political plane, the Puritan move toward constitutionalism in ecclesiastical matters had an analogue in the movement by statesmen and common law lawyers for regard for fundamental law in governmental and legal affairs. Thus even though the Presbyterian party took the Oath of Supremacy, it was evident that its conception of church polity was irreconcilably at odds with the monarchy.[14]

Professor Perry Miller has reminded us that Presbyterianism involved no contribution to the development of liberty or toleration. If it had been adopted it would have been more repressive than the Anglican polity because it would have added to the political force of the Acts of Supremacy and Uniformity, "the blazing sanctions of the divine command."[15]

Congregationalism

Calvin had envisioned an ideal church membership consisting only of saints. But he recognized that there was no infallible mode of determining who was among the elect. This, along with the sixteenth-century emphasis on the absolute necessity of unity in the state, brought him to make all persons subject to the church. Scottish and English Presbyterians followed Calvin on this point. However, the Pruitan clergyman, Robert Browne, in 1582 formulated a plan of church organization and government which soon gained a good number of adherents among pious believers. His polity, which Miller has called Separatist Congregationalism, was based upon the following four principles, which were intended to implement the basic Protestant doctrine of the priesthood of all believers. First, only persons who could prove to a congregation of the elect that they were "redeemed by Christ unto holiness & happiness forever," could be members of the church. Second, a congregation could be formed only by "visible saints" who, coming together and professing their faith, took a covenant of allegiance to Christ as their king, promising to be bound by His laws. Third, the particular congregations so established on the bases of covenant were to be considered autonomous and not subject to the restraining orders of synods, which were relegated to an advisory role. Finally, the church members were to choose the church officers. Browne thought that these principles could be implemented only after separation from the Anglican Church.[16]

Although the civil magistrate was to be excluded from the internal affairs of the congregations, the Congregationalists still assigned to him the maintenance of the true discipline—Congregationalism. Separation from the "true church" was anathema to them, as was toleration of other sects. The problem of unregenerate men was to be solved by requiring their attendance at church services and by civil punishment of offenses against God's commandments.[17]

Congregationalism was diametrically opposed to the Anglican ecclesiastical polity and fundamentally at odds with the Presbyterian idea of church order. Perceptive supporters of the monarchy saw that the concept of compact as the basis of church society might be used to reinforce the budding notion of the contractual basis of the state and thus undermine the established order. That such a transition could easily be made is evident in the experience of the Pilgrim fathers, the Separatist Congregationalists who after sailing to America in 1620 as a congregation on the *Mayflower*, drew up the Mayflower Compact, their articles of political association, on the basis of the congregational church principle of organization.[18]

Non-Separatist Congregationalists differed from the Separatists in believing that separation from the Anglican Church was political folly.

They rationalized their position by holding that the Church of England was really Congregational in substance and it required only that the bishops surrender their civil power to the civil authorities and become merely ministers of the church. In this light, the answer lay not in separation but in reform and purification of the established church on a Congregational basis. However, after Charles I became king in 1625, it seemed evident that reform of the church was out of the question. In 1629 a body of Non-Separatist Congregationalists, armed with a new strategy, decided to undertake an "errand into the wilderness." They secured a commercial charter from the king which established the Massachusetts Bay Company and authorized that body to govern by orders and statutes not contrary to the laws of England and in consonance with the ancient liberties and immunities of Englishmen. Carrying the charter with them, they sailed with the intention of establishing a Congregationalist church order in Massachusetts in a body politic which would be based upon a system that distinguished between the elect and the unregenerate and that would serve as an example for the completion of the Reformation.[19]

The Federal Theology and Cosmic Government

In Calvin's conception of cosmic government, fallen man was a passive entity subject to the arbitrary rule of the divine, inscrutable, absolute monarch. Although, in general, the practical effect of the belief in total depravity, in limited atonement, in predestination, and in irresistible grace was, paradoxically, an activism which affirmed moral responsibility and political obligation, the doctrine itself provoked grave misgivings in many believers late in the sixteenth and early in the seventeenth centuries. A sympathetic student of Calvinism has summed up the harshness and pervasive pessimism of the doctrine in the following manner:

To represent man as sent into the world under a curse, as incurably wicked, —wicked by the constitution of his flesh, and wicked by eternal decree,—as doomed, unless exempted by special grace which he cannot merit, or by any effort of his own obtain, to live in sin while he remains on earth, and to be eternally miserable when he leaves it,—to represent him as born unable to keep the commandments, yet as justly liable to everlasting punishment for breaking them, is alike repugnant to reason and to conscience, and turns existence into a hideous nightmare. To deny the freedom of the will is to make morality impossible. . . . How are we to call the Ruler who laid us under this iron code by the name of Wise, or Just, or Merciful, when we ascribe principles of action to Him which in a human father we should call preposterous and monstrous?[20]

The orthodox Calvinist position was first challenged within its own ranks by Arminianism, a theology named after the sixteenth-century

Dutch divine, Jacobus Arminius. Arminianism posited universal redemption and salvation conditional upon conversion. Conversion, in
turn, was conceived as dependent not merely upon God's favor but also
upon man's free choice and deserving works. To the Puritan this was
merely a refurbished manifestation of the ancient Pelagian heresy—a
limitation upon God's omnipotence and a denial of original sin.[21]

At the other extreme was Antinomianism, a radical and recurrent
theological position particularly attractive to a minority of zealots in
search of certitude. The Antinomian drew from the Orthodox Calvinist
doctrine of irresistible grace the conclusion that grace comes directly
from God to the elect in the form of a sudden infusion accompanied by
an absolute assurance of salvation. He further concluded that once the
elect have experienced conversion they are no longer subject to law but
stand above both it and nature as predestined receptacles of God's favor.
Thus sanctification was excluded as evidence of justification.[22]

The implications of these extremist positions for civil as well as
ecclesiastical polity were thoroughly abhorrent to the Puritan. Arminianism opened the door to the re-entry of Aristotelian justification of authority in terms of the efficacy of the natural virtues and human reason.
Once these were accepted, what viable justification remained for rule
by the elect and what could prevent the inevitable secularization of
society? Then too, Arminianism was associated with the ascendant
Anglican party of the hated Archbishop Laud* and seemed too com-
fortably close to the discarded Catholic position. Although less heretical
in doctrine, Antinomianism was even more unacceptable politically than
Arminianism. If those who claimed that they were visited by grace and
made instruments of God above any law were to be believed, then
both church and state were superfluous for the regenerate. Internal feeling and unbridled charisma—the essence of "enthusiasm"—would replace reliance upon Scripture and reason; anarchy and chaos, with the
odious example of the Anabaptist regime in Muenster in mind, would
shatter the system of order which most pious Protestants from Calvin
on had labored to construct.

Congregationalist Puritans who desired to make Calvinist doctrine
compatible with moral responsibility were confronted with a formidable
task. They had to inject into the doctrine a heavy dosage of voluntarism
while still preserving the orthodox conceptions of man's utter subjection
to God's will and predestination. In the process they had to steer clear
of the Arminian emphasis on freedom of the will and the efficacy of
good works and the Antinomian emphasis on the passivity of man and

* William Laud (1573–1645) was archbishop of Canterbury. The tyranny of his
courts and identification of the Episcopal church polity with the absolutism of
Charles I, as well as his persecution of nonconformists, evoked strong Puritan opposition.

the irrelevance of good works. Their ingenious answer, which essayed to resolve the fundamental antinomies while yet preserving the truths they embodied, took the form of the federal theology. Devised in England by the great Puritan divines, William Ames, William Perkins, and John Preston, and brought on the *Arbella* to New England where it was further developed by the Puritan fathers, the federal theology drew upon the ancient biblical conception of covenant to achieve a new synthesis. In the beginning, it was held, Adam stood as the "federal" representative of the human race in covenant with God who promised eternal bliss in exchange for Adam's adherence to the moral law—the covenant of works. After Adam broke the contract at the fall, his corrupt nature precluded him and his descendants from fulfilling the law. Salvation could now be realized only as a free gift from God. This was made possible through the covenant of grace whereby God requires that man merely believe in Christ and, in exchange, is promised eternal life. The covenant of grace was made possible by a precedent covenant which from the trinitarian viewpoint involves God contracting with Himself—the covenant of redemption, whereby God the Father agrees with Christ, His Son, that in exchange for Christ's assuming mortal flesh as the new "federal" representative of mankind and atoning through His suffering and death for the sins of man, salvation would be afforded the elect faithful through the covenant of grace.[23]

To obviate the danger of slipping into the Antinomian heresy, the federal theologians held that although justification was by faith through the covenant of grace, the commandments embraced in the covenant of works (but not the covenant itself) were still binding upon regenerate man even though he could not entirely fulfill them. Thus the elect of God would necessarily reflect their rehabilitation in the relative goodness of their works. Good works were not made to serve as the condition of salvation as in Arminianism, but to accompany it as evidence thereof. God's grace was assumed to be available to man through the "means" of His Word and the sacraments. Unlike the sudden infusion of the Antinomians, God's grace was likened to a seed planted in the hearts of men, to be nurtured carefully by them.[24]

The federal theology led to several significant conclusions. Inasmuch as the arbitrary, inscrutable, and omnipotent Calvinist God on his own initiative consented to bind Himself in a legally enforceable contract to abide by rational procedures and rules, the form of cosmic government was transformed by the Absolute Monarch Himself into a constitutional monarchy with mankind granted a nonrevocable spiritual bill of rights. Because the theologians believed that the contractual terms and God's commandments could be vindicated by revivified human reason, it was no longer an absolute necessity to base justice and obligation solely upon arbitrary decree. With his natural faculties purified, regenerate man, standing in a juridical relationship to his Maker, could correctly discern by right reason the laws of nature and morality. The Puritans believed that the contractual and rational grounds of moral obligation were firmly laid within the framework of the orthodox doctrines of God's omnipotence and predestination. However, in order for moral obligation to be attributed to the unregenerate, the Calvinist conception of total depravity was substantially modified. It was contended that man naturally does attain a sufficient knowledge of God's law to rule out the excuse of ignorance and to render all, unregenerate and regenerate alike, culpable, if they break it. But in the process there was tacitly imputed to man a natural capacity of choice which, when informed by grace, leads to salvation. It is true that the federal theologians did not directly preach freedom of the will, a doctrine anathema to orthodox Calvinists. However, as Perry Miller has pointed out, by treating grace as God's readiness to covenant with any man who does not actively refuse Him, the theory declared, in effect, that God had taken the initiative and man can blame only himself if he spurns or ignores the divine offer. Indeed, the theory was ultimately construed pragmatically to the effect that any man who could fulfill the covenant was deemed elected.[25]

In sum, the federal theology was accompanied by a reconsideration of the nature of the rational faculty which was of great portent for the future of Puritanism. Had they left unmodified the orthodox Calvinist doctrine, the Puritan intellectuals would have been led logically to nominalism,* a mode of thought they hated and feared because it precluded a rational basis for nature. The federal theological stipulation that God by voluntary act established rational rules for man, and the insistence that the contractual terms were justified not only in terms of Scripture but by reason as well, allowed for alternatives to nominalism. For some years the Aristotelian-scholastic conception of the intellect as an instrument by which man can abstract essences (general concepts) from sense knowledge, and as a light by which he can consider them, was used by Puritan intellectuals as a supplement to the theology. However, the federal theologians found the logic of Petrus Ramus, a sixteenth-century French philosopher and humanist, more amenable to their system. Although Ramus looked upon the intellect merely as an innate propensity, his disciples came in time to view it more as a Platonic source of innate ideas which are rooted ultimately in the mind of God. Unlike the Aristotelian conception which sees sense knowledge as fundamental, the developed Ramist conception attributed to man an ability directly to apprehend ideal, intelligible forms. However, in both

* See Chapter I, page 6.

approaches the departure from the orthodox Calvinist dogma of total depravity is evident.[26]

Thus the New England Puritan had a twofold conception of reason. On the one hand he saw it as an instrument by which truth is deduced from Scripture and abstracted from sense knowledge. If he put prime emphasis upon the senses, he feared that he would be led ineluctably to nominalism. On the other hand, he saw reason as a source or repository of truth itself, coordinate with Scripture and the senses. He realized that if he pursued this conception exclusively, he might end up embracing the Antinomian heresy of the inner light.[27]

The linchpin of the intricate Puritan synthesis of faith and reason, grace and nature, was the voluntaristic conception of covenant. If the universe is rationally governed, if man's reason is to be trusted, it is only because God willed them to be such. Never could the Puritan dare to assert as did the Thomists and the Anglican, Richard Hooker, that natural law is immutable because it is part of the eternal law of God which flows from His essentially rational nature. God is will; to say otherwise, or more, was to commit the sin of presuming to discern His essence by a blasphemous anthropomorphical projection. God, the omnipotent sovereign, could as readily have chosen to promulgate rules for man and nature which run counter to human reason. As a result, insofar as Puritan thought could finally explain and justify reason, nature, and law only in terms of God's will, it was ultimately theologism. Once the belief in the voluntary basis of cosmic order and in theology as the norm of reason was eroded, empiricism and rationalism, which later formed so shaky an alliance in the thought of John Locke, would unfold, with a consequent secularization of both life and the contractual basis of obligation and order.

Finally, it must be observed that while all systematized theologies more or less employ political terminology to portray essential truths, the Puritan federal theology went beyond the mere employment of symbolism and imagery borrowed from the language of politics. If it is true that in the late sixteenth and early seventeenth centuries the theological concept of covenant was heavily influenced by the political concept of compact, the Puritan federal theology represented a distinct and pervasive politicization of Calvinist theology in the direction of effecting a constitutionalization of cosmic rule. It goes without saying that if theology indicates that the omnipotent Ruler of the universe freely contracted to limit His rule by following rational procedures and laws, then surely it is incumbent upon man to disallow absolute government over himself in both church and state.

If men can believe, or act as if they believe, that theological problems can be treated as political questions to be resolved through the juridical

device of contract, it is apparent that they will also be inclined, or at
least mentally disposed, to conclude that political issues can and should,
for the most part, be reduced to legal formulation and resolution. This
latter propensity, remarked upon so frequently by observers of the
American character, may in some good part be traced to the abiding
influence upon the American mind of the ingenious approach of the
federal theology.

The Puritan Church Covenant

Standing alone the covenant of grace could not resolve the problem
of ecclesiastical order. It could, of course, readily indicate the superiority
of the elect over the damned. But if the buoyant Christian liberty im-
parted to the elect by divine grace was to be canalized and, if also, the
unregenerate masses were to be put in rein, skillful deductions had to
be drawn from the individual contract with God. The production of
convincing arguments that the covenant of grace implied the affirmation
of the Congregational Church covenant, not merely as a social expedient
but as a condition of salvation, is evidence of the statesmanlike ingenuity
of the Puritan mind. Regenerate man, it was reasoned, has duties to God
and to his fellow men which can only be fulfilled in a church. Thus
visible evidence that one was the recipient of grace was held to be contained not merely in the desire to live according to the moral law but
also in the desire to subscribe to the ecclesiastical polity outlined in
Scripture.[28]

The necessity of the visible church for both the regenerate and the
unregenerate was defended by the great Connecticut divine, Thomas
Hooker (1586–1647). Hooker described the covenant of grace as, on the
one hand, containing "the *benefits* of saving grace *given* in it," and on
the other hand, "the *means* of grace *offered*." He concluded that the
church covenant was "contained within the compasse of the covenant
[of grace] in the second sense."[29] Thus the visible church served the
regenerate through the sacraments of Baptism and Holy Communion as
well as the sermon, while it provided, in the form of the sermon, the
"means" through which the unregenerate might be stirred to conversion.
It followed that the unregenerate, although not members of the church,
must be compelled to attend services and pay taxes for its sustenance.
The motivation behind this state-enforced requirement, which to a
modern, secular age seems grossly illiberal, was to afford men every
possible opportunity to save that which alone is immortal in them, their
souls.

Because the Puritan church was both the basis of and the pattern for
the state, the church covenant effected what Perry Miller has called a
social transition from a hierarchy of status to a hierarchy of contract.

The new hierarchy included at the top rung the elected minister and elders of each community church along with the civil magistrates. On the next rung were those who upon affording visible proof of sanctification, covenanted together to form the church, elect officers, and ultimately decide upon admissions and excommunications. This group comprised the freemen of the political community. At the bottom rung was the great body of people in each community who, although required to attend church services, had not yet offered proof of their conversion.[30]

Against charges that the Congregationalist polity contained democratic implications, the Puritan argued that the congregations had no power to make laws but merely to see that all members observed the fundamental law which Christ had promulgated. From its inception the Church in New England was regarded not only as divinely ordained but as possessing a government prescribed by Scripture. As a consequence, any action by church officers or members could be justified only in terms of specific biblical authorization or logical deductions therefrom. Thus a legalistic, literal conception of a higher law informed Puritan church polity and government and inevitably all of life.[31]

In choosing church officers, the members were looked upon merely as agents through whom God registered His choice. The ministers and elders were not regarded as deputies, but as representatives of Christ, with their authority flowing directly from God. Thomas Hooker described the form of church government as "in regard of the body of the people . . . Democraticall, in regard of the Elders Aristocraticall; in regard of Christ, truly Monarchicall."[32]

Synodal, coercive government was, of course, contrary to the Congregationalist principle. However, synods were employed. The Platform of Church Discipline drawn up by the synod in Cambridge in 1648 and ratified by the General Court, declared: "It belongeth unto synods . . . to debate and determine controversies of the faith . . . to bear witness against mal-administration and corruption in doctrine of manners in any particular church; and to give directions for the reformation thereof." Although the Platform held that synodal pronouncements were to be received with "reverence and submission," church independence was maintained by denying to synods power to discipline through church censures. Consociation in a synod or a general meeting of ministers became a necessity to offset centrifugal, separatist impulses latent in the Congregational principle. So great was this danger considered to be that a law was passed providing that no new church could be established in Massachusetts Bay Colony without the approval of the General Court. All this is further evidence of the realistic recognition by the Puritan of the need to structure power in a coordinated system of order.[33]

Given this considerable politicization of religious life, what remained of the Protestant conception of the Christian liberty of the pious believer which pristine Congregationalism had attempted to implement? By 1648 and the Cambridge Platform, it had become reduced essentially to the liberty to subscribe to a church covenant upon proof of faith. Samuel Stone succinctly and accurately characterized the working church polity as a "speaking *Aristocracy* in the face of a silent *Democracy*"; a description which, as we shall see, applies just as fittingly to the Puritan state.[34]

The Puritan State

The New England Puritan justified the state in federal theological terms as a deduction from the covenant of grace and its counterpart, the church covenant; in strict Calvinist terms as a remedy for sin; and in traditional, medieval terms as the instrument for the realization of the common good. In the first and most emphasized approach, the state, which presupposes the church as the basic principle and model of order and its coordinate partner in the fulfillment of the Divine commission, originates in a corporate reaffirmation of the individual religious covenant and a mutual acceptance of common duties and purposes. From this it was further deduced that the particular form of government of the new society and the designation of its officers were also justified only by covenant.[35] Richard Mather expounded, in biblical terms, the nature of the political covenant and its relation to the chain of covenants which linked men to God and men to men in Puritan thought:

When *Jehojada* [the high priest] made a Covenant between the King and the people . . . that Covenant was but a branch of the Lord's covenant with them all, both King and people: for the King promised but to Rule the people righteously, according to the will of God: and the people to be subject to the King so Ruling. Now these duties of the King to them, and of them to the King, were such as God required in his Covenant of him and them.[36]

In Massachusetts the clergy corresponded to the high priest, the magistrates to the king, and the settlers to the people. All covenanted either expressly or tacitly with each other and with God to fulfill religious and political obligations. By contract there was created "one visible body" uniting duties of civil obedience to the designated rulers with obligations of Congregationalist worship.[37]

Ministers as well as magistrates accepted the consensual theory not only on theological but on rational and secular grounds as well. John Cotton (1584–1652), one of the leading clergymen in Massachusetts Bay, expressly cited "the light of nature" as a basis. Thomas Hooker maintained that no man can claim authority over others on grounds of nature except a father over his child, nor can man cite "appointment of God" as a basis, inasmuch as direct revelation no longer occurs. It followed that the foundation of authority is laid firstly in "the free consent" of the people, which to Hooker was "that *sement* which soders" corporate bodies;

the soul "that acts all the parts and particular persons." In a similar
vein, John Winthrop argued that "no man hath lawful power over
another, but by birth or consent." and "the essential forme of a common
weale" lies in "the consent of a certain companie of people to cohabit
together, under one government for their mutual safety and welfare."
When challenged by the claim that such a definition did not apply to a
Christian commonwealth, Winthrop replied: "When I describe a commonwealth in general . . . the churches or christians which are in it, fall
not into consideration . . . for it may be a true body politicke, though
there be neither church nor christian in it. The like may be sayd for the
forme of government, whether it be by patent or otherwise yet it is a
government, so the description of it is safe and true."[38]

Acceptance of the compact theory led to approval of one of its principal implications—the right to resist infringements of the covenant.
Thus John Cotton proclaimed that the people are released from allegiance when they find that their rulers violate "the way of justice and
happiness, which they are sworn to maintain" and go contrary to the
"fundamental Articles of their Covenant." Departing from Calvin's prescription of passive resistance, he thought that in such case it was lawful
for the people "to take up armes of defense."[39]

The fact that men like Winthrop, Cotton, and Hooker could justify the
contractual basis of the state and government on rational and secular
grounds shows how far in this regard they had diverged from the Calvinist conception of total depravity and the explanation of the state solely
as a remedy for sin. If one focuses on this point alone, the difference between John Winthrop and John Wise, who, as we shall see, is celebrated
as an early eighteenth-century proponent of democracy, and even more
between Hooker and Wise, is not great. However, the point can easily
be exaggerated; it must always be remembered that the major emphasis
in the early Puritan thinkers was on the theological aspects of the political covenant establishing a "due form of government," i.e., a Christian
commonwealth.

Under the charter of the Massachusetts Bay Company, John Winthrop
and the ten other stockholders (freemen) who accompanied him to New
England possessed broad authority to establish any form of government
they wished over the other settlers but to make no laws repugnant to the
laws of England. According to Winthrop's most recent biographer, their
dedication to the consensual principle brought them to initiate several
significant changes at the first two meetings of the General Court of the
company. By means of a general vote of all the settlers, the term "freemen" was extended to include all church members. The freemen were
invested under the charter with the power to choose annually the assistants (board of directors) who were now empowered to make laws
and appoint from their membership a governor and a deputy governor.

In 1632 the General Court upon Winthrop's initiative decided that the election of governor and deputy governor should be transferred from the assistants to the freemen. Thus the contractual form was used to transform the joint-stock trading company into a commonwealth and the commercial charter into a political constitution.[40]

Winthrop, of course, was no democrat and no believer in the equality of men. In addition to accepting the distinction between the elect and the unregenerate, he thought that "God Almightie in his most holy and wise providence hath soe disposed of the Condicion of mankinde, as in all times some must be rich some poore, some high and eminent in power in dignitie; others meane and in subjeccion." He believed that the best part of the people was always the least in number. Besides having no warrant in Scripture, he saw democracy as "among most Civill nations accounted the meanest and worst of all formes of government." John Cotton's oft-quoted statement, "Democracy, I do not conceyve that ever God did ordeyne as a fitt government eyther for church or commonwealth. If the people be governors, who shall be governed?" unquestionably summed up the attitude of Puritan clerical and lay leadership. By democracy, however, Cotton and Winthrop understood not popular suffrage but direct popular administration of government. In the words of John Norton they believed that it was "not an Arithmeticall equality but a Geometricall that is to be attended to; that is, not the equality of number but of vertue." In this light, the Puritan leadership aimed at the establishment of a constitutional, aristocratic republic of virtue.[41]

To Winthrop then, the people, or a properly qualified portion of them, possessed only the right to decide the form of government and select their rulers. It must be remembered that the Puritan leaders saw the terms of the political covenant as divinely prescribed. Just as in the church, the people were to be ruled in the state righteously, according to the will of God and in light of His commission to foster the true religion. When in 1639 a public petition was presented to have a state order repealed, Winthrop sternly criticized the action as savoring of resistance to an ordinance of God, "for the people having deputed others, have no power to make or alter laws, but are to be subject; and if any such order seem unlawful or inconvenient, they had better prefer some reasons, etc., to the court with manifestation of their desire to move them to a review, than peremptorily to petition to have it repealed, which amounts to a plain reproof of those whom God hath set over them, and putting dishonor upon them against the tenor of the fifth commandment." In sum, the magistracy was to Winthrop, as it was to Calvin, a divinely appointed office. Combating the "democratic spirit" in 1645 after an unsuccessful attempt to impeach him, he informed the freemen: "The covenant between you and us is the oath you have taken of us, which is to this purpose, that we shall govern you and judge your causes by the rules of God's laws and our own, according to our best skill." Then in a passage which has been called the most skillfully presented enunciation of aristocratic stewardship, Winthrop laid bare the true nature of covenant liberty by joining the political covenant to the covenant of grace and defining both Christian liberty and civil liberty in terms of submission to authority.[42]

There is a twofold liberty, natural (I mean as our nature is now corrupt) and civil or federal. The first is common to man with beasts and other creatures. By this, man, as he stands in relation to man simply, hath liberty to do what he lists: it is a liberty to do evil as well as to do good. This liberty is incompatible and inconsistent with authority, and cannot endure the least restraint of the most just authority. The exercise and maintaining of this liberty makes men grow more evil, and in time to be worse than brute beasts. . . . This is that great enemy of truth and peace, that wild beast, which all of the ordinances of God are bent against, to restrain and subdue it. The other kind of liberty I call civil or federal, it may also be termed moral, in reference to the covenant between God and man, in the moral law, and the politic covenants and constitutions, among men themselves. This liberty is the proper end and object of authority, and cannot subsist without it: and it is a liberty to that only which is good, just, and honest. . . . This liberty is maintained and exercised in a way of subjection to authority; it is of the same kind of liberty wherewith Christ hath made us free. . . . If you stand for your natural corrupt liberties, and will do what is good in your own eyes, you will not endure the least weight of authority . . . but if you will be satisfied to enjoy such civil and lawful liberties, such as Christ allows you, then will you quietly and cheerfully submit unto that authority which is set over you, in all the administrations of it, for your good.[43]

Winthrop made amply clear that the basic terms of the political contract were not established by consent but antedated any agreement as dictates of an absolute moral law reflected in Scripture and reason. From a religious as well as a purely rational point of view his position is unassailable insofar as liberty in an ethical sense cannot be defended as absolute autonomy or spontaneity of choice. Morally speaking, no man has a right (liberty) knowingly to do that which is essentially wrong, unjust, or dishonest. Religiously and ethically oriented persons see themselves liberated and their nature integrated and fulfilled by free adherence to the dictates of moral law. Then, too, Winthrop was on solid ground in holding that men in authority must guide their course by that which is "good, just and honest." What can be objected to in Winthrop's speech is the assumption that the content of what is politically "good, just and honest" and thus binding upon all in the state, can and must be determined solely by the vice-regents of God, the magistrates. Common experience and history inform us that noble and pure men can sharply differ concerning what is right and just in political matters, where the question at issue is seldom so simple that it can be defined in terms of choice between absolute right and absolute wrong. Because of the diversity and complexity of factors involved, a political judgment may be rooted in a more or less informed opinion, intuition, or educated guess of equal worth with any number of alternative courses of action. Recognition of the contingent aspect of politics and the need for settled, known law has prompted the soberest political thinkers from Aristotle on to emphasize both the necessity and desirability of giving to the people a significant voice in their government.

However, to conclude from this that Winthrop sought and practiced "despotic" or "arbitrary" power is unwarranted. He shared John Cotton's Calvinist belief that because "there is a straine in a man's heart that will sometime or other runne out to excesse," it is necessary "that all power that is on earth be limited, Church-power or other." Similarly, he would have undoubtedly subscribed to Samuel Willard's observation: "Where there is Government there must be a Rule." This is borne out in his description of the Massachusetts polity: "The Government of the Massachusetts consists of Magistrates and Freemen: in the one is placed the Aut[horit]ye, in the other the Libertye of the Com[mon] W[ealth] either hath power to Acte, both alone, and both togither, yet by a distinct power, the one of Libertye, the other of Aut[horit]ye: the Freemen Act of them selues in Electinge their magistrates and Officers: the magistrates Acte alone in all occurrences out of Court: and both Acte togither in the Generall Court: yet all limited by certaine Rules, bothe in the greater and smaller affaires: so as the Government is Regular in a mixt Aristocratie, and no waye Arbitrary." Winthrop believed that popular election, the dictates of conscience, the oath of office, the laws of God as contained in Scripture and logical deductions therefrom, as well as the general terms of the political compact, constituted sufficient checks against the magistrates to ensure against arbitrariness. His insistence upon the need for prompt and flexible treatment of problems was based upon the probably correct judgment that a perfectionist pursuit of excessive purity and not excessive liberality posed the greatest danger among the elect in Massachusetts. Thus he argued cogently for leniency and magisterial discretion rather than legislative exactitude. Perry Miller writes that this kind of discretion was not the same as the Stuart claim of prerogative because it did not regard itself as either above the law or as the source of law. Instead, "it was an exercise of rational discipline, of logic and human wisdom, within the broad limits of fundamental law, exactly as orthodox theology was the exercise of logic and intelligence within the confines of revelation."[44]

The movement for codification of the law in Massachusetts was a reaction, easily understood in men of Anglo-Saxon heritage, to the authoritarian, discretionary rule of the magistrates. In valiantly bucking the irresistible tide, Winthrop argued in the spirit of a common law lawyer, maintaining that a code was not feasible because of the lack of sufficient experience of the nature and disposition of the people, the condition of the country and other circumstances which required "that such laws would be fittest for us, which should rise pro re nata. . . ."[45]

Thomas Hooker, whose *Survey of the Summe of Church Discipline* was the most celebrated defense of Congregationalism in New England, and whose thought probably inspired the Fundamental Orders of Connecticut (the contractual basis of that colony's existence as a body politic), took sharp issue with Winthrop. Hooker drew deductions from the concept of covenant which differed from Winthrop's in placing heavier emphasis upon the role of the people (the elect) in both church and state and assigning a more limited role to the magistrates. He attacked discretionary authority as "a way which leads directly to tyranny" and regarded it essential that magistrates be guided by promulgated law which "is not subject to passion" and "not to be taken aside with self seeking ends." In addition, he counseled that the magistrates consult with the people and bow to their judgment "in matters of greater consequence, which concern the common good."[46]

The codification movement resulted in adoption by the General Court of the *Body of Liberties* in 1641 and the *Lawes and Liberties of Massachusetts* in 1648. The *Body of Liberties* resembles the Bills of Rights in present American Constitutions but extends beyond them in describing in one hundred provisions the entire legal system of the colony in terms of "liberties" of freemen, magistrates, churches, women, children, servants, foreigners, and even animals. Guarantees of due process of law, equal justice and freedom from cruel and barbarous punishments, impressment, bond slavery (with certain conditions), arbitrary arrest and imprisonment were provided. The law went in advance of contemporary English liberties in treating of a limited freedom of speech and assembly; in stipulating the number of witnesses requisite to conviction for a capital crime; in providing against double jeopardy in civil courts and for bail; and in pronouncing a restricted privilege against self-incrimination. It also assured the existing system of freehold tenure of land by proscribing the incidents of feudalism. Town government, that unique form of local self-government which had sprung up as a counterpart to the freehold land system in Massachusetts, was also afforded the freemen, along with power to choose annually "select persons" to "order the planting or prudential occasions of (the) Town."[47]

The Code of 1648 (*The Lawes and Liberties of Massachusetts*) reenacted the guarantees of 1641 and codified all existing laws along with new provisions. In one authoritative source, this first comprehensive modern code of laws provided for basic liberties, the conduct of government, commerce, military affairs, church-state relations, as well as the substantive law of crime, property, tort, and domestic relations. The influence of the Bible upon the code was heavy, particularly in regard to the criminal law. However, English local law and customs and the dictates of "the clear light of nature in civil nations," which happily demonstrated that "there is no humane law that tendeth to common good . . . but the same is mediately a law of God . . . ," were of equal importance.[48]

We are admonished by the most recent historian of the development of the law in Massachusetts to disregard previous appraisals of the early period as one "of rude, untechnical, popular law" and one in which "the Scriptures were an infallible guide for both judge and legislator." Instead, the process of growth of the law at this stage "was one of syncretizing, on the basis of reason and experience, traditional English ideas with the precepts of the Bible, with a view always to the urgency of fulfilling the dictates of God's special commission of His commonwealth."[49]

The conservative, Anglo-Saxon character of the New England Way was best indicated in the preamble to the Body of Liberties:

The free fruition of such Liberties, Immunities, Privileges, as Humanity, Civillity and Christianity call for, as due to every Man in his Place and Proportion, without Impeachment and Infringement, hath ever been, and ever will be, the Tranquility and Stability of Churches and Common-wealth, and the denyall or deprival thereof, the disturbance, if not ruine of both.[50]

It will be noted that the liberties and immunities were justified in terms of communal peace and stability and that humanity, civility, and Christianity, in that order, were listed as the bases of the stipulated freedoms. Then, too, the *Body of Liberties* as Perry Miller describes it, was not a declaration of righteousness but a prevention of abuses. In light of these points it is inaccurate to describe Massachusetts as merely a "Bible Commonwealth." However, as in the case of the contractual theory, the document should not be read outside of the context of the federal theology as a prefiguration of Locke, Jefferson, or even John Wise. The secular, rationalistic orientation of a later age could come about only after theology was either placed in a position subordinate to reason or ignored or dismissed.

Finally, the codification movement can be construed as having been motivated by a psychology of legalism which stemmed not only from the Anglo-Saxon heritage of the Puritan but from his federal theology as well. If God voluntarily made his terms explicit in the Covenant and the Bible, why then should man not be governed by an explicit, precise, detailed code of laws? What men like Winthrop regarded as in good part political questions to be dealt with on an *ad hoc* basis by magisterial discretion, the freemen of Massachusetts chose to resolve as legal points.

Puritan Church-State Relations

In tune with the ancient Gelasian theory of the two swords,* the New England Puritan distinguished between church and state on a functional basis while staunchly insisting upon their partnership in the fulfillment of the divine commission to create the true Christian society. The Cambridge Platform declared that church and state must "both stand together and flourish, the one being helpfull unto the other in their distinct and due administrations."[51]

As already mentioned, in the first two generations after the founding of Massachusetts, church members alone could vote. In Connecticut although there was no similar explicit restriction of the suffrage, the same end was achieved by effective ministerial supervision of the electorate. While they were prohibited from holding civil office, ministers and church officers exerted an enormous influence upon the state not only through their sermons but as advisors of civil magistrates and arbitrators of disputes. Winthrop summed it up by remarking, "Ministers have great power with the people, whereby throughe the good correspondency between the magistrates and them they are the more easyly gouerned."[52]

In tune with the principles of Congregationalism, magistrates were forbidden to compel their subjects to become church members and "to meddle with the work proper to church officers." On the other hand, the end of the magistrate's office consisted in "not only the quiet and peaceable life of the subject in matters of righteousness and honesty, but also in matters of godliness." As in Calvin's Geneva, he must enforce the duties prescribed in the first as well as the second table of the Decalogue. John Cotton put it this way: "It is a carnall and worldly, indeed, an ungodly imagination, to confine the Magistrates charge, to the bodies and the goods of the Subjects, and to exclude them from the care of their soules." This did not mean, as the Cambridge Platform made clear, extension of magisterial power to "things meerly inward . . . as unbelief, hardness of heart, erroneous opinions not vented, but only such things as are acted upon by the outward man." But such external actions included idolatry, blasphemy, heresy, "venting corrupt and pernicious opinions . . . open contempt of the word preached, prophanation of the Lord's-Day," and "disturbing the peaceable administration and exercise of the holy things of God." In addition, the magistrate was expected to compel church attendance, collect taxes for church support, and restrain schismatic churches. He also assumed jurisdiction over the recording of

* The two swords theory, propounded by Pope Saint Gelasius I (d. 496), held that spiritual and temporal authority though proceeding from God, are distinct yet not separate, with the spiritual authority possessing greater dignity.

births, marriages, and deaths as well as performing the marriage cere-
mony and granting divorces—all of which in contemporary England
were under ecclesiastical control.[53]

Although much of everyday life came under the restraints of rules of
conduct enforced by the churches, and the institution of the "holy
watch" permitted what by present standards can only be described as an
unwarranted invasion of personal privacy, the relative importance of
church and state renders doubtful the characterization of Massachusetts as a "theocracy," if by that is meant a government wherein the
controlling authority is invested in the clergy. If one notes the facts that
permission to establish new churches had to come from the magistrates,
approval of the magistrates' choice of church officers was customary,
ministers whose pronouncements were displeasing to the magistrates
were subject to censure, and excommunication entailed neither civil dis-
abilities nor deposition from civil office, a plausible case can be made for
the contention that civil authority was ultimately supreme. However,
such contention must always be accompanied by the recognition that
magistrates and ministers were dedicated copartners in the promotion
of a "holy experiment."[54]

Because the Puritan, like most men of the seventeenth century, believed that religion is the formal cause of the state and that uniformity
of belief is a precondition of political unity and sound policy, toleration
of other beliefs was anathema to him. Heresy was a word with a specific
content because truth was plainly evident to the piously informed. Thus
Nathaniel Ward (1578–1652), the conservative clergyman who was
chief compiler of the *Body of Liberties,* maintained that "the State that
will give Liberty of Conscience in matters of Religion must give Liberty
of Conscience and Conversation in their Morall Lawes." Likewise a "State
which will permit Errors in Religion, shall admit Errors in Policy un-
avoydably." Sounding a note which accorded with the thought of non-
perfectionists like Winthrop, Ward declared: "Experience will teach
Churches and Christians, that it is farre better to live in a State united,
though somewhat Corrupt, than in a State, whereof some Part is Incorrupt, and all the rest divided."[55]

Perfectionism implied unqualified separatism and anarchy with all
of their baleful consequences for social and religious order. The Puritan
leaders had no intention of presiding over the dissolution of their "due
forme of Government" into an unstructured babel of small sects of
"saints" seeking perfection in this world or acting as a law unto themselves. They had long since opted for the unity embodied in the spotted
actuality of the state against the uncompromising purity of an insular
sectarianism. It is in light of these points that the expulsions of Roger
Williams and Anne Hutchinson and the proscriptive laws against Baptists and Quakers must be viewed.

The Antinomianism of Anne Hutchinson (1591–1643), a brilliant woman greatly influenced by the sermons of John Cotton, which she interpreted literally, struck directly at the heart of Puritan orthodoxy and
convulsed the colony by denying that God's revealed will can be discovered only through the Bible, and asserting the heresy of immediate
personal revelation. Maintaining that sanctification (good works) could
not constitute evidence of justification, Mrs. Hutchinson and her avid
followers contended that any justified person could readily perceive if
another person was divinely elected. For those visited directly by the
Holy Spirit and thus justified, the implication was that they were no
longer subject to the law—moral or civil. Thus the court which tried her
declared that "she walked by such a rule as cannot stand with the
peace of any State; for by such bottomlesse revelations . . . if they be allowed in one thing, must be admitted a rule in all things: for they being
above reason and Scripture, they are not subject to controll."[56]

Along with the Baptists and Quakers, Anne Hutchinson had a conception of conscience radically different from that of the federal theologians. Hers was akin to a mystical, intuitive insight; theirs relied on the rational faculty, which can be informed from without. If we empty the
term of its original pejorative content, Anne Hutchinson, the Quakers
and the Baptists, and to a lesser degree, Williams, can legitimately be
called enthusiasts. Ronald Knox tells us that the essence of enthusiasm is
"ultrasupernaturalism" in that the enthusiast expects more evident results from God's grace than do most Christians. The enthusiast notes
what effects religion *can* have in completely altering a man's life and sets
up these exceptional cases as the standard of religious achievement. He
has ever before him as a model the primitive church visibly informed by
supernatural influences. He is long on piety and short on theology.
Whereas to the Congregationalist Puritan, the Bible, subject to scholarly
interpretation, was infallible, to the enthusiast the Bible is infallible only
when interpreted by a divinely inspired person. Similarly, whereas the
Puritan looked to a learned ministry, the enthusiast looks to a prophetic
one. The ideal of the enthusiast is a society of the pure who are moved
solely by the grace of God. The visible church and state are compromises
with corruption, at the most to be tolerated, never to be completely accepted. The state stands in the corrupt realm of nature; the community of saints is in the sublime realm of grace. If one accepts the
premises of the Puritan leaders, all of these considerations render understandable their strong reaction to any manifestation of enthusiasm.[57]

Samuel Eliot Morison reminds us that to duplicate in modern times
the offense of Anne Hutchinson, one must think of a female preacher
propounding communism and free love, attacking the churches, the
Constitution, and the courts, and with a following composed of four-
fifths of the people in the Boston metropolitan area, including a goodly

number of zealots ready to act to implement her teaching. Even given a very liberal interpretation of the "clear and present danger" test, it is difficult to imagine such a person escaping conviction in the 1950's under a state criminal anarchy law or the Smith Act.[58]

It should also be noted that Winthrop's victory at the trial has recently been called "an unsavory triumph of arbitrary power." Doubtless, by present standards her trial fell far short of procedural fairness. But by the standards of early seventeenth-century English law wherein a criminal trial was essentially a contest between the accused and the prosecutor and his witnesses, and the rules of evidence were strongly weighted against the accused, she was afforded more than a "fair" trial.[59]

Roger Williams: Prophet of Religious Liberty

The separatist perfectionism of Roger Williams (1603–1683) the clergyman-founder of Rhode Island and protégé of the great British jurist, Sir Edward Coke, rang out strongly in his admonition to John Winthrop: "Abstract yourself with a holy violence from the Dung heape of this Earth." Williams' quest for purity brought him not merely to challenge the church in Massachusetts for not separating from the "antichristian" Church of England and enlisting the aid of the state, but also for enforcing the first table of the Decalogue and tendering oaths to unregenerate men. Tenaciously adhering to these convictions, he was banished in 1635 as a subverter of both polities. In Rhode Island Williams initially pursued his separatism to the point of refusing to receive Communion with anyone but his wife, of whose Christian purity he probably had good reason to be assured. Had he gone further he would have reached the *reductio ad absurdum* of separatism—religious and social solipsism.* But he chose not to withdraw from the "dung heap"; instead he strove to find the means to restrain the state from polluting the neverending quest for perfection and truth of the individual Christian.[60]

Contrary to commonly entertained opinion, the categories of Williams' mind were theological and not social in nature. We distort the truth if we paint his portrait with the brush of modern liberalism. He was ever a convinced Calvinist who did not proceed, as one of his biographers claims, from a newly found faith embodying "the certainty of uncertainty" and "disbelief in the unproved." His "seekerism" extended only to the question of the character of the true church, its organization, its form of worship, and its discipline. Though he believed God's favor had granted him adequate light to reject any unseparated church body, he lamented that he had not been sufficiently enlightened to detect the true church. As a consequence he advocated a prophetic rather than a "hire-

---

* Solipsism is the theory that the self can know only its own states or that the self is the only existent thing.

ling" ministry, a ministry which was before and independent of any organized body of believers. It followed that a marked inequality existed among Christian believers, with one's rank in the scale dependent upon the degree of enlightenment afforded him. Similarly, the democratic principle of compact could not be accepted as a vehicle by which the true church was born or properly governed. Williams' theology, like that of the men of Massachusetts, was aristocratic and definitely not democratic. However, unlike Cotton and Winthrop, he was not led to construct a blueprint of civil polity in accordance with this view. Not that he did not ultimately justify his political thought in terms of theology, but that to him the aristocracy of the virtuous was limited to the order of grace.[61]

Williams' case for separation of church and state and freedom of conscience and toleration of all beliefs or unbeliefs which do not manifest themselves in external acts inimical to public peace rested on the following two distinctions. First, toleration must be afforded by the Christian to unbelievers because of the unique character of the Christian faith, the impossibility of compelling God to bestow His grace upon any but those of his choice, and because the end of the state is peace and order. Second, concerning Christians themselves, "God's people were and ought to be Nonconformitants" and toleration should be afforded all, not because of the essential equality of all faiths but because the nature of the true church is as yet unknown and every good Christian must be presumed to be seeking it. Even if the character of the true church were known, because the realm of man's spirit is sacrosanct and never to be invaded by the restraining power of the state, separation of church and state and civil toleration would still be required.[62]

Williams' nonhistorical, typological reading of the Bible brought him to reject the notion that a covenanted chosen people could exist after the resurrection of Christ. Cutting directly athwart the thought of Winthrop, Cotton, and Hooker, who saw the Old Testament as a guidebook of correct political organization and conduct, Williams maintained that the New Testament substituted ministerial spiritual condemnation for state punishment of violations. In the new dispensation the magistrate exists to preserve peace and order, being concerned only with the external acts of men as they bear upon that end. On these grounds Williams engaged in his polemical jousts with John Cotton over conscience and toleration. His perfectionism is clearly mirrored in a letter answering Cotton in 1644, wherein he proclaimed: "When they have opened a gap in the hedge or wall of Separation between the Garden of the Church and the Wildernes of the world, God hath ever broke down the wall itself, removed the Candlestick . . . and made his Garden a Wildernesse, as at this day. And that therefore if he will ever please to restore His Garden and Paradice again, it must of necessitie be walled in peculiarly unto himselfe from the world; and that all that shall be saved out of the world are to be transplanted out of the Wilderness of the world, and added unto his Church or Garden."[63]

In his works on the "Bloudy Tenent" of persecution, Williams answered Cotton's contention that because the few essentials of true doctrine are so clear and simple that any man of reason will embrace them upon proper explanation by a competent minister, if a person after twice being correctively instructed and admonished persists in obdurate error, he must be prosecuted by the state not for the cause of conscience but for sinning against his own conscience. Basing his rebuttal on Scripture, the secular end of the state and expediency, Williams went on to assert that a church stood juridically as one among many voluntary associations within the body politic:

The *Church* or *company of worshippers* (whether true or false) is like unto a Body or Colledge of *Phystians* in a *Citie;* like unto a *Corporation, Society,* or *Company* of *East-Indie* or *Turkie-Merchants,* or any other *Societie* or Company in London: which Companies may hold their *Courts,* keep their *Records,* hold *disputations;* and in matters concerning their *Societie,* may dissent, divide, breake into *Schismes* and *Factions,* sue and implead each other at the *Law,* yea wholly breake up and dissolve into pieces and nothing, and yet the *peace* of the *Citie* not be in the least measure impaired or disturbed; because the *essence* or being of the *Citie,* and so the *well-being* and *peace* thereof is essentially distinct from those particular *Societies;* the *Citie-Courts, Citie-lawes, Citie-punishments* distinct from theirs. The *Citie* was before them, and stands absolute and *intire,* when such a *Corporation* or *Societie* is taken down.[64]

The following points are evident upon analysis of the above quotation and its implications.

1. The state, which is in the order of nature, exists to promote the common good ("well-being and peace") of its members, irrespective of their voluntary associations and the particular ends thereof.

2. The common good presupposes the voluntary principle, not only as the source of public authority and the foundation of the state's legitimacy, but as the basis of less inclusive or nonpolitical associations as well.

3. The common good of the state is distinct from the birth and dissolution of voluntary associations.

4. Each of the voluntary religious associations is to be held equal before the law.

5. The common good demands separation of church and state.

Williams was Calvinistic in regarding the state as necessary because of man's wickedness, Aristotelian in viewing it as a natural entity, and modern and secular in departing from the Augustinian ideal of a *Respublica Christiana.* However, a strong case can be made for the contention that he posed too sharp a disjunction between the state and religion.

If, as men like Winthrop and Cotton believed, a political order, unless imposed or maintained by constraint alone, is an institutionalized representation of a basic truth or body of related truths, much, if not all, depends upon the underlying beliefs of a people. Accepting this, one would have to conclude, using an example cited by Williams, that once the worship of Diana was removed in Ephesus that city was restructured —clearly or confusedly, it matters not—upon a new principle or principles, and thus radically transformed. Coming closer to home, just as the Massachusetts due form of civil government represented the truth embodied principally in the federal theology, Rhode Island reflected Williams' theological belief that because Christ severed religion from the state, civil toleration and freedom of conscience constitute necessary conditions of the true faith and church. Although his "Bloudy Tenent" indicated that the Christian magistrate has the same duties as a non-Christian or pagan ruler, a frequently overlooked work of his, *The Hireling Ministry none of Christ's,* published in 1652, propounded a view which puts his earlier pronouncement more squarely in consonance with his theology:

The first grand design of Christ Jesus is to destroy and consume His mortal enemy, AntiChrist. This must be done by the breath of His mouth in His Prophets and Witnesses: Now the Nations of the world have impiously stopt this heavenly breath, stifled the Lord Jesus in his servants. Now if it shall please the civil state to remove the state bars, set up to resist the holy spirit of God in his servants (whom yet finally to resist, is not in all powers of the world) I humbly conceive that the civil state hath made a fair progress in promoting the Gospel of Jesus Christ.[65]

It would seem to follow logically that because the Christian is interested in promoting the Gospel of Christ and because civil tolerance and freedom of conscience further that end, a Christian magistrate is duty-bound to establish freedom of conscience as a civil norm, with separation of church and state as its necessary, implementing corollary. That this is a correct construction of Williams' thought is evident in his amplifying remarks, wherein he stated that "the civil state is bound before God to take off that bond and yoke of soul-oppression and to proclaim free and impartial liberty to all the people . . . to choose and maintain that worship and ministry their souls and consciences are persuaded of." He deemed this "an act most suiting with the piety and Christianity of the holy testament of Christ Jesus." The state was also expected to provide for the security of all the respective consciences in their respective assemblies. Finally, Williams thought it to be "the duty of all that are in authority . . . to countenance, encourage, and supply such true volunteers as give and devote themselves to the service and ministry of Christ Jesus in any kind." In such manner he believed that peace and unity would be furthered and that the criticism that his views were disruptive of both was effectively rebutted.[66]

Liberty of conscience, although fundamental to Williams, did not justify defiance of rightly constituted authority. Instead of being an absolute right or license, Williams saw it as limited in its application by the just demands of the state in the promotion of the common good:

There goes many a ship to sea, with many hundred souls in one ship, whose weale and woe is common, and is a true picture of a commonwealth, or a human combination or society. It hath fallen out sometimes, that both papists and protestants, Jews and Turks, may be embarked in one ship; upon which supposal I affirm, that all the liberty of conscience, that ever I pleaded for, turns upon these two hinges—that none of the papists, protestants, Jews, or Turks, be forced to come to the ship's prayers or worship, nor compelled from their own particular prayers of worship, if they practice any. I further add, that I never denied, that notwithstanding this liberty, the commander of this ship ought to command the ship's course, yea, and also command that justice, peace and sobriety, be kept and practised, both among the seamen and all passengers. If any of the seamen refuse to perform their services, or passengers to pay their freight; if any refuse to help, in person and purse, towards the common charges and defence; if any refuse to obey the common laws and orders of the ship, concerning their common peace or preservation; if any shall mutiny and rise up against their commanders and officers; if any should preach or write that there ought to be no commanders and officers, because all are equal in Christ, therefore no masters nor officers, no laws nor orders, nor corrections nor punishments;—I say, I never denied, but in such cases, whatever is pretended, the commander or commanders may judge, resist, compel and punish such transgressors, according to their deserts and merits.[67]

Like his fellow New England Calvinists, Williams believed that rightly constituted authority was established by consent of the governed. The people as artificers of government erect the form they regard as most fitting their civil condition. Such governments possess no more power and for no longer time than the people by consent agree upon. He considered this as "cleere not only in *Reason,* but in the experience of all commonweales, where the people are not deprived of their *naturall freedome* by the power of Tyrants." Because Williams rejected the federal theology and espoused liberty of conscience, his political contractualism, although recognizing that all authority is ultimately from God, differed from that of the Puritan Congregationalists in putting more emphasis upon reason and experience. As already mentioned, he would not implement politically his conception of spiritual aristocracy. To him, men stood in relation to the state not as believers or nonbelievers nor as saints or sinners, but simply as men. Spiritually unequal, they must be treated as political equals if the Christian Gospel is to be effectuated and promoted and reason satisfied. If a distinction was to be made between men, Williams would allow that men as heads of families alone be given the suffrage.[68]

Williams' notion of contractualism and his rejection of ecclesiastical polity as a model for the state precluded an acceptance of the mixed state. The establishment by "the major parte of the Colonie" in 1647 of a "DEMOCRATICALL" form of government, that is, "a Government held by ye free and voluntarie consent of all, or the greater parte of the free Individuals," without religious qualifications, reflected his thought. Annually elected officers possessed executive and judicial duties but the General Court became the superior agency of government, and a primitive form of initiative, referendum, and recall was instituted for use by the component towns. At this time a general code of laws and liberties was also drawn up and promulgated. A striking feature of this code was that it refused to allow any semblance of regal or magisterial prerogative; its framework was regarded as containing a complete listing of laws; any subsequent modifications by the legislature were to represent merely further attempts to state, within the outline of the code, the nature of laws adaptable to the colony. The influence of Williams is most particularly evident in the fact that the Bible was not used as a source; instead English precedents served as the basis.[69]

Two other facets of Williams' thought as exemplified in the institutions of Rhode Island deserve mention. In order that they endure and work he believed that democratic government, separation of church and state, and liberty of conscience needed to be supplemented by equality of opportunity in ownership of land and by the spirit of compromise as embodied in arbitration of disputes without governmental sanctions. In regard to land, Williams appears to have anticipated the thesis of the British thinker James Harrington that the manner in which land is distributed in society greatly influences, if not determines, the form of government. Political democracy, in Williams' eye, could not flourish without a broad distribution of land. Concerning compromise through arbitration, Williams demonstrated political sagacity in perceiving that the motley, roisterous, pluralistic, open society of Rhode Island could not well function without the give and take of mutual accommodation.[70]

We are told by a recent commentator that in establishing a separation of church and state Williams "solved the most perplexing political problem of his age by demonstrating that it was not political at all."[71] He urged secularization of the state in the hope that man's natural conscience would serve as a sufficient foundation for civil order. And yet, given his temper of mind and intensely religious disposition, it was but natural that the virtues he demanded of society remained staunchly Christian. A nonreligious society as the underpinning for the secular state appears never to have entered into his calculations. In light of all these factors, it is quite unwarranted to explain Williams' thought in terms of modern liberal and democratic theory.

In conclusion, it must be said that if Roger Williams was a democrat it was primarily because he regarded political democracy as the most feasible mode of government to implement the all-important principle of liberty of conscience. Because the state confronts only the natural man and has no concern with the order of grace, liberty of conscience and its adjunct, separation of church and state, could best be implemented in a political system which, given the conditions of Rhode Island, regarded all men as equal.

The Decline of the City

Congregationalism in New England was an attempt to institutionalize outwardly the ranks of the invisible church by bringing proven saints into a church covenant and polity and giving them the reins of political government. It was thought that this arrangement, effected through the voluntary principle, would coordinate in the "City upon a Hill" Christian liberty and social order. However, doubts about the infallibility of the means of identifying the elect were present from the beginning in New England. Given man's capacity for self-delusion and his propensity to dissemble, it was inevitable that hypocrisy would intrude to threaten the basic premise. Recognizing the existence of hypocrisy, John Cotton attempted to rationalize it on religious and expediential grounds, maintaining that "Hypocrites give God part of his due, the outward man, but the prophane person giveth neither outward nor inward man," and that while hypocrites maintain their hypocrisy, they are "serviceable and useful in their callings." Thus hypocrisy could be used in the City on a Hill for the benefit of society! Such an attitude led inevitably to a formalism which the Congregationalist Puritan abominated when manifested in similar manner in Presbyterianism and Anglicanism.[72]

The early expectation that the main problem in Massachusetts would be to keep people out of the church was upset within a generation by the need to sustain the life as well as the purity of the church. Acceptance by the English Puritan Independents of a limited principle of toleration dropped the intolerant New England Congregationalists from their proud position in the forefront of Protestantism to a defensive posture which made it necessary to keep and extend a strong church membership. The Cambridge Platform, which admitted the possibility of hypocrisy, provided that "the weakest *measure* of faith" is sufficient for admission to church membership and admonished against "severity of examination." In the second half of the seventeenth century the so-called half-way covenant allowed baptized but unconverted children of church members to make upon adulthood an external acceptance of the covenant in order to bring about the baptism and church membership of their own children. By 1684 the principle was extended to permit into half-way membership those who theretofore were outside the covenant, but who now were prepared to make the external profession of obligation. Thus the descendants of the early settlers, who believed their errand into the wilderness was made to set up a society which distinguished between the elect and the unregenerate while not losing sight of man's omnipresent imperfections, under the press of circumstances made concessions which saved the form of church membership while surrendering much of its substance.[73]

Economic factors also played an important role in the reshaping of the colony and the church. After the first decade of the settlements, in which the colonists lived principally off the specie and goods brought in by immigrants, a pressing problem was posed when the civil wars in the homeland shut off immigration. By necessity the New Englanders turned diligently to trade and, in Perry Miller's words, the "sacred cod" became a symbol second only to the Bible. Commerce, ever a deadly enemy of a closed, static society, worked to open up the tightly knit community and by 1675 the sumptuary laws and the fixing of wages and prices, which had been insisted upon so forcibly by John Cotton in the early days, had become anachronisms and lapsed into desuetude.[74]

As the growing merchant class became a powerful vested interest so did the clergy, and a heavier premium came to be put upon power rather than upon purity. After the ministers through deft political maneuvering influenced an election in 1671, they found many of their church members intractable. The lay leaders began to use their power to influence the church despite, and independently of, the ministers. As Urian Oakes saw it, the form of the church polity remained, but the rule of the clergy had become a shadow.[75]

Thus by the turn of the century the city on a hill was in embattled disarray, besieged by a rationalism that was eroding the central idea that theology is the norm of reason, and by economic and political forces, and sapped by a worldly lust for power and a never-ending need to compromise on fundamentals. The external call, even without the internal efficacy of grace, was now sufficient for church membership. Toleration of Protestants was required by the new charter of 1691 and church membership was prohibited as a qualification for suffrage. Christian liberty, the foundation upon which the founders established New England, existed on a precarious basis in a society of church and state which was realistically recognized as standing midway between the endpoints of sin and salvation. In this attitude the city no longer could pretend to be the beacon lighting the way for the fulfillment of the Protestant promise.

Contributions of Puritanism to American Political Thought

The Puritan was prompted by his theology, by his social outlook, and by his considerations of sound policy, to reject outright the basic liberal values of the equality of men, toleration of diverse religious beliefs, and what he called "mere democracy" as a desirable form of government. Concentration on these points alone would render purely antiquarian any study of Puritan political thought. However, even the most unfavorable judge of the Puritans among American intellectual historians, Vernon Louis Parrington, could not lose sight of their emphasis upon such progressive values as individualism and the covenant theory of church and state. He attempted to explain the apparent incongruity by citing a suggestion of Harriet Beecher Stowe to the effect that the Puritan immigrants inherited their theology from the sixteenth century and their politics from the seventeenth century. A "reactionary theology" thus "snuggled down side by side in their minds with a later democratic conception of state and society."[76] Outside of the false identification of New England theology with sixteenth-century Calvinism, Parrington's observation is in error because, as we have seen, it was not a question of two incompatible approaches juxtaposed in the mind, but of theology and political thought reciprocally influencing and reinforcing each other. In the process Puritan political thought was appreciably theologized and Puritan theology considerably politicized. Consequently, one cannot be studied or considered apart from the other, and credit and discredit cannot be parceled out by labeling "political," what one deems "liberal" in Puritan thought, and "theological" what one considers "reactionary" or "absolutist."

Nor can one overlook the fact that New England Puritan thought was a European import, modified as time went on by the reactions of the settlers to the new and greatly different environment. But one must take care to stop short of declaiming that changes were effected because the land gave its law to the settlement. As others have pointed out before, if this were true, why did not the land give the same law to the French settlers in Quebec? The most satisfactory explanation of the development and decline of American Puritan thought lies in the interplay of the imported ideas, institutions, and traditions with the land and with the challenge of new ideas.

In light of these considerations, an appraisal of the contributions of Puritanism to constitutional-democratic thought and practice in America must emphasize the following points:

1. Although the Puritan spurned the idea of the equality of all men, he did emphasize as a Christian *the dignity of each individual* and *the ultimate autonomy of the individual conscience.*

2. The Puritan usually identified the conscience with the rational faculty which can be informed from without. This allowed for the *recognition of an objective higher law* which he equated with the divine law as specifically enunciated in Scripture and as supplemented by the deductions of reason. In no sense was law conceived of as merely the product of the will of the sovereign; instead, the test of positive law was its agreement or disagreement with the higher, divine law.

3. Political authority, to the Puritan, derived from the political compact as an analogue of the church covenant and as a dictate of reason. The principle of the *consent of the governed* as the basis of legitimacy in American political thought goes back, in part, to the theological conception of covenant. Every responsible Puritan leader paid at least lip service to this principle; Hooker and Winthrop in Connecticut and Massachusetts Bay used it either to establish or to give legitimacy to their bodies politic. Thus in the state as well as the church, the Puritan turned from a hierarchy of status to a hierarchy of contract.

4. Recognition of the dignity of the individual together with the conception of a higher law with a specific content underlying the terms of the political compact resulted in the idea of *limited government,* which is the essence of *constitutionalism.*

5. These points, when added to the lingering Calvinist conception of total depravity and the notion of the mixed church polity as a model, led to acceptance of a "balanced aristocracy" as the best form of government. In this manner, at the very beginning of American history, great emphasis was put upon the need for adequate institutional arrangements to arrest, check, and canalize the ubiquitous lust for power in men.

6. The *moral right to resist* unjust exercises of governmental power was deduced from the ideas and principles underlying and informing constitutionalism. If a political command contravened the higher law and thus went beyond the limit of contractually designated power, the people had no recourse as Christian men but to resist.

7. Emphasis upon the Bible as the primary guide for human activity led to a *literalism* in approach which pervaded all of life, including the political. The American propensity to emphasize and rely upon the written word of basic law can be traced back, at least in part, to this aspect of Puritanism.

8. A heavy reliance upon the federal theology, upon a literal interpretation of the Bible, and upon his Anglo-Saxon legal heritage, led the Puritan to *legalism.* Legalism issued in a heightened emphasis upon the *rule of law* and a firm desire to limit the discretion of officials to a minimum. The eminent English historian, Sir Lewis Namier, once sagely remarked that "the Anglo-Saxon mind, like the Jewish, is inclined to legalism." This observation particularly fits the Puritan, whom Parrington correctly characterized as a "Hebraized Englishman."[77] The legalistic

concept of contract, which bound both God and man, and the insistence upon detailed codes of positive law were expressions of this disposition. The American tendency to reduce political issues to legal questions to be resolved definitively by courts of law has its roots in this psychology. To conclude further that the doctrine and practice of judicial review also spring from the attitude would strain the truth somewhat. However, acceptance of a promulgated higher law, plus an emphasis upon the terms of the compact and the colonial charter as fundamental, when enlivened by a psychology of legalism, indicates a stage on the way to the ultimate acceptance of that later great invention of American political science, judicial review.

9. Rejection by the Puritan of a feudal, hierarchical society and establishment by him of the institution of *freehold land tenure* provided an *economic basis for free government,* which appears to have been most realized in town government.

10. Because he rejected "enthusiasm" and valued the intellect as a means by which the divine plan could be both better known and propounded by him, the Puritan emphasized the need for *general public education.* Thus a vital *intellectual and moral precondition of free government* was institutionalized early in New England.

One is sorely tempted to add to the above list the willingness to compromise, which was exemplified in John Winthrop and in the later measures taken to maintain a high church membership. However, Winthrop was limited in his discretion by the successful codification movement and the membership compromises were not peculiar to Puritanism but were concessions on fundamentals dictated by necessity. Thus, at best, compromise as a vehicle of adjustment in life can only be conjecturally imputed to the New England Puritan.

An appraisal of the contributions of Puritanism to American constitutional-democratic thought and practice must also point up the legacy left by such dissenters as Roger Williams, who shared the same basic theological premises as the men of Massachusetts and Connecticut but differed concerning their implementation. Williams emphasized primarily *religious toleration* and *separation of church and state.* If the institutions of Rhode Island are a valid criterion, he also evidenced a more favorable attitude toward a rudimentary *political democracy* along with a greater readiness to compromise than did his contemporaries to the north. One is again tempted to conclude that Williams showed us the way in which people of diverse religious beliefs can live together in a semblance of order. But it appears that his conceptions of toleration and separation of church and state, which, it will be remembered, flowed from his religious seekerism, had little influence upon the later development and fructification of those important principles of contemporary American life.

In sum, then, with the exception of dissenters like Williams, New England Puritan thought pointed away from democracy in disdaining the principles of the equality of men, religious toleration, and the democratic form of government and in emphasizing in its early phases, broad magisterial discretion. It pointed toward democracy in emphasizing individualism, the political compact, freehold land tenure and general education. More importantly, it pointed toward modern American constitutionalism by emphasizing individualism, the higher law, the political compact, limited government, the mixed state, the moral right to resist, the rule of law, and a literalistic, legalistic approach to affairs of government. In light of these points, one must conclude that the contribution of Puritanism to American constitutional democratic thought is indeed considerable.

NOTES

1. "A Modell of Christian Charity," *Winthrop Papers* (Mass. Historical Society, 1931), II, 295, 293.
2. "The Babylonian Captivity," *American Edition of Luther's Works*, J. Pelikan and H. Lehman (eds.), 55 vols. (in preparation) (St. Louis and Philadelphia), XXXVI, 70.
3. Sheldon Wolin, *Politics and Vision* (Boston, 1960), p. 171. I am particularly indebted to Wolin's interpretation. For other general treatments of Luther's thought see J. W. Allen, *A History of Political Thought in the Sixteenth Century* (London, 1060), pp. 15–30 and D. B. Forrester "Luther and Calvin," in L. Strauss and J. Cropsey (eds.), *History of Political Philosophy* (Chicago, 1963), pp. 277–313, and William A. Mueller, *Church and State in Luther and Calvin* (Garden City, 1965).
4. See Luther's "Disputation Against the Scholastic Theology," in T. G. Tappert, ed., *Selected Writings of Martin Luther, 1517–1520* (Philadelphia, 1967), pp. 29–42.
5. Calvin, *Institutes of the Christian Religion*, trans. John Allen (Philadelphia, 1936, 2 vols.), II, 478 (iv, x, 29); the second quotation from Calvin can be found in Perry Miller, *The New England Mind: From Colony to Province* (Boston, 1953, paperback 1961), p. 103. For general treatments of Calvin see Wolin, *op. cit.*, pp. 165–194; Allen, *op. cit.*, pp. 49–72; Forrester, *op. cit.*, and Mueller, *op. cit.* For a convenient collection of Calvin's remarks on the political order, see John T. McNeill (ed.), *John Calvin on God and Political Duty* (New York, 1956).
6. *Institutes*, I, 294 (II, ii, 13).
7. *Institutes*, II, 772, 773, (IV, xx, 1).
8. *Ibid.*, pp. 770–806 (IV, xx, 1–22).
9. Richard Hooker, *Of the Laws of Ecclesiastical Politie* (London, 1617), 8 books.
10. On Puritanism in general see especially Michael Walzer, *The Revolution of the Saints* (Cambridge, Mass., 1965); William Haller, *Liberty and Reformation in the Puritan Revolution* (New York, 1955); Alan Simpson, *Puritanism in Old and New England* (Chicago, 1955); Perry Miller, *The New England Mind: The Seventeenth Century* (New York, 1939), and *The New England Mind: From Colony to Province* (Cambridge, Mass., 1953); Stow Persons, *American Minds* (New York, 1958), 3–43; and Ralph Barton Perry, *Puritanism and Democracy* (New York, 1944, paperback 1964), pp. 62–116.
11. Perry Miller, *Orthodoxy in Massachusetts (1630–1650)* (Cambridge, Mass., 1933), p. 53.
12. *Ibid.*, pp. 38, 39.

13. Cited in *ibid.*, p. 34.

14. *Ibid.*, p. 47.

15. *Ibid.*, p. 36.

16. *Ibid.*, pp. 54, 55, 56, 58; for a statement of Browne's congregational principles see Williston Walker, *The Creeds and Platforms of Congregationalism* (New York, 1893), pp. 1–27.

17. *Ibid.*, pp. 63–64.

18. The Mayflower Compact (Nov. 11, 1620) can be found in B. P. Poore (ed.), *The Federal and State Constitutions,* Part I, p. 931.

19. Miller, *Orthodoxy in Massachusetts,* pp. 83, 87, 91, 100; The First Charter of Massachusetts (March 4, 1629) can be found in F. N. Thorpe (ed.), *Federal and State Constitutions,* III, 1846ff.

20. J. A. Froude, "Calvinism," in *Short Studies on Great Subjects* (New York, 1871; second series), pp. 10–11.

21. Perry Miller, *The New England Mind: The Seventeenth Century,* pp. 367–369, 373; Perry Miller, *Errand Into the Wilderness* (Cambridge, Mass., 1956, paperback ed., 1964), pp. 56–58.

22. *The New England Mind: The Seventeenth Century,* pp. 369–371, 373.

23. *Ibid.*, pp. 374–378, 405, 407; *Errand Into the Wilderness,* pp. 60–63.

24. *The New England Mind: The Seventeenth Century,* pp. 384, 389.

25. *Ibid.*, pp. 379–384, 395; *Errand Into the Wilderness,* pp. 63–68.

26. *The New England Mind: The Seventeenth Century,* pp. 397, 142–143, 192; *Errand Into the Wilderness,* pp. 70–71, 82.

27. *The New England Mind: The Seventeenth Century,* pp. 157, 193–194.

28. On the Puritan church covenant see *ibid.*, pp. 432–462.

29. Thomas Hooker, *A Survey of the Summe of Church Discipline* (London, 1648), Part I, p. 78.

30. *The New England Mind: The Seventeenth Century,* p. 444.

31. *Orthodoxy in Massachusetts,* pp. 168, 172–173.

32. *Ibid.*, p. 178; the Hooker quotation can be found in Persons, *op. cit.*, p. 30.

33. "The Cambridge Synod and Platform," in Walker, *op. cit.*, pp. 233–234; *Orthodoxy in Massachusetts,* pp. 191–193.

34. *Orthodoxy in Massachusetts,* p. 186; *The New England Mind: The Seventeenth Century,* p. 452.

35. *The New England Mind: The Seventeenth Century,* pp. 416–417.

36. Cited in *ibid.*, p. 415.

37. *Ibid.*

38. *Ibid.*, p. 423, 408–409; *A Survey of the Summe of Church Discipline,* Part I, p. 50; R. C. Winthrop, *Life and Letters of John Winthrop* (Boston, 1864–1867), II, 432; *The Hutchinson Papers* (Albany, 1865) I, 97. See also T. H. Breen, *The Character of a Good Ruler* (New Haven, 1970), a study of Puritan ideas which came to my attention too late to be drawn upon in writing this chapter.

39. Cited in *The New England Mind: The Seventeenth Century,* p. 410.

40. Edmund S. Morgan, *The Puritan Dilemma: The Story of John Winthrop* (Boston, 1958), pp. 84, 85, 89, 90, 91–94.

41. John Winthrop, "A Modell of Christian Charitie," *Winthrop Papers,* II, 282; Letter of John Cotton to Lord Say and Seal (1636), in Lawrence Mayo, ed., *Hutchinson's History of Massachusett's Bay* (Cambridge, Mass., 1936), I, 415; Norton's statement is cited in George Lee Haskins, *Law and Authority in Early Massachusetts* (New York, 1960), p. 46. See also Katherine B. Brown, "A Note on the Puritan Concept of Aristocracy," *Mississippi Valley Historical Review* XLI (1954), 105–112, for a clarification of Cotton's and Winthrop's conception of democracy.

42. *The Journal of John Winthrop* (May 22, 1639), in E. F. Jameson (ed.), *Original Narratives of Early American History* (New York, 1908, 2 vols.), I, 303; II, 238; Vernon Louis Parrington, *Main Currents in American Thought* (New York, 1927, 1930, 3 vols.), I, 49.

43. *Journal of John Winthrop* (May 14, 1645), II, 238f.

44. John Cotton, "Limitation of Government," in *An Exposition Upon the Thir-*

teenth Chapter of Revelation (London, 1655), pp. 71–73, reprinted in Perry Miller and Thomas H. Johnson (eds.), *The Puritans* (New York, 1938, paperback ed., 1963), p. 213; Willard is cited in *The New England Mind: The Seventeenth Century*, p. 410; *Winthrop Papers*, IV, 482; *The New England Mind: The Seventeenth Century*, p. 424. See discussion in Haskins, *op. cit.*, pp. 120–121.

45. *Journal of John Winthrop* (September, 1639), I, 323f.

46. Hooker to John Winthrop, May, 1637, *Winthrop Papers*, IV, 81, 82. Hooker is celebrated as a democrat by Parrington, I, 53–62, and by James T. Adams in *The Founding of New England* (Boston, 1921). Perry Miller shows the great similarity in thought between men like Winthrop and Hooker in his "Thomas Hooker and the Democracy of Connecticut," in *Errand Into the Wilderness*, pp. 16–47. Clinton Rossiter attempts to sketch Hooker midway between the two viewpoints in his *Seedtime of the Republic* (New York, 1953), pp. 159–178.

47. *The Body of Liberties* can be found in W. H. Whitmore (ed.), *The Colonial Laws of Massachusetts* (Boston, 1887), pp. 22–61; *The Laws and Liberties* (1648) can be found in M. Farrand (ed.), *The Laws and Liberties of Massachusetts* (Cambridge, Mass., 1929), Chap. 8.

48. *Laws and Liberties*, Epistle, cited by Haskins, *op. cit.*, at p. 160.

49. Haskins, *op. cit.*, pp. 7, 188. See also Thorp L. Wolford, "The Laws and Liberties of 1648," in David H. Flaherty (ed.), *Essays in the History of American Law* (Chapel Hill, 1969), pp. 147–185.

50. William Whitmore (ed.), *The Colonial Laws of Massachusetts*, p. 1; *The New England Mind: The Seventeenth Century*, p. 410.

51. Walker, *op. cit.*, p. 235.

52. *Winthrop Papers*, IV, 493.

53. Walker, *op. cit.*, pp. 236, 237; Haskins, *op. cit.*, pp. 61–63.

54. Haskins, *op. cit.*, pp. 89, 62, 63. Mention should be made of theoretical conceptions of government put forth by John Eliot and John Davenport. Eliot (1604–1690), the Puritan missionary to the Indians, wrote *The Christian Commonwealth: or, The Civil Policy of the Rising Kingdom of Jesus Christ* (1659), in which he argued that Scriptures provide a frame of civil government. Davenport (1607–1670), a founder of New Haven, wrote a pamphlet entitled *Discourse about Civil Government in a New Plantation*, which was printed in 1663, arguing that divine law be made binding on state as well as church.

55. *The Simple Cobler of Aggwam* (London, 1647), reprinted in Miller and Johnson, *op. cit.*, pp. 230, 231.

56. *The New England Mind: The Seventeenth Century*, pp. 389–391; *Orthodoxy in Massachusetts*, p. 164. See also Morgan, *The Puritan Dilemma*, pp. 134–154.

57. *Errand Into the Wilderness*, p. 192; Ronald Knox, *Enthusiasm* (New York, 1962), pp. 2, 134, 137.

58. Book review by Samuel E. Morison, *New England Quarterly*, 3 (July, 1930), 360–361.

59. Morgan, *The Puritan Dilemma*, p. 153; Haskins, *op. cit.*, pp. 49–50. For an evaluation contrary to Haskins', see Edmund Morgan, "The Case Against Anne Hutchinson," *New England Quarterly*, 10 (1937) 635–649, and Emery Battis, *Saints and Sectaries: Ann Hutchinson and the Antinomian Controversy in the Massachusetts Bay Colony* (Chapel Hill, 1962).

60. *The Puritan Dilemma*, p. 130 (for citation) and p. 131; for considerations of Williams' thought, see especially Perry Miller, *Roger Williams* (New York, 1962); Samuel H. Brockunier, *The Irrepressible Democrat, Roger Williams* (New York, 1940); James E. Ernst, *The Political Thought of Roger Williams* (Seattle, 1929); Mauro Calamandrei, "Neglected Aspects of Roger Williams' Thought," *Church History*, XXI (1952), 238–258; Rossiter, *Seedtime of the Republic*, pp. 179–204; Alan Simpson, "How Democratic Was Roger Williams?" *William and Mary Quarterly*, XIII (1956, 56–67; Parrington, *Main Currents in American Thought*, pp. 62–75, and H. B. Parkes, "John Cotton and Roger Williams Debate Toleration," *New England Quarterly*, IV (1931), 735–756. I am particularly indebted to the Miller and Calamandrei interpretations.

61. Brockunier, *op. cit.*, p. 123; Calamandrei, *op. cit.*, pp. 245, 246.

62. Roger Williams, *The Bloudy Tenent of Persecution, for cause of Conscience, discussed, in A Conference between Truth and Peace* (London, 1644), reprinted in Samuel L. Caldwell (ed.), *Publications of the Narragansett Club* (Providence, 1867), III, 72; Calamandrei, *op. cit.*, p. 247.

63. Miller, *Roger Williams*, pp. 34ff, 44; Roger Williams, "Mr. Cotton's Letter Examined and Answered," *Publications of the Narragansett Club* (Providence, 1866), I, 108.

64. *The Bloudy Tenent, Publications of the Narragansett Club*, III, 73–74.

65. *The Hireling Ministry none of Christ's*, appendix to A *review of the Correspondence of Messrs, Fuller and Wayland on the subject of American Slavery* (Utica, 1847), p. 179, cited in Miller, *Roger Williams*, p. 204.

66. *Ibid.*, pp. 204, 205.

67. Roger Williams to the Town of Providence, in John R. Bartlett (ed.), "The Letters of Roger Williams," *Publications of the Narragansett Club* (Providence, 1874), VI, 278–279.

68. *The Bloudy Tenent, Publications of the Narragansett Club*, III, 249–250.

69. The code can be found in *Records of the Colony of Rhode Island and Providence Plantations in New England* (Providence, 1856–1865, 10 vols.), I, 157ff. It is discussed in John T. Farrell, "The Early History of Rhode Island's Court System," *Rhode Island History*, IX, X, 1–31; Brockunier, *op. cit.*, pp. 174–177.

70. Brockunier, pp. 102ff, 174.

71. Rossiter, *op. cit.*, p. 198.

72. *The New England Mind; From Colony to Province* (Boston, 1953, paperback, 1961), pp. 79, 68–81.

73. *Creeds and Platforms*, p. 222; on the half-way covenant see *The New England Mind: From Colony to Province*, pp. 91–104, and Edmund S. Morgan, *Visible Saints* (New York, 1963), pp. 120–138.

74. *The New England Mind: From Colony to Province*, pp. 43, 45ff, 41, 50.

75. *Ibid.*, p. 111.

76. Parrington, *op. cit.*, I, 12–13.

77. Quoted in Ved Mehta, "Onward and Upward with the Arts," *The New Yorker* (Dec. 15, 1962), p. 108.

Chapter 3

THE HOLY EXPERIMENT: QUAKER POLITICAL THOUGHT

My friends that are gone or are going over to plant and make outward plantations in America, keep your own plantations in your hearts with the spirit and power of God, that your vines and lilies be not hurt.

GEORGE FOX

In writing of the charter granted to him in 1681 by the king to establish a settlement in the new world, William Penn (1644–1718) professed that he "eyed the Lord in obtaining it," and "was drawn inward to look to him, and to owe it to his hand and power." He desired to use it to "answer his kind Providence, and serve his truth and people," in order that *"an example may be set up to the nations."* In America rather than England, he believed, "there may be room . . . for such an *holy experiment.*" There, as he had earlier remarked concerning the Quaker settlement in New Jersey, he would attempt to "lay a foundation for after ages to understand their liberty as men and Christians, that they may not be brought in bondage but by their own consent," because, he emphasized, the Quakers "put the power in the people."[1]

Quaker Beliefs

The Society of Friends, commonly known as the Quakers, was founded in England in 1647 by George Fox (1624–1691) as a reaction to formalism in religion and to compromise in Puritanism. The Friends liked to think of themselves as "Children of Light," a characterization which pointed up their basic tenet. Disdaining externalities, whether in the form of sacraments, rites, creeds, or churches, Fox and his followers emphasized the need for men to follow the "Inner Light" of Christ. This light was held to burn as a divine emanation in all men, even though in some it might be the faintest of flickers. It was deemed to manifest itself

69

initially as a judging or condemning principle and, after obedience was learned, as an illuminating and guiding principle. To blaze forth in an inspired, virtuous life, the Inner Light needed only to be fanned by rectitude of disposition, desire, and will.[2]

The idea of an infallible Inner Light rendered superfluous theological speculation on the nature and efficacy of divine grace and the relative roles of grace and works in the reconciliation of man to God. Its faithful pursuit placed man in the spiritual position of Adam before the fall. The Puritan legalistic conception of salvation as a contractual transaction could have no place in this simple mystical approach. Such illuminism issued logically in the notion that all men are potential prophets and consequently must be considered equal. These considerations ruled out acceptance of a ministry on a "hireling" as well as a sacerdotal basis.

Thus the Quakers could legitimately claim to be the true heirs of the Lutheran idea of the priesthood of all believers in the invisible church of Christ. Like the Anabaptists before them, they drew to the fullest the logical implications of that tenet. Whereas Luther qualified his position by pointing to Scripture as the sole controlling authority for Christian men, the Quakers regarded Scripture not as the fountain of truth but as one issue of that fount. If necessary, they believed, the Inner Light must be preferred to the admittedly weighty authority of the Bible. As Robert Barclay, an English Quaker theologian put it, the dictates of Scripture constitute "a secondary Rule subordinate to the Spirit from which they have all their Excellency and Certainty."[3] In fairness it must be said that the Quakers did not see this as a problem. They reasoned that because truth is one, the truth in Scripture could not conflict with its source or other products of that source. While the Calvinist would insist that no divine revelation had been given man since Apostolic times, and while the Catholic would maintain that although revelation has occurred since then, what is truly revealed is determined solely by the infallible church; the Quaker saw each person, when moved by the Spirit, as a temple of divine inspiration.

To the sceptic, questions immediately arise in connection with the Inner Light. If individual Inner Lights conflict, who or what is to decide which is right? If the full individualism of the doctrine is to be preserved there would appear to be no answer and thus no bond of community or safeguard against anarchy. Then, too, if Christ speaks in every person who aspires to Him, is not such person in a sense divine and consequently perfect and above the law—both divine and human? Antinomianism was one of the accusations legitimately made against some of the early Quakers. It must be remembered that tradition, Scripture, and an authoritative church alike were ruled out by the Friends as ultimate, controlling guidelines. Similarly, given the fundamental mysticism of the Inner Light doctrine, reason could not logically be summoned into service as a check. Because the Light is above and beyond reason, the latter was reduced to at best a mere pragmatic tool. Being religious enthusiasts, the Friends conceived of conscience as noncognitive, the dictate of the Inner Light. This should not be taken to mean that to them such dictates had no rational or objective content. On the contrary, they believed that the Light prompted them to accept the counsels of the Sermon on the Mount as basic, universal norms of conduct.[4]

The strong centrifugal impulse of the Inner Light doctrine was dealt with on the ideal level of Quaker thought by the heavy stress put upon the assumptions that truth is forever one, and that sincere men guided by the Light and moved by charity and humility, ultimately arrive at that same truth. In addition, and more importantly, Fox transformed the doctrine to take on a corporate aspect, a reformulation rooted in part in the premise that all men are social by nature. His conception of the "meeting," whether it be for worship or for Society business became, on the formal plane of Quaker thought, second in importance to the central concept of Inner Light. In fact the meeting was seen as an instrument by which the Light could become more fully manifest. As one of his biographers relates, Fox's original contribution lay in the idea that inspiration may be the property not of an individual but of an assembled group. The Spirit of God evidencing itself in the corporate assembly was to Fox the unifying communal bond. The corporate judgment arrived at in "the sense of the meeting" was deemed to have greater validity than the individual Inner Light. In effect, a superior corporate Light with the stamp of divinity upon it was assumed to be the mystical, motive principle of the meeting.[5]

Quaker Organization and Procedure

The principal internal problems of early Quakerism were prompted by the need for correct coordination of the spiritual guidance of the individual with the spiritual sense of the community. As early as 1666 a group of Quaker leaders pronounced that where individual judgment conflicted with the church, the individual must submit, "for of right the elders and members of the church, which keep their habitation in the Truth, ought to judge matters and things that differ; their judgment to stand good and valid." However, the strong enthusiasm in the corporate fellowship originally brought the Quaker to see no need for anything beyond self-discipline in the acceptance of decisions. And yet, if the corporate meeting was intended to serve as a centripetal institutional arrangement for facilitating the Inner Light and offsetting the attendant outward pull of individualism, it soon became evident that difficulties endemic to the individual level intruded themselves on the corporate plane as well. As it is for individuals, so is it possible for diverse collective assemblies to differ. This made necessary a broader assembly whose determinations were viewed as authoritative. Thus the meetings which originally sprang up among Friends as *ad hoc* reactions to immediately felt needs and problems, became, after 1675, regularized as a hierarchy of meetings which resolved points of discipline and inquired into religious practice in daily life. In this fashion the invisible church became more and more visible.[6]

Quaker church organization was based on the congregational principle without the Puritan conception of contract and proof of divine election. The sole prerequisite for membership was the voluntary recognition of, and desire to listen to, the Inner Light, and to live accordingly. The First-Day Meetings of each week were for worship. The Monthly Meetings attended to the business of local congregations in particular areas. At this level elders were chosen, disciplinary action was taken, overseers were appointed to visit all homes and keep a close watch over the lives of members, provision was made for education of the young and relief of the poor, and arbitration was urged upon Friends in their disputes which otherwise would have ended in a civil court. The Monthly Meeting was intended not only to aid in spiritual progress and to attend to Society business but to serve as a vehicle by which Friendly resort to the political and juridical orders could be minimized. Representatives from Monthly Meetings met in Quarterly Meetings, which combined worship with attendance to Society business and hearing appeals from the Quarterly Meetings. At the apex the Yearly Meeting stood in the same relationship to the Quarterly Meetings as did the latter to the Monthly Meetings. In it was invested the power of general superintendence of Quaker affairs for the entire country. Although in local matters American Quaker meetings were autonomous within their limits, they all accorded great respect to the letters of Fox and the official epistles of the London Yearly Meetings. The number of these became so great that in 1703 a committee of the Yearly Meeting codified them. This code became the basis for the discipline which thenceforward became obligatory upon all meetings.[7]

The mode of procedure at a Quaker Meeting was calculated to operate in complete consonance with the Inner Light doctrine. Majority rule was proscribed and consensus aimed at. Any member was allowed to speak as the Spirit moved him. There was no presiding officer; instead a clerk adjudged the weight of each speaker in terms of his arguments and standing. In this way he arrived at what was called "the sense of the meeting," or what also could be called the dictate of the corporate Inner Light. When opinion was so divided that the clerk could not find a formula which gained assent, a representative committee was appointed to draft an understanding. If this failed, discussion was postponed. It is to be noted that no vote was ever taken; the Quaker was supremely confident of the sufficiency of the method. And in truth it did work; it remains even today the method of the Friends. It operated more slowly than the method of voting, but with less friction. It necessarily assumed a spirit of humility, deference, and compromise as well as a strong corporate feeling, but the end result of unanimity justified any inconvenience. Undoubtedly it would not have been able to function in the absence of a broad consensus without running continually afoul of a *liberum veto*. Then, too, from the 1670's on, it operated at the lower levels within the framework of a hierarchical organizational system.[8]

Quaker Political Attitudes and Ideals

Given the Quaker illuminism, perfectionism, ethical absolutism, and novel conception of corporate procedure, it would seem that, like the Anabaptists before them, the Friends logically would have been led to separate from the rest of men and establish a theocracy based on the New Testament ethic and ruled by those who walk righteously in the Light and above the law. However, the strong separatist impulse was effectively countered by Fox who stressed that God's will must be carried out among all men and that there must be no retreat from what Roger Williams called the dung-heap of this world. It was somewhat different with the kindred tendency toward political antinomianism which, as mentioned above, showed up frequently among Friends in the early period. In 1672, Roger Williams, who allowed the Quakers free rein in Rhode Island, attacked their religion as tending "to reduce persons from Civility to Barbarism," and as leading "to an arbitrary Government and the Dictates and Decrees of that *sudden spirit* that acts them." This anarchical tendency was also finally checked by the leadership of men like Fox who saw nothing in Quakerism which should interfere with the ordinary duties of citizenship. Thus Fox exclaimed: "Any such as cry away with your laws, we will have none of your laws, are sons of Belial." Stress was put more and more upon peaceful submission to temporal authority. As a leading historian of the Quakers has expressed it, the Friends in England rendered rigid obedience to laws which did not affront their consciences and adamant nonviolent refusal to those which did. They chose to be imprisoned indefinitely rather than take an oath or remove their hats in court. But having been put in jail by lawful powers, they considered themselves bound in conscience not to attempt escape. In time they embraced the idea that they had no responsibility for the creation of any government and that their sole duty was to be obedient to the existing form. They were fervent believers in resistance to unjust rule but, because of their uncompromising pacifism, they were staunch opponents of the use of any form of violence to produce political change. Thus they maintained that "the setting up and putting down of governments is God's peculiar prerogative." Consistent with this sentiment, as their history in England and America amply shows, they readily transferred their allegiance as soon as a revolution was successfully consummated. This strong disdain for active participation in government hung over even in the thought of William Penn who, despite the fact that he had earlier contended that government is a part of religion, after some bitter political experiences admonished his children: "Meddle not with government; never speak of it, let others say or do as they please; . . . I have said little to you about distributing justice, or being just in power or government, for I should desire you should never be concerned therein."[9]

The apolitical impulse was not so deeply ingrained in the Quaker to preclude him from strongly believing that the Inner Light embodied a spiritual prescription which could revolutionize everyday life, society, and government, and ultimately bring about a new Eden. What could not be accomplished in the Old World, with its test-oaths, proscriptions of dissenters, and its wars and calls to arms, might conceivably be effectuated in the New. Primitive Christianity implemented in a primeval province—that was in the realm of the possible. Thus Penn could look upon the huge tracts of land granted to him as a setting in which the "Holy Experiment" could be conducted. Therein virtuous men (Quakers) might establish, on the basis of the teachings of the fifth chapter of the Gospel according to St. Matthew and the twelfth chapter of St. Paul's epistle to the Romans, a government in which virtue would rule and the ideals of brotherhood, equality, liberty of conscience, simplicity and purity of life and manners, the sovereignty of the Inner Light, and peace and nonviolence might be realized for all men, regardless of religious persuasion. One of the settlers expressed the idealism of the expedition as follows: "Our business . . . here, in this *new land,* is not so much to *build houses,* and *establish factories,* and promote *trade* and *manufacturies* that may enrich ourselves (though all these things, in their due place, are not to be neglected) as to erect temples of *holiness* and *righteousness,* which God may delight in; to lay such lasting frames and foundations of *temperance* and *virtue,* as may support the superstructures of our future happiness, both in this, and the other world." Penn put it more succinctly when he said, "Mine eye is to a blessed government, and a virtuous, ingenuous and industrious society."[10]

William Penn's Political Thought

The political implementation in the Holy Experiment of fundamental Quaker ideals and attitudes necessarily entailed a reasoned justification of government and a sober consideration of means. Because the Quakers abjured a double standard of morality, believing that the norms of moral behavior for individual man apply as strictly to political man, the means chosen must not violate the teachings of the Sermon on the Mount. As founder and Proprietor of Pennsylvania and thus subject to political pressures, William Penn assumed the formidable task of definition. If it is true that he was a principal in the formulation of the basic law of West Jersey in 1676, he was not without experience. He was also peculiarly qualified because of his deep education in the classics. Besides, he was a friend of, and possibly a collaborator with, Algernon Sidney, and apparently was influenced by James Harrington's *Oceana*, and had followed closely political events in England.[11]

Penn faced the crucial question of whether government is a dictate of nature and reason or of the Inner Light and mysticism. Given the Quaker disjunction between nature and the Light, it is obvious that if his answer were given wholly in terms of the former, the conclusion would have to be made that government, as such, is foreign to Quakerism and at best, a necessary evil—a mere concession to the spiritual and moral frailty of most men. If his answer ran wholly in terms of the latter, the model of government must be the Quaker meeting, and coercion, in all its forms, must be completely disavowed.

In the Preface to his first *Frame of Government*, the fundamental law which he drew up for Pennsylvania in 1682, Penn used basic Quaker doctrine to arrive at an answer which justified government both in terms of man's nature and as a part of religion itself. In the beginning, he reasoned, God made man his deputy to rule the world, endowing him not only with skill and power, but with integrity to use them justly. In this state of "native goodness," man had no need of coercion or compulsion because divine love and truth burned brightly within him. This primal order was breeched when lust prevailed against duty, whence man became subject to the external law which theretofore had no power over him. From this point Penn's presentation proceeded in accordance with the Quaker conception that Adam's original sin is not inherited by his progeny, but that men sin by their own original, individual responsible acts, from which corruption they can be raised by their own volition in pursuit of the gracious Inner Light to the spiritual state of Adam before the fall. Thus Penn distinguished between Adam's "disobedient posterity," those men who do "not live comformable to the holy law within," and "the righteous man," who does. The former alone fall "under the reproof and correction of the just law without." Did this mean that the righteous are beyond the embrace of government? Not at all, Penn argued, because government has two ends, the first, to "terrify evildoers," and the second, "to cherish those that do well." In the latter sense government has "a life beyond corruption," and must be considered "a part of religion itself, a thing sacred in its institution and end," and "as

capable of kindness, goodness and charity, as a more private society."
In both its constraining and promotive aspects, government is an emanation of God and thus, in the Pauline sense, exists by divine right. Answering those who contend that government is but a necessary evil, a
mere remedy for sin, Penn declared: "They weakly err, that think
there is no other use of government than correction, which is the
coarsest part of it; daily experience tells us that the care and regulation
of many other affairs, more soft, and daily necessary, make up much of
the greatest part of government." If Adam had never fallen from grace,
Penn contended, government in this sense would still have been necessary.[12]

Government stands then as a necessity for the Children of Light as
well as the Children of Darkness. Even in its coercive aspect, Penn believed, it can be productive of much good by compelling men to do
what they inwardly know is right. In 1693 he wrote:

Government, then, is the prevention or cure of disorder and the means of
justice, as that is of peace. For this cause we have our sessions, terms, assizes,
and parliaments to overrule men's passions and resentments, that they may
not be judges in their own cause nor punishers of their own wrongs, which as
it is very incident to men in their corrupt state, so, for that reason, they would
observe no measure, nor on the other hand would any be easily reduced to
their duty. Not that men know not what is right, their excesses, and wherein
they are to blame, by no means; nothing is plainer to them. But so depraved
is human nature that, without compulsion some way or other, too many would
not readily be brought to do what they know is right and fit, or avoid what
they are satisfied they should not do.[13]

In the first *Frame of Government* Penn fixed upon this point to explain why men, although agreeing that the end for man is happiness,
disagree on the means to its realization. The cause is "not always want
of light and knowledge, but want of using them rightly." Men "side with
their passions against their reason, and their sinister interests have so
strong a bias upon their minds, that they lean to them against the good
of the things they know." It is for this reason that men also differ on the
question of the best form of government. Thus Penn wrote: "*Any government is free to the people under it* (whatever be the frame) *where the
laws rule, and the people are a party to those laws.*" Inasmuch as he had
already talked of government as "the just law without," it is clear that he
meant that not all that passes for law is law in the ethical sense and
that the ultimate norm of legality is the inward moral law. In any
case, "governments rather depend upon men, than men upon governments." If men are good, their government cannot be bad; if they are
bad, no matter how admirable the governmental form, "they will endeavor to warp and spoil it. . . ." Penn was here evincing his disapproval of many of his contemporaries in Europe who believed that the

key to good government lay in the formal institutions and laws of the state. He would concede that good institutions and laws have a beneficial effect and are vitally necessary, but the character of men is the decisive factor because "good men will never want good laws, nor suffer ill ones." A good constitution is the product of "men of wisdom and virtue." And because these qualities must be transmitted in order to continue the righteous constitution, it is imperative that there be "a virtuous education of youth." This then was to be the main ingredient of the "Holy Experiment"—government established in virtue and wisdom and ensured for posterity by the education of youth in virtue. There can be no doubt that Penn had in mind more than the mere natural virtues and wisdom emphasized in classical political thought, and that he believed that the Friends, above all Christian people, possessed these spiritual qualifications to make the great experiment a successful example to all mankind.[14]

While formulating the first *Frame of Government,* Penn wrote in a private letter: "For the matters of liberty and privilege, I propose what is extraordinary and to leave to myself and successors no power of doing mischief, that the will of one man may not hinder the good of an whole country." In the last paragraph of the Preface, he pronounced the principle underlying this self-denying sentiment. The great end of all government and the purpose of the Frame itself, is *"To support power in reverence with the people, and to secure the people from the abuse of power."* This in order that the people "may be free by their just obedience, and the magistrates honourable for their just administration: for liberty without obedience is confusion, and obedience without liberty is slavery." Civil liberty thus consists in ready obedience to just law on the part of rulers and ruled alike.[15]

One notes a fundamental agreement of Penn's conception of civil liberty with that of Winthrop. Both men maintained that magistrates and people are morally limited in their acts by truth and justice and that a cheerful conformity to both spells liberty in the ethical sense. The difference between them lay in their answers to the crucial question, who is ultimately to decide what is politically "good, just and honest"? Winthrop leaned in the direction of magisterial prerogative, whereas Penn, even though he may at times have acted otherwise as proprietor of Pennsylvania, emphasized the need for settled, known, just laws based on the consent of freeholders. Then, too, good Quaker that he was, Penn ultimately relied upon the inward voice of the individual conscience, informed by the injunctions of the Sermon on the Mount. Winthrop, of course, also emphasized conscience, but conscience informed by Scripture as interpreted by the Puritan spiritual and political authorities. Perhaps the most accurate description of Penn is that given by a student of his social thought: "When he philosophized calmly, his

political Utopia tended in some respects to approach the ideals of
[Roger] Williams; when he found himself confronted by practical
necessities of action, he was sometimes inclined, like Winthrop, to make
short shrift of democratic vagaries."[16]

Although Penn aimed at a government by men of virtue, he proceeded to implement the basic Quaker ideals and principles upon the
quite un-Friendly Classical Republican premise that every man must be
presumed a knave even though such is not true in fact. Except that he
did not use the terminology of natural rights, the basic rights and procedures outlined by him for Pennsylvania were for the most part consonant with contemporary Whig conceptions. However, the tendency
toward government by assembly found in the Quaker laws of West
Jersey was replaced in Pennsylvania by emphasis on balanced government and enhancement of the power of the council as against the
assembly. In great similarity to the ideas of Harrington, balance in the
machinery of government was effected through three branches: the
governor (who had no veto power), the annually elected council (which
proposed laws and aided the governor in administration) and the
annually elected assembly (which approved or disapproved proposed
laws). Overlapping, staggered terms, rotation in office, and the property
qualification for the franchise aimed not only at preventing men from
judging in their own cases, but at a wide popular participation and
education in government.[17]

Penn's constitutions and laws were designed to ensure realization of
three basic rights which he justified in terms of religion and English
history, and the importance of which he had learned through hard
personal experience as a dissenter in the homeland. They were the right
to liberty and estate, the right to take part in legislation through the
vote, and the right to be protected by and to participate in the judicial
and executive functions through the jury system. Of all liberties, Penn
saw liberty of conscience as the most important. In his illuminating
essay, *The Great Case of Liberty of Conscience,* which he wrote in
England in 1670, he defined freedom of conscience as "not only a mere
Liberty of the Mind in believing or disbelieving this or that principle or
doctrine, but 'the exercise of ourselves in a visible way of worship upon
our believing it to be indispensably required at our hands, that if we
neglect it for fear or favor of any mortal man we sin and incur divine
wrath.'" He adduced detailed proof of this proposition in terms of
"the honor of God, the meekness of the Christian religion, the authority
of Scripture, the privilege of nature, the principles of common reason,
the well-being of government, and apprehensions of the greatest person-
ages of former and latter ages." To guard against accusations that his
position encouraged anarchy in the name of religious freedom, Penn
added that the lawfulness of any meeting to worship God did not imply

license to bring about or abet "any contrivance destructive of the government and laws of the land tending to matters of an external
nature. . . ."[18]

In the case of West Jersey, liberty of conscience was defined in the
negative sense as freedom from compulsion and in the positive sense
as the right to worship. Under such guarantees, it appears that, as in
the case of Rhode Island, even an atheist was protected. In the Pennsylvania Frames and Charters only those who believed in God were assured this protection and only those "who profess faith in Jesus Christ"
were made eligible for office. Why then the apparent retreat from the
broad New Jersey guarantee? Apart from the great possibility that
Penn had no hand in writing the New Jersey provision, a plausible explanation is that in his "Holy Experiment" he wanted inhabitants who
were on the road to virtue and wisdom, and rulers who to some degree
already possessed these qualities. Because he construed virtue and
wisdom in a religious and, at their highest, in a Christian sense, he expected belief in God from all and faith in Christ from officeholders. To
admit atheists to office would have meant conceding the sufficiency and
efficacy of mere natural virtue and wisdom. Nonetheless, when one
regards Penn's provisions against the contemporary background of intolerance elsewhere in the New World, one must remark their generous
liberality. It must be remembered that Penn was under heavy pressure
to restrict officeholding to Quakers. To this he replied: "We should look
selfish and do that which we have cried out against others for, namely,
letting nobody touch government, but those of their own way." Later he
explained his action as follows: "I went thither to lay the foundation of
a free colony for all mankind, more especially those of my own profession; not that I would lessen the civil liberties of others because of
their own persuasion, but screen and defend our own from any infringement on that account."[19]

Formally speaking, Penn established separation of church and state
in Pennsylvania. But this was in the expectation that society would
embody the essential religious principles of Quaker Christianity, which
in turn would be reflected in the tone and actions of government. He
would have regarded separation of church and state for the purpose of
secularization of life as blasphemous. To him, as to Roger Williams,
liberty of conscience and separation of church and state were conclusions
drawn from essentially religious premises. In reality Quakerism was
reflected in the basic laws and public practices of the commonwealth,
as witness the provisions concerning marriage, the use of affirmation
instead of oath, the provision that arbitrators be attached to the regular
courts, the failure to provide a militia, the laws punishing "all such
offenses against God, as swearing, cursing, lying, prophane talking,
drunkenness, drinking of healths," use of obscene words, sex crimes,

murders, "stage plays, cards, dice, May games, gamesters, masques, revels, bull-baitings, and the like, which excite people to rudeness, cruelty, looseness and irreligion." Much more blue-nosed than the grossly maligned Congregationalists to the north, Penn also stipulated that a Committee on Manners, Education and the Arts be set up in the Council "that all wicked and scandalous living may be prevented and that youth may be successfully trained up in virtue and useful knowledge and arts."[20]

In conclusion it must be noted that Penn's political thought proceeded from and culminated in an implied eschatology which envisioned that as time went on and government by virtuous men produced an ever-increasing number of virtuous constituents, constraint would gradually diminish until one day government would no longer exist to terrify non-existent evildoers and the coercive state would have withered away. With all men in the spiritual state of Adam before the fall, government in the purely directive, promotive, and spiritual sense would alone obtain and the mystical kingdom of God would be established on the basis of universal, joyful acceptance of the teachings in Matthew and Paul. In this light the religious and Whiggish pessimism which gave rise to Penn's acceptance of internal coercive powers, government by balance, etc., can be seen to be restricted to the conception of man in his depraved stage of development. To be fully understood this pessimism must be viewed within the framework of a philosophy, or rather an unsystematized theology, of history which was ultimately optimistic in regarding man as a free agent who can choose to follow the directions of the Inner Light and thus realize the ideal. In this perspective, the "Holy Experiment" was a utopian attempt to demonstrate how men can progress toward the goal of elimination of constraint and the universalization of the Quaker way, in a society guided by divine Light and ordered within the framework of the Meeting House.[21]

The Failure of the Holy Experiment

By 1756 Quaker rule was officially at an end in Pennsylvania, never to be recaptured. It was broken on the reefs of contest for political power and material gain and a spiritual pride which produced an uncompromising perfectionist absolutism.[22] As a squalid, besieged minority without political power in England, the Quakers had frowned upon politics; in Pennsylvania with the reins of government firmly in their hands, the Friends, as true sons of Adam, broke into factions and jockeyed for power. More in anguish than anger, Penn, who lived to see his balanced council-dominated government changed, to his chagrin, to unicameral rule by the assembly, pleaded with them to "be not so governmentish." Then, too, given the fact that the Quaker, as much as, if not more than, the Puritan, absorbed the Calvinistic economic ethic of the "calling" and advancement in wealth, it is no wonder that in the new land of great material abundance the counting house came to rival the meeting house. When one adds to this the fact that many of the later Quakers, who came to the faith by birth rather than adult conversion, accepted the Friendly way of life less out of conviction and newborn faith than out of habit and custom, the ultimate end of the holy rule becomes even more understandable.[23]

Of greater interest and more pertinence to our study is the part played in the decline by the adamant stand of the Children of Light on the questions of oathtaking and the raising and bearing of arms. Because they believed the taking and administering of oaths to be contrary to the command of the New Testament as well as against common sense, the Quakers refused to do either, even when they were legally prescribed as a prerequisite or duty of office and to establish competency as a witness in a court of law. An agreement was finally reached whereby an affirmation containing no allusion to the Deity was permitted by the British authorities. To gain this concession the Pennsylvania Quakers gravely undermined the enlightened penal code established under Penn's aegis, which restricted capital punishment to a very few grave offenses, by agreeing as a *quid pro quo* to accept the much more comprehensive British code. Thus to keep their purity on one point, they compromised on another. And withal, as officials, they still refused to administer oaths to officeholders and jurymen, who were either required or desired to take them. This persistent intransigence imperiled the administration of government and justice.[24]

Concerning the raising and bearing of arms, the Quakers subscribed to a literal interpretation of the New Testament injunction regarding the inflicting of violence upon others. The principle of peace, defined in terms of love and nonviolence, was the central tenet of their ethic. Penn was representative of the view taken by most Friends concerning compulsion within the state. As we have seen, he would not dispense with the policeman and punitive sanctions, including the death penalty for men who did not freely follow the Inner Light. But in reference to the use of force against external foes, the case was different. While it is difficult for many men to discern the difference between the application of governmental force to internal violators of the law and preparation for and prosecution of defensive war, the Quaker purists drew an undeviating line, upon which they stood, rigidly refusing to yield an inch. Because Penn was bound by an agreement with British officials to make military preparations and because the settlers on the frontier, who were almost all non-Quakers, exerted increasing pressure upon the Quaker government for military assistance against the Indians, the Quaker position was clearly precarious. As an expedient, the Friends, responding to British demands, resorted to hypocritical departure from pure principle. Thus the deputy governor, who was almost uniformly a non-Quaker, was given certain military duties. At different times, funds manifestly intended for military purposes were appropriated under the designations, "for the Queen's use" or "for other grain." In this same vein, one of the few blemishes upon Penn's otherwise admirable career came when he wrote in 1691 from England to his council that Europe was fated to be weighted with misery in impending war. In light of this he informed his brethren: "Wherefor be wise, and still, and make your advantage by it, at the markets of the world."[25]

Judgment was quick in coming from the Quaker conscience. In 1715 in a pamphlet entitled *Tribute to Caesar,* an anonymous Friend excoriated the expedient of voting funds and argued that because Christ's kingdom is not of this world, the Quakers should quit all affairs of state. In 1741, James Logan, himself a Quaker, argued that defensive war was identical in principle to the use of force within the state. He concluded that those Friends who believed otherwise should be completely consistent and remove themselves from governmental office. The great Quaker preacher, John Woolman, also urged Quaker divorce from governmental power. He presented the absolutist position, saying: "It requires great self-denial and resignation of ourselves to God, to attain that state wherein we can freely cease from fighting when wrongfully invaded, if, by our fighting, there were a probability of overcoming the invaders. Whoever rightly attains to it does in some degree feel that spirit in which our Redeemer gave his life for us; and through Divine goodness many of our predecessors, and many now living, have learned the blessed lesson; but many others, having their religion chiefly by education and not being enough acquainted with that cross which crucifies to the world, do manifest a temper distinguishable from that of an entire trust in God." Of course, this was small solace to the non-Quaker frontiersmen threatened by Indian raids and imperial war.[26]

After 1745 the Philadelphia Yearly Meeting began to reemphasize the example of Christ "who hath commanded us to love our enemies and to do good even to them that hate us." Thus all sincere Friends must "be faithful to that ancient testimony . . . against bearing of arms and fighting." Finally in 1756 under the urging of the London Yearly Meeting and confronted with the necessity to choose between the absolutist position and responsibly meeting the demand of state safety and security, most of the political Quakers refused to seek reelection and thus relinquished the reins of government. Thereafter the Society of Friends pursued humanitarian works, having solved the political problem by repudiating politics itself and following the course of sectarian withdrawal.[27]

Quaker insistence upon absolute adherence to the non oath-taking and pacifist principles aided in undermining the Holy Experiment by demonstrating the incapacity of the Friends to promote order, security and, to a lesser degree, justice, all of which are basic ends of government. Given this attitude, one can see that the experiment was foredoomed to failure as long as it could not be attempted in an insular environment, hermetically sealed off from the sinful world. But more importantly, in pursuit of their insistence upon a single standard of morality for both individual and political man, the absolutist Quakers, if we pursue the logic of James Logan, established a double standard of their own. It seems obvious that if force can legitimately be used to restrain the violater within, it is not only consistent but morally necessary that, in the absence of a rule of law without, the same means be used to restrain the external violater. Absolutist Quakers, however, accepted one of these terms while rejecting the other. Thus they recognized, realistically, the existence of the Old Adam and the consequent need to protect men from his depredations within, while blindfolding themselves to his presence without. Internal policy was predicated on the assumption that sinful men exist in abundance; external policy was predicated in effect on the utopian premise that all men are angels.

A sympathetic historian of Quaker rule in Pennsylvania has recently passed judgment upon the Holy Experiment in terms of Reinhold Niebuhr's discussion of "Moral Man and Immoral Society," maintaining that, given the single ethical standard, the attempt to construct a society on the preachments of the Sermon on the Mount was bound to fail. He relies heavily upon Niebuhr's contention that while the individual can measure up to an exalted standard of altruism, it is impossible for social groups because the collective ego is so strong that it cannot be controlled by the moral norms applicable to individuals. As a result, there exists a tragic yet inevitable disjunction between individual and political conduct. Thus Niebuhr characterizes pacifism as "a parasite on the sins of the rest of us, who maintain government and relative social justice." If the pacifist mixes in government he must either compromise his principle or lead the state to ruin.[28]

Niebuhr's conclusion regarding pacifism appears irrefutable. But is it necessary to conclude, as Niebuhr does not, but many others do, that politics is a necessary but yet morally deficient human exercise? Are we justified in holding that while individual man can be good, society is always, more or less, irretrievably corrupt? In general, it can be said that a double standard of morality cannot be accepted by anyone who embraces the Judaeo-Christian ethic; nor is it acceptable to the classical tradition of natural law. The basic principles of conduct are the same for both individual and political man; the difference lies in the situations and responsibilities confronting each, a point only partially taken into account by the Quakers. Whereas the individual is justified in restraining one who attacks him, he is not justified in lynching him after his apprehension. Similarly, whereas the political rulers, if the state is unjustifiably attacked, are justified in calling upon its resources for its defense, they are not justified in using them to commit wanton aggression. The question, of course, is much more complex and has wider ramifications than these rather obvious examples indicate. But they do point up the line of reasoning which must be used if the single standard is to be saved and politics rescued from being equated with sin.

If what we have remarked is true, it can be concluded that a major factor in the ultimate failure of the Holy Experiment was not, as is usually averred, the Friends' absolutist insistence upon a single ethical standard but, instead, the Friends' actual pursuit of a double standard in government. Their inconsistency was removed only upon their withdrawal from power and political responsibility.

Quaker Contributions to American Political Thought

Because of its essential mysticism, Quakerism gave rise to no well-knit coherent body of political thought, but it left a legacy of ideals, principles, and practices which have a definite political relevance and which have had an abiding influence upon American constitutional, democratic thought.

1. The Quaker affirmed unreservedly the *equality of all men.* His belief in universal redemption precluded the Puritan distinction between the elect and the damned. His sturdy insistence upon social equality precluded acceptance of any distinction between the high and the low born. Similarly, informed as it was by the New Testament emphasis upon universal love and peace, the Quaker belief in equality dictated brotherly, fair and peaceful treatment of the Indians, and nonviolent opposition to Negro slavery. Within the framework of their doctrine of equality, as seen in Penn's thought, the Quaker recognized the validity and desirability of giving political preference to virtuous men. This did not appear a contradiction to him because he believed all men had the capacity ultimately to attain virtue.

2. Because men are basically equal in possession of the Inner Light, the Quaker affirmed the *sovereignty of the individual conscience and the law within.* This, in turn, prescribed limits to government. Because of the Quaker failure to explain the relationship between reason and the Inner Light, a doctrine of natural moral law as the foundation of constitutionalism was not fully developed. But the Quaker inward, higher law was given substance by the teachings of the Sermon on the Mount. Thus we see that whereas the Puritan conscience was basically informed by the Old Testament, the Quaker conscience was informed by the New. In any case, the religious notion of a higher law, although upheld

on somewhat different bases by Quaker and Puritan, supplemented in both cases the English conception of fundamental law in providing a basis for American constitutionalism.

3. *Liberty of conscience* was, to the Friends, first and foremost among basic liberties. Although most reflective men in the Judaeo-Christian tradition accepted this theory, it is to the credit of the Quakers that, along with Roger Williams, they were among the first to seek its political implementation. Although it is arguable that religious freedom is not necessarily impaired by a state establishment of a particular religion, the Pennsylvania Quaker believed that a *separation of church and state* was requisite to its full realization.

4. The idea of *consent of the governed* was subscribed to by Penn on the theoretical plane as a counterpart of the principle of equality. This was implemented in his submission of the first *Frame of Government* to the first assembly of all freemen in 1682 and in provisions for annual elections, wide popular participation in the governmental process, and in the amendment of the fundamental law.

5. Penn's idea of *balance in government* was a derivative of the ancient conception of the balanced state, as well as the religious recognition of the ubiquity of sin. His conviction that no man should be judge in his own case, as reflected in the idea of balance, proceeded from the premise that unregenerate man is not to be trusted with unqualified power. In this regard although his Pennsylvania settlers changed to unicameralism, he was as one with the principal Puritan thinkers. Admittedly the later American conception of separation of powers owes as much, if not more, to evolutionary colonial practice and later compromises, but the fact is that Penn attempted an institutional implementation of the idea of balance which left its mark upon practice.

6. The Quaker believed strongly in *individual self-reliance.* This was reflected on the corporate level in the practice of leaving to lesser societal institutions than the state, such as the local meetings, the performance of functions which they could amply meet. This presaged the later American pluralism and pursuit of the political principle of devolution of authority. Alongside these considerations must be placed the teaching of Penn that government in its noncoercive sense is a positive good and necessary not only for a well-ordered social life but as a condition of spiritual life. Although the slogan that government is at best a necessary evil is part of American folklore, it must be remembered that the mercantilist emphasis on governmental regulation and intervention in the economy was the rule rather than the exception in America in colonial days and perhaps until well into the nineteenth century. Penn's position on this point affords an able theoretical justification to this day.

7. Finally, the Quaker emphasis on *nonviolence* disabled many Friends from participating in and even supporting the American Revo-

lution, but it must not be seen as a quietistic passivism. Refusal to obey unjust laws was not opposition to change, as such. In this regard the Quaker tradition, as much as the philosophy of Thoreau, remains an abiding influence in American political life.

NOTES

1. Penn to James Harrison, Aug. 25, 1681, reprinted in Robert Proud, *The History of Pennsylvania* (Philadelphia, 1797), I, 169; Penn and partners to Richard Hartshorne, June 26, 1676, cited in Amelia M. Gummere, "The Early Quakers in New Jersey," in Rufus Jones (ed.), *The Quakers in the American Colonies* (New York, 1962), p. 365.

2. Concerning Fox see Rachael Knight, *The Founder of Quakerism* (London, 1922). Regarding the Friends, their origins and beliefs, see William Penn, "A Key," in *The Select Works of William Penn* (London, 1782, 5 vols.), V, 1–36; William C. Braithwaite, *The Beginnings of Quakerism* (Cambridge, 1955); Jones, *op. cit.*, xvi–xxxii; Ronald Knox, *Enthusiasm* (New York, 1950), pp. 144–167; Isaac Sharpless, "The Basis of Quaker Morality," in *Quakerism and Politics* (Philadelphia, 1905), pp. 202–220; Ernst Troeltsch, *The Social Teaching of the Christian Churches* (London, 1931, 2 vols.), II, 780–783.

3. Robert Barclay, *An Apology for the True Christian Divinity* (1680), II, 67, cited in Frederick B. Tolles, *Meetinghouse and Countinghouse* (Chapel Hill, N.C., 1948), p. 5.

4. Barclay did see human reason as a secondary light and regarded it to be "fit to order and rule Man in things Natural." Later Penn appealed at least twice to right reason to establish his doctrine of the Inner Light which he asserted to be "most Reasonable." He also encouraged the scientific study of nature as allowing for a better understanding of the work of God. See "The Sandy Foundation Shaken" and "The Christian Quaker and his Divine Testimony," *Select Works of William Penn*, I, 21–57, 145–291 and Tolles, *op. cit.*, pp. 210–211. For a discussion of Barclay's thought, see William C. Braithwaite, *The Second Period of Quakerism* (Cambridge, 1961, H. J. Cadbury (ed.), pp. 385–392.

5. Knight, *op. cit.*, p. 37; Tolles, *op. cit.*, p. 7; Jones, *op. cit.*, p. 136, 140–141.

6. Arnold Lloyd, *Quaker Social History* (London, 1950), pp. 6, 7ff., 175, 176. See also Braithwaite, *The Second Period of Quakerism*, pp. 251–260 and Knox, *op. cit.*, pp. 166, 167.

7. Jones, *op. cit.*, pp. 136–146, 438; Lloyd, *op. cit.*, pp. 129–144; Edwin B. Bronner, *William Penn's "Holy Experiment"* (New York, 1962), pp. 50–54.

8. Lloyd, *op. cit.*, pp. 23–24.

9. Roger Williams, "George Fox Digged Out of his Burrows," *Narragansett Club Publications*, V, 5, 5; G. P. Gooch, *English Democratic Ideas in the Seventeenth Century* (Cambridge, 1927), p. 231; Jones, *op. cit.*, pp. 459–460. The above quotations can be found cited in Jones at pp. 461 and 462.

10. Cited in Tolles, *op. cit.*, p. 63; Penn to Thomas Janney, August 21, 1681, cited in Catherine Peare, *William Penn* (Philadelphia and New York, 1957), p. 221.

11. Edward C. O. Beatty, *William Penn As Social Philosopher* (New York, 1939), pp. 9–12. It was formerly thought that Penn drafted the Concessions and Agreements of West Jersey, but see to the contrary, John E. Pomfret, "The Problem of the West Jersey Concessions of 1676/7," *The William and Mary Quarterly*, V, 3rd Ser. (1948), 95–105. On the development of Penn's political ideas see Mary Maples Dunn, *William Penn: Politics and Conscience* (Princeton, 1967), pp. 3–107.

12. Preface, "The Frame of Government of Pennsylvania (1682)," F. E. Thorpe (ed.), *The Federal and State Constitutions* (Washington, 1909), V, 3052–3053.

13. "An Essay Towards the Present and Future Peace of Europe," in Frederick

Tolles and E. G. Alderfer (eds.), *The Witness of William Penn* (New York, 1947), p. 144.

14. Thorpe, *op. cit.*, pp. 3053, 3054.

15. Penn to Turner, Sharp and Roberts, Apr. 12, 1681, cited in Peare, *op. cit.*, p. 216; Thorpe, *op. cit.*, p. 3054.

16. Beatty, *op. cit.*, p. 41.

17. Mary Maples, "William Penn, Classical Republican," *The Pennsylvania Magazine of History and Biography*, 81 (1957), 138–156; Beatty, *op. cit.*, pp. 9, 68–69. Concerning Penn and politics, see John E. Illick, *William Penn the Politician* (Ithaca, N.Y., 1965).

18. Maples, *op. cit.*, p. 146; *Select Works of William Penn*, III, 11.

19. Chapter XVI, "The Charter or Fundamental Laws of West New Jersey Agreed Upon, 1676," Thorpe, *op. cit.*, p. 2549. The Penn quotations can be found in Jones, *op. cit.*, pp. 463, 465, 477.

20. "Laws Agreed Upon in England," Thorpe, *op. cit.*, p. 3063. See also Beatty, *op. cit.*, p. 293.

21. Tolles, *op. cit.*, p. 10.

22. See Guy F. Hershberger, "Pacifism and the State in Colonial Pennsylvania," *Church History*, VIII (1939), 54–74.

23. Jones, *op. cit.*, p. 475ff.; Troeltsch, *op. cit.*, p. 781.

24. Isaac Sharpless, *A Quaker Experiment in Government* (Philadelphia, 1898), pp. 138–153; Daniel Boorstin, *The Americans: The Colonial Experience* (New York, 1958), pp. 40–47. See also Gary B. Nash, *Quakers and Politics* (Princeton, 1968).

25. Sharpless, *op. cit.*, pp. 185–225; Boorstin, *op. cit.*, pp. 48–54; Hershberger, *op. cit.*, pp. 58–74; Penn to Pennsylvania Council, cited in Hershberger, *op. cit.*, p. 60.

26. Hershberger, *op. cit.*, pp. 65, 66; Thomas S. Kepler (ed.), *The Journal of John Woolman* (Cleveland, 1954), pp. 80–81.

27. Hershberger, *op. cit.*, pp. 67, 70, 71; see also Boorstin, *op. cit.*, pp. 58–63.

28. Hershberger, *op. cit.*, pp. 71–72.

Chapter 4

ANGLICANISM AND AMERICAN POLITICAL THOUGHT

*Wee doe specially ordaine, charge, and require [that] the
. . . president and councells, and the ministers of the said
several colonies . . . doe provide, that the . . . Christian
faith be preached . . . within every of the said several colonies
. . . according to the doctrine, rights, and religion now professed and established within our realme of England.*

JAMES I (1606)

When Puritanism became a strong force in late sixteenth-century England, the Anglican divine Richard Hooker (1554–1600) answered its
claims and defended the episcopal form and ecclesiastical laws of the
Church of England, as well as the Tudor constitution. In the *Laws of
Ecclesiastical Polity*, he used the Thomistic approach to nature, grace,
and law to reject the voluntarism of the Puritan Reformers, who saw
God as will and the universe and its order as His arbitrary product. By
emphasizing the rational basis of law, Hooker attempted to refute the
Calvinist claim that Scripture is the sole source of law for man. Following
St. Paul he believed that men who possess no written law of God to show
what is good or evil, have like all of mankind the law of reason written
in their hearts. In this light the state is justified on rational grounds: man,
who is social by nature, forms bodies with his fellow men on the basis of
mutual consent. The essential aspect of the state is its right to make
laws, which it derives from the law of reason. The obligation of the
subjects is rooted in the consent or recognition which forms and sustains
the state under the law of reason.[1]

Hooker argued that the church, besides being divinely instituted, is
a natural society with natural functions and needs not defined in
Scripture. He also maintained that in England church and state are two

aspects of one society, with identical membership. Departing from Thomism, Hooker drew upon the medieval thinker Marsilius of Padua*to conclude that in ecclesiastical questions the human legislator acts as the church just as in civil questions he acts as the state. From his belief that society can have but one head, who can abide no division of his sovereignty with either Pope or congregation, it followed that the monarch in Parliament possessed supreme binding power in both church and state. Thus in the English *Respublica Christiana,* ecclesiastical as well as civil laws derived their force from the power which the corporate people originally possessed by nature and which, by mutual consent they delegated to the sovereign. Hooker, however, did not believe that the state legitimately could disavow Christianity. Nor was he an advocate of divine right monarchy, as his rather imprecise medieval consensual theory demonstrates.

When it became obvious that Parliament, under Puritan influence in the seventeenth century, was overwhelmingly hostile to the established church, Anglicans put Hooker aside and took up the Stuart conception of the divine right of kings, with its corollary, the duty of subjects to render passive obedience. Thus did the English church embrace after Hooker's death a political theory tied to the political fortunes of a royal line of succession. This theory was successfully challenged and the conception of Hooker reinstituted in the Whig victory and settlement of 1689.[2]

The Church of England in the American colonies never attained full institutional form; no diocese was ever set up, even where Anglicanism, as in Virginia, was the established church. Supervision was placed in a commissary responsible to the Bishop of London. Most significantly, however, clergy and laity in America subscribed to the Anglican idea of the primacy of political authority in all church matters except where such exercise ran counter to self-evident truth or the explicit teachings of Scripture. This was manifested in colonies where Anglicanism was established, in a republican church polity quite different from that of the mother country and very similar to that of New England.

Virginia: "Pious and Christian Plantation"

There is general agreement that the Puritans in New England and the Quakers in Pennsylvania sought to build their societal and political orders in accordance with their notions of religious truth. On the other hand, it has long been a common belief that the settlement of Virginia

* Marsilius of Padua (d. 1343?) held that authority in both church and state derives from the corporate people (the human legislator) and not from some "higher law."

by the London Company in 1609 was conceived and executed by men of commerce solely in quest of profit. A contemporary historian has recently remarked that Virginia involved "no grandiose scheme, no attempt to rule by an idea, but an earthy effort to transplant institutions."[3] There can be no denying the great importance of the mercantile motive and the practical acceptance of English institutions. These, however, must be considered within the framework of the fact that the members of the company, its promoters and the settlers, were children of an age in which religious faith was yet the uppermost consideration.

Perry Miller has shown, in his survey of early Virginia literature, that religion was indeed a pervasive force in the Virginia enterprise. Where generally the dissimilarities between Massachusetts Bay and Virginia are stressed, Miller emphasizes the fundamental similarities. He tells us that those who see in the founding of Virginia a manifestation of individualism fail to take into account the cosmology of the original colonists, while those who see in it an incipient capitalist imperialism ignore the teleological orientation of the time. Virginia's colonists were militant Protestant Christians dedicated to the missionary goal of converting the Indians. As "low-church" Anglicans they saw their settlement as a holy endeavor dictated by Providence; an example, as John Smith remarked, of God's will in action. They shared with the Puritans an acceptance of the Protestant conceptions of original sin, predestination, and regeneration through divine election. Although, unlike the Puritans, they did not regard themselves as "saints" and thus did not restrict membership in the church to the "elect," they closely regulated their lives by the church. Their cosmology and theory of history also paralleled that of the Puritans on most points. Central to all was God's will which gives rise to the "law of nature," which, contrary to Hooker, God in His omnipotence was deemed free to disregard. Like the Puritans, the Anglican Virginians emphasized divine power above divine reason and the dictates of Scripture above the dictates of human reason. Consequently from the cosmic viewpoint if they quested for profit they concluded that, as Christians, they must do so in the spirit of faith; if they regarded only selfish desires and the law of nature, God would visit them with a curse in the outward sign of bankruptcy. To get them to do what must be done, God was conceived of as luring them on with the promise of material success. Underlying this psychology was the biblical idea of covenant, which shortly thereafter, in more extensive form, permeated the New England mind. Like Abraham of old, the settlers saw themselves going forth under the sanction and prescription of a covenant with God whereby, if they served Him well, He would reward them with success. Thus they went "by way of marchandizing and trade" to buy from the Indians earthly pearls and to sell to them "the pearles of heaven." In this spirit John Rolfe described the migration to

Virginia as that "of a peculiar people, marked and chosen by the finger of God."[4]

Like most of his fellow Christians of the seventeenth century, the Anglican Virginian believed that the structure of society must reflect and protect the truths of religion. As it turned out, this resulted in an acceptance of basically English forms, which the environment and conditions in the New World helped to reshape.

Political Thought of Early Virginia

The political thought of early Virginia was part and parcel of the prevailing Protestant outlook. The fallen nature of man explained the necessity for government, which was seen as a checkrein upon the human propensity for evil and as a means to bring men to virtue. Absent was the later notion that the state exists merely to guarantee and promote liberty and equality. Thus the magistrate possesses more than police powers; he is responsible for the moral welfare of the community, the maintenance of true religion and the repression of heresy. The harsh Virginia legal code, *The Lawes and Orders, Divine, Politique and Martiall*, which was occasioned by catastrophic events of 1607–1609, and which obtained until 1619, was informed by this conception of order. Its theological tenor rings out in the proclamation that the king in his own realm has the duty of caring for true religion and giving reverence to God, which obligation falls with equal force upon his generals and governors. The magistrate was charged with the punishment of that which is "contrary to the divine prescriptions of Piety and Religion." This because Virginia has "no other ends but such as may punctually advance the glory, and propagation of the heavenly goodness," and because success can come only from "the King of Kings." With a liberal use of the death penalty as a sanction, blasphemy, derision of God's word or the Trinity, sacrilege, slander, bearing false oath or witness, and violation of the Sabbath were among the many things proscribed. In this strict manner, the "pious and Christian plantation" was to be maintained.[5]

The organic, hierarchical conception of society, which informed the code, was based upon a positive affirmation of the inequality of men as a divine mandate. Although he spoke later in the colonial period, Anglican Commissary James Blair caught the spirit of this view when he preached: "It was never our Saviour's Design to set all Men upon the Level, by taking away all Distinction between Princes and Subjects, Masters and Servants, Parents and Children, and in short, between also Superiors and Inferiors. This levelling Principle has no Countenance . . . from . . . any . . . Text in Scripture; and would occasion all manner of Anarchy and Confusion in the World."[6]

The provision of the Charter of 1609 placing absolute executive and martial power in the Virginia Governor, who was appointed for life and was subject only to the company council in England, was abolished along with the code in 1619. A form of government was established which comprehended civil magistrates, English common law, and a representative legislature—the General Assembly, consisting of the governor's council selected by the company, and the House of Burgesses, elected by the freemen. This arrangement was in imitation of the existing structure of the parent joint-stock London Company. Thus was the first English colonial representative assembly brought into existence. The new and more liberal form of government, reemphasizing the traditional rights of Englishmen, must not be ascribed to a repudiation of the basic religious, social, and political thought, but to the abuse of executive power and a woeful lack of prosperity, which was piously read as a sign of divine disapproval. When, by 1624, success was still not forthcoming, the king dissolved the company and issued a royal charter for the colony, under which recognition was eventually given to the assembly, which thereafter remained the viable center of government in Virginia.[7]

The significance of the failure symbolized in the dissolution of the Virginia Company, according to Perry Miller, lies not in a nonexistent victory of Stuart "tyranny" over a nascent republican "liberalism," but in the destruction of a colonial venture pursued in terms of an hierarchical, providential universe. The rejection of this basic idea transformed Virginia from a holy endeavor into a commercial enterprise. Unlike New England, Virginia did not gradually evolve into a competitive society, but was made such by a "dramatic failure" which undercut the underlying teleology. The missionary spirit waned as Providence appeared to beckon men to walk, not in the path of the Apostles, but in pursuit of freedom and material abundance. As Miller puts it: "In simple fact, the glorious mission of Virginia came down to growing a weed." God's will having become obscure to human eyes, the sole remaining certainty was the traditional rights of Englishmen exercised and safeguarded in the elective assembly. In this way the spirit of competition became predominant in Virginia long before it did in the mother country.[8]

It would be a mistake to conclude that religion became a secondary consideration in the life of Virginians or that the organic conception of society was erased. Louis B. Wright has recently reminded us that the ruling class of planters remained vitally interested in religion throughout the colonial period. A civilization without religion was to them a contradiction in terms. And yet their great interest was not theological but ethical, with religion seen as a guide to a holy life. "Practical godliness" was considered the substance, doctrines and ceremonies, the shell.

Similarly, the traditional Anglican spirit of moderation was enhanced by the necessity of adjusting to the new environment. Proceeding on the ancient premise of one society comprehending church and state, the parish with its vestry was an important cog of social and political order, assisting the civil government, enforcing morality, providing for the poor, and staffed by the same small group of men who held the principal political offices. The absence of a resident bishop created a vacuum of power which was filled by the vestries with the approval of the assembly. Ministers, who because of the absence of a bishop had to be ordained in England, were chosen by the congregations. In effect Virginia had a Congregational church polity which differed from that of New England principally in that it had no consciously articulated theological justification. The Anglican Church in Virginia was comprised of independent parishes governed by the assembly in temporal matters of church and state, with the governor and council having jurisdiction over clergymen in all civil and ecclesiastical causes.[9]

The effect on the church of the great expanse of land, the dispersed settlements and the absence of large towns, was remarked by a devout Anglican minister in 1661. He saw it as robbing God "of that publick Worship and Service . . . he requires to be constantly paid to him, at the time appointed for it, in the publick Congregations of his people in his House of Prayer." This he deemed the prime cause of the lack of prosperity, Christian neighborliness and education, and the difficulty of ministerial detection of vice as well as the scandal afforded to the Indians. Before Virginia could become a "well-ordered Christian Society," the people would have to build towns, after which a resident bishop could be appointed to one as his see. Underlying the argument was the assumption that if the English Church and civilization were to be faithfully reproduced in America, it would be necessary to arrest the centrifugal impulses of a plantation economy and to duplicate the English scene.[10]

The vast spaces and the thin spread of the population aided in bringing about religious toleration. Although heresy was proscribed and dissenters put under penalty at various times, Virginia was destined to effect *de facto* toleration long before the Revolution of 1776. Preoccupied with their plantation economy, the hard-working men of affairs who ruled the colony were guided by a pragmatic psychology which brought them to ignore speculative questions of church and state and to dwell upon practical means of adjustment within the framework of basic British institutions.

By the start of the eighteenth century, Virginia had evolved a social order steeped in the spirit of moderation, dominated by the landed gentry, and accepted generally by the populace. Politically, the colony was near to being an agrarian republic with suffrage limited to free-

holders and with the principal organs of government—the parish
vestry, the county courts and the assembly—controlled by the large
landholders who disdained demagoguery and looked upon their representative function in the lofty Burkean sense.

Just as no speculative theology was produced in colonial Virginia, so
was no systematic political theory expounded before the Revolutionary
period. When that time arrived, the practical planters could generalize
in terms of their long-existing republicanism and localism in both church
and state, having no fear of the people as a "great beast," a "rabble" or
an irrational mob, because there existed no large city to spawn such
an entity in the whole of Virginia's history.[11]

The Episcopate Dispute: Prelude to the Revolution

Pressure by American High Anglican churchmen after 1763 for the
establishment of an American episcopacy provoked strong colonial
dissent. As Carl Bridenbaugh, the latest historian of the episode has
described it, the colonial high churchmen failed to discern that toleration
in America was gradually being transformed into an ideal of religious
freedom. The dominant sectarianism and republicanism in church
government was influencing a growing sentiment for more republicanism
in civil government and moving toward an ultimate assertion of complete
separation of church and state. In Virginia the episcopate question was
joined with the issue of toleration of the increasing number of religious
dissenters above the fall line and the growing attack on the establishment itself, to become a principal factor leading to the religious liberty
clause in the Virginia Bill of Rights of 1776, the bill for disestablishment
of the same year, and to the statute for religious freedom of 1786.[12]

Finally, the dispute over the episcopate served to bring the colonial
dissenters and most of the Southern Anglican clergy and laity together
before the programs of British politicians provoked moves for colonial
political unity. In this light it has been considered an essential part of
the American Revolution. Like its later political counterpart, the American opposition was a successful effort to conserve what had long been
practiced. John Adams' observations, made long after the event, illustrate the point.

Where is the man to be found at this day . . . who will believe that the apprehension of Episcopacy contributed fifty years ago, as much as any other
cause, to arouse the attention, not only of the inquiring mind, but of the
common people, and urge them to close thinking on the constitutional authority of parliament over the colonies. . . . The objection was not merely
to the office of a bishop, though even that was dreaded, but to the authority
of parliament, on which it must be founded. . . . All sensible men knew that

this system could not be affected but by act of parliament; and if parliament could do this, they could do all things.[13]

The Anglican Division: Jacob Duché (1738–1798) and Jonathan Boucher (1738–1804)

Illustrative of the division in the ranks of American Anglican clergy-men just before the Revolution are the positions taken by Jacob Duché and Jonathan Boucher regarding the consensual theory of government. Duché, a Pennsylvania Whig who became a loyalist after the Declaration of Independence, proceeded in a sermon in 1775, from the Pauline text, "Stand fast, therefore in the liberty wherewith Christ hath made us free," to hold that civil liberty is as much a gift of God from Christ as is spiritual liberty. He contended that "it must surely have been this Wisdom of the Father that first taught man, by social compact, to secure to himself the possession of those necessaries and comforts which are so dear and valuable to his natural life." Though no particular mode of government is pointed out to man in the Gospel, "yet the benevolent spirit of that gospel is directly opposed to every other form, than such as has the Common Good of mankind for its end and aim." Because the common good is a "matter of common feeling," Duché asserted, "true government can have no other foundation than Common Consent." It followed that where rulers "abuse their sacred trust" by attempts to oppress and injure persons from whom, under God, their power is derived, the demands of humanity, reason, and Scripture dictate that Christians "stand fast in that Liberty wherewith Christ . . . hath made them free." Concerning the scriptural injunction so heavily emphasized by proponents of passive obedience, "Submit to every ordinance for the Lord's sake," Duché contended that no submission to unrighteous ordinances of unrighteous men could be "for the Lord's sake."[14]

Boucher, an English-born Maryland divine, was a staunch Tory who returned to England after the outbreak of the Revolution. His thought was a conflation of Protestant pessimism concerning human nature, the Stuart divine right and patriarchal theories of authority and obedience, the traditionalist's dread of change and the conservative's conception of the organic, hierarchical social order, epitomized in an established church. Boucher maintained that if, as Duché had argued, the common good is a matter of "common feeling," it did not follow that it must be instituted by common consent. He would not, however, accept the premise, contending that if by "common feeling" is meant common sense, the assertion is meaningless or false, because men have never agreed "as to what is, or is not, 'the common good.'" Addressing himself to the equalitarian assumption underlying the consent theory, he declared that not only are men by nature unequal but there can be no government "without some relative inferiority and superiority."[15]

To explain the origin of government Boucher borrowed liberally from Robert Filmer's *Patriarcha,* which Locke had attacked, to maintain that the first father was the first king and that monarchy is the most ancient and divinely prescribed form of government. With monarchical government dictated by Scripture, history, and reason, its cornerstone is the "principle of obedience for conscience sake." Christianity and human interest forbid resistance to authority; nonresistance is "the true doctrine of the Church of England agreeable to God's word." Besides, it is impossible to administer any government framed with the reserved right of resistance; to resist government is to destroy it. Thus each subject owes his government obedience, an obedience which is active, "where the duty enjoined may be performed without offending God," and passive, "where that which is commanded by man is forbidden with God." Boucher believed that the preaching of the right of resistance was breeding disrespect for authority in general and pulling society apart at the seams.[16]

Given Boucher's divine right, patriarchal justification of monarchical government and the attendant duty of nonresistance, his conception of civil liberty followed in train. As he saw it,

True liberty . . . is a liberty to do everything that is right, and the being restrained from doing anything that is wrong. So far from our having a right to do everything that we please, under a notion of liberty, liberty itself is limited and confined—but . . . only by laws which are at the same time its foundation and its support.[17]

Because liberty ultimately consists in subservience to God, to respect the laws is to respect liberty. Man is free insofar as he is governed by law and not by arbitrary will. The more carefully the laws are drawn and the more rigorously they are executed, the greater degree of civil liberty. To Boucher the mixed British Constitution was the most splendid frame ever devised to guarantee freedom.

Boucher's definition of liberty squares with the earlier conceptions of the Puritan, John Winthrop, and the Quaker, William Penn, insofar as all agree that liberty entails a right only to do that which, in Winthrop's words, is "good, just and honest." They agree that liberty is possible only under just law. However, whereas Winthrop leaned in the direction of magisterial prerogative in the determination of the political good, and Penn emphasized consent of the governed, Boucher exalted monarchical prerogative, and allowed for representative government only to the degree permitted by the monarch. All three admitted the ultimate sovereignty of the individual conscience, but while Penn focused on the Inner Light, Winthrop emphasized conscience informed by Scripture as interpreted by the Puritan authorities, and Boucher pointed to both Scripture and ecclesiastical law as authoritatively determined. Concerning resistance to unjust laws, Boucher was probably closer to Penn than to Winthrop. It is true that Penn subscribed to the consent theory; but as a devout Quaker he never drew out the full implications of this theory in the form of active resistance. Winthrop, it appears, would have, albeit guardedly and somewhat grudgingly, admitted the necessity of active resistance in certain situations. Boucher would only allow for passive submission, which entailed mere peaceful refusal to comply with a positive law contrary to the law of God and an acceptance of the attendant penalty.

Boucher's critique of the contract and resistance theories, like that of Filmer from whom he drew, has been generally ignored, peremptorily rejected, or dismissed by dint of its association with the patriarchal theory. And yet it has substance in pointing out not merely inadequacies of the contract theory as an explanation of the historical origin of government but as a theory of moral right and obligation. Particularly is the latter true if the theory is extended to mean that *all* authority is validated only in terms of consent. Even Locke admitted the existence of a law of nature in his state of nature which cannot, morally speaking, be abrogated by consent upon or after the establishment of the political state. Then, too, if one proceeds from the tenets of individualism, natural freedom and equality, and the contract theory, Boucher and Filmer would argue that to be logical one must agree that (1) individual consent must be given to specific laws and ordinances as well as to the initial establishment of government; (2) neither one's parents nor a majority legitimately can bind an individual; to conclude as Locke does that an original consent to adhere to majority rule is thereafter binding, is to relinquish the original principle of equality; (3) it cannot be maintained that acquiescence implies consent because acquiescence may issue from impotence or incapacity with the result that any existing government which can maintain its power is legitimized; (4) the same principle of equality that exempts one from being governed without his consent entitles one to recall and resume that consent when he sees fit.

The Significance of Anglicanism in the History of American Political Thought

Where the established church in colonial America was Anglican, it was composed of low churchmen unencumbered in the exercise of their beliefs and practices by a resident hierarchy. The European Hookerian formulation, insofar as it stressed the ultimate sovereignty of the human legislator designated by consent in both church and state, was indeed compatible with the corresponding religious and civil policies of the southern colonies, although there is no evidence it was ever consciously used as a rationale. The Stuart formulation, with its emphasis upon divine right monarchy, nonresistance, and episcopal government as a necessary counterpart, was fundamentally incompatible with the jealously guarded republicanism which evolved in both church and state. If, then, we equate Anglicanism with the high church Stuart conception, which was adhered to by men like Boucher, we must consign it to the category of lost causes. If, however, we define Anglicanism to include all those who chose to regard themselves as members of the Church of England, the appraisal must differ. But we must remember that in doing this, we are emptying the term of substantive content and reducing it to something almost purely nominal.

The Anglican Virginian and the New England Puritan had much in common. Their principal difference was temperamental in nature; the Virginian, perhaps because of the traditional Anglican proclivity toward compromise, was possessed, to a higher degree, of the quality of moderation. Thus he was neither given to theological speculatio₁ nor to reflective political thought apart from successful political practice in the effective implementation of traditional rights of Englishmen. It should be remembered that Virginia was established before the Stuart formulation was officially adopted and effected in England. This factor, along with the absence of a hierarchy, and the different environment with its vast spaces and thin spread of population, provided the conditions in which the republicanism inherent in church government by vestry and civil government by assembly could develop. Thus there existed, when the time was ripe, no religious impediment to acceptance by Virginians of the consent and resistance theories. It was no accident that a majority of the signers of the Declaration of Independence were at least nominal members of the Anglican communion.

NOTES

1. *The Laws of Ecclesiastical Polity* consists of eight books; the first four were published in 1593, the fifth in 1597 and the last three after Hooker's death in 1600. On Hooker and Aquinas see Peter Munz, *The Place of Hooker in the History of Thought* (London, 1952), pp. 29–67 and F. J. Shirley, *Richard Hooker and Contemporary Political Ideas* (London, 1949), p. 90ff.

2. On Hooker and Marsilius see Munz, *op. cit.*, pp. 68–109, and Shirley, *op. cit.*, pp. 112–125.

3. Daniel Boorstin, *The Americans: The Colonial Experience* (New York, 1958), p. 97.

4. Perry Miller, "Religion and Society in the Early Literature of Virginia," in *Errand Into the Wilderness* (Cambridge, Mass., 1956, Harper Torchbook paperback, New York, 1964), pp. 99–141. The first quotation above is cited in the Miller article on page 122 and the Rolfe quotation is at page 119.

5. "Lawes Divine, Morall and Martiall" (1612), in Peter Force (ed.), *Tracts and Other Papers*, III, No. 2; Miller, *op. cit.*, pp. 132–133.

6. James Blair, *Sermons* (London, 1740), IV, 179.

7. See Richard L. Morton, *Colonial Virginia* (Chapel Hill, 1960, 2 vols.), I, 51–105; Miller, *op. cit.*, pp. 126–134.

8. Miller, *op. cit.*, p. 138.

9. Louis B. Wright, "Pious Reading in Colonial Virginia," *Journal of Southern History*, VI (1940), 383–392; Boorstin, *op. cit.*, pp. 123–131.

10. "Virginia's Cure," in Force, *op. cit.*, III, No. 15.

11. Boorstin, *op. cit.*, pp. 116, 117.

12. Carl Bridenbaugh, *Mitre and Sceptre* (New York, 1962), pp. 57, 312. See also Arthur L. Cross, *The Anglican Episcopate and the American Colonies* (New York, 1902), and E. B. Greene, "The Anglican Outlook on the American Colonies in the Early Eighteenth Century," *American Historical Review* (Oct., 1914), 64–85.

13. C. F. Adams (ed.), *The Works of John Adams* (Boston, 1850–1856, 10 vols.), X, 185.

14. Duché's sermon can be found in Miscellaneous Pamphlets, Vol. 669 in the rare book room of the Library of Congress.

15. Boucher's sermon replying in 1775 to Duché's can be found in his book, *A View of the Causes & Consequences of the American Revolution* (New York, reproduced from the original edition of 1797 and published in 1967), pp. 495–560. The quotations above can be found on pages 513–515.

16. *Ibid.*, pp. 525, 306, 487, 546.

17. *Ibid.*, p. 511.

Chapter 5

THE NEW ENGLAND CLERGY AND THE ENLIGHTENMENT

There is no escaping church-tyranny, but by asserting the right of private Judgment, for every Man in the Affairs of his own Salvation.

COTTON MATHER

The eighteenth-century Enlightenment turned the critical eye of reason upon existing institutions, practices, and traditions, seeking to bring life into accord with a concept of nature divorced from theological considerations. Its key philosophical symbols were reason, nature, experience, and humanity; the symbols of its political mythology were state of nature, law of nature, natural rights, and social contract. Because the American manifestation of the Enlightenment had deep roots in Anglo-Saxon empiricism, experimentalism, and experience in limited government, it put less emphasis upon abstract reason than did European thought. The same symbols were used but they appeared to the American generally to confirm historical experience and consequently constituted less a revolutionary threat than an affirmation of practice. Within memory men had formed civil societies by mutual compact; their colonial charters assured them enjoyment of the rights and liberties of Englishmen, which, almost imperceptibly, became identified with natural rights; the law of God, which all pious colonists acknowledged, tended to become assimilated to the law of nature as the deity became more and more naturalized and nature deified; and the growing material abundance, the advance of commerce and the arts, and the extension of civilization, afforded pragmatic proof of the fruits of liberty, and made self-evident the Lockian end of government —preservation of life, liberty, and property.

After the grant of a royal charter to Massachusetts in 1691, the principal clergymen still optimistically believed that despite the winds of rationalism, politics could be kept subservient to theology in the definition of social order. It was not long, however, before the charter and the interpretations given its grant of liberties and privileges were accepted by many as justified in themselves. Although the theory that church and state were partners in the maintenance of social order was still generally accepted, there was a major shift in emphasis: religion was no longer uniformly viewed as the all-pervasive, predominant force, and the church came to be regarded by many as a vested interest to be measured chiefly in terms of its utility. In the first half of the eighteenth century, the theocentric New England society gradually became secularized, and reason became more than a mere supplement to revelation.

Crucial questions going to the heart of the official Puritan theology and social theory arose to challenge the ingenuity of the generally conservative clergy. Were the newly guaranteed liberties of conscience and religious toleration compatible with the idea of total depravity? Or, for that matter, was the conception of a rational, social state of nature? Could the original aim of the founders of the "City upon a Hill" be furthered by a regime constructed on Whig principles and dedicated in practice to minimizing executive authority? The Whig doctrine emphasized happiness as the end of government and implied that its content could be discovered by all well-disposed men, particularly the propertied, through individual reason. If men, whether of the elect or not, can naturally discern what their own happiness consists in, then, again, how can they be considered depraved? Similarly, the Whig concept of the contractural origin of the state ran athwart the Puritan consensual theory. As has been seen, popular consent, to the Puritan fathers, merely served as the vehicle by which the authorities, who have their ordinance from God, were designated. How could the Whig doctrine of popular sovereignty be squared with the official theory that the responsibility of political rulers is to God in the service of the objective good? How could a "silent democracy in the face of a speaking aristocracy," be preserved on Whiggish grounds, unless perhaps the propertied elect was substituted for the religious elect?

When Massachusetts was a century old, the deviation from the original purpose was so considerable and the challenge of reason, utility, and material interest so strong that Congregational ministers could be found justifying Christianity on the ground that it "hath a natural tendency to promote civil Peace and Order; to make a People prosperous in their trade and business." To understand the nature of these changes, and the deviations from, and modifications of, Puritan theory, this chapter will examine the thought of the most significant clerical spokesmen of eighteenth-century New England.[1]

John Wise (1652–1725)

Moses Coit Tyler, the perceptive literary historian of the American colonial period, called John Wise "the first great American democrat" and "the most powerful and brilliant prose-writer produced in this country during the colonial time."[2] Even though Wise's ideas had little influence upon the later development of American democratic thought and the Revolution, his rationalist defense of the Congregational ecclesiastical polity, and his departure from the theologically oriented political thought of the Puritan fathers render him significant.

Wise was a courageous minister in rural Ipswich, Massachusetts, who first gained attention in 1687 when he was jailed and forbidden to preach for persuading townsmen not to comply with a tax which had been levied by the autocratic Governor Edmund Andros without the approval of the assembly. In 1692 he stoutly opposed the current persecutions for witchcraft. His claim to fame, however, lies in his replies to an unsigned document drawn up in 1705 by an association of Boston ministers, which threatened the independence of the Congregationalist churches by proposing a synodal Presbyterian type of church government.[3] *The Churches Quarrel Espoused* (1710) was a satirical treatment of the proposal and *A Vindication of the Government of New England* (1717) was a defense of democratic ecclesiastical polity.

The *Vindication* contains five "demonstrations," including arguments from Scripture, history, and reason. The argument from reason and nature was not original, being borrowed copiously from the German jurist, Samuel von Pufendorf (1632–1694), who in his *De Jure Naturae et Gentium,* expounded a natural law doctrine similar to Locke's. Because Wise based his case for democracy in church government on the notion that the church polity should be in imitation of the best form of civil polity (an approach diametrically opposed to that of the Puritan fathers), he examined closely the principles of civil government.

Waiving consideration of "Man's moral turpitude," he looked upon man in non-Calvinist fashion as a creature "furnished essentially with many ennobling immunities, which render him the most august animal in the world." Although "a principle of self-love and self-preservation is very predominant in every man's being," he has a "sociable disposition" and "an affection or love to mankind in general." In the state of nature man owes homage "to none but God himself." His original "natural" liberty, besides being external in the sense of freedom "not to be controlled by the Authority of any other," is internal in the sense of the free use of the mind in tune with "the tyes of reason and the laws of nature." All else, Wise declared, is "brutal, if not worse." And yet, although man can through his reason discern the laws of nature, he is "often found to be malicious, insolent and easily provoked," a fact which endangers him and others. To preserve himself "it is necessary that he be sociable . . . that he be capable and disposed to unite himself to those of his own species, and to regulate himself towards them, that they may have no fair reason to do him harm, but rather incline to promote his interests, and secure his rights and concerns." Consequently, it is "a fundamental law of nature, that every man as far as in him lies, do maintain a sociableness with others." And "from the principles of sociableness it follows as a fundamental law of nature, that man is not so wedded to his own interest, but that he can make the common good the mark of his aim."[4]

Accordingly, men who are by nature free, equal, and sociable do by covenant: (1) "join in one lasting society, that they may be capable to concert the measure of their safety by a public vote"; (2) set up a particular form of government; (3) form an agreement "whereby those upon whom sovereignty is conferred engage to take care of the common peace and welfare," and whereby the subjects "promise to yield them faithful obedience." As in Locke, but in contrast to Hobbes, man gives up to civil society only as much of his natural liberty and equality as is required by the public good. It follows that man's original liberty, "under due restrictions," should "be cherished in all wise governments; or otherwise a man in making himself a subject . . . alters himself from a freeman into a slave, which is repugnant to the law of nature." Nevertheless, even bad government may be preferred to none at all. Striking a Hobbesian note, Wise maintained that "a churlish tyranny is better than an insolent anarchy, where men are without law, and all hail fellows, not well, but badly, met."[5]

The secular logic of Wise's thought reached its high point in his definition of the end of government, which makes no mention of religion: "The end of all good government is to cultivate humanity, and promote the happiness of all, and the good of every man in all his rights, his life, liberty, estate, honor, etc., without injury or abuse to any." In both its origin and content, government is dependent upon the popular will. Monarchy and aristocracy are unsuitable forms, and although the English mixed constitution is most praiseworthy, democracy is the most ancient form and "a very honorable and regular government according to the dictates of right reason." Wise would subscribe to no "silent democracy in the face of a speaking aristocracy," but extolled government by general assembly of all the people with majority rule as the moving and binding principle.[6]

Because democracy is the most reasonable form of civil government, Wise concluded that it is also justified as a legitimate church polity. Thus on a purely secular and rational basis, he vindicated congregationalism. Perry Miller comments: "The uniqueness of his treatment consists in his isolating the rational proof, of allowing it to stand entirely by itself; in daring to dispense, if only for the moment, with Biblical and historical evidences, he established the philosophy so firmly upon a secular basis of nature that all other testimonies were reduced to subsidiary confirmations." Reason could now stand independent of and apart from theology as an autonomous voice to be heard and solemnly regarded.[7]

The boldness of Wise's formulation is pointed up by a comparison of his conception of liberty with that of Winthrop. To Winthrop natural or original liberty spelled a brutish anarchy; to Wise it was epitomized in a prepolitical life in accordance with reason and natural law with "all the rest" deemed "brutal, if not worse." He thus imputed brutality to rulers who in the manner of Winthrop define, independently of the people, a policy of the true, the good, the honest. He believed that the people must not only by contract establish the state and its governors, but decide by themselves the content of law and policy. Consequently his view closely approximated what Winthrop (and Cotton) had earlier condemned as "mere democracy."[8]

At bottom Wise's thought is somewhat ambivalent. The norm is original or natural liberty under the law of nature, but the fact is that men are impelled to civil society to preserve themselves. His state of nature is at once benevolent and dangerous. To effect the jump from the state of nature to civil society the trait of sociability is imputed to man. Wise had never read Locke, but he may have read Hobbes; certainly he absorbed much of Hobbes through Pufendorf. His difficulties concerning natural man flow from his acceptance of modern natural law thought which uses as the primary datum not man as a political animal but man as an individual without the state. Conceding these points, however, it does not follow that one is left with Winthrop's aristocratic principle as the sole alternative, nor is democracy necessarily precluded. It is to Wise's credit that although he wrote under the insufficiencies of Pufendorf's natural law formula, he employed it, unlike Pufendorf who advocated enlightened despotism, ably to argue the reasonableness of democracy in state and church.

Jonathan Edwards and the Great Awakening

The Great Awakening was the American counterpart of the evangelical fervor which swept over England and a good part of Western Europe from 1730 to 1760. An attempt to revive the old zeal and piety, the movement appealed basically to the emotions in the hope of evoking a concretely evident experience of conversion in the individual.

Jonathan Edwards (1703–1758), Congregationalist minister in the Connecticut Valley of Massachusetts, played a leading role in the revival in America, though he was neither a fanatic nor an emotional zealot. Far from being the anachronism which Parrington, because of Edwards' reaffirmation of pure Calvinism, chose to call him, Edwards used Lockian psychology and Newtonian physics to attempt to resolve knotty theological problems which preoccupy men even today. His empirical, mechanistic orientation brought him to discard teleology, final causes, and intelligible forms, and to chuck the old Ramist logic* of the Puritan fathers. Following Locke, he preached that God does not implant ideas or obligations in man, but operates upon him through sensations. Thus he believed that a man is predestined to be as he perceives.[9]

Rejecting completely the federal covenant theology, Edwards substituted experience for legality and reasserted God's sovereign omnipotence. He maintained that men had come to construe the covenant of grace not in terms of what God mercifully bestowed, but of what He was bound to grant. With him, facts, not prescriptive charters or legal instruments, were the decisive factors. Thus theology must proceed not from logic but from experience. Similarly, God is not bound by any promise or contract; all that preserves men is His arbitrary will and uncovenanted forbearance.[10]

Edwards went further than other contemporary colonial Lockians in holding that an idea is not only a perception but an emotion. In this light, the mystery of grace is dissolved; grace is naught but a "simple idea" which can be learned from experience, that is, perceived intellectually and felt emotionally. Conversion is thus a sensible experience and oratory is a vehicle to evoke it. Then, too, the mind communes with God, not by way of inward perfection, but by contemplating nature. In reading the emotional into the rational, the supernatural into the natural, and in reducing all to perception, Edwards sought to make comprehensible, within terms of the new science, the grave and awesome realities of God's omnipotence, of predestination, and of human pride and sin.[11]

Edwards' thoughts about political rule were shaped by his Lockian psychology and his experience in the Great Awakening. Despite the broadsides of John Wise, the social theory of the New England ministry remained much the same in Edwards' time as Winthrop had stated it. The people must be told by minister and magistrate what to do and what not to do, without consideration of immediate interest. Since Winthrop's day, however, the long-time practice of renewing the covenant of grace had resulted in a situation which ran contrary to the theory. As Perry Miller explains it, the minister found that instead of standing in the pulpit and saying: "I speak, you keep quiet"; he was gradually brought to a point where he, in effect, pleaded, "Come, and

---

* Ramist logic has been discussed in Chapter 2, p. 40.

speak up." Thus under the impact of the Great Awakening the democracy no longer remained silent before the speaking aristocracy.[12]

The logic of the revival movement forced Edwards and other ministers
not only to grant admission to church membership to those who desired
it, but to arouse as many people as possible to insist upon admission.
Edwards perceived that no longer could a religious or political leader
follow Winthrop in dictating the eternally good, just, and honest; instead
he had to mingle with people and persuade them to his position. He
held that political rulers above all must be men of "great ability for the
management of public affairs." They must have developed "great
natural abilities" by study, observation, learning, and, most of all, skill.
They must be able to discern "those things wherein the public welfare
or calamity consists, and the proper means to avoid the one and promote the other." Similarly, they must have "a great understanding of
men and things, a great knowledge of human nature, and of the way of
accommodating themselves to it." Edwards was contending that rulers
must adjust to actual human and social experience. His consideration of
government was almost completely in terms of utility; piety and good
breeding, which loomed large in Winthrop's idea of qualifications, were
brought in ancillary to utility. On this empirical ground there was no
room in Edwards' eyes for a statecraft of preconceived, logically exact
ethical postulates.[13]

Edwards recognized that the economic and social order of New
England, with its increasing emphasis upon rationalism in thought, and
commerce, profit, and speculation, was in contradiction to the orthodox
theology. Instead of renouncing Calvinism, as the growing numbers of
Arminians were to do, he condemned sharp practices. In speaking to
the merchants, speculators, and traders of his congregation, he declared
that a ruler must, in the service of welfare, oppose all persons "of a mean
spirit" who seek by trick and intrigue "to promote their private interest"
and who "take advantage of their authority or commission to line their
own pockets with what is fraudulently taken or withheld from others."
Two years after exalting leadership by skill and experience and not by
the accumulation of wealth, and after condemning men of commerce in
terms of public welfare and calamity, Edwards was forced out of his
pulpit.[14]

Although Edwards was no democrat, the conception of rulership
which arose out of his sensationist psychology and his experience in the
Great Awakening is strikingly modern not only in its secularism but
in its utilitarian emphasis upon accommodation, skill, and experience in
the service of public welfare. His prodigious effort to reconcile theory
and practice and to counter the growing smug and comfortable materialism by demonstrating the truth of the old Calvinist dogmas, the
insecurity of life and the uncertainty of salvation, in terms of Locke's

psychology and Newton's physics, ran counter to the main current of contemporary life. The shrewdly practical Benjamin Franklin, not the profoundly speculative Jonathan Edwards, was to be the exemplar for America.

Arminianism: Charles Chauncey and Jonathan Mayhew

Arminianism has already been explained as a recurrent reaction to the rigorous insistence in Calvinist theology upon predestination, total depravity, limited atonement, and the inability of man by his own effort to gain God's favor. Instead it emphasized God's goodness, love and mercy, and man's moral free agency and goodness. With this generous conception of human nature, reason was exalted and the emotions distrusted. Arminianism in eighteenth-century New England appealed to practical and affluent men of common sense and was drawn upon more and more by many of the clergy who were repelled and shocked by the "enthusiastic" emotionalism of the Great Awakening. Among the leading Arminians was Charles Chauncey (1705–1787). A Boston Congregationalist minister and a great antagonist of Edwards and the emotionalism of the revival, Chauncey wrote in 1739: "As men are rational, free Agents, they can't be religious but with the free Consent of their Wills; and this can be gain'd in no Way, but that of Reason and Persuasion." Believing that happiness is realized through the restraint of reason upon the passions, he pronounced: "The plain Truth is, an enlightened Mind, not raised Affections, ought always to be the Guide of those who call themselves Men." Chauncey defined the virtues of a Christian in terms at odds with the mystical and somewhat egalitarian notions of the revivalists. He emphasized lowliness, patience, meekness, gentleness, contempt of the world, resignation to God, sobriety, moderation, chastity, and contentedness with one's condition. Placed alongside his stress upon reason, moral free agency, personal responsibility, God's benevolence, etc., his list of virtues indicates that he may have used enlightened ideas to defend the *status quo*.[15]

In an election sermon of 1747 Chauncey explained the origin of government in terms of the reason of things and the will of God. God wills that some must rule and others be ruled so that "men's lives, liberties and properties" might be protected. Rulers, especially in a mixed state, must stay within the limits of power prescribed to them by the constitution. They must protect the basic liberties and rights of the people against arbitrariness and sedition. Especially must these rights be safeguarded against the depredations of those seeking power who "strike in with the popular cry of liberty and privilege."[16]

A staunch Whig, Chauncey, in his old age, was a friend of such revolutionary leaders as Samuel and John Adams. He led the Boston ministers in 1774 in refusing to read any proclamations of the governor and council and served as a voluble proponent of the cause of independence.

More well known and more important among Arminians was Jonathan Mayhew (1720–1760), a Boston Congregationalist minister, who, like his contemporary, Jonathan Edwards, saw clearly the contradiction between the accepted Puritan social theory and the economic and social practices in eighteenth-century New England. Unlike Edwards, he did not preach a return to pristine Calvinism, but rejected it root and branch. To the consternation of many of his clerical colleagues he openly and fully embraced Arminian theological principles and Whig political philosophy. In the 1740's he preached a religious and political doctrine congenial to rational and commercial Boston. Believing that "truth and moral rectitude are things fixed, stable, and uniform, having their foundation in the nature of things," and that man, because of his rationality, can freely choose, Mayhew concluded that those who strive to be good, with Christ as their example, have divine grace within them. Practice, not speculation, deeds, not words, private judgment, not authoritarian pronouncement, were most heavily stressed by him. His powerful opposition to the establishment of an Anglican episcopate in the colonies flowed from these sentiments.[17]

Mayhew's political thought, although rendered in terms of Scripture, was, in good part, an amalgam of the thought of Locke, Milton, Algernon Sidney and Benjamin Hoadly, the Anglican bishop from whose work he freely borrowed. It embraced these principles: (1) man is by nature essentially good; (2) government is established by consent of the people; (3) government is a trust, instituted for the common good; (4) insofar as government is just and aims at the common good, it is sacred and obedience is a Christian duty; (5) when rulers habitually act contrary to the common good, popular, active resistance is not only moral but required; and (6) the people, not the rulers, are the ultimate judges as to whether the common good is violated or not.

In his published sermon of 1750, *A Discourse Concerning Unlimited Submission and Non-Resistance to the Higher Powers,* Mayhew spoke on St. Paul's epistle to the Romans which enjoins men to be submissive to their lawful superiors because all authority issues from God. He made clear against the literalists that St. Paul meant submission not to all who bear the title of ruler but only to those "who *actually* perform the duty of rulers, by exercising a reasonable and just authority for the good of human society." Lest this be identified with a holy rule or a rule in Winthrop's sense, Mayhew asserted that "by *good rulers* are not intended such as are good in a *moral* or *religious,* but only in a *political* sense; those who perform their duty so far as their office extends; and so

far as civil society, as such, is concerned in their actions." The test is
thus secular and utilitarian. Laws must be "attempered and accomo-
dated to the common welfare of the subjects." When rulers act contrary
to the common welfare "they immediately cease to be the *ordinance* and
ministers of God; and no more deserve that glorious character than
common *pirates* and *highwaymen.*" Furthermore, the form of government matters not, so long as the end is subserved. Absolute monarchy,
however, is the most "unlikely " of all to realize the end.[18]

Mayhew's argument was rooted in the medieval and Whig conception
that what purports to be law must be inherently just. It is never law
merely because the sovereign wills it. He assumed a higher law of justice
which can be used as the standard. Because government exists to promote the common good, acts which defeat that end violate natural law.
Mayhew concluded from this, as had Locke, that resistance to unjust
rule is morally justifiable. The content of the critical norm, common
good, was also supplied by Mayhew in Lockian terms. In the election
sermon of 1754, after declaring government "a blessing to the world,"
he stated: "It is instituted for the preservation of men's persons,
properties and various rights, against fraud and lawless violence; and
that, by means of it, we may both procure, and quietly enjoy, those
numerous blessings and advantages, which are quite unattainable out
of society."[19]

To the difficult question of the precise point in time and the particular
circumstances in which resistance is justifiable, Mayhew, again like
Locke, was able to give but an approximate answer. He related, approvingly, that some men think active resistance warrantable "in cases
of very great and general oppression, when humble remonstrances fail
of having any effect; and when the public welfare cannot otherwise be
provided for and secured." He added that there must be a habitual
pattern of action by the rulers "which plainly shows, that they aim at
making themselves great, by the ruin of their subjects." He was fully
aware that "turbulent, vicious-minded men, may take occasion from this
principle . . . to raise factions and make disturbances in the state; and
to make resistance where resistance is needless, and therefore, sinful."
He also conceded that because rulers, being men, are fallible, it cannot
be expected that public affairs "should be always administered in the
best manner possible, even by persons of the greatest wisdom and
integrity." If resistance were justifiable upon mere mismanagement,
"it is scarcely supposeable that any government at all could be supported or subsist." To refute the charge that acceptance of the moral
right of revolution injects anarchy and confusion into the body politic,
Mayhew argued that men, in general, possess "a disposition to be . . .
submissive and passive and tame, under government. . . ." Nor will
people complain until they find themselves greatly abused and op-

pressed. Finally, he made the familiar point that because government is a trust wherein rulers are engaged to secure the common good, to say that the people in general are not the proper judges of the case "is as great *treason* as ever man uttered." It is the most vicious type of treason because it is directed not against a single man but against the entire body politic. As with Locke, the right to resist tyrannical rule was to Mayhew a conservative force. The real traitor is the tyrant; the "appeal to Heaven" has as its end his ouster and the reestablishment of lawful government.[20]

Mayhew went far beyond Wise in clearly and positively developing the right of resistance. For his work he was later praised by John Adams as one of the leading figures in the "awakening and revival of American principles and feeling," in the fifteen years preceding the Revolution.[21] Adams' choice of words was coincidental, but it does no violence to them to say that the end sought by the speculative Edwards in the "awakening and revival" of stark, unadulterated Calvinism, was replaced by the "awakening," if not "revival," of the practical, political, rationalist, libertarian design of Mayhew. Both he and Chauncey finally cut the last, tenuous connection with the austere Puritan past. Private judgment, religious toleration, separation of church and state, and the Whig principles of government were the values Mayhew held most high. That he was not irresponsible in his pronouncement of these beliefs is evident in the stirring concluding passage of his sermon of 1750:

Let us learn to be *free*, and to be *loyal*. Let us not profess ourselves vassals to the lawless pleasure of any man on earth. But let us remember, at the same time, that government is *sacred*, and not to be trifled with.[22]

The New England Clergy and the American Revolution

In her authoritative study, *The New England Clergy and the American Revolution*, Alice Baldwin remarks: "No one can fully understand the American Revolution and the American constitutional system without . . . realizing that for a hundred years before the Revolution men taught that these rights [life, liberty, and property] were protected by divine, inviolable law."[23]

From the beginning, New England clergymen and prominent laymen like Winthrop had propounded, under the legalistic federal theology, the primacy of the revealed law of God as the fundamental law of the universe. They also talked of, but emphasized less, a law of nature, which regenerate reason could discern, even though they thought of reason principally as an instrument by which to interpret the Bible. The conception of compact as the formative principle in church and state and rule by objective norms of justice were also essential elements of their political thought. These basic ideas, wedded closely to theology and ecclesiology, were, as the years went on, refined and developed. Under the impact of rationalism stress was placed increasingly upon reason as an autonomous instrument of justification. And yet, even in such Arminians as Chauncey and Mayhew, reason was employed within the context of biblical texts and an affirmation of the law of God as basic.[24]

The annual election sermons in both the seventeenth and eighteenth centuries were heard by many clergymen and laymen and served as "text books of politics." Their principal source was the Bible, supplemented by classical literature. The influence of Locke is evident even before he was quoted by name for what was apparently the first time in 1738. After 1763 allusions to his work and ideas were very frequent. Alice Baldwin relates that before 1763, at one time or another, New England ministers had preached the following as natural rights: "The right of a church to choose its own minister; the right of having the various kinds of religious covenants preserved, unless by proper judges one party had been found guilty of breaking them; the right to read and interpret the Bible for oneself and the right to a complete freedom of conscience, . . . the right to freedom of reading and of speech, to the sacredness of compacts, to the choice of officials, to the right of trial and appeal, to the fruits of a man's labor, unless given up with his own consent, to taxation for the good of the whole levied by the people themselves, to all the rights of Magna Charta and, implied in all these, the right to resist any encroachment upon these rights and . . . the right to all necessary means of defence."[25]

Thus the seeds of the great ideas asserted by Americans in the Declaration of Independence—law of nature, natural rights, consent of governed, rule of law, right of resistance to unjust rule—were sown and had taken firm root in the New England mind before they were refined and secularized in the language of rationalism. Furthermore, they were not expressions of utopian idealism nor were they the product of speculation; instead they were, in good part, generalizations from experience.

In conclusion, it can be said that although New England clergymen played an active political role in the Revolution, serving on committees of correspondence and as delegates to assemblies and constitutional conventions, Mayhew and Chauncey were the last of the line of great New England clergymen going back to John Cotton, to have a significant effect upon American political thought and life. What Parrington called the age of theology was replaced, as the eighteenth century moved on, by an age of politics. Given the development of modern science and the growth of commerce, with their great impact upon the minds of men, it is difficult to say whether Wise, Mayhew, and Chauncey did more than merely reflect the transformation to rationalism. But it can be stated with assurance that after them theology took a back seat to politics as the integrative force in American social life and thought. The lawyer came to the fore to replace the divine; the pulpit gave way to the courtroom, assembly room, and platform.

NOTES

1. Perry Miller, *The New England Mind: From Colony to Province,* pp. 376, 380, 381.

2. Moses Coit Tyler, *A History of American Literature* (*1607–1765*), originally published in 1878 (Ithaca, N.Y., 1949), pp. 359, 350.

3. On Wise's life and thought see, George A. Cook, *John Wise, Early American Democrat* (New York, 1952); Clinton Rossiter, *Seedtime of the Republic* (New York, 1953), pp. 205–226; Vernon Louis Parrington, *Main Currents in American Thought,* I, 118–125; Perry Miller, *The New England Mind: From Colony to Province,* pp. 288–302.

4. John Wise, *A Vindication of the Government of New England Churches* (Boston, 1772), pp. 22–25.

5. *Ibid.,* pp. 29, 40; John Wise, *The Churches Quarrel Espoused: Or, a Reply* (Boston, 1772), p. 99.

6. Wise, *A Vindication,* pp. 40, 31–33, 44.

7. Miller, *The New England Mind: From Colony to Province,* pp. 296–297, 298.

8. *Ibid.,* pp. 298–299.

9. Stow Persons, *American Minds* (New York, 1958), p. 106; Perry Miller, *Jonathan Edwards* (New York, 1949, paperback, 1959), pp. 55, 56, 65.

10. Miller, *Jonathan Edwards,* pp. 77, 78, 147, 31.

11. Perry Miller, "The Rhetoric of Sensation," *Errand into the Wilderness,* p. 179; Miller, *Jonathan Edwards,* pp. 186–187.

12. Miller, *Errand into the Wilderness,* pp. 161, 162.

13. *Ibid.,* quotation at pp. 164, 165.

14. *Ibid.,* quoted at p. 165.

15. Miller, *Jonathan Edwards,* quoted at pp. 165 and 176; Persons, *op. cit.,* pp. 92, 96.

16. Alice Baldwin, *The New England Clergy and the American Revolution,* quoted at pp. 43 and 44.

17. Rossiter, *Seedtime of the Republic,* quoted at pp. 235, 236.

18. Jonathan Mayhew, *A Discourse Concerning Unlimited Submission and Non-Resistance to the Higher Powers* (Sermon of Jan. 30, 1750), in Bernard Bailyn, ed., *Pamphlets of the American Revolution 1750–1756* (Cambridge, Mass., 1965), I, 226, 226n., 228, 233–234n.

19. Rossiter, *op. cit.,* quoted at p. 238.

20. Bailyn, *Pamphlets,* I, 186, 236, 237–238n.

21. Adams to Hezekiah Niles, Feb. 3, 1818, in C. F. Adams (ed.), *The Works of John Adams* (Boston, 1851, 10 vols.), X, 284.

22. Bailyn, *Pamphlets,* I, 247.

23. Baldwin, *op. cit.,* p. 39.

24. *Ibid.,* pp. 13–20.

25. *Ibid.,* pp. 6, 7, 82.

PART THREE

COLONIAL AND REVOLUTIONARY THOUGHT

Chapter 6

PARLIAMENTARY POWER AND THE RIGHTS OF ENGLISHMEN

JOHNSON: *The first Whig was the Devil.*
BOSWELL: *He certainly was, Sir. The Devil was impatient of sub-ordination; he was the first who resisted power. "Better to reign in Hell than to serve in Heaven."*
JAMES BOSWELL, *Life of Samuel Johnson*

The American Declaration of Independence was a political act which followed more than a decade of unresolved differences between the British authorities and the colonists concerning the true nature of the British Constitution and the Empire. In the first phase of this controversy, the issue was whether Parliament (King-in-Parliament) was limited in its authority and if so, to what degree, and what legal remedies existed for redress of alleged violations; in the second the question was whether the colonies were a part of the realm or separate dominions subject only to the royal prerogative. This chapter will be concerned principally with the first period.

The British conception of Parliamentary sovereignty which merged the absolutism of Hobbes with the emphasis of Locke upon legislative supremacy, grew out of the settlement of 1688. Drawn to its logical conclusion by great jurists such as Mansfield and Blackstone, Parliamentary sovereignty, when applied to imperial relations allowed the colonies no legal status between absolute dependence and absolute independence except by sovereign concession. Thus Mansfield proclaimed that "the British Legislature, as to the power of making laws, represents the whole British Empire, and has authority to bind every part, and every subject without the least distinction, whether such subjects have the right to vote, or whether the law binds places within the realm or without." Although most English Whigs believed that the power of Parliament, while absolute, should not be arbitrary, they regarded Parliament itself to be the supreme judge of the matter. The great English Tory, Samuel Johnson, defined most succinctly the indivisibility of sovereignty when he said: "In sovereignty there are no gradations." It was from this premise that Thomas Hutchinson, the native-born royal governor of Massachusetts, proceeded when he told the General Court in 1773 that he knew of "no line that can be drawn between the supreme authority of Parliament and the total independence of the colonies."[1]

The American colonists came to adhere to a conception of the British Constitution as a fundamental, immutable body of principles, rooted in divine and natural law, and binding on king and Parliament alike. As Samuel Adams put it in 1768: "The constitution is fixed; it is from thence that the supreme legislature as well as the supreme executive derives its authority." Likewise, applying the Whig conception of history to their situation, they tended more and more to analogize themselves to the ancient Saxons who upon their migration from the continent established their own free constitution. Finally, concerning the crucial question of the legal remedy for redress from an unconstitutional act, the Americans first put their faith in petition, remonstrance, and the broadcasting of their position in the press, with one or two significant figures contending that the executive courts possessed the authority to refuse to enforce an unconstitutional act. But as these means proved ineffectual, they resorted to economic reprisal, noncompliance, and ultimately violence and revolution.[2]

On the level of political theory, whereas the English Whigs of 1689 had addressed the Lockian natural rights doctrine against the royal prerogative, the colonists addressed the same theory, with a significant correction of focus away from Locke's stress upon legislative supremacy to the earlier emphasis of Richard Hooker on the sovereignty of higher law, against parliamentary sovereignty as well. They were influenced in this direction by the English "eighteenth-century commonwealthmen," particularly John Trenchard and Thomas Gordon (the authors of the widely read *Cato's Letters*) and Bishop Benjamin Hoadly, who though not original thinkers, believed that Parliament, as well as the Crown, should be limited. Flowing from the constitutional and political theory of the principal antagonists was a difference in jurisprudential outlook which grew wider as events brought them to press the logic of their positions to ultimate conclusions. In line with the modern monistic conception of sovereignty, English leaders came to accept a definition and justification of law in terms of its source—the will of Parliament. In line with the more ancient tradition of Fortescue, Bracton, St. Germain, and Coke, the colonists believed that law must ultimately be defined and justified in terms of its essence—its inherent rationality and conformity to fundamental principles.[3]

Then, too, by 1765 the Americans had long lived under what has been called a "practical constitution." This arrangement embodied customary rules of operation which had developed pragmatically on the basis of the colonial charters within the colonial governments and in their relations to British authorities, which added up to a *de facto* home rule.* In light of this it might be said that while the British had the logic of sovereignty on their side, on theirs the Americans had established practice, an ancient, albeit superseded tradition, and the reality of geographical separation.

The Issue of Parliamentary Taxation

When Parliament, desirous of making the colonists contribute to the costs of colonial defense at the end of the French and Indian War, enacted novel legislation in the form of the Sugar Act (1764), a customs tax for revenue purposes, and more particularly the Stamp Act (1765), a direct tax on instruments used in colonial transactions, it disrupted the "practical constitution" which the colonists assumed to be the proper order of the day. The issue soon became joined on the lines of constitutional principle. As the colonial objectors saw it, the new legislation, by taxing them without their consent, violated an ancient liberty of Englishmen, which was protected by the constitution and colonial charters, affirmed by the hoary precept, *Quod omnes tangit, ab omnibus approbetur,*† bolstered by the Whig view of history, and sanctioned by traditional practice.

---

* Colonial *de facto* home rule developed after 1680 within the framework of a few general British regulatory statutes such as the navigation and trade acts, along with the royal authority expressed in commissions and instructions to royal governors, review of court decisions by the judicial committee of the Privy Council, and review of colonial legislation by the Board of Trade. Concerning the internal colonial governments it must be remembered that structurally they resembled the English government with an assembly (chosen by an electorate based upon property and religious qualifications) alongside a governor and his appointed council in a bicameral legislature (except for Pennsylvania). In each colony the governor, whether appointed or elected was dependent upon the legislature for his salary. The legislatures, through their control of the purse, not only appropriated funds but supervised their expenditure, thus invading executive authority. For a colonial governor's appraisal of the colonial political mind, see Thomas Pownall, *The Administration of the Colonies* (1764), excerpted in Merrill Jensen (ed.), *English Historical Documents*, Vol. IX, *American Colonial Documents to 1776* (New York, 1955), 272.

† What touches all, is to be approved by all. This principle evolved from a technicality of the Roman law of co-tutorship into a legal theory of the right relationship between Popes and general councils in the works of canon lawyers writing around 1200. It then appeared in official documents convoking church councils and by the end of the century it appeared in writs of summons to secular representative assemblies. See Brian Tierney, "Medical Canon Law and Western Constitutionalism,"

The broadest official statement in opposition to the Sugar Act came from the New York Assembly. Asserting that exemption from the burden of "involuntary Taxes" must be "the grand principle of every free State" the legislators observed:

Without such a Right vested in themselves, exclusive of all others, there can be no Liberty, no Happiness, no Security; it is inseparable from the very Idea of Property, for who can call that his own, which may be taken away at the Pleasure of another? And so evidently does this appear to be the natural Right of Mankind. . . .[4]

In the official pronouncements of colonial opposition to the Stamp Act, the general tendency to identify constitutional right with the dictates of natural law is best illustrated in the Massachusetts Resolves. Declaring that "certain essential Rights of the *British* Constitution . . . are founded in the Law of God and Nature," the statement concluded, in part, that (1) "no Law of Society consistent with the Law of God and Nature" can rightfully divest men of these rights; (2) because "no Man can justly take the Property of another without his Consent" there exists the "Right of Representation in the same Body, which exercises the Power of making Laws for levying Taxes"; (3) this right and all other English liberties have been confirmed to the people by *Magna Carta* and later acts of Parliament; (4) and, consequently, "all Acts made, by any Power whatever, other than the General Assembly of this Province, imposing Taxes on the Inhabitants are Infringements of our *inherent* and *unalienable* Rights, as *Men* and *British Subjects,* and render void the most valuable Declarations of our Charter."[5]

Where the question of securing representation in the British Parliament was officially considered, it was rejected as impracticable. For remedies, the colonies trusted to the legal technique of remonstrance and petition, with two significant exceptions. Thus New York contended that the colonies "owe Obedience to all Acts of Parliament not inconsistent with the essential Rights and Liberties of *Englishmen*," implying that acts inconsistent therewith were not binding. Rhode Island directed its officers to proceed as usual and assured them indemnification if charged with nonenforcement.[6]

The declarations of the intercolonial Stamp Act Congress in 1765, while admitting subordination to Parliament, proclaimed: the Stamp Act violated a right of Englishmen; the people of the colonies could not "from their local Circumstances" be represented in the House of Commons; the only representatives of the colonial peoples are those chosen by them for

---

Catholic Historical Review, 52 (Apr., 1966), 13ff. For a thorough study of this concept as it affected English law and practice, see the article, "A Roman-Canonical Maxim, *Quod Omnes Tangit,* in Bracton and in Early Parliaments," by Gaines Post in his *Studies in Medieval Legal Thought* (Princeton, 1964), pp. 163–238.

their respective legislatures who alone can constitutionally tax them; and "the Increase, Prosperity and Happiness of these Colonies, depend on the full and free Enjoyment of their Rights and Liberties, and an Intercourse with *Great Britain* mutually Affectionate and Advantageous." The emphasis in the Declarations was not upon natural rights but upon legal rights supplemented by an argument of mutual self-interest.[7]

A recent study of the Stamp Act crisis argues persuasively that the colonists never accepted the distinction between internal and external taxes which allowed Parliament the power to impose the latter. Of the fifteen official statements of colonial rights at this time, only three could be construed as implying an acceptance of this distinction. Two of these were clarified in the following year by statements denying that Parliament had any authority to tax the colonies. Similarly, in the pronouncements of the significant colonial publicists, although a confusing terminology was at times used, the same rejection of Parliamentary power to tax was maintained. The distinction was really an English, not an American one; as a result the American position, in the period from 1764 to 1774, had a greater measure of consistency than is generally realized. When the Townshend duties were levied by Parliament in 1768 on the basis of this distinction, the argument brought against them by the colonists involved no unprincipled shifting of ground. In attempting to draw a line the colonists generally conceded the authority of Parliament to regulate trade and to legislate for the whole empire, but not to tax.[8]

Although the Stamp Act was repealed in 1766, Parliament at the same time passed the Declaratory Act which asserted its sovereign power to legislate for the colonies "in all cases whatsoever." This was the official British answer to the question as to where a line was to be drawn. It was fixed upon by astute observers in the colonies who were not diverted by the repeal of the Stamp Act, as a pronouncement which, if fully implemented, would reduce the colonists from freemen to slaves.[9]

The development of American political thought during this period can best be observed by considering the contributions of four principal figures—James Otis, Daniel Dulany, Richard Bland, and John Dickinson —all of whom were practical men of affairs, learned in the law, and drawn to questions of constitutional and political thought by the concrete problems which confronted them in public life.

James Otis (1725–1783): The American Coke

Otis was educated at Harvard, where he concentrated in classical and English literature. Thereafter he studied in the law office of Jeremiah Gridley, acquiring proficiency in the common law and admiralty law.

Gridley had as a maxim: "A lawyer ought never to be without a volume of natural or public law, or moral philosophy, on his table or in his pocket." Following this advice, Otis gained a scholar's knowledge of the history of law, jurisprudence, and ancient and modern political philosophy.[10]

Erratic in his brilliance and reckless in expression, Otis was nonetheless praised by such a formidable opponent as Governor Thomas Hutchinson as a pleader who "defended his causes solely on their broad and substantial foundations." His place in the history of American political thought is attested to, perhaps too lavishly, by John Adams who saw all that is of substance in the declaration of rights issued by Congress in 1774, in the Declaration of Independence of 1776, and in the writings of Richard Price, Joseph Priestley, and Thomas Paine, as already present in Otis' pamphlet of 1762, *A Vindication of the House of Representatives.* This tract was an able defense, along lines of Whig political theory, of the stand taken by the House against the governor's action in expending public money without previous authorization by the House. This work, along with the more celebrated *The Rights of the British Colonists Asserted and Proved* (1764), written in response to the Sugar Act, and the lesser known *A Vindication of the British Colonies* (1765), constitute Otis' principal contributions to American political literature.[11]

The bases of Otis' political thought are most clearly revealed in the *Rights.* In discussing the question of the origin of government, he rejected explanations in terms of (1) *grace* (because it is "so absurd" and "the world has paid so very dear for embracing it, especially under the administration of the *Roman pontiffs*"); (2) *force* (because it "overturns all morality" and "leads directly to *skepticism,* and ends in *atheism*"); (3) *compact* (because it is subject to the charge that it is "unsupported by reason or experience," and it raises more questions than it answers); and (4) *property* (because it is "a very absurd way of speaking to assert that *one* end of government is the foundation of government," and though, as Harrington has argued, property generally does confer power, "it will never follow from all this that government is *rightfully* founded on *property* alone").[12]

Otis believed that government possesses "an everlasting foundation in the *unchangeable will of God,* the author of nature, whose laws never vary." By natural attraction men form families, then societies of families and communities. "*Government* is therefore most evidently founded *on the necessities of our nature.* It is by no means an *arbitrary* thing depending merely on *compact* or *human will* for its existence." Political authority flows from God, who alone has supreme power, to the people as a whole. Thus in the natural order there stands immediately under God a simple democracy on the authority of the whole over the whole. The people can devolve authority on others on a fiduciary basis to promote the end of government; that is, "the good of mankind," particularized as "the security, the quiet, and happy enjoyment of life, liberty and property." The specific form of government is legitimately to be determined only by popular consent, manifested in a compact, even though, historically speaking, for each time it has been so decided, it has a hundred times been decided by *"fraud, force, or accident."*[13]

Otis was simply saying, in contrast to the more individualistic of the Whigs, that men do not freely originate society and determine whether or not there shall be government as such. As he saw it, man is, as he was to Aristotle, a political animal by nature. What men can legitimately do is designate a particular form of political order under which to live. He did not, however, see this as precluding the possibility of a state of nature whenever men separate from a society for a good cause with the design to form another. "If in such case," he wrote, "there is a real interval between the separation and the new conjunction, during such interval the individuals are as much detached and under the law of nature only as would two men who should chance to meet on a desolate island."[14]

Regarding the best practicable form of government, Otis maintained that except for small states where a single democracy or "a tolerably virtuous *oligarchy* or a *monarchy*" can suffice, a balanced or mixed state combining the three pure forms of government is most desirable. The latter, he thought, was most admirably exemplified in the British Constitution and best sketched in Harrington's *Oceana.* In any case "the same law of nature and of reason is equally obligatory" on all forms of government, and "whenever the administrators in any of those forms deviate from truth, justice and equity, they verge towards tyranny, and are to be opposed; and if they prove incorrigible they will be *deposed* by the people, if the people are not rendered too abject."[15]

Because the law of nature is not of man's making, it cannot be superseded by prescription, no matter how ancient. The law of nature is the fount of natural rights, which are "the grant of God Almighty." Furthermore, and this was a major premise in Otis' thought, the law of nature and derivative natural rights are at the base of the British Constitution.[16]

Otis saw Parliament as possessed of "undoubted power" and "lawful authority" to pass laws which by naming the colonies are binding upon them. But the colonists are entitled to all the rights of Englishmen, with or without charters, "by the law of God and nature, by the common law, and by Act of parliament." And yet, "the power of parliament is uncontrollable, but by themselves, and we must obey. They can only repeal their own acts." Otis' basic conservatism shows broadly in his remark: "There would be an end of all government, if one or a number of subjects or subordinate provinces should take upon them so far to judge of the justice of an act of parliament, as to refuse obedience to it."[17]

The key to an understanding of Otis' conception of Parliamentary power lies in his belief that such power, while admittedly absolute, must not be arbitrary. His natural law approach could not admit the full implications of the Hobbesian conception of sovereignty.

The Parliament cannot make 2 and 2, 5; Omnipotency cannot do it. The supreme power in a state is *jus dicere* only; *jus dare*, strictly speaking, belongs only to God. Parliaments are in all cases to *declare* what is for the good of the whole; but it is not the *declaration* of Parliament that makes it so: There must be in every instance a higher authority, viz., GOD. Should an act of parliament be against any of *his* natural laws, which are *immutably* true, *their* declaration would be contrary to eternal truth, equity and justice, and consequently void: and so it would be adjudged by the Parliament itself, when convinced of their mistake.[18]

Underlying this view is the classical-medieval assumption that law is found and not made, that it must be defined in terms of its essence and not its source.

On the taxation question, Otis saw the right to be taxed only by one's consent or by one's representatives as a natural right of all men and a constitutional right of Englishmen. He distinguished between Parliamentary prohibitions as valid regulations of trade, and Parliamentary taxation of the colonies. He rejected the English contention that the colonists were virtually represented in Parliament and maintained that representation should be afforded them.

Given his full acceptance of Parliamentary sovereignty, Otis could only speak of the colonial assemblies as subordinate bodies existing not by inherent right but by sovereign concession. This placed him in the position where, logically speaking, the most he could do was to beg renewed concessions or reinstatements of lost privileges. Thus he admonished his fellow colonists: "Therefore let the Parliament lay what burdens they please on us, we must, it is our duty to submit and patiently bear them till they will be pleased to relieve us."[19] Petition and remonstrance, and trust in the ultimate wisdom of Parliament in the correction of an unconstitutional act constituted the principal recourse as he saw it.

But alongside this, Otis stressed what at first glance appears to be a contradictory view. In 1761, in his argument in the famous writs of assistance (general, unsigned search warrants) case, he contended that the writs were unconstitutional, violating the rights of Englishmen and natural justice. Drawing upon Coke's dictum in *Bonham's* case, he stated:

An act against the constitution is void; an act against natural equity is void; and if an act of Parliament should be made, in the very words of this petition, it would be void. The executive courts must pass such acts into disuse.[20]

In the *Rights* he repeated this, saying that "if the reasons that can be given against an act are such as plainly demonstrate that it is against *natural* equity, the executive courts will adjudge such act void." Later in the same treatise he attempted to merge his two views within the framework of a conception of the British Constitution as a self-correcting mechanism.

The supreme *legislative* and the supreme *executive* are a perpetual check and balance to each other. If the supreme executive errs it is informed by the supreme legislative in Parliament. If the supreme legislative errs it is informed by the supreme executive in the King's courts of law.[21]

There appear, then, to be two ultimate irreconcilable principles in Otis' thought—the uncontrollable, absolute character of parliamentary power on the one hand, and the right of the courts to determine the validity of an act of Parliament against constitutional standards on the other. The anomaly can only be resolved if we remember that Otis was attempting to apply the assumptions which informed Coke, under quite different conditions and involving private law in the previous century, to contemporary constitutional questions. Like Coke, he saw Parliament as the "high court" of justice, as well as a legislative body. Despite his rhetorical flourishes, he also appears to have seen fundamental law as the standard of legislation not in the sense of providing judges with grounds for declaring acts void because they conflicted with it, but as supplying judges with interpretive principles by which they could mitigate flagrant inequities and resolve contradictions between two sets of law. In this view Parliament was assumed to be the highest judicial body, one which was responsive to the admonitions of other courts and was ever concerned with the implementation of principles of justice. By Otis' day, however, Parliament was no more a judicial body but a sovereign legislature; it was no longer the discoverer but the creator of law and thus, in theory, arbitrary as well as absolute.[22]

In later pamphlets Otis proceeded from the same conception of the British Constitution as a self-adjusting and self-limiting entity which he stressed in the *Rights*. In the *Vindication* (1765), determined to scotch assertions that he had denied Parliamentary sovereignty over America, he put stronger emphasis upon the power of Parliament. For example, he argued that although Parliament has the authority to tax the colonies internally as well as externally, it would be "matter of wonder and astonishment" if it did so in the absence of actual colonial representation. Similarly, Parliament "remains the supreme judge, from whose final determination there is no appeal," in regard to its power over the colonies. If it so decided, Parliament might "abrogate and annihilate all colony or subordinate legislation and administration." But, Otis would add, power is not right, the principles of natural justice and law should not be violated.[23]

In succeeding writings, Otis, under heavy attack, engaged in wild invective and vilification, endorsing complete Parliamentary sovereignty in the process. At one point he reversed his previous position by maintaining that "the *colonists are virtually, constitutionally, in law and in equity, to be considered as represented in the honorable House of Commons.*"[24] His arguments had by now become quite confusing to his contemporaries and he was assailed from both sides. His effective public life ended in 1769 when an officer of the crown struck him on the head with a weapon during a tavern brawl. Thereafter he became insane; he lived on until 1783 when he was struck dead by a bolt of lightning.

Any appraisal of Otis' political thought must note that his legal arguments moved beyond the traditional reliance upon charters as the principal source of colonial rights. More importantly, his major premise—the law of nature is a part of the British Constitution and of the common law—though not original with him, is evidence that he saw the truths of political theory as merged, in the Anglo-Saxon experience, with concrete constitutional and legal tradition, precedent, and practice. Although his conception of natural law drew heavily, in terms of specifics, upon Locke, it probably owed much to the older English view typified in Hooker, insofar as it recognized law as basic and not merely a series of deductions from a fundamental right. Consequently his conception of political order and of obligation flowed from the idea of a divinely instituted natural law.

Otis' works undoubtedly contain flagrant inconsistencies. But restricting one's view to his major contributions, the *Rights* and the *Vindication,* it can be said that the same basic approach underlies both; the difference is one of emphasis. The most recent analyst of Otis' thought has stated that Otis' failure to apply to the eighteenth century political and legal conceptions which had furthered liberty in Coke's day was "dramatically instructive." It showed the need to abandon the notion of indivisible sovereignty and to confront Parliament with "some line drawn between powers it could in right exercise and those it could not. . . ."[25]

Daniel Dulany (1722–1797): The Attack on Virtual Representation

Among those seeking to draw such a line was Daniel Dulany who was born in Maryland, the son of an illustrious father who bore the same name. In 1728 the older Daniel Dulany wrote *The Rights of the Inhabitants of Maryland to the Benefits of English Laws.* This was an able answer, based on arguments drawn mainly from Coke and Locke, to the veto by the proprietary governor of an attempt by the assembly to apply English statutes and the common law to Maryland.[26] The younger Dulany was educated in England where, following his father's lead, he read law and was called to the bar. Returning to Maryland, he became a leading political figure and, in the words of Charles Carroll, "indisputably the best lawyer on this continent."[27] His chief claim to historical notice is his *Considerations of the Propriety of Imposing Taxes in the British Colonies,* which he wrote during the Stamp Act crisis. In this pamphlet Dulany attacked the British contention that the colonists were virtually represented in the House of Commons. In a prefatory statement he included observations on representation which deserve mention because of the high premium put by the colonists on instructions to their representatives. He declared that even if one admits that a representative cannot be bound by the instructions of his constituents, such instructions do have an influence upon him; if he acted against their explicit recommendations he "would most deservedly forfeit their regard and all pretension to their future confidence." Thus the electors in England have notice of proposed laws and may "in the plainest language," without restraint, show "every dangerous tendency" they detect in them. Similarly, when a law in its execution is found to be repugnant to liberty or productive of hardship or inconvenience, they may instruct their representatives to work for its repeal. In the exercise of this right, "THEY are exposed to no danger in explaining their reasons—THEIR situation does not become so delicate as to make it prudent to weaken by not urging them with their full force, and to their utmost extent." But the colonies have no representatives. To them there is available only the right of petition, which demands a reserved style. In this situation, Dulany concluded, the liberty of the press must be fully exploited by the colonists.[28]

Dulany argued in terms of positive law, simple logic, and economic interest. In but one short passage there is what could have been, if fully developed, an appeal to natural law. He stated, as had Otis before him: "In the opinion of a great lawyer, an act of Parliament may be void; and of a great divine, 'all men have natural, and freemen legal rights, which they may justly maintain, and no legislative authority can deprive them of.'" Dulany believed, however, that "unless there should be very peculiar circumstances," these principles should not be relied upon in practice. No more is heard of them thereafter in his essay.[29]

As Dulany saw it, the colonists derived their right of exemption from all taxes imposed without their consent "from the common law, which their charters have declared and confirmed." Since the English insistence that the colonists were virtually represented in Parliament assumed the validity of the asserted right, his task was to demonstrate the falsity of their contention.[30]

In Great Britain, he maintained, the interests of nonelectors, electors, and representatives are the same. Any oppression exercised by Parliament will fall upon all. Then, too, if the nonelectors were not taxed by Parliament, "they would not be taxed *at all;* and it would be iniquitous as well as a solecism in the political system that they should partake of the benefits resulting from the imposition and application of taxes and derive an immunity from the circumstance of not being qualified to vote." Because of this identity of interests, a virtual representation of British nonelectors in the House of Commons may be reasonably supposed.[31]

The colonists live in a dissimilar situation, and are incapable of being electors. If every inhabitant of America held the requisite freehold, they could not vote, except by becoming residents of Great Britain. Instead the colonial legislatures possess "a regular, adequate and constitutional authority to tax them." Above all, "there is not that intimate and inseparable relation between the *electors* of Great-Britain and the *inhabitants of the Colonies,* which must inevitably involve both in the same taxation."[32]

In sum, Dulany contended that the mutuality of interest which obtained between representatives and nonelectors in Great Britain justified the claim of virtual representation of the latter; the lack of such mutuality of interest between British members of Parliament and American colonists showed the invalidity of such claim when applied to the latter.

If, however, an American could give his consent in no other manner than through his representatives in the colonial assemblies, what power remained to Parliament regarding the colonies? Dulany's answer was pragmatic and, whether he knew it or not, in conflict with one of the main attributes of the jealous concept of sovereignty, indivisibility: "May not then the line be distinctly and justly drawn between such acts as are necessary or proper for preserving or securing the dependence of the colonies and such as are not necessary or proper for that very important purpose?" This implied a distinction between the powers of taxation and legislation, precluding the former, which Dulany confusedly called "internal taxation," but allowing the latter, in the form of general acts such as trade regulations, to the Parliament.[33]

Dulany's pamphlet effectively destroyed the argument of virtual representation of the colonies. It went on to suggest a line between the powers of Parliament and those of the colonists which assumed that the latter limited the former and that matters of a general concern alone are in the orbit of Parliamentary authority. Dulany never directly discussed the question of sovereignty which his contentions in effect abridged. He apparently regarded the arrangements embodied in the "practical constitution," which obtained before the Parliamentary exercise of the taxing power and which left questions of "internal polity" and taxation to the colonies, as normal and used them to determine the line of demarcation. Although he never departed from the ideas put forth in the *Considerations,* he could not accept the claim of colonial independence of either the Parliament or of the king, nor could he brook armed resistance. When the Revolution came he remained loyal to Britain.[34]

Richard Bland (1710–1776): Virginian Legislator

Bland was one of the most prominent figures in the Virginia House of Burgesses from 1742 to 1775, serving on its important committees, writing many of its memorials, petitions, and resolutions, and performing executive functions under its authority. An expert on English and Virginian constitutional history, he argued as early as 1753 in a dispute with the governor that taxation must be with the consent of those taxed; consequently, it can only legitimately be exercised by the legislature.[35]

In 1764 he wrote *The Colonel Dismounted, or the Rector Vindicated,* a pamphlet occasioned by a dispute between the House of Burgesses and the clergy. Its significance lies in its treatment of the question of the constitutional relationship of Virginia to Great Britain. The original colonists, Bland argued, were freemen entitled to the rights of Englishmen, including the benefits of laws made with their consent. Considering the question as one not of power but of "constitutional right," Bland distinguished between laws for internal government and laws for external government, admitting Parliamentary authority only in reference to the latter. He was quick to add that this did not exclude from the colonies the common law, which is binding by "the common consent of the people from time immemorial," and follows Englishmen wherever they go, nor did it exclude the English statutes in force at the time of the establishment of Virginia, to which prior consent had been given.[36]

The right of the colonists to legislate regarding internal policy Bland saw as deriving from the British Constitution and as confirmed by the charters as well as prescriptive use. In view of this, submission even to the king is not the whole duty of a citizen; "something is likewise due to the rights of our country, and to the liberties of mankind." Royal instructions bind a governor but not the assembly; they cannot be considered law to be obeyed without reserve. To say otherwise "is, at once to strip us of all the rights and privileges of British subjects . . . for what is the real difference between a French edict and an English instruction if they are both equally absolute?"[37]

Although it was not much more than a statement of principle, Bland's argument in *The Colonel Dismounted* was, like Dulany's, in advance of that of Otis in regarding the rights of the colonial governments to regulate internal affairs as inherent and, as such, a limitation upon the

Parliament; it also was noteworthy in its refusal to distinguish on this point between the powers of taxation and legislation.

The Stamp Act evoked Bland's more celebrated essay, *An Inquiry into the Rights of the British Colonies,* which he published in 1766, and which Thomas Jefferson lauded as the "first pamphlet on the nature of the connection with Great Britain which had any pretension to accuracy of view on that subject."[38] Bland's approach in the *Inquiry* was again legalistic and historical, but unlike the earlier work, within the framework of the notion that the British Constitution is founded upon the principles of natural law.

Treating of virtual representation in Parliament, Bland went beyond Dulany in using Lockian principles to answer the crucial question of the obligation of British nonelectors to obedience to the acts of Parliament. Nonelectors are bound to obey not because of the fallacious notion of virtual representation, but because they choose to remain in Britain and to benefit by its laws, thus consenting to them. But there is a natural right of migration. Men are under no obligation to remain in a state longer than "they find it will conduce to their Happiness, which they have a natural Right to promote." Having chosen to migrate, the colonists owed no obligation to Parliament to whose rule they had never given consent. From this, and in view of Virginia history, Bland concluded that the colonists comprised distinct states independent as to internal government, but united with the kingdom in its determination of external policy.[39]

Bland had now reached the brink. If America was in internal affairs no part of the kingdom of Great Britain, then what rightful authority could the legislature of that realm, in which it lacked representation, have over it? He refused to make the leap; instead, as Jefferson put it, he started back in alarm, unwilling to renounce outright the supremacy of Parliament.[40] In any case Bland gave evidence in his *Inquiry* that a new concept of imperial relations was emerging. In but a few years it was to be warmly embraced and adopted by many Americans as their view.

John Dickinson (1732–1808): Proponent of Limited Sovereignty

Like the younger Dulany, Dickinson was born in Maryland, the son of a wealthy lawyer. He studied law in the London Inns of Court, was a member of the Delaware Assembly, the Pennsylvania Assembly, and the Continental Congress. He wrote the preliminary draft of the Resolves of the Stamp Act Congress and of the Articles of Confederation, became successively governor of Delaware and Pennsylvania, helped draft the Articles of Confederation, and served as a member of the Constitutional Convention of 1787.

Dickinson has been called "the penman of the American Revolution";

in fact he should be called, as Benjamin F. Wright has observed, the penman of the period from 1765 to 1774. He was perhaps the most widely read of the American statesmen of this time in the literature of law, politics, and history—with the possible exception of John Adams. His writings are replete with allusions to and quotations from classical authors, particularly Tacitus, Cicero, Livy, and Sallust. From them, along with his personal observations of corruption in British political life, he drew the moral of the debasing influence of unchecked power and its threat to liberty. Like John Adams, he tended to measure problems and practices at hand against historical examples, assuming the unchangeableness of human nature and universal laws of human behavior.[41]

In 1764 Dickinson demonstrated his allegiance to the principle of the consent of the governed when he fought the attempt of a coalition headed by Benjamin Franklin to get the Pennsylvania Assembly to request a royal charter from the Crown. He based his opposition chiefly upon these grounds: (1) In appealing directly to the Crown for the new charter the assembly was, in effect, surrendering the fundamental rights of the Pennsylvania Charter of Liberties of 1701 for an unknown quantity. (2) The assembly had no right to change the government under which authority was delegated to it except by "*the almost universal consent of the people* exprest in the plainest manner."[42]

In his *Address to the Committee of Correspondence in Barbadoes* (1766), he expounded the theoretical basis from which he proceeded to protest Parliamentary taxation: The rights essential to human happiness, which is the end man strives for, are divinely bestowed, inhere in man's nature, and are the dictates of "the immutable maxims of reason and justice." Having "a right to be happy" man has a right to be free. This assumes a right to be secure in his property which in turn implies a personal exclusive right to determine who shall tax such property.[43]

In 1767 and 1768 Dickinson wrote *Letters from a Farmer in Pennsylvania to the Inhabitants of the British Colonies,* a series which was widely read and heralded throughout America. His main target was the Townshend Acts, through which Parliament, on the basis of the distinction between internal and external taxation, levied customs duties on certain goods for revenue purposes. Dickinson held the distinction to be invalid, maintaining that although Parliament had the authority to regulate the trade of the Empire, and to tax incidentally to that purpose, it could constitutionally levy no tax, as such, upon the colonies in the absence of their consent. "No free people," he wrote, "ever existed, or can ever exist, without keeping 'the purse strings' in their own hands. Where this is the case *they* have a *constitutional* check upon the administration, which may thereby be brought into order *without violence.* But where such a power is not lodged in the *people,* oppression proceeds uncontrouled in its career, till the governed, transported into rage, seek redress in the midst of blood and confusion."[44]

Drawing upon David Hume's emphasis on the influence of custom, opinion, and habit in government, Dickinson warned that "when an act injurious to freedom has been *once* done, and the people *bear* it, the *repetition* of it is most likely to meet with *submission*." He thought that "nations, in general, are not apt to *think* until they *feel*" and thus they lose their liberty; "for as violations of the rights of the *governed,* are commonly not only *specious,* but *small* at the beginning, they spread over the multitude in such a manner, as to touch individuals but slightly." From these reflections he concluded "that every free state should incessantly watch, and instantly take alarm on any addition being made to the power exercised over them."[45]

Dickinson strongly disavowed any resort to arms, contending that "the cause of *liberty* is . . . of too much dignity to be sullied by turbulence and tumult." He reminded his readers that all governments at some time or another take erroneous steps. "Those may proceed from mistake or passion. But every such measure does not dissolve the obligation between government and the governed. The mistake may be corrected; the passion may subside. It is the duty of the governed to rectify the mistake, and to appease the passion." Only when it becomes clear beyond doubt "that an inveterate resolution is formed to annihilate the liberties of the governed" can forcible resistance be resorted to. With prudence and caution as his note, Dickinson declared that "the constitutional modes of obtaining relief" must be pursued, that is, "petitions of our assemblies, or where they are not permitted to meet, of the people, to the powers that can afford us relief."[46]

The *Farmer's Letters* put the stamp of approval on the theretofore not always clearly expressed contention of the colonists that all taxation of the colonies by Parliament without colonial consent was unconstitutional. The work was unjustly characterized by Jefferson years later, as "an *ignis fatuus,*" misleading the colonists "from true principles."[47] Of course, Dickinson did not share the premise later held by Jefferson and others, that Parliament had *no* authority over the colonies; he attempted to draw a line in the *Letters* without entangling himself in a direct consideration of sovereignty and without openly invoking natural law, by distinguishing between taxation and legislation and precluding Parliament from the former.

After the passage of the Intolerable Acts, Dickinson suspected a design to enslave the colonies. In 1774 he wrote *An Essay on the Constitutional Power of Great Britain Over the Colonies in America,* a final attempt on his part to define constitutional principles upon which reasonable men might agree. He described the laws of the constitution as "grounded on reason; full of justice and true equity, mild, and calculated to promote the freedom and welfare of men." He maintained that "the happiness of the people" is the end of government, as well as "the body of the constitution," whereas "freedom is the spirit or the soul." Just as the individual soul has a right to prevent or relieve any mischief to the body "so the soul, speaking of the constitution, has a right to prevent, or relieve any mischief to the body of society, and to keep that in the best of health." The body of the constitution was ill; Dickinson would activate the soul, freedom, to draw out right from wrong.[48]

In this task he confronted directly the logic of absolute sovereignty as embodied in the Declaratory Act and commented sardonically upon it: "*Because* the constitution has not 'expressly declared' the line between the rights of the mother country and those of her colonists, *therefore,* the latter have *no rights.*—a logic, equally edifying to the heads and hearts of men of sense and humanity." As he saw it, "liberty, life, or property, can with no consistency of words or ideas, be termed a *right* of the *possessors,* while *others* have a right of taking them away at pleasure." A power of government which in its nature tends to the misery of the people and is unlimited, that is, a power in which the people have no share, "cannot be a *rightful* or *legal* power."[49]

Dickinson momentarily pursued this reasoning to its inexorable conclusion, declaring that the just inference from these premises would be "an exclusion, of *any* power of parliament over these colonies, rather than the admission of an unbounded power." But he was no man to be pushed to extremes; he still believed that a line could be drawn short of either of the poles. Thus he hastened to disavow a claim of total independence, stating that a submission to the parent state is what "our reason approves, our affection dictates, our duty commands, and our interest inforces." Such submission, however, must proceed from the proposition that the colonial legislatures, "founded on the immutable and unalienable rights of human nature, the principles of the constitution, and charters and grants," and subject to the control of the crown, possess the exclusive right of internal legislation. If the claim of Parliament to such right were admitted, the colonists would be placed in the same situation as would the English people had James I succeeded in his scheme of arbitrary power. The British claim was not only inconsistent with the law of nature and the precepts of Christianity, but constituted "a dreadful novelty" and "the walls of the constitution must be thrown down before it can be introduced among us."[50]

On the basis of the principle of the consent of the governed, Dickinson indicated where the line should be drawn: "To be subordinately connected with England, the colonies *have contracted.* To be subject to the general legislative authority of that kingdom, they *never contracted.* Such a power as may be necessary to preserve this connection she has. The authority of the sovereign, and the authority of controlling our intercourse with *foreign nations* form that power. . . . The sovereignty over the colonies must be limited."[51]

The concept, "limited sovereignty," a contradiction in terms to the logical purist, encapsulates the whole of Dickinson's developed constitutional thought. With it as the major premise, a viable federal conception of empire, based on past practices, geopolitical reality, the need to implement the rights of Englishmen, and a mutual spirit of adjustment and accommodation could follow freely. Dickinson had faced up to the question of sovereignty and shown both its impracticality and its unacceptability to free men of Anglo-Saxon heritage. Parliamentary authority was limited by the inherent power of the colonies to tax themselves and to regulate their internal politics. And yet, Parliament had a legislative authority to deal with the important matters of general concern to the Empire as "the supreme legislative and full *representative* of the parent state, and the only judge between her and her children in commercial interests."[52]

Dickinson's caution and his desire to leave no stone unturned in the quest for a just accommodation brought him to oppose the move for a declaration of independence in July, 1776. After an "Olive Branch Petition" which he drew up, again presenting the colonial grievances to the king, was ignored, he resigned himself to the inevitability of independence but opposed the declaration itself on the grounds that an alliance with France should first be effected, along with intercolonial governmental agreements. Because of this stand he was visited with obloquy and a sharp decline in his once-great popularity. But once the decision was made, in accordance with a principle he later proclaimed —that the will of a society, once decided, if just, should be followed—he enlisted in the Continental Army and comported himself, despite the undeserved vilification, with dignity.[53]

A final observation must be made regarding Dickinson's political theory. Although his principal work, the *Farmer's Letters,* proceeded on legalistic and historical lines of argument, his other writings are ample evidence of his reliance upon a natural law philosophy. By itself, his pointing to happiness as the end of government might lead one to conclude that he was, at bottom, a utilitarian. But happiness was defined by him against the background of a conception of natural law which, in its invocation of rights, followed the lead of Locke, but which in its fundamentals was rooted in the earlier English tradition of Richard Hooker upon whom he heavily relied. Thus Dickinson saw the law of nature as stemming from God who has implanted in man a desire for happiness which must be sought for in God's way and not in man's, and which cannot be attained without the acquisition of virtue. As Otis had also argued, he saw the origin of political authority as divine and as vested originally in the people, who designate the political order they wish—an order which must be in accord with natural justice. On this basis and to the end of happiness, with liberty as its precondition and with private property as a precondition of liberty, government must be constructed and conducted. These conceptions were taken up by Dickinson's brilliant pupil, James Wilson, who fully developed and articulated them after the adoption of the American Constitution of 1787 in his great exposition of the legal philosophy of the democratic, federal republic.[54]

Conclusions

The documents and pamphlets written by Americans during the dispute with Britain illustrate the essentially technical, legalistic, constitutional nature of the dispute. Behind the American position, however, were some important assumptions, unifying ideas and attitudes which might be called categories of the Whig mind. First was the conception of time embodied in the *Whig theory of history* which propounded the myth of Saxon democracy with an elective monarchy and annual parliaments, and no feudal land tenure, no standing army, and no established church, as a norm to be realized anew. Second was the *Whig constitutional theory* which emphasized legislative supremacy, with Parliamentary power held to be absolute, but not arbitrary, and limiting the royal prerogative. Third was the *Whig normative political theory* of the primacy of natural law and natural rights and the explanation and justification of government in terms of contract and the promotion of the common good. Fourth was the *Whig tendency to identify legal rights and natural rights*. Fifth was the *Whig structural political theory* which, in its American manifestation, emphasized the balanced state with particular emphasis on the popular branch of the legislature.

American Whigs came to deviate from their English brethren in holding that Parliament, as well as the king, was limited in power. This led them to formulate a conception of the British Constitution as fixed fundamental law limiting the branches of government. This was accompanied by a tendency to emphasize more strongly the notion that the law of nature was a fundamental part of the British Constitution.

Within this framework there was a progression of steps in the colonial argument. Thus Otis, on constitutional and natural law grounds, stressed no taxation without representation; Dulany exposed the invalidity of the idea of "virtual representation"; the arguments of Dulany and Bland led the English to make a distinction between internal and external taxation, which the colonials would not accept. Dickinson, Bland, and others maintained that taxation in any guise was impermissible, but admitted the right of Parliament to legislate for imperial purposes. The inner logic of the dispute was to drive the colonial Whigs more and more back to first principles while retaining as much as possible the legalistic rhetoric. Thus the next step, to which we now turn, was to assert colonial independence of Parliament on legal, constitutional, and philosophical grounds.

NOTES

1. Hansard, *Parliamentary History*, XVI, Feb. 24, 1766, cited in Randolph G. Adams, *Political Ideas of the American Revolution* (New York, 3rd ed., 1958), pp. 50–51. Samuel Johnson, *Taxation No Tyranny* (London, 1774), reprinted in J. P. Hardy (ed.), *The Political Writings of Dr. Johnson* (New York, 1968), p. 108; Alden Bradford (ed.), *Speeches of the Governors of Massachusetts, from 1765 to 1775* (Boston, 1818), p. 340, cited in Adams, p. 115. On the attitude of English Whigs to the question, see G. H. Gutteridge, *English Whiggism and the American Revolution* (Berkeley, 1942).

2. Samuel Adams to Rockingham, Jan. 22, 1768, *Mass. State Papers*, 142, cited in Adams, p. 138.

3. On the constitutional and legal questions, see besides R. G. Adams, Charles Howard McIlwain, *The American Revolution* (New York, 1923); Charles F. Mullett, *Fundamental Law and the American Revolution* (New York, 1933); R. L. Schuyler, *Parliament and the British Empire* (New York, 1929); Andrew C. McLaughlin, *The Foundations of American Constitutionalism* (New York, 1932); and Bernard Bailyn's introduction (Chapter VI) to his edition of *Pamphlets of the American Revolution* (Cambridge, Mass., 1965), I, 90–138. For an early, interesting discussion of colonial governmental problems see the anonymous work, *An Essay upon the Government of the English Plantations On the Continent of America* (1701), Louis B. Wright (ed.), (Huntington Library, San Marino, California, 1945).

4. The New York Petition to the House of Commons, Oct. 18, 1764, reprinted in Edmund S. Morgan (ed.), *Prologue to Revolution* (Chapel Hill, N.C., 1959), p. 9.

5. The Massachusetts Resolves, Oct. 29, 1765, *ibid.*, pp. 56–57.

6. The New York Resolves, Dec. 18, 1765, *ibid.*, p. 61; The Rhode Island Resolves, Sept., 1765, *ibid.*, p. 51.

7. The Declarations of the Stamp Act Congress, Oct., 1765, *ibid.*, pp. 62–63.

8. Edmund Morgan, "Colonial Ideas of Parliamentary Power, 1764–1766," *William and Mary Quarterly*, V, 3rd Ser. (July, 1948), 311–341.

9. For a comprehensive study of the period see Edmund and Helen Morgan, *The Stamp Act Crisis* (Chapel Hill, N.C., 1953).

10. The Gridley maxim can be found in a statement by John Adams, cited in Bernard Bailyn, *Pamphlets*, I, 410.

11. Hutchinson is quoted in William Tudor, *The Life of James Otis* (Boston, 1823), p. 36. Adams' appraisal can be found in Charles F. Adams (ed.), *The Works of John Adams*, X, 310–311, 262–266.

12. James Otis, "The Rights of the British Colonies Asserted and Proved," (Boston, 1764), reprinted in Bailyn, *Pamphlets*, I, 419, 420, 421, 422, 423. For a short analysis of Otis' thought, see Ralph K. Huitt, "The Constitutional Ideas of James Otis," *Kansas Law Review* (Dec., 1953), pp. 152–173.

13. *Ibid.*, pp. 423, 424, 425, 426.

14. *Ibid.*, p. 439.

15. *Ibid.*, pp. 428, 429, 427.

16. *Ibid.*, pp. 444, 446; "A Vindication of the British Colonies," *ibid.*, pp. 558, 559, 560, 563.

17. Otis, "Rights of the British Colonies," p. 448.

18. *Ibid.*, p. 454.

19. *Ibid.*, p. 448.

20. Adams, *Works*, II, 521–525. The quotation is at p. 522.
21. Otis, "Rights," pp. 449, 455.
22. For a discussion of these questions see Bailyn, *Pamphlets*, I, 411ff., and 91ff.
23. Otis, "Vindication," Bailyn, *Pamphlets*, I, 564, 563.
24. *Brief remarks on the Defence of the Halifax Libel on the British-American Colonies* (Boston, 1765), p. 27, cited in Bailyn, *Pamphlets*, I, 550.
25. Bailyn, *Pamphlets*, I, 551.
26. The elder Dulany's work is discussed in Benjamin F. Wright, *American Interpretations of Natural Law* (Cambridge, Mass., 1931), pp. 57–61.
27. Cited in Bailyn, *Pamphlets*, I, 603.
28. Daniel Dulany, *Considerations on the Propriety of imposing Taxes in the British Colonies* (1765), Bailyn, *Pamphlets*, I, 608, 609.
29. *Ibid.*, p. 609.
30. *Ibid.*, p. 632.
31. *Ibid.*, p. 612.
32. *Ibid.*, p. 615.
33. *Ibid.*, p. 620.
34. See the able discussion of Dulany's arguments in Morgan, *The Stamp Act Crisis*, pp. 71–87.
35. Clinton Rossiter, *Seedtime of the Republic* (New York, 1953), pp. 253–255.
36. Richard Bland, *The Colonel Dismounted* (1764), in Bailyn, *Pamphlets*, I, 320.
37. *Ibid.*, p. 324.
38. Jefferson to Wm. Wirt, Aug. 5, 1815, cited in Rossiter, *Seedtime of the Republic*, p. 261.
39. *An Inquiry Into the Rights of the British Colonies* (1766), pp. 9, 10, 14, 15. I have used an abridged edition of the *Inquiry* found in Merrill Jensen (ed.), *Tracts of the American Revolution* (Indianapolis, 1967), pp. 108–126.
40. Jefferson to Wm. Wirt, Aug. 5, 1815, cited in Rossiter, *Seedtime of the Republic*, p. 261.
41. On Dickinson's life see Charles Stille, *The Life and Times of John Dickinson* (Philadelphia, 1891), and David L. Jacobson, *John Dickinson and the Revolution in Pennsylvania* (University of California Publications in History, Vol. 78, Berkeley and Los Angeles, 1965).
42. John Dickinson, "Speech on a Petition for a Change of Government of the Colony of Pennsylvania, May 24, 1764" in Paul T. Ford (ed.), *The Writings of John Dickinson* (Philadelphia, 1895), pp. 34–37, 44. See also Jacobson, *op. cit.*, pp. 9–26 for a full discussion of the incident.
43. Dickinson, *Writings*, p. 262.
44. Dickinson, Letter IX, *Writings*, p. 364.
45. Dickinson, Letter XI, *Writings*, pp. 388, 389, 390.
46. Dickinson, Letter III, *Writings*, pp. 324, 325, 327.
47. Jefferson to Wm. Wirt, Aug. 5, 1815, cited in Rossiter, *Seedtime of the Republic*, p. 261.
48. *The Political Writings of John Dickinson* (Wilmington, 1801, 2 vols.), I, 330, 332.
49. *Ibid.*, I, 340.
50. *Ibid.*, I, 343, 347, 361, 362, 363, 364, 366, 367, 373, 385.
51. *Ibid.*, I, 386.
52. *Ibid.*, I, 401.
53. Stille, *op. cit.*, 196ff. Dickinson's speech opposing the Declaration can be found in Merrill Jensen (ed.), *English Historical Documents*, IX, *American Colonial Documents to 1776* (New York, 1955), pp. 873–876.
54. A full consideration of Dickinson's thought must take into account his *Letters of Fabius* in 1788 and 1797. See *Political Writings*, Vol. II.

Chapter 7

THE COMMONWEALTH
THEORY OF EMPIRE

JOHNSON: *I regret that the king does not see it to be better for him to receive constitutional supplies from his American subjects by the voice of their own assemblies . . . than through the medium of his British subjects. I am persuaded that the power of the crown . . . would be greater when in contact with all its dominions than if 'the rays of legal bounty' were to 'shine' upon America through that dense and troubled body, a modern British parliament.*

JAMES BOSWELL, *Life of Samuel Johnson*

Attempts of Americans to make a practical definition of a line between parliamentary power and the power of the colonial legislatures were succeeded by the adherence of many to the concept of an empire of independent states united by allegiance to a common monarch. This theory first came strongly to the fore in a public exchange of views between Governor Thomas Hutchinson and the Massachusetts legislature in 1773. Starting from the premise that from the nature of government there must be one supreme authority, Hutchinson concluded that no line could be drawn between the sovereignty of Parliament and colonial independence. In answer to the commonwealth theory he maintained that the authority granted in the Massachusetts charter derived not from the king as a person, but from "the crown of England," which entailed subjection to "the supreme authority of England," Parliament. The Massachusetts House of Representatives used an interlaced argument of legal precedent and political theory to contend that acquired territories were possessions of the British monarch and not of the English realm, unless annexed thereto. It followed that since no formal annexation had ever been made, the colonists owed allegiance only to the king personally and that their legislatures were independent of the British Parliament.[1]

After the Boston Tea Party, Parliament, in the spring of 1774, enacted the "Coercive Acts"—the Boston Port Bill, the Administration of Justice Act, the Government of Massachusetts Act, and the Quartering Act. These acts closed the Boston harbor to commerce; allowed, under certain conditions, the shifting of court trials to England; provided for royal appointment of the Massachusetts Council as well as the appointment and removal by the governor of some judges and officers of law enforcement; prohibited the holding of town meetings except with the approval of the governor; and authorized the quartering of troops in private homes. Together with the Quebec Act, which because of its recognition of Catholicism in that province was regarded by the colonists as a threat to religious liberty, these acts were collectively called the "Intolerable Acts," being seen by many as ample evidence of a British conspiracy to reduce the colonists to servitude.

The first Continental Congress convened in September, 1774, and in the next month formally adopted the theory implicit in the reply of the Massachusetts lower house to Governor Hutchinson. In a resolution which was principally the work of John Adams it was declared that the foundation of English liberty and all free government is a right of the people to be represented in their legislatures. Because Americans are not and cannot feasibly be represented in Parliament, "they are entitled to a free and exclusive power of legislation" in their own legislatures "in all cases of taxation and internal polity," subject only to the royal veto. Reversing the British view, and that of men like Hutchinson, which saw the provincial legislative powers existing only by sovereign Parliamentary concession, the resolution added:

But, from the necessity of the case, and a regard to the mutual interest of both countries, we cheerfully consent to the operations of such acts of the British Parliament, as are *bona fide*, restrained to the regulation of our external commerce, for the purpose of securing the commercial advantages of the whole empire to the mother country, and the commercial benefits of its respective members; excluding every idea of taxation, internal or external for raising a revenue on the subjects in America without their consent.[2]

Thus was the legal argument wedded to the consensual theory to deny legal power to Parliament to legislate for the colonies and to permit that body power in matters of external concern only when agreed to by the American legislatures.

We now turn to an examination of the political thought of the principal American figures who propounded the commonwealth theory of empire and later opted for independence. Throughout the discussion of this theory it must be kept in mind that students of the subject are divided in their views on the historical validity of the colonial legal position. Suffice it to say that that position was not without a strong basis in legal history and, given the assumptions of the consensual theory, an even stronger basis in political theory. But we do an injustice to the colonial position, and that of its principal proponents, if we divorce one from the other. The American argument was at once legal and philosophical with these elements not juxtaposed, but interwoven.[3]

Samuel Adams (1722–1803): Agitator and Propagandist

Unlike most colonial political leaders of his time, Samuel Adams was no lawyer. A leader in the Massachusetts House of Representatives from 1764 on, he wrote many of its resolves and reports, serving as the champion of colonial interests in struggles with governors, the Parliament, and finally with royal authority itself. Above all, he was a superb organizer, popular agitator and propagandist, deftly using caucuses, town meetings, committees of correspondence, newspapers and circular letters to advance the cause. Uncompromisingly honest and stubbornly unyielding, the ascetic Adams, always following his maxim, "keep your enemies in the wrong," gained the admiration, however grudging, even of his enemies. Governor Francis Bernard once cried out in pain, "Damn that Adams, every dip of his pen stings like a horned snake." Joseph Galloway observed: "He eats little, drinks little, sleeps little, thinks much, and is most decisive and indefatigable in the pursuit of his objects." His cousin, John Adams, commented: "Adams, I believe has the most thorough understanding of liberty and her resources in the temper and character of the people, though not in the law and the Constitutions; as well as the most correct, genteel, and artful pen. He is a man of refined policy, steadfast integrity, exquisite humanity, genteel erudition, obliging, engaging manners, real as well as professed piety, and a universal good character, unless it should be admitted that he is too attentive to the public, and not enough so to himself and his family."[4]

Neither a profound nor an original political thinker, Adams never wrote a book or a pamphlet; his thoughts on government must be gleaned mainly from letters in newspapers, his correspondence, and his public statements. These show his thought to be almost completely derivative; he was closely acquainted with the classics of political thought and history, but he relied, for the most part, upon Locke, or popularizations of Locke's thought, differing only in his application of principles along more democratic lines.

As early as 1743 Adams gave evidence of his political beliefs when, in his master's dissertation at Harvard, he answered affirmatively the question: "Whether it be lawful to resist the Supreme Magistrate, if the Commonwealth cannot be otherwise preserved?" No copy of the work remains but it is probable that his conclusion was implementive of the value which he placed first and foremost during his public life—liberty. In a series of articles in his newspaper in 1749 he explained the meaning of liberty and related values. Liberty distinguishes men from beasts. It can exist in the state of nature if men are not constrained by external force and by "irregular and inordinate passions." Similarly, it is enjoyed in government "when neither legislative nor executive powers . . . are disturbed by any internal passion or hindered by any external force from making the wisest laws and executing them in the best manner." Individual man possesses liberty "when he freely enjoys the security of the laws and the rights to which he is born; when he is hindered by no violence from claiming those rights and enjoying that security. . . ." Unfortunately, Adams lamented, the form of liberty often exists without its substance. Just as men may be free from external violence but yet be slaves to their passions, so can a whole people make their own laws and be "blinded by prejudice and diverted by undue influence from uniformly pursuing their own interest."[5]

Adams saw "true loyalty" as "founded in the love and possession of liberty." Because "the true object of loyalty is a good legal constitution," the question of the best form of government is most relevant. At this time (1749) he thought that the English Constitution (which he believed was improved upon by the Massachusetts colonial constitution), with its admirable adjustment of the powers of government and the rights of the governed, most closely approximated the ideal. He especially approved the two institutions which are rooted in the consensual principle, Parliament and the juries, inasmuch as "power intrusted for a short time, is not so likely to be perverted, as that which is perpetual." But because the form of the constitution (external freedom) must be accompanied by civic virtue (internal freedom), Adams warned that "neither the wisest constitution nor the wisest laws will secure the liberty and happiness of a people whose manners are universally corrupt." A true friend to the liberty of his country will work "to promote its virtue, and . . . so far as his power and influence extend, will not suffer a man to be chosen into any office of power and trust who is not a wise and virtuous man."[6] In addition he will be ever watchful of those invested with power. Adams' comment on this point, made in 1771, could very well be a description of the course he personally pursued throughout his long life.

. . . the true patriot will constantly be jealous of those very men, knowing that power, especially in times of corruption, makes men wanton, that it intoxicates the mind; and unless those with whom it is entrusted are carefully watched—such is the weakness or perverseness of human nature,—they will be left to domineer over the people, instead of governing them according to the known laws of the state, to which alone they have submitted. If he finds, upon the best inquiry, the want of ability or integrity, that is, an ignorance of, or a disposition to depart from, the Constitution . . . he will point them out loudly and proclaim them. He will stir up the people incessantly to complain of such men, till they are reformed or removed from the sacred trust. . . .[7]

Adams' conception of "the people" indicates his democratic leaning. All the members of society are equally within its embrace irrespective of social or economic position: "He that despises his neighbor's happiness because he wears a worsted cap or a leathern apron, he that struts immeasurably above the lower size of people, and pretends to adjust the rights of men by the distinctions of fortune, is not over loyal." The "people" whom Adams would "stir up" comprised "no contemptible multitude"; it is for their sake that government was instituted. Men did not submit to government to become subordinate. "Mankind have entered into political societies rather for the sake of restoring equality," the lack of which rendered existence in the state of nature where the weak are subordinate to the strong, "uncomfortable and even dangerous." Adams specifically disavowed "levelling principles" but added that the "constitution of civil government which admits equality in the most extreme degree consistent with the true design of government is the best." And yet, "subordination is necessary to promote the purposes of government." The subordination to which he objected was that which did not conduce to the "welfare and happiness of the whole," in short, a tyrannical rule.[8]

As the Massachusetts Stamp Act resolves and many other utterances of Adams amply show, he saw, as had Otis, divine and natural law as the foundation of the British Constitution, and Lockian natural rights as basic rights of Englishmen: "The British Constitution is founded in the principles of nature and reason. It admits of no more power over the subject than is necessary for the support of government, which was originally designed for the preservation of the inalienable rights of nature." As the Massachusetts Circular Letter of 1768 indicates, although Adams then like Otis admitted Parliamentary authority as "the supreme legislative Power over the whole Empire," he departed from Otis in proclaiming the fixed nature of the British Constitution. On this view Parliament was a creature of the constitution and subordinate to it. In like fashion Adams argued that the colonial charters, like *Magna Carta,* limited Parliament.[9]

In 1771 there was a significant change in Adams' constitutional theory. He now argued, on the grounds of the natural rights of men, that Parliament possessed no authority over the colonies. Relying principally on Locke, supplemented by Hooker and Emmerich de Vattel, a Swiss political theorist, he maintained: (1) express consent alone makes a man a member of a commonwealth; (2) mature men can decide to migrate from, and renounce allegiance to, a commonwealth; (3) the original colonists left England with the consent of the king, and contracted with him to become his subjects, not his slaves. They did not promise to obey any acts of Parliament without their consent; (4) the legislative power must be supreme in any commonwealth; and (5) "If the people of this Province are a part of the body politic of Great Britain, they have as such a right to be consulted in the making of all acts of the British Parliament, of what nature soever. If they are a separate body politic, and are free, they have a right equal to that of the people of Great Britain to make laws for themselves, and are no more than they subject to the control of any Legislature but their own." Now because Adams had consistently, since 1765, asserted the impossibility of effective colonial representation in Parliament, the implication was inescapable—the colonies are separate bodies politic united by a common monarch.[10]

It is probable that Adams' first draft of the reply to Governor Hutchinson's address in 1773 was based on this reasoning. When John Adams was called in to peruse it he objected to it as "full of very popular talk and those democratical principles which have done so much mischief in this country." After getting them expunged, he gave Samuel Adams and the committee the legal references and constitutional arguments which became the core of the reply. The reply, agreed to by both men, denied principally on legal, historical, and constitutional grounds the authority of Parliament over the colonies. This view was not held for long by the older of the two—he soon became an advocate of complete independence and deployed his considerable talents in that revolutionary direction.[11]

In 1790, when the French Revolution was convulsing Europe, the two Adamses engaged in a celebrated correspondence which brought out the significant difference between them on the subject of government. While John Adams emphasized structural principles, Samuel Adams stressed the need for virtue and wisdom, maintaining anew that "the best formed constitutions that have yet been construed by the wit of men have, and will, come to an end,—because 'the kingdoms of the earth have not been governed by reason.'" Believing that "the love of liberty is interwoven in the soul of man, and can never be extinguished," he urged:

Let divines and philosophers, statesmen and patriots, unite their endeavors to renovate the age, by impressing the minds of men with the importance . . . of inculcating in the minds of youth the fear and love of the Deity and universal philanthropy, and in subordination to . . . the love of their country; of instructing them in the art of self-government, without which they never can act a wise part in the government of societies, great or small; in short, of leading them in the study and practice of the exalted virtues of the Christian system, which will happily tend to subdue the turbulent passions of men, and introduce that golden age . . . when the wolf shall dwell with the lamb.[12]

From first to last, then, Samuel Adams believed that liberty is not solely, or even mainly, a function of structural principles of civil government (although these are necessary conditions), but that it depends principally upon individual government of the self through the acquisition of virtue and wisdom. Popular sovereignty and democratic government, as he saw it, presuppose the education of all and a pious practice of the truths of religion. He strove mightily to discipline himself to the demands of a true democratic citizenship, and to alert his countrymen in that direction. He could again have just as well been describing himself when he concluded the correspondence by declaring: "The truly virtuous man and real patriot is satisfied with the approbation of the wise and discerning: he rejoices in the contemplation of the purity of his own intentions, and waits in humble hope for the plaudit of his final Judge."[13]

John Adams (1736–1826): Student of Government

Early in life John Adams resolved: "Aim at an exact knowledge of the nature, end, and means of government. Compare the different forms of it with each other, and each of them with their effect on public and private happiness." Never tiring in this life-long pursuit, he later confessed that to him "no romance was more entertaining" than "the divine science of politics." Steeped in the classics, well versed in the history and practice of law, Adams also possessed a thorough knowledge of political philosophy, with a preference for Aristotle, Cicero, Polybius, Machiavelli, Harrington, Locke, Sidney, and Milton as against "metaphysicians" such as Plato and the French *philosophes*.[14]

Ambitious, crotchety, and not above jealousy and envy, Adams was withal a man of solid integrity. His long life in politics, from the lawyer patriot to the revolutionary statesman, the drawer of blueprints of government, the republican diplomat, the Vice-President and President of the United States, left him at its end with his great desire for popularity unsatisfied. For all of his practical activities, there was an air of impracticality about him, the air of the man who is more at home looking in on a great game rather than being a part of it.[15]

Whereas cousin Samuel had an instinctive grasp of politics, John's was reflective. His method was experimental, built upon his studies in history, his own experience and personal observations. While the New England town meetings were subjects of manipulation to Samuel Adams, to John they were laboratories in which to make discoveries. Therein he attempted to identify the "springs of action" moving men, their aims, ambitions, strengths, and weaknesses. He once advised his son that the practical politician and the student of politics must learn "the machines, arts, and channels by which intelligence and reports are circulated throughout the town," and the people who are "the makers and spreaders of characters." He must study the desires and inclinations of men in all walks and levels of life as well as all the professional and social clubs. Through close observation and systematic study one could discover "the wheels . . . cogs in pins, some of them dirty ones, which compose the machine and make it go."[16]

Adams' first political essay, written in 1765, *A Dissertation on the Canon and Feudal Law*, might be called a secularized portrait, in light of the Whig view of history, of John Winthrop's "City Upon a Hill." America, he contended, could realize and extend freedom, the highest political value, because it did not bear the dead weight of the European past—the unrestrained expression of the "desire of dominion," the canon and feudal law: "I always consider the settlement of America with reverence and wonder, as the opening of a grand scene and design in Providence for the illumination of the ignorant and the emancipation of the slavish part of mankind all over the earth."[17]

Against this background Adams treated in broad and grossly oversimplified terms the relationship of man's development to different forms of government. In the earliest ages, absolute monarchy, based on "a cruel tyranny over the people," who were but little more intelligent than brutes, was probably universal. In the European Middle Ages, although people became more intelligent, the twin tyrannies of the feudal and canon law emerged and soon joined in a "wicked confederacy." After the Reformation, knowledge gradually spread in Europe, particularly in England, issuing in the struggle against the Stuarts and the migration to America of a people moved by a love of religion and a hatred of the two tyrannies.[18]

The settlers of Massachusetts, faithful to classical principles, saw clearly "that popular powers must be placed as a guard, a control, a balance, to the powers of the monarch and the priest, in every government." Discarded were the divine right theory and the doctrines of passive obedience: "They knew that government was a plain, simple, intelligible thing, founded in nature and reason, and quite comprehensible by common sense." With this realization the aura of mystery which for so long had deflected men from the truth was dissolved. History and experience told them that "nothing could preserve their posterity from the encroachments of the two systems of tyranny . . . but knowledge diffused generally through the whole body of the people." For this reason they took the unprecedented step of providing for general public education.[19]

In contrast to his later primary emphasis on a balanced or mixed government as the precondition of liberty, Adams, in the *Dissertation,* stressed the priority of knowledge. God has given men "a desire to know" which must be nourished. Most particularly, "they have a right . . . to that most dreaded and envied kind of knowledge, I mean, of the characters and conduct of their rulers." Political authority derives from the people who depute it on a fiduciary basis to rulers who are accountable to them for their trust. Having followed Locke on this point, Adams departed from him to contend, as had his cousin, Samuel, that "the preservation of the means of knowledge among the lowest ranks, is of more importance to the public than all the property of all the rich men in the country." Just as knowledge through education is the condition of liberty, so the most sacred means of information is a courageous, free press. It followed that a free, intelligent people cannot ever stand in an inferior relationship to another, particularly when the latter, like Britain, is suspected of trying to reimpose upon them the two tyrannies.[20]

Turning to constitutional questions, Adams, the political scientist, demonstrated his preoccupation with structural forms, or what he later called "principles of political architecture." In that year (1765) he contended that Parliamentary taxation of the unrepresented, and placement of the colonies under admiralty courts, were "inconsistent with the spirit of the common law, and of essential fundamental principles of the British Constitution." Like Otis he thought that perhaps the Stamp Act "ought to be waived by the judges as against natural equity and the constitution." More significantly, the following year he expounded his views on the nature of the British Constitution. Some men, he declared, have identified it with the practice of Parliament, others, with the judgments and precedents of the king's courts; but both views make it "a constitution of wind and weather, because the parliaments have sometimes voted the king absolute, and the judges have sometimes adjudged him to be so." Still others identified it with custom, "but this is as fluctuating and variable as the other." And some have called it "the most perfect combination of human powers in society which finite wisdom has yet contrived and reduced to practice for the preservation of liberty and the production of happiness." But this is merely a just observation, rather than a definition of the Constitution. Finally, some have declared it to be "the whole body of the laws," while others maintain that the "king, lords, and commons, make the constitution." Adams admitted that, in light of these definitions, he was at a loss as to what a man meant when he spoke of the British Constitution.[21]

Comparing the Constitution to the human body and to a mechanism, Adams attempted his own description. The physician studies the constitution of the human body before him and administers to it to preserve and protect life and health. And yet there are certain parts of the body which the physician in no case has any authority to destroy or deprive—the *stamina vitae*—the essentials of the bodily constitution. Similarly, a clock has certain fundamental parts which cannot be taken away without destroying it. The same applies to government which is "a frame, a scheme, a system, combination of powers for . . . the good of the whole community." The British Constitution has liberty as its end and its use. To effect this end it provides a popular check in the legislative and the executive branches of government. The popular vote for the members of the House of Commons and the jury system are essential to the great end of the Constitution—the preservation of liberty: "These two popular powers, therefore, are the heart and lungs, the mainspring and the centre wheel, and without them the body must die, the watch must run down, the government must become arbitrary, and this our law books have settled to be the death of the laws and constitution."[22]

By distinguishing between the *stamina vitae*, the principles which are essential to the realization of the end of the constitution, and the parts, practices, customs, and procedures which are not, Adams expressed a view which in emphasis, if not in its elements, departed sharply from the prevalent English conception. As he saw it, the Constitution was the embodiment of certain fixed, basic principles which were paramount to and binding upon Parliament.[23]

In 1767 Adams denied the contention that the British Constitution was a self-correcting mechanism. The end of the Constitution, he argued, is liberty, but the Constitution cannot preserve itself; the remedy is constant attention by the people and their tribunes to the first almost imperceptible encroachments upon their liberties. *Obsta principiis* (oppose in the beginnings), he declared, must be the motto and maxim of the spirit of liberty and thus the true insurance of the preservation of the Constitution.[24]

In 1768, in the instructions which Adams drafted for the Town of Boston to its representatives, he stated: "Under all these misfortunes and affliction, however, it is our fixed resolution to maintain our loyalty and duty to our most gracious Sovereign, a reverence and due subordination to the British parliament, as the supreme legislative in all cases of necessity, for the preservation of the whole empire. . . ." Governor Hutchinson called this statement "a singular manner of expressing the authority of parliament." Which, indeed, it was. Implied in it was the theory of empire which Adams would soon make explicit, a theory which saw the colonies as separate states united with Britain by their allegiance to a common monarch, and which denied to Parliament all authority over the colonies except that to which they specifically agreed. This theory, as has been seen, was the crux of the

answer of the Massachusetts House of Representatives to Governor
Hutchinson in 1773, the legal arguments having been supplied by
Adams. In 1774 it became the official view of the colonies when the
Continental Congress approved Adams' resolution to that effect.[25]

Shortly thereafter, in a series of published letters, Adams answered
the contentions of the Massachusetts Tory, Daniel Leonard (1740–
1829). Leonard argued on legal grounds the authority of Parliament
and on practical grounds that English liberties were better assured to
the colonists under Parliamentary authority than by the king alone.
Adams' arguments were the fruit of a decade of legal research. He
dismissed outright the distinction between taxation and legislation made
by Dulany and Dickinson, calling it "a distinction without a difference."
His premise was now simply, no legislation without American consent.[26]

The conceptions of the origin and of the fiduciary basis of political
authority, which Adams had earlier defined as part of the British Constitution, were now put forth by him on natural law grounds. He
called them "the principles of Aristotle and Plato, of Livy and Cicero,
of Sidney, Harrington, and Locke, the principles of nature and eternal
reason; the principles on which the whole government over us now
stands." With them as norms, he reasoned that "a settled plan to
deprive the people of all the benefits, blessings, and ends of the contract, to subvert the fundamentals of the constitution, to deprive them
of all share in making and executing laws, will justify a revolution."[27]

Adams was not now interested in asserting revolution, however. He
believed he had constitutional history, theory, and law on his side.
The truth is, he declared, the general authority of Parliament was
never acknowledged in America. The examples of Massachusetts and
Virginia were cited in substantiation. "We have by our own express
consent contracted to observe the Navigation Act, and by our implied
consent, by long usage and uninterrupted acquiescence, have submitted
to other acts of trade. . . ." This practice he thought might be compared to "a treaty of commerce by which those distinct states have been
cemented together in perpetual league and amity." By what law, he
asked, has Parliament authority over America? It has none by divine
law nor by the law of nature and nations. The common law does not
provide it inasmuch as it never extended beyond the four seas. Finally,
it has none by statutory law "for no statute was made before the settlement of the colonies for this purpose."[28]

With Leonard's assertion that two supreme and independent authorities cannot exist in the same state, Adams agreed, but added:
"our provincial legislatures are the only supreme authorities in our
colonies." It is they and not Parliament which make the concessions.
Whereas men like Dickinson had argued that Parliament had inherent
authority to legislate for the general concerns of empire, Adams denied

that right, but maintained that its power to act could be conceded by the colonies. The bond between the colonies and Great Britain is the king, in his natural person; America had never been joined to the realm.[29]

James Wilson (1742–1798): Legal Scholar

Born in Scotland, educated at the Universities of Andrews, Glasgow, and Edinburgh, in an atmosphere heavily influenced by the critical spirit of Hume, the commonsense psychology of Thomas Reid, and the social thought of Adam Smith and Adam Ferguson, Wilson came to Philadelphia in 1765. He studied law in the office of John Dickinson and soon became prominent at the bar and in Pennsylvania politics. A master of the history and philosophy of law, the scholarly young Scot, moved by the colonial cause, read assiduously the works of Hooker, Hume, Locke, Montesquieu, Bolingbroke, Blackstone, and Sidney, among others.[30]

Wilson's pamphlet, *Considerations on the Nature and Extent of the British Parliament,* the first draft of which he wrote as early as 1768, and which he published in 1774, denied the legislative authority of Parliament over the colonies *"in every instance."* He began by declaring that he had undertaken the study with the object of tracing "some constitutional line between those cases in which we ought, and those in which we ought not, to acknowledge the power of Parliament over us." His researches, however, had "fully convinced" him that such a line does not and cannot exist. That he was in agreement with Hutchinson and in disagreement with men like his mentor, Dickinson, on the principle involved, is evident from his statement: "There can be no medium between acknowledging and denying that [Parliamentary] power in all cases." But unlike Hutchinson he pointed to the British as the violators of the Constitution. Thus it was British infractions that brought Americans to work to regain the rights that were theirs by the "laws of nature," and "the fundamental principles of the British Constitution."[31]

Wilson argued that Parliamentary supremacy could only be justified if it tended to promote the ultimate end of government. Drawing particularly upon the Swiss legal theorist, Burlamaqui, and probably also influenced by his mentor Dickinson on this point, he defined that end as follows:

All men are, by nature, equal and free: no one has a right to any authority over another without his consent: All lawful government is founded on the consent of those who are subject to it: such consent was given with a view to ensure and to increase the happiness of the governed, above what they

could enjoy in an independent and unconnected state of nature. The consequence is, that the happiness of the society is the *first* law of every government.[32]

In light of this, the basic question, as Wilson saw it, was, will it ensure and increase the happiness (liberty, security, common good) of the
American colonies if "the parliament of Great Britain should possess
a supreme, irresistible, uncontrolled authority over them." If public
happiness is dependent on liberty and liberty is dependent on consent,
since the colonists were unrepresented in Parliament the answer is
obvious on Wilson's natural law premises. On psychological grounds
he further argued that motives of self-interest and love of fame in
members of Parliament militated against the interests of the nonrepre-
sented colonists. Similarly, he asserted that to depend upon a regard
in Parliament "for the dictates of natural justice" would be dangerously
naïve, inasmuch as "a very little degree of knowledge in the history of
men will sufficiently convince us that a regard to justice is by no
means the ruling principle in human nature." In light of this he concluded that no viable force operated to persuade the members of
Parliament to promote the happiness of Americans.[33]
    Wilson turned next to "books of law" to show that his interpretation
of the British Constitution was upheld by British courts in decisions
"which show expressly, or by a necessary implication, that the colonies
are not bound by the acts of the British Parliament; because they have
no share in the British legislature." Among other cases he cited a decision of the reign of Richard III which held that the people of Ireland,
being unrepresented in Parliament, were not bound by English statutes,
although they were subjects of the king. From this he concluded (ignoring a decision made in the following year reversing this judgment)
that "parliamentary authority is derived *solely* from representation" and
that "allegiance to the king and obedience to the parliament are founded
on very different principles," the former being based on "protection,"
and the latter on "representation." The colonies and Great Britain
were linked together by a common monarch and not by the authority
of Parliament. In fact the colonial assemblies are the constitutional
equals of Parliament.[34]
    In his speech to the Pennsylvania Convention in 1775, Wilson again
expounded the theme that acts of Parliament are not binding upon the
colonies unless consented to. Speaking of the Intolerable Acts, he further
developed previous colonial expressions of the fixed nature of the British
Constitution by holding it to be fundamental law by which the validity
or invalidity of Parliamentary and executive acts is determined. The
act of Parliament revoking the Massachusetts charter was void because
it was contrary to the principle of liberty guaranteed in the British Con-

stitution. Since the regal prerogative is limited by the same principle, its similar use is unjustified. Because "a void act can confer no authority upon those, who proceed under colour of it," all attempts at enforcement in courts or without, amount to "force employed contrary to law." It follows "that to resist such force is lawful: and that both the letter and the spirit of the British Constitution justify such resistance." It will be noted that not only did Wilson here aim at Parliament but also at the king and thus did he elaborate a justification for resistance, if not revolution, a year and a half before the Declaration of Independence. Missing from the institutional apparatus available legally to effect Wilson's constitutional ideas was that which was and is foreign to the British Constitution, a final court of appeals which weighs the validity of governmental acts in accordance with a fixed, fundamental law.[35]

In sum, Wilson's case was built upon the following logic: The British people had established representative government to secure their natural right to freedom and to promote public happiness; Americans, as Englishmen, possessed the right in positive law to representative government; no viable principle of motivation existed in Parliament to promote the interests of the unrepresented colonies; therefore the Americans possessed a right in English law, sanctioned ultimately by natural law, to be independent of the authority of Parliament, a conclusion that he saw amply confirmed by historical precedents and legal decisions. Like John Adams, Wilson employed the rhetoric of natural law but preferred to seal his case with concrete citations of positive law.

Alexander Hamilton (1757–1804): Youthful Advocate

Born in the West Indies, Hamilton came to New York in 1772. His early preoccupation with politics is evidenced by his pamphlets *A Full Vindication of the Measures of Congress* and *The Farmer Refuted*, written in 1774 and 1775, when he was but seventeen and eighteen years old, in answer to the *Letters of a Westchester Farmer*, the work of the New York loyalist, Samuel Seabury (1729–1796). Both works show the young Hamilton's acquaintance with the works of Locke, Blackstone, Hume, Montesquieu, Pufendorf, and Grotius. The principal reliance is on natural law, supplemented by arguments from human motivation, particularly self-interest, and by the demands of public policy.[36]

In *A Full Vindication* Hamilton gave the familiar argument that freedom exists where men are governed by laws to which they give their individual or deputized consent. The right of the colonists to be so governed was indicated by "natural justice," and confirmed by "the fundamental principles of the English constitution " and the colonial charters. Because remonstrance and petition to Parliament have proven unavailing, no recourse was left but trade restrictions or a resort to arms.

In choosing the former, the Continental Congress conformed not only to "the strictest maxims of Justice," but to "the sanction of good policy" which demands three things: "First, that the necessity of the times require it: Secondly, that it be not the probable source of greater evils than those it pretends to remedy; And lastly, that it have a probability of success."[37]

Having argued in terms of natural justice and public policy, Hamilton turned to interest, on the assumption that "a vast majority of mankind is intirely biassed by motives of self-interest." If the colonists were to agree to be vassals of England, he stated, like Dulany and Wilson had, that the members of Parliament, with a view to their own and their constituents' ease and advantage, "would oppress and grind the Americans as much as possible."[38]

Challenged by Seabury to declare explicitly his idea of the natural rights of mankind, Hamilton, in *The Farmer Refuted,* answered by attacking the Hobbist conception embraced by Seabury. Hobbes, Hamilton wrote, disbelieved in God, the author of the "eternal and immutable law which is indispensably obligatory upon all mankind, prior to any human institution whatever." After reciting Blackstone's definition of the law of nature, he went on to state that natural rights proceed therefrom. The Supreme Being endowed man with the rational faculty "to discern and pursue such things, as were consistent with his duty and interest, and invested him with an inviolable right to personal liberty, and personal safety." In a state of nature, "no man had any *moral* power to deprive another of his life, limbs, property, or liberty; nor the least authority to command, or exact obedience from him; except that which arose from the ties of consanguinity." Thus the legitimate basis of civil government must be a voluntary compact between rulers and ruled "for the security of the *absolute rights* of the latter."[39]

On this theoretical ground Hamilton rebutted the theses of Seabury. The English king is king of America not by virtue of the Parliamentary Act of Succession but by compact between the colonies and the king, which implies no subordination to Parliament. Both the law of nature and the British Constitution confine allegiance to the person of the king. And concerning the question of representation, frequent direct election ensures the protection of life and property. Hamilton's justification, which is similar to Wilson's, runs along the lines of Hume's analysis of motivation: "The representative . . . is bound, by every possible tie, to consult the advantage of his constituents. Gratitude for the high and honorable trust reposed in him demands a return of attention, and regard to the advancement of his happiness. Self-interest, that most powerful incentive of human actions, points and attracts towards the same object." But when there is imputed to the British House of Commons a jurisdiction over the colonies, the reverse is true. "All these kinds of security immediately disappear; no ties of gratitude or interest remain. Interest, indeed, may operate to our prejudice. . . . But what merits still more serious attention is this. There seems to be already a jealousy of our dawning splendor." Then Hamilton quoted from Hume a passage which ever after remained at the foundation of his political thought.[40]

Political writers . . . . have established it as a maxim, that, in contriving any system of government, and fixing the several checks and controuls of the constitution, *every man* ought to be supposed a *knave;* and to have no other end, in all his actions, but *private interest.* By this interest we must govern him; and by means of it, *make him cooperate to public good,* notwithstanding his insatiable avarice and ambition. Without this, we shall in vain boast of the advantages of *any constitution;* and shall find in the end, that we have no security for our liberties and possessions except the *good will* of our rulers, that is, we should have *no security at all.*[41]

Thus Hamilton answered Seabury's attack on his original argument regarding representation by turning from a mere assertion of Lockian natural rights to Hume's stress upon self-interest. America is without those checks upon the representatives in Great Britain which alone can make them subserve the protection of rights and advancement of the happiness of the governed. "The direct and inevitable consequence is," he concluded, *"they have no right to govern us."*[42]

On the question of sovereignty, Hamilton agreed with Seabury that "in every government there must be a supreme absolute authority lodged somewhere." Employing the mode of logical analysis used by Hume (without mentioning Hume), Hamilton went on to say: "But no use can be made of this principle beyond matter of fact. To infer from thence, that unless a supreme absolute authority be vested in one part of an empire over all the other parts, there can be no government in the whole, is false and absurd." Two or more distinct legislatures cannot exist in the same individual community, but they can exist in one state which comprehends a number of individual societies united under one common head. The king shares in the sovereignty of both Britain and America, and is "the only Sovereign of the empire."[43]

Hamilton, again using Humean reasoning, further contended "that the authority of the British Parliament over America would, in all probability, be a more intolerable and excessive species of despotism than an absolute monarchy." This because "the power of an absolute prince is not temporary but perpetual. He is under no temptation to purchase the favour of one part of his dominions at the expence of another; but, it is his interest to treat them all, upon the same footing."[44]

Turning to an historical examination of the colonies, Hamilton sought to show that the charters granted them by the monarch assuring them the rights of Englishmen would have been condemned as unconstitutional by Parliament, had their grant been beyond royal authority. But because New York had no charter, he returned to the argument from natural rights. With youthful enthusiasm he exclaimed: "The sacred rights of mankind are not to be rummaged for, among old parchments and musty records. They are written, as with a sun beam, in the whole *volume* of human nature, by the hand of the divinity itself; and can never be erased or obscured by mortal power."[45]

That Hamilton still sought to link natural rights with the British Constitution is evident in his summation: "I will now venture to assert, that I have demonstrated, from the voice of nature, the *spirit* of the British constitution, and the charters of the colonies in general, the absolute non-existence of that parliamentary sovereignty for which you contend."[46]

In conclusion it might be stated that Hamilton's arguments in these early pamphlets contain all of the elements which went into his mature political thought. But whereas the boy put primary stress on Locke and secondary emphasis on Hume, the man reversed the relative stress, although never discarding any of the component elements in the process. Once independence was achieved and the task of constructing a viable political order was at hand, the emphasis on rights and principles was overshadowed in his mind by preoccupation with policies and institutional forms.

Thomas Jefferson (1743–1826): "A Summary View"

Born in Albermarle County, Virginia, Jefferson grew up among self-reliant planters, farmers, and frontiersmen whose spirit became his own. Intellectually, however, he was nurtured in the European classical and humanistic tradition. Having attended William and Mary College from 1760 to 1762, he studied law under the direction of the great lawyer and scholar, George Wythe, and was admitted to the bar in 1767. In 1769 he was elected to the Virginia House of Burgesses, serving in that body until its demise in 1775.[47]

In July, 1774, Jefferson wrote a series of resolutions (which were adopted by the freeholders of Albermarle County), the first of which summed up the thesis of his *A Summary View of the Rights of British America* which he published a month later: "That the inhabitants of the several states of British America are subject to the laws which they adopted at their first settlement, and to such others as have been since made by their respective legislatures, duly constituted and appointed with their own consent; that no other legislature whatever may rightfully exercise authority over them, and that these privileges they hold as the common rights of mankind, confirmed by the political constitutions they have respectively assumed, and also by several charters of compact from the crown."[48]

A Summary View was not Jefferson's ablest work, having been written, as he later confessed, "in haste, with a number of blanks, with some uncertainties and inaccuracies of historical facts."[49] Unlike Adams' *Novanglus* or Hamilton's *A Full Vindication*, it is not polemical, nor is it, like Wilson's *Considerations*, a closely reasoned essay. Instead, it constitutes for the most part a preliminary Bill of Indictment, a listing of the wrongs done to the colonies. Much of its substance as well as its rhetoric is suggestive of the Declaration of Independence.

His main charge was against Parliament, "the legislature of one part of the empire," which has attempted "many unwarrantable encroachments and usurpations . . . upon those rights which God and the laws have given equally and independently to all." His arguments for complete colonial independence of Parliament run essentially in terms of natural right and constitutional principles. Like their Saxon forbears, who left the continent, the American colonists, having been free inhabitants of England, had a natural right to emigrate and establish new societies "under such laws and regulations as to them shall seem most likely to promote public happiness." America was conquered and settled at the expense of individuals, not of the British public. Once settled, the colonists agreed to adopt the English system of laws and to continue the union with Britain, "by submitting themselves to the same common sovereign, who was thereby made the central link, connecting the several parts of the empire thus newly multiplied." On this basis the exercise of a free trade by the colonies with all the world was theirs "as of natural right." But the Stuarts, with their "arbitrary power" were succeeded by Parliament and its "uncontrouled power," in the unjustifiable imposition of trade regulations and practices on the colonies. "History has informed us," Jefferson remarked, "that bodies of men as well as individuals are susceptible of the spirit of tyranny." He insisted, however, that these facts were not being pointed out to the king with the intent to rest the case on the principle of justice, "but to shew that experience confirms the propriety of those political principles, which exempt us from the jurisdiction of the British Parliament." The acts are "void" because Parliament "has no right to exercise authority over us." Thus, "not only the principles of common sense, but the common feelings of human nature must be surrendered up, before his Majesty's subjects here can be persuaded to believe that they hold their political existence at the will of a British parliament."[50]

Having stated the grievances against Parliament, Jefferson went on to criticize the king for "his deviations from the line of duty," in failing to protect the interests of the colonies, rejecting "salutary" laws, permitting colonial laws to be neglected in England for years, and dissolving a colonial legislature. Although the veto power had fallen into disuse, Jefferson urged that the king exercise it as the common sovereign to prevent the passage of laws "by any one legislature of the empire which might bear injuriously on the rights and liberties of another." Finally, he stated, kings are "the servants, not the proprietors of the people." The doctrine of consent of the governed precludes any *jure divino* conception of monarchical authority.[51]

Jefferson thought these observations to be obvious. Thus he addressed the king: "The great principles of right and wrong are legible to every reader; to pursue them requires not the aid of many counsellors. The whole art of government consists in the art of being honest. Only aim to do your duty, and mankind will give you credit where you fail. No longer persevere in sacrificing the rights of one part of the empire to the inordinate desires of another; but deal out to all, equal and impartial right."[52]

With all its limitations, *A Summary View* has great relevance to the student of American political thought not only for its assertion of the dominion theory of empire, but as a foreshadowing of Jefferson's greatest work, the *Declaration of Independence*. Like the latter, it is addressed to the king; the dominion theory, which it justified on the consensual principle, based the king's authority on colonial consent. Having accepted the king as a servant, it followed that if he abused his trust as a matter of policy, the colonists could, with moral justification, cut him off—an act accomplished by the Declaration.

Finally, the natural rights theory underlying *A Summary View* anticipated the great second paragraph of the Declaration. In the latter Jefferson talked of "self-evident truths"; in the former he spoke of "the principles of common sense" and "the common feelings of human nature." He believed that both the unsophisticated and the sophisticated, if rightly disposed, are readily capable of discerning "the great principles of right and wrong."[53] This involves no ratiocination nor refined deduction nor an intricate epistemological explanation. Jefferson, like Shaftesbury, Hutcheson, and, more particularly, Henry Home (Lord Kames), believed that by the constitution of human nature men possess a moral sense whose authority lies in the fact that they feel an act to be right or wrong. Although education and experience may aid its development, they are not creative of the faculty itself. Thus it was but natural for him to write in oversimplified fashion that "the whole art of government consists in the art of being honest," i.e., following the moral sense.

Conclusions

Having propounded the commonwealth theory, leading Americans left behind them the important challenges to the concept of indivisibility of sovereignty. They now conceded its indivisibility, agreeing on formal theoretical grounds with the logic of Mansfield, Blackstone, and Hutchinson, but disagreeing with the British authorities concerning the locus of indivisible sovereignty. Thus they claimed sovereignty for their colonial legislatures under the Crown, equal to that of Parliament in England. To explain previous Parliamentary exercise of authority in the colonies for trade or imperial purposes, the American theorists, like John Adams, talked in terms of colonial assent in such instances, and the "necessity" of the case. The identification of sovereignty with legislative bodies, and the generally held Whig conception of legislators as representing the common interest of a people, made it impossible for men to accept the notion of two legislative assemblies, such as Parliament and the colonial bodies, exercising the same powers. Only after the derivative nature of legislative authority was more greatly emphasized and legislative representatives came to be rgarded as agents of the people in their peculiar local interests could the full implications of popular sovereignty as the basis of governmental power be realized.

Finally, one can focus on particular facets of the colonial debate with the English in the decade after 1765 to the point of magnifying the differences in colonial Whig arguments. They were consistent in denying throughout the period Parliamentary power to tax them internally or externally; they were consistent in their willingness to adhere to Parliamentary supervisory legislation for the whole empire. Within these principles they did change in moving to the position of denying Parliamentary power to legislate internally as well as to tax.[54]

NOTES

1. The exchange between Hutchinson and the legislature can be found in Alden T. Vaughan (ed.), *Chronicles of the American Revolution: originally compiled by Hezekiah Niles* (New York, 1965), pp. 42–62, 73–76.

2. Jensen, *Documents*, No. 148, p. 807.

3. The principal authority backing the colonists' legal position on this point is McIlwain; the principal authority in opposition thereto is Schuyler.

4. Moses Coit Tyler, *The Literary History of the American Revolution* (New York, 1957, 2 vols.), II, 11; C. F. Adams (ed.), *The Works of John Adams*, III, 425–426; "Joseph Galloway on the First Continental Congress (1780)," in Jensen, *Documents*, No. 146, p. 801; Adams, *Works*, II, 162.

5. William V. Wells, *The Life and Public Services of Samuel Adams* (Boston, 1865, 3 vols.), I, 10, 6, 19, 20, 21.

6. *Ibid.*, pp. 16, 17, 21, 22.

7. *Ibid.*, p. 331.

8. *Ibid.*, pp. 17, 331, 332.

9. *Ibid.*, p. 97, "Massachusetts Circular Letter, Feb. 11, 1768," Jensen, *Documents*, No. 120, p. 714.

10. Wells, *Life*, I, 429–430.

11. Adams, *Works*, II, 310. An opposite view of the influence of John Adams in the instance is given in Wells, *op. cit.*, II, note on pp. 34–40.

12. Samuel Adams to John Adams, Oct. 4, Nov. 20, 1790, in Wells, *Life*, III, 301–302.

13. *Ibid.*, 314.

14. Diary, *Works of John Adams*, II, 59; "Thoughts on Government," *Works*, IV, 193; J. Adams to Alexander Jardine, June 1, 1790, *Works*, IX, 567.

15. On Adams' life see Page Smith, *John Adams* (New York, 1962, 2 vols.).

16. John Adams to John Quincy Adams, Sept. 13, 1790, cited in *ibid.*, I, 112.

17. Adams, *Works*, III, 449, 452 (footnote).

18. *Ibid.*, pp. 448, 450, 451.

19. *Ibid.*, pp. 452–453, 454, 455, 456.

20. *Ibid.*, pp. 456, 457.

21. *Ibid.*, III, 466; II, 157; III, 477–478.

22. *Ibid.*, III, 478, 479, 480, 481, 482.

23. Bailyn, *Pamphlets*, I, 46.

24. Adams, *Works*, III, 489, 490.

25. *Ibid.*, III, 502. Hutchinson's comment is in a footnote on p. 502; Smith, *op. cit.*, p. 182.

26. Adams, *Works*, IV, 113. Leonard's arguments can be found in John Adams and Daniel Leonard, *Novanglus and Massachusettsensis* (Boston, 1819).

27. *Ibid.*, 15, 16.

28. *Ibid.*, 113–114, 37.

29. Adams, *Works*, IV, 105. For a full discussion of Adams and the constitutional issue see R. G. Adams, *op. cit.*, pp. 107–127, and Mullett, *op. cit.*, pp. 179–188.

30. Concerning Wilson's life and work see Charles Page Smith, *James Wilson* (Chapel Hill, 1956); Robert Green McCloskey, *The Works of James Wilson* (Cambridge, Mass., 1967, 2 vols.), I, 1–48 (hereinafter cited as *Works*); and R. G. Adams (ed.), *Selected Political Essays of James Wilson*, (New York, 1930), pp. 1–42.

31. Wilson, *Works*, II, 721.

32. Wilson, *Works*, II, 723.

33. Wilson, *Works*, II, 723–724, 734.

34. Wilson, *Works*, II, 735, 736–737, 745. Concerning Wilson's oversight of the case reversing that which he cited, see Schuyler, *Parliament and the British Empire*, pp. 63–64.

35. Wilson, *Works*, II, 752–754, 755, 756, 758.

36. Concerning Hamilton's life and work see John C. Miller, *Alexander Hamilton* (New York, 1959); Clinton Rossiter, *Alexander Hamilton and the Constitution* (New York, 1964); and Gerald Stourzh, *Alexander Hamilton and the Idea of Republican Government* (Stanford, 1970). Seabury's arguments can be found in Clarence Vance (ed.) *Publications of the Westchester County Historical Society* (White Plains, N.Y., 1930), vol. 8.

37. Harold C. Syrett (ed.), *The Papers of Alexander Hamilton* (New York, 1961–1969, 15 vols. completed), I, 47, 52.

38. *Ibid.*, I, 53, 54.

39. *Ibid.*, I, 87, 88.

40. *Ibid.*, I, 90, 91, 92, 93.

41. *Ibid.*, I, 94–95.

42. *Ibid.*, I, 95.

43. *Ibid.*, I, 97, 98, 99.

44. *Ibid.*, I, 100.

45. *Ibid.*, I, 122.

46. *Ibid.*

47. Concerning Jefferson's life, see Dumas Malone, *Jefferson and His Time* (Boston, 1948–1970, 4 vols.)

48. "Resolutions of the Freeholders of Albermarle County," July 26, 1774, Julian P. Boyd (ed.), *The Papers of Thomas Jefferson* (Princeton, 1950– , 17 vols. in print), I, 117.

49. P. L. Ford (ed.), *The Writings of Thomas Jefferson* (New York, 1892–1899, 10 vols.), I, 421.

50. *Papers*, I, 121, 122, 123, 124, 125, 126.

51. *Papers*, I, 129, 134.

52. *Papers*, I, 134.

53. *Papers*, I, 126.

54. Morgan, "Colonial Issues of Parliamentary Power," *op. cit.*, p. 341.

Chapter 8

THE DECLARATION OF INDEPENDENCE

Here English Law and English thought 'Gainst the self-will of England fought.

JAMES RUSSELL LOWELL

After hostilities broke out in 1775 there remained in the colonies a strong hope of ultimate reconciliation with the mother country. The legal arguments had been drawn as far as possible in the common-wealth of nations theory; to go beyond meant leaving the law and re-sorting to revolution by cutting the admitted tie to the common mon-arch. It is true that some prominent Americans, notably the Adamses, advocated independence before 1776, but there was lacking a spark to ignite the fuse which would arouse men to make the break. In January, 1776, this deficiency was supplied by a man not yet two years in Amer-ica, Thomas Paine, with his powerful, widely read pamphlet *Common Sense*.

Thomas Paine (1739–1809): The Call to Action

Born in England in lowly circumstances, the self-educated Paine developed a dislike of the English social and political systems. After having been twice discharged from a minor government job, he came to America in 1774 with a letter of introduction from Benjamin Frank-lin describing him as "an ingenious worthy young man," who might be employed as "a clerk, or assistant tutor in a school, or assistant sur-veyor." It may be that Paine really intended, as was thought, to estab-lish a ladies' seminary, but he was born with a desire to move men and he could best do this with his pen. Thus shortly after settling in Phila-delphia he became editor of a journal, publishing many articles in it and elsewhere. Convinced by the resort to arms of the necessity and desirability of American independence—a conviction which was reinforced by his republicanism—he wrote *Common Sense* to break the jam.[1]

Common Sense is less a contribution to political thought than an agitator's impassioned call to action. It is neither scholarly nor profound; Paine appears to have had but slight acquaintance, if any, with the classics of political thought.[2] Similarly, it is utterly devoid of the legalism which informed so much of the previous colonial political literature. A clue to Paine's approach might be gotten from a slightly later statement of his: "When precedents fail to spirit us, we must return to the first principles of things for information; and *think*, as if we were the *first men* that *thought*."[3] *Common Sense*, however, is evidence enough that Paine was not a powerful thinker, and that what he lacked intellectually he more than supplied in intensity and feeling. The work is at once hortatory and abrasive, inspiring and inflammatory, persuasive and vituperative. A rough-hewn genius, Paine was an extraordinarily facile phrasemaker, a master of invective, uncanny in the effective choice and coinage of metaphors and similes, both felicitous and vulgar. As a result his evocative rhetoric at times outran his logic, which served his purpose well, for he seems to have sensed that men are more stirred by appeals to the heart than to the mind. He seems also to have realized that to move a nation one must oversimplify and limn the adversary and his institutions in the darkest hues. Thus there is no mistaking the villain, "the royal brute," who sits on the English throne, and there is no confusion between hereditary monarchy as the principle of evil and republicanism as virtue's soul. Similarly, there is a root and branch rejection of the British Constitution, something which no other prominent American pamphleteer, no matter how corrupt he thought the Constitution had become, dared to do. In short, because of his rejection of the past, of the traditional legalism of the American public mind, and of the tendency to equate natural rights with constitutional rights, Paine was more of the European rationalist than the American traditionalist and empiricist. A born revolutionist, he played a significant active role in American life only as long as the revolution lasted.

He began with a discussion of the origin and end of government, using his celebrated distinction: "Society is produced by our wants and government by our wickedness; the former promotes our happiness *positively*, by uniting our affections, the latter *negatively* by restraining our vices." Society is always "a blessing," but "government, even in its best state, is but a necessary evil." "Government, like dress, is the badge of lost innocence." If men were truly good there would be no need for it; they consent to establish it to gain security and freedom.[4]

Paine then presented a natural history of democratic-republican government (the only just form). Originally a democracy of the whole by dint of necessity, it issues in the deputization by individual consent of the legislative power to representatives who are frequently called to account at elections to ensure "the *strength of government, and the happiness of the governed.*" Paine regarded this as the dictate of "the simple voice of nature and reason," concerning the origin and end of government. History's complexities are now dispelled: "I draw my idea of the form of government from a principle in nature, which no art can overturn, viz., that the more simple any thing is, the less liable it is to be disordered, and the easier repaired when disordered."[5]

In light of nature's norm, he proceeded to arraign the British Constitution. He saw it as a confusion of republican and monarcho-aristocratic principles. The hereditary branches "contribute nothing toward the freedom of the State." The doctrine of reciprocal checks and balances is "farcical"; the same Constitution which assumes the House of Commons to be wiser than the king by giving it a power to withhold supplies, also gives the king a power to check the Commons through the veto power, thus supposing that "the King is wiser than those whom it has already supposed to be wiser than him." Paine asked: *"How came the king by a power which the people are afraid to trust, and always obliged to check?* Such a power could not be the gift of a wise people, neither can any power, *which needs checking,* be from God; yet the provision which the Constitution makes supposes such a power to exist."[6]

It is evident that not only was Paine somewhat ignorant of the existing British Constitution but that his bias against checks and balances was in contradiction to his basic tenet that government exists solely as a restraining force upon men's propensity to err. His choice is clearly that of most popular revolutionists throughout the ages—government by assembly, albeit, in his case, within the framework of a constitution. There was no question, however, in his mind that *"it is wholly owing to the constitution of the people, and not to the constitution of the government* that the Crown is not as oppressive in England as in Turkey."[7]

Paine aimed his principal shafts at the principles of monarchy and hereditary succession: "It is the pride of kings which throws mankind into confusion." Government by kings constitutes "the most prosperous invention the devil ever set on foot for the promotion of idolatry." The first monarch was "nothing better than the principal ruffian of some restless gang." Concerning England and the claim of monarchical right going back to William the Conquerer: "A French bastard, landing with an armed banditti, and establishing himself King of England against the consent of the natives, is in plain terms a very paltry rascally original." And finally, "of more worth is one honest man to society, and in the sight of God, than all the crowned ruffians that ever lived."[8]

But there are insightful nuggets buried in the diatribe. Thus hereditary monarchy, instead of ensuring a race of good and wise men, "opens a door to the *foolish,* the *wicked,* and the *improper.*" Nature disapproves it, "otherwise she would not so frequently turn it into ridicule by giving mankind an *ass* for a *lion*." Similarly, "men who look upon themselves born to reign and others to obey, soon grow insolent; selected from the rest of mankind, their minds are early poisoned by importance; and the world they act in differs so materially from the world at large, that they have but little opportunity of knowing its true interests, and when they succeed to the government are frequently the most ignorant and unfit of any throughout the dominions." But most telling, monarchy "first excludes a man from the means of information, yet empowers him to act in cases where the highest judgment is required." The final blast was more dubious: monarchical governments are warlike, republican governments, peaceful.[9]

Turning to the American connection with Britain, he asserted that the protection provided by Britain was motivated by *"interest* not *attachment";* that the concept of parent country was "jesuitically adopted by the King and his parasites, with a low, papistical design of gaining an unfair bias on the credulous weakness of our minds," and had no validity because Americans came from many European countries; and that it embroils American trade in wars. But most of all: "It is repugnant to reason, to the universal order of things, to all examples from former ages to suppose that this continent can long remain subject to any external power. . . . In no instance hath nature made the satellite larger than its primary planet; and as England and America, with respect to each other, reverse the common order of Nature, it is evident that they belong to different systems. England to Europe: America to itself."[10]

Paine left America in 1787 for Europe where he played a role as a constitutional republican in the French Revolution and published his more famous works *The Rights of Man* and *The Age of Reason*. He came back to America in 1802. Over the years he had acquired, mostly unjustifiably, many enemies. John Adams contemptuously called him "the filthy Tom Paine," and others reviled him for his rationalist reduction of Christianity. On the other hand, Thomas Jefferson, in 1821, observed: "No writer has exceeded Paine in ease and familiarity of style, in perspicuity of expression, happiness of elucidation, and in simple and unassuming language." In the words of Paine's most recent biographer, "the great contribution of *Common Sense* was in preparing the minds of plain men for independence and in shifting their loyalty from the British Crown to the American republic."[11]

The Ideas in the Declaration

The Declaration of Independence, which was drafted by Thomas Jefferson and approved in Congress on July 4, 1776, was essentially a moral and legal justification of the rebellion and the political act of withdrawal from the authority of Great Britain. It assumed the validity of the commonwealth of nations constitutional theory and thus ignored the Parliament and addressed the king. Against the king and in justification of its position it employed natural law theory, using specific instances of monarchical violations of law to substantiate the argument from general principles. Its purpose was stated in the opening paragraph:

When in the Course of human events, it becomes necessary for one people to dissolve the political bands which have connected them with another, and to assume, among the Powers of the earth, the separate and equal station, to which the Laws of Nature and of Nature's God entitle them, a decent respect to the opinions of mankind requires that they should declare the causes which impel them to the separation.

The second paragraph lays down the philosophic principles and norms underlying government.

We hold these truths to be self-evident, that all men are created equal, that they are endowed by their Creator with certain unalienable Rights, that among these are Life, Liberty, and the pursuit of Happiness; that to secure these rights, Governments are instituted among Men, deriving their just powers from the consent of the governed; that whenever any Form of Government becomes destructive of these ends, it is the Right of the People to alter or to abolish it, and to institute new Government laying its foundation on such principles and organizing its powers in such form, as to them shall seem most likely to effect their Safety and Happiness.[12]

The "self-evident" truths—the equality of men, natural rights, and securing of natural rights as the purpose of government, the consent of the governed as the principle of political legitimacy, and the moral right to revolt when natural rights are abridged—were, of course, not original with the Declaration. As Jefferson stated in 1825 his purpose was

Not to find out new principles or new arguments never before thought of, not merely to say things which had never been said before; but to place before mankind the common sense of the subject, in terms so plain and firm as to command their assent. . . . Neither aiming at originality of principle or sentiment, nor yet copied from any particular and previous writing, it was intended to be an expression of the American mind. . . . All its authority rests then on the harmonizing sentiments of the day, whether expressed in conversation, in letters, printed essays, or the elementary books of public right, as Aristotle, Cicero, Locke, Sidney, etc.[13]

To grasp the full meaning and intent of the Founding Fathers we will first analyze the basic concepts in the Declaration and then relate them to the specific charges made against the king.

One people. This term reflects the identity of interest and common experience and purpose which tied Americans together as "United Colonies" and justified their concerted action in a new political entity known as "the united States of America." "One people" was organized in thirteen "Free and Independent States" whose representatives met in "General Congress, Assembled." "One people" must not be seen as synonymous with "nation," a nineteenth-century term, because, as used in the Declaration, it lacked the connotation of homogeneity. Furthermore it assumed a degree of political sophistication and maturity not necessarily embodied in "nation." Consequently the conception of self-determination implicit in the Declaration must be understood in the above sense of "one people" rather than in the later sense of "nation."

Laws of nature. Generally speaking, men of the eighteenth century considered nature as a mechanism whose essential workings are conformable to the human mind. As Carl Becker, a historian of the Declaration put it, they tended to deify nature and denaturalize its author, God. Thus alongside and coordinate with "Nature's God" the Declaration used as justifying independence the term "laws of nature." "Laws of nature" was used in the eighteenth century indiscriminately to include descriptive statements of natural processes, principles of human nature and of social relations, as well as prescriptive statements of right and justice.[14] As a consequence, statements of principles of right and justice could confusedly be identified ·as scientific assertions, a practice which, as has been seen, Hume had attacked. Although some leading Americans tended to regard the law of nature as severed from eternal and divine law and thus autonomous, others such as Otis, Dickinson, and Wilson, as already seen, appear to have been more influenced by the older conception handed down to them through Hooker. In any case, most Americans considered the law of nature, in its application to politics, in terms of their Anglo-Saxon legal heritage.

A decent respect to the opinions of mankind. The Declaration assumed that justice has an objective basis and that men are equally possessed of a moral sense by which they can discern its dictates. For this reason "a decent respect to the opinions of mankind" demanded a clear exposition of the moral reasoning and the principle of political legitimacy underlying the break from England. Similarly, the signers of the Declaration all agreed that government ultimately is rooted in opinion. In this light the Declaration was an appeal not only to the world at large but to Americans themselves.

Self-evident truths. As the signers of the Declaration used the term, "self-evident," it lacked the precision which it possesses when used in reference to mathematical or logical first principles. The truths of the Declaration were "self-evident" because they were, as Jefferson described them in his *Summary View,* "principles of common sense," or as he later called them, "terms so plain and firm as to command assent," or as Franklin saw them, dictates of common experience. As first principles dictated by nature and discernible by all possessed of reason, they needed no demonstrative proof; they constituted obvious points of departure, axioms from which to proceed or moral imperatives deriving from the essential nature of man, upon which to act.

Equality. Although factual inequalities among men were not denied, the Founding Fathers stressed the moral equality of all men in the possession of a common human nature and an ability to discern the principal dictates of moral law. As Jefferson earlier explained it, there is a common capacity in men to discern "the great principles of right and wrong." Taught by the precepts of their religion, by the ancient idea of equality before the law, and by the emphasis of Locke on the mind as a "tabula rasa" and on the state of nature as one of equal natural freedom, Americans could draw on significant phases of their historical experience for confirmation of these tenets. Against the conservative doctrine of the equality of men in depravity, the liberal conception in the Declaration meant concretely equal possession of natural rights, elimination of artificial distinctions between men, equal treatment under law, equal right to the fruits of one's labors, and equal right to participate in the determination of the form of government and in the formulation of its laws. In good part the concept of equality was expressed in a formal as distinguished from a substantive sense. It was assumed that equality under law meant that the laws would be just and equal. Similarly, equal opportunity was deemed by many then as now to be essential, but it was assumed that once artificial restraints and privileges were removed all would, roughly speaking, start from a similar position. In fact the liberal conception of equality, emphasizing as it does formal equality, can and has been used to rationalize substantively unjust and unequal social conditions. Then, too, while no distinction was verbally drawn in the Declaration between the races of men, in fact a goodly number of the signers owned Negro slaves. It would be presumptuous to impute hypocrisy to them for this; many hoped for the eventual elimination of all involuntary servitude. Nevertheless the tension between profession of the principle of general equality on the one hand and practice on the other has ever since been at the center of American life and culture.[15]

Unalienable rights. Unalienable or natural rights were axiomatically regarded as inhering in man because of his nature as a rational, moral being. Possessed by man in the state of nature, they cannot legitimately be renounced or suppressed in the formation and governance of political society. The state of nature was regarded as existing whenever men live together under the law of nature but without a common superior judge. In this view it is not necessarily a primitive or warlike condition, but one which exists whenever men are without political rule, a situation not unfamiliar in the American past. Accordingly, the twin concepts of state of nature and natural rights could be adhered to by men who believed that man is political by nature as well as those who did not. Thus, "unalienable rights," as used in the Declaration, at once precede, limit, and supply purpose to government. Whether they are the principle or the dictate of the law of nature was a point of difference. Even though many gave lip service to the primacy of law over right, they tended to make natural rights the substance of the law of nature as applied to man. In any case, the overwhelming tendency was to equate natural rights in the concrete with British constitutional and legal guarantees, that is, historical rights won dearly by their ancestors and passed on to them as their birthright.

Life, liberty, and the pursuit of happiness. The generic natural rights specifically mentioned in the Declaration were life, liberty, and the pursuit of happiness—a modification of the Lockian triad—life, liberty, and property. This change was not as significant as is sometimes believed. It did not mean that property was not considered a natural right; on the contrary, property was all but universally regarded as a necessary instrument to the realization of the three rights named.

Looked at in reverse order of statement, the pursuit of happiness presupposes liberty and life, while liberty presupposes life. Ideally speaking, life presupposes the others but practically speaking it can exist without them. Then, too, the terms have both an individual and public dimension. The Declaration speaks both of "Men" and "the People." Consequently the natural right of individuals to life is paralleled by the right of "the People" to exist in independence and security. The right to liberty on an individual basis means minimally freedom from restraint which interferes with choice. On a moral basis, as we have seen in the case of men like Winthrop and Penn, it means freedom to do what the objective moral law prescribes, as well as the condition ensuing therefrom. On the collective level it then meant establishment by popular consent of a government dedicated to the preservation and furtherance of individual natural rights.

The phrase "the pursuit of happiness" presents certain difficulties concerning the meaning of its two nouns. The conventional interpretation of "pursuit" has been that of a "seeking" or a "quest." Nonetheless, as Arthur Schlesinger, Sr. has reminded us, the term has also the meaning of "practice," and certain prominent Americans of that era probably understood it as such.[16] If the latter interpretation is accepted, then man has not merely the right to seek happiness but to "practice" it; that is, he has a natural right to happiness. And because the Declaration also talks of the "happiness" of "the People," the same applies to the collectivity. In other words, government in this view has not only the duty of preserving and effecting the natural right of individuals to happiness but also that of the people as a whole.

It seems strained, however, to conclude that the Founding Fathers, in referring to government and the "happiness" of "the People," meant more than the duty of the former to respect, protect, and preserve what John Dickinson earlier called *"the rights essential to happiness."* Nevertheless it is at least plausible to argue that implied in their statement is the duty of government to promote the material conditions for general "happiness." Finally, in interpreting the word "pursuit" it should be remembered that Locke used the phrase "pursuit of happiness" in the sense of a "quest" of that which is inherently elusive.[17] He, as well as Adam Smith, and the Americans Benjamin Franklin and John Adams, saw life as an attempt to satisfy recurring uneasiness. As a recent study suggests, liberalism was touched from the beginning by anxiety and entertained a conception of restless, anxious man. If this is true, then "pursuit" is an endless "quest," happiness is at best a proximate condition, and life is constant movement to allay anxieties.[18]

Turning to the term "happiness," it should be remembered that either in its reference to the individual or the public, it was used, for example, in colonial public pronouncements, and in the works of the two Adamses, Bland, Dickinson, Otis, Wilson, and Paine. The concept is, of course, of great antiquity and it is a mistake to identify it as such with utilitarianism or hedonism. Aristotle propounded it as the end for man; Epicureans equated it with pleasure, or the absence of pain, and deemed it the goal of human endeavor. Besides Locke we find the term used during the eighteenth century by Burlamaqui, Samuel Johnson, Wollaston, Bolingbroke, Hutcheson, Adam Smith, Priestley, and Beccaria, among others.[19]

Because the Declaration put prime emphasis on the individual pursuit of happiness and nowhere mentions civic duties and virtues, it has a pronounced individualistic tone. Then, too, because it provided no definite content to the term "happiness" and because individual conceptions thereof greatly differ (St. Augustine once pointed out that the Roman scholar, Varro, had counted 288 different opinions of its meaning), the result tends toward subjectivism. This is not to deny that the term can be supplied objective content: Aristotle defined it as rational activity of the soul in accordance with virtue in a complete life, and John Dickinson, to take just one American as an example, saw it, as we have seen, as consisting in the following of God's way in the acquisition of virtue. Many Americans probably thought of happiness in this fashion, others probably equated it with pleasurable activity, while yet others probably saw it embodied in the agrarian life of simple virtues. Doubtless some also saw it, as had Hobbes, "not in the repose of a mind satisfied," but as "a continual progress of the desire from one object to another."[20] In any case, it is most probable that the fathers, following liberal impulses and assuming the acceptance of moral law, wished to leave to each individual the right to pursue his own conception of happiness.

That Jefferson thought in this manner seems certain. A recent student of his thought has written that Jefferson believed that "to grant freedom and happiness to the greatest number of individuals should be the common concern of all of them." To him "each individual was an independent unit, and the formation of his personality was the free development of his natural gifts."[21] The egalitarian and liberal implications of such position are obvious. If the individual pursuit of happiness is an ultimate right to be secured by government, and government, although providing for its protection and its conditions, is precluded from affixing to happiness (and virtue) an objective content, then one man's conception is as valid as another's and each should have an equal voice in government. Similarly, the burden for his development lies on each individual's shoulders. He who is made free must assume the awesome responsibility of such freedom. Government then exists to provide the legal conditions of freedom and not to make men good; the American brand of political hedonism relies upon the individual to do the latter for himself.

Consent of the governed. The Founding Fathers believed that a political regime is legitimate if it originates in, and remains subject to, the consent of the governed. This is not the corporate consent stressed by Cicero and Hooker, for example, nor is it a contract agreed to by a select few such as the "saints" in the Puritan concept. Instead, because all men are equal and possess natural rights, the consent must be on an individual basis. It was generally agreed that although men are social by nature, the bond of political unity lies in the consent of individual wills. Thus the contract assumed by the American consensual theory was not constitutive of society but of the state. Whether such contract was creative of political authority or merely indicative of the way such authority should be exercised was a question upon which men divided. An unqualified political hedonism can admit only the former. On the other hand, it is probable that most Americans, following the lead of men like Otis, Dickinson, John Adams, and Hamilton, saw political authority as implicit in the divinely created nature of man.

The right of the people to alter, abolish, and reinstitute government. It followed from the consensual principle that when government acts violative of its end—the securing of natural rights—it can be changed by popular consent. The Founding Fathers disclaimed this as an incendiary doctrine, contending that prudence dictates that long-established governments not be changed for "light and transient causes" and that experience showed "that mankind are more disposed to suffer, while evils are sufferable, than to right themselves by abolishing the forms to which they are accustomed." It is only "when a long train of abuses and usurpations, pursuing invariably the same Object evinces a design to reduce them under absolute Despotism," that it becomes their right (and duty) to employ the necessary means to alter or abolish such government. Nowhere in the Declaration or in any other contemporary American political document is there an advocacy of revolution *per se.* Instead the doctrine is broached in highly qualified moral terms. The principal practical difficulty of the doctrine centers on the questions, who or what constitutes the people and how is the decision to be made by them to take the fateful step? Obviously the fathers did not subscribe to the need for unanimous consent; their acceptance of the "Glorious Revolution," which David Hume once remarked was the work of 700 men in a nation of ten million, shows that they did not believe that an active majority was a moral requisite. Probably they believed that an active minority with widespread moral support constituted a sufficient basis. It is interesting to note that John Adams estimated that one-third of the American people in the Revolutionary period was loyal to the Crown, one-third was in rebellion, and one-third was neutral.* In any case it was a principle which the signers pronounced,

---

* A recent historian of the subject has written that it is better to say that the Loyalists comprised one-third and the Revolutionists two-thirds of the politically active population. Despite common belief, it appears that outside of royal officeholders and Anglican clergymen who remained loyal, the rank and file of the Loyalists contained many more yeomen, cordwainers, tailors, laborers, masons, and blacksmiths than gentlemen, esquires, and merchants. Loyalist strength existed along the sparsely settled western frontier and the maritime regions of the middle colonies, both of which suffered from, or were threatened by, the political and economic domination of the more affluent adjoining areas. Similarly, Loyalist sympathy was more evident among religious groups such as the Quakers and Anglicans who believed in nonresistance, and non-Anglicized cultural minorities such as the Dutch, Germans, Scots Highlanders, Indians and, perhaps, Negroes, who feared the American majority more than British rule. That Loyalist dedication was deep is evidenced by the fact that in 1780 there were 8,000 Loyalists among the British regulars, while Washington's army numbered only 9,000 men. Finally, it should be said that the idea that for society to be well ordered, power must be wielded by the rich and the wise, was as much adhered to by the considerable number of American Whig oligarchs who supported the Revolution as by Tory Loyalist oligarchs. The difference between them was that Loyalist oligarchs were more dependent upon British support than were the Whigs. Most of the prominent Loyalists in colonial political life opposed the Stamp Act; many disbelieved the theory of virtual representation and thought British policy wrong. A few, like Thomas Hutchinson of Massachusetts, focused on the psychological factor, contending that colonial disorders from 1765 on were due to British neglect in allowing the notion of Parliamentary supremacy "to go off from the minds of the people." Others like Leonard and Seabury echoed British constitutional arguments. Still, others like Dulany and Duché were Whigs who stopped short of rebellion. In fact, all Loyalists thought it unconscionable to attempt to effect American independence by revolutionary act. See W. H. Nelson, *The American Tory* (Boston, 1964), pp. 92, 86, 87, 89–91, 3;

one which they were implementing in the Declaration itself, and one which they believed to be essentially conservative.

The statement of principles in the opening paragraphs of the Declaration is succeeded by the listing of specific accusations against the king which added up, in the minds of the Founding Fathers, to a concerted design to reduce them to slavery. Assuming the validity of the commonwealth theory of empire, the fathers were saying, in effect, that it was the king who violated the constitution and was traitorous to its principles. In this light, as Daniel Boorstin has remarked, the Declaration takes on the form of a document of imperial legal relations.[22]

If one reads the document as a coherent whole, one realizes that its opening statement of abstract principles and rights is given concrete meaning in the particular charges. Some of the popular rights which the king and, by implication, Parliament, were accused of violating, are the rights to be represented in government, to assemble peaceably and without interference in a legislative assembly, to possess unimpeded judicial tribunals, to have the civil authority in supremacy over the military, to trial by jury of one's peers in the vicinage, and to the privileges listed in the colonial charters. This listing renders it most likely that when the Founding Fathers used the abstract terms, "equality, unalienable rights, life, liberty and the pursuit of happiness, and the consent of the governed," they meant specifically the right to equal protection and enjoyment of the common law and concrete legal and political rights historically claimed and enjoyed by Englishmen. Contrary to the philosophy of the French Revolution, over a decade thereafter, they were less concerned with man as man than with man as heir to the Anglo-Saxon legal and political tradition.

The Declaration of Independence is at once a proclamation of the independent existence of a "people," a pronouncement of the fundamentals of the American political creed and a manifestation of its great faith in the ability of Anglo-Saxon man, at least, to assume the responsibilities of self-government. Having traversed the long path of justification of self-rule from the argument of a constitutionally limited government, through the commonwealth theory, to the claim of complete independence, Americans turned to devise the institutional forms within which this freedom was to be assured.

Wallace Brown, *The King's Friends* (Providence, 1965), p. 249. See also C. H. Van Tyne, *The Loyalists in the American Revolution* (New York, 1929) and W. A. Benton, *Whig-Loyalism* (Rutherford, N.J., 1969). For a concise statement of Tory thought, see L. W. Labaree, *Conservatism in Early American History* (New York, 1948), pp. 143–170.

NOTES

1. Alfred Owen Aldridge, *Man of Reason: The Life of Thomas Paine* (Philadelphia, 1959), pp. 28, 31, citation at 29.

2. *Ibid.*, p. 40. In 1807 Paine wrote: "I never read Locke nor ever had the work in my hand. . . ." *Ibid.*, p. 309.

3. "The Forester's Letters," No. 4, *Pennsylvania Journal,* May 8, 1776, D. E. Wheeler (ed.), *Life and Writings of Thomas Paine* (New York, 1908, 10 vols.), II, 245.

4. *Ibid.*, II, 1.

5. *Ibid.*, II, 2–4, 5.

6. *Ibid.*, II, 7, 8, 9.

7. *Ibid.*, II, 10.

8. *Ibid.*, II, 13, 21, 22, 28.

9. *Ibid.*, II, 20, 24, 8, 51.

10. *Ibid.*, II, 32, 33, 41–42, 43.

11. Cited in Phillip Foner (ed.), *The Life and Major Writings of Thomas Paine* (New York, 1945), xliv; Aldridge, 43. Regarding attacks on Paine in America, see Aldridge, pp. 273–278. Adams' characterization can be found in Parrington, *op. cit.*, I, 328.

12. The text of the Declaration used here can be found in F. N. Thorpe (ed.), *Federal and State Constitutions*, I, 3ff.

13. Jefferson to Henry Lee, May 8, 1925, *Writings*, X, 343.

14. Carl Becker, *The Declaration of Independence* (New York, 1922), pp. 51, 39–40; B. F. Wright, *op. cit.*, p. 331.

15. For a recent thorough study of the history of the concept of equality, see Sanford A. Lakoff, *Equality in Political Philosophy* (Cambridge, Mass., 1964). See also R. Pennock and J. W. Chapman, *Equality* (New York, 1967).

16. Arthur M. Schlesinger, "The Lost Meaning of the 'Pursuit of Happiness,'" *William and Mary Quarterly*, XXI (July, 1964), 325–327. For a thorough study of the history of the phrase, see H. L. Ganter, "Jefferson's 'Pursuit of Happiness' and Some Forgotten Men," *William and Mary Quarterly*, XVI (July–October, 1936), 422–434, 558–585.

17. John Locke, *An Essay Concerning Human Understanding* (Oxford; 1894, 2 vols.); A. C. Fraser, ed., II, xxxi, 51–53.

18. Sheldon Wolin, *Politics and Vision* (Boston, 1960), pp. 314–331.

19. Ganter, *op. cit.*, pp. 565–585.

20. Hobbes, *Leviathan* (Oxford, 1957), Michael Oakeshott, ed., Chap. XI, paragraph 1, p. 63. See also Cecilia M. Kenyon, "Republicanism and Radicalism in the American Revolution," *William and Mary Quarterly*, XXII (1962), 153–182, especially 173, 177.

21. Karl Lehmann, *Thomas Jefferson: American Humanist* (Chicago, 1947, paperback, 1965), p. 3.

22. Daniel Boorstin, *The Genius of American Politics* (Chicago, 1953), p. 84. For a general survey of American political thought during this period see Clinton Rossiter, *The Political Thought of the American Revolution* (New York, 1963), published originally as Part Three of his *Seedtime of the Republic*, cited above.

PART FOUR

THE MAKING OF CONSTITUTIONS

Chapter 9

EARLY AMERICAN CONSTITUTIONS AND UNDERLYING PSYCHOLOGY

You and I . . . have been sent into life at a time when the greatest lawgivers of antiquity would have wished to live. . . . When before the present epocha, had three millions of people full power and fair opportunity to form and establish the wisest and happiest government that human wisdom can contrive?
JOHN ADAMS *to* GEORGE WYTHE, *January, 1776*

The reconstitution of government on the principles of political legitimacy enunciated in the Declaration of Independence brought Americans to confront basic questions of structural political theory. In this chapter we will discuss the uses made of the contract theory in reference to constitutions; provisions of the early state constitutions and the Articles of Confederation; contemporary criticisms of these instruments of government; and most particularly the underlying theory of human nature held by early constitution builders and its relation to their notions of politics and governmental forms.

The Early State Constitutions

In the dispute with England the contract theory was exploited by Americans as a critical tool and a justification of resistance; in the formulation of the early state constitutions the concept of contract came to be identified not only as the creative act by which the state is legitimately established but in its specific terms as the constitution or fundamental law itself. In their original efforts Americans made no clear distinction between constituent and legislative assemblies and did not submit their constitutions for popular approval. This brought strong protests from men like Jefferson. The requirements to realize legitimacy were stated by a South Carolinian as follows: "The constitution should be the avowed act of the people at large. It should be the first and fundamental law of the State, and should prescribe the limits of all delegated power. It should be declared to be paramount to all acts of the Legislature, and irreparable and unalterable by any authority but the express consent of a majority of the citizens . . ."[1]

In accordance with these standards the following procedure, which later became the norm, was followed by Massachusetts in 1780: (1) popular election of deputies to a convention called for the sole and specific purpose of drawing a constitution; (2) formulation of a written constitution by the convention; (3) submission of the proposed constitution to the people for approval or disapproval. Steps one and three were derived from the notion that to be binding upon individuals a contract must have their particular consent. It was assumed that a majority could decide the whole, the requirement of individual consent supposedly being saved by the idea that mere participation in a vote implied an agreement to abide by a majority determination. The fact that this involved glossing over a contradiction gave rise to no significant comment. It must be regarded as at best a practical solution to a problem which stands insoluble on the theoretical level. Step two was justified on the following grounds by the Concord (Massachusetts) town meeting in 1776: Because a constitution embodies a system of principles to secure men in their rights against governmental encroachments, and because the same body which formulates a constitution has the power to alter it, a constitution drawn by and subject to alteration by the legislature is no security against governmental encroachments.[2]

Such reasoning became generally accepted only after the Whig conception of the legislature as the voice of the people and the locus of sovereignty was replaced by the notions that legislatures are derivative in their authority, that the interest of the legislature is not necessarily identical with that of the people, and that the legislature and its members are agents of the sovereign people. Thus step two was necessary for two related reasons which were regarded as vital to liberty; first to distinguish clearly between the state and government, and second, to preserve the distinction between fundamental and ordinary law.* It follows that there is no need for a separate governmental contract between rulers and ruled, since the constitution embraces both within its terms. Government then can be considered to be, as Locke put it, fiduciary, not contractual, in its nature. The people, the trustor, organ-

---

* Steps similar, though not always identical, to the three listed above were ultimately deemed necessary in the amendment of constitutions.

ized under a constitution in a body politic, designate a trustee—officials of government to administer public affairs in accordance with the fundamental law in the interest of the beneficiary—the people again. It should be remembered that in the English law of trusts, the trustor and beneficiary possess rights; the trustee has only obligations. On the other hand, a contract involves a consideration between at least two parties with resultant mutual rights and obligations.

A difficulty arose because of the almost universal belief in another of Locke's tenets, that liberty and rights exist antecedent to the formation of political authority. If this is so, many concluded, the state arises by contract at the cost of liberty and it can only be a necessary evil to which as little of natural liberty as possible should be relinquished. Discussing this question in 1793, the New Hampshire jurist, Nathaniel Chipman, whose work will be examined later, argued that natural and civil liberty are identical because man, being social by nature, possesses rights which are not "exclusively and independently in himself," but "arise in society and are relative to it." The conception of a political contract drawn and agreed to by the people, Chipman maintained, renders unnecessary any notion of a consideration entailing obedience to its terms because such duty derives from "the inviolable obligation arising from the laws of social nature." Although Chipman was not cognizant of it, the removal of any "consideration" from the notion of contract eliminates not only the old rulers-ruled contract but also the necessity of calling the constituent act which establishes the state, a contract. It remained for John C. Calhoun, two generations later, to pursue this logic to its end and officially discard the contract theory.[3]

Turning to the content of the new state constitutions, it can be said that in general there were at least two sometimes conflicting and often coinciding tendencies discernible therein. For purposes of exposition, it is convenient to call one the *classical republican* tendency, and the other, the *radical democratic* tendency. Both were compatible with the consensual theory and the idea of a written constitution as fundamental law. They also shared a distrust of political power, were amenable to written bills of rights, and tended to identify liberty with the popular legislative house. They diverged principally in institutional principles. The classical republican, epitomized in John Adams, emphasized separation of powers, bicameralism, checks and balances, and property qualifications for the suffrage and office-holding. The radical democrat epitomized in Thomas Paine, Benjamin Franklin, and the formulators of the original Pennsylvania and Vermont constitutions, emphasized unicameralism, legislative supremacy, majority rule, and universal manhood suffrage or its closest approximation. The classical republican regarded "nature" as the ground of his institutional principles, and experience, embodied in history, particularly of the colonial governments, as confirming nature's dictate. The radical democrat tended to call upon "reason" to draw the full implications of the principle of popular sovereignty, although he could also recur to the colonial experience of Pennsylvania to find substantiation of his preference for unicameralism. Then, too, while the classical republican and radical democrat shared belief in some aspects of the Anglo-Saxon myth, the latter tended more greatly to stress Saxon localism, sense of common interest, broad popular participation in a hierarchy of republics based on consent, and unicameralism. In fact, it might be said that while the classical republican looked to Sparta, Rome, or Venice as model, the radical democrat was enamored of Saxon government.[4]

In general, the new constitutions were not radical departures from the past; their basic structural principles were essentially the same as those which underlay the colonial governments. The important differences lay in the relative allocations of power.

1. The fact that the constitutions were written followed not only from the American conception of the contract theory and the need for an immediate conscious reconstruction of the state, but also from the fact that the colonial charters and compacts were written.

2. Although some of the constitutions dilated upon principles, particularly in preambles, they were, as a whole, brief, because they were essentially pronouncements of general principles. It was not until the nineteenth century that the state constitutions, because of a growing distrust of legislatures, began to take on, to use a phrase of John Marshall's, "the prolixity of a legal code," and thus blurred the distinction between fundamental and ordinary law.

3. The constitutions generally adhered at least verbally to the classical republican principle of separation of powers as a condition of liberty.

4. Primarily because of the sad experiences with colonial governors, the new constitutions followed the radical-democratic direction in their great distrust of executive power. In eight states governors were elected by the legislatures on an annual basis. With few exceptions, the governors were afforded no veto power and were limited in their appointive powers.

5. Except for Pennsylvania, Georgia, and Vermont, the classical republican principle of bicameralism was formally followed. Even though extra property qualifications were required in most states for election to and membership in upper chambers, the American balanced state was not mixed in the old sense of being class based. Upon the institution of constitutions by popular consent and the extension of the elective principle to all branches of government, the people no longer were identified with one branch, but placed at the base of government.

In this light the upper chambers came to be justified in terms of a check on the lower branch.

6. The classical-republican principles of separation of powers and checks and balances were, except in a few states, vitiated by the operative ascendancy of the radical-democratic principle of legislative dominance. With the governors in most states constituting what James Madison called "ciphers," and the judges elected by the legislatures or appointed for limited terms by governors elected by the legislatures, no viable checks on legislative majorities existed.

7. On the basis of the Whig principle, "Where annual elections end, tyranny begins," terms of office were short, and were supplemented in most cases by the principle of rotation in office. In view of the fact that John Adams, at this stage of his life following the preachments of James Harrington, subscribed to these principles, it can be seen that classical-republicans could share belief in them with radical-democrats.

8. The constitutions generally stipulated property qualifications for the suffrage and for office-holding. By themselves, the property qualifications stand as an implementation of the classical-republican view; in fact, given the broad ownership of land, they may not have been important limiting factors.[5]

9. Most of the constitutions contained bills of rights, or statements of guarantees of rights within the body of the constitution, based on the philosophy of the Declaration of Independence and embracing specifically the traditional procedural and substantive rights of Englishmen. Establishment of the Protestant religion was continued in some states as were, more generally, religious qualifications for the suffrage. It remained for Virginia, in the statute of religious liberty, written by Thomas Jefferson in 1785, to provide an example to other states by implementing the Lockian notion of a church as a voluntary body through its disestablishment of the Episcopal Church.[6]

10. Concerning the question of which governmental branches were restricted by constitutional statements of rights, it is true that initially the traditional view that the offender was always the executive and not a popularly based assembly was in the ascendancy. Thus the legislature was looked upon as the protector of the rights of the collective people. But as the full implications of American republicanism became more evident and the legislature became identified more and more as just one of the branches serving as an agent of the people, and less and less as the immediate popular voice, the attitude grew that all branches of government were equally subject to the constitutional limitations. It must be remembered that as early as 1774 Thomas Jefferson was saying that "bodies of men as well as individuals are susceptible of the spirit of tyranny."[7]

The Articles of Confederation

Turning to the question of the central government of the states, the old unresolved problem of the proper relation of the whole to the parts was first dealt with in the Articles of Confederation, adopted in 1781. This original constitution of the "one people" may be called a contract which stipulated terms of legal association, with the states as parties. Because of strong particularist sentiments, pervasive distrust of central authority stemming from the colonial experience, and a tendency to equate local self-government with democracy, the Articles constituted more of a league or alliance of sovereign states than a sovereign central government. Thus the document stipulated: "Each state retains its sovereignty, freedom and independence." It followed that all the states must be treated as legally equal. Similarly, because it was a confederation of states which was formed, the general government was made to operate in internal affairs on the states and not directly on individuals.[8]

The structure was simple: the unicameral Congress, set up along the lines of the existing Continental Congress, was composed of delegates elected and paid by, and subject to, the instructions of the respective state legislatures, with each delegation allowed but one vote. A fusion of powers was established, with the administration of foreign and domestic affairs carried on by committees or boards of Congress. The intention originally was that all powers of general concern be delegated to Congress, but this was spelled out in terms of "expressly" delegated particular powers. Thus Congress was given the powers to conduct foreign relations, declare war, control the army and navy, decide interstate disputes, operate a postal system, coin and borrow money, regulate the value of currency, establish a common system of weights and measures, and regulate Indian affairs.

Although this division of powers foreshadowed that of the Constitution of 1787, Congress lacked three of the essential means of effective government—the power to tax individuals, to regulate interstate and foreign commerce, and to coerce compliance with its resolutions and requisitions. Consequently it depended on the willingness of states to uphold their obligations which, too often, was not forthcoming. Because of these factors, the Articles fell short as a general system of government.

Failure, however, did not mean that Congress was without accomplishments in this period. The achievement which most concerns the development of American political thought lay in the area of what can best be called colonial policy. In the Ordinance of 1787, which dealt with the Northwest territories, Congress proceeded from two fundamental principles, first put forth by Thomas Jefferson in a plan presented in 1784. These were: (1) the providing of temporary government in a territory; and (2) the ultimate admission of the territory into the Confederacy on an equal basis with the older members. Thus there was to be no hierarchy of status among the states, old or new, in American public law, and one of the most crucial aspects of the old imperial problem was settled on the basis of the principle of ultimate equality.[9]

Contemporary Criticisms of the Early Constitutions

The most trenchant criticisms of the revolutionary state constitutions and the Articles of Confederation which were made previous to the Convention of 1787 can be found in the writings of Jefferson, Hamilton, and Madison. All three agreed that inexperience in the affairs of constitution-making and the conduct of government was a major cause of the shortcomings. Hamilton and Madison went beyond this, the former emphasizing provincial particularism, an excess in the spirit of liberty, and "an extreme jealousy of power" attendant "on all popular revolutions," and the latter characteristically pointing to "a mistaken confidence that the justice, the good faith, the honor, the sound policy of the several legislative assemblies would render superfluous any appeal to the ordinary motives by which the laws secure the obedience of individuals."[10]

In his *Notes On the State of Virginia* (1782) Jefferson used the democratic principle to find inequitable the suffrage and districting provisions of the Virginia Constitution. Then, using classical-republican norms, he proceeded to analyze the governmental structure. Although the constitution formally expounded the principles of bicameralism and separation of powers, he found them nonoperative in fact. The Senate, he observed, was too "homogeneous" with the House of Delegates. Whereas some of the states established a lower house to represent persons, and an upper house to represent property, in Virginia "wealth and wisdom have equal chance for admission into both houses." Consequently, he added, "we do not, therefore, derive from the separation of our legislature into two houses, those benefits which a proper complication of principles is capable of producing, and those which alone can compensate the evils which may be produced by their dissensions." It can be seen that Jefferson then was not averse to the separate representation of the property interest in one of the legislative houses. In fact he saw it, or a similar arrangement, as essential to bicameralism.

Besides an inadequate implementation of the principle of bicameralism, Jefferson concluded that the Virginia Constitution in fact established a fusion rather than the formally prescribed separation of powers. Concentration of legislative, executive, and judicial powers in the legislature, he declared, "is precisely the definition of despotic government." This shortcoming was not mitigated by the fact that "the powers were exercised by a plurality of hands, and not by a single one," inasmuch as "173 despots would surely be as oppressive as one." He advised the legislators not to be deluded by "the integrity of their own purposes," but instead to look forward to a not distant time, "when a corruption in this, as in the country from which we derive our origin, will have seized the heads of government, and be spread by them through the body of the people; when they will purchase the voices of the people and make them pay the price." Jefferson regarded this as a very real possibility because "human nature is the same on every side of the Atlantic, and will be alike influenced by the same causes."[11]

The principles of strong, energetic, unified government and administration which underlay Hamilton's developed thought were already present in his criticisms of government in this period. Looking at the Congress, he found it inadequate because of its timidity in the use and construction of its powers but more particularly in its lack of the powers to tax, to regulate trade, and effectively to conduct foreign affairs. "In a government framed for durable liberty," he proclaimed, "not less regard must be paid to giving the magistrate a proper degree of authority, to make and execute the laws with rigour, than to guarding against encroachments upon the rights of the community."[12]

The paper written by Madison just before the Convention of 1787, entitled *Vices of the Political System of the United States,* was based on the same realistic analysis of government in terms of human motivation and the principles of classical-republicanism which characterized his later speeches in the Convention and his contributions to the *Federalist* papers. He saw eleven principal evils in the existing system, including lack of coercive central power, trespasses of the states on the rights of each other, and lack of guarantee in the states against internal violence and governmental injustice. Because he saw the injustice of state laws as bringing into question "the fundamental principle of republican Government, that the majority who rule in such governments are the safest Guardians both of public Good and private rights," Madison concerned himself with the causes of this evil and its remedies. Adumbrating the analysis later presented in fully developed form in the tenth *Federalist* paper, he concluded that (1) "the great desideratum in Government is such a modification of the sovereignty as will render it sufficiently neutral between the different interests and factions, to control one part of the society from invading the rights of another, and at the same time sufficiently controlled itself, from setting up an interest adverse to that of the whole Society," and (2) "an extensive Republic," because it "meliorates the administration of a small republic," can best supply the remedy.[13]

In sum it can be said that whereas Jefferson emphasized the need for a more democratic suffrage and a more equitable system of districting along with a full implementation of the structural principles of bi-cameralism and separation of powers in order to guarantee liberty on the state level, and Hamilton focused on the need for a vigorous central authority with sovereign powers operating on individuals, Madison attended to the requirements of both power and liberty, going beyond an analysis in terms of the lack of powers in the central authority and the formal principles of bicameralism, separation of powers, and checks and balances, to indicate a territorial-sociological principle which might serve as the ultimate guarantee against the evils of partiality and factionalism.

Political Psychology of Early Constitution Builders

An understanding of the conception prevalent among American con-stitution builders of the relationship of human nature to politics can be gained by a comparative analysis of the thought of Benjamin Franklin (1706–1790), whose preferences were in the radical-democratic direc-tion, and John Adams, the classical-republican. Although they agreed essentially concerning human nature, they differed markedly in re-lating that conception to structural principles of government, with Franklin serving as a strong backer of the democratic provisions of the Pennsylvania Constitution of 1776, and Adams as the author of the first draft of the Massachusetts Constitution of 1780. Adams was a more consistent and systematic thinker whose adherence to what he believed to be eternal "principles of political architecture" bordered on the dogmatic, while Franklin, although a unicameralist, was basically a pragmatist ever willing to submerge his own views to the end of ac-commodation through compromise.

Benjamin Franklin (1706–1790)

Throughout his long life Franklin emphasized the primacy of self-love in man. At the age of sixteen he described the form of pride, which has been recently called "emulative self-esteem," as follows: "The proud Man aspires after Nothing less than an unlimited Superiority over his Fellow-Creatures. He has made himself a King in *Soliloquy;* fancies himself conquering the World; and the Inhabitants thereof consulting on proper Methods of acknowledging his Merit." In 1730 he commented on the human desire to be praised and admired, an aspect of pride which has been called "approbativeness" or, when manifested in the desire to bring others to confirm one's own conception of one's su-periority, "emulative approbativeness." He declared: "Would you win the Hearts of others, you must not seem to vie with, but admire them: Give them every Opportunity of displaying their own Qualifications, and when you have indulged their Vanity, they will praise you too in Turn, and prefer you over others, in order to secure to themselves the Pleasure your Commendation gives." All men possess the desire "of being taken Notice of and regarded." Thus Franklin, following the English poet Edward Young, concluded in 1751 that "the Love of Praise . . . *reigns more or less in every Heart,*" although men hypocritically tend to disregard it.[14]

Looking at the baneful implications of self-love, Franklin stated: "Men will always be powerfully influenced in their Opinions and Actions by what appears to be their particular Interest." A Newtonian and a Deist, he saw nature ruled by law, but in contrast to the prevailing Shaftesburian optimism, he declared ruefully: "Whatever may be the Musick of the Spheres, how great so ever the Harmony of the Stars, 'tis certain there is no harmony among the Stargazers; but they are perpetually growling and snarling at one another like strange Curs." Consequently he concluded that Hobbes' conception "is somewhat nearer the Truth than that which makes the State of Nature a State of Love." That he never abandoned this dim view is evidenced by his remark made in 1782 that the more he observed men, the more he was disgusted, because he found them to be "a Sort of Beings very badly constructed, as they are generally more easily provok'd than reconcil'd, more disposed to do Mischief to each other than to make Reparation, much more easily deceiv'd than undeceiv'd, and having more Pride and Pleasure in killing than in begetting one another."[15]

Although Franklin assumed reason to be the ideal ordering principle in moral life to enlighten and direct primal self-love to virtue and the general good, he saw it playing a purely instrumental role in the service of the passions in most men. Thus in his *Autobiography* he stated that it was convenient to be a "reasonable creature" because "it enables one to find a reason for everything one has a mind to." And in 1769 he remarked the inefficacy of reason: "Our Reason would still be of more Use to us if it could enable us to *prevent* the Evils it can hardly enable us to bear.—But in that it is so deficient, and in other things so often misleads us, that I have sometimes been almost tempted to wish we had been furnished with a good sensible Instinct instead of it." As a consequence, Franklin could not attribute to the moral sciences the progress he saw in the natural sciences. In 1780 he lamented: "O that moral Science were in as fair a way of Improvement, that Men would cease to be Wolves to one another, and that human Beings would at length learn what they now improperly call Humanity!"[16]

Given the power of self-love and the general debility of reason, Franklin believed that very few men, if any, could be moved to acquire virtue from a regard for the true and the good, as such. He appears to have thought, however, that by playing skillfully upon men's pride, a greater number might be persuaded to seek virtue and use reason as a means to that end. As early as 1728 he observed that approbativeness, in any of its forms, is a "laudable Ambition" but that men generally are unacquainted with the "only infallible method" of satisfying it, the acquisition of virtue, which is admired by all men. The passage implies that virtue can be inculcated if the motive spring of self-love is touched and attuned to it. Because he thought that he knew the "infallible Method" and because he believed that few can be permanently deflected from satisfying their desire for praise and approval in mistakenly pursuing objects other than virtue, it is very probable that his projected "Art of Virtue" was intended for the minority who might be moved.[17]

Franklin's moral theory also implied, as his own pursuits assumed, that the observant, reflective man can acquire, through experience and a study of the springs of human action, not only insight into character, but a knowledge of the uniformities of human behavior. Such knowledge leads, in the Baconian sense, to the ability to move and control men, by playing on their passions and desires. But it appears that Franklin again thought that only a relatively small number of men were properly situated and perceptive and industrious enough to attain such knowledge, or, if in possession of it, to use it effectively.

Franklin's thought on these points issued in distinctions which he drew throughout his life between "wise and good men" and "common people" and, although he did not specifically use the term until late in life, "artful men." In 1785 he wrote: "It is unlucky, I think in the Affairs of this world, that the Wise and Good should be as mortal as Common People and that they often die before others are found fit to supply their Places." As he saw it, the "wise and good" are firmly grounded in virtue and in that knowledge which, when informed by virtue and experience, is ripened into wisdom. On the other hand, "common People" proceed upon prejudices derived from custom, example and education, from habits issuing from their pursuits, and from tradition and opinion. The great proportion of mankind, he declared in 1786, are weak and selfish and in need of "the Motives of Religion to restrain them from Vice." Finally, "artful Men" are those who while in possession of a knowledge of human nature, use it for narrowly selfish purposes, unlike the "wise and good" who are dedicated to the common good.[18]

Thus Franklin, while a staunch believer in the self-evidence of the truth, "all men are created equal," as shown by his correction of Jefferson's draft of the Declaration of Independence, recognized that men do not develop equally in the possession of virtue, wisdom, and knowledge. The masses of men stand in need of moral and political leadership; their receptivity to wise leadership depends upon a variety of factors, ranging from the nature of extant common opinion through the habits induced by their way of life and education, to the rough virtues, if any, which they might possess.

Franklin thought that Americans were peculiarly fit for self-government. There existed among them no great social differences; their principal pursuit, agriculture, was most conducive to the development of the desirable qualities of self-reliance, frugality, honesty, and independence. And he foresaw America as a great continental power where land would always be readily available to a growing population and society would be fluid.[19]

Franklin's conception of the purpose of government is most clearly revealed in his comments on political parties. Like most erudite men of the eighteenth century, he regarded party as synonymous with faction and saw membership therein as incompatible with what he called "the public good." Thus Poor Richard observed in 1748: *"Party, says one, is the madness of many for the gain of a few:* To which may be added, *There are* honest *men in* all *parties,* wise men *in* none: Unless those may be call'd *wise,* for whose profit the rest are *mad."* To counteract this state of affairs, Franklin urged in 1731 the formation of a "United Party for Virtue," by gathering good men of all nations into a regular body "to be govern'd by suitable good and wise rules, which good and wise Men may probably be more unanimous in their Obedience to, than common People are to common laws." In 1750 he reemphasized the point: "Wise and good men are . . . the *strength* of a state: much more so than riches or arms, which, under the management of Ignorance and Wickedness, often draw a destruction, instead of providing for the safety of a people. And though the culture bestowed on *many* should be successful only with a *few,* yet the influence of those few and the service in their power, may be very great."[20]

The vehicle by which Franklin brought into a cohesive relationship his emphases upon equality, opinion, the primacy of self-interest in man, the common good, and his vision of the American destiny, was the program of the eighteenth-century French political economists, the Physiocrats.* He praised physiocracy for its "freedom from local and national prejudices and partialities," and hoped it would "grow and increase till it becomes the governing philosophy of the human species, as it must be that of superior beings in better worlds."[21]

If, as the Physiocrats argued, land is the sole source of wealth, and the pursuit of individual interest is the primary bond of a society wherein all men are treated equally and monopoly and special privilege are excluded, it follows that the pursuit of individual interest in a

* The Physiocrats were political economists who saw an inherent natural harmony of interests as properly governing society; thought land to be the basis of wealth; and advocated free trade.

basically agrarian society is equivalent to the public good and civic virtue. The task of government is then mainly to repress all encroachments on persons and property. Assuming the validity of these principles, Franklin could conclude that the otherwise deficient expressions of human nature would, in the providential Arcadian setting of America, be their own remedy.

It is in light of the physiocratic conception of state policy, supplemented by the distinctions which he drew between wise and good men, common people and artful men, that Franklin's numerous strong condemnations of rulers and governments after 1765 must be read. A case in point is his criticism of legislative assemblies which he made in 1784.

We assemble parliaments and councils, to have the benefit of their collected wisdom; but we necessarily have, at the same time, the inconvenience of their collected passions, prejudices and private interests. By the help of these, artful men overpower their wisdom, and dupe its possessors; and if we may judge by the acts, *arrets*, and edicts, all the world over, for regulating commerce, an assembly of great men is the greatest fool on earth.[22]

As a realist who recognized human fallibility and the pull of the selfish passions as the stuff of politics, Franklin accepted the inevitability of conflict and difference in a free society. In the Constitutional Convention of 1787, after having successfully invoked compromise, he exhorted his colleagues to accept the Constitution even if it was imperfect, reminding them that "when you assemble a number of men, to have the advantage of their joint wisdom, you inevitably assemble with those men all their prejudices, their passions, their errors of opinion, and their selfish views." His postrevolutionary attitude toward political parties also reflects this acceptance of reality. He admitted that they will exist wherever there is liberty, and that each of them attempts to realize what it believes to be the public good. Because "Things, Actions, Measures, and Objects of all kinds, present themselves to the Minds of Men in such a Variety of Lights," he concluded, parties are "the common Lot of Humanity."[23]

Although Franklin clearly recognized and accepted the realities of politics, he never abandoned the ideal of promotion of the public good through leadership of the wise and good. It is the task of these men, if common opinion stands to the contrary, to convince "common People" that their interest will be promoted by desirable changes, a task which involves reason and persuasion and "is not the Work of a Day." In this light, politics is primarily an educative process whereby those who address themselves seriously to "the Knowledge of the true Interest of one's Country," which Franklin once called the most "useful and commendable" science, employ their political skills and knowledge of human nature to attempt to persuade their fellow men to the pursuit of their policies. Unfortunately, "artful men" work upon popular passions and prejudices to subserve their own, or their parties' limited ends and defeat the good of the whole.[24]

Franklin distinguished between types of political leaders, in 1772, in a passage which has great relevance for our discussion:

> To have *good Ends* in view, and to use *proper Means* to obtain them, shows the Minister to be both *good* and *wise*. To pursue *good Ends* by *improper Means* argues him, tho' *good* to be but *weak*. To pursue *bad Ends* by *artful Means* shows him to be *wicked*, tho' *able*. But when his *Ends* are bad and the means he uses *improper* to obtain these ends, what shall we say of such a Minister?[25]

"Good Ends," to Franklin, are those promotive of the general good or interest, while "bad Ends" are those indicated by local, factional, or narrow self-interest. "Proper Means" are those which are fitting to the realization of an end, while "improper Means" are not. "Artful Means," though fitting to the realization of an end, are morally wrong since they involve playing adroitly upon base passions, prejudices, and interests. Franklin thus saw true statesmanship as consisting in the pursuit of good ends by proper means—the work of "wise and good men"—and he excluded, by implication, the pursuit of good ends by "artful means." If confronted, however, with a choice between a minister who consistently and unsuccessfully pursued good ends by "improper means" and one who consistently and successfully pursued the same ends by "artful means," it seems likely that, as a realist, he would have swallowed hard and opted for the latter, while justifying his choice as the lesser of two evils.

In considering Franklin's preferences of governmental institutions we are confronted with what appears to be a contradiction between his dim view of human nature and his emphasis on leadership by the wise and good, on the one hand, and his advocacy of unicameral democracy, which has usually been associated with an optimistic view of man and a belief in the natural political wisdom of the people, on the other. To understand how he attempted to reconcile these principles requires a consideration of his statements in the Constitutional Convention of 1787 and his defense of unicameralism in Pennsylvania in 1789.

In his speech in the Constitutional Convention declaring his opposition to the payment of salaries to the executive (which he thought should be plural and elected each year, probably by a unicameral legislature elected annually by universal manhood suffrage), Franklin voiced sentiments which he had previously expressed in his observations on British governmental corruption. He argued that men are moved by ambition and avarice, which when united in terms of the same object, are very powerful. Thus if official positions of honor are made at the same time a "place of profit," struggle, factionalism, even war, ensue. He maintained that it would not be "the wise and the moderate," but "the Bold and the Violent," who would strive for salaried executive office. To get "wise and good men" to serve, ambition should be pitted against avarice by making "every place of *honour* a place of *burthen.*"[26]

Franklin's argument is clearly based on the premise that leadership by the wise and good is essential if democracy is to subserve the public good and if what he called a natural popular tendency to monarchy is to be arrested. Whether his plan would have resulted in such wise men actually filling the executive office is open to question. In any case, it is evident that in proposing that the executive be established on the principle that passion check passion, and in the belief that its members would watch each other in the task, Franklin did not ignore his theory of human nature.

Concerning the apparent inconsistency between Franklin's unicameralism and his view of human nature, it is certainly true that his strong opposition to separate representation of property in a second chamber flowed from an overriding desire for equality, a dislike of special privilege, and a belief that possession of property is not in itself a sign of wisdom and goodness. This is, however, only a partial explanation of his opposition to bicameralism and one which does not remove the apparent inconsistency. An examination of Franklin's arguments in 1789 against a proposed change to bicameralism in Pennsylvania discloses that his points against bicameralism as an instrument of class rule or of separate representation of property are preceded by arguments which apply to equalitarian, democratic bicameralism as well. Franklin asked, is it not true that: (1) the putative wisdom brought to the legislature by each member may be as effectual a barrier against the impulses of passion and self-interest when the members are united in one body as when they are divided; (2) if one house can control the operation of the other, may not passion, faction, interest, and the spirit of encroachment in one house obstruct the good proposed by the other; (3) in Pennsylvania the unicameral legislature has remedied, or can easily remedy, important errors; (4) if the wisdom brought by the members to the assembly were divided into two branches, might it not be too weak in each to support a good measure, or obstruct a bad one?[27]

It will be noted first that Franklin did not believe that the self-interested passions and prejudices which issue from man's prideful nature can be effectively checked by bicameralism of any type; instead, he believed that their influence might be extended by it. Second, he assumed a limited fund of available wisdom, which would be further diminished by diffusion if the restricted number of men of wisdom were divided into two chambers. If one interprets this in light of his belief that democratic government can be truly effective only if wise and good men serve as political leaders and educators, one can see why he might regard bicameralism as antithetical to that end. Third, because Franklin saw practical politics as rooted in a pragmatic spirit of compromise and adjustment, it is probable that he thought that this delicate work would be jeopardized by requiring its duplication in a second chamber. Because of this it might be maintained that his espousal of unicameralism was an application of the principle of Occam's razor* to political institutions. Finally, Franklin apparently believed that democratic unicameralism was feasible for America because he assumed that elections would be dignified, incorrupt, and quiet, and that the electorate would honor those who were most worthy and did not clamor for office.[28]

If this analysis is correct, it can be concluded that in his treatment of the executive and the legislature Franklin might be challenged, not because he ignored his skepticism about human nature, which he did not, but because he believed that his plan was as good as, if not more efficacious than, bicameralism in dealing with factionalism, and that it was a better instrument for affording the framework for the necessary leadership by the wise and good.

Franklin resembled the seventeenth-century English political thinkers, John Milton and Algernon Sidney, whom he greatly admired, in his conviction that popular election is a way by which the "best men" might be selected to govern, and in seeing the people ideally as a community led by a natural elite. He departed from them in holding that all men must be regarded as equal, and, as such, participate in the frequent selection of their rulers. Whereas they were advocates of an aristocratic republic, he was an advocate of aristocratic democracy. While quite skeptical of human nature, he was more of a pragmatist than a rationalist, and assumed that through democratic processes a natural aristocracy could most readily arise in America to guide the people toward the realization of their country's "true interest."

John Adams (1735–1826)

Because of his overriding interest in politics, John Adams was a lifelong student of human nature.† The main elements of his treatment of human motivation, found in his *Discourses on Davila* (1790), were already present, in unsystematized form, in his pre-Revolutionary writings. Like Franklin, the young Adams believed that reason ought to rule over the passions. He saw truth and the good for man, not as variants of historical relativity, but as given in the nature of things, and thus

---

* The philosophic principle that entities should not be multiplied unnecessarily.
† See the preceding treatment of Adams in Chapter 7.

discernible by unbiased, dispassionate minds. But, again like Franklin, he thought that all but a few men are blinded or perverted by passion and prejudice emanating from self-love. His treatment of this question in his essay, "On Self-Delusion" (1763), followed in good part Adam Smith's reasoning in his *Theory of the Moral Sentiments.* Because truth and virtue are admittedly "the means of present and future happiness" and "the only objects that deserve to be pursued," Adams declared, "the multiplied diversity of opinions, customs, laws and religions that have prevailed," must be imputed to "the capacity to delude one's self." Self-deceit brings men to reduce reason to rationalization and to mistake the impulse of passion for conscience. "For these reasons," he concluded dolefully, "we can never be secure in a resignation of our understandings, or in confiding enormous power . . . to any mortal, however great or good."[29]

In words which recall Franklin's observations on man's prideful propensity to see himself as "a king in soliloquy" (emulative self-esteem), Adams observed early in the Revolutionary period, that "there is no one Principle which predominates in human Nature so much in every stage of life . . . as this Passion for Superiority. . . . Every human being compares itself in its own Imagination, with every other round about it, and will find some Superiority over every other real or imaginary or it will die of Grief and Vexation."[30]

More significant for society, however, is emulative approbativeness, which Adams, in his early period, called the "love of fame" or the desire for "popularity." Regarding it as a principal source of discord, he remarked that it reduced "men of the most exalted Genius and active minds" to "perfect slaves." In 1759 he indicated its social value in a significant passage of his *Diary.* Popularity, he observed, "the Way to gain and figure," ought to be aimed at, after wisdom and virtue, because "it is the Dictate of Wisdom, and is necessary to the practice of Virtue in most." Implied in this statement is the proposition, which was fully developed in his mature thought, that for men generally the motive to virtue is a desire for the approval and regard of others.[31]

Although he maintained that men should pursue virtue for virtue's sake, or, at least, for the sake of popularity and approval, Adams noted in 1760 that:

. . . all Magistrates and all civil officers, and all civil Government, is (sic) founded and maintained by the sins of the People. All armies would be needless if Men were universally virtuous. Most Manufacturers and Tradesmen would be needless; nay some of the natural Passions and sentiments of human Minds, would be needless upon that supposition . . . No man upon that supposition, would ever give another, a just Provocation. And no just Resentment could take Place without a just Provocation. Thus, our natural Resentments are founded on the sins of the People, as much as the Profession of the

Law, or that of Arms, or that of Divinity. In short Vice and folly are so interwoven in all human Affairs that they could not possibly, be wholly separated
from them without tearing and rending the whole system of human Nature,
and state. Nothing would remain as it is.[32]

Two observations on this passage are in order. First, the Calvinist explanation of sin as the reason for government is quite evident. Absent is
a belief in the necessity of the directive, promotive, noncoercive aspects
of government even if men were universally virtuous. It follows that
the more that men are elevated morally, the less the need for government. In this light government is truly, at best, a necessary evil, an
evil which Adams thought would remain because man will never become universally good. Second, a realistic, Mandevilleian* recognition of
the importance of vice, folly, and luxury in the overall economy of life
informs Adams' commentary. Once having fully drawn out and accepted
its implications, he could never condone utopian schemes involving the
remaking of society on the premise of the natural goodness of man.
But this did not mean that he necessarily embraced pessimism; on the
contrary, his treatment in his *Dissertation on the Canon and Feudal
Law* of the "love of power," which he called an "aspiring, noble,
principle," and "the cause of freedom," when it is "founded in benevolence, and cherished by knowledge," shows him to have been a
meliorist.†[33]

It is thus evident that when Adams turned during the Revolution to
the formulation of a proposed plan of government for the new states he
already had articulated the principles of his skeptical conception of
man. These principles, along with his later discussion of forms of the
balanced state, must be understood in light of the following view of
social change which he outlined in 1770: "In Times of Simplicity and
Innocence, Ability and Integrity will be the principal Recommendations
to the public Service, and the sole Title to those Honours and Emoluments, which are in the Power of the Public to bestow." However, when
"Elegance, Luxury and Effeminacy begin to be established," the prerequisites are distributed to "Vanity and Folly." Finally, "when a
Government becomes totally corrupted," the rules of government are
reversed and "Virtue, Integrity, and Ability . . . become the Objects
of the Malice, Hatred and Revenge of the Men in Power, and folly,
Vice and Villany" are "cherished and supported."[34]

Taking as his principal sources "nature and experience" along with
the ideas of Harrington and Montesquieu, Adams wrote his *Thoughts
on Government* (1776), a plan to guide the rebellious colonies in the

---

* Bernard De Mandeville, a British satirist, argued in his *Fable of the Bees* (1714)
that "private vices" themselves, or "by the dextrous management of a skillful
politician" can be "public virtues."

† A meliorist believes that man has the power to aid in the betterment of the
world.

construction of new governments. Asserting that "the divine science of politics is the science of social happiness," and that "the blessings of society depend entirely on the constitutions of government," he proclaimed that "nothing is more certain, from the history of nations and the nature of man, than that some forms of government are better fitted for being well administered than others." Because the end of government is "the happiness of society," it follows that "the form of government which communicates ease, comfort, security . . . to the greatest number of persons, and in the greatest degree, is the best." And because the happiness of man consists in "virtue," Adams searched for a form of government with virtue (which he considered as superior to, and yet embracing within itself, "honor"), as its principle.[35]

Regarding as axiomatic the necessity, if liberty and order are to obtain, of a separation of legislative, executive, and judicial powers, and institutional checks and balances, Adams put forth a plan wherein a popularly elected assembly and a governor elected by the legislature and armed with the veto and appointive powers would be mediated by an upper house elected by the lower house and also possessed of a negative power. It is to be noted that Adams did not specifically require particular property qualifications in connection with the second chamber.

Adams never departed from his emphasis on the necessity of a balanced state with a bicameral legislature based on separation of powers and checks and balances. In accordance, however, with his views on changes in the objects of emulation at different stages of human progression or retrogression, he allowed specifically for alterations in the methods and terms of elections, and by implication, the composition of the upper house. That he believed that Americans in 1776 were basically honest and virtuous explains the absence in the *Thoughts* of a preference for a class-based version of the balanced state.[36]

Shays' Rebellion and attacks upon property and the principle of balance in the state constitutions brought Adams to write his two principal works, *A Defence of the Constitutions of the United States of America* (1786, 1787) and the *Discourses on Davila* (1790). The former, although for the most part an unacknowledged compilation of excerpts from the writings of others, contains the conclusions drawn from his historical studies of republics, ancient and modern; the latter, in its most significant chapters, gives the conclusions of his psychological studies and their application to politics.

The *Defence* is not a radical departure from the *Thoughts on Government;* the main structural principles of government outlined in the latter as dictates of nature and experience are reaffirmed. The emphasis, however, is changed in that qualitative differences among men are now taken into consideration; the separation of powers principle is supple-

mented by the class-based, mixed state concept; and the form of republicanism which is preferred, is constructed not upon *virtue* as a
principle but upon *honor* (emulative approbativeness). The basic assumption of the work is that which Adams defined in a letter to Jefferson
in 1815: "The fundamental article of my political Creed is, that Despotism, or unlimited Sovereignty, or absolute Power, is the same in a
Majority of a popular Assembly, an Aristocratical Counsel, an Oligarchical Junto and a single Emperor."[37]

If there is to be free government, Adams argued, there is need of a
democratic branch of the legislature, representing the people, a strong
independent executive armed with the veto power, an independent
judiciary, and an "aristocratical" upper legislative house. The reason for
the latter is that because "the rich, the well-born, and the able, acquire
an influence among the people that will soon be too much for simple
honesty," the "most illustrious of them" must be separated and placed
in an upper house. Thus it can be seen that while Franklin put his hopes
in the leadership of "wise and good men" in a unicameral legislature,
Adams would "ostracize" to a separate chamber outstanding and superior men, whether they be the rich, the well-born, the famous, or the
wise and good, because of their inordinate influence over the people.[38]

In both the *Defence* and the *Discourses* Adams put an even heavier
emphasis on the role of the passions in relation to reason in political
life than he did earlier. Most emphatically did he pronounce it to be
an egregious error to equate man's nature with his reason. If men would
at all times consult reason and follow conscience, he remained confident
that the objective moral law could alone suffice for their government.
But the constitution of the human mind and heart and the uniform
experience of the species afforded him unassailable proof that the law
of nature, the Decalogue, the dictates of religion and civil laws, will be
freely flouted if men's passions are not effectively checked. Unlike many
contemporary optimists, he could see no mental connection by which
science can extinguish or diminish passion. It followed that although
knowledge and benevolence must be encouraged, it is folly to assume
their primacy in the establishment of social and political order. Like
Hume, whom he approvingly cited on the point, Adams regarded man's
natural generosity as confined, seldom extending beyond the limits of
family, friends, and neighbors. Illustrative of this is the pungent
marginal note which he later wrote in his copy of Mary Wollstonecraft's
book on the French Revolution: "None but an idiot or a madman ever
built a government upon a disinterested principle."[39]

As the mature Adams saw it, the passions are all infinite because if
they were restricted they would soon become extinct. Being at once
ineradicable, unlimited, and insatiable, they are the primary motive

springs. What is more, their power increases with their exercise. In the *Defence* he focused on the love of gold, the love of praise, and ambition for power, which he called "aristocratical passions" because they subdue all others. The chapters on human psychology in the *Discourses,* however, represent his most considered thought on the relation between the affections and morality and politics. In them he brought together under one generic passion the springs of action he had previously separately stressed. Despite his sometimes unrestrained language, he strove primarily to understand and to explain man's moral and political behavior in terms of a theory of human motivation propounded by many influential British thinkers of the seventeenth and eighteenth centuries, the fundamental elements of which he had adumbrated in his earlier thought. Thus he relied heavily upon Pope's *Essay on Man,* the writings of Samuel Johnson, and Edward Young's *Of the Love of Fame;* Mandeville's *Fable of the Bees* peeks through without being mentioned; but the principal source is again Adam Smith's *Theory of the Moral Sentiments.*

Adams called the generic affection upon which he based his political psychology, the "passion for distinction" (emulative approbativeness) which he defined as man's "desire to be observed, considered, esteemed, praised, beloved, and admired by his fellows." In all its forms, Adams contended, this egotistic passion paradoxically constitutes "a principal source of the virtues and vices," and of man's sociability, as well as "the happiness of human life." In fact, the history of mankind "is little more than a narration of its operations and affects."[40]

Men seek to satisfy the passion for distinction in different ways. Not a few commit crimes and cultivate vices to gain attention. The greater number of men, however, seek attention "by riches, by family records, by play, and other frivolous personal accomplishments." Finally, a very few "aim at approbation as well as attention . . . at admiration and gratitude as well as congratulation." In this category are patriots, heroes, and most of mankind's greatest benefactors. But, Adams hastened to warn, even among these "the passion, although refined by the purest sentiments . . . is a passion still; and therefore, like all human desires, unlimited and insatiable."[41]

Given this universal human propensity as the primary datum, Adams was left with the task of explaining how society as a collection of individuals proceeding in their conduct from nonaltruistic motives can be cohesive. Again following Smith, he saw the answer in what might be called, in paraphrase of Hegel, "the cunning of nature." Because reason is a weak spring to virtue, Adams argued, nature compensates by implanting in man the desire and need for the consideration of his fellows, the proper pursuit of which brings the pleasurable rewards of acceptance, congratulations, esteem and admiration, and the ill or non-pursuit of which brings the painful, and, to most men, unbearable sanctions of neglect, disregard, rejection, and contempt.

The language of nature to man in his constitution is this—"I have given you reason, conscience, and benevolence; and thereby made you accountable for your actions, and capable of virtue, in which you will find your highest felicity. But I have not confided wholly in your laudable improvement of these divine gifts. To them I have superadded in your bosoms a passion for the notice and regard of your fellow mortals, which, if you perversely violate your duty, and wholly neglect the part assigned you in the system of the world and the society of mankind, shall torture you from the cradle to the grave."[42]

Neither knowledge nor art can displace this "great leading passion of the soul." As a great antagonist of the French *philosophes* and what he regarded as their unseemly pride in their "genius," Adams asserted that although "A sense of duty; a love of truth; a desire to alleviate the anxieties of ignorance may, . . . have an influence on some minds . . . the universal object and idol of men of letters is *reputation*." The more that knowledge is diffused, the more furiously do the passions grow. Because of this, "Emulation next to self-preservation will forever be the great spring of human actions," and "the theory of education, and the science of government may be reduced to the same simple principle, and be all comprehended in the knowledge of the means of actively conducting, controlling, and regulating the emulation and ambition of the citizens."[43]

Thus the passion for distinction acts as a kind of substitute intelligence in man, a compensatory self-regarding motivational spring to social cooperation and civility. It is equivalent to the instinct which Franklin wished to exist in place of man's weak reason. Under its proddings society exists not in Aristotelian terms for the good life, but as a fulfillment of universal egotism. Adams could not forebear commenting on the irony of nature, in words which recall his statement of 1760 on the significance of vice for society. Because of this passion, he declared, "men of all sorts, even those who have the least of reason, virtue or benevolence, are chained down to an incessant servitude to their fellow creatures; laboring without intermission to produce something which shall contribute to the comfort, convenience, pleasure, profit, or utility of some or other of the species, they are really thus constituted by their own vanity, slaves to mankind."[44] In terms of the Aristotelian definition, "the man is free . . . who exists for his own sake and not for another's," Adams' characterization of men as "slaves to mankind" is peculiarly apt.[45] In unending search of approval and praise, men generally act not toward an end in virtue of an intrinsic rational principle, but from what Adams called an "impulse" which is "irresistible." He regarded it as "folly" and asked: "On a selfish system, what are the thoughts, passions, and sentiments of mankind to us?" The desire for regard and approval issues in a morality not based upon rational intuition of the objective good, but upon the reflected sentiments of one's fellows. Adams believed that the latter should never be more than supplementary to the former, but he conceded that, except for the few who have sufficient strength of character to make and act upon independent judgments, the latter actually replaced the former. It is precisely this substitution which he must have seen as reducing individual men to slaves of the species.[46]

Adams appears to have been heavily influenced on this point not only by Smith but also by Pope, who, following Mandeville, had sounded essentially the same note in a couplet Adams undoubtedly knew. Pope declared that through man's happy frailties,

> Virtue's ends from vanity can raise,
> Which seeks no interest, no reward but praise.[47]

Both Pope and Adams treated vanity, which Pope equated with the desire for praise, and which Adams, in this context, equated with the passion for distinction, as conducive to social accord. They were as one on this point with Hume, who defined vanity as "a social passion, and a bond of union among men."[48] In light of this, the task of statecraft would seem simple and clear—to provide incentives and inducements, whereby the socially beneficial possibilities of this basic desire can be maximized. Government might then be consigned, as the cynical Mandeville put it, to the "skillful management of wary Politicians, who by superimposing flattery upon men's pride, beget the moral virtues and civility."[49] Although as we shall see, Adams did not overlook these important considerations in his political prescriptions, he trusted not the uncircumscribed workings of the passion for distinction in rulers or ruled. Like Pope, he looked to the principle of counterpoise to effect the end where "jarring interests of themselves create the according music of a well-mixed state."[50] But unlike Pope, whom he earlier excused on this point because "poets attend to fanciful images, not the effects of social institutions," he did not dismiss institutional forms as of no moment, so long as the state is well administered. On the contrary, they assumed an even greater importance than before in his political thought, standing as the indispensable means by which the passion for distinction is made to act as the motive principle of the state and as a check upon itself. Like Hume, Adams sought to effect the general good not by altering the motives of men, but by changing the situation in which they find themselves; each branch of government must be set up to be immediately interested in checking the encroachments of the other branches. On this basis, contrary to the thesis of Montesquieu, which he had expounded in the *Thoughts on Government*, republican virtue is a result and not a principle. Thus Adams concluded in the *Discourses:* "The best republics will be virtuous and have been so; but we may hazard a conjecture, that the virtues have been the effect of a well ordered constitution, rather than the cause." So efficacious did he deem balanced government that he asserted that "perhaps it would be impossible to prove that a republic cannot exist even among highwaymen, by setting one rogue to watch another; and the knaves themselves in time may be made honest men by the struggle."[51] Just as nature prods men to virtue and civility through the passion for distinction, so does the balanced state canalize it by making the pursuit of vice unprofitable. In reality, however, because in both instances the immediate motive is a selfish one, it is only the appearance of virtue, albeit a viable substitute, which initially results. But it would be incorrect to call such a motive necessarily vicious and to regard the resultant, as did Mandeville, as merely a concealed indulgence of the passions. As Adams later put it, in one of his marginal notes: "Selfish principles, love of glory are not absolutely and universally to be condemned. They are to be condemned when they do wrong but not when they do right."[52]

Although Adams never relinquished his original conviction that all men, because of their common nature and inherent dignity, are deserving of equal rights and equal treatment under law, he did not consider them equal, physically or intellectually. "God in the constitution of nature, has ordained that every man shall have a disposition to emulation, as well as imitation, and consequently a passion for distinction; and that all men shall not have equal means and opportunities of gratifying it." He saw among men an unavoidable aristocracy whose five pillars are beauty, wealth, birth, genius, and virtue, and thought it a melancholy fact that "Any one of the three first can, at any time, overbear any one or both of the last." Thus among the generality of men "there is less disposition to congratulations with genius, talents, or virtue, than there is with beauty, strength and elegance of person; and less with these than with the gifts of fortune and birth, wealth and fame." From this he concluded that distinctions and orders are at once inevitable and necessary in society, and that government, to be viable and an adequate guarantor of liberty, must take cognizance of them.[53]

Alongside this emphasis upon the political value of birth, wealth, and fame, Adams stressed as a fundamental political fact the inevitability of class differences between the few and the many, a factor he had not stressed in his earlier thought. Even with all the encouragements of general education, he averred, "the laboring part of the people can never be learned." This because "leisure for study must ever be the portion of a few." Like it or not, "the controversy between the rich and the poor, the laborious and the idle, the learned and the ignorant . . .

distinctions which no art or policy nor degree of virtue or philosophy can wholly destroy, will continue, and rivalries will spring out of them." "The great art of lawgiving" consists in protecting property, and thus liberty, by "balancing the poor against the rich in the legislature, and in constituting the legislative a perfect balance against the executive power, at the same time that no individual or party can become its rival."[54]

In his letters to John Taylor, in 1814, in which he answered criticism of the *Defence,* Adams defined an aristocrat as anyone who can and will control one more vote than his own, and asserted that an aristocracy of leaders will naturally manifest itself in any assembly of men, no matter how chosen. By equating aristocracy with personal qualities conducive to leadership, rather than the traditional class distinction, Adams appears to be in agreement with Franklin. If aristocracy is simply the ability to lead and control, then Franklin's broad democracy, as the matrix from which a natural elite of leaders can best arise, and not the class-based, balanced state would seem to be indicated. Adams appears to have been conscious of the implications of his definition; in his letter to Taylor he qualified the equation of aristocracy with leadership by not only reiterating but extending his previous emphasis on the overriding advantage of conspicuous birth. "Birth is naturally and necessarily and inevitably so connected and blended with property, fame, power, education, genius, strength, beauty, learning, science, taste, figure, air, attitudes, movements, etc. . . , that it is often impossible and always difficult to separate them." Birth and wealth are almost inextricably "entangled together," but birth generally prevails over all other qualities including wealth, in effect and power, because it is hereditary.[55]

What we are left with is an admission that aristocracy spells influence, which arises in any group of men, large or small, humble or proud, rich or poor, but that in society at large the most pervasive means of influence have been available to those possessing attributes upon which class distinctions have traditionally been made. The influence of the latter is less in simple, agriculture societies, but decisive in complex, developed societies. By isolating the class-based leaders in a senate, one at once protects their interest and that of the people, and allows for the development of a natural, responsible, popular leadership.

The principle of counterpoise by which passion checks passion, ambition checks ambition, interest checks interest, and class checks class, represents what might be called the negative side of Adams' conclusions from his psychological premises. The positive side is present in his insistence upon the need to excite the admiration and emulation of the citizenry in the interest of the state by marks of distinction and degree, such as titles, symbols, awards, and ceremonies. In 1789 he wrote: "Titles and Ranks are as essential to Government, as Reason and Justice. In short Government is nothing else but Titles, Ceremonies and Ranks. They alone enable Reason to produce Justice."[56]

Such appeals to the imagination, the senses, and the affections were used, Adams noted approvingly, by the Roman Republic, with its distinctions of dress and use of lictors, crowns, chairs, ovations, and parades. He regarded these practices to be "in the true spirit of republics, in which form of government there is no other consistent method of preserving order, or procuring submission to the laws."[57]

Finally, Adams emphasized that the distribution of honors must be separated from the body of the people and the legislature and conferred upon the executive. "Uniformity, consistency, and subordination" may be hoped for "when the emulation of all the citizens looks up to one point," but "deformities, eccentricities and confusion" can be expected, when the citizens "look up to different individuals, or assemblies, or councils." It is not difficult to understand how this statement could lead people to conclude that he was a monarchist at heart.[58]

Whether Adams personally desired adoption in America of the hereditary principle is a question which has divided authorities. It appears that his personal choice was against its adoption but that his political science indicated not merely its desirability but its utter necessity at certain stages of social development, if liberty is to be preserved. By 1790 the doubt which he entertained concerning the American character was reinforced by his interpretation of events and his historical studies of politics. He charged that Americans were more avaricious than any other nation, and that they were more disposed to corruption in elections than he had thought in 1776. It is in this light that one must view his assertion that "America must resort to . . . [hereditary monarchy and aristocracy] as an Asylum against Discords, Seditions, and Civil War, and at no very distant Period of time."[59] This was a dictate of his political science which, as some have alleged, was perhaps too closely tied up with European experience and forgetful of the uniqueness of America as expounded by Adams himself in his youthful *Dissertation On the Canon and Feudal Law*.

In any case, Adams' political thought was essentially consistent from first to last. The basic structural principles of government outlined in the *Thoughts On Government*—separation of powers, checks and balances, bicameralism, a coordinate executive power—were supplemented by the emphasis in the *Defence* on a balance of classes, and a shift from the earlier emphasis on the upper house as mediator between the executive and the lower house to a stress on the executive as mediator between the two legislative houses. This was accompanied in his psychological theory by his constant emphasis on the primacy of the emulative propensity, which changes only in terms of the objects it pursues. If profit, fame, power, and luxury succeed virtue and learning as objects, then the form of the balanced state must change accordingly.

NOTES

1. Quoted in Gordon S. Wood, *The Creation of the American Republic* (Chapel Hill, 1969), p. 281. For Jefferson's objection see his "Notes on the State of Virginia" (1782), in P. L. Ford (ed.), *The Writings of Thomas Jefferson* (New York, 1892–1899, 10 vols.), III, 228. Concerning the contract theory, see Thad Tate, "The Social Contract in America, 1774–1787," *William and Mary Quarterly*, XXII (July, 1965), 375–391, and A. C. McLaughlin, *The Foundations of American Constitutionalism* (New York, 1932), pp. 63–84.

2. Resolves of the Concord Town Meeting, Oct. 21, 1776, in H. S. Commager (ed.), *Documents of American History* (New York, 1948), No. 68, p. 105.

3. J. W. Gough, *The Social Contract* (Oxford, 1957), pp. 143, 232–233; Nathaniel Chipman, *Sketches of the Principles of Government* (Rutland, Vt., 1793), pp. 22, 23, 74, 75, 110, 111, 113, 115. See also Wood, *op. cit.*, pp. 282–305.

4. See the anonymous pamphlet used in Pennsylvania by radical democrats, *The Genuine Principles of the Anglo-Saxon, or English Constitution* (Philadelphia, 1776), discussed in Wood, *op cit.*, p. 226ff.

5. Concerning this question within the framework of the larger question of the degree of democracy then existing in America, see for arguments that democracy was extensive, Robert E. Brown, *Middle Class Democracy and the Revolution in Massachusetts* (Ithaca, N.Y., 1955) and Robert E. and Katherine Brown, *Virginia (1705–1796): Democracy or Aristocracy* (East Lansing, Mich., 1964). To the contrary, see J. R. Pole, "Historians and the Problem of Early American Democracy," *American Historical Review*, LXVII (Apr., 1962), 626–646, and Merrill Jensen, "Democracy and the American Revolution," *The Huntington Library Quarterly*, XX (Aug., 1957), 321–341. See also Wood, *op. cit.*, pp. 167–168.

6. The statute is reprinted in Commager, *op cit.*, No. 80, pp. 125–126.

7. Jefferson, "A Summary View," *Papers*, I, 124. For a discussion of developing American theory regarding the legislature, see Wood, *op. cit.*, especially parts III and IV.

8. The text of the Articles of Confederation can be conveniently found in Commager, *op. cit.*, No. 72, pp. 111–116.

9. The text of the Ordinance of 1787 can be conveniently found in Commager, *op. cit.*, No. 82, pp. 128–132. Jefferson's report of March 1, 1784, on the Government for the Western Territory can be found in *Writings*, III, 407–410.

10. Jefferson, "Notes on the State of Virginia," *Writings*, III, 222; Hamilton to James Duane, Sept. 3, 1780, and "The Continentalist, No. I," July 12, 1781, in Harold, C. Syrett (ed.), *The Papers of Alexander Hamilton*, II, 401, 649, 650; Gaillard Hunt (ed.), *The Writings of James Madison* (New York, 1900–1910, 9 vols.), II, 364.

11. Jefferson, *Writings*, III, 222, 223, 224, 225.

12. "The Continentalist, No. I," July 12, 1781, *Papers*, II, 651, "The Continentalist, No. IV," August 30, 1781, *Papers*, II, 670.

13. Madison, "Vices of the Political System of the United States," Gaillard Hunt, ed., *Writings of James Madison* (New York, 1900, 1910, 9 vols.), II, 361–369. The quotations can be found on pp. 366 and 368.

14. Leonard W. Labaree (ed.), *The Papers of Benjamin Franklin* (New Haven, 1959, 8 vols.), I, 21, 178, 179; IV, 194, 195. The characterizations of pride above can be found in Arthur O. Lovejoy, *Reflections on Human Nature* (Baltimore, 1961), pp. 145, 129. Concerning Franklin's life and career see Gerald Stourzh, *Benjamin Franklin and American Foreign Policy* (Chicago, 1954) and Paul W. Conner, *Poor Richard's Politics* (New York, 1965).

15. *Papers,* I, 146; II, 3, 185; Albert H. Smyth (ed.), *The Life and Writings of Benjamin Franklin* (New York, 1905–1907, 10 vols.), VIII, 451–452. (Hereinafter cited as *Writings*).

16. *Writings,* I, 267; Carl Van Doren (ed.), *The Letters of Benjamin Franklin and Jane Mecom* (Princeton, 1950), p. 112; *Writings,* VIII, 10.

17. *Papers,* I, 120–121.

18. *Writings,* IX, 330–331; *Papers,* II, 66; *Writings,* IX, 241, 702.

19. Regarding Franklin and the Declaration of Independence, see Carl L. Becker, *The Declaration of Independence* (New York, 1958, Vintage edition), p. 161; *Writings,* IX, 608–609, 614–615; VI, 129; V, 362; *Papers,* IV, 225–234; *Writings,* IX, 245–246.

20. *Papers,* III, 260; I, 193; IV, 41.

21. *Writings,* V, 155–156; *Papers,* II, 223. See also *Writings,* IV, 243–244.

22. *Writings,* IX, 241.

23. *Writings,* IX, 608; X, 120–121.

24. *Writings,* IX, 614, 615; *Papers,* II, 141. See also *Writings,* IX, 702.

25. *Writings,* VI, 212–213.

26. *Writings,* IX, 591–595, 170. See the discussion of this point in Stourzh, *op. cit.,* 18, 19.

27. *Writings,* X, 56–60. After the Federal Constitutional Convention of 1787, Franklin at least twice restated his belief that one chamber would be better than two in the federal legislature. See *Writings,* IX, 645, 674.

28. For Franklin's idealized 1774 view of the American electoral process see *Writings,* VI, 209, 210.

29. L. H. Butterfield (ed.), *The Diary and Autobiography of John Adams* (Cambridge, Mass., 1961, 4 vols.), I, 26 (May 11, 1756); Charles F. Adams (ed.), *The Works of John Adams* (Boston, 1851, 10 vols.), III, 432–435. Adams drew upon Part III, Chapter IV of Smith's *Theory of the Moral Sentiments,* entitled "Of the Nature of Self-deceit and of the Origin and Use of General Rules." Concerning Adams' life and works see Correa M. Walsh, *The Political Science of John Adams* (New York, 1915); Edward Handler, *America and Europe in the Political Thought of John Adams* (Cambridge, Mass., 1964); John Howe Jr., *The Changing Political Thought of John Adams* (Princeton, 1966); Adrienne Koch, *Power, Morals and the Founding Fathers* (New York, 1961), Chap. 4; and Page Smith, *John Adams* (New York, 1962).

30. John Adams to Abigail Adams, May 22, 1777, L. H. Butterfield (ed.), *Adams Family Correspondence* (Cambridge, Mass., 1963, 2 vols.), II, 245–246.

31. Adams, *Diary,* I, 8 (Feb. 19, 1756); I, 96, 69 (Jan., Spring, 1759). For Adams' deep concern for his own reputation and progress, see L. H. Butterfield (ed.), *The Earliest Diary of John Adams; 1753–1754, 1758–1759* (Cambridge, Mass., 1966), p. 77.

32. Adams, *Diary,* I, 184 (Dec. 18, 1760).

33. Adams, *Works,* III, 448.

34. Adams, *Diary,* I, 365 (August 22, 1770).

35. Adams, *Works,* IV, 193, 194.

36. Regarding Adams' views pro and con the virtue of America at the time, see his letters to his wife Abigail in *Adams Family Correspondence,* II, 28, 76, 131, 253 (July 3, Aug. 4, Sept. 22, Oct. 8, 1776, and June 2, 1777).

37. Adams to Jefferson, Nov. 13, 1815, *Works,* X, 174. Also found in Lester J. Cappon, ed., *The Adams–Jefferson Letters* (Chapel Hill, 1959, 2 vols.), II, 456.

38. *A Defence of the Constitutions of Government of the U.S.A.,* in *Works,* IV, 290.

39. *Defence, Works,* VI, 114–115, 141; John Adams to Samuel Adams, Oct. 18, 1790, *Works,* VI, 415; quoted in Zoltan Haraszti, *John Adams and the Prophets of Progress* (Cambridge, Mass., 1952), p. 220.

40. *Discourses, Works,* VI, 232, 233.

41. *Discourses, Works,* VI, 248, 249.

42. *Discourses, Works,* VI, 246.

43. *Discourses, Works,* VI, 240, 275, 279, 248.

44. *Discourses, Works,* VI, 245.

45. Aristotle, *Metaphysics,* I, 982b.

46. *Discourses, Works,* VI, 245, 246, 234.

47. "An Essay On Man," in *Alexander Pope: Selected Works* (Modern Library Edition, New York, 1948), Epistle II, p. 114.

48. David Hume, *Treatise of Human Nature,* in *Hume's Philosophical Works* (Boston, 1854, 4 vols.), II, 257.

49. Bernard de Mandeville, *A Fable of the Bees,* cited in Lovejoy, *op. cit.,* 173.

50. Adams placed lines from the third epistle of the "Essay On Man," including those quoted above, on the title page of *Discourses, Works,* VI, 223.

51. Adams, *Works,* VI, 219.

52. Haraszti, *op. cit.,* 204.

53. *Discourses, Works,* VI, 271, 272, 288; John Adams to Thomas Jefferson, Sept. 2, 1813, *Works,* X, 65 and *Adams–Jefferson Letters,* I, 371; *Discourses, Works,* VI, 253. See also John Adams to Samuel Adams, Oct. 18, 1790, *Works,* VI, 418–419.

54. *Discourses, Works,* VI, 280.

55. John Adams to John Taylor, Apr. 15, 1814, *Works,* VI, 451–458, 501.

56. John Adams to Benjamin Rush, July 24, 1789, *Old Family Letters: Copied from the Originals for Alexander Biddle* (Philadelphia, 1892, 2 vols.), I, 47.

57. *Discourses, Works,* VI, 243.

58. *Discourses, Works,* VI, 256.

59. John Adams to Benjamin Rush, April 4, 1790, *Old Family Letters,* I, 57, 60, 37–38.

Chapter 10

THE CONSTITUTION
OF 1787

*This admirable federal constitution of ours . . . is superior to
the wisdom of any or all of the men by whose agency it was
made. The force of circumstances, and not foresight or wisdom,
induced them to adopt many of its wisest provisions.*

JOHN C. CALHOUN

Rationalists such as Thomas Paine thought that the construction of a
government was a simple proposition; the Constitution of 1787, however, as Madison stated, was not "the offspring of a single brain" but
"the work of many heads and many hands," which established a political
system that was at once novel and complex. In it, pragmatic men of
vision defined structural forms and allocated, divided, and limited
governmental power in an attempt at once to implement the ideals of
the Revolution and to establish a central authority which would solve
the old imperial problem of the relation of the whole to its parts. In this
chapter we will examine the purposes of the Convention, the varieties of
thought presented therein, the main issues and their resolution, the contemporary critical and favorable literature on the Constitution itself,
and the contributions of the Founding Fathers to political science.

The Convention: Purposes, Sources, and Setting

The Founding Fathers, in the words of Madison, aimed at "framing
a system which we wish to last for ages."[1] Translated into the terms of
the finished constitution, their purposes were (1) to form a more perfect
union, (2) to establish justice, (3) to ensure domestic tranquility,
(4) to provide for the common defense, (5) to promote the general
welfare, and (6) to secure the blessings of liberty. It is noteworthy that
the Articles of Confederation failed to mention purposes two and three.
Thus it might be said that the fathers believed that if left solely to the

states not only would these objectives not be properly realized, but the moral authority of the central government would be insufficient. In other words, they thought that a vital national common interest in the full implementation of the above purposes had evolved.

The convention delegates represented the cultural and political elite of America. We are so far removed from their day, with our heavy emphasis upon specialization and technical proficiency, that it is hard to realize that the nation's best minds were then attracted to politics and assumed positions of leadership. Except for such dissenters as John Hancock, Samuel Adams, Patrick Henry, and Richard Henry Lee, and men who were abroad in the service of their country, such as Thomas Jefferson and John Adams, America's great men were at the Convention.

Most of the delegates were lawyers, and by our standards, young— they averaged just about forty years of age. As men of affairs they viewed politics in terms of concrete problems and issues. Although they almost universally subscribed to the natural rights philosophy, they were distrustful of abstractions. John Dickinson stated the point in the Convention: "Experience must be our only guide. Reason may mislead us."[2] As the primary source, experience embraced: (1) personal experience; (2) the experience of history, particularly previous efforts in colonial times and since independence to solve the vexing imperial problem; (3) the traditional Anglo-Saxon legal and political heritage. This is not to say that the men of intellect in the Convention turned aside from ideas. All their deliberations were against a background compounded of the ideas of political theorists such as Aristotle, Polybius, Cicero, Hooker, Machiavelli, Hobbes, Harrington, Milton, Locke, Montesquieu, and Hume.[•] As practical men, however, the Founding Fathers saw ideas as relevant in terms of the specific issues. If a realist is a man who operates from a keen knowledge of human motivation, the lessons of experience, and the possibilities of the people whose problems constitute his focus and for whom he prescribes, the fathers were realists.

Reason, then, was seen by the fathers not as a faculty operating from and upon a *tabula rasa* but as a temper or mood, which, as Franklin stated, proceeded from a consciousness of fallibility, and issued in a spirit of compromise and adjustment.[3] Thus it was not the spirit of an Abbé Sieyes which moved the Convention but that of a David Hume, who equated reasonable action with conduct in accordance with the calm, as opposed to the violent, passions. As has recently been shown, the Convention can more fully be appreciated if viewed as a "reform-caucus" with the attendant implications of bargaining, dealing, and accommodation.[4] Finally, it should be added that the delegates deliberated in secret, a procedure which, however admirable, would be impossible to pursue today. Had the procedure been otherwise, it is doubtful that an agreement could have been realized. Demagogy was unprofitable and candor at a premium where men gathered in a small hall to address each other and reason together in conversational tones.*

Varieties of Political Thought in the Convention

Analysis of the Convention proceedings reveals five principal conceptions of governmental order among the delegates. For purposes of exposition they will be presented logically, not chronologically, in a spectrum ranging from the most extreme nationalist formulation to the plan which assumed retention of the Articles of Confederation.

Aristo-Monarchic, Consolidated Nationalism

Alexander Hamilton. Although Hamilton was outvoted in the New York delegation, he was listened to closely by the Convention, even though the specific plan which he introduced, after the Virginia and New Jersey plans had been submitted, was disregarded.

Short of an exact copy of the British Constitution, which was his model, Hamilton wished to effect an embodiment of its structural principles, consolidated powers, and mode of operation, within a nominal republican framework. In this spirit he outlined what he called "the great and essential principles necessary for the support of Government," namely: (1) "an active and constant interest in supporting it"; (2) "the love of power"; (3) "an habitual attachment of the people"; (4) *"a coercion of laws, or a coercion of arms";* and (5) *"influence."* As the situation then stood, he observed: "All the passions . . . of avarice, ambition, interest, which govern most individuals, and all public bodies, fall into the current of the States. . . ." The evils could be remedied only by injecting "such a complete sovereignty in the general Government as will turn all the strong principles and passions . . . on its side." He conceded that subordinate authorities would be necessary but merely as "corporations for local purposes." Although he later attempted to qualify this remark in the direction of a retention of the states, there can be no doubt that a great consolidation of authority at the center was what he deemed both requisite and desirable.[5]

Seeing society in terms of contending interests and conflicting human passions, he reduced the significant political interests to two, which he called the *few* (the rich and the well born) and the *many* (the poor).

---

* That there was disagreement among Americans on this practice is evident in a letter Jefferson wrote to John Adams, August 30, 1787 wherein he says: "I am sorry they [the Convention] began their deliberations by so abominable a precedent as that of tying up the tongues of their members. Nothing can justify this example but the innocence of their intentions and ignorance of the value of public discussions." *Papers,* XII, 69.

Because if power is given to either it will oppress the other, Hamilton prescribed a class-based balanced state, with a Senate appointed for life and a lower house elected by the people for a short term. The Senate would play the role of the House of Lords, which "having nothing to hope for by a change, and a sufficient interest by means of their property, in being faithful to the national interest, . . . form a barrier against every pernicious innovation." But at the center of the Hamiltonian plan was an executive elected indirectly by the people for life and possessed of strong powers, including an absolute veto. Hamilton thus primarily aimed not at a balance of interests as such but at their representation and positive enlistment in the mobilization of a general will effecting a consolidation of power. Because he believed that "a reliance on pure patriotism had been the source of many of our errors" he could not be a republican in the ideal sense of one who held virtue (devotion to the common good) to be the principle of a republic. Thus Hamilton argued: "We must take man as we find him, and if we expect him to serve the public, must interest his passions in doing so." A government which frankly recognized in its institutions the two social classes and enlisted their passions in its cause was his answer.[6]

Gouverneur Morris. While propounding conceptions of aristocracy and political psychology quite similar to those of John Adams, Morris' views on government were generally the same as Hamilton's with some qualifications regarding consolidation of power and governmental structure.

Morris believed aristocracy to be inevitable in society and that one should aim "to keep it as much as possible from doing mischief." Because the rich are impelled by a desire to "enslave the rest" and will establish an oligarchy if they mix with the poor in a commercial country, they should be given separate lifetime representation in the Senate. Unlike Madison, Morris believed that "the schemes of the rich will be favored by the extent of the country." By giving them separate representation, the pride of the aristocrat, which tends to the abuse of authority, will be checked by the pride of the poor which resists authority.[7]

Morris urged the establishment of a vigorous independent executive which, like Hamilton, he believed should control the legislature. Because the Senate was meant to serve as a check "on the abuse of lawful powers, on the propensity in the first branch to legislate too much, to run into projects of paper money, and similar expedients. . . ." Morris declared, "the Executive . . . ought to be so constituted as to be the great protector of the mass of the people." Popular election of an executive personifying the public interest and armed with the absolute veto was his prescription. He believed that the people would never fail to select a "man of distinguished character, or services; some man . . .

of continental reputation," whereas if the national legislature were to make the selection, it would "be the work of intrigue, of cabal, and of faction."[8]

If Hamilton's watchword was what we might call "Prosperity and freedom through national power," Morris' was "Protection of property through national power and the balancing of classes." In arguing that property should be a factor in the apportionment of representation, he maintained that the preservation and protection of property was the main object of society and government. He further contended that new western states should not enter the Union on an equal footing with the original states. An advocate of a commercial republic, he thought that "the Busy haunts of men not the remote wilderness, was the proper school of political Talents." A republican mixed state depended, in his mind, on class distinctions which were nonexistent in the undeveloped West.[9]

Democratic Nationalism

James Wilson. No delegate propounded the democratic and nationalistic principles more effectively and consistently in the Convention than did James Wilson. Speaking directly to Morris' point, he declared that he "could not agree that property was the sole or primary object of Government and society." Instead, "the cultivation and improvement of the human mind was the most noble object." He concluded that "numbers were surely the natural and precise measure of representation." Thus Wilson espoused raising "the federal pyramid to a considerable altitude, and for that reason [he] wished to give it as broad a basis as possible," through direct popular election of the bicameral legislature and the executive. This because "the government ought to possess not only . . . the *force*, but . . . the *mind* or *sense* of the people at large." The Legislature "ought to be the most exact transcript of the whole Society," because representation "is made necessary only because it is impossible for the people to act collectively."[10]

Replying to men like Hamilton, Wilson argued the impropriety of the British Constitution as the basic model. "Our manners, our laws . . . the whole genius of the people, are opposed to it." Through the broadly based democratic pyramid he would effect a strong, vigorous central government, which preserved the states by restricting them to limited orbits, and which operated directly upon individuals. Like Morris, he deemed essential a popularly elected, single, independent and powerful executive armed with an absolute veto, but he would make the suffrage as broad as possible.[11]

Wilson's nationalism is evidenced in his agreement with Madison on the necessity of a general, unspecified grant of powers to the central government and on a national negative on the states which he called "the key-stone wanted to complete the wide arch of Government, we are raising." Because of his basic democracy, he could not, however, accept the Madisonian conception of indirect elections except as a second best means. Whereas Madison, Hamilton, and Morris saw society in terms of contending interests, Wilson saw it as a collection of individual wills, pursuing happiness not in the acquisition of property or self-aggrandizement but in the "cultivation and improvement of the human mind." He would agree to neither state sovereignty nor national sovereignty, nor a class-based, mixed state. His polestar was popular sovereignty; a national government, to be effective, must be based upon, and be reflective of, the wills of the individuals in the society it represents.[12]

While Madison emphasized liberty, and Hamilton and Morris, property, and all three feared "a levelling spirit," Wilson emphasized numerical equality. He was at one with Hamilton and Morris in seeking the realization of a corporate will in government—but whereas Hamilton and Morris would effect this through enlistment of the passions and interests (particularly commercial), Wilson sought its realization through a democratic majority.

Democratic Nationalism: Government by Assembly

Benjamin Franklin. It will be recalled that Benjamin Franklin advocated unicameral democracy as most conducive to rule by "wise and good men." Except for the mutual check of avarice and ambition within his plural executive, Franklin saw no need for institutional checks and balances (counterpoise). Thus although he was as democratic and almost as nationalistic as Wilson, he did not subscribe to Wilson's views on institutions. Franklin, of course, differed from proponents of the New Jersey plan who also were unicameralists, in his firm espousal of greatly broadened national powers, and in his experimentalism.

Republican Nationalism

James Madison. In a letter to Edmund Randolph just before the Convention, Madison stated that he held it to be "a fundamental point, that an individual independence of the states, is utterly irreconciliable with the idea of an aggregate sovereignty." He thought, however, that "a consolidation of the States into one simple republic is not less unattainable than it would be inexpedient." Consequently, he urged that an attempt be made to find "a middle ground" which "will at once support a due supremacy of the national authority, and leave in force the local authorities so far as they can be subordinately useful." He then outlined the principles which were thereafter embodied in the Virginia plan presented to the Convention by Randolph.[13]

Madison's "middle-ground" was fundamentally national in substance and republican in form. He aimed at withdrawing from volatile majorities within the states the jurisdiction over matters which affected the union and which were the source of enervating disputes and violations of fundamental rights. This was illustrated in the course of debate in the Convention when after Roger Sherman of Connecticut declared that the objects of the union were defense, domestic order, treaties, regulation of foreign commerce and revenue, Madison objected that this omitted the need for "providing more effectually for the security of private rights, and the steady dispensation of Justice."[14] By rights Madison meant property rights, the security of which he deemed essential to life and liberty. By "the steady dispensation of Justice" he meant the ending of legislative determinations of judicial questions. At the same time he sought to neutralize and insulate, as much as possible, the inevitable clash of contending interests and to bring about ultimate determination of national issues not by a Hamiltonian or Wilsonian general will but by patriotic men of elevated minds and established character comparable to Franklin's "wise and good men." Thus he aimed at (1) a general grant of power to the central government and (2) institutional arrangements designed to minimize politics (in the sense of bargaining and dealing) and to effect the ascendancy of republican virtue (dedication to the common good) over self-interest.

Madison's main implementive principles were: (1) enlarging the territorial spheres of constituencies and of republican jurisdiction; (2) separation of powers, checks and balances, an independent non-political executive, and bicameralism; (3) the "filtration" and "refining" of opinion; (4) operation of the central government directly upon individuals; and (5) a national veto over state laws.

The principle of enlargement of the sphere, which Madison saw as "the only defence against the inconveniences of democracy consistent with the democratic form of government," had been sketched by him, as we have seen, in an earlier paper, and was fully elaborated by him after the Convention in number ten of the *Federalist* papers.[15] He considered the belief that the legislature ought to be as exact a reflection of society as possible to be a principal of disruption. Instead he believed that sizable electoral districts in an extensive republic could aid in preventing the evils issuing from the majoritarian principle without the abandonment of the principle itself.

Madison would put into effect his principle of "refining the popular appointments by successive filtrations," through the representative principle and the selection of the members of the upper house by members of the lower house. He believed that this would result in the selection of "a portion of enlightened citizens, whose limited number, and firmness might interpose against impetuous counsels."[16]

Madison deviated from the recommendation in the Virginia plan of indirect election of the national executive. Like Morris, he believed that direct election would better suffice because the people at large "generally could only know and vote for some Citizen whose merits had rendered him an object of general attention and esteem." But what he conceded on the one hand, he greatly qualified on the other. Thus because he believed that republican government could not give an individual citizen that "settled preeminence in the eyes of the rest, that weight of property, that personal interest against betraying the national interest, which appertain to an hereditary magistrate," and because "the executive magistrate would be envied and assailed by disappointed competitors," he deemed it necessary to associate a portion of the judiciary with him in a Council of Revision to exercise the veto.[17]

Republican Qualified Nationalism

George Mason. The author of the Virginia Bill of Rights confessed in the Convention of 1787 that he had "for his primary object—for the pole-star of his political conduct, the preservation of the rights of the people." Because he believed the Articles of Confederation incapable of remedy, he urged a central government which would operate directly on individuals as in the Virginia plan.[18]

Mason advocated popular election of the lower house on the principle that "it ought to know and sympathize with every part of the com munity." He admitted that the country had been "too democratic," but he feared a reaction "into the opposite extreme." And yet he proposed a property qualification for all members of Congress. Unlike Madison, Morris, and Wilson, he deemed direct popular election of the executive impracticable, holding it to be "as unnatural to refer the choice of a proper character for chief Magistrate to the people, as it would, to refer a trial of colors to a blind man." This because "the extent of the Country renders it impossible that the people can have the requisite capacity to judge of the respective pretensions of the Candidates." Although he desired election of the executive by the legislature, he opposed rendering him "the mere creature" of the legislature. In line with his emphasis on the priority of human rights he contended that "the great officers of State, and particularly the Executive, should at fixed periods return to that mass from which they were at first taken, in order that they may feel and respect those rights and interests which are again to be personally valuable to them."[19]

Mason differed from Madison (and the Virginia plan) principally in doubting the advisability of a national negative on state acts, and in ultimately concluding that the states must have the means of "self-defence." For the latter, he proposed a Senate chosen by the state legislatures, with equal representation afforded each state. Presaging his later opposition to the Constitution, he stated in the Convention his belief that it should contain a Bill of Rights, because if it along with national laws was to be paramount and controlling, the state bills of rights could conceivably be superseded.[20]

Amendment of the Articles of Confederation

The New Jersey Plan. Based upon the principle of state sovereignty, the New Jersey plan proposed retention of the unicameral Congress with equality of state representation and voting power. It would have added a plural executive (with no veto power) elected by Congress and removable by that body on application of a majority of the state governors. More importantly, it granted power to Congress (1) to levy taxes on imports, and (2) to regulate foreign and interstate commerce. Most significantly, it answered the question of enforcement by opting for the coercion of law. Thus though the state judiciaries were to be the instruments of enforcement, the acts of the United States were defined as "the supreme law of the respective States."[21]

Jealous of preserving the foci of politics within the states, advocates of the New Jersey plan cannot be dismissed as men who did not recognize and attempt to solve the basic problems of government under the Articles. Had the Congress been provided with the powers to tax and regulate commerce, and had the enforcement been through state courts bound to recognize the federal acts as supreme, it is hard to say that such an arrangement would have been unworkable. The one readily apparent difficulty—the possibility of conflicting interpretations of federal acts and laws—would not have been insurmountable since conceivably the federal court, also provided for by the plan, could have been given power to make final determinations in such cases. When measured against Madison's views, and those embodied in the final draft of the Constitution, the most significant omission of the New Jersey plan was its failure to withdraw from state majorities the power to enfringe individual rights and the course of justice.

Main Issues and Their Resolution

None of these views was accepted as a whole by the Convention. Thus although there was fundamental agreement on such principles as a stronger national government and a formal separation of powers, the finished Constitution was, in good part, the product of compromise and adjustment.

1. *Federalism.* The question of the position of the states in the Union, was resolved by establishing the *national* principle of proportional representation in the lower house of the Congress and the *federal* principle of equality of the states in the Senate. Logically speaking,

Madison's and Wilson's firm advocacy of proportional representation for both houses should have carried the day. Madison's principle was: "In all cases where the General Government is to act on the people, let the people be represented, and the votes be proportional. In all cases where the Government is to act on the States as such . . . let the States be represented, and the votes be equal." Because he could see no instance in which the government was not to act on the people individually, he thought there was no basis for equal representation of the states in the Senate.[22] The issue, however, was not logical, but political, and could only be resolved through mutual accommodation. Similarly, Madison's desire for a general grant of power to the national government ran athwart the determination to define more exactly those powers. Article I, Section 8 of the Constitution, which lists the specific powers of the Congress and culminates in the "necessary and proper clause," represents the limits of political concession.

Thus it can be seen that the first of America's great contributions to political science, its peculiar type of federalism, was less the product of conscious creative statesmanship than the result of the interplay of contending forces within the Convention Hall.

2. *The Executive.* Article II of the Constitution reflects the reassertion of executive power in America. In line with the teaching of John Adams, most delegates saw the need to establish a strong executive as a principle of balance. But the final product went beyond this. The emphasis of Wilson on the need for "energy," "dispatch," and "unity" was reflected in the vesting of all executive power in a single individual, the President. Rejected was the Madisonian recommendation of a Council of Revision; the President was to exercise the veto power alone. The Hamiltonian emphasis on executive initiative was reflected in the power granted the President to recommend measures to the legislature. The provision for the selection of a president by an electoral college was an awkward, makeshift compromise between the positions of advocates of popular election and the advocates of election by the national legislature. The American Presidency was thus built upon Adam's notion of balance, Wilson's conception of unity, and Hamilton's idea of leadership. Preceding in its inception the modern distinction between "chief of state" and "head of government," it fused both. In a material sense, the office is monarchical; in a formal sense, given the mode of selection, it is republican. In any case, the office represents the greatest of all American contributions to political science.

3. *The Judiciary.* The great contribution of the New Jersey plan to the Constitution was the "supremacy clause." The definition of federal law as supreme and thus binding on state and federal judges provided an alternative to Madison's national negative on state laws. The establishment of a federal judiciary, capped by a Supreme Court, whose

appellate powers were to be defined by Congress, rounded out the formal conditions within which judicial review could develop. Although it was not specifically provided for, judicial review was implied in the above provisions. Then, too, statements either directly or indirectly suggesting some form of judicial review were made in the Convention by such men as Luther Martin, George Mason, John Rutledge, and Gouverneur Morris.[23] It might then be said that the Convention Fathers formulated an instrument of government which presupposed at least a minimal power of judicial review, America's unique contribution to political science.

4. *Democracy.* It must be remembered that the Convention Fathers met to draw a blueprint of government which would provide both for liberty and order. Within this framework, they allowed for democratic development. Thus the qualifications of electors for members of the lower house were left to the determination of the states, insofar as the same electors who chose members of the most numerous branch of the state legislatures were declared to be eligible to select members of the national House of Representatives. Although members of the Senate were to be chosen by the state legislatures, even though the Convention Fathers probably did not have it in mind as a possibility, there was no obstruction put in the way of the legislatures delegating the real choice to the people. Finally, the provision for an electoral college to elect the President allowed the state legislatures to designate the manner of choosing electors, including direct popular election.

The Constitution did not, in any case, require property or religious tests as a qualification for holding office. In fact, religious tests were specifically forbidden. All in all, even though the democracy of James Wilson was not established, the terms of, and qualifications for office were closer to his position than to that of Hamilton and Morris.

The resolution of the western lands question in favor of the principle of equality of new with old states was a victory for democracy and a defeat for the oligarchical view of Morris. In reaffirming the dictate of the Northwest Ordinance, the Convention precluded the possibility of future differences in status among the United States.

The decision for ratification of the Constitution by popularly elected conventions within at least nine states rather than by the state legislatures was also democratic in spirit. Of course, the provision was extralegal in the sense that the Articles of Confederation were circumvented in their requirement of unanimous approval by state legislatures for their amendment. Analysis of the convention debates on the point shows that the postrevolutionary concept of the means by which legitimate constitutional government is established greatly influenced the rhetoric of the delegates. Thus Mason distinguished between the powers of the legislatures as mere creatures of the state constitutions and the constituent power itself, which he declared must reside in the people. Madison stated that it would be "a novel and dangerous doctrine that a Legislature could change the constitution under which it held its existence." He saw the difference between a system founded on the legislatures only, and one founded on the people, as "the true difference between a *league* or *treaty*, and a *Constitution.*" While speaking in opposition to ratification by conventions, Oliver Ellsworth testified to the full development of the new principle of legitimacy. He observed that "a new set of ideas seemed to have crept in since the Articles of Confederation were established. Conventions of the people, or with power derived expressly from the people, were not then thought of."[24]

It is not too much to say that the Convention, no matter how mixed its motives in deciding for ratification by popularly elected state conventions, regarded the principle of popular sovereignty as supreme over the legal requirements of the Articles of Confederation. The American political mind had advanced to the full acceptance of the mode of constitution making first followed by Massachusetts. The procedure stands as the fourth great American contribution to political science.

5. *The Form of the Constitution.* Partly because of the need to be vague in order to gain agreement, partly because of a desire to avoid inflexibility, and partly because of an intention to write a document to endure for the ages, the fathers made the Constitution, in good part, a statement of broad principles. Although a formal amendment process was provided for, the Constitution as a statement of principles at once vague and general, and yet ample as points of departure, represents in its essence an instrument capable of growth, amplification, and interpretation in view of changed conditions. As such, it could assume not only a lasting but also a symbolic value. Thus the Constitution, as a relatively brief, uncluttered statement of basic principles, represents American creative statesmanship at its best. As fundamental law defining and delimiting governmental powers and serving always as the ultimate positive norm, the Constitution of 1787 was the culmination of an experimental process of development beginning in the colonial past, reaching a point of definition in the period just preceding the Revolution, and coming first to fruition in the state constitutions.

The Anti-Federalists

Opponents of the proposed Constitution, who numbered about one-half of the active white population of the country, were handicapped by the dubious name, "Anti-Federalist." The proponents of the Constitution had deftly appropriated to themselves the favorable term "Federalist" which theretofore had connoted a supporter of the Confederation. Cast in a negative role and outmaneuvered politically by the Federalists, the Anti-Federalists included in their ranks such eminent men as George Mason, Patrick Henry, and Richard H. Lee of Virginia, George Clinton and Robert Yates of New York, Eldridge Gerry of Massachusetts, and Luther Martin of Maryland, all of whom were local rather than national leaders.[25]

Although attempts have been made to show a basis in class differences for allegiance to the Anti-Federalist or Federalist causes, no unqualified statements to that effect can be made. The most recent historian of Anti-Federalism has concluded that areas of subsistence farming tended to be Anti-Federalist, whereas commercial areas and areas of farmers dependent upon commercial markets tended to be Federalist. Suffice it to say that in the ranks of the Anti-Federalists were men of means and men of commerce, as well as men of "middling" and low ranks. If we may apply to this situation the terms of John Adams, there were many "gentlemen" and "simplemen" on both sides, with a proportionally greater number of the latter among the Anti-Federalists.[26]

It is common in discussing the thought of Anti-Federalists to stress their differences from the Federalists. A more accurate picture can be presented, however, if one shows differences within the framework of shared principles and objectives. In this manner one can see that the points of difference mainly concerned means and not ends.[27]

1. *Free Government (Republicanism)*. Both parties equated free government and republicanism. The Anti-Federalists took a conservative position, however, in relying upon their reading of Montesquieu and the lessons of history to conclude that free government could function only in a small territory with a homogeneity of interests and population. Thus they believed that the Federalists projected a Constitution which was a radical innovation, contrary to a law of political science and human experience. Whereas the Federalists looked at America and glimpsed a nation, the Anti-Federalists saw a pluralistic collection of established, sovereign republics joined together for limited common purposes. In the eyes of the latter, a republican government over the whole could only evolve into a despotism enforced by a large standing army.[28] James Winthrop of Massachusetts stated this point:

The idea of an uncompounded republick, on an average one thousand miles in length, and eight hundred in breadth, and containing six millions of white inhabitants all reduced to the same standard of morals, of habits, and of laws, is in itself an absurdity, and contrary to the whole experience of mankind.[29]

That the Constitution really embraced a "consolidated" government, most Anti-Federalists were certain. To prove their point they singled out Article I, Section 8, most particularly the taxing and "necessary and proper" clauses; Article II, Section 2, which conferred military powers on the Congress and President; and the supremacy clause (Article VI, Clause 3). These provisions, they believed, when brought together, spelled consolidated power and the loss of liberty (individual rights as well as local sovereignty).

2. *Conception of Human Nature.* Just as strongly as the Federalists, most Anti-Federalists believed man to be motivated principally by self-interest. George Mason, for example, talked of "the natural lust of power so inherent in man." Patrick Henry remarked "the predominant thirst of dominion in man which has invariably and uniformly prompted rulers to abuse their power," concluding that in government "all checks founded on anything but self-love, will not avail." Robert Lansing of New York declared that the object of government "is to restrain and punish vice; and all free constitutions are formed with two views—to deter the governed from crime, and the governors from tyranny." Suspicious of man and of power, the Anti-Federalists regarded the Federalists as naive in not providing in the Constitution more adequate guards against man's avarice, ambition, and thirst for glory. Similarly, many Anti-Federalists doubted the ability of people at large to withstand being duped in their judgment of the Constitution. Thus one Pennsylvanian commented: "If it were not for the stability and attachment which time and habit give to forms of government, it would be in the power of the enlightened and aspiring few, if they should combine, at any time to destroy the best establishments, and even make the people the instruments of their own subjugation."[30]

3. *Consent of the Governed.* Being republicans, both parties subscribed to the consent of the governed as the principle of political legitimacy. Whereas Federalists insisted on establishing the Constitution on the will of the people, Anti-Federalists believed that state sovereignty, based on popular consent, demanded that a central authority rest upon the authority of the states. This view was of one piece with the notion that the Constitution was a prescription of consolidated power. For example, when Samuel Adams read the words "We the People," in the Preamble, he remarked: "As I enter the Building I stumble at the Threshold." He thought that if the government were truly to be federal, it should read, "We the States." In a similar vein, Patrick Henry declared that the phrase indicated that the Constitution established "most clearly a consoldiated government." Anti-Federalists generally believed that the American states became sovereign and independent in 1776, while many Federalists like James Wilson, relying upon a literal reading of the Declaration of Independence, saw "We the people of the United States" as the sovereign entity.[31]

On the question of representation, the Anti-Federalists believed that the popular branch of the legislature should reflect as accurately as possible the divisions and interests within the community, a fact which demanded small districts. The implementation in the Constitution of the

Madisonian principles of "filtration" and "enlargement of the sphere" in the ratio of representatives to population, was attacked as aristocratic in its tendency. It was argued that they would preclude election of men from the middle and lower orders, and, as Henry remarked, lead the common man to ask a man of influence "how he is to proceed, and for whom he must vote." The government would be impersonalized by its removal from direct contact with the people. Similarly, the Anti-Federalists feared that large districts would be to the advantage of the rich because of the need for organization. Anti-Federalists also decried the lack of a rigid scheme of rotation in office for the President and Senators and a power in state legislatures to recall Senators. These devices accorded with their conception of representation, which regarded the elected officials as instruments or delegates of the electorate. The fact that rotation in office conflicted with the democratic notion that the people should have a free choice was overcome in their minds by the desirability of precluding a professional political class.[32]

4. *Constitutional Limitations*. Anti-Federalists, even though they believed in a legislative predominance in government, criticized the Constitution not because of its separation of powers but for what they saw as violations thereof. They urged, for example, an executive council to share with the President the treaty-making and appointive powers, which the Constitution, in violation of separation of powers, stipulated that he share with the Senate.[33]

Similarly because of their jaundiced view of human nature, Anti-Federalists complained that the limitations in the Constitution were neither precise, numerous, nor detailed enough. If they had had their way, the federal constitution might have taken on the "prolixity of a legal code," which John Marshall later warned against, and which was the fate of state constitutions in the nineteenth century. Anti-Federalists were thus strong advocates of strictly defined and narrowly circumscribed power.

The most powerful criticism of the Constitution put forth by the Anti-Federalists was that it did not contain a Bill of Rights. Their arguments, already stated in some part by Mason in the Convention, made the Federalists' contention that a Bill of Rights was by definition unnecessary in a Constitution of defined, limited powers, appear weak. A Bill of Rights was necessary, the Anti-Federalists believed, not merely because the supremacy clause threatened states' bills of rights, but because government (power), whether it be by one, few, or many, is not to be trusted. Because the Constitution probably could not have been ratified without an implied understanding that a Bill of Rights would be added, it can be stated that the Anti-Federalists in effect contributed one of its most vital parts to a Constitution which they opposed.[34]

Concerning the limitations on the states in Article I, Section 10, it appears that there was no great opposition to them manifested by Anti-Federalists. The most thorough analyst of Anti-Federalist thought has concluded that "the response of the Anti-Federalists to these important limitations on the power of the states can accurately be described . . . as one of over-all approbation tempered by some doubts caused by fear that they would be applied retroactively." Similarly, although there was objection to the clause allowing the establishment of lower federal courts, there was none concerning the possibility of judicial review. In fact, a statement of Patrick Henry at the time can be taken as an endorsement of the principle of judicial review.[35]

In conclusion, it must be said that the Anti-Federalists, generally speaking, did not believe that the country was declining so rapidly that abandonment of the Articles of Confederation was indicated. For the most part their positive program of reform was the same as that of the New Jersey Plan. Jealous of preserving political power in the localities, convinced that a concentration of power at the center meant the end of liberty, they identified state sovereignty with freedom. While believing in legislative supremacy, they wished restraints and limitations to be placed on all power-wielders. Theirs was a philosophy of free government which they were convinced could only flourish when it was close to, if not identical with, the local community. They had learned well from the Revolution the lesson of liberty as identified with local self-government. As Thomas Tredwell of New York put it, the Constitution "departed widely from the principles and political faith of '76, when the spirit of liberty ran high, and danger put a curb on ambition."[36] In this light the Anti-Federalists, as opponents of innovation and guardians of the Revolutionary settlement, were conservatives; the Federalists were the radicals.

The Federalist

The eighty-five *Federalist* papers, which were written for the primary purpose of gaining ratification of the Constitution in New York, exemplify the general tendency of American political thought to elucidate principles within the framework of a polemical discussion of practical problems and specific issues. Using the pseudonym "Publius," after Publius Valerius Publioca who, according to Plutarch, saved a republic, Alexander Hamilton wrote fifty-one papers, John Jay, five papers, and James Madison, seventeen papers without assistance, nine more which are presumptively his work alone, and three in which Hamilton gave some assistance.[37]

The basic theme of the *Federalist* is the justification of constitutional representative government manifested in an extensive federal republic. Accepting the notion of equality in the possession of rights, the *Federal-*

ist turns aside from the mixed-state principle of separate representation of classes as propounded by John Adams in his writings and by Hamilton and Morris in the Convention. Finally, it assumes the natural rights philosophy and the contract theory of the state, along with the ultimate moral right of revolution, but argues less in terms of man as the bearer of abstract rights than man as moved by interest, passion, and prejudice. In short, it is concerned more with the *how* than the *why* of constitutional government. Accordingly, its principal sources appear to have been the great structural political theorists—Machiavelli, Hume, Harrington, Montesquieu—and jurists such as Coke and Blackstone. A central premise is Machiavelli's principle, seconded by Hume, that in setting up a governmental institution one should presume every man to be a knave. The emphasis of Harrington on the primacy of self-interest in man and the consequent need for counterpose in institutions, along with Montesquieu's stress on separation of powers and checks and balances, are of great importance. But perhaps more influential was David Hume, whose "science of human nature" posited reason in the service of the passions, and prescribed the following to render government effective: (1) enlistment of the passions; (2) changing the situation of men so as to make their immediate interest coincide with their duty; and (3) extending the territorial sphere to blunt the thrust of factionalism.[38]

The tone of the *Federalist* is definitely Humean in its appeal to the calm passions and in its disdain of demagogy. If the calm passions are in truth a surrogate, if not a synonym, for reason, the embodiment of a temper of moderation, and a suspension of judgment until all arguments are heard, the *Federalist* is an appeal to reason. This approach, when considered along with the focus on the concrete and the particular, puts the *Federalist* outside the pale of abstract theory, ideology, and mere propaganda. The *Federalist* thus presupposes civility; it relies upon reasoned discourse, tolerance, and temperance. It is less a public philosophy than an expression of a public spirit and attitude indispensable to free government. This is illustrated by Hamilton's remarks in the opening paper.

So numerous indeed and so powerful are the causes, which serve to give a false bias to the judgment, that we upon many occasions, see wise and good men on the wrong as well as on the right side of questions, of the first magnitude to society. This circumstance, if duly attended to, would furnish a lesson of moderation to those, who are ever so much persuaded of their being in the right, in any controversy. And a further reason for caution, in this respect, might be drawn from the reflection, that we are not always sure, that those who advocate the truth are influenced by purer principles than their antagonists. Ambition, avarice, personal animosity, party opposition, and many other motives, not more laudable than these, are apt to operate as well upon those who support as upon those who oppose the right side of a question. Were there not even these inducements to moderation, nothing could be more ill judged than that intolerant spirit, which has, at all times, characterized political parties. For, in politics as in religion, it is equally absurd to aim at making proselytes by fire and sword. Heresies in either can rarely be cured by persecution.[39]

With the same consciousness of human shortcomings, Madison listed the difficulties involved in accurately defining the principles and conclusions of political science: (1) the complexity and indistinctness of the object of study; (2) the imperfection of the organ of conception; and (3) the inadequacy of the vehicles of ideas (words). Adding to these the play of passion and self-interest in men, Madison asked: "Would it be wonderful [surprising] if under the pressure of all these difficulties, the Convention should have been forced into some deviations from that artificial structure and regular symmetry, which an abstract view of the subject might lead an ingenious theorist to bestow on a Constitution planned in his closet or in his imagination?"[40]

Hamilton, in turn, remarked the ability of *unprejudiced* men to arrive at a firm knowledge of principles. First, he talked of abstract, general principles of politics and morals, akin to those of geometry, which command the immediate assent of the mind, except where there is intruded "a defect or disorder in the organs of perception," or "some strong interest, or passion, or prejudice." In this category he listed such "maxims" as "there cannot be an effect without a cause"; "the means ought to be proportioned to the end"; "every power ought to be commensurate with its object"; and "there ought to be no limitation of a power destined to effect a purpose; which is itself incapable of limitation." Second, Hamilton talked of truths of political science, which are "direct inferences" from the above axioms, and are "so obvious in themselves, and so agreeable to the natural and unsophisticated dictates of common sense, that they challenge the assent of a sound and unbiased mind, with a degree of force and conviction almost equally irresistible." Among such theorems we might place Hamilton's emphasis on the propriety and necessity of a general power of taxation in the national government, along with the control of foreign affairs, the power to use means necessary and proper to effect the ends of government and the supremacy of national law. Third, Hamilton mentioned principles of republican government which are more strictly the lesson of human experience— truths which he stated were either unknown or only imperfectly known to the ancients. These include: "The regular distribution of power in distinct departments—the introduction of legislative balances and checks —the institution of courts composed of judges, holding their offices during good behaviour—the representation of the people in the legislature by deputies of their own election," and the "ENLARGEMENT of the ORBIT" of republican rule. Although Hamilton qualified his statements by asserting that "it cannot be pretended that the principles of moral and political knowledge have in general the same degree of certainty with those of mathematics," he added that "the obscurity is much oftener in the passions and prejudices of the reasoner than in the subject." Hamilton's intuitive-deductive approach ought not be underestimated; nonetheless, for the most part, the principles from which he, and more particularly Madison, proceeded were dictates of their experience as students of history and participant observers in politics, as well as their desire to construct an effective general government. To Hamilton experience was the "best oracle of wisdom;" to Madison it was "the oracle of truth."[41]

The common first principle of politics taught by experience to Hamilton and Madison was that man was moved less by reason than by passion and interest, less by benevolence than by self-love (a view which they shared with John Adams, Franklin, and the Anti-Federalists). Thus Madison asked: "But what is government itself but the greatest of all reflections on human nature? If men were angels, no government would be necessary. If angels were to govern men, neither external nor internal controls on government would be necessary." In a similar vein, Hamilton asked: "Why has government been instituted at all? Because the passions of men will not conform to the dictates of reason and justice without constraint." Because self-love is basic in man, self-interest is fundamental. The *Federalist*, however, distinguishes (1) between man's "immediate interests," which are generally informed by passion, and his "true interests," which are laid bare by "the mild voice of reason" and (2) between the "transient impulse" of the community and its "deliberate sense." Interest thus has a rational dimension which points to freedom, peace, and security as political ends. The rational basis of interest, in turn, assumes that passion can have a rational character. Thus man's "temporary delusion" is distinguished from his "cool and sedate reflection," a synonym for Hume's "calm passion."[42]

Because men, particularly when grouped together, generally follow immediate interests and violent passions, the *Federalist* maintains that it is reason's task to devise governmental institutions which will neutralize their effects or enlist their energy in the cause by redirection.[43] Neutralization can be effected by: (1) pitting passion against passion (e.g., ambition *v.* avarice); (2) causing passion, through a change in its objects, to check itself (e.g., ambition *v.* ambition); and (3) opposing interest to interest (e.g., counterpoise through checks and balances and enlargement of the geographic sphere of rule). Enlistment through redirection can be effected, not by conversion, but by the technique of changing the situation so that it becomes one's immediate interest to work for the public good. As Hamilton put it: "The best security for the fidelity of mankind is to make . . . interest coincide with . . . duty."[44]

The *Federalist* nonetheless is neither so naive nor so cynical as to assume that mechanical contrivances balancing and enlisting the selfish mainsprings of human action, are alone capable of effecting viable and just government. Both Hamilton and Madison, but more particularly the latter, talk of the need for "virtue" (regard for the public good) in the populace, and for the selection of able and good men as rulers. Madison summed up the point neatly when he wrote: "As there is a degree of depravity in mankind which requires a certain degree of circumspection and distrust: So there are other qualities in human nature, which justify a certain portion of esteem and confidence. Republican government presupposes the existence of these qualities in a higher degree than any other form." Hamilton echoed: "The supposition of universal venality in human nature is little less an error in political reasoning than the supposition of universal rectitude. The institution of delegated power implies that there is a portion of virtue and honor among mankind, which may be a reasonable foundation of confidence. And experience justifies the theory: It has been found to exist in the most corrupt periods of the most corrupt governments." From which it can be concluded that Madison and Hamilton were neither rigidly Hobbesian nor Pelagian* in their view of man.[45]

The Constitution is explained and justified in the *Federalist* in terms of the theory of human motivation outlined above. Within this framework the discussion turns for the most part upon the aforementioned institutional principles of political science which Hamilton saw as either unknown, or only confusedly known, to the ancients. Added to these, of course, was the American conception of federalism, which had been worked out as a compromise in the convention. A few of the principal arguments will now be considered.

1. *The Question of an Extensive Federal Republic.* In the tenth *Federalist* paper, Madison answered the principal Anti-Federalist argument that free government cannot effectively operate over a large territory. Extending his earlier remarks concerning "enlarging the sphere," he shows not merely the utility but the necessity of an extensive republic of republics in checking factionalism within the United States. He defines faction as a majority or minority of men "united and actuated by some common impulse of passion, or of interest, adverse to the rights of other citizens, or to the permanent and aggregate interests of the community." The mischiefs of faction can be cured either by removing its causes or controlling its effects. Madison disavows removal of the causes of faction as an answer because it involves either destroying liberty or giving all citizens the same opinions, passions, and interests. The

---

* A Pelagian is one who denies original sin and holds that man has perfect freedom of the will.

latter would run athwart the natural diversity of human faculties, the protection of which is the first object of government. Although religion, government, parties, and attachment to different leaders are sources of faction, "the most common and durable source . . . has been the various and unequal distribution of property." Madison speaks of creditors, debtors, landed, mercantile, monied, and manufacturing interests as dividing men "into different classes, actuated by different sentiments and views." He concludes: "The regulation of these various and interfering interests forms the principal task of modern Legislation, and involves the spirit of party and faction in the necessary and ordinary operations of Government."[46]

Because neither "enlightened statesmen" nor "moral and religious motives" can be relied upon to control faction, the control of its effects depends upon enlarging the sphere in the establishment of governmental institutions. Refinement and enlargement of public views are first effected through representation, "by passing them through the medium of a chosen body of citizens, whose wisdom may best discern the true interest of their country, and whose patriotism and love of justice, will be least likely to sacrifice it to temporary or partial considerations." Just as a representative republic is superior in this regard to a pure democracy, a large republic is superior to a smaller one. Madison admits that by enlarging the number of electors for each representative, the latter might be rendered "too little acquainted with all their local circumstances and lesser interests." But the Constitution, he believed, had struck a happy mean, with "the great and aggregate interests being referred to the national, the local and particular, to the state legislatures." His principal point, however, is that by an extension of the sphere, "you take in a greater variety of parties and interests; you make it less probable that a majority of the whole will have a common motive to invade the rights of other citizens; or if such a common motive exists, it will be more difficult for all who feel it to discover their own strength, and to act in unison with each other." The evils of faction are thus cured and free government may ensue in an extensive, representative republic comprehending many diverse interests which because of their number and the difficulties of communication are unlikely to form, singly or in combination, a majority acting to the detriment of the whole or to the rights of individuals.[47]

2. *Separation of Powers.* Madison justifies the separation of powers in the Constitution against the Anti-Federalist charge that the principle was violated by the vesting of legislative powers in the executive and vice versa, by explaining Montesquieu's doctrine as meaning that "where the *whole* power of one department is exercised by the same hands which possess the *whole* power of another department, the fundamental principles of a free constitution are subverted." Both he and Hamilton

believed that "the tendency of republican governments is to an aggran-
dizement of the legislative, at the expense of the other departments,"—
a fact requiring adequate checks to keep the departments in their constitutional spheres. He asserts: "Ambition must be made to counteract
ambition. The interest of the man must be connected with the constitutional right of the place." Dividing the legislature into two branches adds
a necessary internal check on that potentially overbearing branch. The
executive has for his defense the qualified veto; the judiciary is unmen-
tioned, but Madison's principle implies judicial power to deny validity
to acts of the other branches interfering with its defined sphere.[48]

3. *Representation.* In answering the charge of the Anti-Federalists
that the small ratio of representatives to the population would result in
an oligarchy not in sympathy with the people, Madison first expresses
his basic view of representation: "The aim of every political Constitution is or ought to be first to obtain for rulers, men who possess most
wisdom to discern, and most virtue to pursue the common good of the
society; and in the next place, to take the most effectual precautions for
keeping them virtuous, while they continue to hold their public trust."
Since the Constitution required no qualification of wealth, birth, religion,
or way of life, "every citizen whose merit may recommend him to the
esteem and confidence of his country" may be the object of popular
choice. Their fidelity to the public will be ensured by (1) recurrent
elections, (2) the generally valid presumption that because they have
been chosen they possess qualities promising "a sincere and scrupulous
regard to the nature of their engagements," (3) their sense of gratitude,
(4) their pride and vanity which attach them "to a form of government
which favors [their] pretensions," and (5) the fact that the laws they
pass will affect them as well as others. Madison emphasizes that "government is instituted no less for protection of property, than of the persons of individuals." Because "the rights of property are committed," by
the Constitution, "into the same hands with the personal rights," he
asserts, "some attention ought therefore to be paid to property in the
choice of those hands." He thinks this is effected by the fact that although "an opulent citizen" possesses but a single vote, "the respect and
consequence which he derives from his fortunate situation, very frequently guide the votes of others to the objects of his choice." In any case,
Madison is concerned throughout with justifying representative institutions which do not reflect, but blunt or enervate the thrust of interests. As such, he and the Constitution were at variance with the popular
revolutionary belief that the representative must be the instrument by
which the instructions of his constituents are presented and acted
upon.[49]

Hamilton's view of representation proceeded from his premise that
"the idea of an actual representation of all classes of the people by per-

sons of each class is altogether visionary." Where elections are free the representative body will inevitably be composed of landholders, merchants (the natural representative of manufacturers, and artisans, as well as commercial interests), and men of the learned professions. Justice will result from the fact that the latter will act as impartial arbiters between the first two. By men of the learned professions Hamilton most probably meant lawyers. If this is so, we can conclude that he saw lawyers as the instruments of justice in the promotion of the common good in the legislature as well as the guardians of property. The Hamilton of the *Federalist* papers, unlike the Hamilton of the Convention, does not talk in terms of representation of the many and the few but, in effect, imputes to the learned professions either an exemption from the ordinary pull of self-interest, at least when the other two classes are at odds, or an identification of their immediate interest with the general good.[50]

4. *The Executive.* Hamilton insists that "energy in the executive is a leading character in the definition of good government." Its ingredients are "unity," "duration," "an adequate provision for its support," and "competent powers." Unity makes for concentrated responsibility and accountability and a nondiffused focus of public censure. Duration is a condition of personal firmness in the execution of powers and stability in administration. Hamilton sees the executive as a guardian of the people's interests, particularly when they are "at variance with their inclinations." Duration, of a considerable extent, "is necessary to give to the officer himself the inclination and the resolution to act his part well, and to the community time and leisure to observe the tendency of his measures," while reeligibility "is necessary to enable the people, when they see reason to approve of his conduct, to continue him in the station, in order to prolong the utility of his talents and virtues, and to secure to the government, the advantage of permanency in a wise system of administration." Restriction to office for a limited period "would be a diminution of the inducements to good behaviour." The incentives of the desire of reward and the love of fame would be lacking as would "the best security for the fidelity of mankind," which is "to make their interest coincide with their duty." Then, too, the community would be deprived of the experience gained by the chief magistrate, particularly in time of emergency, and a principle of instability would be intruded.[51]

Possessing unity, duration, and the financial support necessary for independence, the executive can vigorously exercise the powers which are vested in him by the Constitution, to effect external security, to prevent through the veto unwise acts of the legislature, to develop effective administration, and to promote public good and order. Although Hamilton's voice is somewhat muted in comparison with both his earlier and later remarks, it is still evident in the *Federalist* that he believes the executive must be the principle of vigorous leadership.

5. *The Judiciary.* To Hamilton, "the judiciary, from the nature of its functions, will always be the least dangerous to the political rights of the constitution," because it has "neither Force nor Will, but merely judgment; and must ultimately depend upon the aid of the executive arm even for the efficacy of its judgments." The judiciary must therefore be independent that it might fulfill the function of "an intermediate body between the people and the legislature," in order, among other things, to keep the latter within the limits assigned to their authority.[52]

Because the Constitution is fundamental law, the judges, in the course of their duty, must prefer it to contravening statutes. Hamilton justifies judicial review in the following train of reasoning.

1. Every act of a delegated authority, contrary to the tenor of the commission under which it is exercised, is void.
2. No legislative act therefore contrary to the constitution can be valid.
3. It is not otherwise to be supposed that the constitution could intend to enable the representatives of the people to substitute their *will* to that of their constituents.
4. The interpretation of the laws is the proper and peculiar province of the courts.
5. A constitution. is in fact, and must be, regarded by the judges as a fundamental law.
6. It therefore belongs to them to ascertain its meaning as well as the meaning of any particular act proceeding from the legislative body. [In case of conflict, they must prefer the former.][53]

Hamilton is clear that the courts alone determine *conclusively* the question of the constitutionality of laws. By imputing *judgment* to them and *will* to the political branches, he is able to see the judiciary as unbiased. How far was this power to extend? Hamilton mentions certain specified exceptions in the Constitution to legislative authority, such as the bill of attainder and *ex post facto* clauses. He goes on to say: "Limitations of this kind can be preserved in practice no other way than through the medium of the courts of justice; whose duty it must be to declare all acts contrary to the manifest tenor of the constitution void." The statement is equivocal in that the specific limitations mentioned are definite and precise, while the phrase "manifest tenor of the constitution" offers room for ranging more widely.[54]

The Federalist: *A Split Personality?*

Within a framework of general agreement there are differences in emphases between Hamilton and Madison in the *Federalist* which have brought forth the claim in recent years that the papers evidence a split personality.[55] If we take the positions expounded by the two men in the Convention as truly indicative of their views, we can conclude first of all that their respective contributions to the *Federalist* represent modifications thereof, and that these contributions were bound at some points to reflect, at least in terms of relative emphasis, their true differences.

It has already been mentioned that although both men were skeptical concerning human nature and warned against the identification of certitude with certainty, Hamilton viewed political science as ultimately based on intuited principles which the few men who are unbiased can discern, while Madison appears to have adhered almost exclusively to principles rooted in experience. Then, too, although both men accepted and acted upon the Humean psychology, embodying what Madison called "inventions of prudence," Hamilton stressed more the enlistment and redirection of passion and interest, while Madison stressed balancing, offsetting, and neutralizing them.[56]

Both men accepted and defended the federal principle of the Constitution. But while Madison saw federalism as an instrument for the establishment of a power equilibrium among the states, Hamilton emphasized it as an instrument for the establishment of a strong national government. In other words, Madison focused more upon federalism as a balancing factor, Hamilton focused upon it as an empowering factor.[57]

Similarly in regard to the principle of separation of powers, Madison tended to stress the power balance between branches, whereas Hamilton, while welcoming the broad grants of power to the legislature, saw the principle mainly as a means of limiting the legislature in the interest of the other two branches.[58]

Both men agreed on the need for a national government stronger than that of the Articles of Confederation. But while Madison argued that the Constitution proposed change which "consists much less in the addition of NEW POWERS to the union, than in the invigoration of its ORIGINAL POWERS," Hamilton saw those changes as embodying powers commensurate to the end of an "unconfined authority, as to all those objects" entrusted to the central government.[59]

Most significantly, they differed on the question of the nature of the Union to be established by the Constitution. Hamilton saw the Constitution, if adopted, as established by "the consent of the people," thus precluding the notion that "a party to *a compact* has a right to revoke that *compact.*" The authority of the union was extended "to the persons of the citizens—the only proper objects of government." On the other hand, Madison's view on this point reflects the fundamental ambiguity of the Constitution itself. It was not the undifferentiated people of the nation as a whole which established ratification, and thus served as the principal, but the people of "the distinct and independent states to which they respectively belong." Ratification was thus not "a national but a federal act."[60]

Madison's language can be interpreted in two different ways, depending upon one's predispositions. Many proponents of the South, before the Civil War, held that the Constitution was a compact, the principals of which were the people of the separate states, who, consequently, could withdraw consent when the terms of the agreement were not met. On the other hand, the nationalist position, as put forth by Chief Justice John Marshall in *McCulloch v. Maryland*, in 1823, is based on a distinction between the form and essence of ratification. Speaking of the people, Marshall wrote that "when they act, they act in the States. But the measures they adopt do not, on that account, cease to be the measures of the people of the nation, or become the measures of the State governments."[61]

The *Federalist* thus not only is marked by different emphases on some significant points but by ambiguity and equivocation. This has allowed men to use it to give substance to their differing positions on such fundamental points as the nature of the union and the conflicting constitutional doctrines of nationalism and dual federalism. But this is due primarily to the fact that the Constitution itself is ambiguous and susceptible, in its general principles, of interpretation along different lines.[62] The result has been twofold. First, American political thought developed principally on dualistic lines and second, political differences reflected in political thought have tended to be expressed in the rhetoric of the law. As the Constitution became an accepted symbol of union, its generality and ambiguity allowed contending parties to claim an undeniable basis for their positions in the fundamentl law. Thus American political arguments were foreordained, for the most part, to be constitutional arguments.

Conclusions

No systematic theory was formulated during the period of constitution-making which began with the Revolution and culminated in the work of the Philadelphia Convention. Nevertheless, political science was enriched by the attack upon concrete problems and the writings issuing therefrom. The period began in a popular psychology which (1) was suspicious of centralized power and jealous of local prerogatives, (2) regarded as next to certain the impossibility of an extensive, free republic, (3) conceived of government as a ruler-ruled relationship, (4) generally identified the members of the lower legislative house as alone representative of the people, (5) was greatly distrustful of executive power, (6) strongly supported annual elections and rotation in office, and (7) tended to envision society in terms of class divisions. Upon the changes in, and the development of, state constitutions during the period, and most particularly, upon the ratification of the Federal Constitution of 1787, it was evident that significant changes had come about. These included: (1) replacement of the notion of government as the ruler-ruled relationship with the notion of rulers as representative of the sovereign people; (2) the consequent full realization that a constitution, as Madison observed, was no longer to be seen as a charter of liberty granted by power, but as a charter of power granted by liberty; (3) the extension of the term "the people" to include all classes; (4) the consequent abandonment of the notion of the class-based mixed constitution and the broadening of the concept of representation of the people to include the upper legislative house and the executive; (5) the replacement of the notion of the people at large by the conception of the people comprising many and conflicting group interests; (6) the drawing of a clear distinction between a constituent assembly (Convention) and a legislative assembly; (7) the qualification of the idea of republican government as rooted in "virtue" by the notion of enlistment of "self-interest" to the cause; (8) the acceptance of the establishment of an extensive republic bearing directly upon the people, with specific powers to make laws defined as supreme over the state constitutions and laws; (9) the articulation of a new conception of "federalism" fusing elements theretofore considered as separate and antagonistic; (10) the circumscription of legislative power on the basis of an increased suspicion of majority rule; (11) the abandonment of annual elections as a general norm and the diminution of the rotation principle; (12) the enhancement of executive power and authority; and (13) the establishment by popular approval of a federal constitution capable of growth and adaptation by amendment and the interpretation of general principles.*

---

* A word must be said concerning the motivation of the Convention Fathers and the thesis of Charles Beard, the most influential historian and student of government in the early twentieth century, whose interpretation was accepted without significant challenge for almost forty years. Rejecting the naive nineteenth-century conception of the Constitution as the will of the undifferentiated people and the product of disinterested patriots, Beard, pursuing Madison's resolution of society into conflicting interests, but focusing upon the economic motive, concluded that the Constitution was created by four groups of personal interests adversely affected under the Articles of Confederation—money, public securities, manufactures, trading and shipping. He concluded that the Constitution was thus an *economic document* designed to protect property interests through the vital powers to tax, regulate commerce and dispose of western lands, and the prohibitions upon the states to issue paper money and impair the obligation of contracts. He further concluded that because the Constitution withdrew these powers from popular majorities and established a viable separation of powers and checks and balances, it was undemocratic in essence. Aside from the fact that Beard's analysis and conclusions have been recently strongly challenged on factual grounds, it can be said that to argue that the Constitution was in the personal economic interest of the fathers does not warrant a conclusion that it was formulated solely or even primarily for that reason. This would involve a denial that the principles of ordered liberty, internal peace, stability in the institution and transference of property, along with the obligation of contract, due process of law, and external security, can be vindicated and acted upon on grounds of the common good, apart from per-

sonal gain. Carried to its logical conclusion, an unqualified economic interpretation leads to the proposition that if it is in one's selfish economic interest to opt for a principle, one's choice of such principle is the result of economic interest. Were this true how could one explain the goodly number of men who had the same economic interests and vigorously opposed the Constitution? Just as it is fallacious to conceive of the fathers, who well knew that reason in most men is reducible to rationalization in service of selfish passions, desires and interests, as disinterested spirits, so it is fallacious to conclude that one must be a disinterested spirit to proceed from patriotic motives. In fact, because the motives of men, generally speaking, are mixed and irreducible one to the other, and because the Founding Fathers were men of intellect, character, dedication, and vision, it is incumbent upon the student of political ideas, until it is solidly proven to the contrary, to assume that they meant what they said and were neither disguising nor rationalizing selfish designs in the ideological garb of public purpose. In this view the vitally interested fathers believed that there was not merely a common interest in, but an absolute need for, a viable union. Thus envisaged, the Constitution stands out as a *political document*, a framework of order and a vehicle of change, allocating and delimiting powers and establishing offices, to the end that the common purposes proclaimed in the preamble could be realized. Beard's work is *An Economic Interpretation of the Constitution* (New York, 1913). He has been challenged by Robert E. Brown, *Charles Beard and the Constitution* (Princeton, 1956), and Forrest McDonald, *We the People* (Chicago, 1958). See also Lee Benson, *Turner and Beard—American Historical Writing Reconsidered* (Glencoe, Ill., 1960).

NOTES

1. *Notes of Debates in the Federal Convention of 1787 Reported by James Madison*, reprint of C. C. Tansill edition (Athens, Ohio, 1966), p. 194. Hereinafter cited as *Notes*. All abbreviations in the original text are expanded in my quotations thereof, and archaic spelling is modernized.

2. *Ibid.*, p. 447.

3. *Ibid.*, pp. 653–654. See also Roland Bainton, "The Appeal to Reason in the American Constitution," in Conyers Read (ed.), *The Constitution Reconsidered* (New York, 1938), pp. 121–130. For recent treatments of the ideas of the fathers, see Paul Eidelberg, *The Philosophy of the American Constitution* (New York, 1968) and David G. Smith, *The Convention and the Constitution* (New York, 1965).

4. John P. Roche, "The Founding Fathers: A Reform Caucus in Action," *American Political Science Review* (March, 1962), LVI, 799–816.

5. *Notes*, pp. 130–132, 134, 152.

6. *Ibid.*, pp. 135, 138, 175.

7. *Ibid.*, pp. 251, 233, 234, 235.

8. *Ibid.*, pp. 323, 306.

9. *Ibid.*, pp. 244, 271.

10. *Ibid.*, pp. 287, 40, 42, 48, 74.

11. Ibid., pp. 85, 61.

12. *Ibid.*, pp. 518, 287, 97–98, 74.

13. James Madison to Edmund Randolph, April 8, 1787, reprinted in Jonathan Elliot (ed.), *Debates of the Adoption of the Federal Constitution* (Philadelphia, 1937, 5 vols.), V, 107; The Virginia Plan can be found in *Notes*, pp. 30–33.

14. *Notes*, pp. 74, 75–76.

15. *Ibid.*, p. 76.

16. *Ibid.*, pp. 40, 194.

17. *Ibid.*, pp. 327, 79.

18. *Ibid.*, p. 371.

19. *Ibid.*, pp. 39, 49, 308–309, 56, 371.

20. *Ibid.*, pp. 190, 630.

21. *Ibid.*, pp. 118–121.

22. *Ibid.*, p. 294.

23. *Ibid.*, pp. 340, 341, 343, 305, 342.

24. *Ibid.*, pp. 348, 352, 350–351.

25. Jackson Turner Main, *The Anti-Federalists* (Chapel Hill, 1961), pp. xi–xii, 249, 252. For treatments of the Anti-Federalist cause and the movement for ratification, see also Cecelia M. Kenyon (ed.), *The Anti-Federalists* (Indianapolis, 1966), Robert A. Rutland, *The Ordeal of the Constitution* (Norman, Okla., 1965), Wood, *op. cit.*, pp. 519–562, and Cecelia M. Kenyon, "Men of Little Faith: The Anti-Federalists on the Nature of Representative Government," *William and Mary Quarterly*, XII, 3rd Ser. (Jan., 1955), 3–43.

26. Main, *op. cit.*, pp. 263–281.

27. See the discussion of points of agreement in the introductory essay by Cecelia Kenyon in her edition of *The Anti-Federalists*, pp. xxvi–xxix.

28. See the discussion in Wood, *op. cit.*, pp. 499–501.

29. James Winthrop, "The Letters of Agrippa" (Dec. 3, 1787), in Kenyon, *The Anti-Federalists*, p. 134. For a full discussion of Anti-Federalist objections, see Main, *op. cit.*, Chapters 6 and 7.

30. Kenyon, "Men of Little Faith," p. 14; Kenyon, *The Anti-Federalists*, p. 4.

31. Samuel Adams to R. H. Lee, Dec. 3, 1787, quoted in Main, *op. cit.*, p. 122; Henry's quote is cited in Kenyon, *The Anti-Federalists*, p. 239.

32. Kenyon, "Men of Little Faith," pp. 10–13, 28–29.

33. Kenyon, "Men of Little Faith," p. 42.

34. *Ibid.*, pp. 35–36. For specific arguments on the point, see Kenyon, *The Anti-Federalists*, pp. 46–47, 54–59, 98–99, 120–122, 141, 152–160, 193–233, 363, 411–413.

35. Kenyon, "Men of Little Faith," p. 31, 32, 30.

36. Quoted in Kenyon, *The Anti-Federalists*, p. 399.

37. *Plutarch's Lives* (New York, Modern Library ed.; undated), pp. 117–130; concerning the authorship of the papers, see J. E. Cooke (ed.), *The Federalist* (Middletown, Conn., 1961), pp. xx–xxx, and Douglass Adair, "The Authorship of the Disputed Federalist Papers," *William and Mary Quarterly*, I, 3rd Ser. (1944), pp. 97–122, 235–265. The Cooke edition of the *Federalist* is used throughout the treatment above.

38. For discussions of *The Federalist* see Gottfried Dietze, *The Federalist: A Classic on Federalism and Free Government* (Baltimore, 1960); Martin Diamond, "Democracy and *The Federalist*," *American Political Science Review*, LIII (March, 1959), 52–68; James P. Scanlon, "The Federalist and Human Nature," *The Review of Politics* (Oct., 1959), 657–677; Maynard Smith, "Reason, Passion and Political Freedom in *The Federalist*," *The Journal of Politics* (August, 1960), 525–544; and Benjamin F. Wright, "*The Federalist* on the Nature of Political Man," *Ethics*, LIX (1949), 1–31.

39. *The Federalist*, No. 1, pp. 4–5.

40. *Ibid.*, No. 37, pp. 235–238.

41. *Ibid.*, No. 31, pp. 194–195; No. 9, pp. 51–52; No. 15, p. 96; No. 20, p. 128.

42. *Ibid.*, No. 51, p. 349; No. 15, p. 96; No. 6, p. 31; No. 42, p. 283; No. 71, pp. 482–483. See the discussion in Smith, *op. cit.*, pp. 527–529.

43. Concerning an assembly's greater proneness to passion, see Madison's remarks in *ibid.*, No. 58, pp. 395–396.

44. *Ibid.*, No. 72, p. 488.

45. *Ibid.*, No. 56, p. 378; No. 76, 513–514.

46. *Ibid.*, No. 10, pp. 57, 59.

47. *Ibid.*, No. 10, pp. 60, 61, 62, 63, 64.

48. *Ibid.*, No. 47, pp. 325–326; No. 49, p. 341; No. 51, p. 349.

49. *Ibid.*, No. 57, pp. 384, 385, 386; No. 54, p. 370.

50. *Ibid.*, No. 35, pp. 219, 220–221.

51. *Ibid.*, No. 70, pp. 471, 472; No. 71, p. 482; No. 72, pp. 487, 488.

52. *Ibid.*, No. 78, pp. 522–523, 525.

53. *Ibid.*, No. 78, pp. 524–525.

54. *Ibid.*, No. 78, p. 524.

55. Alpheus T. Mason, "The Federalist—A Split Personality," *American Historical Review*, LVII (1952), 625–643; Dietze, *op. cit.*, pp. 265–275; Adair, *op. cit.* But see to the contrary, Clinton Rossiter, *Alexander Hamilton and the Constitution* (New York, 1964), p. 58.

56. *The Federalist*, No. 51, p. 349.

57. Dietze, *op. cit.*, pp. 268–269; Mason, *op. cit.*, pp. 639–640.

58. Dietze, *op. cit.*, pp. 269–270; Mason, *op. cit.*, p. 641.

59. *The Federalist*, No. 45, p. 314; No. 23, p. 150; Mason, *op. cit.*, p. 641.

60. *Ibid.*, No. 23, p. 146; No. 15, p. 95; No. 39, p. 254; Mason, *op. cit.*, pp. 639–640.

61. Wheaton, 316, 402 (1819); Dietze, *op cit.*, pp. 261–262.

62. Dietze, *op. cit.*, pp. 273–275.

Chapter 11

AN AMERICAN SCIENCE OF POLITICS AND LAW

The government most conformable to nature is that which best agrees with the humor and disposition of the people in whose favor it is established.

MONTESQUIEU

In 1787 there was formed in Philadelphia a Society for Political Enquiries, with Benjamin Franklin (its president) and Thomas Paine as its principal originators. The charter, written by Paine, proclaimed that inquiry into political subjects was most important to Americans because their habitual disposition to look to Europe for their "laws . . . opinions and . . . manners" had brought them to retain "with undistinguished reverence" the "errors" of European nations, as well as their "improvements," thus blending "with [their] public institutions the policy of dissimilar countries." Having effected political independence, the American Revolution will be complete only when Americans have freed themselves, "no less from the influence of foreign prejudices than from the fetters of foreign powers." In effect, the charter asked for an intellectual, or more precisely, a psychological act of independence, by which Americans would break "through the bounds in which a dependent people have been accustomed to think and act," and thus "adopt those maxims of policy" suited to their "new situation." This entailed redirecting "the associated labours of learned and ingenious men" from "objects of subordinate importance" to "the arduous and complicated science of government," a pursuit which "has been generally left to the care of practical politicians, or the speculations of individual theorists." The society was thus established for "mutual improvement in the knowledge of government, and for the advancement of political science."[1]

The two related notes sounded in the charter, the need for an in-

dependent American mind reflected in a citizenry educated in republicanism, and for the articulation of a true science of government, were
strongly stressed by others in the infant republic. George Washington, in
his will, lamented that young men had to be sent abroad for their
education, where they contracted "not only habits of dissipation and
extravagance, but principles unfriendly to Republican government and
the true and genuine liberties of mankind." Washington wanted a national university established which, among other things, would stress
"acquiring knowledge in the principles of politics and good government."[2]
Similarly, James Wilson in 1790 declared:

The foundations of political truth have been laid but lately: the genuine
science of government, to no human science inferior in importance, is indeed,
but in its infancy: and the reason of this can be easily assigned. In the whole
annals of the Transatlantic world, it will be difficult to point out a single
instance of its legitimate institution: I will go further, and say, that among all
the political writers of the Transatlantic world, it will be difficult to point out
a single model of its unbiased theory.[3]

Nathaniel Chipman (1752–1843), Chief Justice of Vermont, wrote in
reference to the American governments in 1793: "We ought to know
their principles, to study well their tendency, and to be able both in
theory and practice to exclude all foreign principles."[4] And, in 1798,
Jesse Root (1736–1822), Chief Justice of Connecticut, stated: "Let us,
Americans then, duly appreciate our own government, laws, and manners, and be what we profess—an independent nation—and not plume
ourselves upon being humble imitators of foreigners, at home and in our
own country. But let our manners in all respects be characteristic of the
spirit and principles of our independence."[5]

The idea of a science of politics, arrived at through the experimental
method, had been tied, as we have seen, in the thought of the most
influential Founding Fathers, to the "science of human nature," propounded principally by David Hume and Adam Smith. John Adams,
James Madison, and Alexander Hamilton saw "experience," as evidenced in history and the actions of men, as the norm, and believed that
men had progressed to the knowledge of certain psychological, structural, and operational principles whose implementation could best work
to ensure liberty, justice, and order. Adams, who was influenced more
by Harrington and Smith than by Hume, prescribed the principle of
balance either between governmental branches, or between classes, depending upon the moral and socioeconomic state of the country, as well
as the manipulative use of the emulative propensity in man; Hamilton
emphasized a strong corporate will, the enlistment of the passions, and
a concentration of power; and Madison pointed to the balancing of interests and institutional devices to refine opinion and blunt the thrust of

group interests. All three men could follow the Humean depreciation of reason just short of declaring moral norms to be merely subjective emotional reactions. Although they fondly embraced experimentalism, they were as wary of falling prey to its Humean philosophic source—skepticism—as the Puritan fathers were of Antinomianism. As a consequence, theirs was no "value-free" political science; they stressed with varying emphases the twin ends of liberty and the public good. The philosophy of natural law, in its classical or modern form, or a confusion of both, loomed always in the background of their studies, indicating objectives, standards, and criteria of relevance.

The purified American political science called for by the Philadelphia Society, Chipman, and Wilson ostensibly would have regarded aspects of the political science of Madison, but more particularly, Adams and Hamilton, as derived from European experience, social conditions, and prejudices, and thus, in good part, inapplicable to American republicanism.

The type of studies contemplated by Franklin's Society embraced "essays, facts, or observations . . . or political queries." This most probably included not merely historical studies and papers attacking particular problems but statistical surveys and projections, like Franklin's demographic study of 1752, "Observations Concerning the Increase of Mankind."[6] It is also likely that the approach was to be similar to that pursued by Franklin's American Philosophical Society, which undertook "philosophical experiments to let Light into the Nature of Things . . . increase the Power of Man over Matter, and multiply the conveniences and Pleasures of Life." And yet, assuming a possible behavioral tendency in the Society's orientation, there can be no doubt that all of its inquiries were to have been made on the assumption of freedom as the individual value and democratic republicanism as its governmental counterpart.[7]

The Society for Political Enquiries never realized its promise; with it died whatever desire existed to construct a behavioral or problem-oriented political science. Instead, Americans were to use the Declaration of Independence, the Constitution, and other state papers, along with *The Federalist,* as their principal sources. By identifying political science with free government, and free government with essential American practice, early American study of politics tended to merge the "is" with the "ought." It taught maxims and principles as intuitively or experientially derived, and after allowing for residues of European "prejudice" and "bias," it found verification in existing institutions and practice.[8]

It was in this setting that James Wilson and Nathaniel Chipman attempted an elucidation of the principles of American government as a manifestation of natural public law. In their approach experimentalism was relegated to an ancillary position; the conception of the clash of interests as the subject matter of politics and the previous preoccupation with structural forms were overshadowed by the explanation of government in terms of juridical principles. Both men, but most particularly Wilson, drew on the strain of influence in American political thought exerted by the Anglican, Richard Hooker, to explain man as a social and political animal under cosmic law. Classical natural law was merged with the teachings of the Scottish commonsense school, to overcome Humean skepticism and provide a philosophical basis for popular sovereignty by showing the interdependence of liberty and law. Sensing the tendency to political hedonism inherent in a revolutionary emphasis on liberty, the two jurists pointed up the necessity of a sense of responsibility and obligation as the condition of democratic government. Seeking to purify the science of government and, more particularly, jurisprudence, of alien residues, the natural target of both men was Blackstone.

Chipman, a veteran of the Continental Army who had experienced the hardships of Valley Forge, wrote, in 1793, *Sketches of the Principles of Government*. Although he was a Federalist and admirer of Alexander Hamilton, his book was held in high esteem by both Jefferson and Madison.[9] Believing that the revolution in America had opened "new avenues to the science of government," a science which consists neither in "arbitrary" principles nor "the reveries of metaphysics." Chipman proposed "to find the leading Principles of Government in the laws of social nature, and to trace them into exercise, in the establishment of civil institutions." He saw man as (1) a creature of God whose law is prescribed in man's nature; (2) a social and political animal; and (3) a person to be viewed not merely in light of what he was or is, but what he can be by improvement, and is intended by the Deity to become. On this basis he found that "the pursuit and attainment of happiness, is agreeable to the laws of man's nature, and dictated by them." As men develop in knowledge, in the extension of their faculties, powers, and mental comprehension, they extend their human associations. The "natural history of the human mind," he suggested, can be studied experimentally by observing man in various stages of development. Such observation precludes celebration of the primitive stage as one of virtue and happiness. In fact, man's possession of a moral sense, whose promptings are implemented by reason, attests to his social nature.[10]

Because man is a political animal, Chipman contended, Thomas Paine and Locke were in error in holding that man surrenders certain rights when he establishes the state. Indeed, Chipman admitted, man "gives up" the right of judging in his own cause; but this is a "juvenile right" which has no meaning when he comes to political, and thus natural maturity. Chipman held that "to give up the performance of any action, which is forbidden by the laws of moral and social nature, cannot be deemed a sacrifice." It follows that "all of the rights of man are relative to his social nature," and "exist only in a coincidence with the rights of the whole, in a well-ordered state of society and civil government."[11]

Chipman retained the concept of the social contract as constitutive of the state, but as we have seen,* unknowingly rendered it superfluous by denying the necessity of a contractual "consideration." More importantly, he contended that the "laws of social nature" are the basis of all legitimate government, which must promote the good of the whole, while not violating the natural rights of man. Applying his historical approach, he talked of progressive stages of human development, which issue in the various forms of government. He believed that "certain degrees of improvement, in science, in morals, in manners, and sentiments, will tend to an abolition of every other form of government; and to the establishment of Democratic Republics, in which alone, . . . natural principles can have any general operation."[12]

The American Constitution, as Chipman saw it, is of such kind. It is based on a science of natural principles of government centered on the revolutionary precept "that all legitimate government is founded in the rights of the people; that it is an institution for their convenience and happiness." The European political science, which imputed all power and right to rulers, and nothing but duty to subjects, is supplanted by a political science which sees at the base of government, man as a bearer of both rights and duties. Most particularly is the American Constitution unique because it can be amended to allow for the progress and improvement of its citizenry. As a result, it alone is based on true principles of natural law.[13]

Turning to the question of principles of legislation and the common law, Chipman lamented the fact that the American law student had available to him only Blackstone's *Commentaries.* That treatise, he thought, is excellent as an exposition of the elements of the British system, but is in good part inapplicable to America, and inadequate in critical analysis. Chipman was concerned with the question of the moral obligation to obey law. He found Blackstone's distinctions between offenses which are *mala in se,* avoidance of which is binding in conscience, and those which are merely *mala prohibita,* acts having reference to conscience only insofar as they direct submission to a penalty in case of their breach, as owing to the confusion of principles in the British Constitution. Blending Montesquieu's relativism with the concept of the moral sense expounded by the Scottish philosopher, Lord Kames, Chipman wrote: "Those actions are right in any society, constituted upon natural principles, which are conformable to the principles and nature of that

* In Chapter 9.

society." It follows that "if laws command that, which is absolutely indifferent to the state, they deviate from the true spirit and principles of legislation in a free government," whereas when they conform, "they are strictly binding on the consciences of men." British law has erected crimes "upon actions wholly indifferent to society," such as those favoring a particular class or supporting a monopoly. "In such cases, unable to find any moral restraint, men learn to make a distinction [such as Blackstone's], between what is morally, and what is only politically wrong."[14]

It is clear that Chipman sought to find a basis for rendering *all* law morally binding. He believed that this can be achieved only by a government which is rooted in "natural" principles. To justify this he posited three levels of principles of natural law. First, he mentioned principles which dictate duties and bind all men independent of social relations or degree of development. Contrary to Blackstone, he saw these as very few in number, embracing reverence to God and self-preservation, infractions of which are alone *mala in se*. Second, Chipman talked of unchanging principles and relations common to men in all societies and governments. Third, he wrote, "in the natural course of human improvement" arise new principles and relations which vary according to the degrees of progress. These also are "laws of nature, and natural duties," and thus morally obligatory.[15]

The concept of natural law as that conforming to man's nature in its stages of development was Chipman's critical tool. With it he measured and found wanting governments based on the principles of fear and honor, neither of which "have any principal regard to the happiness of the citizens, or to the interests of morality." The democratic republic alone is "uncontrovertibly good" because its principles dictate those laws, and those only, which are adapted to the present state of men and manners, and tend to social improvement, which are influenced by a sense of moral obligation, and sanctioned by the laws of nature, not of savage solitary nature, but of social nature, in its improved and improvable state.[16]

On this basis, Chipman turned aside from his fellow Federalists John Adams and Hamilton and dismissed the class-based mixed state and the British Constitution. He agreed with Montesquieu that a democratic republic, such as the United States, must be based on the principle of *virtue* (dedication to the public weal) and cannot allow for the intervention of *fear* or *honor*.[17]

Finally, Chipman called for "a system of laws applicable to our governments, and a train of reasoning congenial to their principles." Although years may be necessary for its completion, "genius is not wanting in America," and "he who shall only prepare the rudiments, will deserve highly of his country."[18]

It is interesting to observe that the first attempt to restate the common law in America, along lines called for by Chipman, ended, in effect, in the realization of a tendency implicit in his thesis. The restatement by Judge Root of Connecticut, in 1798, of that state's common law, ended up by equating it with the law of nature and thus assimilating the "is" to the "ought." English common law, on this view, insofar as it derives from feudalism, is alien to American experience and the American spirit.[19]

Three years before Chipman wrote, James Wilson, who was a member of the Society for Political Enquiries, a justice of the U.S. Supreme Court, and like Chipman a member of the Federalist party, gave a series of lectures on government and law in Philadelphia. In a key passage he identified the elements which he saw standing in the way of a true science of man and of government.

Despotism, by an artful use of "superiority" in politics, and scepticism, by an artful use of "ideas" in metaphysics, have endeavoured . . . to destroy all true liberty, and sound philosophy. By their baneful effects, the science of man and the science of government have been poisoned to their very foundations.[20]

Wilson attempted to solve the related problems of "scepticism" and "despotism" by joining the metaphysics of Hooker with the common-sense psychology of the Scottish philosopher, Thomas Reid.[21] He believed that only by overcoming the subjectivism implicit in the two elements could the American principles of popular sovereignty, republicanism, and representation be vindicated, and the science of man and government placed on a communicable foundation in truth.

Wilson pointed to Locke as the source from which issued the unacceptable Humean identification of reality with "ideas"* and the equally unacceptable later identification by Joseph Priestley of "ideas" with matter. Locke was wrong in not admitting that we directly perceive objects which become the measure of truth. This is a first fact of consciousness, an intuition made certain "by the constitution of our nature." The first principles of being and of morality are likewise self-evident, because directly intuited, and are called by Wilson "common sense." Reason subserves these principles and inclinations by drawing conclusions therefrom and applying them to particular circumstances. Just as the perception of moral principles is not to be identified with reason, in the sense of comparison of ideas, so is it not to be identified with utility. Even savages apprehend the *"communes notitiae"* (common notions, or first principles of morality), although their application of

* "Ideas" to Hume have validity only if capable of reduction to discrete impressions of sensation and/or impressions of reflection. In either case there is no proof of the reality of an extramental universe, or of the self.

them "is often extremely irrational and absurd." The sharing of common first principles thus provides the moral basis for community and its articulation in law.[22]

On the basis of this refutation of scepticism and assertion of an objective basis for morality and law, Wilson turned to Hooker's metaphysical teaching, proclaiming: "Order, proportion, and fitness pervade the universe. Around us, we see; within us, we feel; above us, we admire a rule, from which deviation cannot, or should not, or will not be made." Using Hooker's formulation of Aquinas' division of law, Wilson talked of (1) the eternal law of God, from whence all direction flows, (2) the celestial law, which pertains to purely spiritual beings, (3) laws of nature, which inform physical and irrational creation, (4) the law for man in his present state, which is known through reason and conscience. The latter, as pronounced in Scripture, is revelation; as addressed to men through the moral sense and reason, it is the law of nature; as addressed to political societies it is the law of nations. Finally, (5) there is human positive law which applies the principles and conclusions of natural law to particular circumstances. All law ultimately is related to the eternal law; none is autonomous. Its divine injunction is "Let man pursue his own perfection and happiness." Its fundamental maxims are: "no injury should be done," and "a lawful engagement, voluntarily made, should be faithfully fulfilled." The first principles of the law of nature are alone immutable; because man is capable of improvement, the law of nature is "progressive in its operations and effects." Similarly, one looks not to a primitive stage for norms; instead "it is but candid to consider human nature in her improved, and not in her most rude or depraved forms." Finally, Wilson broke completely with the theological voluntarism of his Calvinist forebears by proclaiming that since God "is the author of our constitution; he cannot but command or forbid such things as are necessarily agreeable or disagreeable to this very constitution. He is under the glorious necessity of not contradicting himself."[23]

On this philosophic basis, Wilson proceeded to attack the main obstacle to a true science of government and law—the voluntaristic and despotic use of the notion, "superiority." The Blackstonian conception of law as a "rule of action which is prescribed by some superior, and which the inferior is bound to obey," was his principal target. He agreed that the definition is relevant to divine law (natural law and revelation), but he saw it as completely inapplicable to human (positive) law. Central to the question was the issue of political obligation. Relying again on Hooker, Wilson insisted that in reference to positive law, obligation rests on consent. He declared: "If a man cannot bind himself, no human authority can bind him. . . . The consequence necessarily is, that if a man can be bound by any human authority, it must be by himself." Men, who by nature are equal in regard to rights, are destined to live under political rule in society. But since government exists to secure and to enlarge the exercise of the natural rights of its members, their consent is required. Human laws are not the commands of a superior but the application of natural law principles to particular circumstances. The dichotomy superior/inferior is a residue of the "divine right" concept of rulership which is not only alien to America but contrary to natural law.[24]

Wilson went on to trace the course of the consensual principle in the form and order of American government and law, which he saw as based on "the just and genuine principles of society." The Constitution, as reflective of natural public law, embraces the revolutionary principle of popular sovereignty which is "not a principle of discord," but of "melioration, contentment, and peace." Representative democracy is established on the theory that the representative should express the same sentiments which the represented, if possessed of equal information, would express. The United States of America thus meets the requirements of a true state—"a complete body of free persons, united together for their common benefit, to enjoy peaceably what is their own, and to do justice to others." Drawing on the old Whig myth, Wilson maintained that America's legal system is superior to that of England because in its principles and many particulars it bears "a stronger and fairer resemblance to the common law as it was improved under the Saxon, than to that law, as it was disfigured under the Norman government," with its system of feudal tenures.[25]

The principle of popular sovereignty, reflected in a democratic republic, which Wilson had emphasized previous to and in the Constitutional Convention, is thus central in his treatise. The notions of a ruler-ruled relationship (which keeps the conception of "superiority") and of the people as represented only in the lower legislative house, are dissolved; the people undergird and are represented in all branches of government. Because the law of nature is observed and men are regarded as essentially equal there is no class representation in America; the upper legislative chamber, the executive, and even the judiciary, in terms of ultimate source, derive their authority from the product of the people, the Constitution.

Alongside popular sovereignty Wilson advocated judicial review. Positive law, which is made by the representatives of the people, and the common law, which is rooted in popular consent, are both obligatory insofar as they conform not only to the Constitution but to the law of nature. Consequently he maintained that although "the general and most important principles of law" can be known by all mature citizens, it is ultimately the right and the duty of courts to decide in case of conflicting opinions. The conclusion that such duty involves interpretation of the Constitution in terms of principles of natural law is implicit in Wilson's treatise and in his pronouncements as a member of the Supreme Court of the United States. In this view it would seem that there are limits to popular sovereignty and majority rule which are traceable to the same source from which Wilson thought true democracy issued—the law of nature.[26]

Wilson's treatise is evidence that the common unqualified conception of American political thought as merely derivative from Locke is in error.[27] Lockian constitutionalism, with its emphasis on the natural right of property, however broadly considered, its individualism, and its tendency toward hedonism, was, and is, a strong, abiding influence. It is to Wilson's credit that he discerned its philosophic and practical insufficiencies for a free government which assumes duties as well as rights, and which recognizes a common good broader than the protection of property. His constitutionalism was thus ultimately Aristotelian. It recognized man's natural end, happiness, which Wilson saw as the cultivation of the mind in knowledge and virtue, as well as the natural associations, and institutions, which men form, such as the family, the state, and private property, as fixed, ethically limiting factors. Popular sovereignty, as expressed in majoritarian decisions must, to retain its legitimacy, subserve and enhance these ends. A constitutional representative democracy deriving from the consensual principle was to Wilson the dictate of the law of nature. Finally, Wilson agreed with Montesquieu in identifying "virtue" as the republican principle. Unlike Chipman, however, he was unwilling to dismiss "honor" as a factor. He proclaimed that republican government is attached to that honor "whose connection with virtue is indissoluble." And what is prescribed in theory exists in practice in America where, because "the doors of public honors and public offices are, on the broad principles of equal liberty, thrown open to all," a "laudable emulation . . . may prompt a man to legislate, not merely for a single State, but for the most august Union that has yet been formed on the face of the globe."[28]

Conclusions

Chipman and Wilson attempted to consolidate on the theoretical level the significant changes wrought in the formative period of American government. Their concern was not only to explain and relate fundamental principles but to justify these principles as dictates or implementations of the law of nature. Classical natural law was extended from its ethical focus and used by Wilson to attempt to purge American political thought of Lockian philosophical insufficiencies. Representative constitutional democracy, as essentially established in the United States, was pronounced to be most in accordance with man's developed nature. Upon this basis the politicized law of nature, as used particularly, but not solely, by judges, posited as the high controlling norm of public law the concept, "the nature of free government," which became conveniently equated with "the nature of American institutions."

Within this framework the old questions were resolved. No longer need there be talk of "divided sovereignty," because natural law dictates that except for its prescriptions, free and equal individuals are not bound except by their consent. Consequently the ultimate (sovereign) authority to determine institutions and positive law lies in the people. The jump from the notion of a pure democracy to that of a democratic republic is effected by a realization that the new concept of representation which sees all jurisdictions and branches of government stemming ultimately in their authorization and personnel from the sovereign popular source erases the need to distinguish between rulers and ruled on the basis of the principle of "superiority."

It follows that American government, reflecting in its principles natural public law, should be studied in order to develop the only valid political science. Artificialities indeed remain, particularly in the realm of psychology. With proper education in government and the law, men will recognize and eradicate them. Similarly, particular changes in structure might be dictated by inevitable societal developments; but this involves at most a reapplication of the immutable first principles. Consequently, it might be said, American government, born of the revolutionary principle of popular sovereignty, stood at the end of the eighteenth century as the refurbished "City On a Hill," and the notion of a purified political science existed in relation thereto as did theology to the earlier Puritan ideal. Thus envisaged, the new American political science, based on institutions born in good part of compromise, takes on a dogmatic and moralistic tone. It is then no cause for wonder that, for the most part, what passed as American political science for decades thereafter was an amalgam of jurisprudence, civic education, and political ethics.

Finally, it should be remembered that in expounding popular sovereignty, Wilson and Chipman assumed a cultural milieu in which men agreed essentially on morals, or what Walter Lippmann has recently called a "public philosophy." Without such a generally shared ethical view or communion in objective truth, Wilson would maintain, "scepticism" with its attendant "subjectivism" would ultimately render popular sovereignty impossible; "superiority," would reassert itself to restore order out of the subsequent chaos and the American Revolution would have been in vain.

NOTES

1. *Rules and Regulations of the Society for Political Enquiries* (Philadelphia, printed by Robert Aitken, 1787). A copy of the charter can also be found in W. Van

der Weyde (ed.), *The Life and Works of Thomas Paine* (New Rochelle, N.Y., 1925, 10 vols.), IV, 311–315. Van der Weyde, in his introductory remarks preceding the charter identifies Paine as its author.

2. Washington Chauncey Ford, *Wills of George Washington and His Immediate Successors* (Brooklyn, N.Y., 1891), pp. 90, 91; cited in Bernard Crick, *The American Science of Politics* (Berkeley, 1959), p. 4.

3. James Wilson, *Lectures on the Law*, in J. D. Andrews (ed.), *The Works of James Wilson*, (Chicago, 1896, 2 vols.), I, 20, 21. The lectures are in McCloskey's aforementioned edition of Wilson's *Works*, I, 59–435, II, 441–707.

4. Nathaniel Chipman, *Sketches of the Principles of Government* (Rutland, Vt., 1793), p. 236.

5. Jesse Root, *The Origin of Government and Laws in Connecticut*, reproduced in part in Perry Miller (ed.), *The Legal Mind in America* (Garden City, N.Y., 1962), pp. 38–39.

6. Leonard Labaree (ed.), *The Papers of Benjamin Franklin* (New Haven, 1959), IV, 225–34.

7. *Ibid.*, II, 382; Philip Foner, *The Life and Major Writings of Thomas Paine* (New York, 1945), pp. 407–408n states that Paine delivered a paper before the Society advising against the incorporation of towns. The Society had 42 members; its meetings were sparsely attended; one of the members talked incessantly. In 1787 Benjamin Rush, famed physician, read a paper to the Society entitled, "An Enquiry into the Effect of Public Punishments Upon Criminals and Upon Society." In a letter of Feb. 14, 1787, to Richard Price, Rush stated: "A society has likewise been established among us for 'political enquiries.' The objects of this society are the advancement of the science of Government, and the promotion of human happiness. It is considered in the manner of the Philosophical Societies in Europe; we expect to publish our communications annually, and thereby preserve in volumes many invaluable essays, which might perish in the newspapers." Rush's comments are reprinted in *Pennsylvania Magazine of History and Biography*, LXXVIII (Jan., 1954), 29. See also Albert Post, "Early Efforts to Abolish Capital Punishment," *Pennsylvania Magazine of History and Biography*, LXVIII (January, 1904), 41. Professor Aldridge states that the Society provides a clue to the political philosophy of Franklin, inasmuch as its name suggests Franklin's pragmatic approach which emphasized instead of expediency the application of common sense and disciplined thought to particular problems. A. O. Aldridge, *Benjamin Franklin, Philosopher and Man* (Philadelphia and New York, 1965), p. 390.

8. Bernard Crick, *The American Science of Politics* (Berkeley, 1959), pp. 7, 8. It has been suggested by Foner that the Society for Political Enquiries was a precursor of the Democratic-Republican Societies which sprang up throughout the country in the wake of the French Revolution and in opposition to Aristomonarchic tendencies and programs of leading Federalists. It is true that Thomas Paine was the lodestar of most of these clubs and that he maintained that "The moral principle of revolutions is to instruct not to destroy." Then, too, the clubs were interested in emphasizing the democratic features of republicanism to the point of reducing representatives to mere popular agents, and they were called "Schools for Political Knowledge." Also, the Baltimore Republican Club probably typified many others in proclaiming politics a science to be studied like astronomy or mathematics. Nonetheless, it appears that, unlike the two Federalists Chipman and Wilson, no republican club member, with the possible exception of Paine who was out of the country at the time, can be said to have produced a reasoned treatise of republican government. Information was disseminated, civic education and general education were promoted, the works of Paine and others were disseminated, and political activities engaged in. Thomas Jefferson used these clubs to his political advantage, but he himself produced no work on government or the science of politics. Instead people could look to the Declaration of Independence, which he drafted, for principles to be propagated. For a treatment of these questions, see Eugene P. Link, *Democratic-Republican Societies, 1790–1800* (New York, 1942).

9. R. J. Honeywell, "Nathaniel Chipman, Political Philosopher and Jurist," *New England Quarterly*, V (July, 1932), 555–584.

10. Chipman, *op. cit.*, pp. 13, 15, 71, 72, 32, 33ff, 51ff. Chipman distinguished his practical use of the term "principles" from Montesquieu's use, by talking of (1) those comprehending "not only the laws of mechanics, but those, rules, by which the relative proportions of the several parts, are determined to direct the motions to a certain end" ("Principles of construction"), and (2) rules "by which the moving force is applied, and made to operate on the machine, with a view to the end proposed" ("Principles of Operation"). *Ibid.*, p. 17.

11. *Ibid.*, pp. 106, 110, 74, 77.

12. *Ibid.*, pp. 113ff, 98ff, 102.

13. *Ibid.*, pp. 289ff, 105.

14. *Ibid.*, pp. 216–223.

15. *Ibid.*, pp. 220–227.

16. *Ibid.*, p. 233ff.

17. *Ibid.*, p. 237.

18. *Ibid.*, p. 238.

19. Root, *op. cit.*, pp. 32–40.

20. James Wilson, "Discourses upon Jurisprudence and the Political Science," J. D. Andrews (ed.), *The Works of James Wilson* (Chicago, 1896, 2 vols.), I, 60.

21. On the Scottish background of Wilson's thought, see, Arnaud B. Leavelle, "James Wilson and the Relation of the Scottish Metaphysics to American Political Thought," *Political Science Quarterly*, 57 (1942), 394–410. On the medieval background of Wilson's thought see, William F. Obering, S. J., *The Philosophy of Law of James Wilson* (Washington, 1938). On Wilson's public life, see Page Smith, *James Wilson* (Chapel Hill, 1956).

22. *Works of Wilson*, I, 233–252, 109–121.

23. *Ibid.*, I, 49, 91–94, 99, 127, 115, 124.

24. *Ibid.*, I, 59, 159, 179, 193, 198.

25. *Ibid.*, I, 3, 18, 271, 445.

26. *Ibid.*, I, 27, 415–418, 7.

27. For an interpretation of American political thought in terms of Locke, see Louis Hartz, *The Liberal Tradition in America* (New York, 1955). See also Bernard Crick, *The American Science of Politics* (Berkeley, 1959), pp. 10, 11.

28. *Works*, II, 313; I, 11.

PART FIVE

FEDERALIST AND JEFFERSONIAN THOUGHT

Chapter 12

FEDERALIST POLITICAL THOUGHT

A wise prince will seek means by which his subjects will always and in every possible condition of things have need of his government, and then they will always be faithful to him.

MACHIAVELLI

Alexander Hamilton: Creative Statesman

Hamilton believed that "with governments as with individuals, first impressions and early habits give a lasting bias and character." Consequently he urged Washington to serve as first president of the republic because "it is of little purpose to have *introduced* a system, if the weightiest influence is not given to its first *establishment* in the outset."* Behind these statements lay a conception of leadership which is best summed up by a quotation from Demosthenes that Hamilton took for his own: "As a general marches at the head of his troops, so ought wise politicians . . . march at the head of affairs. . . . they ought not to await the event, to know what measures to take; but the measures which they have taken ought to produce the *event*."[1]

Thus it was that as Secretary of the Treasury in Washington's cabinet, Hamilton played, in effect, the role of prime minister. By bold, energetic, and imaginative leadership he established a pattern of practices, policies, and precedents which gave substance to the new Constitution. Having been unable to effect adoption in the Convention of 1787 of the consolidated aristocratic balanced state, which he held as the best regime, he resigned himself to republicanism as most fitting to the American situation, and as the only practicable alternative to an incipient anarchy. But at the same time he attempted to breathe into its forms and policies much of the spirit and substance of the principles he had propounded earlier in Philadelphia.

* See the previous discussion of Hamilton's thought in Chapters 7 and 10.

Convinced that "the centrifugal is much stronger in these States than the centripetal," his primary objective was a vigorous, respected and predominant central government. He labored "to establish in this country principles more and more *national* and free from all foreign ingredients, so that we may be neither 'Greeks nor Trojans,' but truly Americans." He defined his political creed as embracing, "first, the necessity of *Union* to the respectability and happiness of this country, and second the necessity of an *efficient* government to maintain that Union." As he saw it, "a weak and embarrassed government never fails to be unpopular," because "it attaches to itself the disrespect incident to weakness." Whereas "too much power leads to despotism, too little leads to anarchy, and both eventually to the ruin of the people."[2]

The objective of a strong national government was comprehended in Hamilton's notion of the "public good," a generic, normative, yet objective concept which he believed was distinct from, and superior to, the sum of individual or class interests, as well as the Madisonian idea of the reconciliation or neutralization of conflicting group interests. Although his political psychology was premised on the primacy of egoism, his conception of the community was corporate. The national community, as yet inchoate, was to him an objective common good, which in its demands and requirements could be known only by an enlightened, dedicated few led on by the love of fame. Thus despite his belief in the great influence upon man of economic forces, Hamilton valued more the great legislators, or state-builders, who use power to effect public tranquility, order, prosperity, and progress. The acquisition and successful use of power, Hamilton thought, involved, (1) the recognition that "men are rather reasoning than reasonable animals, for the most part governed by the impulse of passion," and (2) the consequent deft deployment of Humean principles. Enlist the passions, make it the immediate interest of men to support the public cause, work to make beneficial practices habitual dispositions in men; these, together with a Hobbesian emphasis on the strength which evokes fear, comprised the manipulative devices of Hamilton's applied political science.[3]

To detach the strong connection of passion and interest from the state governments and transfer it to the national government was Hamilton's principal aim. This entailed giving both the rich and well born, on the one hand, and the many, on the other, a strong discernible stake in the new national government. In actuality, Hamilton appealed almost exclusively to the former. As legislator he deemed that the national public good presupposed a unified economic order and used as his examplar the Whig program of fiscal reform effected earlier in Britain. In this view an equal distribution of the favors of government would not achieve the end of economic unity and development. Hume had neatly captured the rationale of this position when he noted that capital little benefits the economy and the state "if it is dispersed into numberless hands, which either squander it in idle show and magnificence, or employ it in the purchase of the common necessaries of life."[4] Because the United States contained but few large concentrations of capital, Hamilton concluded that the government must basically concern itself with those possessing capital which could be used for its support and for national development.

Hamilton's "First Report on the Public Credit" (1790) which recommended funding the national debt at par, and the assumption of state debts, was based on the principle enunciated by him years before: "The only plan that can preserve the currency is one that will make it the *immediate* interest of the monied men to cooperate with government in its support." The private interest of the wealthy must be joined with the national interest in the realization of economic unity, stability, and growth. Maintenance of the public credit was to Hamilton at once a prerequisite of good, respectable government, a dictate of morality as well as expediency, the price of liberty, the condition of public confidence and national strength, and the means to the procuring of advantages "to every class of the community."[5]

The report is an excellent example of Hamilton's propensity to think first and foremost in terms of the nation, and of individuals only insofar as they might be used to this end. His bias in this regard is manifest in the statement that "those who are common creditors of a nation are, generally speaking, enlightened men." Brought to choose between establishing the financial authority and sobriety of the nation and correcting the inequities attendant upon a policy of noncompensation to original holders of securities, including the soldiers of the Revolution, he opted for the former. In light of this it is understandable that he regarded Talleyrand as "the greatest of modern statesmen," because "he had well known it was necessary both to suffer wrong to be done and to do it."[6]

On the basis of the established credit of the country Hamilton, in his "Report on Manufactures" (1791) laid bare his plan for the development of the national economy. Mercantilist in its assumptions, the report recommended governmental encouragement through duties, prohibitions, and subventions. That the plan would redound to the benefit of the Northeast section of the country by making it America's workshop did not deter Hamilton. Again he saw the plan as dictated by the common good, and promotive of national strength, by making it the "immediate interest" of an influential segment of Americans to adhere to it.[7]

A principal revenue measure enacted under Hamilton's leadership was an excise tax on liquor, the incidence of which was greatest upon Westerners. Upon the outbreak of the Whisky Rebellion in 1794, which was, characteristically, put down by a firm use of national force,

Hamilton wrote a series of letters under the pseudonym, "Tully," defending the administration and attacking what he regarded as a strong tendency toward anarchy. He extolled the rule of law as the common bond of protection, and the sole alternative to force: "Those, therefore, who preach doctrines, or set examples which undermine or subvert the authority of the laws, lead us from freedom to slavery; they incapacitate us for a GOVERNMENT OF LAWS, and consequently prepare the way for one of FORCE, for mankind must have GOVERNMENT OF ONE SORT OR ANOTHER." Civil war, though a great evil, "is incomparably a less evil than the destruction of government." Anarchy was Hamilton's *bête noir*, a malignant disease which must be forcefully excised from the body politic at its first appearance, if it is to be checked at all.[8]

The display of force visited upon the so-called rebels may have been disproportionate to the infraction. The authority of the central government was, however, upon its first major challenge, vigorously vindicated. A firm and abiding precedent was set, upon which have been based in recent years similar manifestations of the assertion of national authority. In such cases, Hamilton undoubtedly thought, it is better to err on the side of excess than deficiency. Well versed in the teaching of Machiavelli, he could conclude that a government must not allow itself to be despised and that it is much safer to be feared than loved.

Hamilton based his program on a broad construction of the Constitution. His reasoned arguments justify calling him the first great expositor of the fundamental law as a viable instrument of government. While men like Adams and Madison viewed the Constitution as a mechanical contrivance checking, balancing, exploiting, and neutralizing human passions and interests, he looked upon it as an organism capable of growth in the application of its general principles.

Hamilton's opinion on the constitutionality of the national bank, which was established as an instrument for the central control of credit, is the classical example of his approach. His articulation of the doctrine of implied powers contrasted sharply with Jefferson's restriction of Congress to powers specifically mentioned in the Constitution and those indispensible to carry them into effect. Two passages deserve quotation as illustrative of his argument.

Now it appears to the Secretary of the Treasury, that this *general principle* is *inherent* in the very *definition* of *Government,* and *essential* to every step of the progress to be made by that of the United States; namely—That every power vested in a Government is in its nature *sovereign,* and includes by *force* of the *term,* a right to employ all the *means* requisite, and fairly *applicable* to the attainment of the *ends* of such power; and which are not precluded by restrictions and exceptions specified in the constitution; or not immoral, or not contrary to the essential ends of political society.

[The] criterion is the *end,* to which the measure relates as a *mean.* If the end be clearly comprehended within any of the specified powers, and if the measure have an obvious relation to that end, and is not forbidden by any particular provision of the constitution—it may safely be deemed to come within the compass of the national authority.[9]

These statements are remarkable for two reasons. The first is the spirit of liberality in interpreting the Constitution, which was consistent with the theme of national power central to Hamilton's thought. The second, and equally important in the sequel, is the clear affirmation that limitations on governmental power include not only those specifically defined in the Constitution but by natural law as well. When this fact is joined to Hamilton's espousal of judicial review in *Federalist* number 78, it can fairly be inferred that, as did James Wilson, he believed that the judiciary is not restricted to positive law in its duty to expound the Constitution.

Hamilton's interpretation of the "general welfare" clause of the Constitution was in this same spirit. Contrary to Madison, who declared that the Congressional power to spend for the general welfare could only be exercised in pursuit of the other specifically defined powers, Hamilton put forth the view, which is now accepted doctrine, that the power is an independent grant, embracing "a vast variety of particulars, which are susceptible neither of specification nor of definition."[10] Whatever concerns the public or common good is covered by it.

The realistic principles of foreign policy laid down by Hamilton were grounded in the conviction that international politics constitute a constant power struggle and that a viable policy cannot be built on moral principles divorced from considerations of national interest and power. After great opposition arose to Washington's Proclamation of Neutrality in the war between the coalition powers and the Revolutionary French regime in 1793, Hamilton, in a series of papers written under the pseudonyms Pacificus and Americanus, defended the action against the charges that it abridged the Treaty of Alliance with France of 1778; that it was an unconstitutional exercise of Presidential power; and that it violated the obligation of contract, the dictate of gratitude, and the affinity of liberty between nations with republican institutions.[11]

Concerning the constitutional grounds, Hamilton held that since the Presidency is (1) the organ of intercourse with foreign nations, (2) the interpreter of national treaties, (3) the executor of laws, of which treaties are a part, (4) the vehicle of public force, and (5) the seat of all executive power (limited only by the constitutional provisions that treaties and ministerial appointments must be made with senatorial concurrence, and that war can only be declared by the Congress), the chief executive alone can declare neutrality when the engagements of the nation permit, and its interests so require. Although this interpretation was attacked by Madison as smacking of the British prerogative, it has never successfully been challenged. That the President today serves ultimately as the formulator and voice of American foreign policy is owing, in good part, to the precedent set by Washington and defended by Hamilton.[12]

Hamilton further argued that the proclamation did not violate the treaty of alliance, principally because the war was offensive on France's part and the alliance was defensive in nature. Any offensive alliance is detrimental, he declared, because it "subjects the peace of each ally to the will of the other, and obliges each to partake in the other's wars of policy and interest, as well as in those of safety and defense, of the other." Then, too, "there would be no proportion between the mischiefs and perils to which the United States would expose themselves, by embarking in the war, and the benefit *which the nature of their stipulation aims at securing* to France, or that, which it would be in their power actually to render her, by becoming a party."[13]

The core of Hamilton's arguments against the charge of immorality is contained in the following statement:

Self-preservation is the first duty of a nation; and though in the performance of stipulations relating to war, good faith requires that its *ordinary hazards* should be fairly encountered, because they are directly contemplated by such stipulations, yet it does not require that *extraordinary* and *extreme* hazards should be run, especially where the object for which they are to be run, is only a *partial* or *particular* interest of the ally, for whom they are to be run.[14]

Hamilton saw as the precondition of gratitude "a benefit received or intended which there was no right to claim, originating in a regard to the interest or advantage of the party on whom the benefit is or is meant to be conferred." But "if a service is rendered from views *chiefly* relative to the immediate interest of the party who renders it, and is productive of reciprocal advantages, there seems scarcely in such a case, to be an adequate basis for a sentiment like that of gratitude." In fact, the rule of morality in this respect differs between individuals and nations.

The duty of making its own welfare the guide of its actions is much stronger upon [nations] than upon [individuals]; in proportion to the greater magnitude and importance of national compared with individual happiness, and to the greater permanency of the effects of national than of individual conduct. Existing Millions, and for the most part future generations are concerned in the present measures of a government; While the consequences of the private actions of an individual ordinarily terminate with himself, or are circumscribed within a narrow compass.[15]

Thus an individual may indulge his gratitude even at the expense of his own interest; rulers of a government, who are "only trustees for the happiness and interest of their nation," cannot. This is not to recommend an absolutely self-interested policy for nations, "but to shew that a policy regulated by their own interest, as far as justice and good faith permit, is, and ought to be the prevailing policy." In short, nations cannot afford to be "self-denying" and "self-sacrificing" if such course violates their fundamental interest.[16]

Finally, Hamilton addressed himself to the claim that America's liberty was at stake because if France fell, the enemy "will never forgive in us the origination of those principles which were the germs of the French Revolution," and "will endeavour to eradicate them from the world." He replied that (1) if this is so, "our interference is not likely to alter the case" and that "it would only serve prematurely to exhaust our strength," and (2) distinctions must be made between America's case and that of France so Americans might not "pervert or hazard our own principles by persuading ourselves of a similitude which does not exist."[17]

Washington's Farewell Address of 1796, which, for the most part, was the work of Hamilton, summed up the ideals of the Federalists, warned of present and impending dangers to the republic, and advised concerning sound principles of government and policy. The context of the address was the development of an organized opposition party, headed by Jefferson and Madison, and the parallel division of the attitudes toward revolutionary France.[18]

The address strongly criticized political parties and the dissension they engender. Although they may have value in governments with "a monarchical cast," this is not so in governments based on the elective principle, where there is "constant danger of excess." The party spirit "serves always to distract the public councils and enfeeble the public administration. It agitates the Community with ill founded jealousies and false alarms; kindles the animosity of one part against another; foments occasionally riot and insurrection" and "opens the door to foreign influence and corruption." Although it is "inseparable from our nature, having its root in the strongest passions of the human mind," it is "a spirit not to be encouraged." Similarly, because "time and habit are at least as necessary to fix the true character of governments as of other human institutions," it is necessary to resist "the spirit of innovation," invoked by factions.[19]

Hamilton tended to equate "faction" with "party," seeing the former as a group of men inimical to the common voice of the nation. By definition, party entailed the pursuit of private or group interest, and the equation of a particular will to the general will. Refusing to see the movement he led as a party, he regarded it as, at most, a group of patriots held together by a common regard for the public good, effected through the deployment of the manipulative principles of politics.[20]

The Address further spoke of the necessity to maintain the salutary separation of powers in government, but put prime emphasis on "religion and morality" as "indispensable supports" of "political prosperity." Conceding that morality might be maintained without religion among a few "of refined education" with "minds of peculiar structure," it declared that "reason and experience both forbid us to expect that national morality can prevail in exclusion of religious principle." Because virtue is "a necessary spring of popular government," there ought be promoted "institutions for the general diffusion of knowledge," which will aid in the development of an "enlightened" public opinion.[21]

The principles of foreign policy put forth in the Address are rooted ultimately in the same conception of the overriding primacy of national interest articulated earlier by Hamilton. "Good faith and justice towards all Nations," the cultivation of "peace and harmony with all" were particularized in the advice to avoid "permanent, inveterate antipathies against particular nations and passionate attachments for others."[22]

In connection with the question of foreign policy it should be mentioned that both Hamilton and Jefferson, who served as Secretary of State in Washington's cabinet, entertained a conception of "empire." While Jefferson, however, emphasized internal development and westward expansion in the building of an agrarian, pacifist, isolationist "Empire of Liberty," Hamilton looked outward, hoping, as did Washington, that one day America "will have some weight in the scale of Empires."[23]

Significance of Hamilton's Thought

The impress of Hamilton's thought is great in American constitutional law, public policy, and political practice. And yet, it is difficult to dismiss as completely hyperbolic John Adams' remark that Hamilton knew "no more of the sentiments and feelings of the people of America than he did of those of the inhabitants of one of the planets."[24] Unattached by birth, blood, or sentiment to any locality or state, he poured all his energies in the cause of the nation at a time when American loyalties were divided between state and nation, with priority generally given to the former. Insofar as Hamilton regarded local attachments and loyalties as potentially subversive, Adams' stricture has weight. The same might be said of Hamilton's economic program. Concerned with making it the "immediate interest" of men to support the national government, he chose to use the carrot to entice the "rich and well-born" and, when he deemed it necessary, the stick to coerce the many. In the process there resulted a sharp division of men along economic and sectional lines and the development of an organized opposition party —the eventualities he had most feared and least wanted. That he realized this in later years is evidenced by the fact that around the turn of the century he advocated road building and the encouragement of agriculture and the arts, on the ground that such a program would appeal to those classes whose benefits from government had been least manifest.

Nonetheless, Hamilton's policy was thoroughly consistent with his most candid exposition of his political thought, his speech to the Constitutional Convention in June 1787. Therein, he had argued that the rich and well-born must be given a permanent share in the government, as a bulwark against precipitous popular change in the maintenance of good government.[25] After the Convention foreclosed the possibility of institutionalizing the rich and well-born in a separate branch of government, Hamilton sought to bind them to the new government through his financial program, which appealed not to their patriotism or virtue, but to their immediate self-interest. With the rich and well-born won over to the national cause, Hamilton could believe that the base had been laid for stable government and national economic development beneficial to all. But for the latter to be obvious to all, particularly those not originally directly benefiting, demanded time. To point to a general prosperity was not sufficient; the day had not yet arrived when Americans were to regard the condition of the national economy as the responsibility of the administration in power.

Hamilton's political thought was compounded of two apparently incompatible elements, the conception of the corporate community as an organic unit embodying an objective common good, on the one hand, and the conception of man as an egotistic animal moved principally by the desires for wealth, power, and esteem, on the other. The former supplied Hamilton's normative principle, the latter is the source of his realistic manipulative techniques. They are mediated to each other by the notion of the legislator, state-builder, or "wise politician" who, motivated by the love of glory, transcends immediate personal or group interest, discerns the common good, translates it into law, and solidifies allegiance thereto by joining men's passions and identifying their interest with the cause.

A recent study of Hamilton concludes that he failed in his career on two levels. First, he failed as a manager of "party politics," because he regarded himself as a founder and disliked the task of organization as well as the recurrent compromises demanded by "popular politics." Second, he fell short as an officer under the Constitution because as a self-appointed founder of an empire he regarded the task of correctly plotting and guiding the course of the new nation as superior to a strict regard to constitutional rules. Because of the latter, he engaged in the recently revealed passage of state secrets to the British behind the back of the President, and unsuccessfully attempted to effect a disregard for the New York state constitution in reference to the Presidential election of 1800.[26]

Angered by the French Revolution and its extension to American politics, comprehending but late the effect of ideology upon people at large, and ever distrustful of democracy, Hamilton, to his credit, wrote in warning to his fellow Federalists on the day before he was killed in his duel with Aaron Burr: "Dismemberment of our Empire will be a clear sacrifice of great positive advantages without counterbalancing good; administering no relief to our real disease, which is Democracy; the poison of which, by a subdivision, will only be the more concentrated in each part, and consequently the more virulent."[27] From first to last Hamilton remained a strong unionist, nationalist, and elitist thinker. Even today, however, when his nationalism and "realism" have gained wide attention and regard, when the debt which is owed him is broadly appreciated, he has captured the nation's grudging admiration and gratitude, but not its heart. Thus he sits uneasily in the American pantheon, a foreign import in mind and temperament, who is celebrated not as Jefferson, for an exposition of first principles of free government, nor as Adams and Madison for an exposition of structural principles, but because he symbolizes the importance in government, of men, power, and policies.

John Marshall (1755–1835): Creative Jurist

Born in a log cabin near the Virginia frontier, Marshall, a distant cousin of his later great antagonist, Thomas Jefferson, learned his nationalism as a soldier in the Continental Army, enduring the terrible winter of 1777–1778 at Valley Forge. Having read Blackstone early in life, he attended lectures on the law given by George Wythe in 1780. He served in the Virginia House of Delegates, was a firm supporter of the Constitution in the debate over ratification, represented the new nation in France, was Secretary of State in the last year of John Adams' Presidency and was appointed Chief Justice of the Supreme Court of the United States in the waning hours of Federalist power after Jefferson's victory in 1800.[28]

Possessing neither judicial experience nor a broad legal education, Marshall labored for thirty-four years on the Court to write Hamiltonian principles into American constitutional law, influencing his colleagues by his strong will, dedication to duty, and single-minded sense of purpose. His approach is best summed up in a statement from one of his opinions: "In exploring an unbeaten path, with few, if any aids, from precedents or written law, the court has found it necessary to rely much on general principles."[29] The articulation of the doctrines of judicial review, implied powers, and vested rights are among his main contributions.

1. *Judicial Review.* In *Marbury v. Madison* (1803), Marshall, relying essentially upon the logic of Hamilton's *Federalist* number 78, formally pronounced the doctrine of judicial review of the constitutional validity of acts of the political branches of the government. He reasoned as follows: The Constitution is either a superior, paramount law, unchangeable by ordinary means, or it is on the same level as ordinary acts of the legislature and thus alterable by the latter. Written constitutions, however, are intended to be paramount, controlling law, a fact confirmed by the supremacy clause of the Constitution. The Court is the guardian of the Constitution because not only do the judges swear to uphold it but "it is emphatically the province and duty of the judicial department to say what the law is." In case of an asserted conflict between an executive or legislative act and a provision of the Constitution, it is the function of the judiciary to decide the question on the basis of the primacy of the fundamental law.[30]

Although Marshall undoubtedly intended that the judiciary act as the ultimate expositor of the Constitution, his statement of judicial review was not dissimilar to that advocated by his political enemies, the Jeffersonians. For example, in introducing the Bill of Rights in the first Congress, Madison had stated that the courts would "consider themselves in a peculiar manner the guardians of those rights; they would be an impenetrable bulwark against every assumption of power in the Legislative or Executive; they will be naturally led to resist every encroachment upon rights expressly stipulated for in the Constitution by the declaration of rights."[31] Federalists and Jeffersonian Republicans did not differ over judicial review, as such, but over its binding effect on other branches of government. Whereas Marshall apparently assumed that the political branches were bound by judicial pronouncements, Jeffersonians believed that each of the three branches could make independent judgments of constitutionality. Acceptance in American constitutional law of the former view was a later development.

2. *Implied Powers and Broad Construction.* In *McCulloch v. Maryland* (1819), which affirmed the constitutionality of the establishment of the United States Bank, Marshall followed the reasoning of Hamilton's earlier opinion given to Washington on the question: The Constitution emanates from the will of the people of the United States and not from the states. It created a national government of enumerated powers supreme in its sphere of action. The doctrine of implied powers

derives from the "necessary and proper" clause, as well as general principles. And in a key passage, Marshall felicitously paraphrased Hamilton's earlier observation.

Let the end be legitimate, let it be within the scope of the Constitution, and all means which are appropriate, which are plainly adapted to that end, which are not prohibited, but consist with the letter and spirit of the Constitution, are constitutional.[32]

3. *Vested Property Rights.* In an opinion solicited from him as a private attorney, in 1795, Hamilton had written of vested property rights as being protected against state revocation by "natural justice" and the obligation of contract clause in the federal Constitution.[33]

Relying on these principles, Marshall followed a trend of decisions and reasoning already established by the Supreme Court before his appointment, in pronouncing upon the sanctity of property rights, the obligation of contract, the contractual nature of state grants and of corporate charters. Justice William Paterson had stated in 1795 that "the right of acquiring and possessing property, and having it protected, is one of the natural, inherent and inalienable rights of man," which precludes legislative authority to divest a citizen of his freehold and vest it in another without just compensation. Similarly, Justice Samuel Chase declared three years later: "There are certain vital principles in our free Republican governments, which will determine and overrule an apparent and flagrant abuse of legislative power; as to authorize manifest injustice by positive law; or to take away that security for personal liberty, or private property, for the protection whereof the government was established."[34]

Such assertions should be understood against the background of more general Federalist declarations of higher law evoked by the French Revolution and its peculiar version of popular sovereignty. A statement by John Quincy Adams in 1791 is illustrative.

This principle, that a whole nation has a right to do whatever it pleases, cannot in any sense whatever be admitted as true. The eternal and immutable laws of justice and morality are paramount to all human legislation. The violation of those laws is certainly within the power of a nation, but it is not among the rights of nations. The power of a nation is the collected power of all the individuals which compose it. . . . If, therefore, a majority . . . are bound by no law human or divine, and have no other rule but their sovereign will and pleasure to direct them, what possible security can any citizen . . . have for the protection of his inalienable rights? The principles of liberty must still be the sport of arbitrary power, and the hideous form of despotism must lay aside the diadem and the scepter, only to assume the party-colored garments of democracy.[35]

Although Marshall asserted the vested rights principle in *Marbury v. Madison,* his main pronouncements came in cases involving state action. In *Fletcher v. Peck* (1810), which arose from the same controversy to which Hamilton earlier addressed himself, Marshall vacillated between the contract clause and absolute principles of justice to pronounce unconstitutional the revocation of a state legislative land grant. In *Dartmouth College v. Woodward* (1819), he extended the interpretation of the contract clause to include corporate charters, a ruling which was bypassed by the inclusion of reserve clauses allowing for revocation either in general legislation or in the charters themselves. And in two other cases, Marshall succeeded in holding retrospective bankruptcy laws to be violative of the contract clause, but failed to get the Court to agree to his contention that prospective bankruptcy laws were likewise unconstitutional. Had his position been accepted, it would have constituted perhaps an even greater limitation upon state legislative power than that assumed later in the nineteenth century by the Court in reference to the due process clause of the Fourteenth Amendment.[36]

Marshall's jurisprudence, it might be said in summary, had two main sources: the *positive* principle of national power and supremacy and the *restrictive* doctrine of vested rights. Coupled with the fundamental principle of judicial guardianship of the Constitution, they comprised essential elements of Federalist doctrine which helped shape the political life of the new nation.

John Adams: Patriot Executive

Federalists of the old school such as John Jay of New York, George Cabot and Theodore Sedgwick of Massachusetts, Gouverneur Morris of Pennsylvania, Daniel Carroll of Maryland, and Washington himself: (1) thought more in terms of society than of the individual; (2) viewed government in a positive enlarged sense; (3) wished to maintain a ruling elite with popular consent by the reinforcement of the colonial social deferential spirit; and (4) opposed the spirit of political party.[37]

John Adams, the second Federalist President, differed considerably from these views. As has been seen, he did not view society as a harmonious whole and he regarded aristocracy not in the hereditary but the natural sense of talent and qualities which afford influence over others.* He distrusted both the aristocrats and the people. His concept of the Presidency was that of a disinterested executive who would mediate differences above the haul and pull of partisanship and act for the good of the country.

* See the discussion of Adams' thought in Chapters 7 and 9.

The difference between Adams and Hamilton on the question of the best regime is succinctly portrayed in the report by Jefferson of a colloquy between the two in which Hamilton reiterated the opinions of Hume and Blackstone.

[The] conversation . . . was led to the British Constitution, on which Mr. Adams observed, 'purge that constitution of its corruption, and give to its popular branch equality of representation, and it would be the most perfect constitution ever devised by the wit of man.' Hamilton paused and said, 'purge it of its corruption, and give to its popular branch equality of representation, and it would become an *impracticable* government: as it stands at present, with all its supposed defects, it is the most perfect government which ever existed.'[38]

Adams also differed with Hamilton on economic grounds, seeing agriculture as "the most essential interest of America." Although he approved Hamilton's funding and assumption program and spoke of the importance of commerce, he differed on fiscal and banking policy.[39]

During the early years of the federal republic Adams was most concerned with checking the tendency toward popular assumption of power; as time went on he concluded that the balance was becoming overweighted in the opposite direction. True to his principles, he attempted as chief executive to redress the balance, which brought fellow Federalists to question his sanity. He replied characteristically by cursing their "stiff-rumped stupidity."[40] With the Federalist house divided and with the continued growth of a strong popular opposition under the leadership of Jefferson, Adams was unable to play effectively the role of mediator. Having the courage of his convictions, he well served the public interest by preventing a war with France desired by many Federalists, with Hamilton in the forefront.

The most vital question relating to American political thought during Adams' tenure grew out of the Sedition Act of 1798, which was directed in particular against anti-Federalist editors and pamphleteers. The part of the act which is relevant to us made it a crime to write, print, utter, or publish "any false, scandalous and malicious writing . . . against the government of the United States, or either house of Congress . . . or the President . . . with intent to defame . . . or to bring them . . . into contempt, or disrepute; or to excite any unlawful combinations . . . for opposing or resisting" the authority of the United States.[41]

Because it is a common belief that the act was unconstitutional and in view of the fact that it served as the occasion for the birth of a more libertarian conception of the freedoms of speech and the press, it is incumbent upon us to examine the main outlines of the tradition of free expression in the background of the act itself.

The common law of seditious libel, as described by Blackstone, held that utterances were to be free from prior restraint but subject to prosecution if false, malicious, or having a bad tendency. The truth was not a defense and questions such as intent were left to the determination of the judge, with the jury merely deciding whether or not the utterance was made by the accused.

A recent study of the development of free expression in the United States questions the validity of many widely held conceptions. It shows first of all that it is not true that an object of the Revolution was to eliminate the common law of seditious libel. In only two of the original state constitutions (Pennsylvania in 1776 and Vermont as an independent republic in 1777 and in its constitution of 1791 as a member of the Union), was free speech elevated to a constitutional right. This, however, did not prevent at least one of these states, Pennsylvania, from thereafter applying the common law restraints. Thus twelve states left speech without constitutional protection and four of these (Connecticut, Rhode Island, New York, and New Jersey) afforded no constitutional guarantee of freedom of the press.[42]

The Virginia Statute of Religious Freedom, drawn by Jefferson in 1785, though referring specifically to religious opinions, by implication embraced oral and written speech. The preamble to the act specifically rejects the bad-tendency test and replaces it with another.

. . . to suffer the civil magistrate to intrude his powers into the field of opinion and to restrain the profession or propagation of principles, on the supposition of their ill tendency is a dangerous fallacy, which at once destroys all religious liberty, because he being of course judge of that tendency will make his opinions the rule of judgment, and approve or condemn the sentiments of others only as they shall square with or differ from his own; that it is time enough for the rightful purposes of civil government for its officers to interfere when principles break out into overt acts against peace and good order.[43]

Despite this language, the overt-action test was not applied in Virginia regarding certain political utterances prohibited by the legislature. Similarly, twelve states, including the nine with constitutional provisions for a free press, stipulated in their constitutions or statutes that the common law of England before the Revolution was to be in effect unless contrary to another constitutional or statutory provision. In each instance it is most probable that there was no contradiction seen between a guarantee of free press and *post-factum* prosecution for seditious libel.

The correspondence of John Adams and William Cushing, Chief Justice of the Massachusetts high court, in 1789, is of great relevance to the question. Replying to Cushing's queries concerning the meaning of the free speech provision of the Massachusetts Constitution, Adams, who had drafted the provision wrote:

The difficult and important question is whether the truth of words can be admitted by the court to be given in evidence to the jury. . . . In England

I suppose it is settled. But it is a serious Question whether our Constitution is not at present so different as to render the innovation necessary? Our chief magistrates and Senators etc. are annually eligible by the people. How are their characters and conduct to be known to their constituents but by the press? If the press is stopped and the people kept in Ignorance we had much better have the first magistrate and Senators hereditary. I, therefore, am very clear that under the Articles of our Constitution which you have quoted, it would be safest to admit evidence to the jury of the Truth of accusations, and if the jury found them true and that they were published for the Public good, they would readily acquit.[44]

Clearly Adams favored modification of the common law of seditious libel to allow a defense of truth. Truth, however, goes to *knowledge* whereas political utterances go to *opinion*, a fact which Adams did not mention. A charge of bribery differs substantially on evidentiary grounds from an imputation of gross incompetency, of pursuing a policy contrary to the public good or, to use a modern term, of "un-Americanism." The human tendency, especially in public life, is to equate one's own political opinions with the truth. With the development of sharp partisan differences, the opinions of one's most articulate and critical opponents understandably can become identified with falsity or "bad tendency." In light of this what was necessary was not merely a reform of the common law procedure but a recognition of freedom of expression of *opinion* as such.

Turning from the states to the level of the new federal republic, it will be remembered that the Convention Fathers maintained that because the authority of the new government was limited to its stipulated powers, no specific bill of rights was necessary. In the debates on ratification, the Anti-Federalist demands for a bill of rights were singularly vague in defining what was meant by freedom of speech and press. Of the twelve states which ratified the Constitution before the First Amendment was added, only Virginia, North Carolina, and New York sought to secure a guarantee of free expression of opinion against the federal government. This probably was motivated by the desire to preserve state rights in the field. Similarly, the debates in the first Congress shed no light on the extent and fundamental meaning of vital freedoms. Thus there is no hard evidence that the framers of the First Amendment understood the guarantee of free speech and press to preclude future prosecutions of seditious utterances. Despite the assurances of the fathers in the debate over ratification of the Constitution that repression of utterances was not within the competence of the federal government, after the First Amendment was adopted many of them acted and spoke as if speech and press could be prosecuted, not necessarily by statute, but under a federal common law of crimes. Thus federal judges, as early as 1792 and continuing through the decade, operated on the assumption of the existence of a federal criminal common law. Even before the Sedition Act there were federal prosecutions for seditious libel.

Against this legal background the Sedition Act was passed. It had the strong backing of Hamiltonian Federalists, with the sole exception of John Marshall, who doubted the wisdom of the action. Because it allowed for the truth as a defense and granted to the jury the right to determine intent, it could be pointed to as a reform of the Blackstonian procedure.

Although Adams had not personally pressed for the law, he acquiesced in its severe application. Nowhere does one see the shortsightedness of Federalist views more clearly than in the harsh uses of the Act. Political opponents could understandably interpret this conduct as an attempt to eliminate criticism, and to establish, in effect, a one-party press. The record, however, is not one-sided. After the Jeffersonians came to power, they began to institute proceedings under state law against Federalist editors for their attacks upon Jefferson. The tables had turned, and now Federalists posed as champions of free expression. The culmination of this development came in 1804 when Hamilton, in his last great speech before his death, argued before the New York Court of Appeals that truth be made a defense in seditious libel cases, and that the jury be allowed to determine the truth and the law. Shortly thereafter New York adopted this reform and other states followed in train.[45]

The Decline of Federalism

The New England politician, Fisher Ames (1758–1808), illustrates a transitional phase in the history of Federalist political thought. Although sounding generally like a sententious village scold, he differed from many of the older Federalists in recognizing the obvious. Noting the important changes in American political life brought about by a rising democratic mood, he urged his party to revitalize itself.[46]

Staunchly conservative, Ames entertained a notion of the end of government which was an attenuation of the Hamiltonian ideal. The protection of property, the promotion of peace, and the preservation of liberty, through the "just subordination" of the many to the few, were to him the foundation of good order. Liberty was prior to equality, consisting "not so much in removing all restraint from the orderly, as imposing it on the violent." Equality embodied not "an equal right to all things" but equal protection of whatever men had a right to. "Republicanism," defined as popular deference to an elite, was to him an honorific term; "democracy" which he equated with the identification of right with the popular will, was a pejorative epithet. He further distinguished between "democrats" and "jacobins," seeing the former as idealistic believers in the notion that it is easy to govern without a government, and the latter as politicians, who like Franklin's "artful men," exploit human credulity and passions for their own purposes.[47]

Upon the growth of the Jeffersonian party and its superior organization, Ames, like Hamilton, became disenchanted with the assumption of the older Federalists that the people would resume a deferential attitude toward their "natural leaders." He summed up his attitude in 1805: "Federalism was . . . manifestly founded on a mistake, on the supposed existence of sufficient political virtue, and on the permanency and authority of the public morals." While Federalists indulged their error, Jeffersonians "acted on the knowledge of what men actually are, not what they ought to be."[48]

The old Federalist belief had been summed up by George Cabot in 1797: "Popular gales sometimes blow hard, but they don't blow long. The man who has the courage to face them will at last out-face them." Ames in 1801, advised this substitution: "We must court popular favor. We must study popular opinion and accommodate measures to what it is." Whereas party was equivalent to faction in Ames' early thought, he came to see it as a necessity: "Party is an association of honest men for honest purposes, and, when the State falls into bad hands, is the only efficient defense."[49]

Ames' note was picked up by younger Federalists. Thus in 1803 William Plumer declared, while asking that Ames, Hamilton and others be abandoned: "We must have a new set of leaders. . . . Let us have men who can relax their principles of morality as occasion may require and adapt themselves to circumstances." The new leaders emulated the Jeffersonians in developing party organization, in electioneering techniques, in the foundation of benevolent societies and of a partisan press, to the end of reestablishing elitism through popular appeals.[50]

In basic agreement with the new approach, Hamilton suggested a scheme which would play on a factor which the deist Jefferson studiously forebore from exploiting. He proposed a nation-wide Federalist "front" organization, the Christian Constitutional Society, whose purpose was to be threefold: (1) to diffuse information; (2) to use all lawful means to effect the election of proper men; and (3) to promote charitable and useful institutions in populous cities for the relief of immigrants and for education. Fortunately this plan to use religion for political purposes never got off the ground.[51]

The significant aspect of the Federalist reorientation was the impact upon the party of the growing democratic sentiment. Rule by an elite remained the goal, but it was to be realized through recognition of the wishes, interests, and desires of an active multitude, as evidenced in later Federalist appeals to minorities and exploitation of the notion of a popular will. Failure to find an issue strong enough to bring them success, however, turned the party after sixteen years of defeat into a

regular loser, and the name "Federalist" into an invidious epithet. Opposition to the Republican policy of embargo, and the War of 1812 with
Great Britain, which issued in a secessionist movement, reinforced Republican equations of Federalism with Monarchism, Toryism, and
Anglophilism. As stated by the recent historian of later Federalism, the
unlucky coincidence of the Peace of Ghent, the victory at New Orleans,
and the ill-advised Hartford Convention of 1815, rendered it the *coup
de grâce.** The War of 1812 stands as the sole war in American history
not succeeded by a strong trend toward conservatism; the opportunity
existed but the party of the conservatives was no longer a vital entity.[52]

* The Hartford Convention report, after stating that the states should defend their
citizens against unconstitutional federal acts and that defense should be left to the
states, asked amendment of the Constitution to apportion taxes and representation in
proportion to the number of free persons, to prohibit embargoes longer than sixty
days, to require a two-thirds Congressional vote for a declaration of war, to limit
foreign trade, preclude naturalized citizens from federal office and limit the Presidency
to one term. For a full discussion see Marshall Smelser, *The Democratic Republic*
(New York, 1968), pp. 298–299.

NOTES

1. Second Letter from Phocian (1784); Hamilton to Washington, Aug. 13, 1788;
and "Pay Book," 1777, Harold C. Syrett and Jacob E. Cooke (eds.), *The Papers of
Alexander Hamilton* (New York, 1961–1969, 15 vols.), III, 556, V, 202, I, 390.
Hereinafter cited as *Papers*.
2. Hamilton to Rufus King; Dec. 16, 1796, Henry Cabot Lodge (ed.), *The Works
of Alexander Hamilton* (New York, 1904, 12 vols.), X, 217. Hereinafter cited as
Works. Hamilton to Edw. Carrington, May 26, 1792, *Papers*, XI, 426; Hamilton, "The
Continentalist," No. 1, *Papers*, II, 651.
3. Hamilton to James Bayard, April 1802, *Works*, X, 433. For a discussion of
Hamilton's conception of "public good," see Cecelia Kenyon, "Alexander Hamilton:
Rousseau of the Right," *Political Science Quarterly*, LXXIII (June, 1958), 161–178,
and Clinton Rossiter, *Alexander Hamilton and the Constitution* (New York, 1964),
pp. 142–147.
4. Hume, as cited in John C. Miller; *Alexander Hamilton, Portrait in Paradox*
(New York, 1959), p. 233.
5. *Papers*, II, 244.
6. Hamilton, "First Report on the Public Credit" (1790), *Works*, II, 227–291;
Hamilton, cited in Miller, *op. cit.*, pp. 237, 234.
7. *Papers*, X, 230–340.
8. "Tully," Aug. 28, 1794, *Works*, VI, 419, 422.
9. *Papers*, VIII, 98, 107.
10. *Papers*, X, 303.
11. A full consideration of Hamilton's conception of foreign policy in a republican
government can be found in Gerald Stourzh, *Alexander Hamilton and the Idea of
Republican Government* (Stanford, Calif., 1970), pp. 126–170.
12. *Papers*, XV, 33–43.
13. *Papers*, XV, 66, 62.
14. *Papers*, XV, 66.
15. *Papers*, XV, 84, 85.
16. *Papers*, XV, 85n., 86.
17. *Works*, V, 89, 96.
18. Hamilton, First Draft of Washington's Farewell Address, *Works*, VIII, 187–214.

19. Richardson, *Messages and Papers of the Presidents*, I, 213ff.
20. *Papers*, I, 84. For discussions of Hamilton's view of parties see Stourzh, *op. cit.*, pp. 110–120 and Rossiter, *op. cit.*, pp. 147–149.
21. Richardson, *Messages and Papers*, I, 230.
22. *Ibid.*
23. Stourzh, *op. cit.*, pp. 191–195.
24. Quoted in Rossiter, *op. cit.*, p. 14.
25. *Papers*, IV, 185, 192, 200; *Works*, IV, 109.
26. Stourzh, *op. cit.*, 203–204. For the story of Hamilton's dealings with the British, see Julian P. Boyd, *Number 7* (Princeton, N.J., 1964).
27. Hamilton to Theodore Sedgwick, July 10, 1804, John C. Hamilton, *History of the Republic of the United States of America as Traced in the Writings of Alexander Hamilton and of His Contemporaries* (New York, 1857–1864, 7 vols.), VII, 823–824.
28. For Marshall's life see Albert J. Beveridge, *The Life of John Marshall* (Boston and New York, 1916, 4 vols.). For a recent study of Marshall's thought see Robert K. Faulkner, *The Jurisprudence of John Marshall* (Princeton, N.J., 1968).
29. *Marbury v Madison*, 1 Cranch 137, 155 (1803).
30. *Marbury v. Madison*, 1 Cranch, 137, 177 (1803).
31. *Annals U.S. Congress*. 1st Congress (1789–91), I, 440.
32. 4 Wheaton 316 (1819).
33. See B. F. Wright, *The Contract Clause of the Constitution* (Cambridge, Mass., 1938), p. 22. For a full consideration of the development and nature of the vested rights doctrine see Edward S. Corwin, "The Basic Doctrine of American Constitutional Law," *Michigan Law Review*, XII (Feb., 1914), reprinted in A. T. Mason and G. Garvey, *American Constitutional History: Essays by Edward S. Corwin* (New York, 1964), pp. 25–45.
34. *Van Horne's Lessee* v. *Dorrance*, 2 Dallas, 304, 310 (1795); *Calder v. Bull*, 3 Dallas 386, 388 (1798).
35. "Columbian Centinel," June 11, 1791, W. C. Ford (ed.), *The Writings of John Quincy Adams* (New York, 1913–1917, 7 vols.), I, 70, 71.
36. 6 Cranch 87 (1810); 4 Wheaton 518 (1819); *Sturgis v. Crowninshield*, 4 Wheaton 122 (1819); *Ogden v. Saunders*, 12 Wheaton 213 (1827).
37. For a discussion of the views of the old Federalists see D. H. Fischer, *The Revolution of American Conservatism* (New York, 1965), pp. 1–17, 20.
38. Jefferson, "The Anas," A. A. Lipscomb and A. E. Bergh (eds.), *Writings of Thomas Jefferson* (Washington, 1905, 20 vols.), I, 279; See also Stourzh, *op. cit.*, pp. 83–84.
39. Quoted in Manning Dauer, *The Adams Federalists* (Baltimore, 1953), p. 55.
40. Fischer, *op. cit.*, p. 19.
41. *U.S. Statutes at Large*, I, 596–597.
42. Leonard W. Levy, *Freedom of Speech and Press in Early American History: Legacy of Suppression* (Cambridge, Mass., 1960). I am indebted to Levy's discussion in the presentation which follows.
43. Boyd, *The Papers of Thomas Jefferson*, II, 546.
44. Quoted in Levy, *op. cit.*, pp. 195–196.
45. See Hamilton's speech in *People v. Croswell*, *Works*, VIII, 387–425.
46. Ames to Theodore Dwight, March 19, 1801, Seth Ames (ed.), *Works of Fisher Ames* (Boston, 1854, 2 vols.), I, 293.
47. *Ibid.*, II, 210, 221, 109ff. See also Ames' essay, "The Dangers of American Liberty," *ibid.*, II, 344ff.
48. *Ibid.*, II, 204, 205, 379.
49. Cabot is quoted in Fischer, *op. cit.*, p. 150; Ames to Theodore Dwight, March 19, 1801, *Works*, I, 293.
50. Quoted in Fischer, *op. cit.*, p. 45.
51. Hamilton to James A. Bayard, Apr. 1802, *Works*, X, 435–437.
52. Fischer, *op. cit.*, p. 181.

Chapter 13

THE POLITICAL THOUGHT OF THOMAS JEFFERSON

Nothing then is unchangeable but the inherent and unalienable rights of man.

THOMAS JEFFERSON

Thomas Jefferson: Homo Americanus

Alexis De Tocqueville called Jefferson "the most powerful advocate democracy has ever had," and Abraham Lincoln later declared that "the principles of Jefferson are the definitions and axioms of free society."[1] Because Jefferson never wrote a systematic study of politics, the arguments of the champion of popular government must be gleaned from the great state papers and laws which he drew; his only book, *Notes on Virginia;* his early pamphlet, "A Summary View";* and the thousands of letters which he wrote during his long life as revolutionist, legislator, governor, diplomat, president, educator, and retired statesman.

Capping his early intensive education in the classics, natural science, and mathematics with a thorough study of law, Jefferson's interests were universal and his whole life was involved in the omnivorous pursuit of knowledge. His approach to his studies was dictated by a peculiarly American concentration on the concrete, an intense concern with the task at hand, with the useful, with the challenge of the environment—in other words by a conviction that the practical life is paramount to the speculative, and action is superior to contemplation.[2]

Principles and Presuppositions of Jefferson's Thought

Although he disdained metaphysics, disliked speculative thinkers such as Plato and regarded the empiricists Bacon, Newton, and Locke as the

* See the previous discussion of Jefferson's thought in Chapter 7.

267

greatest men who ever lived, Jefferson's democratic thought was posited on the following principles, the truth of which he in good part presupposed.[3]

1. *Cosmology.* Rejecting chance and blind necessity as ultimate principles, Jefferson assumed, in eighteenth-century fashion, a creator of man and the universe, whom he saw in the image of an architect. Nature, the divine plan, was to him the product of the Creator's art. In this view, all existence is understood in terms of nature; the concrete, material world, the world of external "facts," and of tangible experience is the real world.[4]

2. *Epistemology.* Because the nature of the Creator's plan can be seen in the visible world, sense knowledge is alone reliable. Jefferson remarked: "When once we quit the basis of sensation, all is in the wind. To talk of *immaterial* existences, is to talk of *nothings.*" Then, too: "The moment a person forms a theory, his imagination sees in every object only the tracts which favor that theory." He concluded: "A patient pursuit of facts, and cautious combination and comparison of them, is the drudgery to which man is subjected by his Maker, if he wishes to attain sure knowledge." Ideas have significance only to the degree that they affect human conduct or external reality. Thus it is man's external relation to the paradigm, nature, rather than inward reflection, contemplation, or abstraction, which serves as the Jeffersonian point of departure and of reference.[5]

3. *Man.* Jefferson saw man, like other animals, as explicable in purely naturalistic terms, i.e., biologically organized matter. Mind is a function of brain; thought is "an action of a particular organization of matter formed for that purpose by its Creator." The dualism of body and soul is overcome by a reduction of the latter to the former. Man, however, is above the rest of creation, in that he is its center. Men are not equal in the sense that they possess an immortal spiritual soul but in their equal creation and their biological unity as a species. The various races of men are explained in terms of their adaptations to the different environments. In fact, adaptability is not only man's basic characteristic but an empirical verification of his fundamental equality. Human nature is fixed, but because man is educable he is capable of improvement.[6]

Although men are created equal, their minds are differently shaped, inevitably and necessarily giving rise to variations in ideas and opinions. As Jefferson put it: "Differences of opinion . . . like differences of face, are a law of our nature, and should be viewed with the same tolerance." Consequently, "our opinions are not voluntary." It followed that it is not what a man believes but his honest profession of his beliefs which is important. Man is thus not answerable for the "rightness" but for the "uprightness" of his choices.[7]

4. *Morality.* Jefferson's belief in the biologically determined diversity

of minds precluded acceptance of "right reason" as the objective ground of moral judgments. Instead, he saw all men endowed with a moral sense which he defined as a function of feeling rather than reflection. The dictates of the moral sense, he believed, were essentially the same in all men.

Man was destined for society. His morality therefore was to be formed to this object. He was endowed with a sense of right and wrong merely relative to this. This sense is as much a part of his nature as the sense of hearing, seeing, feeling; it is the true foundation of morality. . . . It is given to all human beings in a stronger or weaker degree. It may be strengthened by exercise, as may any particular limb of the body. This sense is submitted indeed in some degree to the guidance of reason; but it is a small stock which is required for this: even a less one than what we call Common sense. State a moral case to a ploughman and a professor. The former will decide it as well, and often better than the latter, because he has not been led astray by artificial rules.[8]

What men generally feel is right was accepted as such by Jefferson and attributed to a common determination of the species by the Creator. He thus rejected explanations of morality in terms of truth, taste, or self-interest. Admitting imperfections in the moral sense of some men as departures from "health," he believed they could be corrected by education, appeals to reason, utility, interest, legal sanctions, exploitation of the natural desire to please others, and the fear of divine punishment.

The end for man, as Jefferson saw it, is happiness, which besides connoting material security and prosperity entails individual virtue and presupposes liberty. Believing that every mind finds pleasure in doing good to others, Jefferson defined the latter as virtue. He found his prescriptions for personal self-government in the stoicism of Epictetus and the refined hedonism of Epicurus; for one's duties to others, he could find no teacher superior to the nondivinized Christ. And he knew "but one code of morality for men, whether acting singly or collectively."

Jefferson came to qualify his moral sense doctrine by utilitarian considerations. In 1814 he wrote: "The answer is that nature has constituted *utility* to man, the standard and test of virtue. Men living in different countries under different circumstances, different habits and regimens, may have different utilities; the same act, therefore, may be useful, and consequently virtuous in one country which is injurious and vicious in another differently circumstanced." Utility, however, was to him not egoistic hedonism; instead it was subordinate to the controlling norm—the happiness of others. Speaking of human conduct, he wrote: "If it is to effect the happiness of him to whom it is directed, it is virtuous, while in a society under different circumstances and opinions, the same act might produce pain, and would be vicious. The essence of virtue is in doing good to others, while what is good may be one thing in one society, and its contrary in another."[9]

5. *Religion.* The essence of religion to Jefferson is morality, or action, in contrast to theology, which he classified as "opinion." Dogmas and revelations are products of "the varieties in the structure and action of the human mind," and thus, if they do not influence moral behavior adversely, socially irrelevant. He concluded: "We should not inter-meddle with the particular dogmas in which all religions differ, and which are totally unconnected with morality."

The fundamental truth of any particular creed consists in those teachings it shares with others. As in questions of morality, the *consensus gentium* is central to Jefferson. "He who steadily observes those precepts in which all religions concur, will never be questioned at the gates of heaven as to the dogmas in which they all differ." That religion is good "which produces an honest life." True Christianity follows Christ in proclaiming God's goodness and perfection, but not defining Him. It teaches men to be "of one sect, doers of good, and eschewers of evil."[10]

6. *Natural Rights.* Having been "created equal," "born free," and endowed by their Maker with a moral sense which ensures that "the great principles of right and wrong are legible to every reader," men by their common nature possess inalienable natural rights. These are based on Jefferson's notion of "rightful liberty" as "unobstructed action according to our will within limits drawn around us by the equal rights of others," and include: (1) the most fundamental of rights such as freedom of the mind, conscience, religion and self-government; (2) rights involving motion, including freedom of movement, migration, communication, commerce, work, and the enjoyment of its fruits; (3) rights deduced from those above, including equal protection of laws, property, revolution against oppression, trial by jury, and recognition of the will of the majority as "the natural law of every society of men."

While Jefferson's early formulation of his natural rights doctrine was principally in moral terms, or "the common sense of the subject," he re-shaped it later in terms of biological needs and wants, thus integrating it more closely with his naturalistic approach to man. In this view each natural right is rooted in a basic natural want or need, the denial of which entails an unwarranted violation of nature's plan.[11]

Although Jefferson spoke of the "law of nature" in the Declaration of Independence, and elsewhere mentioned it as part of the "law of nations," his use of the term, in its moral sense, was infrequent when compared to his use of "natural rights." It does no violence to his thought if one states that applied to man, the content of his "law of nature," or "natural law" is essentially "the natural rights of man."

7. *Society.* In his original draft of the Declaration of Independence,

Jefferson wrote that "all men are created equal and *independent*." Elsewhere he stated that "experience declares that man is the only animal which devours his own kind," and talked of men as divided into "sheep" and "wolves." Independent men, possessed of idiosyncratic minds, conflicting opinions, predatory inclinations, and equal natural rights, can hardly be said to possess the nucleating ties and duties which are the prerequisites of communal life.[12]

On the other hand, Jefferson was "convinced man has no natural right in opposition to his social duties"; he considered man "as formed for society, and endowed by nature with those dispositions which fit him for society." Society is "one of the natural wants with which man has been created." Although he put forth no positive notion of community, he did postulate human propensities and faculties which might produce shared objectives and bonds of unity. As we have seen, he thought that nature has given men a common moral sense testifying to their sociability, and prescribing obligations the performance of which is accompanied by a feeling of pleasure. Similarly, the natural reliability of sense knowledge, placed against the challenge of the environment, brings men together in the common patient pursuit, combination and comparison of "facts," issuing in a body of tested and useful practical truths, whose application brings material prosperity, security, and happiness. Then, too, differences of opinion can be socially advantageous, particularly in religion, where "the several sects perform the office of a *censor morum* over each other."[13]

Jefferson believed that a true society is a "healthy" society in the biological sense of the term. Nature is thus the model for society and the indicator of its ends. In providing the environmental setting it defines common problems which give rise to shared objectives. Nature likewise unfailingly supplies society with a "natural aristocracy" whose grounds are "virtue and talents." Jefferson considered the natural aristocracy "the most precious gift of nature, for the instruction, the trusts, and government of society." Indeed, he added, "it would have been inconsistent in creation to have formed man for the social state, and not to have provided virtue and wisdom enough to manage the concerns of the society." At the same time he assumed that the people in a society would defer to their naturally appointed leaders.[14]

For people in general, agriculture is the pursuit which is most in accordance with nature and thus productive of social, political, and individual "health." "Cultivators of the earth are the most valuable citizens. They are the most vigorous, the most independent, the most virtuous, and they are tied to their country and wedded to its liberty and interests by the most lasting bonds." In fact, "those who labor in the earth are the chosen people of God, if ever He had a chosen people, whose breasts He has made His peculiar deposit for substantial and genuine virtue."[15]

The factor of environment as a societal influence was complemented by Jefferson's emphasis upon what has been called "presentism" as the vital temporal factor. Thinking again in basic biological terms, Jefferson postulated "generations" as the vehicles of society. Having put prime emphasis on rights rather than duties, Jefferson saw members of the contemporary generation but loosely linked. He saw, however, *no* bonds in the form of duties between the present generation, on the one hand, and the past, on the other. And the obligation of the present to the future consists only in the duty not to pass on to it any incurred debt. Thus *"the earth belongs in usufruct to the living"* and "no man can by *natural right* oblige the lands he occupied, or the persons who succeed him in that occupation, to the payment of debts contracted by him." And, "what is true of every member of the society individually, is true of them all collectively, since the rights of the whole can be no more than the sum of the rights of the individuals." Consequently, the present generation is never bound by traditions, inherited institutions, and ancient customs and practices, but can and should remake society as it wishes. Simply put, "no society can make a perpetual constitution, or even a perpetual law," because "the earth belongs always to the living generation." The present generation, with its bounds and tasks defined by the environment and its ends implicit in nature, forms the substance of society, whose "natural law" is the "law of the majority." For the will of the majority to be "rightful" however, Jefferson insisted that it must be "reasonable," i.e., not violative of natural rights. Jefferson thus defined "rightful liberty" quite differently than did Winthrop, Penn, and Boucher, as "unobstructed action according to our will within limits drawn around us by the equal rights of others."[16]

Finally, although the species is essentially fixed, man's "mind is perfectible to a degree of which we cannot as yet form any conception," and "this whole chapter in the history of man is new." The present generation of Americans lives in a republic, whose "great extent" and "sparse habitation" are new. Thus the contemporary American generation, unlike that of ancient Europe with its feudal inheritance, confronts a continent which is a "tabula rasa," upon which it can freely experiment.[17]

Jefferson's Political Thought: The Empire for Liberty

Jefferson's comparative evaluation of the three main types of society which he saw extant in the world further illustrates his penchant to regard nature as a model. First, he talked of societies without government, exemplified in the American Indian; second, societies under governments wherein every person has a just influence, exemplified in a limited degree in England, and to a great degree in the United States; and third, societies with governments based on force, exemplified in all other monarchies than England, and in most republics. Of the three,

Jefferson was "not clear" in his mind that the first condition "is not the best," although he thought it inconsistent with a large population. He admired in it the absence of coercive governmental power and the control exerted by manners, social sanctions, public opinion, and the moral sense. He greatly preferred this condition to rule by "too much law, as among the civilized Europeans." He added significantly, "It will be said, the great societies cannot exist without government. The savages, therefore, break them into small ones."[18]

Much of Jefferson's political thought is implicit in these statements. Convinced that man is a social animal, he seems always to have harbored a strong doubt that nature intended man to be a political animal. His ideal apparently was a natural society without formal government, but he saw this as limited in terms of progressive advancement, and impossible of realization in a large geographical area. Thus he looked to the development of political institutions which would aid in realizing a situation most closely approximating the "free" natural state, while preserving the advantages of civilization. Indian society was, in this sense, a favorable evaluative norm to him. Proclaiming, in 1787, against those who saw government under the Articles of Confederation as bad, he asserted: "The only condition on earth to be compared with ours, in my opinion, is that of the Indians, where they have still less law than we."[19]

Jefferson regarded European nations as divided, "under pretence of governing," into two classes, "wolves and sheep." America was not immune to this condition because "human nature is the same on every side of the Atlantic, and will be alike influenced by the same causes." He did not think "that fourteen out of fifteen men are rogues"; but in matters governmental, he "always found that rogues would be uppermost," unless safeguards were provided. Thus he warned that the time to guard against corruption and tyranny is before they take hold.[20]

Government then was to Jefferson a necessary evil which should subserve the fundamental end of individual freedom. "Free government," he wrote in the Kentucky Resolutions of 1798, "is founded in jealousy, and not in confidence. . . . In questions of power, . . . let no more be heard of confidence in man, but bind him down from mischief by the chains of the Constitution." Government must be reduced to the task of securing "our just rights," as indicated by man's biological and psychological needs. The notions of a substantive "public good" and "energetic government," propounded by Hamilton and Wilson, were alien to Jefferson's mind. He admitted to being "not a friend to a very energetic government," thinking it "always oppressive." He summed up his thought on the point in his first Inaugural address, stating: "A wise and frugal government which shall restrain men from injuring one another, which shall leave them otherwise free to regulate their own pursuits of industry and improvement, and shall not take from the mouth of labor the bread it has earned. This is the sum of good government, and this is necessary to close the circles of our felicities."[21]

To check the wolves and preserve freedom the sheep must have power. Popular sovereignty and republicanism are the resultant Jeffersonian prescriptions. It would be a great mistake to think that Jefferson ever equated *vox populi* with *vox dei;* that was the work of a later age. He indeed believed that the people "are the only safe, because the only honest, depositories of the public rights and should . . . be introduced into the administration of them in every function to which they are sufficient." He also thought that "in general they will elect the wise and good," i.e., the natural aristocracy. And, above all, the people are simply too numerous to be bought.[22]

The consensual principle is thus championed by Jefferson as the instrument for establishing legitimate government and as its *modus operandi,* not because the people are necessarily wise and good, but because obligation is based on consent and the people are the only effective check on rulers bent on limiting freedom. The Declaration of Independence attests to his adherence to popular sovereignty; his theory of republicanism attests to his affirmation of democratic government. "Purely and simply," he said of a republic, "it means a government by its citizens in mass, acting directly and personally, according to rules established by the majority; and that every other government is more or less republican, in proportion as it has in its composition more or less of this ingredient of the direct action of the citizens." The full implementation of this norm he saw impracticable outside of areas like the New England townships. Beyond this, republicanism shades off into types "where the powers of the government, being divided, should be exercised each by representatives chosen either *pro hac vice,* or for such short terms as should render secure the duty of expressing the will of their constituents."[23]

An ancillary Jeffersonian principle was the gradation of authority in accordance with competence.

We think experience has proved it safer, for the mass of individuals composing the society, to reserve to themselves personally the exercise of all rightful powers to which they are competent, and to delegate those to which they are not competent to deputies named, and removable for unfaithful conduct, by themselves immediately. Hence with us the people . . . being competent to judge of the facts in ordinary life . . . have retained the functions of judges of the facts, under the name of jurors; but being unqualified for the management of affairs requiring intelligence above the common level, yet competent judges of human character, they chose, for their management, representatives, some by themselves immediately, others by electors chosen by themselves.[24]

Jefferson nevertheless believed with Madison that a representative republic "must be so extensive as that local egoisms may never reach its greater part; that on every particular question, a majority may be found in its councils free from particular interests, and giving, therefore, an uniform prevalence to the principles of justice."[25]

Jefferson's theory of "wards" is not only illustrative of how he brought together his ideas of democratic republicanism, the territorial devolution of authority, and the practicality of an extensive representative republic, but represents his conception of how political man can most closely approximate the order of freedom indicated by nature. The basic unit, the ward, a territory about six miles square, was described as a small republic, in the purest sense of the term wherein all members would transact a great portion of its business. The majoritarian principle would be the motive force in this direct democracy. The functions of each ward would include provision for an elementary school, a company of militia, a justice of the peace, police, care of the poor, sanitation, roads, and election of jurors as well as all governmental functionaries. The basic idea apparently was to reform the southern county system of government with an infusion of New England democracy by relieving the county of most of its business and having it better done "by making every citizen an acting member of the government." The county government would, in turn, be controlled by justices elected in the wards and would deal with matters of general concern to the county. The theory is summed up in Jefferson's statement:

The way to have good and safe government, is not to trust it all to one, but to divide it among the many. . . . Let the national government be entrusted with the defence of the nation, and its foreign and federal relations; the State governments with the civil rights, laws, police, and administration of what concerns the State generally; the counties with the local concerns of the counties; and each ward direct the interests within itself. It is by dividing and subdividing these republics from the great national one down through all its subordinations, until it ends in the administration of every man's farm and affairs by himself; by placing under every one what his own eye may superintend, that all will be done for the best.[26]

To effect a removal of obstructions to the individual's free pursuit of his natural rights was the Jeffersonian justification of government. Republicanism built upon the pure democracy of the agrarian wards and extended upward in pyramidal fashion through the county, state, and federal representative democracies was an indispensable means.

Equally important to Jefferson was the right of rebellion, and the need for its recurrent exercise. Using again the analogy with nature he wrote in 1787: "I hold it that a little rebellion now and then is a good thing, and as necessary in the political world as storms in the physical.

. . . It is a medicine necessary for the sound health of government."
Referring to Shays' rebellion, he wrote: "God forbid we should ever
be 20 years without such a rebellion. . . . The tree of liberty must be
refreshed from time to time with the blood of patriots and tyrants. It is
its natural manure." Rebellion is, in effect, purgative, bringing men back
to the first principles of nature from which they can start anew and
unencumbered.[27]

Because it is the living generation which alone has rights—"one
generation is to another as one independent nation to another"—and
because Jefferson computed that a generation lasts nineteen years, he
concluded that "every constitution . . . and every law, naturally expires
at the end of 19 years." Wedding the doctrine of rebellion to that of the
present generation, it follows that each generation not only possesses
the right but the duty to detach itself, by force, if necessary, from the
shackles of the past. In this fashion will they find themselves in the same
favorable situation as Americans in 1776 who appealed to "the laws and
institutions . . . of nature."[28]

Jefferson used the rhetoric of exaggeration to declare that each
generation must be free to return to first principles.* He extolled rebellion but admitted that the peaceful making of a new constitution, or
even an election, served the purpose as well. Thus he considered his
election in 1800 as great a revolution in the *principles* of government as
the revolution of 1776 was in the *form* of government.[29] Like Chipman
and Wilson, Jefferson regarded the provisions for amendment in the
American constitutions as instruments by which could be gained peacefully what otherwise would be effected only extralegally and perhaps
by force. If the "wolves" are apprised that not only are the "sheep"

---

* In 1816 Jefferson explained that he was no advocate of change for its own sake:
"I am certainly not an advocate for frequent and untried changes in laws and constitutions. I think moderate imperfections had better be borne with; because, when
once known, we accommodate ourselves to them, and find practical means of correcting
their ill effects." (Jefferson to Samuel Kercheval, July 12, 1816, *Writings*, XV, 40–41.)
Similarly, Jefferson's circumspection is illustrated by his action along with other members of a committee on the revision of the laws in 1777. In that regard he wrote, "at
the first and only meeting of the whole committee . . . the question was discussed
whether we would attempt to reduce the whole body of the law into a code, the text
of which should become the law of the land? We decided against that, because every
word and phrase in that text would become a new subject of criticism and litigation,
until its sense should have been settled by numerous decisions, and that, in the
meantime, the rights of property would be in the air. We concluded not to meddle
with the common law, i.e., the law preceding the existence of the statutes, further than
to accommodate it to our new principles and circumstances; but to take up the whole
body of statutes and Virginia laws, to leave out everything obsolete or improper, in-
sert what was wanting, and reduce the whole within as moderate a compass as it
would bear, and to the plain language of common sense, divested of the verbiage, the
barbarous tautologies and redundancies which render the British statutes unintelligible." (Jefferson to Skelton Jones, July 28, 1809, *Writings*, XII, 298–299).

watching them, but that they also possess a constitutional means for change, and behind that the moral right to revolt, there will be less inclination to mischief.

After the Declaration of Independence, Jefferson was a principal figure in the task of clearing the ground of residues of what he called the "patrician order" and the "aristocracy of wealth" to bring about an "aristocracy of virtue and talent." The repeal of the laws of entail and primogeniture, though probably not much more than a formalization of existing practice, was seen by him as an "enlargement" of natural right, in that it worked toward an equalization of property, an elimination of the dead hand of the past, and a basis for a more solidified republic of rural landholders.[30] He also urged, unsuccessfully, that slavery be gradually eliminated by requiring that all Negroes born after a certain date be freed and deported. Gradual emancipation and subsidized colonization were his lifelong themes. He tried hard to stifle doubts he had concerning the equal potential of the Negro; he did not, however, think that the black and white races could live tranquilly together on the level of equal freedom.

Nothing is more certainly written in the book of fate, than that these people are to be free; nor is it less certain that the two races, equally free, cannot live in the same government. Nature, habit, opinion have drawn indelible lines of distinction between them. It is still in our power to direct the process of emancipation and deportation, peaceably, and in such slow degree, as that the evil will wear off insensibly, and their place be . . . filled up with free white laborers.[31]

Because he saw the people as the "only safe depositories of government," Jefferson concluded that "to render even them safe their minds must be improved to a certain degree." His early plans for public education for all white males through three levels of schools, according to competence, and his later founding of the University of Virginia, attest to his keen concern with education on a secular basis, as the foundation of democracy. The same animus which informed Washington, Wilson, and Chipman against sending Americans to Europe to be educated prompted Jefferson to declaim against it. Education in the principles of republicanism was basic in his scheme; but education was more than just a precondition of good government—it was also "the resource most to be relied on for ameliorating the condition promoting the virtue, and advancing the happiness of man." In this spirit he also strongly opposed Blackstone's *Commentaries* as the embodiment of Norman, Tory, monarchical influences, as against the Whiggism of Coke's *Institutes* and reports.

Having sworn "eternal hostility against every tyranny over the mind of man," and believing that "the varieties in structure and action of the human mind as in those of the body, are the work of our Creator, against which it cannot be a religious duty to erect the standard of uniformity," Jefferson espoused freedom of conscience, toleration of all religions, and a strict separation of church and state. His "Act for Establishing Religious Freedom" with its substitution of the test of "overt action" for that of "bad tendency," which was passed into law in Virginia in 1786, has already been commented upon.* It should be added that although the law allowed no public purpose for religion and established a secular state, it freed religion from ties to government, allowing its unrestrained exercise and propagation so long as its principles do not "break out into overt acts against peace and good order."[32]

Jefferson's notion of the diversity of minds and the involuntary nature of options allowed him also to give a naturalistic explanation of political parties.

Men have differed in opinion, and been divided into parties by these opinions, from the first origin of societies, and in all governments where they have been permitted to think and to speak. The same political parties which now agitate the United States, have existed through all time. Whether the power of the people or that of the *aristoi* should prevail, were questions which kept the States of Greece and Rome in eternal convulsions, as they now schismatize every people whose minds and mouths are not shut up by the gag of a despot. And in fact, the terms of whig and tory belong to natural history as well as to civil history. They denote the temper and constitution of mind of different individuals.[33]

We find no condemnation in general of parties and factions in Jefferson's writings, such as that made by most Federalists, but a recognition of their inevitability and desirability as a fact of natural history. As Jefferson said in 1811 concerning his past differences with John Adams: "Our different views of the same subject are the result of our difference in our organization and experience." The two parties issuing from nature comprehend "those who fear and distrust the people," and "those who identify themselves with the people," i.e., in contemporary terms, Federalists and Republicans.[34]

Jefferson is rightly regarded as America's foremost proponent of freedom of the mind and freedom of expression. He maintained, on the one hand, that "our opinions are not voluntary," and, on the other, that "difference of opinion leads to inquiry, and inquiry to truth."[35] We have seen how, assuming the natural reliability of sense knowledge in the attack on practical problems, he believed that men, through cooperative effort, could arrive at useful, practical, and communicable truths. We

* In the previous chapter.

also have remarked how he disdained metaphysics, theology, abstract theories or dogmas of any kind. It is this latter realm, as well as that of party preference, to which he more properly meant to apply the term opinion. It was different with scientific theories; he regarded Newton's theory as proven by "reason and experiment," i.e., it was empirically verifiable. He also thought that certain political principles had been experimentally elevated in America above mere "opinion" into truth; most particularly, "that man can govern himself," and "that religious freedom is the most effectual anodyne against religious dissension."[36]

It can be concluded that Jefferson believed that it is not only a dictate of natural right but of progressive society that all men should be allowed freely to propound their naturally diverse opinions, that government censorship or acceptance of an official creed is an intrusion at once deleterious and unhealthy ("[were] the government to prescribe to us our medicine and diet, our bodies would be in such keeping as our souls are now"), and that the ultimate test of truth is not abstract reason or passion (opinion) but empirical verification. It is in this sense that we must interpret his Miltonic affirmation in his "Act for Establishing Religious Freedom."

. . . . truth is great and will prevail if left to herself, . . . she is the proper and sufficient antagonist to error, and has nothing to fear from conflict, unless by human interposition disarmed of her natural weapons, free argument and debate, errors ceasing to be dangerous when it is permitted freely to contradict them.[37]

Finally, Jefferson did not believe that democracy was realizable only in America. American republicanism was to him like John Winthrop's "City Upon a Hill."

A just and solid republican government maintained here, will be a standing monument and example for the aim and imitation of the people of other countries; and I join . . . in the hope and belief that they will see, from our example, that a free government is of all others the most energetic; that the inquiry which has been excited among the mass of mankind by our revolution and its consequences, will ameliorate the condition of man over a great portion of the globe.[38]

Jefferson's Constitutional Thought

Jefferson considered a constitution to be a compact, which, ideally speaking, is renewed or revised by each generation. He saw certain structural and operational constitutional principles, such as the provision for amendment, as necessary to free government. Thus he wrote John Adams: "The first principle of a good government is certainly a distribution of its powers into executive, judiciary, and legislative, and a subdivision of the latter into two or three branches." He was as much an enemy of the tyranny of a majority as a tyranny of one. In 1789 he remarked: "The executive in our governments is not the sole, it is scarcely the principal object of my jealousy. The tyranny of the legislatures is the most formidable dread at present, and will be for long years." Similarly did he insist on the implementation of the principle of equality, in the form of equal districting and extension of the suffrage to "every man who fights or pays." In a draft of a Constitution, which he drew for Virginia in 1776, he included a provision to grant a fifty-acre freehold to every propertyless male citizen. Of central importance to Jefferson was the elective principle. On the state level he advocated popular election of legislators, governors, juries, and although originally he urged appointment of judges for life, he later advocated their election for limited terms also.[39]

Most particularly did Jefferson insist on the inclusion of a Bill of Rights as an integral part of a constitution, particularly one which did not qualify its grant of powers by the term "expressly." He asserted that "a bill of rights is what the people are entitled to against every government on earth, general or particular; and what no just government should refuse, or rest on inference." In 1787 he urged that the federal constitution be amended to include guarantees of "freedom of religion, freedom of the press, protection against standing armies; restriction of monopolies, the eternal and unremitting force of the habeas corpus laws, and trials by jury in all matters of fact triable by the laws of the land and not by the laws of Nations."[40]

Jefferson's differences with the Federalists came to a focus in their conflicting interpretations of the nature of the federal Constitution and its ultimate arbiter. He opposed Hamilton's broad construction with the principle that the framers of the Constitution "intended to lace [Congress] up straitly within the enumerated powers, and those without which, as means, these powers could not be carried into effect." Specifically, he considered the establishment of a national bank unconstitutional because the "general welfare" clause implied no such broad power, and the word "necessary," in the "necessary and proper" clause of the Constitution must be construed as including only those means "without which the grant of power would be nugatory," and not including those which are merely "convenient."[41]

Jefferson saw his election in 1800 as an overwhelming popular rejection of the Federalist policy of "consolidation," a Republican victory which, however, was blunted by the fact that the Federalists remained entrenched in the only nonelective branch of the government, the judiciary. He did not, however, disbelieve in judicial review. Arguing for the inclusion of a Bill of Rights in the federal Constitution, he praised "the legal check which it puts in the hands of a judiciary," which he thought must be "independent and kept strictly to their own department." Although he came greatly to distrust the Federalist judges and what he considered to be a tendency on their part to expand their jurisdiction, he never abandoned the concept of judicial review rendered limited in a government of coordinate branches responsible ultimately to the people. His principle regarding who shall adjudge the constitutionality of questions denied exclusive power to the judiciary by holding "that each department is truly independent of the others, and has an equal right to decide for itself what is the meaning of the Constitution in the cases submitted to its action; and especially, where it is to act ultimately and without appeal." Thus although the federal judges could legitimately enforce the Sedition Act of 1798 as a constitutional exercise of power, Jefferson, when President, did not feel bound thereby and released or pardoned those imprisoned under it, on his independent judgment of the unconstitutionality of the act.[42]

Jefferson proposed to rectify the irresponsibility of the federal judges to the people by rendering them subject to the elective principle. That left the question of who was ultimately to decide constitutional questions in cases of conflicting interpretations between the nation and the states. His original answer came in the form of a draft of the Kentucky Resolutions of 1798 which laid the groundwork for the theory of state nullification of federal law which was fully developed later by John C. Calhoun. Seeing the federal Constitution as a compact between the states, Jefferson declared that the federal government, being merely the creature, cannot be the final judge of the extent of its powers, "but that as in all other cases of compact among powers having no common judge, each party has an equal right to judge for itself as well of infractions as of the mode and measure of redress." And "where powers are assumed which have not been delegated, a nullification of the act is the rightful remedy." In other words, Jefferson thought that each state has "a natural right" to judge whether a case is violative of the compact, and then "to nullify of their own authority" attempts at enforcement within their limits. Still more remarkable, in light of Jefferson's professed devotion to the people as ultimate judges, the Resolutions assume that the legislature, as well as the people of a state, can nullify federal law.[43]

Clearly the irreconcilable conflict in constitutional theory concerning the nature of the Union between the views expressed by Chief Justice Marshall in *McCulloch v. Maryland* and Jefferson in the Kentucky Resolutions, was not merely reflective of the deep division between Federalist and Republican but of a fundamental ambiguity in the Constitution. Jefferson later reformulated his position, asserting that the ultimate arbiter in case of a conflict between nation and states was "the people of the Union, assembled by their deputies in Convention, at the

call of Congress, of two-thirds of the States." With this no one could differ because it is prescribed specifically in the Constitution; its principal
shortcoming of course lay in the fact that a general convention could
not serve as a practical mechanism to solve each recurrent federal-state
difference. In any case, Jefferson loved the Union, thinking that its dissolution would be "among the greatest calamities," but adding that an
even greater calamity would be "submission to a government of unlimited powers."[44]

Jefferson's Principles and Practice

Men of action, confronted with the burden of decision, find of necessity that a pure application of general principles, no matter how dearly
held, is seldom possible. Prudence, or correct practical judgment about
things to be done in the welter of complex, concrete circumstances and
competing demands, is the supreme political virtue, one which is quite
incompatible with slide-rule morality. Men of equal rectitude and wisdom may act prudentially in different ways in similar political situations.
One cannot then expect a rigid consistency between the general principles and the practice of a man who is at once a political thinker and a
politician.

So it was with Jefferson, a practical politician whose ability is attested
to in his collaboration with Madison in the formation of the successful
Democratic-Republican party, and in his steering the United States successfully through eight troubled years as President. "No maxim," he
declared, "can be laid down as being wise and expedient for all times
and circumstances." All is changeable except "the inherent inalienable
rights of man." Consequently, Jefferson was not deterred by his principle of strict construction of the Constitution from the purchase of the
Louisiana territory, from continuing part of the Hamiltonian program,
or from establishing a rigid embargo which touched the table of every
American family. Similarly in 1776, despite his rhetorical calls to return
to nature's principles, Jefferson, in his monumental revision of Virginia's
laws, opposed abolishing the old system and preparing one completely
new, preferring to "preserve the general system, and only modify it to
the present state of things," because, among other things, it would result
in endless litigation and render property uncertain.[45]

In fact, like any responsible statesman, Jefferson subscribed to the
primacy of the ancient principle *salus populi suprema lex.* He wrote in
1810: "A strict observance of the written laws is doubtless *one* of the
high duties of a good citizen but it is not the *highest.* The laws of necessity, of self-preservation, of saving our country when in danger, are of
higher obligation. To lose our country by a scrupulous adherence to
written law, would be to lose the law itself, with life, liberty, property

and all those who are enjoying them with us; thus absurdly sacrificing the end to the means."[46]

If we keep these factors in mind, along with the vitally important knowledge that the period of Jefferson's public life from the 1760's through the first decade of the nineteenth century and beyond was beset by crises, going many times to the heart of the state, it is easier to understand the allegedly unprincipled actions, for which he has been recently heavily indicted. The charge is that "Jefferson at one time or another supported loyalty oaths; countenanced internment camps for political suspects; drafted a bill of attainder; urged prosecutions for seditious libel; trampled on the Fourth Amendment; condoned military despotism; used the Army to enforce laws in time of peace; censored reading; chose professors for their political opinions; and endorsed the doctrine that the means, however odious, were justified by the ends." Among other things it is claimed that Jefferson never protested against the law of seditious libel during the Sedition Act controversy; his great call for freedom of the press in the Kentucky Resolutions was based on a belief that the Sedition Act was an unconstitutional federal invasion of an area properly left to the states; as President he condoned a prosecution under the very concept of a federal common law of seditious libel against which he had proclaimed in 1798; he refused as President to observe a federal court order and was rebuked thereupon in the name of the law and the Constitution by the federal judge, one of his own appointees and sympathizers; and he sought to make the University of Virginia an instrument of his political party and its doctrines.[47]

Indeed, the apotheosized Jefferson, the anachronistic creation of the twentieth-century libertarian, is tarnished by such charges. The flesh-and-blood Jefferson, the eighteenth-century Whig who attempted to purge free government of feudal and monarchical residues and to preserve it by all means at his disposal, remains a man of his times, but in the forefront thereof.

Significance of Jefferson's Thought

Although his interests were as broad as nature, Jefferson focused on man, whom he regarded as the most exalted member of nature's kingdom, and on the liberty which he believed to be the condition of man's "pursuit of happiness." As a result he could study and explain man at once naturalistically and humanistically. Neither profound enough nor temperamentally disposed to be a philosopher, he was rather an Anglo-Saxon American politician who was also a *philosophe* in the eighteenth-century sense of one concerned with studying man and improving his lot, uninhibited by scholastic, feudal, or regal prejudices and preconceptions. He differed, however, from the continental *philosophes* in that although they used (although never as felicitously as he) the same rhetorical abstractions—nature, reason, natural rights, happiness—he saw them ultimately reducible to concrete, substantive historical content. At the same time that he could talk of a "natural right" of the present generation to return to natural principles, he, as the greatest student of the past of all the Founding Fathers, could urge the study of history for a deeper understanding of man, speak admiringly of the common law (as expounded by Coke) as basically worthy of retention, and strive to refine and reshape the Whiggish approach to government. At the same time that he exalted popular rule and the will of the majority as a law of nature, he expressed as great a distrust of legislative majorities as he did of executives, or later, the judiciary. At the same time that he, like Franklin before him, could exalt democracy as the dictate of nature and the only effective means by which "the wise and good" can rise to leadership, he, unlike Franklin, espoused bicameralism separation of powers and checks and balances as restraints upon the "natural aristocracy." His aphoristic incantations of liberty were specifically calls for *independence* for individuals, i.e., freedom from dependence on others, a condition which entailed the possession of property, the performance of productive work, the right to form and live by one's own conscience, and the right to free expression. More particularly, Jefferson's "natural rights" were reducible in good part to the historic common law rights of Englishmen, which time had verified as commensurate to their basic needs.

Symbolic of this was Jefferson's proposal in 1776 that the shield of the United States bear the faces of the children of Israel and the ancient Anglo-Saxon chiefs, Hengist and Horsa. Americans were to him the chosen people who had recaptured their prefeudal Saxon birthright. The Saxon myth is as important to a full understanding of Jefferson's thought as is the myth of a future golden age to that of Condorcet. Above all it symbolizes the Anglo-Saxon cultural matrix from whence sprang Jefferson's basic impulses and aspirations, and in terms of which his universalized abstractions must be understood.

Because Jefferson's whole approach to government was from the angle of the realization of freedom and the preservation of natural rights, his political thought is greatly exaggerated in that direction. Concretely speaking, Jefferson believed that political liberty could be preserved through representative republics checked principally by strong local self-government and an electorate of vigilant, *independent* producers. He departed from the Whiggish emphasis on legislative supremacy to stress the primacy of a written constitution based on popular consent and assuring the preservation of natural rights. So insistent was he upon the implementation of the elective principle that his constitutional theory fell short of defining a viable substitute for the judiciary as the ultimate and definitive *governmental* expounder of the constitution.

In like vein, his emphasis upon freedom brought him to see government as limited merely to the preservation of natural rights. Just as there is no real conception of "community" in Jefferson's thought, so is there no conception of a "common good" which goes beyond the realization of freedom nor is there a consideration of duty, or, for that matter, of the nature of political order.

What then, in short, were the Jeffersonian principles which Lincoln saw as "the definitions and axioms of a free society?" Jefferson anticipated that question by indicating what he wished inscribed on his tombstone.

Here was buried

Thomas Jefferson

Author of the American Declaration of Independence

of the Statute of Virginia for religious freedom
& Father of the University of Virginia

The principles of the declaration—equality, natural rights, consent of the governed, and the moral right to rebel against oppression—provide the general basic framework. The statute for religious freedom represents the freedom of the mind which was fundamental to all other rights to Jefferson. It also represents the closest analysis he ever made of a basic right, one which he may have refrained from applying to other rights because of his tendency as a lawyer and an heir of the Anglo-Saxon tradition to identify natural rights with specific historic rights, and because other natural rights have more immediate social consequences which render them, in their interrelations, more complex. The founding of the University of Virginia indicates the importance Jefferson attached to public secular education as necessary to a free society. More particularly did it reaffirm his belief in a natural aristocracy of virtue and talent, which must be the ultimate fruit of the educational process and to which, he always assumed, the people at large will naturally defer.

Finally, Jefferson's thought is thoroughly American not only because it at once emphasizes ideals and practice but because of its underlying optimism and inner certitude. Missing from it is the note of the tragic, of the doubt and anguish which come from the consciousness of the chasm separating ideals from harsh reality which characterizes contemporary thought and which did not wholly escape John Adams. Gilbert Chinard has characterized Jefferson as a "practical idealist," and thus the essential American. The epithet cannot be improved upon.[48]

NOTES

1. Alexis De Tocqueville, *Democracy in America,* Phillip Bradley, ed. (New York, 1945, 2 vols.), I, 270; Lincoln to H. L. Pierce, Apr. 6, 1849, Roy F. Basler (ed.), *Abraham Lincoln: His Speeches and Writings* (New York, 1946), p. 489.

2. Concerning Jefferson's education and classical background see Karl Lehmann, *Thomas Jefferson: American Humanist* (Chicago, 1947).

3. I have found particularly helpful in writing this section Daniel Boorstin's *The Lost World of Thomas Jefferson* (Boston, 1948), and Adrienne Koch, *The Philosophy of Thomas Jefferson* (New York, 1943).

4. Jefferson to John Adams, Apr. 11, 1823, August 15, 1820, A. A. Lipscomb and A. E. Bergh (eds.), *The Writings of Thomas Jefferson* (Washington, 1905, 20 vols.), XV, 425–430, 273–276; Boorstin, *op. cit.,* 54–56, 125–129.

5. Jefferson to John Adams; August 15, 1820, *ibid.,* XV, 274; Jefferson to Charles Thompson, Sept. 20, 1787, *Papers,* XII, 159; "Notes on the State of Virginia," Query VI, *Writings,* II, 97n.

6. Jefferson to John Adams, Aug. 15, 1820, *Writings,* XV, 273–276; Jefferson's early draft of the Declaration of Independence talks of the "equal creation" of men. See Julian P. Boyd, *The Declaration of Independence* (Princeton, 1945), p. 19; Boorstin, *op. cit.,* pp. 61–67.

7. Jefferson to Benjamin Rush, Dec. 5, 1811, *Writings,* XIII, 116; Jefferson to E. Gerry, Jan. 29, 1799, *Writings,* X, 85, 74–86; Jefferson to T. J. Randolph, Nov. 24, 1808, cited in Adrienne Koch (ed.), *The American Enlightenment* (New York, 1965), p. 349; Jefferson to Benjamin Rush, March 6, 1813, *Writings,* XIII, 225; Jefferson to Peter Carr, Aug. 10, 1787, *Papers,* XII, 17.

8. Jefferson to Peter Carr, Aug. 10, 1787, *Papers,* XII, 15.

9. Jefferson to John Adams, Jan. 11, 1817, *Writings,* XV, 99–100; Jefferson to Wm. Short, Oct. 31, 1819, *Writings,* XV, 219–224; Jefferson to Thomas Law, June 13, 1814, *Writings,* XIV, 138–144; Jefferson to James Madison, Aug. 28, 1789, *Writings,* VII, 449–450; Jefferson to John Adams, Oct. 14, 1816, *Writings,* XV, 76–77.

10. Jefferson to James Fishback, Sept. 27, 1809, *Writings,* XII, 315–316; Jefferson to John Adams, Jan. 11, 1817, *Writings,* XV, 99–100; Jefferson to Wm. Canby, *Writings,* XIII, 377–378; Jefferson to M. King, Sept. 26, 1814, *Writings,* XIV, 197–198; Jefferson to E. Styles, June 25, 1819, *Writings,* XV, 203–204.

11. Jefferson to Noah Webster, Dec. 4, 1790, *Writings,* VIII, 113; Jefferson to D. Humphreys, March 18, 1789, *Papers,* XIV, 678–679; Jefferson to James Monroe, Sept. 7, 1797, *Writings,* IX, 422–424. Concerning Jefferson's identification of right with need, see Koch, *The Philosophy of Thomas Jefferson,* pp. 142, 143.

12. Jefferson to Edward Carrington, Jan. 16, 1787, *Papers,* XI, 49.

13. Reply to address of the Danbury Baptist Association, Jan. 1, 1802, *Writings,* XVI, 282; Jefferson to Wm. Mumford, June 18, 1799, reprinted in Koch (ed.), *The American Enlightenment,* p. 340; Jefferson to Dupont de Nemours, Apr. 24, 1816, *Writings,* XIV, 490–491; Jefferson to Peter Carr, Aug. 10, 1787, *Papers,* XII, 14–15; Jefferson to John Adams, Oct. 14, 1816, *Writings,* XV, 76–77; "Notes on the State of Virginia," Query XIX, *Writings,* II, 223.

14. Jefferson to John Adams, Oct. 28, 1813, *Writings,* XIII, 395–396.

15. Jefferson to John Jay, August 23, 1785, *Papers,* VIII, 426; "Notes On the State of Virginia," Query XIX, *Writings,* II, 228–230.

16. Jefferson to James Madison, Sept. 6, 1789, *Papers,* XV, 392–397; Jefferson, Opinion on the Constitutionality of the Residence Bill, July 15, 1790, *Papers,* XVII, 195; Jefferson, First Inaugural Address, March 4, 1801, *Writings,* III, 318; Jefferson to Isaac Tiffany, Apr. 4, 1819, in Edw. Dumbauld (ed.), *The Political Writings of Thomas Jefferson* (Indianapolis, 1955), p. 55.

17. Jefferson to Wm. Mumford, in Koch (ed.), *The American Enlightenment,* 340; Jefferson to Jos. Priestley, March 21, 1801, *Writings,* X, 229.

18. Jefferson to James Madison, Jan. 30, 1787, *Papers*, XI, 92–93; Jefferson to F. W. Gilmer, June 7, 1816, *Writings*, XV, 25–26.

19. Jefferson to Rutledge, Aug. 6, 1787, *Papers*, XI, 701.

20. Jefferson to Edw. Carrington, Jan. 16, 1787, *Papers*, XI, 49; Jefferson to Mann Page, Aug. 30, 1795, *Writings*, IX, 306–307.

21. See Jefferson's Draft of the Kentucky Resolutions, *Writings* XVII, 379–391; Jefferson to James Madison, Dec. 20, 1787, *Papers*, XII, 442; Jefferson, First Inaugural Address, *Writings*, III, 320–321.

22. Jefferson to John Adams, Oct. 28, 1813, *Writings*, XIII, 394–403; Jefferson to A. Coray, Oct. 31, 1823, Dumbauld, *Political Writings*, p. 90; Notes On the State of Virginia," Query XIV, *Writings*, II, 207–208.

23. Jefferson to John Taylor, May 28, 1816, *Writings*, XV, 19.

24. Jefferson to Dupont de Nemours, April 24, 1816, *Writings*, XIV, 487–488.

25. Jefferson to d'Ivernois, Feb. 6, 1795, in Dumbauld, *op. cit.*, p. 54.

26. Jefferson to Samuel Kercheval, Sept. 5, 1816, *Writings*, XV, 70–72; Jefferson to Joseph Cabell, Feb. 2, 1816, *Writings*, XIV, 421; Jefferson to John Adams, Oct. 28, 1813, *Writings*, XIII, 397–401; Jefferson to John Cartwright, June 5, 1824, *Writings*, XVI, 44–48.

27. Jefferson to James Madison, Jan. 30, 1787, Dec. 20, 1787, *Papers*, XI, 93, XII, 442; Jefferson to Wm. Smith, Nov. 13, 1787, *Papers*, XII, 356.

28. Jefferson to James Madison, Sept. 6, 1789, *Papers*, XV, 392–397; Jefferson to J. Cartwright, June 5, 1824, *Writings*, XVI, 44.

29. Jefferson to Spencer Roane, Sept. 6, 1819, *Writings*, XV, 212.

30. Jefferson, Autobiography, *Writings*, I, 54.

31. *Ibid.*, pp. 72–73. See also "Notes on the State of Virginia," Query XVIII, *Writings*, II, 225; Jefferson to B. Banneker, Aug. 30, 1791, *Writings*, VIII, 241; Jefferson to Gregoire, Feb. 25, 1809, *Writings*, XII, 254; Jefferson to Edw. Coles, Aug. 25, 1814, Koch (ed.), *The American Enlightenment*, p. 361; Jefferson to Miss Wright, Aug. 7, 1825, *Writings*, XVI, 119; Jefferson to Dr. T. Humphreys, Feb. 8, 1817, *Writings*, XV, 102; Jefferson to Jared Sparks, Feb. 4, 1824, *Writings*, XVI, 8.

32. Jefferson to Benjamin Rush, Sept. 23, 1800, *Writings*, X, 175; Jefferson to J. Fishback, Sept. 27, 1809, *Writings*, XII, 315; "An Act for Establishing Religious Freedom Passed in the Assembly of Virginia (1786)," *Papers*, II, 543–553; "Notes on the State of Virginia," Query XVII, *Writings*, II, 217ff.; Jefferson to Rev. S. Miller, Jan. 23, 1808, *Writings*, XI, 428–430; On Jefferson and Blackstone, see Julius Waterman, "Thomas Jefferson and Blackstone's Commentaries," in David Flaherty (ed.), *Essays in the History of Early American Law* (Chapel Hill, 1969), pp. 451–488.

33. To John Adams, June 27, 1813, *Writings*, XIII, 279–280.

34. Jefferson to Benjamin Rush, Dec. 5, 1811, *Writings*, XIII, 116; Jefferson to H. Lee, Aug. 10, 1824, *Writings*, XVI, 73–74.

35. Jefferson to Benjamin Rush, March 6, 1813, *Writings*, XIII, 225; to Wendover March 13, 1815, *Writings*, XIV, 283.

36. "Notes on the State of Virginia," Query XVII, *Writings*, II, 222.

37. "An Act for Establishing Religious Freedom," *Writings*, II, 302; "Notes on the State of Virginia," Query XVII, *Writings*, II, 221–222.

38. Jefferson to John Dickinson, March 6, 1801, *Writings*, X, 217.

39. Jefferson to John Cartwright, June 5, 1824, *Writings*, XVI, 45ff.; "Notes on the State of Virginia," Query XIII, *Writings*, II, 162ff.; Jefferson to John Adams, Sept. 28, 1787, *Papers*, XII, 189; Jefferson to James Madison, March 15, 1789, *Papers*, XIV, 661; "Notes on the State of Virginia," Query XVII, *Writings*, II, 148; Jefferson to Samuel Kercheval, July 12, 1816, *Writings*, XV, 32–44; Draft of a Constitution for Virginia (1776), *Papers*, I, 344; Jefferson to George Wythe, June[?], 1776, *Papers*, I, 410; Jefferson to the Abbé Arnoux, July 19, 1789, *Papers*, XV, 283; Jefferson to John Pleasants, April 19, 1824, *Writings*, XVI, 26–30; Jefferson to W. T. Barry, July 2, 1822, *Writings*, XV, 388.

40. Jefferson to James Madison, Dec. 20, 1787, *Papers*, XII, 440; Jefferson to James Madison, March 15, 1789, *Papers*, XIV, 659–662.

41. Opinion on the Constitutionality of a National Bank, Feb. 15, 1791, Ford (ed.), *Writings of Thomas Jefferson*, V, 286, 287.

42. Jefferson to James Madison, March 15, 1789, *Papers*, XIV, 659; Jefferson to Wm. C. Jarvis, Sept. 28, 1820, *Writings*, XV, 276–279; Jefferson to Spencer Roane, Sept. 6, 1819, *Writings*, XV, 214; Jefferson to Wm. H. Torrance, June 11, 1815, *Writings*, XIV, 304–306.

43. Kentucky Resolutions, *Writings*, XVII, 379–391.

44. To Wm. Johnson, June 12, 1823, *Writings*, XV, 451; Proposed Declaration and Protest of Virginia (1825), Dumbauld, *op. cit.*, p. 168.

45. Autobiography, Koch (ed.), *The American Enlightenment*, p. 296.

46. Jefferson to John Colvin, Sept. 20, 1810, *Writings*, XII, 418.

47. Leonard W. Levy. *Jefferson and Civil Liberties: The Darker Side* (Cambridge, Mass., 1963), 18 and *passim*.

48. Gilbert Chinard, *Thomas Jefferson: The Apostle of Americanism* (Boston, 1929), pp. 86, 87, 275.

Chapter 14

JEFFERSONIAN–REPUBLICAN POLITICAL THOUGHT

Virtue in a republic is a most simple thing; it is a love of the republic; it is a sensation, and not a consequence of acquired knowledge and may be felt by the meanest as well as by the highest person in the state.

MONTESQUIEU

James Madison: Republican Statesman

In contrast to Jefferson, who had the appearance of a "tall, large-boned farmer," and who was careless of dress, Madison, who succeeded Jefferson as President, was a small, unassuming man who "always appeared neat and genteel, and in the costume of a well-bred and tasty-old-school gentleman."[1] These contrasting characteristics were reflected in the different interests and approaches of the two scholarly Virginians, who complemented each other in what was perhaps the most compatible and successful political partnership in American history. Jefferson's rambling humanistic concerns brought him to focus more strictly upon ends; Madison, always primarily concerned with politics, concentrated upon precise, detailed analysis and exposition centering upon the institutional devices which might render representative republican government effective and secure. As President, however, Jefferson proved himself the more effective political leader.

Madison's Political Thought: The Workshop of Liberty

Cool and deliberate of judgment and moderate in manner, the meticulous Madison effected a balance in his character and private life which mirrored the operational value which he deemed essential to the realization of republican liberty.* At base was his notion of man as possessed of "a degree of depravity which requires a certain degree of

---

* See the previous discussion of Madison's thought in Chapter 10.

circumspection and distrust," and of other qualities "which justify a certain portion of esteem and confidence."[2] From this rose his recognition of the need to use power in the service of liberty, his constant emphasis upon finding a ground between polar opposites such as despotism and anarchy, and his prescriptions of the "inventions of prudence" and the extensive republic fully discussed in *Federalist* papers number 10 and 51.

If Hume and Montesquieu principally supplied Madison with institutional ideas, Locke was the source of his conception of the origin and end of government. Madison talked of an original compact, implied or presumed, "by which a people agree to form one society," followed by a second compact "by which the people in their social state agree to a Government over them." These two compacts he saw "blended in the Constitution of the United States, which recognises a union or society of States, and makes it the basis of the Government formed by the parties to it." His position is summarized in his draft of the Bill of Rights in a manner which anticipates Lincoln's famous definition: "That all power is originally vested in and consequently derived from, the people. That government is instituted and ought to be exercised for the benefit of the people . . . that the people have an indubitable, unalienable and indefeasible right to reform or change their government whenever it be found adverse or inadequate to the purposes of its institution." Most important for his constitutional theory was his insistence that a compact, in its very essence, "is equally obligatory on the parties to it and . . . no one of them can be liberated therefrom without the consent of the others or such a violation or abuse of it by the others as will amount to a dissolution of the compact."[3]

Madison defined the end of government as the preservation and protection of property, declaring, "that alone is *a just* government, which *impartially* secures to every man, whatever is his *own*." He construed "property" in the enlarged Lockian sense, embracing "everything to which a man may attach a value and have a right; and *which leaves to everyone else the like advantage*." Thus besides his material possessions, a man has a property in his opinions and their free communication, his religious beliefs, profession and practice, the safety and liberty of his person, the free use of his faculties and the free choice of the objects on which to employ them. "In a word," Madison stated, "as a man is said to have a right to his property, he may be equally said to have a property in his rights."[4]

Believing that "the essence of Government is power," Madison cautioned that because power must be lodged in human hands, it "will ever be liable to abuse." And "where an excess of power prevails, property of no sort is respected," with the consequence that "no man is safe in his opinions, his person, his faculties or his possessions." On the other hand, "where there is an excess of liberty, the effect is the same, tho' from an opposite cause." Thus "it is a melancholy reflection that liberty should be equally exposed to danger whether the Government have too much or too little power, and that the line which divides these extremes should be so inaccurately defined by experience." To harness power in the service of liberty, government must be established not only as an impartial umpire between but as a regulator of contending interests to the end of the protection of the diverse faculties of men and the realization of justice, while, at the same time, it is prevented from setting up an interest adverse to that of the entire society. Essentially government exists "to make people do their duty," because a government which would leave to each man the option to fulfill his duty or not would be "no government at all." As Madison saw it, given the weakness of human nature, controlled power exercised impartially is requisite to ordered liberty. His prescription of institutions, which sought, in the context of liberty, to neutralize, refine, and counteract the drive of self-interest, followed therefrom. While Jefferson proclaimed the necessity and virtues of liberty, Madison tackled the more difficult task of finding the structural and operational framework whereby power might be enlisted in its service.[5]

Madison contended that "conscience is the most sacred of all property." His *Memorial and Remonstrance Against Religious Assessments* (1785) constituted a defense of freedom of religion, and by implication, the separation of not merely church and state, but of religion and the state. Writing against a Virginia bill, backed by such worthy gentlemen as George Washington, John Marshall, and Patrick Henry, which would have provided state support for all teachers of the Christian religion, Madison, starting from the familiar Lockian premise that religion is purely a private concern, stated:

The Religion . . . of every man must be left to the conviction and conscience of every man; and it is the right of every man to exercise it as these may dictate. That right is in its nature an unalienable right. It is unalienable; because the opinions of men, depending only on the evidence contemplated by their own minds, cannot follow the dictates of other men: It is unalienable also; because what is here a right towards men, is a duty towards the Creator. It is the duty of every man to render to the Creator such homage, and such only, as he believes to be acceptable to him. This duty is precedent both in order of time and degree of obligation, to the claims of Civil Society. Before any man can be considered as a member of Civil Society, he must be considered as a subject of the Governor of the Universe: And if a member of Civil Society, who enters into any subordinate Association, must always do it with a reservation of his duty to the general authority; much more must every man who becomes a member of any particular Civil Society, do it with a saving of his allegiance to the Universal Sovereign. We maintain therefore that in matters of Religion, no man's right is abridged by the institution of Civil Society, and that Religion is wholly exempt from its cognizance.[6]

Madison's argument assumed the primacy of the individual's duty to God and the subjective character of that relationship. As such, religion is beyond the bounds of government which is not "a competent Judge of religious truth"; "a just government" is "best supported by protecting every citizen in the enjoyment of his Religion with the same equal hand which protects his own person and his property." Thus he championed a formal separation of religion and the state not because he was motivated against religion but because he believed that its cause and proper influence are harmed by any form of tie with the state. Ancillary to his principal argument but yet of great importance, was his practical proposition that in a pluralistic society such connection would tend to inhibit public peace by destroying "moderation and harmony" among the sects, and that attempts to enforce by legal sanctions acts obnoxious to a great portion of men, "tend to enervate the laws in general, and to slacken the bands of Society."[7]

These arguments, along with Jefferson's statement of principles of religious freedom, are of great significance in the history of American political thought because the Supreme Court of the United States has, since 1947, accepted them as the authoritative interpretation of the clause in the first amendment to the national Constitution prohibiting an establishment of religion.[8]

Madison is regarded as the Father of the Bill of Rights in the federal Constitution, although he was initially less sure of the necessity for its inclusion than was Jefferson. A principal reason he gave was that in American government, "the real power lies in the majority of the Community, and the invasion of private rights is *chiefly* to be apprehended, not from acts of Government contrary to the sense of its constituents, but from acts in which the Government is the mere instrument of the major number of the Constituents." This was plainly a declaration that in a government based on popular consent, unlike a monarchical government, for example, the danger to liberty arises mainly from an interested majority, whose determined will cannot be forestalled by paper guarantees, as such.[9]

Nevertheless Madison saw a bill of rights as "useful" in America for these reasons: (1) "The political truths declared in that solemn manner acquire by degrees the character of fundamental maxims of free Government, and as they become incorporated with the national sentiment, counteract the impulses of interest and passion"; and (2) there may be occasions in which an infringement of rights may spring from the government, i.e., a minority of officials, and not an interested popular majority, against which the guarantee may prove efficacious.[10]

Madison divided governments into three main types: (1) those sustained by military force which have prevailed in every age; (2) those "operating by corrupt influence; substituting the motive of private interest in place of public duty"; and (3) those sustained by "the will of the society," and operating in the interest of the whole. The latter is republican government, which he saw as "the glory of America to have invented," and the best form of government because it is the least imperfect. Concerning the economic basis of republicanism, Madison, like all Jeffersonians, considered the agrarian life as best calculated to realize "*health, virtue, intelligence* and *competency*," qualities which he contended presuppose liberty and result in safety. On the other hand, like the Puritan of old, he looked upon the sailor's life as most devoid of these characteristics. Between the farmer and the sailor he listed "those who work the materials furnished by the earth in its natural or cultivated state." In 1792 he could equate the American situation with the norm by contending that here "so much of the ordinary and most essential consumption, takes place in fabrics which can be prepared in every family, and which constitute the natural ally of agriculture." He concluded: "The class of citizens who provide at once their own food and . . . raiment, may be viewed as the most truly independent and happy. They are more: they are the best basis of public liberty, and the strongest bulwark of public safety. It follows, that the greater the proportion of this class to the whole society, the more free, the more independent, and the more happy must be the society itself." Ultimately, the proponent of the principle of balance could proclaim that no theoretical checks or form of government by itself could render America secure. Like the great democrats, Franklin and Jefferson, he also insisted upon what he called "this great republican principle" that "the people will have virtue and intelligence to select men of virtue and wisdom." To perform this task the people, however, must be, in the main, sober, industrious, independent farmers and planters.[11]

Madison defined "the vital principle of republican government" as the "*lex majoris partis,* the will of the majority." He added that "if the will of a majority cannot be trusted where there are diversified and conflicting interests, it can be trusted nowhere, because such interests exist everywhere." And yet, he would never admit, without great qualification, that the interest of the majority is the political standard of right and wrong. If "interest" is defined as "ultimate happiness," and thus is "qualified with every necessary moral ingredient," he admitted its truth; if it is defined in the "popular sense" as "immediate augmentation of property and wealth" he thought it false, because it would then make force the measure of right. At bottom Madison, like Jefferson, rendered the operative majoritarian principle subservient to the moral primacy of the natural rights of men. He disagreed, however, with Jefferson's description of majority rule as a "law of nature," contending instead that it derives "from compact founded on utility."[12]

Because of the plurality of interests in a political society, Madison contended that, like it or not, parties are inevitable. He prescribed five means "to combat the evil": (1) establish political equality for all; (2) withhold unnecessary opportunities from a few to increase inequality of property by an unwarranted accumulation of wealth; (3) reduce "extreme wealth" and "extreme indigence" by "the silent operation of the laws, while not violating the rights of property"; (4) abstain from measures which operate differently upon different interests; and (5) make one party a check on the other. Like Jefferson, Madison accepted parties as a fact of nature, but unlike Jefferson, who attributed them to temperamental differences, he saw them rooted in interests (most particularly, economic interests) traceable ultimately to the diversity in the faculties of men.[13]

An even more important difference from Jefferson was the position taken by Madison regarding the former's thesis that because the earth belongs to the living, constitutions and laws should automatically expire after nineteen years unless positively reenacted.* Nowhere does the matter-of-fact, skeptical realist and careful, constructive builder stand out in starker contrast to the idealist. Conceding the possible theoretical value of the idea, Madison interposed practical objections. In a manner reminiscent of Edmund Burke he asked: "Would not a Government so often revised become too mutable and novel to retain that share of prejudice in its favor which is a salutary aid to the most rational Government?" Would it not "engender pernicious factions that might not otherwise come into existence?" Would not a government established under such conditions be at the end "too subject to the casualty and consequences of an interregnum?" Going to the heart of Jefferson's thesis, he maintained that the title of the living extends only to the earth's natural state and that the improvements made by the dead constitute a charge upon the living who benefit by them. Thus debts may be incurred for purposes which interest the unborn along with the living, such as "repelling a conquest," or those embodied in the debt of the United States, which far exceeds the ability of one generation to liquidate. Consequently, "all that seems indispensable in adjusting the account between the dead and the living, is to see that the debts against the latter do not exceed the advances made by the former." Similarly, if ordinary laws terminated automatically at a set time and were not renewed, most property rights would become defunct and strug-

---

* Jefferson's reasoning can be found on page 276 in the preceding chapter.

gle would ensue. Then, too, uncertainty whether existing arrangements would or would not be renewed would weaken the regard to obligations, injure the less rather than the more "sagacious part of the Society," and undermine the regard for government, thus rendering it unstable. Following Locke, Madison considered the concept of tacit consent a sounder principle than Jefferson's. Under it, succeeding generations can revise or revoke the work of their predecessors, but if they do not so act, it is necessary to assume their assent to existing arrangements, if the foundation of civil society is not to be subverted.[14]

Of course it is more difficult to effect a positive revocation of existing laws than a renewal or change upon their automatic expiration. Madison believed that property depends upon stability in government and wanted to marshal in that cause the strong conservative forces of habit, custom, attachment, and inertia. Jefferson, with "presentism" as a major premise and nature as paradigm, saw liberty dependent upon the ability of the present generation to wipe the slate clean, if necessary, and start anew from first principles. Thus we must put alongside Madison's contractual conception of the origin of the state and his individualistic conception of the end of government, as well as his mechanical approach to governmental institutions and his analysis of politics into conflicting group interests, a commonsense realization, on the level of practice, of the organic connection in society between the past, the present, and the future as a prerequisite of ordered liberty.

Madison's keen concern with stability and the protection of property rights brought him to pose this dilemma in his consideration of the question of suffrage qualifications: "Allow the right exclusively to property, and the rights of persons may be oppressed. . . . Extend it equally to all, and the rights of property or the claims of justice may be overruled by a majority without property, or interested in measures of injustice." Because the rights of both property and persons must be safeguarded in a just and free government, he concluded that each must have a defense. He appears to have favored a plan which would strike a balance by confining the right of electing members of one house of the legislature to freeholders, and allowing a general suffrage for the election of the other house. He added, however, that if "experience or public opinion require an equal and universal suffrage" for both houses, property might be protected through an enlargement of the electoral districts of one house, as well as an extension of the term of its members. This was based on his belief that large districts are an institutional device favorable "to the election of persons of general respectability, and of probable attachment to the rights of property." If, however, the only choice was between equal, universal suffrage for both houses, and a restriction of the right to a part of the citizenry, he declared that it would be better "that those having the greater interest at stake, namely that of property and persons both, should be deprived of half of their share in the Government; than, that those having the lesser interest, that of personal rights only, should be deprived of the whole."[15]

Madison's Constitutional Thought

The concept of a "middle ground," a balance between localism and nationalism as an instrument of liberty and justice, pervades Madison's constitutional thought. His shifts in emphases from his early nationalism to a states-rights position and back again to a firm insistence on the primacy of the Union, might be called reactions to what he regarded as dangerous tendencies toward imbalance.

In light of Locke, he saw the Constitution as an executed contract, the parties to which are the states. This view precluded acceptance of an organic conception of the Union as older than the Constitution or the states. Unlike the Articles of Confederation which, he declared, set up a league, Madison saw the Constitution as establishing a true state which was unique because it was based on a concept that defied the logical monism of the great jurists—divided sovereignty. Of course what Madison really meant was that political sovereignty in the sense of the constituent power lay in the people organized as political societies in the states, and that the powers of sovereignty were divided between the nation and states in a unique federal system, in which both governments operate directly upon individuals.

Madison's views on constitutional construction were similar to those of Jefferson. He opposed inclusion of the word "expressly" in the Tenth Amendment but maintained that because the federal government was one of specific, enumerated powers, the "necessary and proper" and "general welfare" clauses must be construed in a restrictive sense. He opposed the establishment of the first Bank of the United States on the same grounds as Jefferson; later as President he sustained its existence on the ground that it had been acquiesced in by all the branches of government as well as the states generally. He admitted federal powers by implication, such as the encouragement of navigation and shipbuilding and retaliation against trade restrictions by foreign countries, as well as protective tariffs. He opposed Marshall's dictum in *McCulloch v. Maryland* as potentially subversive of the federal system, and denied the constitutional validity of federal expenditures for internal improvements but, in an action recalling Jefferson's purchase of Louisiana, seized West Florida without constitutional compunction. He insisted, against the Hamiltonian thesis which in 1935 was adopted by the Supreme Court, that the "general welfare" clause constituted no separate grant of power but must be construed in light of the specific powers granted to Congress. Finally, he strenuously opposed the broad Hamiltonian view of the executive power, contending that the Constitution recognized no federal inherent powers. In similar vein he denied the existence of a federal common law. All in all, Madison the nonlawyer, came to be perhaps the most legalistic figure of the Jeffersonian circle, a propensity which hobbled him as President. He departed from legalism, however, in prescribing that in very doubtful cases a line should be drawn so that that government in the federal system which can most ably perform the required or desired action be allowed to do it.[16]

In 1798 when he thought a grave imbalance in the direction of federal power had developed, Madison drafted the Virginia Resolutions, asserting the unconstitutionality of the Alien and Sedition Acts. Whereas Jefferson in his draft of the Kentucky Resolutions had mentioned "nullification" by a single state as one of the remedies, Madison used the word "interpose" and linked it solely to the collective action of the states. His conception of the Constitution as an executed contract incapable of being dissolved by any of its parties unless released by the others precluded acceptance of Jefferson's thesis. "Interpose" to him meant communicating with other states to seek legal redress of an alleged wrong.[17]

Like Jefferson, Madison believed in judicial review within the context of the theory that each department of government has the authority ultimately to define the extent of its powers. He believed that except for extraordinary cases, most federal-state disputes could be settled by the federal judiciary. In fact, his displeasure with John Marshall issued not from the exercise of judicial review, but from what he believed to be the failure of the Marshall Court to declare certain acts of Congress unconstitutional. Most particularly did he, following Jefferson's early lead, believe that the federal courts ought "consider themselves in a peculiar manner the guardian of those rights" guaranteed in the Bill of Rights. The federal judiciary to him was at once an instrument for the protection of private rights as well as the preservation of the federal balance. Nowhere in American political literature is there a stronger assertion of the authority of the federal courts than that made by Madison when he saw the delicate federal balance threatened by the doctrine of nullification: ". . . the Federal Judiciary is truly the *only* defensive armour of the Federal Government, or, rather, for the Constitution and laws of the United States. Strip it of that armour, and the door is wide open for nullification, anarchy, and convulsion. . . ."[18]

Finally, Madison maintained to the end of his life that the collective authority of the states is supreme over the federal and state governments in the "great and extraordinary cases in which all the forms of the Constitution may prove ineffectual against infractions dangerous to the essential rights of the parties to it." Expressed in other terms he held that this ultimate authority can interpose for the protection of the federal balance and the original division of powers. He was vague re-

garding the particular character of this authority but probably equated
it with the constituent power which exists in a majority of the people in
a majority of the states and upon which the Constitution and Union
ultimately rest. In any case, he was most emphatic in his insistence
that though there may be a *natural* right to secession in an intolerable
situation, there is no *constitutional* right, as men like Calhoun contended.[19]

Significance of Madison's Thought

Madison was a practical thinker concerned primarily with the development of institutions and devices whereby the ends of liberty, justice,
and order can best be implemented. His early training under the direction of the Presbyterian theologian John Witherspoon (1723–1794) at
Princeton had given him an appreciation of the religious basis of cosmic
order. His reading in the classics had made him sensible of the principle
of balance as the essence of form. Synthesizing natural theology and
classical formalism, he saw cosmic order imitated by the earthly rule of
law equally applied and posited upon a structure which, within an extensive sphere, refines, checks, and neutralizes self-interested human
propensities epitomized in political factions and willful majorities. His
basic premise, which he shared with all Jeffersonians, was that the
individual concrete person with his creative energies and capacity to
make his own decisions, must always be the fundamental political value.
Thus liberty is the supreme object of government; the common good
extends no farther than provisions for the protection of the free release
of human energy. Thus order is a presupposition of liberty and justice
is its necessary condition. In this light governmment is a framework
stipulating minimal rules and guidelines. Governmental measures are
important, but to a lesser degree than institutions. In essence Madison
believed that although society is organic, government must be a mechanism and never a mold. Because of his preoccupation with form he did
not possess the suppleness and flexibility of mind which marks Jefferson, a factor which probably explains his penchant for legalism. On this
point he relates more closely to John Adams than to Jefferson; the political science of both, although differing in significant details and in the
identification of basic elements, is very similar in its concern with framework as opposed to policies. He is at one with Adams and Hamilton in
identifying interest at the base of politics, but advances beyond them in
his appreciation of interests as multiple and in his advocacy of an extended sphere as an instrument of republican control. In fact, if Madison
had written only *Federalist* papers 10 and 51, he would merit the highest
praise as a political scientist.

Madison's conception of liberty as a by-product of balance has been
characterized as "institutionalized anomie," and it is charged that he

naively assumed a natural harmony in society, a willingness of all groups to play by the rules, and multipolarism. On the other hand, a more recent analyst has reminded us that Madison saw groups as "necessary evils much in need of regulation," whereas to the modern pluralist, "groups are good" and "require accommodation." Whether "regulation," as used by Madison, means merely institutionalized structure, or positive governmental action as well, spells the point of difference in interpretation. Nonetheless, it is true that he did specifically call for regulation of groups.[20]

John Taylor: Doctrinaire Agrarian

John Taylor (1753–1824) was a wealthy Virginia planter and political associate of Jefferson who has rather extravagantly been called the "Philosopher of Jeffersonian Democracy," the author of one of the "two or three really historic contributions to political science which have been produced in the United States," and "the most fruitful of Republican intellects."[21] An unrelenting critic of Hamiltonian policy and a staunch proponent of a *laissez-faire* agrarian, states-rights republicanism, his principal works are: *Arator* (1813), a series of "practical and political" agricultural essays; *An Inquiry into the Principles and Policy of the Government of the United States* (1814), an attempt at a systematic presentation of a political science based on simple principles of morality; and three polemical works attacking tendencies toward consolidation in the federal government and the decisions of the federal Supreme Court—*Construction Construed and Constitutions Vindicated* (1820), *Tyranny Unmasked* (1822), and *New Views of the Constitution of the United States* (1823).

Written generally in a dull, verbose, repetitive, and sometimes incoherent style, Taylor's *magnum opus*, the *Inquiry*, shares the motive, but not the substance, of the earlier attempts by the Federalists, Wilson and Chipman, to propound an American political science. It was directed primarily against the thesis of John Adams' *Defence*, almost thirty years after its publication, as well as the *Federalist* and the Hamiltonian fiscal program.

Taylor thought that a valid political science recognizes that "men are naturally both virtuous and vicious," possessing "a power of regulating motives, or electing principles, which will cultivate either virtue or vice." Man's strongest inclination is to do good to himself, which, in turn, begets a propensity to harm others. These tendencies are responsible for the fact that while power changes moral character, private life regenerates it. When self-interest is pursued without harming others, it is beneficial; when it results in a monopoly or exclusive privilege it is bad. Thus the more that power is divided, the farther is it removed from evil.

Popular sovereignty is indicated by man's propensity to do himself good; responsibility and division of power are suggested, to the exclusion of hereditary monarchy and aristocracy, as well as direct democracy, by his propensity to harm others.[22]

Because government is founded in moral and not natural or physical principles, Taylor considered John Adams' *Defence* to be in fundamental error in arguing the inevitability of a "natural aristocracy." Against such "political predestination," issuing in the prescription of mixed government, he declared that man has been perpetually escaping from all political forms, because government is capable of modification and improvement. Consequently all aristocracies are variable and artificial. The aristocracy of knowledge is leveled by the printing press; the aristocracy of wealth by alienation. Adams was wrong because he proceeded from the assumptions of the old, erroneous European political science, which sees the principles of monarchy, aristocracy, and democracy, or a mixture of them, as comprising "the whole extent of political volition." Thus, Taylor asserted, "whilst the liberty enjoyed by the other sciences, has produced a series of wonderful discoveries; politics . . . remained stationary from the earliest ages, to the American revolution."[23]

The new American political science, as Taylor saw it, rejects the old formal and fatalistic principles, replacing them with "moral principles," based on the recognition that talent, virtue, and wealth are now broadly distributed throughout the nation. As a result, "these ancient sanctions of aristocracy, become the modern sanctions of public opinion." Just as the pernicious principle of pure democracy has been eliminated in America by the elective principle, the principle of responsibility and the division of power replace aristocracy and monarchy. With democracy, aristocracy, and monarchy erased, there exists no rational basis to the classical argument for the mixed state (a balance of orders), with its erroneous assumption of the constancy of human nature propounded by Adams. Because men are not each, everywhere, and at all times morally alike, there can be no timeless prescription of a form of government. Consequently it is not forms of government but principles and policies which have the greatest relevance.[24]

The authors of the *Federalist* fall under the same indictment as Adams. Specifically they were unduly enamored of Montesquieu's principle of the separation of powers and of English government both in their treatment of the executive and in their tendencies toward consolidative nationalism. Being preoccupied with form, Adams' *Defence* and the *Federalist* deal only with what Taylor called "the shadow," in contrast to "measures," which are "the substance of government." Taylor concluded: "Liberty and tyranny are neither of them inevitable consequences of any form of government, as both depend, to a great extent, upon its operations, whatever may be its form."[25]

Taylor saw moral principles in politics as intimately related to economic life. The protection of property is defined as a principal end of government and political liberty is described as consisting "only in a government constituted to preserve, and not to defeat the natural capacity of providing for our own good." The most uncompromising proponent among Jeffersonians of the agrarian life, which he saw as having an identity of interest with labor in general, Taylor extolled it as the life of nature. Government by consent, with equal laws and no monopolies, is most facilely constructed on an agricultural basis. Majority rule is completely compatible therewith in America because agriculture is a national interest which, as such, does not seek to establish monopoly or oppress minorities. Whereas Adams' political theory divides a nation into several interests while uniting power, the politics of agriculture divides power while uniting the nation in one interest.[26]

On this basis Taylor condemned political parties as self-interested factions unresponsive to the good principles of American government such as division of power, responsibility, rotation, and restricted area of action. Because parties foster intrigue and corruption, they are subversive. Speaking of English parties, Taylor wrote: "Representation limited to the alternative of enlisting under one of these parties, ceases to be an instrument of national self government, and dwindles into an instrument of oppression." Faction, instead of being an inevitable phenomenon in free government as Madison had seen it, was to Taylor unnatural to it. In fact, parties in America are principally the outgrowth of Hamilton's immoral financial system.[27]

Following the approach put forth in the *Inquiry*, Taylor severely criticized federal policy, seeing the Federalist program of funding, assumption of state debts, the establishment of the Bank of the United States, and the protective tariff as based upon self-seeking corruption. In the process he did not spare Jefferson and Madison for their concessions to consolidative nationalism during their terms as President. Just as Taylor's prime target in asserting the primacy of policy over form was Adams and the doctrine of a natural aristocracy, so when he turned to specific policies he aimed squarely at Hamilton and the new paper or capitalist aristocracy. The agrarian and capitalist interests, he argued, are fundamentally at odds with each other. Because the aristocracy of credit is based on the evil principle of privilege, it is inimical to the good moral principles of American government and political science. Sound public policy must therefore extirpate this noxious foreign principle by the prompt elimination of all privilege.[28]

Believing in the necessity of a maintenance of government by sound principle, Taylor was inevitably drawn to contend against the constitutional views of John Marshall and the growing nationalism of the country. As he saw it, the federal government, especially the Supreme

Court, was undermining the vital limits on federal power. Rejecting the Madisonian notion of divided sovereignty, he argued that sovereignty is "by its nature a unit," and that the revolution had determined its locus in the people of the several states. The framers of the Constitution had unfortunately overlooked, in their division of powers, the uses of construction as an instrument for the extension of the federal sphere. Focusing on the implied powers doctrine, he asserted against Marshall that when a federal implied power confronts a reserved power of the states, the former must give way. Turning to the Missouri Compromise, he argued presciently that its basic presupposition of a balance of power between North and South would inevitably lead to war. Slavery is a question left by the Constitution to the states, the evils of which will be remedied by an evolutionary process. If the issue remains a basis of sectional change and conflict, the states, whose vital interest is challenged, may draw upon their anterior natural right of self-defense. The assumption of federal competence to deal with the question of slavery was, to Taylor, an inflammatory expression along sectional lines of the underlying class conflict between independent self-reliant agrarian producers and capitalist monopolists.

As with Jefferson and Madison, Taylor's argument with the Marshall Court concerned not so much judicial review, although he denied that the Constitution granted such power, as the lack of its proper use in restraining the federal government in its intrusions upon the rights of the states. No recourse was left, he thought, but to resort to the state governments as "tribunes of the people," exercising a veto upon federal assertions of power, a doctrine later developed by Calhoun as "the concurrent majority." In fact, Taylor was at the other pole from nationalists such as Marshall in assuming that the federal authority was less a government than a league. In light of this we can better understand the position of Madison as *via media* between them.[29]

Significance of Taylor's Thought

Taylor was a political purist who held as the norm a static Arcadian republic of equal self-reliant producers. Thus he could reduce political science to a few simple moral principles in place of the old formal principles. Ultimately he talked of these moral principles in economic terms with emphasis on the right of the individual to be protected in his labor and its fruits against artificially created monopoly, special privilege, and consolidation of power. With this approach he could also maintain a lofty consistency and sit in stern judgment upon deviations therefrom not merely by Hamilton but Jefferson and Madison as well. If he must be characterized, he might best be called a Jefferson denuded of the qualities which the latter derived from a deep sense of history, the burden of political decision, and the necessity of accommodation to change.

It cannot be claimed that Taylor's political science, with its simplistic reduction of American society to two basic economic interests, the agrarian (good) and the capitalist (bad), and of politics as a conflict between them, approached in realism the Madisonian multi-interest and group-conflict analysis even though it presaged the later Populistic and Progressive political evangelism. Nor can his emphasis on America as different from Europe be singled out as original—John Adams himself had made this point long before in his *Dissertation*. Similarly, his denunciation of political parties not only betrays a lack of realism but a sharp difference from both Jefferson and Madison. With politics reduced to a morality play between readily identifiable forces, Taylor's political science takes on the aspect of a caricature of reality.

Despite these drawbacks, there are significant contributions. The principal one is the deemphasis on form and the stress on function, as a counterbalance to the heavily emphasized institutional approach of the Founding Fathers. Principles and policies rather than mechanisms become Taylor's focal points. Coupled with his stress upon interest, the concern with measures gives rise to an analysis of government in terms of the source, substance, and consequences of policies, a point later readily appreciated and exploited by the historian Charles Beard in his study of Jeffersonian Democracy. Second, Taylor's portrayal of the divisions of power in American government as necessary to meaningful self-government posed distinctions and relationships which, though present from the inception of the Constitution, had not been fully brought to the level of concise discussion. Third, Taylor's brief against Marshall's mode of construction of the Constitution embodies a formidable argument which can be read even today with profit not merely for historical reasons but as a background against which one can better appreciate policy alternatives open to the judicial mind, as well as the jurisprudence and workings of the modern Court. Fourth, Taylor correctly anticipated important developments in American political thought and life. He forecast the troubles issuing from the Missouri Compromise and the arguments in the ensuing *Dred Scott* opinion of the Supreme Court. His advocacy in the *Inquiry* of rotation in office and his arguments against the Bank of the United States and federal subventions for internal improvements served the Jacksonians in good stead. His insistence on the indivisibility of sovereignty, against the Madisonian view, along with his identification of sovereignty with the states and his adumbration of a theory of a concurrent majority, served the cause of Calhoun, just as his insistence on popular sovereignty in regard to the slavery question served that of Stephen Douglas.

Finally it must be said that the so-called "Philosopher of Jeffersonian Democracy" was not a philosopher but a publicist and, although a believer in popular sovereignty and representative government, less a democrat and a simple farmer than a landed aristocrat in the traditional Virginian sense of that term.[30] Unable to accommodate the elements of time and change to his thought, despite his belief in man's moral change-ableness, his conception of society remained static and the vital Jeffersonian principles which he embraced tended to be transmuted by him into ideology—the rationalization of the economic interest of a section and the ascendancy therein of the gentleman-planter.

The Democratic–Republican Clubs: "Schools of Political Knowledge"

During the 1790's Democratic-Republican clubs sprang up in communities throughout America. Town and city societies were organized into county associations which, in turn, were joined in state federations. There existed within the clubs a strong desire to extend their organization into an international democratic movement aiming at a world democratic society. Successfully linking together urban and rural areas, the clubs helped lay the groundwork of the Jeffersonian Republican party.[31]

Generally speaking, the clubs went beyond Jefferson and Madison to draw upon Thomas Paine, and more particularly Jean Jacques Rousseau, in emphasizing the continuing primacy of the general will, a factor which caused club members to be labeled "Jacobins" by Federalist opponents. Differing markedly from James Wilson, who while strongly championing popular sovereignty was quite careful to insist upon the duty of the representative to act upon his own reflective judgment and the dictates of the moral law, the clubs tended to regard government as an organ of the general will and the representative as a mere deputy of the people. As one club member put it: "The different members of the government are nothing more than the agents of the people, and as such, have no right to prevent their employers from inspecting into their conduct, as it regards the management of public affairs."[32]

Rejecting the notion of human depravity, the clubs and their principal writers proceeded on the assumption of the capacity of man for indefinite improvement. Their focus was the person; Joel Barlow (1754–1812), the poet, thus declared: "It is the *person*, not the property, that exercises the will, and is capable of enjoying happiness; it is therefore the person, for whom government is instituted, and by whom its functions are performed."[33]

Because they believed in the continuing sovereignty of the general will, the clubs stressed the need for an enlightened public. Their principal emphasis was on two fundamental rights—freedom of inquiry and freedom of oral and written expression. Called by one of their members, "schools for political knowledge," the clubs fostered study groups, educational projects for women as well as men, civic education, academies and colleges, and a public school system which would realize equality by integrating "the unfortunate children of indigence and neglect" with "the children of opulence and vigilance." The typical club studied closely the journals, debates, and laws of Congress, and official records and correspondence, among other sources. As one club statement put it: "On information we will speak; and upon deliberation, we will write and publish our sentiments." The assumption was: "Let the people be led to the means of deliberate, unbiased investigation, and they will decide rightly." Reliance was thus put less upon the aristocratic leader, as in the Virginia of Jefferson, Madison, and Taylor, than the informed public acting on its own.[34]

For inquiry to be free, it was assumed that no institution must be above critical examination. Thus Elihu Palmer (1764–1806) of New York cast doubt upon the dogma of the separation of powers and an independent executive, suggesting instead the possibility of government by a unicameral assembly moved by a majority as most fit for the realization of liberty and equal rights. His main point was the necessity for experiment as the test of institutional efficacy.[35]

One of the main publicists in the movement was Tunis Wortman (d. 1822), of New York, a man who, though not original in his thought, typified the spirit and political theory of the clubs. Believing that "education and habitude" decide whether virtue or vice shall prevail, he concluded that "systems of jurisprudence and forms of government, and not physical causes, have produced that astonishing dissimilarity with which the human character abounds." The key to happiness lies then in free government and education. Speaking of republican government he pronounced: "Under this happy modification of social life, we can only expect to arrive at that ultimate state of perfection of which the human character is susceptible,"[36] His *Treatise Concerning Political Enquiry*, while more journalistic than scholarly, constitutes a plea for the popular right to investigate, communicate, and criticize government. The understanding of government, he maintained, is open to all. Similarly, the study of politics, which he saw then in its infancy, demands unrestrained freedom of inquiry. Operating from these assumptions, Wortman symbolized many members of the clubs in his attack on the notion of seditious libel, a position far in advance of Jefferson's. To erect a crime upon the tendency of words was to him an effort to establish public tranquility "upon the ruins of Civil Liberty." The crime could "never be reconciled to the genius and constitution of a Representative Commonwealth." Only by overt acts, not words, did Wortman believe men should be accused.[37]

The theme of equality which was basic in the political philosophy of the clubs was most eloquently sounded by Barlow in his *Advice to the Privileged Orders*. Seeing the state as the instrument of justice, Barlow argued that justice presupposed equal opportunity, a condition which cannot be realized except by education: "Only admit that original, unalterable truth, *that all men are equal in their rights*, and the foundation of everything is laid." He conceded that "*interested* and *passionate* men" would continue to direct the affairs of the world, but added optimistically, "in national assemblies passion is lost in deliberation, and interest balances interest; till the good of the whole community combines the general will."[38]

In their emphasis on equality, the continuing sovereignty of the general will, the deputy theory of representation, the placing of institutional forms in the background, complete freedom of inquiry and criticism of government, equal secular education at public expense, and the denial of the right of government to institute the crime of seditious libel, the societies generally went beyond both Jefferson and Madison in the direction of an equalitarian and libertarian democracy. Their conception of political education was not dissimilar from Jefferson's in stressing as sources the great American state papers and liberal publicists. Their spirit was, however, even broader in latitude than Jefferson's, as was their faith in the ability of men at large, upon sound inquiry and discussion, to discern clearly the great issues and act intelligently upon them. Following Palmer, who contended that "the moral condition of man will be as essentially renovated by the American Revolution as his civil condition," they looked to the Revolution's fulfillment.[39] That this idea was shared by most Jeffersonians is made evident by the fact that the medical doctor, Benjamin Rush, an adherent to Jefferson's thought and also very probably a club member, attempted to verify the thesis empirically. In his "Account of the Influence of the American Revolution upon the Human Body," Rush argued that although an excess of the passion for liberty had produced in many patriots a form of insanity called "*anarchia*," the American revolutionists generally, in contrast to the "monarchist" on the one hand, and the "anarchists," on the other, kept a remarkable mental and physical health.[40] In a later treatise he further concluded:

In no part of the human species is animal life in a more perfect state than in the inhabitants of Great Britain and the United States of America. With all the natural stimuli . . . they are constantly under the invigorating influence of liberty. There is an indissoluble union between moral, political, and physical happiness; and if it be true that elective and representative governments are most favorable to individual, as well as national prosperity, it follows of course, that they are most favorable to animal life.[41]

Popular government is thus justified naturalistically as well as theoretically. It is an experiment which has been tried and found to work. The Democratic-Republican clubs, fired by this optimism, emphasized the full pursuit of the logic of liberty in the direction of democracy and thus served as a bridge between the formative period of American political thought and its democratic extension in the early nineteenth century.

Conclusions

Jeffersonian-Republican political thought is remarkable for its diversity of emphases within a common acceptance of basic principles by its proponents. Madison stressed political form, Taylor stressed function, while Jefferson embraced both but leaned in the direction of function. Madison was distrustful of man in general; Jefferson was distrustful only of political man. Jefferson was optimistic regarding majority rule but insisted upon a Bill of Rights as protection against its abuse. Madison, while accepting majority rule as a republican principle, distrusted all majorities and relied upon formal institutional checks as a safeguard, seeing a Bill of Rights as efficacious only against minorities. Taylor was quite trustful of an agrarian majority and declamatory against the "capitalist" minority, while the Democratic-Republican Clubs extolled the primacy of the general will. Jefferson and Madison saw political parties as inevitable but Jefferson regarded them as functions of temperament while Madison explained them as rooted in interest. Taylor, on the other hand, agreed with Madison in seeing a conflict between interests at the base of politics but reduced interests to two, and regarded parties as something to be eradicated. Jefferson and Taylor, despite their democratic rhetoric, assumed a natural aristocratic leadership while the clubs went beyond them in pointing toward a more equalitarian politics. The rhetorical Jefferson emphasized abstract rights, man in general, and the sovereignty of the present generation, while Jefferson the statesman and student of history stressed the concrete historical rights of Englishmen and the path of moderation. Madison, while seeing society anomalously as contractual in origin and organic in its link to the past and the future, followed a legalistic path in his political life.

On the constitutional issue Madison saw the federal authority as a government, Taylor regarded it as a mere league, while Jefferson was ambivalent on the point. Madison talked of divided sovereignty, Taylor of the indivisibility of sovereignty. All three criticized the Supreme Court, but Jefferson and Madison accepted a limited judicial review. Madison came to regard the federal judiciary as the only effective defensive arm of the federal government while Jefferson and Taylor laid the basis for the full-blown doctrine of nullification.

The common principles shared by all Jeffersonian-Republicans included:

1. The primacy of the free individual and his basic natural rights.
2. The consensual principle as the vehicle of political legitimacy and the basis of obligation.
3. Majority rule as the principle of republicanism.
4. Liberty as the limited purpose of government, with equality of treatment as its corollary.
5. Popular education as the necessary condition for an enlightened electorate upon which free government ultimately depends.
6. The agrarian life as the politically, morally, and physically "healthful" life and the basis of individual creativity and virtue.

Because of its many facets and its various and shifting emphases, Jeffersonian thought has tended, historically, to be at the service of many interests. Already in its early days, in the writings of Taylor, it ossified into an ideology. Its separate strands have since been fastened on by men and interests justifying their diverse positions in its light. In this manner it has been turned against itself, with its particularism and strict constructionism, for example, pitted against its stress upon human rights and human equality. Although Jefferson saw all his principles as necessarily related, there can be no doubt that he and all other Republican leaders, with the exception perhaps of doctrinaires like Taylor, believed that at the center of their thought as controlling premises and goals were the vital principles of human liberty, equality, and dignity. It is this core of Jeffersonian thought which transcends the tendency of the contemporary conservative to equate Jeffersonianism with strict constructionism and states rights, as well as the tendency of many modern liberals to regard governmental action as the necessary vehicle for the realization of Jeffersonian values.[42]

NOTES

1. Henry Adams, *History of the United States during the Administration of Thomas Jefferson* (New York, 1930), I, 186, 189.
2. The *Federalist*, No. 55, Cooke edition, p. 378.
3. Madison to N. P. Trist, Feb. 15, 1830, *Letters and Other Writings of James Madison* (New York, 1884, 4 vols.), IV, 63; Amendments to the Constitution, June 8, 1789, Gaillard Hunt (ed.), *The Writings of James Madison* (New York, 1906, 9 vols.), V, 376–377. Hereafter referred to as *Writings*.
4. "Property," *The National Gazette*, March 29, 1792, in *Writings*, VI, 102, 101.
5. Speech in the Virginia Constitutional Convention, Dec. 2, 1829, *Writings*, IX, 361; "Property," *Writings*, VI, 101; quoted in Saul Padover (ed.), *The Complete*

Madison (New York, 1953), 16; Madison to Jefferson, Oct. 24, 1787, *Writings*, V, 28–32; *Elliot's Debates*, II, 309.

6. Memorial and Remonstrance Against Religious Assessments, 1785, Padover, *op. cit.*, 299–300.

7. *Ibid.*, 302, 303, 304, 305.

8. *Everson v. Board of Education*, 330 U.S. 1, (1947); *McCullom v. Board of Education*, 333 U.S. 203 (1948).

9. Madison to Jefferson, Oct. 17, 1788, *Writings*, V, 272.

10. *Ibid.*, V. 273.

11. "Spirit of Governments," *The National Gazette*, Feb. 20, 1792, *Writings*, VI, 94; "Republican Distribution of Citizens," *The National Gazette*, March 5, 1792, *Writings*, VI, 96, 98–99; "Power of Judiciary," June 20, 1788, *Writings*, V, 223.

12. Madison to _____ _____, 1833, *Writings*, IX, 528; Madison to James Monroe, Oct. 5, 1786, *Writings*, II, 273; Madison to Jefferson, Feb. 4, 1790, *Writings*, V, 440n.

13. "Parties," *National Gazette*, Jan. 23, 1792, *Writings*, VI, 86.

14. Madison to Jefferson, Feb. 4, 1790, *Writings*, V, 438n–439n.

15. Note to Speech on the Right of Suffrage, *circa* 1821, in Padover, pp. 36–40.

16. E. M. Burns, *James Madison: Philosopher of the Constitution* (New Brunswick, N.J., 1938), pp. 108, 109, 138, 139, 105; Madison to Professor Davis, 1832 (1833?), *Letters and Writings of James Madison*, IV, 240–242; Madison to Spencer Roane, Sept. 2, 1819, *Writings*, VIII, 448–450; James Richardson (ed.), *Messages and Papers of the Presidents*, Veto Message, March 3, 1817, I, 585.

17. Resolutions of 1798, Dec. 21, 1798, *Writings*, VI, 326–331.

18. Burns, *op. cit.*, p. 155; Madison to Spencer Roane, Sept. 2, 1819, *Writings*, VIII, 449–452; Madison to Joseph Cabell, Apr. 1, 1833, *Letters and Other Writings*, IV, 296–297.

19. Report on the Resolutions, 1799, *Writings*, VI, 351; Notes on Nullification, June 1835, *Writings*, IX, 576 581; Outline (on the Constitution), Sept., 1829, *Writings*, IX, 353; Burns, *op. cit.*, p. 122.

20. John P. Roche, "American Liberty: An Examination of the 'Tradition' of Freedom," in Milton P. Konvitz and Clinton Rossiter (eds.), *Aspects of Liberty* (Ithaca, 1958), pp. 140, 144; Theodore J. Lowi, *The End of Liberalism* (New York, 1969), p. 296.

21. B. F. Wright, Jr., "The Philosopher of Jeffersonian Democracy," *American Political Science Review*, XXII (Nov. 1928), 870–892; Charles A. Beard, *Economic Origins of Jeffersonian Democracy* (New York, 1915), p. 323; Albert J. Beveridge, *Life of John Marshall*, III, 58n. For Taylor's thought in general I have been greatly aided by E. T. Mudge, *The Social Philosophy of John Taylor of Carolina* (New York, 1939).

22. *An Inquiry into the Principles and policy of the Government of the United States* (New Haven, 1950), pp. 166, 95, 187, 400ff., 362.

23. *Inquiry*, pp. 36, 37.

24. *Ibid.*, pp. 58, 97, 38–39.

25. *Ibid.*, pp. 167, 466 ff.; *Construction Construed and Constitutions Vindicated* (Richmond, 1820), 13, cited in Mudge, *op. cit.*, p. 77.

26. *Tyranny Unmasked*, p. 28; *Inquiry*, p. 356ff.

27. *Inquiry*, p. 191.

28. Taylor's attack on Federalist policy can be found in *Definition of Parties* (Philadelphia, 1794); *An Enquiry into the Principles and Tendency of Certain Public Measures* (1794); Chapters 4 and 5 of the *Inquiry*; and *Tyranny Unmasked* (Washington, 1822).

29. Taylor's views on the Constitution, sovereignty, and the Supreme Court can be found in Chapters 2, 3, 6, and 9 of the *Inquiry*; *Construction Construed and Constitutions Vindicated* (Richmond, 1820); and *New Views on the Constitution of the United States* (Washington, 1823).

30. Concerning the aristocratic aspects of Taylor's thought see Manning J. Dauer

and Hans Hammond, "John Taylor; Democrat or Aristocrat," *Journal of Politics,* VI (Nov. 1944), 381–403.

31. My principal source has been Eugene Perry Link, *Democratic–Republican Societies 1790–1800* (New York, 1942).

32. Link, *op. cit.,* p. 106.

33. Joel Barlow, *A Letter to the National Convention of France* (New York, 1793), p. 32.

34. Link, *op. cit.,* pp. 164, 161.

35. Elihu Palmer, *An Enquiry Relative to the Moral and Political Improvement of the Human Species* (New York, 1797), pp. 18, 22.

36. Tunis Wortman, *An Oration on the Influence of Social Institutions Upon Human Morals and Happiness* (New York, 1796), pp. 8, 10, 24.

37. Tunis Wortman, *A Treatise Concerning Political Enquiry and the Freedom of the Press* (New York, 1800), pp. 253, 262.

38. Joel Barlow, *Advice to the Privileged Orders* (New York, 1792), Pt. I, pp. 69, 73.

39. Palmer, *op. cit.,* p. 26.

40. Benjamin Rush, *Medical Inquiries and Observations* (Philadelphia, 1915, 4 vols.), I, 127–134, cited in Daniel Boorstin, *The Lost World of Thomas Jefferson* (Boston, 1948), pp. 181–183.

41. Rush, "Inquiry into the Cause of Criminal Life," *Medical Inquiries,* I, 40, cited in Boorstin, *op. cit.,* 184.

42. For a thorough discussion of the historical influence of Jeffersonian thought in America see Merrill D. Peterson, *The Jeffersonian Image in the American Mind* (New York, 1962).

PART SIX

EARLY DEMOCRATIC THOUGHT, ITS CRITICS AND CRISIS

Chapter 15

THE DEVELOPMENT OF DEMOCRACY

The meaning of Democracy is to put in practice the idea of the sovereignty, license, sacredness of the individual.

WALT WHITMAN

Alexis de Tocqueville: Democracy in America

When, in 1835, the Frenchman Alexis de Tocqueville first published his great study of American life, *Democracy in America*, the democratic impulse had effected significant changes in the patterns of political life inherited from the formative period. State constitutions drawn up in the new Western states and revised in some of the old states followed the American-prescribed steps of political legitimacy—submission by popularly elected conventions of constitutions drawn by them to the people at large. Their provisions were generally in the direction of a diffusion of political power through extension of the suffrage, elimination of the representation of property in legislatures, shorter terms of office, popular election of judges, governors, and other officials, and the replacement of legislative caucuses by political party conventions. Similarly, executive authority on both national and state levels was enhanced, with governors and presidents seeing themselves as representatives of the people. At the same time the expansion westward and the growth of industry and commerce brought forth a sense of nationalism and a mood of individualism and equality which exalted a *laissez-faire* approach and decried monopoly and privilege.

De Tocqueville saw America as different because of its democracy, which he regarded as more than a collection of political principles but as a new phenomenon. Thus he stated, in a manner recalling earlier American emphasis on the point, "a new science of politics is needed for a new world." He rejected all analogies with antiquity, holding ancient and modern republicanism so different that none but novel ideas could apply to so novel a condition as that of American society. He summed it up, saying: "To evils that are common to all democratic nations they [Americans] have applied remedies that none but themselves had ever thought of; and, although they were the first to make the experiment, they have succeeded in it."[1]

What had brought this about? De Tocqueville answered that Americans had been allowed, "by their circumstances, their origin, their intelligence, and especially by their morals to establish and maintain the sovereignty of the people." Unlike later historians, he did not regard the frontier and the availability of free land as any more than important conditioning factors. Thus the laws were more influential than the situation, and manners, morals, and customs were more important than the laws. Everything about the pioneer, he declared, may be "primitive and wild," yet "he is himself the result of the labor and experience of eighteen centuries." True information is principally derived from experience and "if the Americans had not been accustomed to govern themselves, their book learning would not help them much at the present day." Generally speaking there existed a social condition in which neither laws nor customs retained any person in his place. Social fluidity made "an easy and unbounded career" seem open to all. American democracy was different because America never had a feudal system.[2]

De Tocqueville believed that American democracy emphasized equality above liberty but aimed at an equality in freedom. The general equality of condition gave the tone to society, public opinion, and government. The West exemplified "democracy arrived at its utmost limits," where the people had escaped "the influence not only of great names and great wealth, but even of the natural aristocracy of knowledge and virtue." Unlike old Europe, "in the United States there is no religious animosity, because all religion is respected and no sect is predominant; there is no jealousy of rank, because the people are everything, and none can contest their authority; lastly there is no public misery . . . because the physical position of the country opens so wide a field to industry that man needs only to be let alone to be able to accomplish prodigies." As a result, individualism, as distinct from egoism or selfishness, stands with equality as a basic aspect of American democracy. And yet, de Tocqueville added: "I know of no country in which there is so little independence of mind and real freedom of discussion as in America." Americans are moved primarily by the insatiable passion for acquiring the good things of this world, the bootless chase of which renders them anxious and restless. Prodded by their condition and culture to a practical conquest of nature, Americans disdain general ideas and theoretical speculations. De Tocqueville concluded that "nothing is less suited to meditation than the structure of democratic society."[3]

Most particularly was the aristocratic de Tocqueville concerned with the possibility of a tyranny of the majority in America. Great men do not come to the fore, he contended, because social conformity visits obloquy and persecution upon the dissenter. A society with no elite as the judge of morals and manners is peculiarly susceptible to the tyranny of opinion which substitutes imitation and image for innovation and character. John Adams' emphasis on "emulative approbativeness" as a basic political and social motive, seen from de Tocqueville's perspective of a democratic society, results in pressure for conformity to mass opinion.[4]

But de Tocqueville saw checks in America upon this tendency. Among these were the liberty and propensity of Americans to associate in groups, the absence of centralized administration and power, the formal checks upon power and the conservative influence of the legal profession, which had taken possession of the government through political positions, the courts of justice, and the practice of judicial review. "The profession of the law," he declared, "is the only aristocratic element that can be amalgamated without violence with the natural elements of democracy. . . ." In America, "scarcely any political question arises . . . that is not resolved, sooner or later, into a judicial question." And yet, judges of the federal Supreme Court are "all powerful as long as the people respect the law; but they would be impotent against popular neglect or contempt of the law."[5]

Perhaps most important as a guarantor of liberty in America, de Tocqueville thought, was religion: "The Americans combine the notions of Christianity and of liberty so intimately in their minds that it is impossible to make them conceive the one without the other." Religious institutions are made wholly distinct from the political so that the laws are changed without shaking belief. A democracy needs religion as its sheet anchor or it degenerates into a strife-torn babel. Fortunately, "the Americans, having admitted the principal doctrines of the Christian religion without inquiry, are obliged to accept in like manner a great number of moral truths originating in and connected with it." There exists a plurality of sects, each respected and none predominant, and a general acceptance of the same basic principles.[6]

De Tocqueville's analysis ties in with the thesis of Ralph Gabriel, the prominent historian of American democratic ideas. Seeing democracy as a secular religion, Gabriel defined it as "a pattern of ideals providing standards of value with which the accomplishments of realistic democracy may be judged." The basic tenets of the pattern are, (1) a fundamental moral order; (2) the free individual, and (3) nationalism, or the mission of America. The life of this secular faith consists in a balance of these doctrines.[7] Each of these tenets, as we have seen, was old in America, having been embraced with varying degrees of emphasis from the beginning. The doctrine of a moral order based on the will of God was common to all Protestant sects. The small but growing number of Catholics in the first half of the nineteenth century may have pointed to divine reason as the source of cosmic law, but saw the content thereof as essentially the same as their Protestant brethren. Then, too, also in substantial agreement, though tending to render human reason autonomous, was the deistic notion of the law of nature. It was evangelical revivalism, however, which supplied the emotional basis for the continuing renewal of religion in contrast to the staid, rationalist Unitarianism which had come to terms with the existing order. Separation of church and state did not mean separation of the state and society from religious influence. In fact the religious conception of a moral order was argued not only as inherently true but necessary for the preservation of government under law. Jeffersonians might assert that Christianity was not a part of the common law and legal commentators like James Kent and Joseph Story might contend that it was, but the fact remained that most Americans assumed it to be at the base of the republic.[8]

From Classical Republicanism to Democracy

American classical republicanism had (1) assumed leadership either by "the wise and good" or "the rich and well-born," (2) equated citizenship with equal rights under the law, while assuming a freehold qualification for the suffrage, (3) emphasized institutional checks and balances and "inventions of prudence" in the structure of government, and (4) generally assumed the need for representation, in some form, of property as well as persons. The rising American democracy of the nineteenth century (1) assumed popular leadership, (2) equated citizenship with the suffrage, (3) stressed the will of the majority as the vehicle of government, and (4) emphasized, in the tradition of Jefferson and Taylor, the removal of privilege and monopoly in the operation and policy of government. Federalists had stressed the role of the national government as a positive instrument in the promotion of a national common good, a position later adhered to by those Jeffersonian-Republicans who became Whigs. Democrats, on the other hand, like the older Jeffersonian purists, thought of national government as having the minimal role of freeing individual energies. Finally, whereas classical republicans distrusted man in general, and Jeffersonians distrusted political man, the new democracy tended to exalt man as such.

The basic differences in viewpoints, particularly those concerning the question of property and government, were reflected in good part in the constitutional conventions held in Massachusetts (1820), New York (1821), and Virginia (1829–1830). The clash over property, its prerogatives and protection, was essentially a sham battle because in America landed property was broadly distributed in ownership and was universally respected. The opposition was not to property but to its special representation. The logic of the drive for equality in freedom argued the full implementation of the natural rights proclaimed in the Declaration of Independence. Thus there were two fundamental and by now traditional American political symbols that tended to be at odds—the conception of a constitution as a balance of forces and the equalitarianism of the Declaration of Independence.[9]

At issue in Massachusetts was the Constitution of 1780, devised on classical, balanced lines by John Adams. Included were the questions of town representation in the lower house, the tax-paying qualification for the suffrage; the independence of the judiciary from accountability through popular election; the foundation of representation in the Senate on property (tax payments), and government support of religion. Although the conservatives won the battle in 1820, the provision for amendment placed in the Constitution provided the means whereby most of the democratic reforms were thereafter realized.

The democratic case was best presented by Henry Dearborn and Levi Lincoln, both of whom were sons of members of Jefferson's cabinet. The core of the former's argument was that property needed no special protection because it "secures respect whenever it is not abused, and the influence of those who possess it is sufficient for its protection." Lincoln, while accepting the notion of checks and balances, contended that representation is founded on the interests or rights of the people and that intelligence and not property can alone sustain a free government. Opposing any unequal principle of representation, he argued that an ample check could be attained by establishing a different mode of representation for the two legislative houses.[10]

For the conservatives Leverett Saltonstall maintained that property should be represented "because it is the greatest object of civil society," and the now venerable John Adams declared that the great object was to render property secure, "because it is the foundation upon which civilization rests."[11] The most important proponents of property, however, were two very prominent representatives of the conservative American legal mind, Justice Joseph Story (1779–1845) of the Supreme Court of the United States, and Daniel Webster (1782–1852), the able barrister and soon United States Senator.

Story admitted that because of the nonfeudal nature of the American statute of descents and distributions and because of the universal interest in property among Americans, "there is not then a conflict but a harmony of interests between them." He added, however, that population is not always the safest and best system of representation, particularly where there exists much poverty. He concluded: "What should be the basis on which representation should be founded, is not an abstract theoretical question, but depends upon the habits, manners, character and institutions of the people, who are to be represented." Citing Jefferson's objections to the homogeneous nature of both houses of the Virginia legislature and his advice that they should reflect the influence of different interests or principles, Story argued for retention of the system of allocation of senators to districts in proportion to the taxes paid therein.[12]

Daniel Webster maintained that there could be no effectual control without some difference between the two legislative houses in origin, character, interest, feeling, or sentiment. He proceeded principally from James Harrington's premise that power, in the absence of military force, naturally and necessarily follows property. Thus forms of government are a function of "those laws which regulate the descent and transmission of property." Looking at American history, Webster described the situation of the colonists as demanding "a parcelling out and division of the lands," in an act which "fixed the future frame and form of their government." In this light, universal suffrage "could not long exist in a community where there was great inequality of property." Webster concluded: "It would seem, then, to be the part of political wisdom to found government on property; and to establish such distribution of property, by the laws which regulate its transmission and alienation, as to interest the great majority of society in the protection of the government . . . With property divided, as we have it, no other government than that of a republic could be maintained, even were we foolish enough to desire it."[13]

Webster's thesis hardly substantiated his conclusion that property needed special protection and representation in American government, for if power is a function of property, and property is widespread in its distribution, the government is inevitably republican, irrespective of the claims of numbers. On this basis there was little for conservatives to fear and the only justification for election of the legislative houses on different principles was to guard against hasty action and to filter opinion.

In the New York Convention of 1821, which formulated a constitution embodying significant democratic reforms, the principal issue was the so-called judicial oligarchy whose most moderate representative was the conservative legal scholar and jurist, Chancellor James Kent, an avid follower of the policies and political philosophy of Alexander Hamilton and a judicial proponent of the vested rights doctrine. In the constitution drawn for New York in revolutionary days, the judges of the Supreme Court and the Chancellor were associated in a council of revision which had veto power on both constitutional and policy grounds over bills passed by the legislature. By 1821, men like Kent realized that direct judicial participation in policy questions could no longer be abided and that it endangered judicial review itself. The new constitution removed the judges from politics by eliminating the Council but, against the desires of radical democrats, it granted the veto power to the governor.

The new fundamental law stopped just short of establishing universal suffrage for white males. Kent had argued that the freehold qualification for the senatorial electorate provided "a sheet anchor amidst the future factions and storms of the republic." As he saw it, universal suffrage was "too mighty an excitement for the moral constitution of men to endure" and would jeopardize liberty and property. Speaking in terms of a class struggle, and assuming a polarized rigidity in American society, he observed: "There is a tendency in the poor to covet and to share the plunder of the rich; in the debtor to relax or avoid the obligations of contracts; in the majority to tyrannize over the minority . . . in the indolent and profligate to cast the whole burthens of society upon the industrious and the virtuous; and *there is a tendency in ambitious and wicked men, to inflame these combustible materials.*" He did not think that Americans could validly deem themselves "a peculiar people," exempt from the passions which mark the rest of mankind, and summed up his position, saying: "Society is an association for the protection of property as well as of life, and the individual who contributes only one cent to the common stock, ought not to have the same power and influence in directing the property concerns of the partnership as he who contributes his thousands."[14]

The most effective answer to Kent came from David Buel, Jr., who, after citing James Wilson in the cause of universal suffrage, argued on sociological grounds that Kent drew a picture "from the existing state of society in European kingdoms, which would be indeed appalling, if we could suppose such a state of society could exist here." Using the same premise as Webster, Buel concluded that Americans were different because real property in America was in the hands of a majority. Then, too, the law of descent, the common school system, and "the universal diffusion of information" preserved Americans from European vices. He further maintained that virtue and intelligence were the bases of republican government and that "our community is an association of persons . . . not a partnership founded on property." Because property is essential to temporal happiness, he admitted that it required protection. On a note reminiscent of John Adams' analysis in the *Defence*, he concluded, without accepting Adams' corresponding institutional prescriptions: "The truth is, that both wealth and talents will ever have a great influence; and without the aid of exclusive privileges, you will always find the influence of both wealth and talents predominant in our halls of legislation."[15]

In the Virginia Convention of 1829–1830 the deceased Jefferson was drawn upon by both democrats and conservatives. While the latter focused on the *Notes On Virginia,* the former proceeded from ideas propounded by Jefferson in two letters which he had written in 1816. Therein he had admitted that some of his earlier suggestions for constitutional reform in Virginia contained "gross departures . . . from genuine republican canons." His "mother principle" was that "governments are republican only in proportion as they embody the will of the people, and execute it." In view of this he recommended: (1) equality of representation in the legislature; (2) the grant of the suffrage to all males who pay taxes or render militia service; (3) abolition of the executive council and popular election of the governor and judges, or appointment of judges by the governor subject to removal upon a vote of both legislative houses; (4) abolition of the oligarchical county courts and transfer of their functions to the people in local "wards"; (5) regular periodic changes of the Constitution.[16]

Even more importantly, democrats could cite Jefferson in the Declaration of Independence and George Mason in the Virginia Bill of Rights and place their case on the ground of natural right. Thus John R. Cooke talked in terms of popular sovereignty, human equality, and the right of the majority to rule. Because, he contended, man is "an *affectionate, a social,* a patriotic, a conscientious, and a religious creature," it is a gross error to conclude that "the love of property" is his "engrossing passion," that the poor will inevitably be the enemy of the rich, that it is the real interest of any class in the community to disregard conscience and the principles of justice. Indeed, "the *very* desire for property implies the desire to possess it *securely,*" a fact which should assure any who believe that equal apportionment of representation according to population will tend to the detriment of property.[17]

The principal speech for the conservatives, who deplored the propensity of the democrats to argue political questions upon deductions from abstract principles, was that of Judge Abel Upshur (1790–1844). Upshur distinguished between a majority in interest and a majority in number, opting for the former on the basis that "those who have the greatest stake in the Government, shall have the greatest share of power in the administration of it." In this view concrete material interests constitute claims to influence in government as good as, if not better than, rights possessed by men simply as persons. Upshur likewise could not accept the notion of the natural right of a numerical majority to control a minority, seeing the law of nature as prescribing only "the right in every creature to use the powers derived from nature, in such mode as will best promote its own happiness." In fact, he pronounced in Hobbesian fashion that the rule of force pervades nature. Men are not bound by any obligation, prior to society, to adopt the majority principle. Admitting a fundamental human equality, he denied, however, that men had ever existed in a state of nature. In opposition to the teachings of Jefferson, Chipman, Wilson, and Madison, for example, Upshur stated: "In truth *there are no original principles of Government at all. . . .* Principles do not *precede*, but spring out of Government." If the democrats were right there would be a natural public law which prescribed but one form of government. On the contrary, "every Government is legitimate which springs directly from the will of the people, or to which the people have consented to give allegiance," because "if the majority possesses all power, they possess the power to *surrender* their power." Consequently, "there is not in nature, nor even in sound political science, any fundamental principle applicable to this subject, which is mandatory upon us. We are at perfect liberty to select our principle." If there exists in society an identity, though not an equality of interests, "the presumption naturally arises, that the greater number possess the greater interest." But there exists no such identity of interest; the difference arising from possession of property demands that it be considered in fixing the basis of representation, along with persons. Because "the safety of men depends on the safety of property; the rights of persons must mingle in the ruin of the rights of property."[18]

In rebuttal Philip Doddridge asked from whence Upshur derived the power in question to the minority. It could not be from nature where, Upshur said, force prevailed, since that was superseded by the existing government, nor from the exigencies of society, the necessities of government, or the constitution and declaration of rights. He concluded: "We are a majority of individual units in the State, and your equals in intelligence and virtue, moral and political. Yet you say we must obey you. You declare that the rule of the minority has never oppressed us, nor visited us with practical evil; but of this we are the best judges."[19]

The Virginia debates presaged the later national discussions on the power of a majority in the federal government to override sectional interests. Upshur's argument points to Calhoun. The abstract individualism issuing from the state of nature postulate was discarded by men concerned with the protection of fundamental interests threatened by a numerical majority. Madison's sociological principle—the extension of the sphere of republican government—was not regarded as an efficacious safeguard by men like Upshur, apart from a specific veto power granted the tidewater property interest, just as it was regarded as unworkable by Calhoun on the national level. Thus their arguments came to emphasize utility and interests above abstract rights. Similarly, many democrats accepted John Adams' thesis that talent, but more particularly, wealth and birth, inevitably make themselves felt as influences upon any government, while rejecting his advice that persons possessing these qualities be placed in a separate chamber of the legislature in the interest of the people at large. Many conservatives, on the other hand, tended to reject Adams' description but embraced his prescription.

The debates in the Massachusetts, New York, and Virginia conventions are important to us today not because of the arguments over the extension of the suffrage but because they put clearly in focus the issue of equitable representation, which within the past decade has been decided by the Supreme Court of the United States on the basis of the principle, "one man, one vote," in favor of equal democratic representation of persons to the exclusion of special representation of property, territory, or any other principle.[20] Opposed to those who today, invoking the reasoning of John Adams' *Defence,* or Thomas Jefferson's *Notes on Virginia,* see the equalitarian principle as contrary to the principle of bicameralism, are the arguments put forth by some democrats in the conventions that differences in sizes of districts and terms of office between the two houses can effect a viable bicameralism and thus preserve an essential truth embodied in classical republicanism.

Finally, it must be noted that in state constitutional conventions before the Civil War there was a gradual abandonment of the compact theory along with a rhetorical deemphasis on natural rights in favor of pragmatic experimentalism. It was not that natural rights were denied; they were instead tacitly assumed. Typical of this mood are the remarks of a Democratic delegate to the Wisconsin Convention of 1846: "Conservatism abhors experiments because simply they are experiments. . . . Democracy lives in experiments; democracy is a creed of progress and progress can come only by experiment. . . . Conservatism asks: Is this or that provision new. . . . On what precedent is it founded? Democracy simply questions: Is it right?"[21]

Jacksonian Democracy

Andrew Jackson (1757–1845) was elected President in 1828 after the legislative caucus system of nomination had been overthrown and significant extensions in the suffrage had been effected. Thus he was less a cause than a result of democracy, elevated to high office with the aid of a new species of politician—the technician of mass leadership. The era of aristocratic republican leadership thus ended with the advent of the political manager and the exaltation of equality and majority rule.[22]

Jackson himself was less a political thinker than a symbol of the new democracy. He and the men about him known as Jacksonians can hardly be said to have had a political philosophy. For the most part they simply and uncritically assumed a natural harmony of economic interests and argued against the monopolistic monetary control exercised by the Bank of the United States, as well as protective tariffs, public debts, and the sale of public lands to provide revenue for government spending. Jefferson had talked in terms of "a wise and frugal Government"; Jackson emphasized one "which shall restrain men from injuring one another," and "shall leave them otherwise free to regulate their own pursuits of industry." Jacksonians looked to the executive and the veto power, rather than the legislature, seeing the former as the tribune of the people. They regarded producers as "the real people," as had Jefferson and John Taylor; but advanced upon them by including in that category not only planters and farmers but mechanics, laborers, and entrepreneurs. Marvin Myers has summed up Jackson's political creed as consisting in, "the Constitution strictly construed; strict observance of the 'fundamental and sacred' rules of simplicity and economy," and "separation of political authority from the conduct of economic affairs." The first principle of his system, Jackson stated in his first message to Congress, is "that the majority is to govern." He regarded government as a simple operation and thought that "the duties of all public officers are, or at least admit of being made so plain and simple that men of intelligence may readily qualify themselves for their performance. . . ."[23]

The urban side of Jacksonian thought was manifested in "locofocoism," an expression of the Workingman's party in New York whose chief expounders were William Leggett (1801–1839) and Theodore Sedgewick (1780–1839). Orestes Brownson aptly described a "locofoco" as "a Jeffersonian Democrat, who having realized political equality, passed through one phase of the revolution, now passes on to another, and attempts the realization of social equality, so that the actual condition of men in society shall be in harmony with their acknowledged rights as citizens." Espousing governmental intervention only to restore the supposed equal competition of the natural order, the locofoco desired to prohibit all banks from issuing notes while most other Jacksonians desired merely the elimination of the central bank in order to remove controls upon their own banking activities within the states. As Bray Hammond, alluding to the latter, has put it: "The Jacksonian revolution was a consequence of the Industrial Revolution and of a farm-born people's realization that now anyone in America could get rich and through his own efforts, if he had a fair chance." The millionaires created by the so-called Jacksonian revolution of "agrarians" against "capitalists" were richer than those they dispossessed.[24]

The most elevated public statement of Jacksonian thought was the pronouncement of Chief Justice Roger Brooke Taney (1777–1864) in the *Charles River Bridge Case* (1837), refusing to enlarge a public grant by implication on the ground that "the object and end of all government is to promote the happiness and prosperity of the community by which it is established; and it can never be assumed that the government intended to diminish its power of accomplishing the end for which it was created." Taney maintained that "the continued existence of a government would be of no great value if, by implications and presumptions, it was disarmed of the powers necessary to accomplish the ends of its creation, and the functions it was designed to perform transferred to the hands of privileged corporations."[25]

While Jacksonians sought a minimization of federal governmental activity, their opponents, the Whigs, following in the train of Hamilton, exalted the state. Edward Everett (1794–1865) declared that "the greatest engine of moral power known to human affairs is an organized, prosperous state." The ablest exponent of nationalism at this time was John Quincy Adams (1768–1848) who preceded Jackson as President. Whereas his father, John Adams, had emphasized an institutional approach to government epitomized in the balanced state, John Quincy Adams talked of a "cooperation of the departments" in the interest of the public. Seeking to rise above party, he held that legislators "should cast all their feelings and interests as Citizens of a single State into the common Stock of the National concern." His fundamental principle was put forth in his first message to Congress as follows: "The great object of the institution of civil government is the improvement of the condition of those who are parties to the social compact, and no government, in whatever form constituted, can accomplish the lawful ends of its institutions but in proportion as it improves the condition over whom it is established." Not only did he espouse national expenditures for internal improvements and the advancement of agriculture, commerce, and manufactures, but moral and intellectual improvement in the arts, literature, and science. His program assumed a sense of nationhood and public interest which outran the realities of political, sectional, and social divisions. The former nationalist turned states'-rightist, John C. Calhoun, later cut down Adams and the Whig exponent of an "American System," Henry Clay (1777–1852), by declaring that "no such political body as the American people collectively, either now or ever, did exist."[26]

The Presidential election campaign of 1840 in which the Whigs successfully used broad uninhibited demagogic appeals signified a shift in their approach. As Louis Hartz has written, they not only stole the Democratic egalitarian thunder but transformed it. While giving up Hamilton's distrust of the people, they retained his capitalism and combined it with the Jeffersonian notion of equal opportunity. The result, Hartz concludes, "was to electrify the Democratic individual with a passion for great achievement and to produce a personality type that was neither Hamiltonian nor Jeffersonian but a strange mixture of them both: the hero of Horatio Alger."[27] The same should be said of the earlier Jacksonian capitalist who, as Hammond has shown, was equally bent on the pursuit of wealth while embracing his egalitarian political creed.

Democratic Protagonists

George Bancroft (1800–1891)

Bancroft, best known for his *History of the United States,* was a strong supporter of Jackson, who extolled equality, the common man and the democratic mission of America. Seeing the popular voice as the voice of God, Bancroft defined democracy, mystically, as "Eternal Justice ruling through the people." He thought that the "common mind" is the infallible oracle to be consulted because it "winnows opinion" and "is the sieve which separates error from certainty." Combining this democratic faith with a belief in the universality of moral law and the all-pervasive influence of a benevolent Providence, Bancroft expounded a conception of progress epitomized in the proposition that the selfishness of evil defeats itself, and God rules in the affairs of man. The Democrats, he proclaimed, constitute the "party of progress and reform," subserving the true end of government—the promotion of the general welfare and happiness. And democracy, by emphasizing equality and the sovereignty of the common mind as the vehicle of truth, is the progressive instrument of Providence. The history of America is thus the story of the progressive realization of freedom and right, and the United States has a divinely ordained mission to spread those principles to mankind at large.[28]

Bancroft's buoyant faith in democracy, the common man, and the common mind, bordered upon political pantheism. And yet it stopped short. In his *History* he had discussed the American Revolution in terms of a conflict between the British assertion of legislative sovereignty and American reliance on the primacy of natural rights. In his social thought he continued to assume that the American "common mind," as expressed in public opinion or through political majorities, would operate on the same premise as that of the Revolutionary Fathers. By identifying the "common mind" with the primacy of natural rights, he never directly confronted the issue arising from a possible conflict between the two which keener analysts of democracy saw quite clearly.

Richard Hildreth (1807–1865)

Bancroft wrote his American history justifying democracy in a spirited though diffuse style; Hildreth's *History of the United States* was a dull, turgid work written from the Federalist point of view. At odds with the bias of Hildreth's *History,* however, was his separately expounded democratic social theory which was unique in America insofar as it was rooted in radical utilitarian, naturalistic premises. Hildreth, a Whig in politics, aimed ambitiously at the ultimate production of a systematic treatment of what he called *The Rudiments of the Inductive Science of Man,* based on the Baconian inductive approach.[29]

Hildreth proposed to analyze the moral, political, economic, intellectual, and aesthetic factors in human life. His *Theory of Morals* and *Theory of Politics* were written in the 1840's; his *Theory of Wealth* and *Theory of Taste* were written later and have been printed but recently. His basic presuppositions were: (1) man is explicable in terms of nature and analyzable by the methods successfully used to investigate nature at large; (2) the supernatural (the realm of religion) is irrelevant to a "scientific" study of man, and should not concern morals and politics; (3) natural rights similarly have no relevance, a meaningful analysis can be made only in terms of "pleasures" and "pains"; (4) civilization is the story of man's progress to an extension and an ever greater balance of "pleasures" over "pains."

Hildreth conceived of "the progress of civilization" as including four dimensions: (1) "the advancement and diffusion of knowledge, which implies a great extension of the range of human pains, pleasures, and desires"; (2) "the accumulation and diffusion of wealth, the chief means of gratifying these new desires"; (3) "the increase of the average force of the sentiment of benevolence, producing what is called the moral advancement of communities," and (4) "an increased sensibility to several pleasures and pains . . . which . . . is commonly designated by the word *Taste.*" It followed that a developed "taste" is the culmination of moral and political progress because "in proportion as a community, or a portion of it, is delivered from that perpetual struggle for the bare means of subsistence in which savage life consists this susceptibility to the beautiful exercises a constant, increasing influence."[30]

Hildreth's utilitarianism, though heavily influenced by Bentham, was more in the direction of Hume. Thus he saw virtuous acts as those which are useful to others and he attributed to men the sentiment of benevolence, defined as the ability to feel pleasure or pain in contemplating the pleasure or pain of others. Unlike Bentham but like John Stuart Mill, he asserted qualitative differences in pleasures, thus undercutting his system by intruding a standard to measure his chosen standard.[31]

Defining government as a "political equilibrium," Hildreth analyzed politics in terms of the ultimate principles, *pleasure* and *pain.* Like John Adams he held "the pleasure of superiority" to be the most prominent psychological force in politics. Because an actual superiority on the part of rulers is the only basis upon which any form of government can securely rest, it can be said that in this sense might makes right. On the other hand, there can never be any "settled obedience or quiet submission on the part of the governed, until the pain of inferiority, which the position of subjects naturally tends to inspire, is counterbalanced or neutralized by the operation of other sentiments." These countervailing motives Hildreth defined as fear, or the "pain of apprehension," admiration for superiors and the pleasure it affords, and the derivative idea of the moral duty of obedience.[32]

Because a stationary political equilibrium is possible only in the speculation of theorists and because the same motives obtain in both ruler and ruled, Hildreth saw two ensuing possibilities. When the motives of the ruled which prompt to obedience are stronger than those which prompt to resistance, the rulers, impelled by the love of power, work to increase their authority until the pain of inferiority in the governed is heightened to the point that they resist until an equilibrium is restored. Similarly, when the movement is contrariwise and the motives prompting to obedience are less intense than those prompting to resistance, resistance occurs until a new equilibrium is established.[33]

On this basis Hildreth advanced a realistic critique of equality and a justification of democracy. If men were equally convinced of their superiority, he maintained, there could be no government. For perfect equality to obtain, men would not only need to be identical but mutually to accept the fact. The primary or intrinsic sources of inequality are strength, skill, sagacity, force, knowledge, eloquence, and virtue. The secondary or extrinsic sources are wealth, traditionary respect, the idea of a property in power, the influence of mystical ideas, and the combination or aggregation of all of these factors.[34]

After explaining the origin and forms of government, Hildreth expounded a test by which the forms must be measured—the degree of pain they inflict, as manifested not in the extent or degree of their power but in the opposition, active or passive, which they encounter. By this canon, democracy emerges as the least oppressive (painful) of governments. Looked at positively, democratic government, unlike other forms, allows for the widest diffusion of the pleasure of superiority. While all of its citizens are obliged to submit to the pain of obedience, they are, at the same time, allowed the pleasure of commanding at the ballot box. Democracy thus satisfies in the vast majority of persons the sentiment of self-comparison by affording them equality. Then, too, superior men, when living under democratic government, are generally its greatest supporters because the road is left open to merit and talent, which evoke admiration, "the true basis of political influence." By allowing all to participate in the pleasure of governing, democratic government in good part neutralizes the pain of obedience and allows superior men peacefully to come to the fore.[35]

Only in a democracy are the means of peaceful change afforded to men. A majority may admittedly be tyrannical but that possibility is a lesser evil than the possibility of a tyrannous minority. In fact, when a democratic majority performs a tyrannical act, it falls into the danger of ceasing to be a majority: "If the pains which the administrators of a democratical government inflict counterbalance the pleasures resulting from their ascendancy, the administration is sure presently to change hands."[36]

And yet, democracy ultimately involves leadership by a few. Its justification lies in the fact that through frequent elections it provides a means for measuring "the natural elements of power, and of consequence the right to rule." It aims at minimizing the power factors of mystical ideas, traditionary respect, and the idea of property in power while allowing the other factors free play. Caucus politicians undertake the aristocratic function of dictating to the people, but at the same time they play "a democratic part, by humbling and restraining within due limits those possessors of the natural elements of power, whom the strong tendency to 'hero-worship,' even in the most democratic communities, might otherwise be likely to elevate to a dangerous authority."[37]

Hildreth also contended that democratic government effects the progress of civilization by increasing and extending knowledge, wealth, and morals. The principle of equality precludes all monopolies, restrictions, and prohibitions; the absence of castes and mysticism produces "a general spirit of humanity and philanthropy"; and in place of a great number of contradictory moral codes, democracy supplies one standard.[38]

While defending democracy as a civilizing influence, Hildreth took sharp issue with de Tocqueville, whom he considered superficial on the subject of American democracy: "It might be as well for the good-natured critics and speculatists of Europe to wait a half century or so longer . . . before coming to any final and dogmatical conclusion as to the . . . [lasting] influences of democracy in these particulars." Specifically Hildreth meant that there were existent in America several "disturbing factors." These included: (1) the English common law which he saw as hostile to democracy and a contrivance for defeating the intentions of legislatures; (2) the presence of "mystical ideas" embodied in "theocratic despotism," which he deemed a "foreign and even hostile ingredient" and which de Tocqueville under the name of religion misconceived as basic to American democracy; (3) chattel slavery; and (4) the fact that America is a new country where the accumulation of wealth is just beginning and the dispersion and poverty of people form serious obstacles in the way of social improvements, especially the cultivation of the arts and sciences.[39]

Looking to the future, Hildreth, after stating there have been in history ages of the clergy, nobles, kings, and burghers, asked, "Is there never to be an *Age of the People*—of the working classes?" He answered that he believed it was beginning, but that no mere redistribution of wealth could effect it. Instead, it depended primarily upon an increase in the productivity of labor and the development of science and industry.[40]

Hildreth's ideas were of no significant influence in his day. His rejection of the natural rights philosophy and attempt to restate democratic theory on purely utilitarian grounds fell as a foreign import on barren ground, while his positivism, implied behavioralism, and naturalism were premature. He stands, however, as an anomalous example of a Whig dissenter from the traditional Lockian approach who justified equality, democracy, individualism, and industrialism as interrelated operational values and vehicles of civilizational progress.

Frederick Grimke (1791–1863)

Grimke is worthy of our attention because of his greatly neglected book *Considerations Upon the Nature and Tendency of Free Institutions* (1848), a reasoned defense of American democracy and a plea for the development of a revised political science in view of the signal contributions of democracy. Political science, Grimke complained, had remained stationary amidst the general progress of the human mind in the previous two centuries. The reason for this he saw as fourfold: (1) the diversity of the facts involved and the difficulty in reducing them to general rules; (2) it is the science not only of what is and what ought to be, but what may be made to be; (3) the traditional secretiveness of government; (4) the greater past and present attraction of the active life to potential scholars. Grimke viewed political science as experimental, deriving, as is all knowledge, from facts, from whence, in turn, principles arise. And yet, he declared, it cannot be divorced from a consideration of what ought to be, based on the objective moral law.[41]

Grimke particularly objected to the overemphasis on institutions and mechanisms in the traditional study of government to the neglect of underlying social structure. All governments, but particularly democracy, he wrote, are "to a great degree dependent upon the manners, habits, and dispositions of the people among whom they subsist." Instead of focusing on the traditional institutional checks and balances, stress should be placed on the balance existing in a "rightly constituted" society (democracy) between the government and "the power out of the government" (society and public opinion). Unlike other forms of government, a representative democracy alone is based on this balance, a "new fact" in the history of political science which heretofore has escaped attention. In this light there is but one legitimate form of government— representative democracy—which when "joined to an upright and enlightened administration of . . . public affairs" promotes and diffuses freedom and intelligence, the arts and sciences and "a vigorous morality." It successfully connects the interests of the people with their improvement in their mutual interdependence, as well as identifying the interests of rulers and ruled. And yet it would be an egregious error to conclude that political institutions can never be made to rise higher than social manners. In fact even in a democracy their influence is reciprocal.[42]

Grimke saw government as a dictate of human nature requiring the instrumentality of a compact to render it legitimate. Majority rule is indicated as its principle of operation because it produces beneficial results. Grimke contended that "whenever a majority is competent to take care of its own interests, it will also be competent to take care of those of the minority," because (1) all the substantial interests in society are included in the majority; and (2) parties in a republic do not occupy fixed positions and classes, but shift grounds. In fact, the constant tendency in a republic is toward the formation of a middle class representing interests common to the whole, as the predominant body. Consequently a majority cannot be formed without being principally composed of that class. Thus where free institutions exist the major interests of minorities will be enclosed in those of the majority, and leaders of one political party will not differ essentially from those of the other. Experience shows that no sooner is the rule of the majority established than it proceeds to prescribe limits to itself on the basis of enlightened self-interest.[43]

Concerning the related factor of public opinion, Grimke declared that above all it contributes to the production of "a just equalization of the moral power of the community," thus superseding resort to physical force. Like De Tocqueville, he remarked: "No one who is an attentive observer of human nature, can fail to be struck with the amazing influence which the opinion of a multitude exercises over the mind." He attributed this to the fact that, (1) the sense of right and wrong is implanted in all men, and (2) conformity is encouraged through training and education and any revolt against it is followed by dread and uneasiness as well as social disapproval. Unlike De Tocqueville, he defended the pressure of public opinion, maintaining that it is highly probable "that the opinion of an individual as to his own conduct is biased, and an equal probability that the sentiment of the body is impartial." In fact, public opinion only tends to be right in proportion as it resembles the opinion of mankind. It follows that to gain a *consensus gentium* it is necessary to maximize the number of men in possession of political liberty. Extended equal liberty plus reflection cause men to modify and limit each other's views and opinions, bringing public opinion into accord with the voice of mankind. Thus "a sort of self-regulative principle" resides in society, "which tends to keep everything in its place." And it is "the partial distribution of the privilege," not its communication to all, which brings disorder and insubordination in society. The resolution of the political problem of how to reconcile popular liberty with political power is best decided in a democratic republic.[44]

It is to be noted that in a democracy not only does public opinion check government but it is the force by which people "are made to act as watches upon each other, to consult each other's temper and disposition, to balance the great advantage of acting from impulse." Each man "acts as a sentinel upon his neighbor, and thus, through the co-operation of all, the private interest of each is rendered as consistent as possible with the interests of all." As the population increases in America, the more will the people be placed in close proximity and "the more rigorous" will be their mutual control.[45]

Regarding the principle of equality, Grimke held that in America it had a natural support in the broad distribution of land and had not been created by law. Should, however, the population become very dense and capital accumulate to create a class society of rich and poor, "the laws, the character of the government, may do much toward either promoting, or preventing the disparity of estates." And yet, the division of labor is basic to civilization and assumes inequality. Thus the complete redistribution of property by law, even if it made all comfortable, "would paralyze the springs of industry." Public virtue is best strengthened by the nourishment of the private affections. Grimke, like most Jacksonian Democrats, assumed a natural harmony of interests in society which demanded a minimum of governmental restraint on individual effort and thus, inevitably, an implied recognition of inequality.[46]

Why then, Grimke asked, do democratic legislators insist upon the maxim that all are equal? He answered:

First. Because to teach and to act upon it is the only way of attaining equality, to the extent to which it is actually attained. Second. Because it is not in the power of government to make anything like an accurate discrimination between the inequalities of different men, and the attempt to do so would be to encroach upon these points in which there is no inequality. Third. Because the principle of equality may very well be recognized as the rule among men as citizens—as members of a political community, although as individuals there may be great and numerous inequalities between them. The utmost which the citizen can demand is that no law shall be passed to obstruct his rise, and to impede his progress through life.[47]

Inequality is thus socially and economically relevant, but politically irrelevant. Equality is at once an unattainable yet necessary norm and an indispensable political operational principle. Thus the property qualification for the suffrage, a residue of the feudal era, is politically indefensible. The true plan of balancing power is to prevent its concentration in the hands of a few and the only way to control rulers is to open the door to all men for the acquisition of property, which, Grimke believed, is most effectively promoted by universal suffrage. Like Hildreth, Grimke observed that landed property was being replaced by industry, sagacity, and enterprise as the chief elements of wealth. In such a situation he thought it necessary to identify the natural and legal majorities.[48]

On the basis of his acceptance of equality, liberty, public opinion, and majority rule, Grimke declared the inevitability and desirability of political parties. Although party strife is an annoyance and inconvenience, "it is a great mistake, with our knowledge of the constitution of human nature, to suppose that society would be better ordered if its surface were a perfect calm." Grimke believed that popular parties take the place of checks and balances which are most fitting in monarchies or aristocracies but which play only a subordinate role in popular government. There is a hint of Madison's sociological principle in his assertion that the wider the area in which parties operate, the more numerous and diverse the persons they comprehend, and thus the less dangerous they are to the state. Parties are a positive good, in that they stimulate conflict of opinion and reflection and serve to ameliorate the sharpness of difference.[49]

Finally, Grimke, in his treatment of the democratic legislature, repeated his doubts about the central necessity of checks and balances by asserting the probability of the greater feasibility of unicameralism. "A single body having the public eye intently fixed upon it, and not distracted by the shuffling and the maneuvering of two chambers, would feel a more thorough, because a more undivided, responsibility to its constituents." To the argument that minorities should be represented in government, he replied that minorities should influence and not govern. When all is said and done, however, Grimke averred, "the sovereignty of the people" and its expression in majority rule is not unlimited, morally speaking, because "there is no power on earth, the people no more than the prince, which can be conceived to be absolved from the eternal principles of justice," which are "not mere arbitrary rules" but "a part of our original constitution."[50]

All the elements predominant in American thought of the middle period—the free individual, the moral law, the mission of America, democracy and the idea of progress, are present in Grimke's political science. He is related to the classical American theorists in his espousal of the experimental method but differs with their emphasis on political institutional mechanisms and techniques. His revised concept of balance in government follows more closely upon Franklin, Jefferson, and even more Taylor, in focusing upon the external check of public opinion. Like them, he assumed a natural order which must not be disturbed but expedited. Thus in the economic world the division of labor is the means of realizing a natural identity of interests; in the social world an extended public opinion naturally restrains men from excesses and promotes accord; and in the political world democratic government, with majority rule and free political parties, naturally tends to an increase in knowledge and happiness and in social equilibrium. It follows that democracy is the dictate of nature and the only principle of political legitimacy.

Walt Whitman (1819–1892)

The "Bard of Democracy" propounded no logical theory but sang exultingly and optimistically of the future of the "new man," the product of democracy extended to all aspects of American life. As the young editor of the Brooklyn *Eagle*, he was greatly influenced by cocofocoism, opposing banks, tariffs, monopolies, and paper money. He thought but one rule necessary regarding government: *"to make no more laws than those useful for preventing a man or body of men from infringing on the rights of other men."* Strongly individualistic ("I am a radical of radicals, but I don't belong to any school"), he urged "positive and vital Democracy" permeating manners and the whole of culture. Defiantly, he wrote: "I want no more of these deferences to authority—this taking off hats and saying Sir—I want to encourage in the young men the spirit that does not know what it is to feel that it stands in the presence of superiors." Applied to American life and letters this led him to conclude: "I hold it should be the glory and pride of America not to be like other lands, but different, after its own different spirit."[51] His fundamental conception of what made America unique is summed up in the following passage:

The meaning of America is Democracy. The meaning of Democracy is to put in practice the idea of the sovereignty, license, sacredness of the individual. This idea gives identity and isolation to every man and woman—but the idea of Love fuses and combines all with irresistible power. . . . A third idea, also, is or shall be put there,—namely Religion,—the idea which swallows up and purifies all other ideas and things—and gives endless meaning and destiny to a man and condenses him in all things.[52]

Individualism, love (or "adhesiveness," as he sometimes called it) and religion were the keynotes of Whitman's thought. Distrusting the "putridity" of political life and the grossness of commerce and wealth, he put faith in that which lay fathoms beneath the surface—"sound men, women and children, of simpler wants, owners of their own homes, of natural talents, untainted with the sick madness which we see." He envisioned the evolution of "a perfect race . . . grandly developed in body, emotions, heroism and intellect—not a select class so developed but the great population." His "final aim" he declared, was to concentrate around him the leaders of all reforms, because "we want no *reforms,* no *institutions,* no *parties,*" but "*a living principle* as nature has, under which nothing can go wrong."[53]

Whitman's lusty, lyrical expression of an indigenous American poetry, *Leaves of Grass,* is, as he described it, a song of "the great pride of man in himself." The individualism which "isolates" is supplemented therein by the "adhesiveness" which "fuses," and the cult of democratic man. At once crudely realistic (he was the first to write sympathetically of the city) and romantically utopian, Whitman advanced beyond the individualism of both Emerson and Thoreau to stress the bond of fraternity. The absolute law of liberty, as he called it, is considered only by the shallow as a release from every constraint, whereas the wise see in it the fusion of the "partial individual law, with those universal, eternal, unconscious ones, which run thru all Time, pervade history, prove immortality, give moral purpose to the entire objective world, and the last dignity to human life." To him there was "nothing in the universe any more divine than man." The new democratic theology, he thought, brings a shift in the previous relative positions, "Man comes forward inherent, superb, the soul, the judge, the common average man advances, ascends to place. God disappears—the whole idea of God, as hitherto presented in the religions of the world for the thousands of past years. . . ." Thus democratic man can brook no superior of flesh or spirit; instead he must assert his own divinity and identity with the cosmic laws. Faith in democracy becomes ineluctably to Whitman synonomous with faith in the sovereignty not of men but of man.[54] Such an outlook, like that of Bancroft, belongs less in the realm of intellect and theory than of emotion and feeling—a hope and trust in democratic humanity of the American stripe, the mission of which is ultimately universal salvation.

Conclusions

Positing the primacy of individual effort and development, proponents of democracy stressed political and legal equality while conceding the inevitability of social and economic inequality. They considered government to be secondary to the free workings of the economy and society, and assigned to it a limited role—the removal of artificial legal restraints and privileges. Majority rule was extolled and, except for the utilitarian Hildreth, all assumed the primacy of moral law. Just as many Americans of the revolutionary period exalted the legislature as the bastion of popular rights, so did most of democracy's proponents exalt public opinion as the ultimate sovereign, guarantor of rights and checkrein upon unrestrained individualism. Public opinion was mediated to the moral law by the notion that the more inclusive the public the closer is public opinion to the *consensus gentium,* an infallible indicator of the content of moral law. Similarly, majority rule was justified on the assumption that an informed public will have regard for the interests of minorities. It followed that the extension of equality in government and the development of a broad public opinion are essentially progressive and lead not only to the cultural but the biological advancement of the race. Public opinion could then in turn be considered as an automatic instrument of social control in tune with, if not identical to, the moral law and thus a surrogate for government. Finally, just as Grimke tended to deify public opinion, Whitman and Bancroft tended to deify democratic man.

NOTES

1. Alexis De Tocqueville, *Democracy in America* (Phillips Bradley, ed., New York, 1945, 2 vols.), I, 7, 315–316, 325.
2. *Ibid.,* 1, 54, 319–323, 316, 317.
3. *Ibid.,* I, 51, 177–178, 263; II, 98, 134, 136, 137, 42.
4. *Ibid.,* I, 200, 202, 254ff.
5. *Ibid.,* II, 125ff; I, 191ff, 271ff, 275, 276, 280, 151.
6. *Ibid.,* I, 306; II, 6.
7. Ralph Gabriel, *The Course of American Democratic Thought* (New York, 1940), pp. 14 25
8. Perry Miller, *The Life of the Mind in America* (New York, 1965), pp. 37, 39, 66ff.
9. The principal arguments in these conventions are conveniently brought together in Merrill D. Peterson (ed.) *Democracy, Liberty and Property* (Indianapolis, 1966).
10. Peterson, *op. cit.,* pp. 68–70.
11. *Ibid.,* pp. 74–76.
12. *Ibid.,* pp. 79, 83, 84.
13. *Ibid.,* pp. 92ff, 98, 99, 100.
14. *Ibid.,* pp. 193, 194, 192, 196.
15. *Ibid.,* pp. 202, 203, 205, 206. The last quotation is not included in Peterson's compilation but can be found in the original source, *Reports of the Proceedings and Debates of the Convention of 1821, Asembled for the Purpose of Amending the Constitution of the State of New York* (Albany, 1821), p. 244.
16. Jefferson to S. Kercheval, July 12, Sept. 5, 1816. Ford (ed.), *The Writings of Thomas Jefferson,* X, 37–45.
17. Peterson, *op. cit.,* pp. 289ff, 302, 303.
18. *Ibid.,* pp. 307, 308, 309, 316, 317–318, 319.
19. *Ibid.,* p. 336.
20. *Baker v. Carr,* 369 U.S. 186 (1962).
21. Remarks of Edward G. Ryan, in Milo Quaife (ed.), *The Struggle Over Ratification (1846–1847)* (Madison, 1920), p. 445.
22. I have relied in good part on the treatment of Jackson in Richard Hofstadter, *The American Political Tradition* (New York, 1948), Chapter 3; Marvin Myers, *The Jacksonian Persuasion: Politics and Belief* (Palo Alto, 1957); and Arthur Schlesinger Jr., *The Age of Jackson* (Boston, 1946).
23. Myers, *op. cit.,* pp. 24, 28–29, 30, 21, 23; James D. Richardson (ed.), *A Com-*

pilation of the Messages and Papers of the Presidents (Washington, 1896), II, 448, 449.

24. Schlesinger, *op. cit.,* p. 313; Bray Hammond, *Banks and Politics in America* (Princeton, 1957), 328.

25. *Charles River Bridge v. Warren Bridge,* II Peters 420 (1837).

26. The Everett, Adams, and Calhoun statements can be found in Herbert Schneider, *A History of American Philosophy* (New York, 1946), pp. 101, 102, 103, 104.

27. Louis Hartz, *The Liberal Tradition in America* (New York, 1955), pp. 111, 112.

28. George Bancroft, *Literary and Historical Miscellanies* (New York, 1855), pp. 415, 422, 426ff.

29. Hildreth to Caroline Weston, Jan. 8, 1841, quoted in Martha M. Pingel, *An American Utilitarian* (New York, 1948), pp. 11, 12.

30. Richard Hildreth, *Theory of Politics* (New York, 1853), p. 230; *Theory of Taste,* printed in Pingel, *op. cit.,* p. 76.

31. Hildreth's views on morality are summed up in "A Joint Letter to Orestes A. Brownson and the Editor of the 'North American Review,'" in Pingel, *op. cit.,* pp. 153–176.

32. *Theory of Politics,* pp. 16, 17, 18–23.

33. *Ibid.,* pp. 23–26.

34. *Ibid.,* pp. 26–28, 31–48, 49–69.

35. *Ibid.,* pp. 233, 254, 255.

36. *Ibid.,* p. 256.

37. *Ibid.,* pp. 259, 67.

38. *Ibid.,* pp. 261, 262.

39. *Ibid.,* pp. 263, 266, 264, 265.

40. *Ibid.,* pp. 267, 268–270.

41. Frederick Grimke, *Considerations Upon the Nature and Tendency of Free Institutions* (Cincinnati, 1848), pp. 1, 2.

42. *Ibid.,* pp. 4, 5, 6, 8, 9, 10.

43. *Ibid.,* pp. 11, 16, 18, 19, 21.

44. *Ibid.,* pp. 108, 109, 110, 111, 112, 113, 114.

45. *Ibid.,* pp. 119, 122, 120.

46. *Ibid.,* pp. 45, 47, 49, 50, 51.

47. *Ibid.,* p. 53.

48. *Ibid.,* pp. 54, 56, 57, 63, 64, 69.

49. *Ibid.,* pp. 92, 94, 95.

50. *Ibid.,* pp. 196, 197, 204, 154.

51. Cleveland Rogers and John Block, *The Gathering of the Forces* (New York, 1920), I, 54; Horace Traubel, *With Walt Whitman in Camden* (Boston, 1906–1964), I, 215; Walt Whitman "Notes for Lectures on Democracy and 'Adhesiveness'," in C. J. Furness (ed.), *Walt Whitman's Workshop* (Cambridge, Mass., 1928), pp. 54, 55.

52. Whitman, manuscript Introduction to *Leaves of Grass,* in Furness, *op. cit.,* p. 171.

53. Furness, *op. cit.,* pp. 56, 57, 62.

54. Whitman, "Introduction to the London Edition of *Leaves of Grass*" in Furness, *op. cit.,* p. 150; Furness, *op. cit.,* footnote 66, p. 221; Whitman, *Complete Prose Works* (Boston, 1898), p. 35; "Notes for Lectures," in Furness, *op. cit.,* pp. 43, 44.

Chapter 16

THE CRITICAL APPRAISAL OF DEMOCRACY

He is the purest democrat who best maintains his rights, and no rights can be dearer to a man of cultivation, than exemptions from unseasonable invasions on his time, by the coarse-minded and ignorant.

JAMES FENIMORE COOPER

As already seen, De Tocqueville had expressed concern over implications of majority rule and a sovereign public opinion for the cause of liberty. Prominent Americans turned to this and related questions. They were concerned with the relationship between equality on the one hand and liberty and property on the other, between conformity to public opinion and individuality, and between majority rule and minority rights. In connection therewith emphasis was put upon providing restraints on an unbounded democratic impulse in the form of religion, or a reassertion of moral law, or the reaffirmation of a fundamental law enforced and guarded by lawyers and judges.

Friendly Critics of Democracy

James Fenimore Cooper (1789–1851)

Cooper, known best for his novels celebrating the free individual ("Natty Bumpo") in tension with the positive law ("Judge Temple"), was a Jacksonian Democrat of aristocratic tastes and great landed wealth, whose father had been a Federalist of the John Adams school. Cooper joined the classical institutional emphasis on checks and balances, which he inherited from his father, to a Jeffersonian preference for the moral and political worth of natural property (land) over artificial property (capital, paper money, securities). In his early work,

Notions of the Americans Picked Up By a Traveling Bachelor (1828),
he defended popular suffrage, equality, and popular education. Attacking the Whig concept of property in government, he characterized
the disfranchisement of the poor as "violence to natural justice." Although he thought that "a trifling *qualification* of property" for the
suffrage may sometimes be useful in certain social situations, he added
that there was "no greater fallacy than its *representation*" in government.[1]

After a trip to Europe, where his observations reinforced his belief
in the wisdom of the American conception of a balanced constitution,
Cooper was affronted by the unpermitted use of a portion of his land
as a public picnic ground. The occasion stimulated him to a reappraisal
of democracy. Thus his book, *The American Democrat* (1838), was
written as both a primer and an important critique of democracy.[2]

Cooper first declared his preference for democracy over other systems
because of "its comparative advantages, and not . . . its perfection."
Simply put, it is less evil than monarchy or aristocracy. Its two main
drawbacks are (1) "a disposition in the majority to carry out the
opinions of the system to extremes," and (2) a "disposition in the
minority to abandon all to the current of the day, with the hope that
this current will lead, in the end, to radical changes."[3]

Unlike such men as Emerson, Thoreau, and Whitman, Cooper did
not assume the goodness of human nature, but like Adams and Madison,
saw government resulting from human weakness. Consonant with the
current belief in the universality of moral law, he declared that laws
must be "founded on the immutable principles of natural justice . . . to
protect the feeble against the . . . strong; the honest from the schemes
of the dishonest; the temperate and industrious from the waste and
indolence of the dissolute and idle." Thus, "the very necessity of a
government . . . arises from the impossibility of controlling the passions
by any other means than that of force."[4]

Cooper distinguished between equality of condition, which he regarded as incompatible with civilization, and equality of rights, which
he saw as the proper dictate of democracy. The rights of property are
"an indispensable condition of civilization," even though they give rise
to inequality of condition. Men are born equal neither physically nor
morally, and the very existence of government indicates inequality. On
this basis Cooper conceded that "there are numerous instances in which
the social inequality of America may do violence to our notions of
abstract justice," nevertheless, "the compromise of interests under which
all civilized society must exist, renders this unavoidable." Consequently, a good government aims "to add no unnecessary and artificial
aid to the force of its own unavoidable consequences, and to abstain
from fortifying and accumulating social inequality as a means of increasing political inequalities."[5]

Similarly, Cooper believed, a perfect and absolute liberty is incompatible with society. He defined liberty as "such a state of the social compact as permits the members of a community to lay no more restraints on themselves, than are required by their real necessities, and obvious interests." Without the power to frame its own laws, no people is free—a conception of liberty effected in America, which Cooper called "new to the world."[6]

Turning to the question of majority rule, Cooper warned that it can be admitted only "with many limitations." Constitutions would be useless if they proceeded from the will of numbers. The majority rules in America only in prescribed cases. He apparently believed that the constituent power must lodge in an extraordinary majority or be qualified by moderation and the spirit of compromise. Constitutions have to do with general principles and must accord with the dictates of natural justice. Cooper declared: "Were it wise to trust power, unreservedly, to majorities, all fundamental and controlling laws would be unnecessary. . . ." Majority rule under a constitution prescribing limits and embodying checks and balances was to him a necessity. Unlike many Jacksonians, he did not deify the majority but held that it was simply less liable to do wrong than minorities. The educated and the affluent, he admitted, are more qualified than the majority to rule, but "all history proves, when power is the sole possession of a few, that it is perverted to their sole advantage. . . ." Thus the same human nature which imposes the need for government indicates that government must be controlled in the last resort by the people at large "as the only lasting protection against gross abuses."[7]

The weakness of majority rule, Cooper thought, is its tendency to violate individual rights. More particularly is public opinion indicted. Cooper deemed it "a great mistake for the American citizen to take sides with the public, in doubtful cases affecting the rights of individuals." Democracy is prone to be influenced by popular impulses arising from imperfect information, "sudden mutations of sentiment," the tendency toward mediocrity, and, in larger states, the influence of "demagogues and political managers." Thus "it is a besetting vice of Democracies to substitute public opinion for law."[8]

Distinguishing between the "political or public" and the "social, or private" stations, Cooper saw them united in monarchies and aristocracies. Because social status is mainly a consequence of property, Cooper stated, "all that democracies legitimately attempt is to prevent the advantages which accompany social station from accumulating rights that do not properly belong to the condition," that is, by denying it "factitious political aids." He believed that "the man of refinement, with his education, tastes and sentiments is superior to all," and denounced "visionary theories" which deny this fact. Thus there exist orders in American society, as in all other countries, but America differs because "the classes run into each other more easily, the lines of separation are less strongly drawn and their shadows are more intimately blended."[9]

The American gentleman, a member of the class which is "the natural repository of the manners, tastes, tone, and to a certain extent, of the principles of [the] country," has the duty of guarding the liberties of his fellow citizens. In this light democracy means only "as equal a participation in rights as is practicable," because "to pretend that social equality is a condition of popular institutions, is to assume that the latter are destructive of civilization." Because it is impossible to raise all men to the highest standard of refinement and development, it does not follow that all should be reduced to the lowest.[10]

Cooper distinguished the "democratic gentleman" from the "aristocratic gentleman." The latter "fortifies his exclusive privileges by positive institutions"; the former "is willing to admit of a free competition, in all things." Though democratic and aristocratic gentlemen are virtually identical in their ordinary habits and taste, they differ in principles and deportment: "The democrat, recognizing the right of all to participate in power, will be more liberal in his general sentiments, a quality of superiority in itself; but, in conceding this much to his fellow man, he will proudly maintain his own independence of vulgar domination, as indispensable to his personal habits." Democracy can legitimately assert the control of the majority in matters of law and not in matters of custom. "He is the purest democrat who best maintains his rights, and no rights can be dearer to a man of cultivation, than exemptions from unseasonable invasions on his time, by the coarse-minded and ignorant." And property is the "ground work of moral independence," as a means of improving the faculties of doing good to others. Finally, Cooper proclaimed, "Individuality is the aim of political liberty."[11]

Cooper's *American Democrat* is of great significance because it is a serious attempt to identify and remove the confusions arising from the unabashed, uncritical exaltation of equality, public opinion, and majority rule by placing them within the composite framework of the classical institutionalism of John Adams and James Madison, the Jeffersonian emphasis on the priority of landed property, and John Adams' assumption of the inevitability of social orders. Natural justice, Cooper thought, indicates both the need for government and limitations thereon, the recognition of the political and civil equality of all, and the inevitable social inequality necessary to civilization brought about by differences in talent, energy, character, birth, and wealth. Democracy and majority rule are advocated not in terms of their inherent worth but as lesser evils. But democracy, majority rule, and public opinion can only be restrained from becoming tyrannical when limited by a constitution not subject to a transient majority, but to checks and balances and the existence in society of men of refined taste, culture, development, and character who are leaders and guardians of the rights of all. Above all, democratic institutions must allow the individual freely to develop without imposing upon him common social norms. Thus Cooper's *American Democrat* represents the most reasoned effort in the Jacksonian period to synthesize the new truth of democracy with the received truth of classical republicanism. In Cooper's thought Adams, Jefferson, and Jackson are rendered mutually compatible.

Ralph Waldo Emerson (1803–1882)

Emerson was the central figure in a group of diverse New England intellectuals who beginning in the 1830's propounded an idealistic approach to life and politics which came to be called Transcendentalism. Critical of the growing materialism of the age and of the crudities of mass democracy, the Transcendentalists, who found confirmation for their thought principally in German philosophy (Kant, Fichte) and in English letters (Coleridge, Carlyle), turned away from the sensationist psychology of Locke and Hume to the mystical recognition of "consciousness," "intuition," or "instinct," as the instrument of truth.

An outgrowth of Unitarianism, which had succeeded to the deistic rationalism of the eighteenth century and which had exalted human nature as good, regarded God not as an arbitrary sovereign but as a loving father, and emphasized personal responsibility, Transcendentalism exalted human nature as divine and stressed the primacy of the developed moral self as the ultimate lawgiver.

Like the rationalist before him, the Transcendentalist invoked "nature" as a norm at once to transcend and judge history and work therefrom to a reconstruction of the moral, social, and political order. But whereas the rationalist identified nature with absolute fixed laws based on self-evidence or generalizations from experience, the Transcendentalist identified it with the divine indwelling in man. He believed that man's spiritual life is independent of history, contingency, and the mediate knowledge of sense experience, because it is identified with ultimate reality. Approached from the angle of the two main traditions of American political thought, that of Locke and that of Hooker, Transcendentalism rejected the empiricism of the former and the analogical use of reason of the latter. Approached from the angle of American religious thought, Transcendentalism stood, in contrast to deism and Unitarianism, in the Antinomian rather than the Arminian tradition.[12]

Transcendental politics subordinated prudence to natural right directly apprehended, seeing the ideas of the Declaration of Independence—equality, unalienable rights, the purpose of government as the protection of all in the enjoyment of these rights—as grasped independently of the senses and controlling. Thus envisaged, the American Revolution and American history constituted attempts "to organize the transcendental idea of politics," and democracy was vindicated as "a government by natural justice." The task of transcendental politics was seen as the implementation of the divine conception of the state based on a morality which regards man as a completely autonomous individual.[13]

Emerson regarded mind as "the only reality" and on this basis sought to free the moral and spiritual life of man from the shackles of any mediatory influences. Thus he indicted the historical church and traditional Christian theology for placing barriers between man's soul and the ultimate transhistorical reality. His conception of "intuition" was not opposed to reason but to authority, tradition, dogma, and custom, terms which all bear strong historical connotations. Intuition goes directly to absolute truth and to spiritual laws which are "out of time, out of space, and not subject to circumstance." Not only is the object of "intuition" above history but so is its manner of operation. Through it subject and object are identified, and man becomes one with the "Oversoul."[14]

Emerson related the individual directly to absolute Being while not destroying individuality by assuming that the full causal power of the former is directed to the actuality of the latter. The individual, if he opens himself to the divine influx, removes himself from contingency while retaining personality. The sensed world of public objects, their successions and interrelations in space and time, are thus merely representative of reality, having but a symbolic character. It followed that he who has the lawgiver within, stands above every written commandment.

On this basis Emerson could talk of three classes of men in the ascendant order of their worth. The first lives according to the utility of the symbol, deeming health and wealth as final goods; the second (poets, artists, naturalists, and scientists) focuses on the beauty of the symbol; and the third rises above the symbol, in Platonic fashion, to the beauty of the thing signified. The levels of common sense and taste are then inferior to that of spiritual perception, which is the property of that toward which nature aims, the wise or cultivated man.[15]

With the wise man (the fully developed individual who is one with the Oversoul) as paradigm, Emerson expounded his conception of politics and his critique of contemporary democracy. In his essay, "Self-Reliance," he declared that "society everywhere is in conspiracy against the manhood of every one of its members" and that "whoso would be a man must be a nonconformist." Because he lives from within, the nonconformist has naught to do "with the sacredness of traditions" but follows in independence only "the eternal law." Self trust is inhibited by the desires for conformity and consistency. Emerson aimed directly at the emulative approbativeness in man which the realist John Adams had put at the base of his political psychology. The want of self-reliance, he argued, brings reliance on property and on government and man the person becomes the slave of things, sacrificing in the process his autonomy.[16]

Emerson's individualism is most pronounced in his critique of reform movements. He wrote: "The criticism and attack on institutions which we have witnessed, has made one thing plain, that society gains nothing whilst a man, not himself renovated, attempts to renovate things around him." In fact, "no society can ever be so large as one man" and "it only needs, that a just man should walk in our streets, to make it appear how pitiful and inartificial a contrivance is our legislation." Whereas "the multitude have no habit of self-reliance or original action," the "cultivated man, wise to know and perform, is the end to which Nature works. . . ."[17]

Emerson believed that democracy has its "root and seed" in the doctrine, "Judge for yourself. Reverence yourself." He thought that its inevitable effect, although rare, is "to insulate the partisan, to make each man a state," while "it replaces the dead with a living check in a true, delicate reverence for superior, congenial minds." It is based "in the sacred truth that every man hath in him the divine Reason," though few men since the creation of the world have lived according to its dictates. In fact this is the only equality which can be imputed to men. At the same time Emerson made it clear that in speaking of democracy he meant not "that ill thing, vain and loud, which writes lying newspapers, spouts at caucuses, and sells its lies for gold; but that spirit of love for the general good whose name this assumes."[18]

Emerson's essay on *Politics* repeats his point that "the highest end of government is the culture of men." Consequently, "the only interest for the consideration of the State, is persons" and "property will always follow persons." Despite "the ignorant and deceivable majority," there exist limits which cannot be transgressed because "things have their laws, as well as men; and things refuse to be trifled with." Thus inevitably property will be protected; under any form of government it; and persons as well, "must and will have their just sway." Then, too, the same necessity "determines the form and method of governing, which are proper to each nation and to its habit of thought. . . ." Thus American institutions "are not better, but only fitter for us." They are not exempt "from the practical defects which have discredited other forms," because "every actual State is corrupt" and therefore "good men must not obey the laws too well."[19]

In Emerson's eyes American radicalism was "destructive and aimless," while American conservatism was "timid, and merely defensive of property." Neither parties nor forms of government can assume importance, however, where "absolute right is the first governor." Because the history of government is the story of attempts by men to bind their fellows, "the less government we have the better," and "the antidote to this abuse of formal Government, is, the influence of private character, . . . the appearance of the wise man, of whom the existing government is . . . but a shabby imitation." The state exists "to educate the wise man," and with his appearance, it expires, because character "makes the State unnecessary." Thus "the wise man is the State"; he needs "no experience, for the life of the creator shoots through him, and looks from his eyes. . . ." Only so long as men remain selfish shall there be coercive government.[20]

In sum, to Emerson government is in the symbolic world of representation and necessary only for men who, operating from common sense, take the symbol for reality, and men who, operating from taste, preoccupy themselves with the beauty of symbols. The wise man, who by intuition goes to the transcendent ultimate reality, is his own law. It follows that the .end of coercive government, in the twofold sense of purpose and termination, is the production of wise men who voluntarily promote the common good. In the interim the idea of the wise man is the critical norm by which government must be judged. And yet the wise man can be produced by self-reliance alone. Thus government must be reduced to a minimum. Neither it nor voluntary cooperative collectivism can substitute for personal responsibility and self-development. The wise man is sovereign, his focus is inward and upward and he must not be deterred by any mediatory forces or forms such as opinion, politics, government, property, or interest. He is interested in justice but only after the realization of self-government within himself. In this light what is important in the American political tradition is not the classical preoccupation with governmental forms and institutional devices nor the principle of majority rule but the individualism of the Declaration of Independence. In contrast to Whitman and Grimke, Emerson thought that not *man* or *socialized humanity*, but *individual men,* fully developed, are of ultimate significance.

Henry David Thoreau (1817–1862)

Thoreau was a Transcendentalist who like Emerson believed that the free moral individual was threatened by materialism, industrialism, and the coercive state. Whereas Emerson preached his philosophy in the midst of men, Thoreau sought solitude and direct communion with nature in order to demonstrate how one might *live* and not merely *exist.* An avid devotee of Oriental thought, Thoreau, unlike most of his fellow Americans, disdained membership in associations and the church, and demonstrated his refusal to come to terms with the state by refusing to pay his poll tax, which brought him to spend a short time in jail.[21]

Of most significance to us is Thoreau's essay, *Civil Disobedience*, which was occasioned by his opposition to slavery and his belief that the American war with Mexico was immoral. Emerson had contended that "that government is best which governs least"; Thoreau went a step further, declaring "that government is best which governs not at all." He did not mean that the state should be immediately dismantled, but that "when men are prepared for it," noncoercive government will be the kind which they will have. It is not government, he maintained, but the character of the American people which keeps the country free, develops the West, and educates. Insofar as it has worth, government is only an expedient. Speaking "practically and as a citizen," Thoreau asked for "not at once no government, but *at once* a better government."[22]

Instead of relying on majorities men should be ruled by conscience. Thoreau remarked: "I think that we should be men first, and subjects afterward. It is not desirable to cultivate a respect for the law, so much as for the right. . . . A common and natural result of an undue respect for law is, that you may see a file of soldiers . . . marching in admirable order . . . to the wars, against their wills . . . their common sense and consciences. . . ." Thus the mass of men serve the state with their bodies, as "machines" and exercise no moral judgment. Legislators, politicians, lawyers, ministers, civil servants, serve the state chiefly with their "heads," rarely making moral distinctions. Only a very few men serve the state with their "consciences and so necessarily resist it for the most part."[23]

Looking specifically at American government in his day, Thoreau declared that a man could not without disgrace be associated with it because it condoned slavery. What then should be done? He excluded resort to the ballot box, saying: "Even voting *for the right* is *doing* nothing for it. It is only expressing to men feebly your desire that it should prevail. A wise man will not leave the right to the mercy of chance, nor wish it to prevail through the power of a majority." Action from principle is indicated in cases where the injustice is of such a nature that it requires a man to be the agent of injustice to another. Specifically, Thoreau advised that in such instances the law be broken and the individual allow his life to serve as "a counter friction to stop the machine." Withdrawal of the support of government both in person and property is prescribed for those who though lacking a majority "have God on their side," because "any man more right than his neighbors constitutes a majority of one already." Fear of imprisonment should not deter, since "under a government which imprisons any unjustly, the true place for a just man is . . . a prison."[24]

Thoreau believed that truth is far stronger than error and that it is both readily known on important issues and commonly shared by men of developed conscience. Thus "a minority is powerless while it conforms to the majority; it is not even a minority then; but it is irresistible when it clogs by its whole weight." He was convinced that if the alternative was "to keep all just men in prison, or give up war and slavery," the state would not hesitate to choose the latter. This, he contended, is "the definition of a peaceable revolution, if any such is possible."[25]

In reality the state is "half-witted" and "timid" and one should not be awed by it. "[It] never intentionally confronts a man's sense, intellectual or moral, but only his body, his senses. It is not armed with superior wit or honesty, but with superior physical strength." Statesmen are governed by expediency not wisdom. It is well for citizens who can ascend no higher to stand by the Bible and the Constitution, but those who behold truth in its ultimate source must act upon it. In fact, although the New Testament was written almost two centuries ago, no legislator is evident "who has wisdom and practical talent enough to avail himself of the light which it sheds on the science of legislation." Thoreau concluded: "There will never be a really free and enlightened State until the State comes to recognize the individual as a higher and independent power, from which all its own power and authority are derived, and treats him accordingly."[26]

Emerson and Thoreau shared an anarchical belief in the ultimate possible elimination of coercive government. As Antinomian archindividualists, they were fundamentally apolitical animals; Emerson preached the irrelevance of politics to self-reliance and Thoreau disdained constitutional processes. Both of them, but more particularly Thoreau, naively assumed that political questions are at base moral questions, the answers to which are readily evident to all truly conscientious persons. In this light they could brook no compromise, accommodation, and mutual concession, seeing them as intrinsically immoral. While Emerson was content with exhortation, Thoreau emphasized passive resistance. Fundamentally they were both proponents of an individualistic moral elitism, a posture which brought Thoreau to withdraw from the world of human frailties and seek the kingdom within while viewing its mirror in nature.

Both men, however, have exerted a significant social and political influence in our day. Their individualism has been borrowed from by adherents of the political right and left, but especially the latter, to put a philosophical base under their protests against the existing establishment, organization, bureaucracy, mass opinion, and conformity. More particularly, the method of passive resistance prescribed by Thoreau has had an inestimable influence in the development of non-violent tactics of opposition and reform employed by contemporary civil rights and anti-war groups.

Utopian Cooperative Reformism

While Emerson and Thoreau emphasized the free moral individual against the numerical majority, conformism, and association as well as competitive conflict, Utopian reformism, which issued in the establishment of almost 100 voluntary communities between 1825 and 1860, stressed cooperation. Many of these societies were religious in orientation, like the Shaker communities, for example, proceeding from the premises of perfectionist separatism and chiliasm* which remained strong traditions within American Protestantism. Others, like the short-lived Brook Farm led by the Transcendentalist George Ripley, were secular, following either the prescriptions of the English reformer, Robert Owen, or the Frenchman, Charles Fourier. Essentially the secular communal Utopians, like Emerson and Thoreau, denied original sin, but unlike the two New England individualists assumed that character is primarily a function of the environment. Thus it is not the individual who bears primary responsibility for his condition, but society. It follows that reform is a collective function aimed at establishing conditions which, assuming the primacy of altruism over egotism, bring to harmonious fruition the social nature of man, with an attendant elimination of crime, poverty, and conflict. Cooperative associative effort and education then comprise the rational alternative to the competitive principle and to the assumption of a natural identity of interests.[27]

The leading expounder of Fourieristic principles in America was Albert Brisbane (1809–1890), who exerted a strong influence on Ripley and the journalist Horace Greeley. Brisbane believed that over the course of history man had moved from savagery to civilization in the development of the arts, sciences, technology, and industry. Whereas until the present the fruits thereof were shared by a few, upon the establishment of cooperative communities the world could be transformed into a paradise of plenty for all. He thought that there were basic laws of human association upon which institutions must be established. Thus the self-sufficient, voluntary "phalanx" of not more than 1600 people comprising all human types, was prescribed as the basic unit to replace the traditional township. People within the phalanx would reside in a common building and engage in intermittent periods of work, play, education, and culture. Such arrangement, Brisbane thought, would spell the end of the conflict of egos and interests which

---

* The belief in Christ's return to earth to reign during the millennium.

is restrictive of true human progress. Government, which he called the "Collective Mind," would aim ultimately at a fixed order based on scientific organization and planning.[28]

The relatively short existence of the secular utopian societies testifies to their basic lack of realism. Their very establishment as separatist entities, however, was a critical commentary upon existing democratic society. Although many adherents accepted the environmentalist assumption, they thought ultimately of the regenerated individual. Brisbane, however, regarded individual man as "a fragment" in "the collective man," a mere part of the whole wherein "all shades of character" are joined to form what he called "integral man." In any case, whereas Emerson and Thoreau tended to lose sight of society in their concentration on the individual, the societies tended to overstress the community. It was to the establishment of an analysis which gives due accord to the influence of each and to their interrelations, that our next subject, Orestes Brownson, addressed himself.

Orestes Brownson (1803–1876)

A few years before his death Brownson wrote: "I have never in my life been able to persuade myself that a principle, really sound and true, will not bear pushing to its last logical consequence." As a result, most of his life was concerned with the critical examination of ideas on what he considered to be related theological, metaphysical, and political planes. His restless probing brought him to move from Congregationalism to Presbyterianism, to Universalism, to Transcendentalism and Unitarianism and finally, in 1844, to Catholicism, which he embraced the rest of his life.[29]

Because Brownson's religious quest entailed the examination of theological and metaphysical ideas which lie at the base of his political thought, it is necessary to give them first consideration. Originally he sought to determine through private judgment alone the historically authentic form of Christianity. When that proved impossible, he, like Emerson, began to doubt history. Unlike Emerson, however, he could not embrace subjective individualism, holding instead that divinity is originally in humanity and not in the individual. This brought him to criticize the principle of private judgment and to propound instead, as criteria of truth, tradition and universal consent.

The doctrine of creation explained to Brownson the ultimate historical character of contingent being. While the Creator is the objective complement of the universe, secondary causes mediate the expression of the absolute creative principle in accordance with the conditions of concrete existence which constitute the order of nature. Thus history was reestablished in his mind as a principle of being, informing nature, humanity, and society. From this he concluded that the individual gains solidarity and actuality under the historical forms of family, nation, and property. On the basis of his belief that human nature logically precedes the individual, and his concept of nature as essentially historical, Brownson denied the Transcendentalist claim of immediate natural access of the individual to the divine; instead, he maintained, the individual soul approaches the divine mediately through history and tradition. Because of this he denied the autonomy of man and of nature, asserting the dependence of all created, i.e., historical being, upon God. Thus he came to emphasize divine providence as the only rational explanation of history. Nature and men are in the dimension of secondary causation, the ultimate purposes of which are providential. Consequently, he distinguished between the purpose of a free human act and the purpose toward which God might direct such an act. Having established the historically mediated connection of man to God, it was logical for Brownson to accept the full implications of the doctrine of the Word made flesh and to embrace the historical institution which he saw divinely established to expound ultimate truth—the Roman Catholic Church.[30]

Turning to Brownson's political thought, which he expounded over the years as editor of the *Boston Quarterly Review, Brownson's Quarterly Review*, and for a short while as a contributor to the *Democratic Review*, it must first be said that on the basis of his conceptions of creation, nature, humanity, history, and providence, he had to conclude that any political thought which ignores historical experience and tradition and depends upon logic alone is in error. He started adult life as a convinced democrat, strongly championing Jacksonian democracy of the locofoco variety. Not accepting, however, the Jacksonian notion of a natural harmony of interests, he determined to push the idea of equality to its political and social conclusions. Thus in 1840, after analyzing America in terms of class warfare, he urged the equalization of property and the removal of all restraints upon democracy. Like the later American progressives, he believed that the defects of bad legislation could not be attributed to democracy, but to the fact that the democratic principle was obstructed, and the will of the people could not have its free and full expression.

The demagogic Whig campaign of 1840 wrought a much greater revolution in Brownson than in the government. Until then he had believed uncritically in democracy and little else. Jolted into a reexamination of his premises, he found them "untenable and absurd." Just as he critically appraised the doctrine of the primacy of private judgment in theology so he questioned the validity of its application to politics. On this ground he came not to reject democracy but to redefine it in terms of ultimate truth. Already in 1838, six years before his religious conversion and two years before the campaign of 1840, he had

attacked the notion of popular sovereignty, maintaining that true
democracy is based on the absolute sovereignty of justice. His most
serious reflections, however, are found in a lengthy series of essays,
The Origin and Ground of Government, which he began to publish in
1843. Because the principal ideas therein are essentially contained in
his book, *The American Republic,* published in 1865, the two works will
be considered together.[31]

He began the essays by lamenting the fact that because of the preoccupation of Americans with practical problems "politics as a science is
almost entirely unknown and unheeded" in America. Except for John C.
Calhoun, he was unaware of a single American who then gave public
evidence of having studied the origin, ground, and constitution of the
state. In fact, he thought, American theory in that regard was strictly
derivative from Hobbes, Locke, Montesquieu, and Rousseau. To George
Bancroft's contention that simple practical planters can surpass the most
profound philosophers in the construction of governments, Brownson
replied: "I must still believe that science is preferable to ignorance, and
the wisdom resulting from it more worthy of reliance than popular
passion, or even popular instinct."[32]

Brownson's reformulation of democratic thought constitutes a critique
of the Lockian tradition in American political thought, exemplified in
Jeffersonianism and vulgarized in Jacksonianism, which postulates the
autonomy of individual reason and sees the state as merely a function
thereof. As such, Brownson's work has a great affinity to the tradition
of Hooker, as exemplified principally in James Wilson, although in its
developed form it is not linked to medieval Aristotelian scholasticism
through Hooker but goes directly to Aquinas and the later scholastics,
Suarez and Bellarmine.

His first point was that just as the individual is not sovereign in
matters religious, neither are the people sovereign in matters politic.
Second, he contended that the people who form a government must
be considered in the corporate or organic sense and never as a mere
aggregate of individuals. Third, he distinguished between the providential constitution of a people, which is expressed in their organic, historical makeup, and their constitution of government, which is a product of
will. Fourth, he distinguished between individualistic democracy (the
Lockian extreme), socialist or humanitarian democracy (the other extreme), and the "territorial democracy" which is the valid *via media*
describing the organic constitution as necessarily rooted in and delim-
ited by a geographical base. Finally, he distinguished between the
"barbarous" or "despotic" conception of authority which makes all human authority, original or derivative, a private or personal right, and the
"civilized" or truly political conception of authority which sees authority
and power as a public trust.

Concerning the social compact theory, Brownson denied on historical and logical grounds the idea of a state of nature. If we found the state in compact, he asserted, "we either leave the individual his natural freedom, and then we have no government; or we subject the individual to the state, and then we have no individual liberty." At this point he directly confronted the Declaration of Independence and did not spare his criticism. He accepted it as "a wise, just, and patriotic *measure*" but held that its "self-evident" principles "were not only not called for as the ground of the justification of the measure, but were . . . of questionable soundness, and have led to the adoption by a large portion of our people, of theories practically incompatible with government itself, and everything like social order." It was not necessary for the colonists to go beyond the valid principle that each people as an organic political community (as opposed to a collection of individuals), has the inherent right to self-government. The assertion, "all men are created equal," is not self-evident since men are obviously created unequal, but it has truth because men are equal as human beings alike accountable to God. We should, Brownson declared, assume the natural inequality of men as the ground of government and make it the duty of government to maintain that equality before the law which men do not hold before nature. The Declaration's assertion of the right of a people to alter or abolish their government has validity only if the term people is understood in the organic and territorial sense. In like vein, the principle of the unalienable rights of life, liberty, and the pursuit of happiness was assailed on the ground that if it were consistently to be maintained, government could never rightfully command the life of an individual, nor restrain his liberty or place any impediment before his pursuit of his subjectively conceived happiness.[33]

In this view the only legitimate vehicle of politics in the establishment, change, or abolition of government is the providentially formed territorial people, who are subject to the natural law, which instead of being the law of a nonexistent state of nature and the simple product of unaided human reason, is the law written into man's social nature by the divine sovereign. The American people have, under God, ultimate authority only when legally assembled in the institution which alone can prescribe the constitution of government and which must act in accordance with their organic, providential constitution—the convention. Thus he juxtaposed the terms convention and caucus, accepting the former and rejecting the latter as a mere vehicle of opinion. Similarly, Brownson could accept majority rule only within the context of constitutional and natural law limitations. To assert majority rule as a natural right was to him reducible to the proposition that might makes right.[34]

In sum, Brownson's essential view of the origin of government was the scholastic conception that political authority derives ultimately from God, and is mediated by the corporate people to an established government, which like the people themselves is ever subject to the commands of natural law. He added to this the notion of the providential constitution of the people which is never the work of deliberation, but always the work of Divine Providence, using men and circumstances as his instruments and which precedes, in both an existential and normative sense, the constitution of government of a people, which is the product of the secondary causation of human will. This led him to an essential conservatism regarding policy and a rejection of the subjectivism and disregard of historical and territorial factors in contemporary humanitarian reformism. Thus the true social reformer "seeks always to heal the disorders of the state without destroying or impairing the constitution." Finally Brownson insisted that because of man's social nature, society has rights not derived from individuals.[35]

Believing in the need for an institution to expound ultimate truth under natural law in the maintenance of a viable democracy, Brownson argued in 1845 that Catholicism was necessary in order to sustain popular liberty. Because *"the people are fallible both individually and collectively, and governed by their passions and interests,"* it is not enough to assert the priority of justice and natural law. Brownson thought that the Catholic Church alone had the power to subdue the barbarous elements in human nature, and to enable men of widely different races, complexions, and characters to live together in the bonds of peace and brotherhood. By this Brownson did not mean that the Catholic Church should be formally established. Instead he argued in his *American Republic* that whereas an establishment of any religion would be a regression into barbarism, all depended upon the nature of the state. In conceiving the Trinity as ultimate reality and "the prototype of all society," he went on to conclude in a tortured, far-fetched argument that the American system with its nonantagonistic division of powers between a general and state governments is in basic attunement therewith. Whereas the English system emphasizes antagonistic elements without the conciliating mid-term, and the French imperial system excludes the elements and embraces only unity, American government embraces democracy within the federal division of powers. Thus, he declared, American government is constructed on civilized, Catholic principles, and the mutual trust and lack of antagonism and freedom afforded to religion allow the Church freely to administer to and instruct individuals.[36]

Brownson was a democrat who believed in the primacy of the corporate people organized under a fundamental law but subject to the natural law which is at once descriptive of rights and prescriptive of duties, and which, unless chaos and discord are to ensue, must be given final statement by an infallible authority above and yet without the state, the divinely instituted Church. The fulfillment of this conception was dependent upon the voluntary acceptance by Americans of the supreme religious institution. In this manner Brownson believed that the anarchy which he saw inherent in the principle of the primacy of individual judgment could be surmounted. The idea bears some resemblance to the emphasis placed by conservative lawyers upon the need for a nondemocratic agency, the judiciary, as the ultimate and definitive expounder through judicial review of the meaning of the Constitution in the light of the common law, a subject which we will consider later.

Francis Lieber (1800–1872)

Lieber was a German liberal nationalist who came to America via England in 1827 after having been arrested by the Prussian police on political charges. From 1835 to 1855 he taught at South Carolina College, after which he joined the faculty of Columbia University in New York.[37] His principal contributions to American political thought are *A Manual of Political Ethics* (1838) and *On Civil Liberty and Self-Government* (1853).[38]

Political Ethics was dedicated to Joseph Story, the American jurist, and Henry Hallam, the English historian, a fact which illustrates not merely Lieber's high regard for the two men but for their disciplines. The work is, however, primarily philosophical in its elucidation of principles, drawing particularly upon Kantian idealism and its postulate of the primacy of man as a moral being. Lamenting that political theory ended with Locke, to be replaced by political economy through Adam Smith, Lieber aimed at a reconstruction of systematic political theory through an exposition of principles which are both morally intuited and empirically verified, in the belief that "nothing can be true in theory without being true in practice."[39] If we use modern terminology we can say that he worked toward a value-oriented empirical political science, geared to the two elements which he thought constitutive of all human progress, "abstract reasoning" and "historical development."[40] His illustrative sources were manifold and not always logically connected—data on primitive tribes and contemporary social phenomena are intermixed with historical allusions, extractions from the Church Fathers, scholastic treatises, Protestant reform tracts, historical works, philosophic and jurisprudential tomes and political literature. Critical contemporary appraisals of the work nonetheless identified it as essentially American. This was possible because Lieber not only freely used American materials but wished to reinterpret American political phenomena in light of his Kantian principles.[41]

Lieber's basic principle was that man is a self-determining being, who can discern the *a priori* self-evident principles of right and wrong and who has within him a feeling of obligation to the right. Whereas the science of ethics stresses duties, the science of natural law emphasizes rights, based on the axiom, "I exist as a human being, *therefore* I have a right to exist as a human being." Natural law must not be seen as the law of a nonexistent state of nature as propounded by Hobbes and Locke; nor must it be associated with primitiveness as in Rousseau. Instead it is "the law, the body of rights, which we deduce from the essential nature of man." No greater mistake can be made, Lieber thought, than to confound the idea of artificiality with that of development; instead it must be remembered that "man was essentially made for progressive civilization, and this, therefore, is *his* natural state."[42]

While natural law concerns principles of right, politics concerns the most feasible means of securing the right on the basis of experience and within the given circumstances. The two sciences are logically distinct yet integrally related. Without "firm and absolute principles" all would be "confusion and insecurity" and power would be established as the foundation of right. To adjudge, however, every political question by theory alone, to the disregard of experience and prudence leads to "tyrannical outrages" justified in the name of "that perfect state to be founded upon absolute theory."[43]

In this light Lieber distinguished the terms "society," "state," and "government." The state evolves progressively in society from the family through the division of labor. The basic idea of the state is justice; it is a jural and moral order demanding of no member an obligation on his side alone but recognizing mutual obligations only. It is the "society of societies," in the Aristotelian sense, containing all the lesser human associations and aiming ultimately at the perfection of mankind. It is rooted in man's nature and its origin cannot be explained in terms of an historical contract.[44]

Lieber discarded the terms "absolute" and "unalienable" in talking of fundamental rights, substituting instead the term "primordial." Among primordial rights are freedom of thought, communication, religion, emigration and expatriation, property, physical integrity, and protection of honor and reputation. His basic conservatism stands out in his statement that "there is no right more essential to man, as man, than that of acquisition—property." And yet, he added, no other right "calls for more modification and regulation by the state, because it relates more than any other right to the material world, and more effects in its enjoyment the jural relations of others."[45]

Lieber saw sovereignty as inherent in society and manifested in public opinion, law, and power. Against the divided-sovereignty thesis of the *Federalist* he argued that sovereignty is indivisible and incapable of being located in any government. But society, he declared in the mood of nationalism, did not comprise Calhoun's conception of the people of the separate states but the organic whole.[46]

Government was defined by Lieber as "that institution or contrivance, through which the state . . . acts in all cases in which it does not act by direct operation of its sovereignty." Expressing the thought which later sparked Brownson to distinguish between the providential and governmental constitutions, Lieber defined legitimate government as that "which exists according to the fundamental laws and usages of the state, i.e. the society; or if these organic laws have been changed, by the existing government, if the people may be considered as having fairly acquiesced in it."[47]

Lieber's critique of democracy in the *Political Ethics* revolved principally around his belief that public opinion and majority rule are not infallible. The value he was concerned with protecting against the absolutism of the one, few, or many was *liberty*, which he contended "exists in the degree in which my action and activity in all just and right things is untrammeled. . . . ." On this ground he distinguished between states which he called "autarchies," wherein the whole public power is vested uncontrolled and unlimited in the one, few, or many, and "hamarchies," polities "in which a thousand distinct parts have their independent action, yet are by the general organism united into one whole." In hamarchies the law is "generated" and modifies itself in its application and operation. Thus the principle of autarchy is sacrifice, that of hamarchy is compromise. Examples of the latter are England with its independent judiciary, corporations, commons, lords and kings, and the American federal government with its pluralism and division of power. It is not the "balance of power," a mechanistic relation, which constitutes a hamarchy but "the generation of power," an interdependent relation of parts in an organic whole.[48]

In his work, *Civil Liberty*, Lieber extended his previous discussion of liberty into a theory of "institutional liberty." His approach was now principally historical rather than philosophical; the focus was the historic rights of Anglo-Saxons rather than the primordial rights of the *Political Ethics*, although there can be no doubt that he thought that the former best institutionalized the latter. He believed in the cultural superiority of "the virile branch of the Teutonic race," the Anglo-Saxons, assuming that diffusion of such culture to other peoples and races, through the progressive civilization which is man's natural state, was possible.[49]

Contrasting "Anglican liberty" (which included "American liberty") to "Gallican liberty," Lieber saw the latter as based on an abstract notion of equality established through "the undivided sovereignty of the people" in an "uncompromising centralism," and the former as "institutional self-government." By "institutional self-government" he meant a government of "a cooperative character," opposed to centralism, based on "articulated liberty" possessed of an "interlimiting" character, "a self-evolving and genetic nature," and embodying "self-reliance and mutual acknowledgment of self-rule." Seeing a mob as "an inorganic multitude, he condemned majority rule through universal suffrage without the institutional framework of "Anglican liberty."[50]

Lieber's organic approach was thus opposed to the rationalist imposition of forms dictated by abstract ideas as well as the structural political science of a John Adams. It also brought him to reject Calhoun's proposal of a check upon the numerical majority through a balancing of interests in an institutional arrangement which would give each major interest a veto power. He regarded this as a throwback to the medieval concept of representation, violative of the principle of national organic self-government, and promotive of "a multitudinous antagonism."[51]

Lieber's emphasis upon the vital character and interdependence of social, cultural, and political institutions, on self-government as implementative of liberty and viable only when the state is seen in the corporate sense, and his stress upon empirical verification through refined methods, including statistics, were important influences in the development not only of American political science but of American sociology and anthropology.

His regard for property as a primordial right, his organicism and nationalism, his emphasis on the great worth of the common law, on the value of judicial review (an opinion he later modified), his strictures on unqualified, unstructured, and unlimited majoritarianism, were in comfortable agreement with the outlook of contemporary American conservatism. Both Joseph Story and James Kent praised his work lavishly. Kent told him unabashedly: "I love your books, I love you; you are so sound, so conservative, you are so very safe."[52]

Law as a Restraint Upon Majority Opinion and the Instrument of Order

Upon returning home from the Continental Congress in 1775, John Adams was greeted by a former client who told him how happy he was that Congress had abolished courts of justice in Massachusetts, adding that he hoped there would never be any others. Adams' somber reaction is recorded in his *Autobiography:*

Is this the Object for which I have been contending? . . . Are these the Sentiments of such People? And how many of them are there in the Country? Half the Nation for what I know: for half the Nation are Debtors if not more, and these have been in all Countries the Sentiments of Debtors. If the Power of the Country should get into such hands . . . to what purpose have We sacrificed our Time, health and every Thing else? Surely We must guard against this Spirit and these Principles or We shall repent of all our Conduct.[53]

This anarchical dislike of law, particularly the English common law, was deeply rooted in many Americans in the early years of the Republic. The common law had been, as we have seen, relied upon by the dissenting colonists in their dispute with Parliament. Upon the consummation of the Revolution, when the common law was no longer considered the source of power or jurisdiction but as a means by which it is to be implemented, the impulse was to discard all foreign institutions and alien imports, among which many included the common law itself. This tendency continued into the Jacksonian period and was met by (1) the efforts of men like James Kent and Joseph Story, who wrote commentaries on the law which supplemented the general reliance upon Blackstone's work, (2) the efforts of barristers like Daniel Webster to persuade courts that the protection of vested rights was the ultimate purpose of the law, (3) the work of judges like John Marshall and Story, on the federal level, and Kent and Ambrose Spencer, on the state level, to implement in their decisions the conservative principles embodied in the common law, (4) the production of law reports upon which a science of the law could be based, and (5) the attempt to establish the practice of the law as a learned profession based on a cosmopolitan jurisprudence and comprising men molded in the image of Kent and Story, whom Andrew Jackson saw as the "most dangerous" men in the country.[54]

Among lawyers there existed a split which might conveniently be characterized as a division between those who saw jurisprudence as the simple expression of "natural" principles, which should give rise to a codified body of law, and those who saw law, as Coke had centuries earlier, as "artificial reason," demanding deep study and sophistication. It has already been shown how James Wilson and Nathaniel Chipman in their treatises, and Jefferson in his correspondence, had criticized Blackstone upon the birth of the Republic, how Chipman called for a body of American law denuded of foreign influences and based on natural principles, and how Judge Jesse Root of Connecticut had identified the common law of Connecticut, as distinct from English common law, as a simple statement of natural principles. As Perry Miller has said, the premise was that the more we perfect our legal system the more natural we shall become, as opposed to English and European artificiality.[55]

In contrast to this "democratic" school of jurisprudence, the conservatives, while admitting the need to eliminate foreign excrescences, nevertheless championed the essential English common law, supplemented by insights from European civil law, as the bulwark against an-

archy and despotism. The aim of this group was threefold: (1) to incul-
cate in the people a respect for law as such; (2) to reduce the popular
periority of the legal profession.[56]
suspicion of the common law; and (3) to establish the intellectual su-

By 1821 Story could report that since the turn of the century over
150 volumes of law reports had been published and that in all of the
twenty-four states, except Louisiana, the common law had been established as the basis of jurisprudence. He could also rejoice in the fact
that the privilege of bringing laws to the test of the Constitution
(which he thought should be interpreted in light of the principles of
the common law) was afforded to every citizen. Judicial review, on
both state and national levels, was the answer to those "visionary statesmen . . . who affect to believe . . . that popular opinion is the voice of
unerring wisdom," and question "this authority of courts of justice," in
contrast to "the wise, and the learned, and the virtuous," who have
nearly unanimously supported that doctrine. Americans must have this
safeguard, he warned, because they are susceptible to "a zeal for untried theories" and lack the checks of habit, national spirit, and institutional aspects present in traditional monarchies. The judiciary, he
added, has little power except the protection of others, operating as it
does "mainly by an appeal to the understandings of the wise and good."
Its chief support, however, is "the integrity and independence of an enlightened bar." In fact, "lawyers are here . . . placed as sentinels upon
the outpost of the constitution; and no nobler end can be proposed for
their ambition or patriotism, than to stand as faithful guardians of the
constitution, ready to defend its legitimate powers, and to stay the
arm of legislative, executive, or popular oppression."[57]

In 1829 Story made explicit what was to be guarded—the "sacred
rights of property," which if unprotected render all other rights "worthless or visionary." This, he added, could not be affected by a system of
law which is reduced to "natural reason," because while the common
law has foundations in natural reason, it is built and perfected by "artificial doctrines adapted and molded to the artificial structure of society."
Both Story and Kent, in their respective *Commentaries,* assumed the
primacy of vested rights. In this view, contrary to the more generous
conception of James Wilson, for example, the requirements of the common good were reducible to protection of individual natural rights, centered around that of property.[58]

By 1845, Rufus Choate, a Massachusetts lawyer, could, in the spirit
of Story and Kent, talk of the American Bar as "an element of conservation in the state," which helps preserve "our organic forms, our civil
and social order, our public and private justice, our constitutions of
government,—even the Union itself." This it did by keeping alive "the
sacred sentiments of obedience and reverence and justice, of the

supremacy of the calm and grand reason of the law over the fitful will of the individual and the crowd." Admitting the need of reform in society, Choate argued like Emerson that it could not be produced by legislation but by inner development in "a more diffused, profound, and graceful, popular and higher culture."[59]

The continuing democratic emphasis upon codification in opposition to the "mystical and cabalistic" common law was put directly by the liberal reformer, Robert Rantoul (1778–1858) in 1836. Describing the common law as "but the glimmering taper by which men groped their way through the palpable midnight" of the Dark Ages, and as suitable only to a stationary society, Rantoul argued that because nothing in America can develop by prescription, resort must be made to the rational statement of law through statute. Particularly did he attack what he called the *ex post facto* judicial legislation necessarily ensuing from a common law jurisprudence, as "subversive of the fundamental principles of a free government, because it deposits in the same hands the power of first making the general laws, and then applying them to individual cases." He epitomized his position by insisting in Jacksonian terms that "we must have democratic governors, who will appoint democratic judges, and the whole body of the law must be codified."[60]

The movement for codification culminated in the learned writings of David Dudley Field (1805–1894), who began his agitation in 1839 and continued his work through the 1850's, during which decade he met with some success in a few states. Field's intimacy with a literary group in New York, called Young America, which dedicated itself to the eradication of English influence from American literature and the creation of an original American genre, attests to the democratic nationalism which informed his effort. He asked for "a book of our own laws, a CODE AMERICAN, not insular but continental, as simple as so vast a work can be made, free in its spirit, catholic in its principles!"[61]

The democratic desire to implement natural justice through precise statutory formulations; to delimit the discretion of the judiciary and to render less mysterious, more democratic and American the reason of the law by eradicating all remains of the English conception of the common law as the source of authority; and at the same time to secularize the priesthood of the law, was destined to meet with but limited success. Symbolic of the tenacity of the common law was the fact that one who was to become democracy's greatest leader—Abraham Lincoln—was nurtured in Blackstone's *Commentaries*. From that work he derived the principle of the irrevocable nature of an executed contract, which was to serve as his major premise in asserting the invalidity of secession. Then, too, if one looks closely at the work of the Jacksonian Democrat, Chief Justice Roger Brooke Taney, and his Democratic colleagues on the federal Supreme Court, one notes that not only

did they for the most part reaffirm the conservative position taken by
the Marshall Court on such key questions as the obligation of contract
and vested rights, but that in 1857, in the *Dred Scott* case, they tragi-
cally presumed that as the umpires of the federal system they could render a judicial settlement of the great political question of slavery in the
territories. It is testimony to the vigor of the conception of law expounded by an independent judiciary and ministered to by a bar nurtured in the common law, that even this heavy blow to judicial prestige
was overcome, so that in the last quarter of the nineteenth century,
the law as a conservative force was to become the most significant element in American political life and the most significant institutional restraint upon the will of the majority.

Conclusions

American democratic thought advanced dialectically in the period
from 1815 to 1816 within the tensions existing between (1) the emphasis on equality of rights in the Declaration of Independence and the
emphasis upon the conception of a Constitution consisting of checks and
balances, and (2) the exaltation of the popular voice in majority rule
and public opinion and the traditional acceptance of the primacy of
the moral law and natural rights. Except for isolated individuals
like the writer Herman Melville, who saw clearly the depths of evil into
which men can and do sink, the general mood was one of almost un-
relieved optimism, of inevitable human progress, with democracy as its
principal vehicle.

Among the unfriendly critics of democracy, Upshur, on the basis of his
assumption of the unchanging nature of the numerical majority and
the primacy of sectional or class interests, discarded natural rights, equality, and majority rule. The friendly critics of democracy, on the other
hand, accepted the broad suffrage and equality in representation and
before the law, but were most concerned with the possibilities of the
tyranny of numerical majorities and the conformism induced by public
opinion. Cooper and Brownson retained the concept of original sin;
for this reason Cooper maintained that democracy can be viable and
just only within the classical check and balance system and when a cultivated class of independent men is developed as leaders. Emerson and
Thoreau rejected the idea of original sin, Lockian sensationalism, dogma
and tradition, and stressed the ultimacy of the individual and his inner
development in wisdom. Both men were at bottom essentially apolitical,
assuming that historically conditioned, political questions are reducible
to moral questions, the answers to which are readily discernible to men
who have the divine dwelling within. The utopian communitarians, on
the other hand, stressed social salvation and the full realization of de-

mocracy through cooperative, socialistic association. Brownson shifted from a radical advocacy of equality, social as well as political, to a critical, conservative advocacy of democracy. He reconstructed his political thought on the basis of the divinely ordained natural law which he saw as the framework within which a just democracy must operate. Discarding the individualistic natural rights assumptions of Locke and Jefferson, along with the Jacksonian assumption of a natural harmony of interests in society, he reinterpreted the Declaration of Independence in light of his metaphysical conception of natural law and his historical, organic approach to politics, concluding finally that because subjective preference cannot be accepted as controlling in either religion or politics, voluntary acceptance of the infallible Roman Catholic Church alone can provide the moral basis upon which democracy can flourish. Lieber essayed a reconstruction of political theory, taking into consideration the American experience, in light of Kantian principles. He retained natural rights while discarding the notions of a state of nature and a historical contract. Rejecting majoritarian absolutism, he argued that only through historically developed and interrelated institutions culminating in the jural order which is the nation-state, can there develop a people whose "organically evolved opinion," as expressed in representative self-government and the law, can serve as the viable basis of democracy.

Finally, the proponents of the primacy of the artificial reason of the law, to be effected through a system of judicial review binding on all branches of government, and a bar whose members were conceived of as sentinels of the Constitution, saw the common law as *the* conservative force to delimit and direct democracy. Challenged by those who wanted a simple written statutory statement of law stemming from natural reason and purged of all alien residues, the conservatives lost some battles but were ultimately to win the war. "Government by judges" was still far in the offing but its direction had been marked and the movement thereto begun. Before that goal could be reached, however, the country had to undergo a convulsive constitutional and moral crisis in which the fate of democracy was in doubt until finally resolved on the battlefield.

NOTES

1. James Fenimore Cooper, *Notions of the Americans; Picked Up by a Travelling Bachelor* (Philadelphia, 1821), I, 265.
2. See Robert E. Spiller's introductory note to the third edition of Cooper's *The American Democrat* (New York, 1956), xvff.
3. Cooper, *The American Democrat*, pp. 4, 5.
4. *Ibid.*, pp. 7, 45.

5. *Ibid.,* pp. 40, 43, 46, 47.

6. *Ibid.,* pp. 47, 48, 49.

7. *Ibid.,* pp. 49, 50, 51.

8. *Ibid.,* pp. 55, 66, 69.

9. *Ibid.,* pp. 75, 76, 80, 77, 78, 81.

10. *Ibid.,* pp. 89, 90, 94.

11. *Ibid.,* pp. 92, 96, 95, 180.

12. For expositions of Transcendentalism, see Ralph Waldo Emerson's essay, "The Transcendentalist," and Theodore Parker's essay, "Transcendentalism," reprinted in George F. Whicher (ed.), *The Transcendentalist Revolt Against Materialism* (Boston, 1949), pp. 18–30, 65–83.

13. *Ibid.,* p. 78.

14. I am greatly indebted in the discussion of Emerson to A. Robert Caponigri's article, "Brownson and Emerson: Nature and History," *New England Quarterly,* XVIII (1945), 368–90.

15. Emerson, "Prudence," in *The Works of Ralph Waldo Emerson* (Black's Readers Service, 1-vol. ed., New York, undated), pp. 158, 159.

16. Emerson, "Self Reliance," *ibid.,* p. 99ff.

17. Emerson, "New England Reformers," *ibid.,* pp. 298, 299, 305; "Power," *ibid.,* p. 327.

18. Emerson, *Journals,* III, 369, 390; IV, 95; cited in V. L. Parrington, *op. cit.,* III, 392.

19. Emerson, "Politics," *Works,* pp. 278, 279, 280.

20. *Ibid.,* pp. 280, 283.

21. See chapter, "Emerson and Thoreau," in Gabriel, *American Democratic Thought,* pp. 31–51.

22. Thoreau, "Of Civil Disobedience," reprinted in Whicher, *op. cit.,* pp. 40, 41.

23. *Ibid.,* pp. 41, 42, 43.

24. *Ibid.,* pp. 43, 45, 46.

25. *Ibid.,* p. 47.

26. *Ibid.,* pp. 49, 53, 54.

27. For an account of these societies see Alice Felt Tyler, *Freedom's Ferment* (New York, 1962), pp. 47–220 and Arthur E. Beston Jr., *Backwoods Utopias* (Philadelphia, 1950). See also Mark Holloway, *Heavens on Earth* (New York, 1966); Wm. A. Hinds, *American Communities* (New York, 1961); and Katherine Burton, *Paradise Planters: The Story of Brook Farm* (New York, 1939).

28. Brisbane's principal work was *The Social Destiny of Man* (Philadelphia, 1840).

29. Henry F. Brownson (ed.), *The Works of Orestes A. Brownson* (Detroit, 1885, 18 vols.), XVIII, 224; Regarding Brownson's life, see Arthur M. Schlesinger, Jr., *Orestes A. Brownson: A Pilgrim's Progress* (Boston, 1939), and Theodore Maynard, *Orestes Brownson: Yankee, Radical and Catholic* (New York, 1943).

30. For a full exposition of Brownson's theological and philosophical ideas see Caponigri, *op. cit.* For an examination of Brownson's political presuppositions, see Stanley J. Parry, C.S.C., "The Premises of Brownson's Political Theory," *The Review of Politics,* XVI (April, 1954), 194–211, and Lawrence Roemer, *Brownson on Democracy and the Trend Toward Socialism* (New York, 1953).

31. *Boston Quarterly Review* July, 1840, October, 1840, III, 358–395, 420–512; *Works,* XVIII, 223, 224; *Works,* XV, 1ff.

32. *Works,* XV, 296, 297, 298.

33. *Works,* XV, 311–313, 316, 329, 330, 331.

34. *Works,* XV, 334, 339–350.

35. *Works,* XV, 392, 361, 570.

36. *Works,* X, 1, 2; XVIII, 208ff., 203–205.

37. On Lieber's life, see Frank Friedel, *Francis Lieber, Nineteenth Century Liberal* (Baton Rouge, 1947); for a discussion of Lieber's thought see Bernard E. Brown, *American Conservatives: The Political Thought of Francis Lieber and John W. Burgess* (New York, 1951); and C. B. Robson, "Francis Lieber's Theories of Society,

Government, and Liberty," and "Francis Lieber's Nationalism," *Journal of Politics,* IV (May, 1942), 227–249 and (Feb., 1946), 57–73.

38. *Manual of Political Ethics* (Boston, 1838–1839, 2 vols.). I have used the single-volume London, 1839, edition of this work. *On Civil Liberty and Self-Government* (Philadelphia, 1853, 2 vols.). I have used the single-volume Philadelphia, 1881, edition of this work.

39. Cited in Brown, p. 26.

40. *Civil Liberty,* p. 260.

41. Friedel, *op. cit.,* p. 149.

42. *Political Ethics,* pp. 28, 60, 61, 62, 134, 136, 137.

43. *Ibid.,* pp. 62, 65, 66.

44. *Ibid.,* pp. 151, 152, 185, 171, 311.

45. *Ibid.,* pp. 214, 207.

46. *Ibid.,* p. 234ff.

47. *Ibid.,* pp. 254, 297, 298.

48. *Ibid.,* pp. 353, 356, 383, 384.

49. Robson, "Francis Lieber's Nationalism," *op. cit.,* p. 58ff.

50. *Civil Liberty,* pp. 279ff, 51ff, 256, 319, 329, 405, 407; Robson, "Francis Lieber's Theories," *op. cit.,* p. 248.

51. Robson, "Francis Lieber's Theories," *op. cit.,* pp. 248, 249.

52. Friedel, *op. cit.,* p. 165.

53. *Diary and Autobiography of John Adams, Adams Papers,* L. H. Butterfield (ed.), (Cambridge, Mass., 1961), III, 326–327.

54. I am indebted in this section to Perry Miller's treatment of the development of the law and the legal mentality in his edited collection of original sources, *The Legal Mind in America* (Garden City, N.Y., 1962), and Book Two of his work, *The Life of the Mind in America,* pp. 99–265.

55. Miller, *The Legal Mind in America,* p. 21.

56. *Ibid.,* p. 119.

57. Joseph Story, "Address Delivered Before the Members of the Suffolk Bar, 1821," in Miller, *The Legal Mind,* pp. 68, 70, 71, 72.

58. Joseph Story, "Discourse Pronounced upon the Inauguration of the Author, as Dane Professor of Law in Harvard University, August 25th, 1829," *ibid.,* 180, 183.

59. Rufus Choate, "The Position and Functions of the American Bar, as an Element of Conservatism in the State," *ibid.,* pp. 258, 260, 263.

60. Robert Rantoul, Jr. "Oration at Scituate," *ibid.,* pp. 222, 223, 225, 226.

61. *Ibid.,* p. 206; David Dudley Field, "Reform in the Legal Profession and the Laws," *ibid.,* p. 294.

Chapter 17

SLAVERY: THE SOCIAL CONTRADICTION

Slavery is founded in the selfishness of man's nature—opposition to it in his love of justice.

ABRAHAM LINCOLN

It has been recently convincingly argued that the individual liberty which was a mark of American society before its urbanization was not a function of any libertarian ideology or paper bills of rights but of the openness and pluralism of that society. Diversity of opinion resulted not from a general tolerance and mutual respect but from the presence within American society at large of many communities with their own canons of orthodoxy in which one had but the liberty to conform or to leave.[1] Against this background, prejudice, hatred, fear and bigotry at times bred on a sectional and even national basis a paranoid approach to politics the essence of which has been defined as belief in "the existence of a vast, insidious, preternaturally effective international conspiratorial network designed to perpetrate acts of the most fiendish character."[2] Thus the frenzy in the late 1790's in New England over a "Jacobin conspiracy," with its resultant reflection in the repressive Alien and Sedition Acts; thus the Anti-Masonic movement in the 1820's and 1830's in many parts of the northern United States, a populist, egalitarian reaction against an imaginary conspiracy of a secret society; and thus in the 1840's and 1850's the nativist suspicion of the "foreigner" (immigrant) and the "Know-Nothing" fear of a Catholic "plot" against the republic and free religion. In each of these pathological phases, although more pronouncedly in the latter two, intolerance manifested itself in mob action, violence, and denials of basic rights.[3]

Most particularly, however, was freedom denied to the Negro who languished in chattel slavery. It is of the greatest importance to realize that the question of the status of the Negro in American life has been from 1776 to the present a perennial issue in American politics and the source of the greatest contradiction between American ideals and American reality. It is of equal importance to recognize the complexity of the problem, a fact attested to by such elevated and upright men as Jefferson, De Tocqueville and Lincoln, each of whom, though desiring emancipation, was uncertain that the two races could live peaceably side by side in freedom.

The politics of both the antislavery and proslavery movements in the nineteenth century were tainted by the conspiratorial psychology and by a fanaticism at the extremes. Attendant upon the proslavery move-ment was the violation of human rights not merely of the enslaved black but also the white and free Negro in both North and South, but par-ticularly in the South, in the form of private and public denials of oral and written expression, academic freedom, the right of petition and un-hampered use of the mails, and in the use of extralegal vigilance com-mittees and "lynch-law." So powerful were the vigilance committees that a historian of the period has remarked: "There can be little doubt that, concerning slavery and related matters, such committees exercised a more powerful control over the life of the white man than any other agency in the South."[4] Thus the question of slavery must be seen not only in terms of its effect on the Negro but on the white man and his ideals as well.

Antislavery Thought

Antislavery sentiment was already prominent in the colonial period in all parts of the country. It was prompted by the Christian emphasis on human equality, as exemplified in John Woolman, and on the natural rights philosophy, as exemplified in James Otis. These two sources, one religious, the other philosophical, became the principal bases upon which the antislavery thought of the nineteenth century was built.

The Declaration of Independence with its emphasis on the equality of all men in the possession of unalienable rights was the basic public documentary source for the nineteenth-century opponents of slavery. It will be remembered that its abstract principles tended to be identified in practice by contemporaries, including its author, Jefferson, with con-crete historical rights. This allowed many of them, and men of succeed-ing generations as well, to circumscribe the universal and abstract pronouncements by concluding that the practical reference was not to the enslaved Negro. Evidence that the rhetoric of the Declaration was construed to mean what it did not say is embodied in the fact that Jef-ferson's condemnation of the king, in the first draft, for violating colonial antislavery acts was eliminated upon southern opposition. Thus at its very inception the Declaration of Independence was at best a pro-nouncement of ideals to be realized, and at its worst a mask covering a basic contradiction in American society. And yet, until the invention of the cotton gin, which made the cultivation of short-staple cotton by slave labor in the vast Southern hinterlands profitable, sentiment both North and South was strong for the gradual elimination of slavery. The Ordinance of 1787 prohibited slavery in the Northwest Territory; seven of the thirteen states provided for emancipation between 1776 and 1804; and while the Constitution of 1787 left control over slavery to the states and provided for interstate rendition of fugitive slaves, it did provide for the elimination of the African slave trade by 1808.

Antislavery thought in the nineteenth century can be roughly divided into three categories: (1) that which aimed at emancipation followed by colonization of the freed Negro in Africa; (2) that which aimed at immediate emancipation; (3) that which aimed at gradual emancipation.

The first was backed by many distinguished men from both North and South whose efforts revolved around the American Colonization Society, which was established in 1817 and articulated into approximately 250 units by 1832. The tacit adherence of the membership either to the notion of the Negro as a "degraded race," or to the belief that the two races could not peacefully live together in freedom, is evident not only in the program to colonize slaves upon emancipation by owners who wished to free them (a program which proved logistically impossible), but to colonize free Negroes of the North as well.[5]

The movement for immediate abolition of slavery was begun by the fiery William Lloyd Garrison (1805–1879), editor of the *Liberator,* who in the belief that history showed that "gradualism in theory is perpetuity in practice," threw down the gauntlet to the Southern slaveholders, proclaiming: "I will be as harsh as truth, and as uncompromising as justice. On this subject, I do not wish to think, or speak, or write, with moderation." *The Declaration of Sentiments of the American Anti-Slavery Convention,* drawn up by Garrison in 1833, epitomized the views of the radical abolitionists. Proceeding from the Christian and natural-rights emphases on equality, it was declared: (1) that there is no difference between the proscribed African slave trade and American slavery; (2) that the slaves ought instantly to be freed and put under the protection of the law, without compensation to owners; (3) that all existing laws admitting the right of slavery are "before God, utterly null and void," being not only "an audacious usurpation of the Divine prerogative," but "a daring infringment on the law of nature" and "a base overthrow of the very foundations of the social compact"; and (4) that any scheme of expatriation of freed slaves is "delusive, cruel and dangerous."[6]

The principal exponent of a moderate approach, the Unitarian minister William Ellery Channing (1780–1842) maintained in his *Essay on*

Slavery (1835) that "the eternal law binds us to take the side of the injured; and this law is particularly obligatory when we forbid him to lift an arm in his own defense. . . ." Channing held specifically: (1) because a man has rights by nature he cannot morally be held as property; (2) the diversities among men are nothing in comparison with the common attributes such as rationality, conscience, and creation in the divine image; (3) man is "an End in Himself," a person who has rights granted by the Creator bound up indissolubly in his moral constitution; (4) governments as well as individuals are bound by the moral law; (5) above the law of the state is a "higher law" to which the former must conform; and (6) slavery, by instilling in masters the habit of command to the complete disregard of obedience, is deleterious to self-government.

Disagreeing with Garrison's "immediatism," Channing held that only the slave states could abolish slavery, that it would be cruel to give to a man immediate full freedom which he is unprepared to understand or enjoy, and that the agitation of the abolitionist begat increased opposition and alienated multitudes. At the same time he asserted: "There is a worse evil than Abolitionism, and that is the suppression of it by lawless force." He urged all friends of freedom to protest mob action because it could lead only to tyranny.[7]

The passage of fugitive slave laws raised the question among Northern opponents of slavery of the obligation to obey them. Generally they justified noncompliance as a dictate of a "higher law" which upon analysis proved to be the moral law indicated by nature and/or God. Thus Willian Hosmer (1814–1877), in his book *The Higher Law* (1852) identified the law of nature with the law of God and pointed to the individual as the "ultimate judge of whether governmental acts were violative thereof." He declared that "when the fundamental law of the land is proved to be a conspiracy against human rights . . . then and in so far, law ceases to be law, and becomes a wanton outrage on society." Senator Charles Sumner (1811–1874), in his speech calling for repeal of the Fugitive Slave Law in 1852, advanced upon this thesis by proclaiming that when human law is contrary to the law of God, then by "the Supreme Law which commands me to do no injustice, by the comprehensive Christian Law of Brotherhood, by the Constitution which I have sworn to support, *I am bound to disobey the act*." In fact, many Northern extremists were willing to condemn the Constitution as such, seeing it, insofar as it permitted slavery in the states and expedited the rendition of slaves, in the words of Garrison, as a "covenant with death and an agreement with hell." Thoreau, for example, declared: "I cannot for an instant recognize that political organization as *my* government which is the *slave's* government also." More precise was the pronouncement in 1838 by the New England Non-Resistance Society, which was sponsored by Garrison and the social perfectionist John H. Noyes (1811–1886). The statement proclaimed that its members could not acknowledge allegiance to any human government, and recommended that they use no force for or against others and refuse to vote, hold office, or resort to the constituted courts. Thus the more radical abolitionists aimed ultimately not only at the freedom of the Negro slave but at "universal emancipation" which meant to them "the emancipation of our whole race from the dominion of man, from the thraldom of self, from the government of brute force, from the bondage of sin."[8]

Abraham Lincoln (1809–1865)

As early as 1837 Abraham Lincoln stated his belief that although "the institution of slavery is founded on both injustice and bad policy . . . the promulgation of abolition doctrines tends to increase rather than abate its evils." In his early years he was most particularly concerned over "the increasing disregard for law," which, arising from or in reaction to abolitionism, pervaded the country. Scoring the "mobocratic spirit" as dissolvent of popular attachment to established government, he warned: "At such a time, and under such circumstances, men of sufficient talent and ambition will not be wanting to seize the opportunity, strike the blow, and overturn that fair fabric which for the last half century has been the fondest hope of the lovers of freedom throughout the world." To check this reaction by men of "towering genius," which "thirsts and burns for distinction," he asked Americans to let "reverence for the laws . . . become the political religion of the nation."[9]

Lincoln the lawyer and proponent of order, unlike activists and fanatics such as Garrison and John Brown, sought to implement the principles of the Declaration of Independence within the political framework of the Constitution, which to him symbolized, even though it was not identical with, his highest political value—the Union and its free democratic institutions. Believing that the Constitution allowed each state to determine whether or not slavery should exist within its confines, he was principally concerned with preventing its extension into the federal territories. He portrayed the slavery issue in terms of the self-interest of the free white laborer. While he could supplement his argument from self-interest with the practical observation that once men are excluded on the basis of color no inner limit exists as a check and a precedent is set for further discrimination, his principal point was the intrinsic injustice of slavery. Thus he declared: "Slavery is founded in the selfishness of man's nature—opposition to it is [in?] his love of justice."[10]

After Chief Justice Taney proclaimed in the *Dred Scott* case that the authors of the Declaration had not intended to include Negroes within its embrace, Lincoln declared:

I think the authors . . . intended to include *all* men, but they did not intend to declare all men equal *in all respects.* They did not mean to say all were equal in color, size, intellect, moral developments, or social capacity. They defined with tolerable distinctness, in what respects they did consider all men created equal—equal with "certain inalienable rights, among which are life, liberty, and the pursuit of happiness." This they said, and this they meant. They did not mean to assert the obvious untruth, that all were then actually enjoying that equality, nor yet, that they were about to confer it immediately upon them. In fact, they had no power to confer such a boon. They meant simply to confer . . . the *right,* so that the *enforcement* of it might follow as fast as circumstances should permit.[11]

Lincoln believed that because the Negro is a man he must consequently be recognized as possessed of certain rights. Against the argument that the principle of the consent of the governed allowed settlers in the territories to determine whether slavery should be instituted, he insisted that although the doctrine of the "sacred right of self-government" is "absolutely and eternally right," it had no just application in the case. If Negroes are men and thus fundamentally equal, it is "a total destruction of self government" to say that they too shall not govern themselves. He freely admitted that his own feelings would not admit of making the Negro a political and social equal. He saw no reason, however, "why the Negro is not entitled to all the natural rights enumerated in the Declaration of Independence."[12]

Lincoln conceived of equality as an ideal to be realized, a view which went beyond the Lockian-Jeffersonian notion of equality as an original property of man in the state of nature. Thus he stated in 1858:

The Savior, I suppose, did not expect that any human creature could be as perfect as the Father in Heaven; but He said, "As your Father in Heaven is perfect, be ye also perfect." He set that up as standard, and he who did most towards reaching that standard, attained the highest degree of moral perfection. So I say in relation to the principle that all men are created equal, let it be as nearly reached as we can. If we cannot give freedom to every creature, let us do nothing that will impose slavery upon any other creature.[13]

In this light equality is a goal to be aimed at, and the Declaration of Independence is not merely a justification of revolution and a statement of the principles of political legitimacy, but a pronouncement of standards to be "constantly looked to, constantly labored for, and even though never perfectly attained, constantly approximated, and thereby constantly spreading and deepening its influence, and augmenting the happiness and value of life to all people of all colors everywhere."[14]

Proslavery Thought

Slavery was justified by Southern protagonists on grounds of natural right, the inferiority of the Negro, certain biblical texts, the experience of ancient Greece, and utility to civilization.[15] For example, Thomas R. Dew (1802–1846), besides arguing in 1833 the economic advantages of slavery, saw it justified in terms of the following: (1) the Old Testament; (2) the fact that "so soon as the private right to property is established, slavery commences," and with it "the cruelties of war begin to diminish"; (3) all writers on the law of nations agree that slavery is just under certain circumstances; (4) the advantages which have resulted to the world according to the Creator's intent, from the institution of slavery; and (5) the fact that slavery is, as evidenced in Athens, Rome, and Sparta, favorable to the republican spirit. Because menial work is performed by the blacks in the South, Dew declared, "there is at once taken away the greatest cause of distinction and separation of the ranks of society." Consequently, in contrast to the North, no Southern white man feels an inferiority of rank: "Color alone is here the badge of distinction, the true mark of aristocracy, and all who are white are equal in spite of the variety of occupation. . . ."[16]

The most influential public figure defending slavery was John C. Calhoun of South Carolina (1782–1851). Calhoun contended that the maintenance of slavery was necessary to the peace and happiness of both races in the South. He thought that slavery aided the Negro not only physically, but morally and intellectually. In the present state of civilization, he proclaimed, where there exist two races of different origin, distinguished by color and other physical and intellectual differences, slavery is "instead of an evil, a good—a positive good." Contending that a wealthy civilized society has never existed historically in which one portion of the community did not live on the labor of the other, Calhoun asserted that in few countries was so much left to the share of the laborer and so little asked of him as in the South. On the assumption that all societies are based on class differences, Calhoun declared that the slave labor system exempted the South from the disorders and dangers of conflict which obtained between capital and labor in the North. Thus slavery was not a moral and political evil but "the most safe and stable basis for free institutions in the world." Indeed, Calhoun, who has been called "the Marx of the Master Class," sought unsuccessfully an alliance of southern planters and northern capitalists, forecasting that if this were not effected, after the planters were eliminated the contest would be between the capitalists and laborers.[17]

Southern protagonists of slavery could draw upon the current anthropological and ethnological literature to give "scientific" evidence of Negro inferiority. By 1850 European students of race were divided into two camps, the monogenists, who asserted a single creation of all races, and the polygenists who taught a separate creation of each race. Generally speaking those proponents of slavery who concerned themselves with "scientific" bases proceeded from the latter position.[18] It should be remembered that what we today call cultural anthropology had not yet been born. Thus factors which now can be analyzed in terms of cultural differences between peoples were then more readily treated as biological differences.

Sociology, Slavery, and Political Thought

The tendency of Americans to equate the factual ("is") with the moral ("ought") order and to argue on empirical rather than metaphysical grounds was evident in the slavery controversy. The study of society, which is today called sociology, is generally considered to have been introduced in America after the Civil War by William Graham Sumner and Lester Ward. In fact it was presaged in the emphases placed on groups and social analysis by Hildreth and Grimke, and its way was further prepared by the development of statistics, particularly in the Census of 1850, which was managed by the Southern journalist J. D. B. DeBow, (1820–1867). Then, too, as Daniel Boorstin has observed, the fact that slavery was established on a regional basis in America made it possible to construct competing concepts of culture, founded on data like that which would interest a modern sociologist.[19]

One of the earliest American sociologists was George Frederick Holmes (1820–1897), a Southern champion of slavery who, believing that a solution of societal ills cannot be found in natural philosophy (physical science), urged that "by a more profound study of the laws and mechanisms of communities, we must probe the wounds of society and discover mendiciments." Attacking individualism, liberalism, and the idea of human perfectibility, he saw himself as one with the French father of sociology, August Comte, in a "common endeavor to discover the true laws of social disorganization, with the design of thence descending to the amelioration of the social distemper of the times."[20]

Most sensational of the Southern "social critics" was the Virginian George Fitzhugh (1806–1881), author of *Sociology for the South or the Failure of Free Society* (1854) and *Cannibals All or Slaves Without Masters* (1859). Explaining that "sociology" had arisen in Europe in response to the social disorder following upon the development of individualism and freedom, he posed in happy contrast to "Free Society," the "Slave Society" of the South. The main thrust of his work was against the liberal assumptions of Locke, Adam Smith, and Jefferson. Disdainful of their arguments from abstractions, he stressed instead actual human behavior and institutional analysis.

Fitzhugh argued that "man is born a member of society, and does not form society. . . . Society is the being—he one of the members of that being." It was not merely that he saw man as a social and political animal but that he envisioned him as merely a part of a whole having no rights whatsoever except those provided him by society.[21]

Second, Fitzhugh argued that "the love of personal liberty and freedom from all restraint, are distinguishing traits of wild men and wild beasts. . . . As civilization advances, liberty recedes: and it is fortunate for man that he loses his love of liberty just as fast as he becomes more moral and intellectual." From this he concluded: "The mass of mankind cannot be governed by Law. More of despotic discretion and less of Law is what the world wants." Contrary to the Declaration of Independence, the principles of which are "at war with all government, all subordination, all order," government is a thing of force, not consent.[22]

Third, Fitzhugh denied the equality of men, asserting that their ineradicable physical, moral, and intellectual differences were increased by the environment. Against Jefferson he contended that the right to life, liberty, and the pursuit of happiness was not inalienable; he would admit only that most men "have a natural . . . right to be slaves." In fact, under competitive liberalism, he stated, most men's happiness consists in destroying the happiness of others. Similarly, he railed against appeals to a "higher law" of justice, noting that no two men agree on its content. Jefferson's "fundamental principles" and William Seward's "higher law" meant "just nothing at all, unless it be a determination to inaugurate anarchy." In fact Jefferson was to him "the genius of innovation, the architect of ruin, the inaugurator of anarchy" whose mission was "to pull down, not to build up." Insofar as American institutions are founded on Lockian-Jeffersonian abstractions, they "are like a splendid edifice built upon kegs of gunpowder."[23]

On these premises Fitzhugh launched a stinging critique of "free society." The unrestrained competition, free pursuit of self-interest, and disregard of man's social nature were, he thought, based on a morality of "simple and unadulterated selfishness" which begat the class war of capital versus labor and rich versus poor. Using as background sources British Parliamentary Reports and the social protest literature of English Christian socialists, he cited crime statistics to show the insufficiency of a society of free labor. He denied that there was such a thing as "society" in so-called "free countries," declaring: "We use the term free society, for want of a better; but like the term free government, it is an absurdity; those who are governed are not free—those who are free are not social." Thus were "free government" and "free society" dismissed as contradictions in terms.[24]

The rise of socialism, which Fitzhugh called "the new fashionable name of slavery," was to him evidence that free Western competitive societies were "unconsciously marching" toward slavery. He welcomed this as in attunement with man's nature and as advancing civilization, but added significantly that it is better to make a man "the slave of one man, instead of the slave of society." Seeing the world divided into "two philosophies," that of free trade and universal liberty, which is concerned with the promotion of the interests of "the strong, the wealthy, and the wise," and socialism, which intends to protect "the weak, the poor and the ignorant," he extolled the Southern social system as beneficient, civilized, and truly democratic inasmuch as it equalized burdens according to capacity and need.[25]

Fitzhugh's equation of government with repression, his belief that "neither individuals nor societies can govern themselves," coupled with his contention that a free man has no responsible master but the state, which is the least humane of masters, led him to conclude the necessity of the replacement of "free labor" by "slave labor," a task in which the South could show the way. Thus he went beyond other Southern defenders of slavery not only by denying free government but advocating an extension of slavery in some form to include not merely Negroes but the mass of mankind.

At the base of Fitzhugh's thought was not merely an assumption of the inferiority of the Negro, but a demeaned conception of man as such, an equation of human society with the society of bees and ants. It is society which alone has being; man is merely a part of the whole, and the whole determines what rights he may have. Because of this some have asserted that he was returning to the political thought of Aristotle. But in identifying the unity which is society with an organism and equating human members with irrational animals moved by the substitute intelligence of instinct, Fitzhugh not only undercut the principles of the Declaration of Independence but also the Aristotelian conception of society as a unity of order wherein the members have an action independent of the whole.

Fitzhugh vainly attempted to deny and overcome the American political, moral, and intellectual heritage of freedom. The whole of modernity—rationalism, individualism, liberalism, democracy, and constitutionalism—was rejected by him in his wish "to roll back the Reformation in its political phases." The Reformation symbolized the triumph of the principle of private judgment, which he believed was corrosive of society. Thus he proclaimed: "Liberty of the press, liberty of speech, freedom of religion, and the unlimited right of private judgement, have borne no good fruits and many bad ones."[26] He would, in effect, chuck Locke for Filmer, Jefferson for Boucher, and substitute the principle of order instituted by an elite few for that of liberty. In this light Fitzhugh's work, stripped of its hyperbole and extravagant rhetoric, though possessed of much cogency in its critique of economic individualism, was in its assumptions and prescriptions a radical departure from the main tradition of American political thought.

While men like Fitzhugh, DeBow, and Calhoun argued the interest of all Southerners in maintaining black slavery, Hinton R. Helper (1829–1909), who had been raised among farmers in the highlands of North Carolina, urged in his *The Impending Crisis of the South* (1857), that the dominance of the slave-holding planter be removed in the interest of free white labor. Although he cited Scriptural passages, churchmen, the Founding Fathers and political theorists on the evil of slavery, he principally undertook, on a statistical basis, using census figures, to survey the relative position of the Northern and Southern states and show that although they had started out on an equal basis, the former had risen "to a degree of almost unexampled power and eminence," while the latter had sunk "into a state of comparative imbecility and obscurity." Helper thought that proof of the economic and social backwardness of the South would reveal the undesirability of slavery, whereas to demonstrate the prosperous nature of the North would show "that free labor is far more respectable, profitable, and productive, than slave labor." His argument contrasted with that of Fitzhugh in that it was less in terms of community than economics. Having shown the uneconomical nature of slavery, he went on to illustrate how the resultant poverty bred illiteracy, ignorance, cultural impoverishment, and wickedness.[27]

Helper's vast array of statistics which, incidentally, were put forth on a selective basis most favorable to his case, was intended to demonstrate the need to end slavery not in the interest of the Negro, whom he, like most of the yeomanry in the South despised and regarded as inferior, but to bring the non-slave-holding Southern whites to boycott the planter oligarchy, capture political power, and eliminate slavery. Although the upland whites were in some part in a depressed condition, Helper assumed erroneously that they would rally to his position. He overlooked the fact that many nonslaveowners strongly believed that they had a direct and great interest in the preservation of "the peculiar institution" because it maintained white supremacy and ensured order by effectively containing 4,000,000 Negroes.[28]

The sociological approach to the slavery controversy was almost as old and as much resorted to as the moral approach. In his *Notes on Virginia* Jefferson had noted the demoralizing effect of slavery on the way of life of the white man. Lincoln was probably most effective in the antebellum years when opposing the extension of slavery in terms of its effect upon the white laborer. Both Lincoln and Fitzhugh agreed that a house divided against itself cannot stand; the nation would have either to be all slave or all free. Thus it became important for both sides to call to their aid the infant science of statistics to prove empirically what could not be effected by moral suasion. The facts would speak for themselves and show the validity of the respective positions. Fitzhugh argued in terms of community, stating that, empirically viewed, men want ordered government, not liberty, and used English reports to buttress his indictment of economic individualism, while unquestioningly accepting the Southern plantation as an example of a true identity of communal interest. Helper, relying much more heavily upon a comparative statistical analysis, made a powerful case for economic individualism and against slavery in terms of production and economic development. He went on, more tenuously, to show what he regarded as the direct results of economic backwardness—cultural, political, and moral impoverishment. Simply put, it might be said that the sociological approach amounted on both sides to an acceptance of the biblical thesis, "By their fruits you shall know them." Results, however, are inevitably measured in terms of what one originally desires. In political and social terms this means that a society adjudges itself in reference to the question of whether its basic values, as articulated in political theory, are realized or not. On this basis it must be said that although both North and South generally accepted the terms of the Declaration of Independence and the values of the Constitution they differed enough in their interpretation of these terms and values for the difference to be significant. As a result neither was convinced by the other. Instead it might be contended that the view taken of the principles of the Declaration and the Constitution was, for the most part, a function of the sectional interest involved. While Fitzhugh's work stands, when deflated of excess, as a cogent indictment of "free" industrial society, it is romanticized nonsense concerning the South. Similarly while Helper's work is a cogent indictment of slavery, it is oblivious of the evils of economic individualism. Finally, Fitzhugh's prescription of universalized slavery and Helper's recommended elimination of slavery by the non-slaveholding Southern white were equally unrealistic.

NOTES

1. John P. Roche, "American Liberty: An Examination of the 'Tradition' of Freedom," in Milton R. Konvitz and Clinton Rossiter (eds.), *Aspects of Liberty* (Ithaca, 1958), pp. 129–150.
2. Richard Hofstadter, *The Paranoid Style in American Politics* (New York, 1965), p. 14.
3. *Ibid.*, pp. 10–23; see also the chapter, "Denials of Democratic Principles," in Alice Felt Tyler, *Freedom's Ferment* (New York, 1962), pp. 351–395.
4. Russell Nye, *Fettered Freedom* (East Lansing, Mich., 1949), pp. 32, 70–82, 94–115, 139–143, 155.
5. *Ibid.*, pp. 3–7, Tyler, *op. cit.*, pp. 476–481.
6. B. F. Wright, Jr., *A Source Book of American Political Theory* (New York,

1929), pp. 434, 435–438. For a sympathetic treatment of Garrison, see John Jay Chapman's essay, "William Lloyd Garrison," in Jacques Barzun (ed.), *The Selected Writings of John Jay Chapman* (Garden City, 1959), pp. 3–152. For a convenient collection of anti-slavery arguments, see W. H. Pease and J. H. Pease (eds.), *The Anti-Slavery Argument* (Indianapolis, 1965).

7. William E. Channing, "Essay on Slavery," reprinted in Wright, *op. cit.*, 439–448.

8. B. F. Wright, Jr., *American Interpretations of Natural Law* (Cambridge, Mass., 1931), pp. 222, 223, 224; *William Lloyd Garrison: The Story of his Life as told By his Children* (New York, 1885), II, 201.

9. Roy P. Basler (ed.), *The Collected Works of Abraham Lincoln* (Rutgers University, 1953, 9 vols.), I, 75, 108–116. Hereinafter cited as *Works*. The most thorough discussion of Lincoln's political thought is Harry V. Jaffa, *Crisis of the House Divided* (Garden City, N.Y., 1959). See also the somewhat different account in Richard Hofstadter, *The American Political Tradition*, pp. 93–196.

10. *Works*, II, 222–223; 247–283, quotation at 271.

11. *Works*, II, 405, 406.

12. *Works*, II, 242–283, III, 16.

13. *Works*, II, 501.

14. *Works*, II, 406.

15. For a convenient collection of pro-slavery writings, see E. L. McKetrick (ed.), *Slavery Defended* (Englewood Cliffs, N.J., 1963).

16. "Review of the Debate in the Virginia Legislature 1831–32," reprinted in B. F. Wright, *Source Book*, pp. 462–465.

17. Richard K. Cralle (ed.), *The Works of John C. Calhoun* (New York, 1854–1857, 6 vols.), II, 630, 631, 633; III, 179–180; Hofstadter, *op. cit.*, pp. 68–92.

18. Harvey Wish, *Ante Bellum Writings of George Fitzhugh and Hinton Rowan Helper on Society* (New York, 1962), p. 12.

19. *The Genius of American Politics*, pp. 102–106.

20. Harvey Wish, "George Frederick Holmes and the Genesis of American Sociology," *American Sociological Review*, 46 (March, 1941), 700, 704.

21. *Sociology for the South* (New York, undated reprint, Burt Franklin: Research and Source Work Series #102), 25, 26.

22. *Ibid.*, pp. 29–30, 175; *Cannibals All*, edited by C. Vann Woodward (Cambridge, Mass., 1960), p. 248.

23. *Sociology for the South*, pp. 177ff., 189; *Cannibals All*, pp. 69, 134, 135.

24. *Sociology for the South*, pp. 20, 22, 33.

25. *Ibid.*, pp. 42, 45, 47, 48, 80.

26. *Cannibals All*, p. 131.

27. *Impending Crisis of the South* (New York, 1857), pp. ii, 12, 41, 31.

28. See the discussion of Helper in Wish, *Ante-Bellum, op. cit.*, p. 125.

Chapter 18

THE ESTABLISHMENT OF NATIONAL SUPREMACY

The Union is older than any of the States, and, in fact, created them as States.

ABRAHAM LINCOLN

The Union, Sovereignty, and the Contract Theory

The interrelated questions of the nature of the Union and the Constitution, and of the locus of sovereignty, were answered in the first half of the nineteenth century, for the most part in terms reflective of sectional interests. Those who were in a majority behind a federal measure generally propounded a nationalist approach, those in a minority, a "states-rights" position. As has been seen, in 1798 Jeffersonian Republicans answered the Alien and Sedition Acts with the Kentucky and Virginia Resolutions, the first of which proposed "nullification" by the states and the second, "interposition." In 1815 when commercial New England states considered the Jeffersonian embargo to be unconstitutional, they declared the right to decide whether the Constitution was violated or not. As the years went on, the tariff, which Southerners saw as oppressive because it aided the North while running athwart their interest in free trade, and the increased agitation to use federal power to eliminate or prevent the spread of slavery, brought men in the South to reassert the doctrine of "states' rights." Sectional economic changes were manifested in the shifts in position of two of the greatest statesmen of the time, Daniel Webster, the New Englander who started political life as a particularist and became a nationalist, and the South Carolinian, John C. Calhoun, who began as a strong nationalist and became a sectionalist.

While sectional interests influenced the answers which men gave to the important constitutional questions, there was also a shift in emphasis in the use of theoretical concepts. First, the rhetoric of natural rights, which in the eyes of dissenters was unable to check oppressive national majority decisions, became overshadowed by an emphasis on states' rights as a protective vehicle for liberty and interest. Second, there was a gradual transition from the mechanistic, analytic approach to government, exemplified in the social contract theory, to the organismic, genetic approach, which substituted explanation in terms of historical development for that of abstract ideas.[1]

There were three basic variations of the contract theory used in constitutional thought during the period. First, Andrew Jackson, following Madison, held that the states were the parties to the contract which is the Constitution and that none of them could dissolve the association without "acknowledging the correlative right in the remainder to decide whether that dissolution can be permitted consistently with the general happiness." Clearly this conception could not consistently accept nullification and secession except as revolutionary rights beyond the pale of the Constitution.[2]

Second, the theory of the Virginians, Jefferson, Taylor, Henry St. George Tucker, and Upshur, and many New Englanders during the Jefferson-Madison administrations, saw the Constitution as a compact with the states as parties and the federal government as the mere creature of the agreement. In this view the states, which had their origin in a social compact, retain ultimate sovereignty in that it is they, as Jefferson declared, who possess "the natural right" of nullification. Taylor thus stated: "In the creation of the federal government, the states exercised the highest act of sovereignty, and they may, if they please, repeat the proof of their sovereignty, by its annihilation."[3]

Third, the legal nationalism of men like Wilson, Marshall, Kent, Webster, and Story stressed "We the people of the United States" as sovereign, i.e., the people of the nation considered either in undifferentiated fashion, or as individuals grouped for mere convenience in the states who in unison contracted to establish the state and federal governments. The Constitution is thus based on a contract between individuals and is a binding, fundamental, supreme law under which sovereign powers are divided by the sovereign people between nation and states. As Webster put it: "The Constitution . . . is not a contract, but the result of a contract; meaning by contract no more than assent. Founded on consent, it is a government proper. . . . The people have agreed to make a Constitution, but when made, that Constitution becomes what its name imports. It is no longer a mere agreement."[4]

Central to the constitutional dispute was the vital question of who possessed the power to judge finally the validity or invalidity of an exercise of governmental power. Because of the general nature of the federal constitutional powers and the possibility of a broad construction thereof, it made no sense to argue to an aggrieved interest or section that the determination of the ultimate validity of an exercise of federal power approved by a majority was in the federal government or a branch thereof. The nationalist argument of Marshall, Webster, and Story, which asserted the unqualified final authority of the Supreme Court on all constitutional questions, an authority binding not only on the parties to a case but in its doctrine on all the branches of government and the states as well, was not only rejected by Southerners but by Abraham Lincoln as well. As unsuccessful attempt to render the ultimate authority of the Supreme Court palatable to all was made within the framework of the old Madisonian theory of divided sovereignty, just before the Civil War, by Chief Justice Taney who contended that the Supreme Court stood in constitutional cases involving federal-state conflict, not as a member of the national authority, but as an impartial arbiter between nation and states.[5]

Many Southern observers and politicians came to believe that instead of a constitutional rule, the rule of force applied by a federal majority had developed in America. Thomas Cooper (1759–1839), president of South Carolina College, restated the natural right doctrine in 1829, in the manner of Spinoza: "No man has any rights but such as depend on his relative force of body or force of mind. The universal law of nature is the law of force," and political rights "are what society acknowledges and sanctions, and they are nothing else." From this he concluded that "the only safeguard in our confederacy, is the absolute inviolability of state sovereignty," which entails "the expressed and declared right of withdrawing peaceably from the Union, whenever circumstances may render it expedient, or the persevering injustice of a majority, may render it necessary to do so."[6]

What was demanded in the interest of the states'-rights position was a precise statement of the nature of the problem, its political and juristic dimensions and implications, and a prescription of a protective principle based not on an ultimate appeal to heaven, natural law, or force, but to constitutional right. It was to this task that John C. Calhoun addressed himself.

John C. Calhoun: The Critical "Restorative" Reconsideration of American Political Thought

Born in 1782 in South Carolina of Scotch-Irish Calvinist parentage, John C. Calhoun attended Yale College where he studied under Timothy Dwight (1752–1817), a caustic Federalist critic of Jefferson and a supporter of secession, after which he was instructed in the law in Litchfield, Connecticut, by Judge Tapping Reeve (1744–1823), and

Judge James Gould (1770–1838), both of whom were, like Dwight, Federalist proponents of states' rights and secession.

In the early years of his public life Calhoun was a war hawk and a strong nationalist who backed a protective tariff, a national bank, and federal expenditures for internal improvements, asserting that he was "no advocate for refined arguments on the Constitution." After South Carolina became a predominantly cotton-growing state and the protective tariff conflicted with its interest in free trade, he became a constitutional strict constructionist. He remained an ardent unionist but shifted from nationalism to sectionalism. A man of strong character, deep intellect, and austere habits who believed "the duties of life to be greater than life itself," he served as Secretary of War in James Monroe's cabinet and was elected Vice President in 1824 and 1828, but resigned this post after the nullification crisis of 1832, and served from then as a U.S. Senator until his death in 1850.[7]

In 1828 Calhoun wrote, without divulging his authorship, the *Exposition and Protest* of the South Carolina legislature, in answer to the so-called Tariff of Abominations of 1828. Proceeding upon the proposition that "no government based on the naked principle that the majority ought to govern . . . can preserve its liberty for a single generation," and on the principle of state sovereignty, he asserted the constitutional right of the states to nullification of federal law within their confines.

Calhoun accepted with reservations the Lockian-Jeffersonian principle of majority rule, but like Madison and John Adams he did not believe that the Jeffersonian prescription of a Bill of Rights and a mere formal separation of powers served as adequate protection against the abuse of majority rule. He changed Jefferson's doctrine of nullification, expounded in the Kentucky Resolutions, from a negative instrument into a positive facet of constitutional government. At the center of his thought was the Madisonian admonition: "In framing a government which is to be administered by men over men . . . you must first enable the government to control the governed, and in the next place oblige it to control itself." Although he agreed with the Madisonian formulation of the problem, he could not accept Madison's sociological principle propounded in *Federalist* number 10; the experience of the majoritarian imposition of the tariffs of 1828 and 1832 were irrefutable evidence to him of its insufficiency. Similarly, although he accepted Madison's "inventions of prudence," John Adams' psychology of emulative approbativeness, and the principle of the negative power propounded in Adam's class-based balanced state, he regarded the former two as important but ancillary, and the substance of the latter as not fitted to a democratic society like America. Thus he sought a formula that would fulfill what he regarded to be the intent of the Constitutional Fathers

—to regard *interests* as well as *numbers* by providing the former with a protective power which would eliminate the possibility of a tyranny of the majority by making accommodation and compromise necessary.[8]

Calhoun's fully matured thoughts were put forth in two works published shortly after his death, *A Disquisition on Government*, which he called "an enquiry into the elements of political science," and *A Discourse on the Constitution and Government of the United States*.[9] The *Disquisition* was at once a *livre de circonstance* and the product of a lifetime of reflection, intended to have universal validity in its principles and conclusions. It differs, formally speaking, from the great works of preceding American scholar-statesmen in that it was written in a more logical and systematic manner.

Underlying Calhoun's political theory is the Aristotelian notion that man is a social and political animal by nature, a view which regards the political community as organic and precludes the notions of a state of nature and a social compact. Man needs association with his fellows "to attain a full development of his moral and intellectual faculties." Similarly, "universal experience" attests that the social state cannot exist without government. Like his classical republican predecessors, Calhoun held that man's "direct or individual affections are stronger than his sympathetic or social feelings." This leads to social conflict and the need for the restraining arm of government. Just as society is necessary to individual existence and development, so government is necessary to society. Were man's sympathetic affections more intense, government would be unnecessary; were man's individual affections even stronger than they are, there could be no society.[10]

On the same principle, governments are comprised of men who, like their fellows, possess stronger individual than social feelings, and thus, as experience shows, are prone to abuse their power, which must be checked by a constitution. Calhoun observed: "Having its origin in the same principle of our nature, *constitution* stands to *government*, as *government* stands to *society*." Whereas necessity renders it not difficult to form a government, "it is one of the most difficult tasks imposed on man to form a constitution. . . ." The ruled must be provided means by which they might peaceably and effectively resist the incursions of the rulers. The democratic principle of the right of suffrage, "the indispensable and primary principle in the *foundation* of a constitutional government," was Calhoun's prescription. By itself, however, the democratic right of suffrage leads to absolutism—the tyranny of the numerical majority which takes cognizance of individuals while overlooking groups and interests. If the entire community, Calhoun argued, had the same interests, "then the right of suffrage of itself, would be all-sufficient to counteract the tendency of government to oppression." And yet, even if this were the fact, a difference in interest would ensue because "the advantages of possessing the control of the powers of the government, and thereby of its honors and emoluments, are, of themselves, exclusive of all other considerations, ample to divide even such a community into two great hostile parties." Although Madison was correct in analyzing the political community in terms of factions or interests, he was otherwise wrong because "the more extensive and populous the country, the more diversified the condition and pursuits of its population; and the richer, more luxurious, and dissimilar the people, the more difficult is it to equalize the action of the government and the more easy for one portion of the community to pervert its powers to oppress, and plunder the other." Thus the right of suffrage, "by placing the control of the government in the community, must, from the same constitution of our nature which makes government necessary to preserve society, lead to conflict among its different interests." Instead of controlling conflict, a government which is checked only by suffrage, extends conflict and ensures the dominance of the strongest. As such it is an *absolute* and not a *constitutional* government.[11]

Calhoun concluded that the principle of the numerical majority must be supplemented by that of the concurrent majority. Neither a written constitution, nor a formal separation of powers is sufficient to supply this inasmuch as a majority can control all branches. It is instead necessary, by dividing and distributing the powers of government, to give to the different "interests, orders, classes, or portions into which the community may be divided," either a concurrent voice in making and executing the laws, or a veto on their execution. Just as the rights of individuals must be protected against the numerical majority, so must their legitimate interests.[12]

In the realistic spirit of Madison and Adams, Calhoun contended that it is folly to conclude that the party in possession of the ballot box and the physical force of the country can be successfully resisted "by an appeal to reason, truth, justice, or the obligations imposed by the constitution." In this light "it is . . . the negative power which makes the constitution, and the positive which makes the government." Whereas government by numerical majority necessarily divides the community into two contending parties, government by concurrent majority prevents strife because it is made the interest of each portion to conciliate and promote the interests of the others.[13]

Calhoun claimed that the beneficial results of government by concurrent majority would extend to the whole community. In an important passage which recalls Adams' emphasis on emulative approbativeness and institutional forms, he stated that the character of a people is shaped mostly by the means necessary to the gaining of power and influence in government because power and influence are the objects most admired and sought. "So powerful," he declared, "is the operation of the concurrent majority, in this respect, that, if it were possible for a corrupt and degenerate community to establish and maintain a well-organized government of the kind, it would of itself purify and regenerate them; while, on the other hand, a government based wholly on the numerical majority, would just as certainly corrupt and debase the most patriotic and virtuous people." He thought that "so great is their difference in this respect, that, just as the one or the other element preponderates in the construction of any government, in the same proportion will the character of the government and the people rise or sink in the scale of patriotism or virtue." Thus Calhoun claimed that the form of government determines not only the objects of emulation but the people themselves.[14]

Calhoun admitted the difficulty but not the impossibility of the construction of a government by concurrent majority, holding that even an approximation thereof was better than the absolute rule of numerical majority. As to the practicability of obtaining concurrent majorities within a constituted system, he insisted that this was likely where there existed a necessity to unite on a common action, a fact which forces compromise. For concrete proof he pointed to the unanimity requirement for juries, the Polish Constitution, the Iroquois Confederation, and the Roman and British Constitutions. Nevertheless, he emphasized the uniqueness of *constitutional* as opposed to *absolute* government. His departure from eighteenth-century rationalism is as pronounced here as in his denial of a state of nature and the social contract. History, organic development, necessity, and, most particularly, the unpredictable play of "fortunate circumstances" replace the explanation of man and government in terms of abstractions. Thus he held that constitutional governments have mostly grown out of struggles between conflicting interests, ending by some "fortunate turn" in compromise giving each a separate voice in government.[15]

Calhoun illustrated his thesis in terms of the historical development of the Roman and British Constitutions which he saw as originating in pressures, occasioned by conflicts of interests between hostile classes or orders, to meet the exigencies of the occasion, with neither party having any notion of the principles involved or of the consequences beyond the immediate concern. The case of America, however, he saw as even more complex, because in the organic American communities— the states—there are no classes, orders, or artificial distinctions, and government is assumed to originate in the will of the people.[16]

In his *Discourse* Calhoun analyzed the American Constitution and government to show that: (1) the fathers intended to establish a government based on the principle of the concurrent majority (for example, the federal House of Representatives, calculated in federal numerical terms, and the Senate, representing the interests of the states regarded in their equal corporate characters, were given concurring vetos upon each other); (2) instead of a contest for power between the federal government and the separate state governments, which the fathers believed would develop, the real struggle had been one to gain control of the federal government, which resulted in a collapse of the balance between the individual states and the federal numerical majority and in the rise of political parties on a geographic basis transcending the old lines of division between national and state governments; and (3) to restrain the advance toward absolute numerical majoritarianism and reestablish the principle of concurrent majority intended by the fathers in light of changed circumstances, the constitutional veto must be redefined.[17]

Asserting the sovereignty of the states and describing the Constitution as a federal compact with the states as contracting parties, Calhoun articulated the *constitutional* right of individual state nullification as a means by which necessity might force protection of major interests through accommodation and compromise or the amending of the Constitution. Thus it was not a mere negative and obstructive doctrine which he propounded, but a serious proposal which could conceivably make, if not for harmony, at least for the fair consideration of significant minority claims. He argued that a state convention especially elected by the sovereign people has the constitutional authority to negate a federal act which it deems unconstitutional. The onus is then put upon the federal government as the agent of the principals to invoke the amending power to back its position. If the extraordinary majorities needed to amend the Constitution prove favorable to the federal government's position, the dissident state can then either accede or secede. Thus secession is the ultimate constitutional prerogative, a reserve power of each sovereign state.[18]

Finally, declaring that when the Constitution was formed, many of the fathers thought that conflict would arise between the larger and smaller states and provided mutual checks to guard against that eventuality, Calhoun, recognizing that the basic conflict was now between two great sections, proposed a dual executive. One president would be elected from the North, the other from the South. One would be in charge of domestic affairs, the other of foreign affairs. Both would have the power to veto proposed laws, and thus protect their vital sectional interests.[19]

In sum, it can be said that Calhoun's political thought was constructed upon the following premises: (1) the self-assertive nature of man; (2) the fundamental inequality of men; (3) the social and political nature of man; (4) the inevitability in life of social exploitation; (5) the organic nature of the community and the nonexistence of a state of nature and a social contract; (6) the denial of natural rights and the assertion of the social origin of rights; (7) the indivisibility of sovereignty and its locus in America in the individual states; (8) the conception of the federal Constitution as a compact agreed to by the sovereign states; (9) the definition of a "people" not as a mere collection of individuals, but of various groups and divisions with specific and sometimes conflicting interests; (10) the notion that a federal union cannot exist if any substantial portion, section, or interest therein feels grossly insecure because it is not equally protected; (11) the absolute and nonconstitutional nature of government by a mere numerical majority; (12) the notion that a constitution incorporating both the numerical and concurrent majority principles is not the product of abstraction but of history and fortuitous circumstance; (13) the idea that such a constitution alone guarantees both liberty and order by making compromise and adjustment, instead of force, its necessary motive power.

Herbert Schneider has stated that "Calhoun's . . . doctrine of the 'concurrent majority' was clearly based on a reversion to Jeffersonian principles and scarcely deserves the recognition it has received as an original contribution to political philosophy."[20] Except for his reformulation of Jefferson's extralegal doctrine of nullification, however, Calhoun, besides rejecting the Jeffersonian ideas of natural rights, state of nature, social contract and human equality, found Jefferson's constitutionalism, which limited majority rule only by a written constitution, a formal and territorial division of powers, and a Bill of Rights, as insufficient. That Calhoun was not basically an original thinker is probably true. He certainly was not the only and first American of his day to reject the social contract theory. Nor was he the first to focus on "groups" and "interests" as basic factors in government, and on compromise as opposed to force as the motive principle of constitutional government. His contribution lies in his reanalysis and resynthesis of classical American republican thought in light of new circumstances and changes. It is tempting to label his thought as simply ideological in the sense of its being merely a rationalization in political theory of a purely sectional interest. The ideological dimension indeed exists in his thought, but to explain him purely as perspective-bound is to do an injustice to a man who was grappling with a problem which confounds us even today and which has only been approximately solved in a small minority of nations in the contemporary world—how to protect the vital interests of substantial minorities within an institutional framework which allows for peaceful progress in freedom. Calhoun rejected Madison's sociological principle and his conception of divided sovereignty but accepted his institutional prescriptions and "inventions or prudence"; he accepted Adams' concept of emulative approbativeness but, because of his qualified acceptance of Jefferson's principle of majority rule and the democratic nature of

American society, rejected the class-based balanced state proposed by Adams, seeing it as embodying the concurrent majoritarian principle in a form proper to Britain but alien to America. His specific prescription of the concurrent majoritarian principle, in terms of the *constitutional* right to nullification and secession, was not intended to promote local interest as such, but to repair the bonds of union by forcing accommodation.

Aside from the fact that Calhoun's prescriptions assume the validity of his constitutional theory, they raise as many questions as they answer. He never defined specifically the groups to be protected by the device of the concurrent majority. At most he talked of "interests, orders, classes, or portions into which a community may be divided." The practical situation brought him to think in terms of geographical sections, which might explain why he added his proposal for a dual executive at the end of his *Discourse*. When is an "interest" or "order" or "class" or "portion of a community" significant enough to benefit from the device of the concurrent majority? Ostensibly when it is able to move the sovereign state or states within which it exists to the act of interposition or nullification or to the threat thereof.

The objections, however, do not vitiate Calhoun's contribution, which lies principally in his concise statement of the problem, his definition of the essence of constitutionalism, and his reexamination of American political thought and government in light thereof. As Upshur had done on the state level, he raised the question of the political reality, or lack thereof, of analyses of the body politic in terms of atomic individuals, or what today is encapsulated in the slogan, "One man, one vote," to the neglect of the groups and interests in which men are nucleated and by which they are divided. His emphasis upon the need for political analysis in pluralistic terms of groups and interests has become, as the work of Arthur Bentley and, more recently, David Truman, shows, a basic aspect of modern American political science. Similarly, the validity of his stress upon the need for a protective device in the hands of substantial minorities as a cement of union and a lever to accommodation and adjustment was borne out after the Civil War by the return to a politics of compromise in the settlement of 1877. Then, too, our written and unwritten constitutions today provide devices within political parties, the electoral, legislative, administrative, executive, and even judicial processes, which organized minorities can and do use to advance and protect their interests. Just as Thoreau believed that a mere counting of heads did not necessarily result in a moral resolution of a problem, and sought to protect the dignity of the individual by vindicating the moral right to civil disobedience, Calhoun rightly believed that a numerical majority could be as tyrannical as an absolute monarch and sought to articulate a constitutional technique by which an aggrieved minority could protect itself and a nation be kept from being torn asunder. In a day such as ours when men on all points of the political spectrum have become increasingly suspect of all forms of consolidated power, Calhoun, minus his racism and his disregard of the rights inherent in rational social beings, has a renewed relevance. What has been learned since from the teacher which Calhoun regarded as supreme —experience—is the necessity for oppressed, aggrieved, threatened, and insecure minority interests to organize politically and assert their power to force the accommodations—formal or informal—upon which viable, peaceful and free government exists.

The Civil War and Reconstruction

Although it is true that with the onset of the Civil War bullets replaced ballots, and political democracy, whose fate hung in the balance, lapsed at least temporarily, there was, generally speaking, a continuity in American political thought. Both sides used the same basic symbols and concepts; the rhetoric was almost exclusively legalistic, being concerned with the great constitutional issue of the right to secession and the presuppositions thereof. Thus, unlike the rhetoric of the American Revolution, which was also heavily legalistic, there was no significant appeal to a universal law of nature or to natural rights. There was instead, as a recent historian has put it, a conflict between two orthodox interpretations of the nature of the American Constitution and of the Union.[21] Human rights of both white and black men were always secondary in Lincoln's mind to the preservation of the condition of freedom, the Union; States' rights were primary to the Southerner. Likewise, appeals were made to both the Declaration of Independence and the Constitution. Jefferson Davis, for example, alluded to the Declaration in his inaugural address, saying: "Our present political position . . . illustrates the American idea that governments rest on the consent of the governed, and that it is the right of the people to alter or abolish them at will whenever they become destructive of the ends for which they were established." The Constitution of the Southern Confederacy was basically the American federal Constitution changed to assert directly the sovereignty of the states and the specific and limited nature of Congressional powers. As Lincoln had predicted, however, the logic of the doctrine of secession was driven to extreme limits by opponents of the Southern central government's inevitable assertion of broad powers to prosecute the war—a fact which inhibited the cause of the Confederacy.[22]

In his first inaugural address Lincoln restated his historical-legal argument that the Union was older than the states and was based on an executed binding contract. He held that: (1) perpetuity is inherent in the fundamental laws of all national governments; (2) the Union was first formed by the Articles of Association in 1774, it was matured and continued by the Declaration of Independence in 1776 and the Articles of Confederation in 1778, and was finally formed into "a more perfect Union" by the Constitution of 1787; (3) no state can legally secede; and (4) on questions where minority rights are not clearly defined, "if the minority will not acquiesce, the majority must, or the Government must cease." In his belief that the preservation of the Union and political democracy—"Government of the people, by the people, and for the people"—was the primary goal, he flagrantly violated the letter of the Constitution by suspending the writ of *habeas corpus*, declaring martial law in areas removed from hostilities and where the civil courts were open, and increasing the military forces without previous Congressional authorization. In answer to Chief Justice Taney's decision that his suspension of *habeas corpus* was unconstitutional Lincoln argued in the spirit of the maxim, *inter arma silent leges*, that it was better for the President to violate a single law "to a very limited extent" than to have all the laws go unexecuted and "the Government itself to go to pieces" through failure to crush the rebellion.[23]

The process of reconstruction after the war and the assassination of Lincoln have been characterized as "a huge social and political revolution under the forms of law."[24] Its main facets were: the Thirteenth Amendment which prohibited slavery; the Fourteenth Amendment, which defined citizenship, made national citizenship primary, and prohibited state action violating the privileges and immunities of citizens of the U.S., depriving any person of the rights to life, liberty, and property without due process of law, or denying any person the equal protection of the law; and the Fifteenth Amendment which prohibited the states from denying a person the right to vote because of race, color, or previous condition of servitude. These amendments were supplemented by many laws, including provisions for military occupation of the South, a good number of which were later declared unconstitutional by the Supreme Court.

Two generalizations can be made concerning these measures. First, they were based on a heightened sense of nationhood. Second, they were motivated on a low level by a desire to ensure the political supremacy of the Republican Party, and on a high level by a desire to guarantee and protect primarily the rights of the Negro but also those of the white men who had suffered before the war under local prejudices and violence.[25] Essentially it might be said that at best these measures represented a desire to nationalize liberty by bringing the Constitution abreast of the universalist implications of the Declaration of Independence. In the process of effecting a social and political revolution there was, however, a disregard of the niceties and of consistency. As one observer has put it:

The policy of Congressional reconstruction was constitutionally inconsistent. The Republican North waged the war on the theory that secession was illegal and impossible, yet proceeded to treat the rebellious states practically as though they had seceded. The people of a state could not secede, but the "state" might do so. The Southern states were recognized as states for the purpose of ratifying the Fourteenth Amendment at the same time that Congress was prescribing conditions for their readmission as states. Besides, the Southern states were required to grant suffrage to the negroes, and at the same time ratify the Fourteenth Amendment, which left the granting of negro suffrage optional with the states.[26]

Reconstruction ended when federal troops left the South in 1877 after the compromise following the disputed election of 1876. The nation was once again united, but at the price of permitting the states to deal with the Negro, who was rendered a "national scapegoat." The general attitude of the country on the racial question was summed up by Justice Bradley who spoke for the Supreme Court of the United States in the *Civil Rights Cases* in 1883: "When a man has emerged from slavery . . . there must be some stage in the progress of his elevation when he takes the rank of a mere citizen, and ceases to be the special favorite of the laws. . . . There were thousands of free colored people in this country before the abolition of slavery, enjoying all the essential rights of life, liberty and property the same as white citizens. . . . Mere discriminations on account of race or color were not regarded as badges of slavery."[27]

The historian C. Vann Woodward has shown how the complete segregation of whites and Negroes in the South and the restrictions on the civil, political, and economic rights of the latter epitomized in "Jim Crow" laws, were a development principally of the 1890's and thereafter. Premised on the assumption of "white supremacy," segregation of the races was declared constitutional by the Supreme Court in *Plessy v. Ferguson* in 1896, on the basis of the "separate but equal" doctrine, which held that separate facilities for the races, if equal, did not violate the equal protection of the law clause of the Fourteenth Amendment. In any case, it is erroneous to assume that the rigid segregation laws, which obtained in the South until recently, and the disenfranchisement of the Negro, were enacted immediately upon the withdrawal of federal troops in 1877 and represent the sole Southern tradition of race relations. Woodward ascribes the South's adoption of a policy of extreme racism to the almost simultaneous decline in the effectiveness of the restraining forces of Northern liberal opinion in the press, courts, and government, and of the internal checks imposed by the prestige and influence of Southern conservatives, as well as the idealism and zeal of Southern radicals.[28]

American Nationalism

American nationalism differs from its European counterparts insofar as it developed in the absence of elements traditionally regarded essential—a common descent of the people, an indigenous language and an initially historically defined territory. In fact American civilization, as De Tocqueville described it, is "the result . . . of two distinct elements, which in other places have been in frequent disagreement . . . the *spirit of religion* and the *spirit of liberty*."[29] A recent student of American nationalism, Hans Kohn, sees it as having three bases: (1) the English tradition of liberty; (2) the thinly populated continent which united Americans in quest of independence, in imperial expansion, and in the establishment of a republic of republics; and (3) a combination of the historical roots and spatial opportunities in the idea of universal liberty and America's ability to assimilate vast numbers of diverse immigrants. Implied in these considerations is the notion of the historic mission of America, stressed by the historian Ralph Gabriel, and the idea of the constantly shifting frontier as a nationalizing force, emphasized by Frederick Jackson Turner.[30]

Although the question of national supremacy was undecided until the Civil War, the "one people" spoken of in the Declaration of Independence had been established as a political entity, and the Constitution which issued in "a more perfect union," had for long been the symbol of unity and the political basis of American nationalism. Before the Civil War, nationalism expressed itself on the political level in the form of Federalist, National Republican, and Whig policies, as well as the stern Jacksonian determination to quash efforts at nullification of federal law; on the economic level in the mercantilism of Hamilton, the embargo policy of the Jeffersonian Republicans, and the programs for internal improvements of various administrations; on the juridical level in the constitutional thought of Hamilton, Marshall, Story, and Webster; on the imperial level in the form of the westward expansion, the War of 1812–1815 and the Mexican War; and on the cultural level in the call for an American literature and a purely American legal system and science of politics.

It might be said that both politically and culturally American nationalism historically has had and still has narrow and universalist manifestations in tension with each other. Thus, for example, when Emerson pleaded for what has been called an intellectual declaration of independence, he urged the scholar to be independent of all but the highest universal standards, predicting that if this were to happen, "a nation will for the first time exist, because each believes himself inspired [not by a national soul but] by the Divine Soul which also inspires all men." On the other hand, Herman Melville expressed a narrower conception when, in addressing Anglophiles, he stated: "You must believe in Shakespeare's unapproachability or quit the country. But what sort of a belief is this for an American, a man who is bound to carry republican progressiveness into Literature as well as into Life?"[31] Both the universalist and narrow expressions of American nationalism have been possessed of the enduring American sense of mission, both have at times issued on the political level in domestic discord and imperial endeavors, and both have been guilty of "moralizing."

The literature on nationalism which appeared in the wake of the Civil War was heavily influenced by the Germanic emphasis in scholarship upon history, organic ties, common purpose, and the "spirit" and "feelings" of a people. Historicism, the movement in thought which assumes the historically determined nature of all sociocultural phenomena and the relativity of all values, was replacing rationalism. The danger was that in the shift in emphasis from "individual" to "group," from "reason" to "feeling," from "nature" to "history," and from "contract" to "organism," the universal ideals of the Declaration of Independence might be either lost sight of or provincialized and rendered subordinate to the all-encompassing mystical whole. Lincoln had struck a balance in his historical-legalistic nationalism which never ignored the service of the nation in the cause of the universal ideals. As we have seen, Lieber, proceeding from Kantian premises, distinguished between a "people" and a "nation," holding that the latter implies not an aggregate of individuals but an organic unity. Similarly Brownson, drawing mainly from French organicist theorists, distinguished between the constitution of a nation rooted in "the genius, the character, the habits, customs, and wants of a people," and the legal charter which is the constitution of a government. Likewise John A. Jameson (1824–1890) distinguished between a constitution as an "organic growth" and constitutions as "instruments of evidence" defining the particular political organization of a state.[32]

Building upon Lieber's work and heavily influenced by the German idea of the state propounded by J. D. Bluntschli, Theodore Dwight Woolsey (1801–1889), in his ponderous treatise, *Political Science*, explained the origin of the state in terms of historical development and the demands of human nature, rejecting the social contract and natural rights theory. Describing the United States as a "State formed by a union without merging the existence of the members in that which they created," he declared that it is bound together not merely by the formal

Constitution but "feelings" of loyalty for the Union, the ties of language, law, civilization and similar political views and experiences as well as reconcilable interests.[33]

Representative of the Hegelian influence on American thought were the works of Elisha Mulford (1833–1885) and John W. Burgess (1844–1931), both of whom had studied in Germany. Following his Teutonic teachers, Mulford portrayed the nation as a mystical entity possessed of a body and spirit. "The Nation," he wrote, "is as old as history. . . . It is a work of God in history. . . . Its vocation is from God, and its obligation is only to God." It is doubtful whether the average American then or now, with his Anglo-Saxon empirical background and his sense of unity in diversity, would have recognized Mulford's characterization as anything but a caricature of the American political community.[34]

Burgess was the most systematic and comprehensive of all the nationalist writers. In his *Political Science and Comparative Constitutional Law* he explained the state historically as it evolved from theocracy, through despotism and absolute monarchy to an elevated constitutional stage. He regarded sovereignty, defined as the "original, absolute, unlimited, universal power over the individual subject and all associations of subjects," as the distinctive aspect of the state. Liberty is not only compatible with absolute sovereignty but assumes it as a necessary condition. Because sovereignty is indivisible and exists in the nation ("a population of an ethnic unity, inhabiting a geographic unity"), organized in a state, a federal state is a contradiction in terms. The United States of America constitutes a dual government based on a sovereign nation in which the states are merely instruments of government for the nation.

Burgess' nationalism merged with a belief in the superiority of Teutonic peoples, an attitude which was shared by many of his scholarly contemporaries in America. Only the Roman and Teutonic peoples, he wrote, have realized the state in its pure (constitutional) form. "From them," he declared "the propaganda must go out, until the whole human race shall come to the consciousness of itself, shall realize its universal substance, and subject itself to the universal laws of rationality." The Teutons, Burgess added, have the highest political psychology because they are the founders of national states.[35]

The Hegelian view, in its exaltation of the state as a supreme moral organism in the realization of national freedom and of the nation as the embodiment of a mystical spirit of the people, was incompatible with traditional American pluralism and emphasis on the primacy of individual rights. It could later be used to justify [or rationalize] the "manifest destiny" of imperial American adventures, but it never was able to secure the hold on the American mind which Puritanism, Rationalism, and domesticated Transcendentalism had before it.

NOTES

1. For a general discussion of the different conceptions of the Constitution, see Charles M. Wiltse, "From Compact to National State in American Political Thought," in Milton R. Konvitz and Arthur E. Murphy (eds.), *Essays in Political Theory* (Ithaca, N.Y., 1948), pp. 153–178; A. C. McLaughlin, "Social Compact and Constitutional Construction," *American Historical Review*, V (April, 1900), 467–490; and E. K. Bauer, *Commentaries on the Constitution* (New York, 1952).

2. Madison, *Letters and Writings*, IV, 390, 391, 63; Jackson (Nullification Address), Dec. 10, 1833, Richardson, *Messages and Papers of the Presidents*, II, 1203–1219.

3. Taylor, *New Views of the Constitution of the U.S.* (Washington, 1823), p. 37.

4. *The Writings and Speeches of Daniel Webster* (Boston, 1903, 18 vols.), VI, 201.

5. *Ableman v. Booth*, 21 Howard 506 (1859).

6. *Lectures on the Elements of Political Economy* (Columbia, 1829, 2nd ed.), pp. 360–361, 365, cited in Wiltse, *op. cit.*, p. 166.

7. For Calhoun's life and career, see Charles M. Wiltse, *John C. Calhoun, Nationalist, 1782–1828* (New York, 1944), *John C. Calhoun, Nullifier, 1829–1839* (New York, 1949), and *John C. Calhoun, Sectionalist, 1840–1850* (New York, 1951). See also, Margaret L. Coit, *John C. Calhoun, American Portrait* (Boston, 1950).

8. See the original Draft of the "South Carolina Exposition" in *The Works of John C. Calhoun*, VI, 1–50. The basic elements of Calhoun's developed thought are present in this document and in his Fort Hill Address of 1831 which can be found in the above volume of his works, pages 59–94.

9. These works are published together in Calhoun, *Works*, I, 1–406.

10. *Ibid.*, pp. 2, 3, 4, 5.

11. *Ibid.*, pp. 7, 8, 12, 13, 14, 15, 16, 17, 18.

12. *Ibid.*, pp. 24, 25.

13. *Ibid.*, pp. 33, 35.

14. *Ibid.*, pp. 50–51.

15. *Ibid.*, pp. 64, 65–66, 71, 72, 78.

16. *Ibid.*, 92ff., 98ff.

17. *Discourse, Works*, I, 169ff, 229ff.

18. *Ibid.*, pp. 241, 242, 263–269, 274–279, 296–301. Calhoun distinguished between amendments to the federal Constitution which are within "the limits of the amending power . . . or with the nature of the system" and those which are not. In the former instance, the state is bound to acquiesce; in the latter it may acquiesce or secede. In any case the state makes the ultimate determination on the point.

19. *Ibid.*, pp. 391–392.

20. Schneider, *A History of American Philosophy* (New York, 1946), p. 104. For a discussion of Calhoun's political thought, see August A. Spain, *The Political Theory of John C. Calhoun* (New York, 1950).

21. Boorstin, *op. cit.*, pp. 121–132.

22. Dunbar Rowland (ed.), *Jefferson Davis: Constitutionalist,* (Jackson, Miss., 1923, 10 vols.), V, 50; "Constitution of the Confederate States of America," in James Richardson (ed.), *Messages and Papers of the Confederacy* (New York, 1966, 2 vols.), I, 37ff.

23. Richardson, *Messages and Papers of the Presidents of the United States*, VI, 5ff.; Message to Congress July 4, 1861, *Collected Works of Abraham Lincoln*, IV, 430.

24. W. A. Dunning, *Essays on the Civil War and Reconstruction* (New York, 1904), p. 250.

25. See particularly, Howard Jay Graham, "Early Anti-Slavery Backgrounds of the Fourteenth Amendment," *Wisconsin Law Review* (May, July, 1950), 479–507, 610–661.

26. Raymond G. Gettell, *History of American Political Thought* (New York, 1928), pp. 386, 387.

27. *Civil Rights Cases*, 109 U.S. 3 (1883).

28. Woodward, *The Strange Career of Jim Crow* (New York, 1957), pp. 51–52.

29. De Tocqueville, *op. cit.*, I, 43.

30. Hans Kohn, *American Nationalism* (New York, 1961), p. 141. See also Gabriel, *op. cit., and* F. J. Turner, *The Frontier in American History* (New York, 1921).

31. Cited in *ibid.*, pp. 68–69, 74–75.

32. John A. Jameson, *A Treatise on Constitutional Conventions* (New York, 1867), Section 63.

33. Theodore D. Woolsey, *Political Science* (New York, 1878), II, 256, 258 and Chapter IV, as quoted in Gettell, *op. cit.*, p. 402.

34. Elisha Mulford, *The Nation* (New York, 1870), p. 358.

35. John W. Burgess, *Political Science and Comparative Constitutional Law* (Boston, 1913, 2 vols.), I, 59–67, 52, 53, 55, 30–39, 67.

PART SEVEN

EVOLUTIONARY NATURALISM AND AMERICAN POLITICAL THOUGHT

Chapter 19

SOCIAL DARWINISM AND AMERICAN POLITICAL THOUGHT

The moment a person forms a theory his imagination sees in every object only the tracts that favor that theory.

THOMAS JEFFERSON

In speaking of his and his family's return to America in 1868 after spending a decade in England, Henry Adams (1838–1918) wrote: "Had they been Tyrian traders of the year B.C. 1000, landing from a galley fresh from Gibraltar, they could hardly have been stranger on the shore of a world, so changed from what it had been ten years before. . . . One could divine pretty nearly where the force lay, since the last ten years had given to the great mechanical energies—coal, iron, steam —a distinct superiority in power over the old industrial elements— agriculture, handiwork, and learning; but the result of this revolution on a survivor from the fifties resembled the action of the earthworm; he twisted about, in vain, to recover his starting-point; he could no longer see his own trail." Adams went on in his autobiography to record his ensuing disillusion with the new America which brought him to renounce his family's long tradition of public service. Commenting on this, Van Wyck Brooks has observed: "The old idealism had been burnt away, the hopes of the patriot fathers, the youthful and generous dreams of the early republic. The war, with its fearful tension, draining the national vitality, had left the mind of the people morally flabby. The indifference to the public welfare was as marked as Henry Adams thought, and a new type of 'business ethics' prevailed over the old ethics, in a larger and larger measure, as time went on."[1]

The Influence of Herbert Spencer

The forces of technology, industrialism, corporate enterprise, exploitation of physical resources, scientific development, immigration, urbanization, and expansive nationalism, which worked to change the face, composition, and mores of America in the last half of the nineteenth century, were accompanied by significant changes in intellectual and theoretical approaches challenging the traditional political ideals upon which the republic had been founded and developed. The successive traditions of the Calvinist religious ethic, which emphasized the primacy of the commands of the stern personal God; the Deistic static "laws of nature" which stressed the natural right of men to life, liberty, and the pursuit of happiness; the classical-republican imitation of the Newtonian mechanistic cosmology in the principle of checks and balances; and the early nineteenth-century evangelical and Transcendental preachments of the primacy of the free individual and the divine moral law remained like geological strata in the American consciousness. They were covered over by, or juxtaposed to, the new emphasis upon evolutionary development, a monistic explanation of life which stressed the uniform rule of biophysical laws of nature. Transformed to the social realm, evolutionary naturalism assumed the possibility of the ultimate reduction of human and social phenomena to biological and thence simple mechanical terms.

The evolutionary theory was popularized in America through the works of the Englishman Herbert Spencer (1820–1903).* Richard Hofstadter has written: "Spencer's philosophy was admirably suited to the American scene. It was scientific in derivation and comprehensive in scope. It had a reassuring theory of progress based upon biology and physics. It was large enough to be all things to all men, broad enough to satisfy agnostics like Robert Ingersoll and theists like Fiske and Beecher. It offered a comprehensive world-view, uniting under one generalization everything in nature from protozoa to politics. . . . Moreover it was not a technical creed for professionals. Presented in language that tyros in philosophy could understand, it made Spencer the metaphysician of the homemade intellectual, and the prophet of the cracker-barrel agnostic."[2]

Whereas Charles Darwin had emphasized natural selection in the evolutionary process, Spencer stressed "survival of the fittest" within the framework of the thermodynamic principle of the conservation of energy. He defined evolution polysyllabically as "an integration of

---

* Between the years 1860 and 1903, 368,755 volumes of Spencer's writings were sold in the United States. See Sidney Fine, *Laissez-Faire and the General-Welfare State* (Ann Arbor, Mich., 1964), p. 41.

matter and concomitant dissipation of motion; during which the matter passes from an indefinite, incoherent homogeneity to a definite, coherent heterogeneity; and during which the retained motion undergoes a parallel transformation."[3] Science delineated a self-contained system (which William James would later satirically call a "block universe") wherein matter and energy are never dissipated but ceaselessly change in form. On this basis man was explained in terms of the natural law of the survival of the fittest in the struggle for existence. The inexorable character of the evolutionary force furnished Spencer with a proscription against social reformism, a naturalistic theodicy (God was relegated to the dimension of the "Unknowable") and a theory of progress. Thus the poverty of the incapable, the distress of the imprudent, the starvation of the idle, and the conquests of the strong, are "the decrees of a large, farseeing benevolence"; progress is "not an accident but a necessity" and "what we call evil and immorality must disappear," in the certainty "that man must become perfect." Because the evolutionary process cannot endlessly move toward increasing heterogeneity, an ultimate state of "equilibration" must be reached which is represented in the individual by death, and on the social level by a harmonious state in which "evolution can end only in the establishment of the greatest perfection and the most complete happiness."[4]

Spencer refurbished the notion of *laissez-faire* expounded in English classical economics, drawing upon Malthus and Ricardo to exalt it as the instrument of progressive development and the means prescribed by nature to realize the "survival of the fittest." He aimed at an ethic and a public policy based on "science" and ultimate law, stressing optimistically that adaptation of human actions to the realities of life would result in the evolution of the moral character of the race in complete adjustment to the requirements of civilization. He rephrased the old doctrine of natural rights by asserting the indefeasible right of each individual to do as he wished as long as he did not violate the equal rights of others. Government exists solely to protect this fundamental right in imitation of nature's unalterable dictate; the state is justified as a means by which artificial impediments to the natural law of the "survival of the fittest" might be removed.

American Evolutionary Studies and the "Science of Man"

Under the influence of positivism and the popularization of the findings of Charles Darwin, "science" became, along with "evolution" one of the key words in the vocabulary of the educated postbellum American. Understood as the gathering of facts from which are deduced "universal laws," science was assumed to provide a methodology as valid for the study of man as for the rest of nature. The universal law or laws which were thought to describe uniformly the workings of all the elements of the cosmos were, however, as applied to political man, in reality less the warranted generalizations of "facts" than the discovery and fitting of "facts" in the mold of preconceived monistic theory. Finally, what was ostensibly descriptive of the "facts," of what is and must be, was at the same time regarded as prescriptive of what ought to be.[5]

One of the first naturalistic analyses illustrative of these points was the work of a New York professor of chemistry and physiology, John W. Draper (1811–1882), *Thoughts on the Future Civil Policy of America* (1865). Draper argued that because "social advancement is as completely under the control of natural law as is the bodily growth of an individual," it is scientifically predictable and "the Historian, who relies on the immutability of Nature [can] predict the inevitable course through which a nation must pass." It is thus "the province of statesmanship to determine how change shall be provided for in political institutions, and what is the true nature of the law by which they shall be modified." Because all of life is "influenced by physical agents and is . . . under the control of law," reformers to the contrary notwithstanding, "there are physical boundaries beyond which society cannot pass" and "ends that no human legislation can accomplish." Physiological laws, for example, preclude the possibility that education can ever establish an intellectual equality among men; because the lower strata of men cannot be educated completely, "their conceptions of political progress dwindle into a change of men" and they erroneously and dangerously conclude "in the face of endless disappointments . . . that they can gain their object by that inadequate device."[6]

Draper emphasized the formative influence in America of climate, immigration, political ideas, and "the natural course of national development." To neutralize the continental climatic differences "which, if unchecked, must transmute us into different nations," he prescribed education, locomotion, and intercommunication. Although he admitted that ideas "govern the world," he added that "nature has prepared the path along which the course must be run." Nature had allowed America to develop without "vast ecclesiastical establishments," which resulted in intellectual freedom. The basic American idea, however, is "that there shall exist on this continent one Republic, great and indivisible, whose grandeur shall eclipse the grandeur of Rome . . . so ruling in truth, in wisdom, in justice, in force, that every human being, no matter how obscure or desolate he may be, may find in it a refuge and protector; that every government, from the Atlantic Ocean . . . to the Chinese Seas, no matter how strong it may be, shall listen with attention to its suggestions." That this was at once a dictate of a deterministic universal law and a moral imperative to Draper is evident in his further comment: "There is a course through which we *must* go. Let us cast from ourselves the untrue, the unworthy belief that the will of man determines the events of this world. National life . . . is shaped by a stern logic of events." He further contended that there are but three powers that can organize the world—theology, literature, and science. Europe had tried and exhausted the first; the Chinese had ultimately failed with the second; America, however, can succeed through science because science can be communicated universally, as long as its social organization, while affording a basic equality of opportunity, is based on superiority and subordination.[7]

More influential in laying the structure and defining the conceptual framework which many Americans would use to form "scientific" explanations of society and politics was the pioneer work of the first great American cultural anthropologist, Lewis H. Morgan (1818–1881). This was *Ancient Society* (1877), the subtitle of which was *Researches in the Lines of Human Progress from Savagery Through Barbarism to Civilization.* Starting from the premise of the intellectual and biological uniformity of mankind and relying on a broad range of ethnological and historical data, Morgan traced the development of man by delineating the growth of (1) intelligence through inventions and discoveries, (2) the idea of government, (3) the idea of the family, and (4) the idea of property. He propounded alongside each other an idealistic and materialistic theory of evolution. The idealism is evident in his claim that the evidence tends "to show that the principal institutions of mankind have been developed from a few primary germs of thought; and that the course and manner of their development were predetermined, as well as restricted within narrow limits of divergence, by the natural logic of the human mind and the necessary limitations of its powers." And yet it was the objective evidence of inventions and discoveries, particularly in technology, which Morgan used to note the advance in phases within the typical stages of natural development and from one stage to another. Thus he declared that "with the production of inventions and discoveries, and with the growth of institutions, the human mind necessarily grew and expanded." But more particularly was this point made in his treatment of the evolution of property. The passion for property, Morgan contended, beginning at zero in savagery, and developing with technological advancement, has now "as the representative of accumulated subsistence," become dominant over the human mind and has "not only led mankind to overcome the obstacles which delayed civilization, but to establish political society on the basis of territory and property." He declared: "There is something grandly impressive in a principle which has wrought out civilization by assiduous application from small beginnings; from the arrow head, which expresses the thought in the brain of a savage, to the smelting of iron ore, which represents the higher intelligence of the barbarian, and, finally, to the railway train in motion, which may be called the triumph of civilization."[8]

Progress is measured ultimately in terms of *technological development* upon which *economic institutions* are constructed and upon which in turn the *superstructure of culture and politics* is erected. Thus changes in property relations bring changes in society and government. Man advanced from primitive communism and elementary democracy in savagery, to the introduction of property and the development of civilization expressed successively in despotism, imperialism, monarchy, aristocratic privilege, and representative democracy. Morgan saw the latter as a peculiarly American development initiated by the Revolution and sealed by the Civil War and the end of black slavery. Just as he saw the Aryan race as representing "the central stream of human progress, because it produced the highest type of mankind, and because it has proved its intrinsic superiority by gradually assuming the control of the earth," he regarded the fluid American society based on private property and the politics of representative democracy as the highest stage of civilizational development. But it was not the ultimate stage; propounding the notion that the system of private property contains contradictions which must lead to its change (a point eagerly pounced upon by Marxists such as Friedrich Engels), Morgan expressed a belief that "democracy in government, brotherhood in society, equality in rights and privileges, and universal education, foreshadow the next higher plane of society." As Ralph Gabriel has put it: "In these phrases Morgan restated in the language of naturalism the old American doctrine of democracy as the salvation of the world." Thus the progress of man through the three stages of development was inexorable; it was only the time of its achievement, not its result, which was subject to fortuitous circumstance.[9]

Although Morgan's anthropology has been greatly altered by more recent discoveries, criticism, and retheoretization, it is significant to us, along with Draper's work, as an indication of the evolutionary naturalistic approach to the study of man. Discernible in Draper's thought is a cluster of ideas which though propounded as scientific can also be called ideological in the sense of the rationalization of a definite conception of public policy and leadership—society as an organism, nationalism as an expansive force sanctioned and sanctified by scientific law, science as the organon of progress, the key to the knowledge of laws of human behavior and the instrument of world organization, statecraft as an exact science, and the elitist hegemony of the scientific expert. Morgan's notions that the law of human progress is indicated in the deterministic terms of stages of technological development, that American representative democracy and freedom are the natural outcome of individualistic property relations, and that universal democracy is inevitable, became fixed categories in the minds of many Americans. They also became important elements in the later development of American social science, providing a convenient means for the classification of cultures and governments and an explanation of the bases of politics.

William Graham Sumner: "Tough-Minded" Individualist

William Graham Sumner (1840–1910) was born in New Jersey, educated in Connecticut, and graduated from Yale College in 1863, after which he went to Europe where he studied in Geneva and at Göttingen. He absorbed and admired the critical German biblical science which taught him "rigorous and pitiless methods of investigation and deduction." Moving on to Oxford, he became interested in the work of the historian Thomas Buckle who he thought properly assumed "that social science must be an induction from history." Ordained a minister in 1869, Sumner's earlier interest in classical political economy was supplemented by his reading of Spencer's essays later published collectively in *The Study of Sociology*. He recorded his reaction as follows: "The conception of society, of social forces, and of the science of society there offered was just the one which I had been groping after but had not been able to deduce for myself. It solved the old difficulty about the relation of social science to history, rescued social science from dominion of the cranks, and offered a definite and magnificent field for work, from which we might hope at least to derive definite results for the solution of social problems."[10]

Designated professor of Political and Social Science at Yale in 1872 by President Noah Porter, a devout man who thought that as a clergyman Sumner was a theologically "safe" appointment, Sumner proceeded to teach his disciplines within the framework of a rigidly naturalistic evolutionary approach, merging classical economics and Darwin, and using Spencer as the midwife to deliver the issue. As he later expressed it: "I never consciously gave up a religious belief. It was as if I had put my beliefs into a drawer, and when I opened it there was nothing there at all."[11]

Sumner's work can be divided into two parts—his essays, including his little book *What Social Classes Owe to Each Other* (1883), which he wrote in good part during his early academic years, and his *magnum opus, Folkways*, published in 1906. Throughout he strove to effect the mood of the sober, unbiased scientist who would expose the truth as he saw it and let the chips fall where they may. As such he rejected all religious, ethical, and political absolutes, dismissing them with the pejorative epithets "metaphysics" or "phantasms."

Sumner defined science as the "knowledge of reality acquired by methods which are established in the confidence of men whose occupation it is to investigate truth." He distinguished between motives and purposes on the one hand, and consequences on the other. Whereas the former "are infected by human ignorance, folly, self-deception, and passion," the latter "are sequences of cause and effect dependent upon the nature of the forces at work." Since consequences, defined as "facts in the world of experience," are "entirely independent of motives and purposes," ethics has no application to consequences. Thus the fashion of injecting ethics into economics and politics "is utterly ignorant and mischievous." It follows that "dogmatic ideals like perfect liberty, justice, or equality," especially in the economic realm, "can never furnish rational or scientific motives of action or starting-points for rational effort." In this fashion did Sumner restate the original Humean distinction between fact and value which lay at the base of positivism and what modern social scientists describe as a "value free social science." He thought it imperative that "in the development of the application of science to human interests," what was most important was "the subjection of societal phenomena to scientific investigation, together with the elimination of metaphysics from this entire domain." And whereas Spencer brushed aside religion as concerned with the "unknowable," Sumner declared that "all religions are creations of fantasy."[12]

The proposition that metaphysics always buries its own undertakers can be amply demonstrated in the thought of Sumner. Aside from his elevation of his conception of science into a self-justifying absolute, most of his essays were built upon Spencerian evolutionary postulates concerning ultimate reality which formed a screen by which he identified "relevant facts." These "truths" (which he never regarded as mere hypotheses) were then expressed by him with the certitude, eloquence, and passionately moralistic fervor of an evangelical preacher. His initial economic determinism and conception of "nature" are particularly illustrative. That which proves successful in an incessant "struggle for existence" and produces "the survival of the fittest" is identified with "good," its opposite with "evil." Reduced to economic terms, this meant that "in any true philosophy, it must be held that in the economic forces which control the material prosperity of a population lie the real causes of its political institutions, its social class-adjustments, its industrial prosperity, its moral code, and its world-philosophy." Thus technology, which issues from human inventive ingenuity responding to the human drives of "hunger, love, vanity, and fear of superior power," is fundamental in relation to morality and politics.[13]

In demographic terms Sumner argued on Malthusian lines that it is the ratio of population to land which determines "the possibilities of human development or the limits of what man can attain in civilization and comfort." But technological improvements serve to multiply the ability of a given amount of land to support more people. Competition within the framework of combined effort, the specialization of function, or "antagonistic cooperation" as he called it, is the instrument of such progress and of civilization. Liberty is necessary to competition, and property and inequality are both necessary to, and conditions of, liberty. In fact all three comprise a cosmic dictate.

The struggle for existence is aimed against nature. It is from her niggardly hand that we have to wrest the satisfaction for our needs, but our fellow-men are our competitors for the meager supply. Competition, therefore, is a law of nature. Nature is entirely neutral; she submits to him who most energetically and resolutely assails her. She grants her rewards to the fittest, therefore, without regard to other considerations of any kind. If, then, there be liberty, men get from her just in proportion to their works, and their having and enjoying are just in proportion to their being and their doing. Such is the system of nature. If we do not like it, and if we try to amend it, there is only one way in which we can do it. We can take from the better and give to the worse. We can deflect the penalties of those who have done ill and throw them on those who have done better. . . . We shall thus lessen the inequalities. We shall favor the survival of the unfittest, and we shall accomplish this by destroying liberty.[14]

Nature is thus a manifold term connoting: (1) the original dominion against which men struggle for existence; (2) a neutral entity, which like Machiavelli's *fortuna* submits to those who most boldly assail her; and (3) experientially learned dictates, such as the principles of competition and antagonistic cooperation, which prescribe means by which nature in its first sense of original dominion might be surmounted while yet remaining in the background as an ultimate sanction to be visited upon those who violate the dictates of experience. In a word, men survive and prosper by rising above nature through a life in accordance with her prescriptions. Logically speaking it would appear that Sumner should have discarded his monistic naturalism and adopted a dualism emphasizing man as the active and nature as the passive principle. He maintained his position, however, by so construing the term "nature" as to make it man's mistress who while being overcome imposes her demands upon him.

Sumner saw liberty not as a right deriving from man's nature as such but as "the security given to each man that, if he employs his energies to sustain the struggle on behalf of himself and those he cares for, he shall dispose of the product exclusively as he chooses." And justice is derivative therefrom. Eighteenth-century concepts such as "state of nature," "social compact," and "natural rights" are "exploded superstitions." Instead of being an original property of man, "liberty is to be found at the summit of civilization, and . . . those who have the resources of civilization at their command are the only ones who are free." Civil liberty "is really a great induction from all the experience of mankind in the use of civil institutions"; it must be defined "not in terms drawn from metaphysics, but . . . from history and law." He explained that the notion of rights as "natural" grew out of the fact that "rights" originate in custom and remain there long before they are articulated philosophically and legally. Thus "it is certainly far wiser to think of rights as rules of the game of social competition which are current now and here." Sumner did not deny an instrumental value to the old "natural rights" doctrine, as expressed, for example, in equality before the law. Nonetheless, he concluded: "We are not free and equal because Jefferson put it into the Declaration of Independence that we were born so; but Jefferson could put it into the Declaration of Independence . . . because the economic relations existing in America made the members of society to all intents and purposes free and equal."[15]

Thus Sumner assumed the absolute necessity of the law of competition and its derivatives, freedom of contract and private property, as prescribing limits to political action. To violate them carried the physical sanction of decline and ultimate social stagnation. Constantly he would thunder against reformers and "the absurd effort to make the world over." If economics is by nature basic and politics secondary, then it is sheer folly to invert the order. In similar vein did he declaim against unqualified majoritarian democracy, which he called "the pet superstition of the age," believing that it had never done anything "in politics, social affairs, or industry, to prove its power to bless mankind." In fact, American democracy could be explained as a form of government attendant upon a low ratio of population to land. The principle of democracy, which he accepted as "partially realizable," was "that each man should be esteemed for his own merit and worth . . . without regard to birth, wealth, rank, or other adventitious circumstance." He called this "a principle of industrialism," proceeding from and intelligible "only in a society built on the industrial virtues, free endeavor, security of property, and repression of the baser vices." Self-government, he contended, cannot be established by political machinery; on the contrary, "the more machinery we have the greater is the danger to self-government."[16]

Government, as Sumner saw it, has merely the duty to protect and secure liberty, property, peace, and equality under law in order to permit the free working of the natural law of competition and the principle of freedom of contract. Charity is confined to the private realm; social classes owe to each other only respect for individual rights. Wealth is an index of success, but the plutocrat (a man of wealth who uses government for his own selfish purposes) is as much to be derided as the utopian democrat; in fact, Sumner ran athwart the desires of most of his contemporary industrialists by condemning Hamiltonian mercantilism and any form of state interference via a protective tariff, subventions or monetary policy favorable to the rich, as energetically as he did socialism and egalitarianism. His hero was "the forgotten-man," the hardworking middle-class individual, who with his nose to the grindstone, asking and giving no quarter, persists in the competitive race, which results in the accumulation of capital and thus the progress of civilization. Sumner's "forgotten-man" can be characterized as the industrial analogue to the independent farmer celebrated in Jeffersonian democracy.[17]

Nonetheless, Sumner in effect canonized wealth and the current "Gospel of Wealth," by asserting: "Wealth, in itself . . . is only power. . . . To prove any harm in aggregations of wealth it must be shown that great wealth is, as a rule, in the ordinary course of social affairs, put to a mischievous use. This cannot be shown beyond the slightest degree, if at all." [18]

Sumner's emphasis on economic causation in his early work was projected to the social-psychological level in the cultural determinism which informs his great anthropological treatise, *Folkways*. In sum, this heavily documented work argued that men are ruled ultimately by the nonrational forces of "folkways" or "mores" which are customs adopted historically by society on the basis of experience. The basic *wants* of hunger, love, vanity, and fear give rise to interests, which are satisfied by *experience* issuing in *folkways*, that is, proven traditional, expediential modes of dealing with the adjustment of interests and resolution of problems, which, when generalized in terms of "right" and "wrong," are rendered into "mores." Morality is thus relative—"the mores can make anything right."[19]

Sumner's description of social classes showed why a true "science of man" must exclude egalitarian democracy. At one social extreme he saw the elite few, the leaders who exercise creative intelligence, whom he collectively called the *classes*. At the other extreme are the defectives, dependents and delinquents. In between are the broad *masses* of people, those who work and are self-supporting but unskilled and illiterate. The masses are anything but the exalted "people" existing in American political mythology. They are traditionally conservative, "the real bearers of the mores of the society." In fact social change occurs only when the masses accept ultimately, gradually, and unconsciously, changes issuing from the gifted few in the classes. Sumner concluded, however, that both classes and masses must cooperate in the rule of society.[20]

Despite its great learning and effort to avoid preconceptions or absolutes, *Folkways*, like Sumner's other works, while admitting inevitable evolution toward a more cooperative society, assumed the ultimacy of descriptive laws of nature which were also prescriptive of what should be. As Robert McCloskey has shown, Sumner really used the term societal welfare as a nonrelative norm of goodness and badness in mores and ideals. Thus "beauty, glory, poetry, and dithyrambic rhetoric" along with ideal "philosophical and ethical generalizations," are merely instrumental at best to "societal welfare." In fact, "societal welfare" was ultimately and primarily understood by Sumner in its material and economic dimensions. And yet, although he assumed an ethics of material welfare it would be erroneous to conclude that he preached, as McCloskey intimates, a mere "success" philosophy. Thus he wrote: "Amongst ourselves now, in politics, finance, and industry, we see the man-who-can-do-things elevated to a social hero whose success overrides all other considerations. Where that code is adopted it calls for arbitrary definitions, false conventions, and untruthful character." Success by whatever means, in the manner of a Jim Fisk or a Jay Gould, could not be justified by Sumner, who, like his "forgotten-man," and despite his professed sceptical relativism, held integrity, duty, and work to be the highest values.[21]

The Burkean nature of Sumner's *Folkways* is most evident in the deemphasis on reason and the stress upon societal evolution of mores. The mores are prior to the state; therefore stateways (laws) cannot without peril be used to change folkways. Because he believed social life is primary and determinative of norms, it is hard to see how Sumner could escape the conservative conclusion that whatever is, is right. In fact it might be argued that he ultimately identified nature (*physis*) and convention (*nomos*). As Bernard Crick has put it in speaking of *Folkways:* "Social laws appear as conventional, as liberty is 'a status created for the individual by law and institutions.' But if they are to be 'good laws,' then they must also, presumably, be in conformity with the law of evolution which is not conventional, but natural."[22]

Sumner saw and protested, however, much that he thought wrong in the developing American society of the twentieth century, particularly the trend toward "state regulation." Presumably he regarded himself and like-minded "social scientists" as members of the gifted "classes" who might work to keep the *nomoi* in line with *physis*. In any case, a sound social science to him was one which indicated empirically the law of the survival of the fittest and prescribed competition and "antagonistic cooperation" through freedom of contract, and governmental action restricted to the protection of rights. But if the mores are determinative of all, if science and reason are restricted to narrow interstices in which the gifted individual can merely propose but not necessarily effect variations, social science can at most state the basic "facts" and "laws" and preach against meddling with "natural processes."

Sumner was impeded by his original premise which he derived from

Spencer—evolution is the ultimate principle and reality must be construed mechanically, with man as its passive object. He thus failed adequately to appreciate man's psychic role in the process as an active subject. If man has the rational faculty and the will to effect change intelligently, it might still be absurd to "attempt to remake the world over" but progress might be made toward its betterment. To Sumner, however, significant beneficial change could be effected only through a change in the mores.

Besides playing a major role in the development of American social science, Sumner was perhaps the most unrelenting and prescient foe of war, imperialism, and militarism of any scholar or publicist of his day. To understand adequately his position on these points mention must first be made of his contemporaries who used the evolutionary hypothesis of survival of the fittest to justify and exalt war, conquest, and the racial superiority of the Teutonic peoples.

In his *Descent of Man* Darwin had talked of the probability of the elimination of backward races upon the advance of higher civilizations. As has been seen, John Draper envisioned American hegemony from the Atlantic to the China Sea and Lewis Morgan proclaimed the superiority of the Aryan race. Similarly John Fiske (1842–1901), in his *American Political Ideas Viewed from the Standpoint of Universal History* (1885), exalted Anglo-Saxon superiority by showing its genetic development from the prehistorical German folkmoot to the New England town meeting. Woodrow Wilson declared American democracy to be an evolutionary development of Teutonic experience, clearly distinguishable from the less desirable French democracy, and Herbert Baxter Adams (1850–1901) influenced a generation of historians by studying Anglo-Saxon democratic institutions and pointing to their beginnings in the German forests.[23]

American "Manifest Destiny," besides being propounded by the politicians Theodore Roosevelt, Henry Cabot Lodge, Albert Beveridge, and John Hay, was given a basis in geopolitical strategy by the naval officer, Alfred Thayer Mahan (1840–1914). Mahan reflected the Darwinian presuppositions of the expansionists in his utterance of 1897: "All around us now is strife: 'the struggle of life,' 'the race of life' are phrases so familiar that we do not feel their significance till we stop to think about them." And even more to the point, the military writer Homer Lea (1876–1912) proclaimed: "As physical vigor represents the strength of man in his struggle for existence, in the same sense military vigor constitutes the strength of nations; ideals, laws and constitutions are but temporary effulgences, and are existent only so long as this strength remains vital. As manhood marks the height of physical vigor among mankind, so the militant successes of a nation mark the zenith of its physical greatness."[24]

Revolted by American expansionism beginning in the 1890's, Sumner castigated war as a violation of the universalized principle of "antagonistic cooperation." Already in 1889 he had written: "When men quarrel with each other, as every war shows, they fall back under the dominion of nature. It is only when they unite in cooperative effort against nature that they win triumphs over her and ameliorate their condition on earth." In a bitterly satirical essay, which he called "The Conquest of the United States by Spain," he argued that the sword of imperialism in 1898 had passed from Spain to America, and that militarism historically had abased "all the products of science and art," while "defeating the energy of the population, and wasting its savings." Thus "expansion and imperialism are at war with the best traditions, principles, and interests of the American people." Standing in almost solitary isolation from his contemporaries who looked to a future of steady progress, he foresaw in the twentieth century an era of nationalist competition propelled by the three ideas of socialism, imperialism, and militarism, summed up in the leviathan state which would trample beneath its hob-nailed boots the notion of the free individual.[25] This was ominous enough, but there were even greater grounds for pessimism if one accepted fully Sumner's social determinism, moral relativism, and ultimate emphasis on the irrational nature of the common lot of men.

The Gospel of Wealth

Sumner's exposition of the struggle for existence, the survival of the fittest, the law of competition, and the acquisition of wealth as cosmic dictates implied their self-justification. An America which had a basically religious and moral tradition, however, sought to go beyond evolutionary naturalism to find a theological and ethical basis for indulging the acquisitive impulse and disposing of its gains. The ancient Puritan ethic and its secularization in Franklin's "Poor Richard" needed a major reformulation to be relevant in an age of industrial development and growing finance capitalism.

Attempts to justify acquisition on theological or religious lines were of two types, dignified and vulgar. Representing the first, Mark Hopkins (1802–1887), president of Williams College, in his *The Law of Love and Love as Law* (1868), stated that "the acquisition of property is required by love, because it is a powerful means of benefiting others."[26] Similarly, Episcopalian Bishop William Lawrence (1850–1941) maintained: "Godliness is in league with riches. . . . In other words, to seek for and earn wealth is a sign of a natural, vigorous, and strong character. . . . Material prosperity is helping to make the national character sweeter, more joyous, more unselfish, more Christlike." By further contending that wealth comes in the long run "only to the man of morality,"

Lawrence apparently sought to preserve the older Calvinist sanctification of property. He failed, however, to take due notice of the fact that riches did indeed come to many in the short run, through cunning, fraud, exploitation, and rapacity.[27] On a lower level, the Baptist minister, Russell H. Conwell (1843–1925), in his oft-repeated popular lecture, "Acres of Diamonds," declared it to be a Christian duty to "get rich," and that "to make money honestly is to preach the gospel." Since money is power one "ought to be reasonably ambitious to have it" because it "printed your Bible . . . builds your churches . . . sends your missionaries . . . and pays your preachers . . . ." Admitting that while men should sympathize with those who cannot help themselves, "let us remember there is not a poor person in the United States who was not made poor by his own shortcomings, or by the shortcomings of someone else." Indeed, "a man can judge very well what he is worth" by "what he receives for his efforts monetarily." And for those who prided themselves on the privilege of casting one vote, he stated: "Unless you can control more than one vote, you will be unknown, and your influence so dissipated as practically not to be felt. This country is not run by votes. . . . It is governed by influence . . . by the ambitions and the enterprises which control votes." The real leaders are those who build the country in an economic sense. Conwell asked: "What would become of this nation if our great men should take office?" He answered: "The great men cannot afford to take political office, and you and I cannot afford to put them there."[28]

An attempt to justify wealth on a purely secular basis was made by the industrialist Andrew Carnegie (1835–1910) who early came to the conclusion that Spencer and Darwin, and not the Calvinist conception of "the harmony of God's Universe," effectively answered the fundamental questions of life. Having accumulated great wealth himself, Carnegie, who in 1868 had written that "the amassing of wealth is one of the worst species of idolatry," wrote in 1889 the essay, "Wealth," an *apologia* for the life of the pursuit and uncontrolled dispensation of riches. Asserting the ultimacy of "the law of competition" as ensuring "the survival of the fittest in every department," Carnegie welcomed as necessary "great inequality of environment" and "the concentration of business . . . in the hands of a few." It followed that the few men who are possessed of the rare talent for organization and management must, "under the free play of economic forces," soon have more money than can be "judiciously expended upon themselves," a law which is "beneficial for the race." Carnegie was asked what is then the proper mode of the distribution of wealth by its few possessors? He answered that leaving wealth to familial descendents is "most injudicious" and the leaving of it at death for public uses is problematic because the real object of the deceased may be defeated and "it requires the exercise of no less ability than that which acquired the wealth to use it so as to be really beneficial to the community." Instead wealth must be administered by its possessors on a philanthropic stewardship basis.

This, then, is held to be the duty of the man of wealth: To set an example of modest, unostentatious living, shunning display or extravagance; to provide moderately for the legitimate wants of those dependent upon him; and, after doing so, to consider all surplus revenues which come to him simply as trust funds, which he is called upon to administer, and strictly bound as a matter of duty to administer in the manner which, in his judgement, is best calculated to produce the most beneficial results for the community—the man of wealth thus becoming the mere agent and trustee for his poorer brethern, bringing to their service his superior wisdom, experience, and ability to administer, doing for them better than they would or could for themselves.

Carnegie was convinced that obedience to the Gospel of Wealth was "destined some day to solve the problem of the rich and the poor, and to bring 'Peace on earth, among men good will.' "[29]

The Gospel of Wealth, as expounded by Carnegie, was an attempt to reconcile individualistic and oligarchic means with democratic ends. Like his earlier work, *Triumphant Democracy* (1888), it sought to show the compatibility of industrial capitalism and democracy. It blinked away the economic and social problems and injustices which were then causing great dislocations in the nation, by either alluding to ultimately beneficent Spencerian laws of nature, or ignoring the very existence of the difficulties. And yet, like the theology of property expounded by Hopkins and Lawrence, it was motivated by a desire to reconcile competitive acquisitiveness with the dictates of moral law, to which most Americans subscribed. If in the process, as Carnegie thought, the inexorable laws of economics could be identified with the traditional moral law, so much the better for all, because men would then confront reality and make moral judgments on the basis of its "laws." In addition, from a political point of view, the state was seen in the manner of Conwell and Sumner, as less in importance than the strong men who through energy and talent rise to the top and must not be interfered with in their awesome responsibility.[30]

Finally, the Gospel of Wealth was not the ideology of an elite few; the broad mass of Americans who lived in the fluid economic society of the day, particularly small entrepreneurs, businessman, shopkeepers, and aspiring energetic youth, subscribed to the same values. The belief that it was through individualism and competitive free enterprise that America was built, and that the man of means can responsibly determine how he will dispose of his gains, was a widely held popular tenet which has broad currency even in our day.

The American Judiciary and the Gospel of Wealth

We have seen that in the early years of the Republic the doctrines of judicial review and vested rights were established in American constitutional law as the answer of the conservative judiciary to the doctrine of legislative supremacy. It will also be remembered that following Locke Americans believed with James Madison that "as a man is said to have a right in his property, he may be equally said to have a property in his rights." The term "property" in its more restricted aspect, however, then had reference to the rights of use, sale, or control of tangible objects. When Chancellor Kent asserted in his *Commentaries* that "the legislature . . . has no right to limit the extent of the acquisition of property," he used the term property in its tangible sense. As Edward S. Corwin has written: "Certainly no one would have thought of suggesting before the Civil War that the right to engage in trade, the right to contract, the right—to employ Madison's phrase—of the individual 'in the use of his faculties' were 'vested rights'. . . . [T]he doctrine of vested rights was interposed to shield only the property right in the strict sense of the term from legislative attack."[31]

Critics of the American judiciary over the years have talked of the tendency of judges "to confuse the legal and the moral." That a distinction must be made between the two is undeniable. It cannot be too greatly emphasized, however, that having been born and nurtured in a natural law tradition which assumes a cosmic constitution under which positive law must be in consonance with "natural justice," Americans, including judges, then, as now, tend to evaluate and interpret written enactments in light of controlling norms provided by their moral and political philosophy. Consequently it is no exaggeration to say that American constitutional law generally reflects those meta-constitutional principles of political theory which obtain at any given time. Difficulties arise not so readily when the judges reflect America sober against America drunk but when they are either far in advance of or far behind the general moral assumptions. In light of this, judges, employing their great power of judicial review of acts of the more strictly political branches of government, a power which, as shall be seen, was greatly extended in the postbellum period, use in certain cases the rhetoric of the law to make prudential judgments by interpreting the facts (including the positive law) in light of the controlling norms indicated by cosmic law. Uneasiness and disquietude occur when abstract principles of justice are not expressed through specific written constitutional provisions. For this reason in the antebellum period the vested rights doctrine was linked, when possible, to the contract clause of the constitution or to the principle of the separation of powers to adjudge the validity of state legislation.

It is undoubtedly true that there was a greater emphasis in the Jacksonian court headed by Chief Justice Taney upon legislative power to regulate individual and corporate action and uses of property in the interest of the public health, welfare, morality, and safety (commonly called the "police power") than in the Hamiltonian court headed by John Marshall. But as Benjamin F. Wright has shown, the Taney court not only retained but reinforced the vested rights doctrine and the contract clause to strike down state legislation.[32]

The postbellum technological, industrial, and commercial developments posed conditions in which the legal meaning of the concept of property was broadened and corporations were assimilated to individuals. The meta-constitutional principles which served as presuppositions to the judiciary were again encapsulated in such terms as "principles of republican government" or "fundamental principles of justice." The specific constitutional clauses which were used much more accommodatingly than the contract clause to incorporate property rights in the written fundamental law, were the "due process" clauses of the Fifth and Fourteenth Amendments and the equal protection clause of the Fourteenth Amendment. The details of the process whereby these changes were effected are more proper to a study of American constitutional history. Emphasis in the following account will consequently be put primarily upon an exposition of the meta-constitutional principles and secondarily upon the specific clauses and cases.

Most influential among writers of legal texts at this time were Thomas M. Cooley (1824–1898), and Christopher G. Tiedeman (1857–1903). Cooley, a law professor at the University of Michigan and a judge on the Michigan Supreme Court, wrote the widely read *A Treatise on the Constitutional Limitations Which Rest upon the Legislative Power of the States of the American Union* (1868), stressing not only explicit but implied limitations. He expounded the so-called "public purpose" doctrine, contending that the "only legitimate object of taxation is the raising of money for public purposes and the proper needs of government." He insisted that not legislatures but courts must make the ultimate determinations in this regard. More importantly, Cooley helped transform the concept of "due process" into a substantive as well as a procedural guarantee, contending that "it is not the partial nature of [a] rule, so much as its arbitrary and unusual character, which condemns it as unknown to the law of the land." Again it was the judiciary to which he consigned the ultimate determination.[33]

Tiedeman's work on the police power was written with the avowed desire "to awaken the public mind to a full appreciation of the power of constitutional limitations to protect private rights against the radical experimentations of social reformers." He saw the police power as confined solely to the protection of individual rights. He advised bench and bar to look for limitations on state regulation in the general clauses of the Constitution such as due process provisions and held it to be strictly a judicial matter to decide if a calling or trade demanded regulation or if a regulation exceeded the necessity of the situation.[34]

Turning to the development of the law in the federal Supreme Court, in *Loan Association v. Topeka* (1875), Justice Samuel F. Miller, one of the most capable jurists of the era, spoke for the Court in holding that a state statute authorizing local governmental units to issue bonds to encourage private business violated the public purpose doctrine. The grounds stated were implied general principles unrelated to any specific constitutional provision: "The theory of our governments State and National is opposed to the deposit of unlimited government anywhere. . . . There are limitations on such power which grow out of the essential nature of all free governments, implied reservations of individual rights without which the social compact could not exist.* [35]

These words, although addressed to a different factual situation, were in good part a restatement of the original rationale of the vested rights doctrine propounded by Justice Samuel Chase in 1795. They are important to us for three reasons: (1) they illustrate the near unanimity of the Court in their acceptance; (2) they were general principles not yet specifically identified with or presupposing a Spencerian or Sumnerian notion of a natural economic order; and (3) they were terms which to be fully efficacious as bulwarks of an extended conception of property rights required association with a specific constitutional provision and with factual circumstances reflecting the changes in society.

Two years earlier in the *Slaughterhouse Cases* the Court had denied the claim that a state statute granting a monopoly violated either the privileges and immunities or the due process clauses of the Fourteenth Amendment.† In a vigorous dissent Justice Stephen Field, a rugged individualist of the frontier West, used terms such as "principles of morality" and "inherent rights" to maintain that all the common rights of citizenship, including those in the Declaration of Independence, were included in the phrase "privileges or immunities of citizens of the United States." In a related case he defined the freedom to pursue one's happiness as "the right to pursue any lawful business or vocation, in any

---

* For a strong opposing view see Justice Clifford's dissenting opinion wherein he said in part: "Such a power is denied to the courts, because to concede it would be to make the courts sovereign over both the constitution and the people, and convert the government into a judicial despotism." *Loan Association v. Topeka*, 20 Wall. 655 (1875), 669.

† "No State shall make or enforce any law which shall abridge the privileges or immunities of citizens of the United States."

manner not inconsistent with the equal rights of others, which may increase their prosperity or develop their faculties, so as to give them their highest enjoyment." He thus proclaimed the liberty of contract and the freedom to accumulate wealth as natural rights while equating the pursuit of happiness with a broad conception of the property right.[36]

Along with Justice Joseph Bradley, Field was groping toward an articulation of the principle of substantive due process. The history of the evolution of the meaning of "due process" in American constitutional law from its original reference to the *procedure* prescribed by common and statutory law to its construction as a limitation on the *substance* of legislation, has been well told.[37] Related to this is the pronouncement of the Court in 1886 that corporations were to be considered as "persons" and thus afforded the *same* protection as individuals under the terms of the due process and equal protection clauses of the Fourteenth Amendment (and by implication the due process clause of the Fifth Amendment).[38] In the following year Justice John Marshall Harlan, in *Mugler v. Kansas,* although ruling in favor of the particular state exercise of police power, warned: "The courts are not bound by mere forms, nor are they to be misled by mere pretenses. They are at liberty—indeed are under a solemn duty—to look at the substance of things, whenever they enter upon the inquiry whether the legislature has transcended the limits of its authority."[39] Finally, in two major cases in the 1890's the substantive conception of due process was employed by the Court in striking down state regulation of railroad rates.[40] Whereas earlier in *Munn v. Illinois* (1877) Chief Justice Morrison Waite had stated that the reasonableness of a rate was a legislative question, the Court now declared it to be a judicial question, with the justices going so far as to stipulate the economic principles which legislatures and commissions must follow in determining rates. Thus did "due process" come to mean, in the interest of corporate combines as well as individuals, a judicial interpretation of the "reasonableness" of governmental regulation; allusions to "natural justice," in cases involving economic and property rights, were no longer necessary, having been assimilated to the concept of "due process." It should be added that in 1897 Justice Field's notion of liberty of contract was incorporated by a unanimous Court in the concept of liberty in the due process clauses.[41]

With the constitutional basis laid, the Court began a long period in which it acted, although not without some vigorous internal dissent, as ultimate censor of state and federal legislation affecting economic and social questions. Sometimes using in addition to the due process and equal protection clauses, the commerce clause, the taxing and spending clause, the separation of powers principle, and the notion of an inherent national power to protect the peace, the Court in reality assumed as basic the conceptions of a *laissez-faire* natural economic order, the re-

stricted state, and the propositions underlying the "Gospel of Wealth."
Thus Justice David Brewer, Field's nephew, speaking in favorable
terms of Herbert Spencer, told a group of lawyers: "It is the unvarying
law that the wealth of the community will be in the hands of the few.
. . . The great majority of men are unwilling to endure that long self-
denial and savings which make accumulations possible." Defending the
broad extension of judicial power, he uttered an "apologia" for what a
foreign observer later called "Government by Judges."

The great body of judges are as well versed in the affairs of life as any, and
they, who unravel all the mysteries of accounting between partners, settle
the business of the largest corporations and extract all the truth from the mass
of sciolistic verbiage that falls from the lips of expert witnesses in patent
cases, will find no difficulty in determining what is right and wrong between
employer and employees, and whether proposed rates of freight and fare are
reasonable as between the public and the owners; while, as for speed, is there
anything quicker than a writ of injunction?[42]

In this spirit, the Court, in the celebrated case, *Lochner v. New York*
(1905), struck down as violative of the liberty of contract embodied in
the due process clause of the Fourteenth Amendment, a state statute
regulating for health purposes the employment hours of bakers. Justice
Peckham opposed the legislative wisdom with the idea of "common
understanding," according to which "the trade of a baker has never been
regarded as unhealthy." Justice Harlan, in dissent, used nonjudicial
sources to show that "the labors of bakers were among the hardest and
most laborious imaginable." In short, he asserted that factual studies and
not judicial notions of "common understanding" should be the test. But
more informative of the assumptions of the Court majority was the dissent of Justice Oliver Wendell Holmes, who charged that the case was
decided "upon an economic theory which a large part of the country
does not entertain." Specifically, he declared, "the Fourteenth Amendment does not enact Mr. Herbert Spencer's Social Statics." Unlike the
majority of the Court, Holmes would presume the reasonableness of
legislative majorities. Nonetheless he accepted the notion of substantive
due process, holding that the word "liberty" in the Fourteenth Amendment is perverted if "it can be said that a rational and fair man necessarily would admit that the statute proposed would infringe fundamental principles as they have been understood by the traditions of our
people and our law." Because Harlan, as shown in the *Mugler* case, also
accepted substantive due process, the quarrel of the dissenters with
the majority really concerned differences over what constituted "reasonableness."[43]

Taking a cue from Harlan's opinion, the lawyer Louis D. Brandeis, who later served with distinction on the Court, accepted the Court's determination to make ultimate findings on policy questions, and developed in future cases the "Brandeis brief," in which he spelled out the factual basis sustaining the pertinent social legislation for the consideration of the judges. Having met with temporary success in the decade before World War I, this approach was generally unsuccessful in the succeeding decade and a half because the meta-constitutional assumptions of a majority of the Court proved stronger than a factual appeal.

Just as Justice Field was most typical of the view which gave primacy to the extended property right before the turn of the century, so Justice George Sutherland was the most able and articulate expounder of a starkly Spencerian theory in the 1920's. Before coming to the Court he had propounded his misgivings for popular majorities and his high regard for judicial review.

It is one of the anomalies of representative government that it is often the people who have themselves established the principle who most strenuously demand its violation. With painstaking care they limit the power of their official representatives by specific constitutional provisions, and then not infrequently turn their best energies in the direction of having the limitations disregarded and abuse those most who most faithfully follow their permanent will and reject their temporary fancies.[44]

In *Adkins v. Children's Hospital* (1923), Sutherland pronounced for the Court the "permanent will" of the people against one of their "temporary fancies" by brushing aside the stacks of sociological data presented by counsel, as "interesting but only mildly persuasive," and striking down as violative of the due process clause a statute regulating women's wages. Although admitting that there is "no such thing as absolute freedom of contract," he added significantly, "freedom of contract is, nevertheless, the general rule and restraint the exception; and the exercise of legislative authority to abridge it can be justified only by the existence of exceptional circumstances." The elucidation of the question of regulation, he added, "cannot be aided by a counting of heads." As his biographer has put it: "Basically the decision in the *Adkins* case was an attack on the very idea of government."[45]

The *Lochner* and *Adkins* cases are illustrative of a conception of judicial review which, in effect, rendered the Court not merely the arbiter of whether a specific constitutional provision was violated by state or federal statute or regulatory action, but of the wisdom of the acts in question. This was an extension of the exercise of judicial power exercised before the Civil War not only because federal laws were now struck down as readily as state laws, but because it involved a final judicial determination of policy—a task traditionally conceived as belonging to the legislative and executive branches. Because determinations of policy involve an act of *will*, a conscious choice made among alternative courses, the charge was made by advocates of judicial self-restraint that the judges had departed their proper domain of impartial judgment and proceeded on the maxim, *sic volo, sic jubeo* (Thus I wish, thus I order). Stung by such attacks, Justice Sutherland declared in 1937: "Self-restraint belongs in the domain of will and not of judgment. The check upon the judge is that imposed by his oath of office, by the Constitution and by his own conscientious and informed convictions; and since he has the duty to make up his own mind and adjudge accordingly, it is hard to see how there could be any other restraint. . . . The judicial function is that of interpretation; it does not include the power of amendment under the guise of interpretation."[46]

Sutherland was simply reiterating the jurisprudential theory which prevailed in America at the turn of the century. According to this conception, which Roscoe Pound lampooned as the "slot-machine" theory of law, judges do not make law but discover and apply it. The Constitution was viewed as immutable, except by amendment, and embracive of fundamental principles of justice which merely required, as Justice Roberts put it as late as 1936, that when an act of Congress is appropriately challenged in the courts as unconstitutional, "the judicial branch of the Government has only one duty,—to lay the article of the Constitution which is invoked beside the statute which is challenged and to decide whether the latter squares with the former."[47]

This mechanical approach to jurisprudence is understandable if we remember that the conservative judiciary interpreted the Constitution in light of a notion of cosmic law which added to the static eighteenth-century conception of a natural harmony of interests in society, the evolutionary hypothesis of survival of the fittest through the unfettered law of competition. The judiciary saw its task as that of applying ultimate principles to the concrete facts, which in the late nineteenth century embraced the new modes of property of finance capitalism and the large corporation along with the accompanying social protest movements. Conceptual forms which had been the bases of an old agrarian and aristocratic democracy were now supplemented by Spencerian Social Darwinism and applied to the institutions and modes of action of a new oligarchical society. In fairness to the Court it must be remembered that politically speaking, there was a significant change in America after the Civil War from an emphasis on the primacy of the principle of freedom through equality, which characterized the Jacksonian period, to a stress on the primacy of the principle of wealth. Joined to the idea of the primacy of the economic over the political order, the principle of wealth, as a goal shared by the many, brought forth a society which can be described as a democracy led by oligarchs. The judges reflected this fact in their decisions and rationalized it in terms of the old republican concepts.

Conclusions

Social Darwinism, as expounded in the new industrial America by Sumner, relegated political thought to a secondary position in the "science of society." It assumed that nature sufficiently explained all of life in terms of the survival of the fittest and the means (laws) by which survival could be reached. The eighteenth-century concept of "nature" embodied *static* cosmic laws, projected on the social level in terms of a natural harmony of interests in society; the Social Darwinist saw "nature" as a *dynamic* evolving force whose dictates were learned by experience summed up in *laissez-faire* approach to society, based on "antagonistic cooperation," and rationalized in terms of "survival of the fittest."

Likewise, the Social Darwinists tended to follow the lead of men like Morgan in accepting a monistic explanation of human development through stages basically determined by economic material factors. They differed from men like Madison, Hamilton, Webster, and Calhoun, who, while emphasizing economic forces as important, regarded them less as determinative than conditioning. Although Sumner's later cultural determinism differed from his early economic determinism, it posed similar problems concerning not merely the range but the very possibility of human freedom and, consequently, of politics as a viable instrument of change. Nevertheless, like the Calvinists before them and the Marxists who were their contemporaries, Social Darwinists did not simply resign themselves to inexorable law but exhorted men actively to promote the dictates of nature. Believing that what nature describes (laws) is what nature prescribes, they denigrated the state, relegating it to the role of protecting those freely following nature's law of competition.

In this context, although the vocabulary of American political thought remained the same, the meaning of ideals and the relative priority of values changed. The concept of natural right lost its earlier moral connotation and was thought of in terms of unhindered participation in the struggle for existence. Whereas the Founding Fathers, particularly the Jeffersonians, who were steeped in classical studies, emphasized human rights, Social Darwinists, who disdained the classics, heavily emphasized the property right. Similarly, liberty, defined ultimately in terms of freedom of acquisition, freedom of contract, and the acquisition and unimpeded disposal of wealth, was elevated above equality, which was reduced in content to equal treatment under law. Thus "the pursuit of happiness," which to the Jeffersonians meant the overall development of individuals living on a roughly equal basis in a rural society, and which to men like James Wilson denoted intellectual excellence, came to mean the pursuit of wealth and its unrestricted use in a society greatly changed in economic foundation from that of the Founding Fathers. Democracy led by a natural aristocracy, which had been emphasized by Franklin, Jefferson, Adams, and Madison, and Jacksonian majoritarian democracy were replaced by the idea of the societal overlordship of oligarchs who because they were concerned with that which is fundamental, the economic material sphere, must not be interfered with by government. In fact, aside from the notion of mere protection of life and property, there existed in Spencerian and Sumnerian Social Darwinism and its offshoot, "The Gospel of Wealth," no true conception of a common good binding men together and providing the end of political action. Although Sumner favored antimonopoly laws, the Social Darwinist, generally speaking, regarded the state as concerned only with its most elemental function, the protection of life, and not with the function which distinguishes it from other basic forms of social organization, promotion of the morally and intellectually good life. Even this is granting too much because the Social Darwinist disdained use of the state to alleviate poverty and social misery as an interference with cosmic law. Reduced to its bare essentials, Spencerian Social Darwinism was an ideology of power which regarded wealth, like the dynamo, steam, or electricity, as a fundamental force and thus a good. Accepting these premises one must also accept their logical conclusions; as Aquinas succinctly put it seven centuries before, if the acquisition of wealth is the purpose of social life then the most affluent men should be kings. In a world defined in terms of basic forces the power of wealth is self-justifying and the oligarch is responsible to no one in its acquisition and use simply because there can exist no real political common good.

Then, too, the old concept of a natural moral law had no relevance in the new "science of society." Seeing the subject matter of politics and ethics as fixed by "scientifically" defined natural movements or forces, the Social Darwinist lost sight of a truth expressed in classical political theory, that nature is seen in political and moral questions at two poles —in the natural powers and passions of individuals, and in the natural associations which preserve life and secure its ends. In this light the subject matter of political and ethical science is concerned not with fixed laws or physical forces but with the particular capacities of men, their possibilities to be ruled, and social conditions as they relate to the realization of the ends of individual and social life. Politics then involves prudential judgments, with the norms which are indicated by human nature in its developed sense applied in light of actual circumstances. Classical economics and Social Darwinism were in fundamental error because they assumed a fixed natural harmony of interests, their difference being that the latter added the notion of natural selection. While classical economics in its emphasis on *laissez-faire* had relevance in a society of independent, basically rural producers, *laissez-faire*, justified in terms of "survival of the fittest" in an industrial and increasingly urban society, denied any meaningful conception of community except the flimsy relations assumed in Sumner's "antagonistic cooperation."

On the level of public law, old legal concepts also received new meanings; "due process" was given a substantive connotation; "judicial review" was extended to comprehend the ultimate and binding judicial determination of the "reasonableness" of policy questions; the term "persons" was extended to cover corporations; "liberty" was interpreted to cover freedom of contract and all but identified with a broadened conception of "property" to cover intangible factors; and emphasis was put on the primacy of the property right. At the same time the Court, as we earlier saw, narrowly construed certain relevant aspects of what we today call "civil rights." Thus the due process and equal protection of the law clauses of the Fourteenth Amendment were broadly interpreted to protect property and corporate interests while they were narrowly construed to condone segregation of the races on the "separate but equal" principle. In fact, the Court generally assumed as a major premise the primacy of the Social Darwinism of Spencer while using the rhetoric of the Declaration of Independence and the Constitution. What had been familiar to the judges (and many Americans in general) was identified by them with the natural. Similarly, Sumner's *Folkways* brought wide acceptance of the thesis that since state-ways can neither change nor make folkways, the law must follow the latter—a factor which prevented major political changes to alleviate the lot of the Negro as well as other less fortunate Americans. The Court, in short, came to regard itself (and was so accepted by many) as the guardian of the vital property right.

NOTES

1. Henry Adams, *The Education of Henry Adams* (Modern Library ed., New York, 1931), pp. 237, 238; Van Wyck Brooks, *New England: Indian Summer* (1946), p. 97.
2. Richard Hofstadter, *Social Darwinism in American Thought* (Boston, 1955), pp. 31–32.
3. Herbert Spencer, *First Principles* (4th American ed., 1900), p. 407.
4. Herbert Spencer, *Social Statics* (New York, 1866); *First Principles*, pp. 496, 530. See the discussion of Spencer's thought in Hofstadter, *op. cit.*, pp. 35–44, and Sidney Fine, *Laissez–Faire and the General Welfare State* (Ann Arbor, Mich., 1967), pp. 32–46.
5. For a discussion of naturalism in American thought, see Stow Persons, *American Minds* (New York, 1958), pp. 217–345.

6. John W. Draper, *Thoughts on the Future Policy of America* (New York, 3rd ed., 1867), pp. iii, iv, 59, 36, 37, 46.

7. *Ibid.*, pp. 82, 84, 85, 197, 179, 235, 236, 239, 240, 241, 250, 251, 267.

8. Lewis H. Morgan, *Ancient Society* (New York, 1877), pp. 17, 18, vii, 6, 553.

9. *Ibid.*, pp. 526ff., 553; Gabriel, *op. cit.*, p. 167.

10. "Sketch of William Graham Sumner," in Albert G. Keller and Maurice R. Davie (eds.), *Essays of William Graham Sumner* (New Haven, 1934, 2 vols.), II, 6, 8, 9–10.

11. Harris E. Starr, *William Graham Sumner* (New York, 1925), p. 543.

12. "The Scientific Attitude of Mind," in Keller and Davie, *op. cit.*, I, 44; "Purposes and Consequences," *ibid.*, pp. 11–19; "Religion and the Mores," *ibid.*, p. 61.

13. "The Absurd Effort to Make the World Over," *ibid.*, I, 101.

14. "Earth Hunger or the Philosophy of Land Grabbing," *ibid.*, I, 174; "The Challenge of Facts," *ibid.*, II, 95.

15. "The Challenge of Facts," *ibid.*, II, 93; "Is Liberty a Lost Blessing?", *ibid.*, I, 285; "Who is Free?," *ibid.*, I, 301; "Liberty and Responsibility," *ibid.*, I, 314; "Rights," *ibid.*, I, 358, 362; "Some Natural Rights," *ibid.*, I, 364–365; "Consequences of Increased Social Power," *ibid.*, I, 458–459.

16. "Earth Hunger or the Philosophy of Land Grabbing," *ibid.*, I, 185; "The Absurd Effort to Make the World Over," *ibid.*, I, 100, 101, 104; "Republican Government," *ibid.*, II, 210; "The Challenge of Facts," *ibid.*, II, 96.

17. William Graham Sumner, *What Social Classes Owe to Each Other* (New York, 1883); "The Forgotten Man," in Keller and Davie, *op. cit.*, I, 466–496.

18. "The Absurd Effort to Make the World Over," *ibid.*, I, 98–99.

19. William Graham Sumner, *Folkways* (New York, 1906), pp. 2–39, 521, para. 572.

20. *Ibid.*, pp. 39–53.

21. Robert G. McCloskey, *American Conservatism in the Age of Enterprise 1865–1910* (New York, 1951), pp. 45–48; *Folkways*, p. 652.

22. Bernard Crick, *The American Science of Politics* (Berkeley, 1959), p. 53.

23. Hofstadter, *op. cit.*, pp. 170–175; Persons, *op. cit.*, pp. 282–283.

24. Quoted in Hofstadter, *op. cit.*, pp. 188, 190.

25. "Who is Free," in Keller and Davie, *op. cit.*, I, 301; II, 293, 295; *Folkways*, pp. 98, 194. See also Sumner's essay "War," in Keller and Davie, *op. cit.*, I, 136–173.

26. Quoted in Gabriel, *op. cit.*, p. 149.

27. Right Reverend William Lawrence, "The Relation of Wealth to Morals," *World's Work* (January, 1901), pp. 286–290.

28. Quoted in Alpheus T. Mason, *Free Government in the Making*, (New York, 1965), pp. 596–599; quoted in Clinton Rossiter, *Conservatism in America* (New York, 1962), pp. 135–136.

29. Andrew Carnegie, "Wealth," *The North American Review* (June 1889), pp. 653–664, reprinted in Andrew Carnegie, *The Gospel of Wealth and Other Timely Essays* (New York, 1901), pp. 1–19.

30. For a full discussion of *The Gospel of Wealth*, see Gabriel, *op. cit.*, Chapter 13, 143–160, and McCloskey, *op. cit.*, Chapter 6, 127–167.

31. Edward S. Corwin, "The Basic Doctrine of American Constitutional Law," *Michigan Law Review*, XII (February, 1914); reprinted in Alpheus T. Mason and Gerald Garvey, *American Constitutional History: Essays by Edward S. Corwin* (New York, 1964), pp. 25–45. All references are to the latter. The quotation from Madison's *Essay on Property* of 1792 can be found in Corwin's essay on pages 41–42; Kent's quotation is on page 39; the statements of Corwin are on pages 42, 43, 44.

32. Benjamin F. Wright, *The Growth of American Constitutional Law* (Boston, 1942), pp. 62–73; See also Wright's more extended discussion in his earlier work *The Contract Clause of the Constitution* (Cambridge, Mass., 1938).

33. Thomas M. Cooley, *A Treatise on the Constitutional Limitations Which Rest Upon the Legislative Power of the States of the American Union* (Boston, 1927, 2 vols.), II, 1026, II, 1026, 986; I, 264, 356; II, 739.

34. Christopher G. Tiedeman, *A Treatise on the State and Federal Control of Per-*

sons and Property in the United States, Considered from Both a Civil and Criminal Standpoint, (St. Louis, 1900).

35. *Loan Association v. Topeka,* 20 Wall. 655, 662–663 (1875).

36. *The Slaughter-House Cases,* 16 Wall. 36, 83–112 (1873); *Butcher's Union v. Crescent City Co.,* 111 U.S. 746, 756–757 (1884). See also Field's dissenting opinion in *Munn v. Illinois,* 94 U.S. 113 (1877). For a biography of Field, see Carl B. Swisher, *Stephen J. Field: Craftsman of the Law* (Washington, 1930).

37. Besides E. S. Corwin's essay on vested rights, see his essays "The Doctrine of Due Process of Law Before the Civil War," *Harvard Law Review,* XXIV (March, 1911), 366, and (April, 1911), 460; and "The Supreme Court and the Fourteenth Amendment," *Michigan Law Review,* VII (June 1909), 643. These are reprinted in Mason and Garvey, *op. cit.* pp. 46–66 and 67–98. See also Howard Jay Graham, "The 'Conspiracy' Theory of the Fourteenth Amendment," *Yale Law Journal,* 47 (1938), 371; "The Early Anti-Slavery Backgrounds of the Fourteenth Amendment" *Wisconsin Law Review* (1950), 610; and "Procedure to Substance—Extra-Judicial Rise of Due Process, 1830–1860," *California Law Review,* 40 (1952) 483.

38. *Santa Clara Co. v. Southern Pacific R. R.,* 118 U.S. 394 (1886).

39. 123 U.S. 623, 661 (1887).

40. *C. M. and St. P. R. R. Co. v. Minn.,* 134 U.S. 418 (1890); *Smyth v. Ames,* 169 U.S. 466 (1898).

41. *Allgeyer v. Louisiana,* 165 U.S. 578, 588 (1897).

42. Cited in A. J. Mason and W. M. Beaney, *American Constitutional Law* (Englewood Cliffs, N.J., 1964), p. 327. See also McCloskey, *op. cit.,* pp. 72–126 and Gabriel, *op. cit.,* pp. 216–233.

43. *Lochner v. New York,* 198 U.S. 45 (1905).

44. Quoted in Joel F. Paschal, *Mr. Justice Sutherland* (Princeton, 1951), p. 110.

45. 261 U.S. 525, 545 (1923); Paschal, *op. cit.,* p. 124.

46. *West Coast Hotel Co. v. Parrish,* 300 U.S. 379, 402, 404 (1937),

47. *U.S. v. Butler,* 297 U.S. 1, 62 (1936).

Chapter 20

THE GOSPEL OF WEALTH: DISSENTING VIEWS

All human institutions . . . are . . . only so many ways of meeting and checkmating the principle of competition as it manifests itself in society.

LESTER WARD

In surveying the American scene in 1888 the English diplomat and student of government, James Bryce, wrote in his *The American Commonwealth* that the United States had reached "the highest level, not only of material well-being, but of intelligence and happiness which the race has yet attained." Hostile to monopoly but not to prominence or wealth, the American people, Bryce remarked, had only one of the faults traditionally charged to democracy—"the disposition to be lax in enforcing laws disliked by any large part of the population, to tolerate breaches of public order, and to be too indulgent to offenders generally." Balancing the virtues and shortcomings of the American version of democracy, Bryce declared that the former included: (1) the stability of the system; (2) a popular disposition to obey law; (3) a simplicity in popular political ideas and in the courage of carrying them out; (4) an absence of the power of official arbitrary interferences; and (5) an absence of a class struggle between rich and poor. The faults were: (1) a lower love of public life than one expects to find in so great a nation; (2) a comparative indifference to political life on the part of the educated and wealthy, and (3) the presence of corruption in official bodies due to the spoils system, machine politics, and business pressure which allows wealth to overcome public virtue, and results in a want of dignity in public life and the prominence of inferior men.[1]

Dissenters to the Gospel of Wealth varied in their conception of the virtues of American life but they agreed essentially with Bryce's focus upon the elevation of mediocrity, the denigration and corruption of political life, and the elevation of the pursuit of wealth above civic virtue and the common good, as major shortcomings. The principal protestors rejected Spencerian and Sumnerian Social Darwinism; some of them proposed alternatives within the framework of a naturalistic approach while others modified or rejected naturalism. They wrote in a social context which embraced the strife-ridden rise of monopolistic finance capitalism and organized labor, the development of a religious social consciousness, the populist revolt, the successful movement for civil service and electoral reform, and the accelerating revolutionary developments in science, technology, and communications which rendered Americans increasingly interdependent.

Aristocratic Dissenters: Henry Adams (1838–1918) and Brooks Adams (1848–1927)

The cultivated descendants of one of America's oldest and most distinguished families, the brothers Henry and Brooks Adams, disagreed sharply with the faith in progress, the primacy of *laissez-faire* and the triumphant nature of democracy propounded in the Gospel of Wealth. Both men appraised public life with the same fundamental beliefs embraced by their Presidential forebears, John Adams and John Quincy Adams. These were: (1) public issues can and must be treated rationally, not emotionally, and government and politics can and must be studied scientifically; (2) a representative republic must have an educated, dedicated, and enlightened leadership; (3) a nation, like an individual, requires continuous self-examination; (4) it is an error to operate on the premise of man's innate goodness; and (5) majorities, like any other self-interested faction such as that of entrenched paper wealth, must be viewed with suspicion and guarded against by institutional checks and balances.[2]

On the other hand, Henry and Brooks Adams came to reject their forebears' belief in the rise of a natural aristocracy, seeing the leadership of their day as plutocratic and consequently inimical to the common good. Likewise, whereas their Presidential ancestors criticized the belief in progress from a cautious meliorist position, they were pessimistic and sceptical regarding the future. Then, too, their assumption that man is explicable in physical terms was contrary to the belief in the primacy of the human spirit accepted by their grandfather and great-grandfather.

Henry was rudely awakened from his early belief in democratic government by the low caliber of men appointed by President Grant to his cabinet. As Brooks put it, Henry "blushed for himself because he had dreamed it to be possible that a democratic republic could develop the intellectual energy to raise itself to that advanced level of intelligence which had been accepted as a moral certainty by Washington, his own grandfather, and most of his grandfather's contemporaries of the eighteenth century." Comparing Alexander the Great and Grant, Henry doubted an evolution of man to a higher level of life.[3]

Turning to historical studies to gain understanding, Henry saw history as proceeding from unity (best epitomized in the Middle Ages and somewhat approximated in the American democratic belief in an over-arching fundamental moral law) to an increasingly confusing multiplicity. Believing that no concrete proof of the Social Darwinian principles of survival of the fittest and natural selection could be adduced, he propounded the negative doctrine of evolutionary regression. Ultimately he came to abandon history (and man) to mathematics and physics, seeing life as subject not to the law of conservation of energy as expounded by Spencer but to the law of the degradation of energy as expounded on a cosmic physical basis by Lord Kelvin. Thus human thought is a form of energy subject like all other aspects of nature to the ineluctable laws of physics. In this view man is merely a force who erroneously assumes that he directs other forces, when in reality the forces of nature capture him.[4]

Because the laws of force and the degradation of energy apply to all phenomena, politics, like man and nature, must be described in physical terms. Adams declared: "Modern politics is, at bottom, a struggle not of men but of forces. The men become every year more and more creatures of force, massed about central power houses. The conflict is no longer between the men, but between the motors that drive the men, and the men tend to succumb to their own motive forces." Finally Adams maintained that democracy had indeed declined, and that the increased acceleration in change joined to the law of degradation pointed to catastrophe in the twentieth century. Because of the inescapable physical determinism underlying his views, he believed that man could do nothing to arrest the decline.[5]

While Henry Adams talked in terms of the law of degradation of energy, Brooks Adams expounded his "law of civilization and decay." He declared that "the law of force and energy is of universal application" and men and the social "organism" move in "obedience to an impulsion as automatic as the impulsion of gravity." Thus thought is a manifestation of human energy which historically is prompted basically by fear or greed. Fear creates a belief in an invisible world, and ultimately produces the religious, military, and artistic mental types. With the advance of consolidation "fear yields to greed, and the economic organism tends to supersede the emotional and martial." When the acquisitive instinct replaces the creative, an age of consolidation replaces the age of imagination. Finally, "when a highly centralized society disintegrates, under the pressure of economic competition, it is because the energy of the race has been exhausted."[6]

Although Brooks Adams' theory posited cyclical change, it also forecast ultimate decay. He relied more on biological and economic forces as determining factors than had Henry, who conveniently simplified Brooks' law as follows:

> All Civilization is Centralization.
> All Civilization is Economy.
> Therefore all Civilization is the survival of the most economical or cheapest.[7]

Brooks Adams agreed with the Darwinist view that life is a struggle for survival although he rejected the belief in progressive evolution. In a passage with which Spencer could have agreed he declared: "Institutions are good which lead to success in competition, and are bad when they hinder. No series of institutions are *a priori* to be preferred to others; the criterion is the practical one of success." In this light he viewed politics as "the struggle for ascendency of a class or a majority." Similarly he regarded democracy, which he saw as in a state of decline in America since 1828 (the year of Jackson's electoral victory over J. Q. Adams) as "an infinite mass of conflicting minds and of conflicting interests which, by the persistent action of such a solvent as the modern or competitive industrial system, becomes resolved into what is, in substance, a vapor, which loses in collective energy in proportion to the perfection of its expansion." Nowhere, however, does his economic determinism come more to the fore than in his statement that "political institutions and political principles are but a conventional dial on whose face the hands revolve which mark the movement of the mechanism within."[8]

Within this framework Brooks Adams criticized the America of his day. His first book, *The Law of Civilization and Decay* (1896) was, in part, an attempt to show by an examination of history the deleterious effect of the money power on the world. His *Theory of Social Revolutions* (1913) concluded that "the extreme complexity of the administrative problems presented by modern industrial civilization is beyond the compass of the capitalist mind." He indicted American capitalism on two grounds: its perversion of the courts and of the law, and its inability to bring forth the needed concentration of energy and centralization of power which is the mark of the administrative or generalizing mind.

Concerning the first count, Adams asserted that when courts attempt to legislate (by exercising will in contrast to judgment) they enter into the struggle for power and become factors in partisan politics. And yet, he admitted, in the American system, "the Constitution . . . is expounded by judges, and this function, which, in essence, is political, has brought precisely that quality of pressure on the bench which it has been the labor of a hundred generations of our ancestors to remove." Consequently, the American judiciary, "because it deals with the most fiercely contested of political issues has been the instrument necessary to political success," and "has always had an avowed partisan bias." American corporate wealth has secured the favor of the courts to the detriment of the majority in the country. Whereas the capitalist uses the Constitution for his own purposes, the American lawyer has "learned to worship it as a fetish."[9]

Concerning the second count, he argued for social consolidation through a concentration of power in men who would protect the whole community, by which he meant a trained body of generalists in a national bureaucracy. In this manner a *laissez-faire* capitalism would be replaced by a centralized planning state. Supplementing this nationalism was Adams' imperialism, [expounded in his *America's Economic Supremacy* (1900) and *The New Empire* (1902)], which proceeded from his belief that to survive in international competition America must gain control of the trade routes of the world. Neither *laissez-faire* nor the worship of abstract ideals as expounded in the Declaration of Independence could serve America well in the Age of Steel. Instead men must regard their government and nation dispassionately: "Americans in former generations led a simple agricultural life. Possibly such a life was happier than ours. Very probably competition is not a blessing. We cannot alter our environment. Nature has cast the United States into the vortex of the fiercest struggle which the world has ever known. She has become the heart of the economic system of the age, and she must maintain her supremacy by wit and by force, or share the fate of the discarded. . . ."[10]

Both Henry and Brooks Adams believed that there are "fundamental facts which are stronger than democratic theories," meaning, of course, the laws which they propounded.[11] The democratic ethos could survive neither the test of Henry's dissolvent law of degradation nor Brooks' economic determinism. In subscribing to theories which ultimately diminished man by reducing him to a force subject to the same laws as the whole of nature, the Adams brothers not only turned away from the faith of their fathers but exemplified the decline of the classical aristocratic intellectual tradition in America as epitomized in such men as John Adams and James Fenimore Cooper.

Utopian Critics: Henry George (1839–1897) and Edward Bellamy (1850–1898)

Henry George, a self-educated native of Philadelphia, took up residence as a young man in San Francisco where he could observe the sudden development of a community from, using Spencer's terms, "incoherent homogeneity to coherent heterogeneity." Himself a victim of want, he undertook to study the paradoxical phenomenon of poverty in the midst of plenty. In this task he was moved by a utopian longing "for the promised Millennium, when each one will be free to follow his best and noblest impulses, unfettered by the restrictions and necessities which our present state of society imposes upon him; when the poorest and the meanest will have a chance to use all his God-given faculties and not be forced to drudge away the best part of his time in order to supply wants but little above those of the animal. . . ." He accepted the evolutionary theory not in the Spencerian sense but as a divinely instituted method of development. Thus he regarded the emphasis on progress through "survival of the fittest" as at best "a sort of hopeful fatalism."[12]

Concerning man, George maintained that "the intelligence which increases all through nature's rising scale passes at one bound into an intelligence so superior, that the difference seems of kind rather than degree." Because "mind is the instrument by which man advances," socioeconomic evils instead of being inevitable "spring from the fact that the application of intelligence to social affairs has not kept pace with the application of intelligence to individual needs and material ends." Particularly did he lament the fact that while "natural science strides forward . . . political science lags."[13]

Believing that "the godlike power of adaptation and invention makes feeble man nature's king," George answered Spencer and Sumner by reasserting the subordination of economics to ethics and the principle of *laissez-faire* (competition) to the principle of the common good (cooperation). A religious man, he believed "that a very kingdom of God might be brought on this earth if men . . . would but acknowledge the essential principle of Christianity, that of doing to others as we would have others do to us, and of recognizing that we are all here equally the children of the one Father, equally entitled to share His bounty. . . ."[14]

In his widely read book, *Progress and Poverty* (1879), George attacked America's plutocratic society and the Gospel of Wealth, proposing a specific remedy to dissolve the social contradiction which saw poverty increase alongside technological progress. Dealing first with the prevailing economic thought, George showed the fallacy of (1) the classical wages-fund theory (wages are derived from a restricted amount of capital) by arguing that wages are drawn not from capital but from production, and (2) the Malthusian theory of population (poverty and other social ills are inevitable results of the tendency of population to increase faster than the food supply) by maintaining that there is no necessary connection between increasing population and poverty and that "the injustice of society, not the niggardliness of nature" is the cause of want and misery. He went on to show that land, which by its very nature is limited in supply, is not the product of labor, nor can it be reproduced like wealth. Thus the landowner, unlike the producers of wealth, can readily siphon off the benefits of labor and capital. Rent advances as population increases. In this view, the crucial difference is not, as in the Marxist thesis, between labor and capital but between labor and capital on one hand, and the landowner on the other.[15]

George concluded that poverty could not be ended unless "the equal right of all men to the use of land" was recognized. He proposed not a confiscation of land itself but of the rent therefrom in the form of a single tax on unearned increment. The governmental appropriation of rent would eliminate the need of any other tax, which in turn would end restrictions on an equitable, natural economic system of *laissez-faire*, and "raise wages, increase the earnings of capital, extirpate pauperism, abolish poverty . . . lessen crime, elevate morals, and taste, and intelligence, purify government" and bring a nobler civilization.[16]

George's single-tax was a panacea, a simplistic solution of societal problems unlocking the door to Utopia. In the perspective of history he is less important for his specific remedy than for the critical attitude he assumed toward the gospelers of wealth and his reassertion of the ability of men to resolve problems through cooperative applied intelligence. Although he was oversanguine concerning the possibility to curb, if not end, evil by changing the economic environment, he saw man not as an object explicable solely in terms of cosmic force but as a moral free agent possessed of an immortal soul. His revision of the law of progress away from the emphasis on technological development to a focus on the person not as a discrete individual but as a participating member of the community assumed the existence of a common good which could be determined and promoted only if a fundamental equality were maintained.

Whereas George would leave the existing mode of production untouched, Edward Bellamy in his widely read utopian novel, *Looking Backward* (1886), projected an America of the year 2000 in which the nation owned and controlled all facets of production and distribution. He studiously avoided use of the term "socialism" because: "In the first place it is a foreign word . . . and equally foreign in all its suggestions. It smells to the average American of petroleum, suggests the red flag with all manner of sexual novelties, and an abusive tone about God and religion, which in this country we at least treat with decent respect." Instead Bellamy used the term "nationalism," rejected the notion of class war, and traced the evolutionary growth of concentration from individual through corporate to national control. The resulting society was free of crime (except for a few infractions due to atavistic "outcroppings of ancestral traits"), want, parties, politics, and politicians as well as lawyers. This obtained not because human nature had changed but because the conditions of human life had been altered and with them the motives of human action. He indicted Americans of the late nineteenth century because "selfishness was their only science, and in industrial production selfishness is suicide." Thus "competition, which is the instinct of selfishness, is another word for dissipation of energy, while combination is the secret of efficient production."[17]

Change in economic conditions was thus crucial; but such change could not come about until men were disabused of the conventional wisdom which proclaimed the necessity as well as superiority of the *laissez-faire* system, survival of the fittest and rule by the rich. In this light Bellamy, looking backward from Utopia, explained: "The folly of men, not their hard-heartedness was the great cause of the world's poverty." For the blunder of competition twentieth-century America substituted brotherhood through equality in cooperative association.[18]

Like George, Bellamy refused to separate the economic and moral realms, believing that "any economic proposition which cannot be stated in ethical terms is false." His cooperative commonwealth was designed not to make men conform to things, as in systems of competitive inequality, but to conform things to men. His "Great Trust," the national state as monopolist owner and director of means of production and distribution, was principally an economic enterprise whose political functions in the traditional sense were minimal. It was based on a universal system of labor service in an "industrial army" of workers from ages 21 to 45 who were assigned jobs according to ability but equally paid. Emulation was encouraged in pursuit of awards and honors, although Bellamy did not think it "a motive likely to appeal to the nobler sort of men." Although he denied that his system of labor service was compulsory, he admitted that "if it were conceivable that a man could escape it, he would be left with no possible way to provide for his existence. He would have . . . committed suicide." Otherwise the nation guaranteed "the nurture, education and comfortable maintenance of every citizen from the cradle to the grave."[19]

All citizens over 45 would be retired from work and rendered active in the limited political sense that remained after nationalization. They alone would choose the President (the general in chief) and the Congress. The Congress would meet once every five years, not to legislate (because the principles of society were settled), but to receive the report of the President (as well as the heads of the ten syndicate departments) and reelect or reject him. The law as a special science would be obsolete; because there would exist a world federation of cooperative commonwealths there would be no armed forces or department of foreign affairs. Similarly because there would be no money economy there would be no Treasury or Internal Revenue Departments. In fact, the function of government in the old sense of the term would be reduced to adjudication and policing. The principal aspects of the new society would be economic at base; lawyers, politicians, and parties would be absent, and technician-administrators would serve as the state's important officials.

After participating in the activities of the great number of Nationalist Clubs in the 1890's which pressed for enactment of practical measures leading to the realization of his utopian vision, Bellamy undertook to answer critical attacks on his thesis in his book, *Equality* (1896). Although less interesting and more of a preachment than his first work, *Equality* is a systematic statement of his fundamental ideas. He particularly explained a point only adumbrated by him earlier, that the right to life, liberty, and the pursuit of happiness talked of in the Declaration of Independence has no real meaning if not implemented in economic equality. In this light he surveyed critically the history of the democratic idea in America. To the signers of the Declaration democracy meant merely a device for ruling without kings. Thus they effected a change only in the form, not in the principles of government. Presaging the later thesis of Charles Beard, Bellamy held that the founders were suspicious of the sovereign people. So little, he wrote, "'were they able to appreciate the logic and force of the democratic idea that they believed it possible by ingenious clauses in paper Constitutions to prevent the people from using their power to help themselves if they should wish to." This *negative* phase of American political thought was regarded by Bellamy as formally democratic in its principles of equality under law, equality of opportunity and equality in the suffrage, but materially undemocratic because the distinction between rich and poor remained and vitiated the ideals.[20]

Bellamy saw the second or *positive* stage of the evolution of the democratic idea in the growing popular awakening to "the use of the collective social machinery for the indefinite promotion of the welfare of the people at large." By ultimately realizing economic equality, a peaceful revolution could be effected with the recognition in practice of the democratic idea of human dignity and the full realization of the common good and the individuality which is suppressed by inequality.[21]

Bellamy believed that not only would Christianity in its essential social message be implemented in his utopia but religion itself would be purified: "Just as the abolition of private capitalism was the beginning of effective wealth production, so the disappearance of church organization and machinery, or ecclesiastical capitalism, was the beginning of a world-awakening or impassioned interest in the vast concerns covered by the word religion." In fact, in the cooperative nationalist commonwealth, the progress of the race and the increase in human happiness would be most manifest "in the science of the soul and its relation to the Eternal and Infinite." *Eritis sicut Deus,** Bellamy exultantly promised his readers.[22]

Bellamy's writings had a great middle-class audience because they were not abrasive or violent in language or substance. He was preoccupied with the realization of the American democratic dream through the extension of equality into the economic realm. While he saw economic conditions as basic to, and determinative of, political conditions and government, he thought that human beliefs and fixed conventional ideas were the main obstructions to, as well as instruments of change. It is doubtful that he would have agreed with the Marxist argument that ideas are epiphenomenal, that is, explicable only in terms of underlying economic conditions.

In any case, he too readily believed that the nationalist commonwealth, by eliminating the motives arising from want and the ability to amass wealth, would eradicate crime, vice, strife, and politics. His reluctant admission that the young men in his utopia were greatly desirous of honors indicates a possible source of conflict. But more important, his conception of the state as an instrument administered by technicians hierarchically organized can be questioned on two counts. First of all, it led in his case to the totalitarian concept of forced labor service. Second, politics reduced to technical administration is a contradiction in terms. The problem of authoritative control and direction of self-willed individuals cannot be solved by asserting that with cooperation established (ostensibly) in the economic realm, it will automatically obtain in all areas of life. The twentieth century, to which Bellamy looked forward so eagerly, has provided ample proof that the political problem is more fundamental, abiding, and complex than the economic.

Marxian Socialist Protest: Laurence Gronlund (1849–1899)

As has been seen, before the Civil War a number of generally short-lived communist communities had been set up in America. Although most were religious in orientation, a good number, following Fourierist and Owenite principles, were secular. The theory underlying these societies was regarded scornfully by Marxists as "utopian" in contrast to their "scientific" brand, which, on the basis of dialectical materialism and economic determinism, predicted that the historical "class struggle" between capital and labor would inevitably result in a revolutionary change wherein the workers would seize the forces of production and socialize the economy.[23]

Marxian socialism was first propagated in America by German immi-

* You will be as God.

grants who fled their country after the revolution of 1848. Although the Marxist approach shared the nineteenth-century emphasis on naturalism and the formulation of laws of historical development, it made no significant impression on the broad mass of Americans. The Marxist idiom was foreign to America; its rhetoric ("class-struggle," "revolution," "dictatorship of the proletariat," "expropriation") was too inflammatory to be readily received by a people with a middle-class psychology; its narrowing down of relevant economic and political interests to two (capital and labor), the conflict between which would finally be resolved by the revolution, was incompatible with the traditional American pluralist conception of society.

Laurence Gronlund, a Danish immigrant, attempted in his *The Cooperative Commonwealth* (1884), to make Marxian socialism palatable to Americans as a form of social criticism and as a prescription for the just society. He disclaimed "any vindictive feelings against *persons* who are from circumstances what they are," appealed to "the reflective minds of all classes," and stated that he wrote to reach and possibly win to his cause "a vigorous minority . . . of intelligent and energetic American men and women."[24]

After first expounding the Marxist labor theory of value and theory of surplus value and, in light of these, criticizing *laissez-faire* capitalism, with its wage and profit system, as leading inevitably to monopoly of the instruments of production by private individuals, the elimination of small employers, the exploitation of labor, economic crises and "social anarchy," Gronlund examined the nature of the state. He cleverly appropriated Spencer's concept of society as a "social organism," to criticize the individualistic notion which saw the state as "merely an organ of Society, synonomous with Government," and to justify his definition of the state as "the organized Society." Rather than being a voluntary association, the state "literally is an *Organism*." Whereas it can never be dissolved without dissolving society, government (the "punishing and restraining authority") might be dispensed with in the future. On this ground Gronlund attacked the theory of natural rights which underlay the Declaration of Independence. Because civil society is "man's natural state," he asserted, there can be neither a state of nature nor natural rights, although both concepts "were good tools to tear down rotten systems." Before any firm foundation can be reached, "the lesson taught . . . in our Declaration of Independence must be unlearned." Instead of men having rights by nature, "*it is Society, organized Society, the State that gives us all the rights we have.*" Established as man's "greatest good," the state "consigns the 'rights of man' to obscurity and puts *Duty* in the foreground." The state has rights, duties, and functions relative to other organisms, "but towards its own members it has only a sphere of activities." Choosing Burke over Jefferson, Gronlund held that the state was a partnership of the living with the dead and the unborn. As such the only "vested right" any man can have "is the right to such institutions as will best promote the Public Good." He declared that the socialist state would be a state of equality helping each individual to attain his highest development, and would "put *Interdependence* in the place of the phrases of our Declaration of Independence." Thus his cooperative commonwealth would be based on the public ownership and control of all instruments of production. Unlike Bellamy, he prescribed no compulsory membership in an industrial army and would mete out material compensation, in his nonmoney economy, on the basis of "deeds" not "needs."[25]

Turning to the essential political problem of how there can be "due subordination in a State where all dependence of one individual upon another is destroyed," Gronlund went on to explain his "political expression of Interdependence"—democracy. Whereas in his discussion of the nature of the state he had attacked the philosophy of the Declaration of Independence, in his exposition of the socialist concept of democracy he criticized the Constitution and political parties. Because "the New Order cannot use a machinery which allows the reigning party to be a master of the situation," it would abide no fixed terms of office, permanent parties, system of representation, chief executives, Senate, coordinate branches and checks and balances, appointments from above, state sovereignty in a federal system, and judicial review.[26]

As a Marxist Gronlund believed that economic conditions, not forms of government, are the basic factor: "We believe . . . that forms of governments, in themselves, amount to nothing; that civil liberty, by itself, is hardly worth the trouble of agitation, that political freedom won, nothing may yet be won—but emptiness." Because economic and industrial relations are "everything," a new socialist constitution "will form itself as naturally as the ice forms upon the water, when the freezing point is reached." The cooperative commonwealth, produced by the inner logic of history, would reflect in its constitution its social organic composition. Thus a constitution rightly considered, is not a "piece of paper" but *"the organic power that makes necessary the institutions which we find."*[27]

Gronlund, like Bellamy, assumed that traditional political functions would be minimal and administrative functions central in a socialist commonwealth. It must be remembered, he declared, that "the '*whole people*' does not want, or need, any '*government*' at all. It simply wants *administration—good* administration." Democracy then means *"Administration by the Competent."* He believed this could be effected in a socialized state through appointment from below with tenure during good behavior in the administrative hierarchy of power, and use of the popular referendum by those directly concerned, instead of representation.[28]

Finally, Gronlund believed that upon the end of the class struggle there would be a "perfect harmony" between "the interests of each citizen and those of the citizen at large," morals would be improved, justice and equality for all (including women) realized, and religion elevated "from being a narrow personal concern between the individual and his maker into a *social concern between Humanity and its Destiny.*"[29]

Because his purpose was to popularize Marxism and fit it to the American situation, Gronlund was even more ambiguous than Marx regarding the transition from capitalism to socialism. He declared that "*the Coming Revolution is Strictly an Evolution,*" by which he meant a complete yet bloodless change, brought about by "the Logic of Events." At the same time, however, he could write approvingly that the "distinguishing trait of Socialists today is that they boldly aim at a *revolution* and care not a jot about *reforms.*" He asked: "How can anyone 'reform' away abuses *that are inherent in the system?*" He appears to have believed that the trend toward consolidation of economic power would facilitate the inevitable bloodless nationalization of the forces of production by the government. And, yet, he stressed the necessity of trained leaders. Thus in the introduction to the 1890 edition of his book he wrote: "Everything is ripe, especially in the United States, for the great change, except leaders. I am convinced they will come out from among the deeply religious minds among us. What is needed is to convince them that coming change is God's will; that the society to be ushered in . . . is, indeed, the Kingdom of Heaven on Earth."[30]

Gronlund's redefinition of democracy as "administration by the competent," his literal equation of the state with an organism and his consequent denial of natural rights, had grave implications for individual liberty. To believe, as Gronlund and most socialists did, that in a socialized cooperative commonwealth all men would think essentially the same, and that conflict and differences would be minimal, is to assume that human nature will be transformed. His attack on the great American symbols, the Declaration of Independence and the Constitution, became necessary once he identified men as merely parts of an organism possessing no rights because of their nature as men but only those accorded to them by the state. His characterization of the theory of checks and balances as "one born of passions, engendered by struggle against arbitrary power; *not* one born of philosophical observations," is entirely correct.[31] His conclusion that it is a misconception and must be discarded, however, demonstrates his great distance from the Founding Fathers. They believed that diverse interests and conflicts will abide as long as men are men and that governmental institutions must be erected accordingly; he believed that because men will ultimately be identical in their basic interests, conflict will end and governmental institutions as such, not merely checks and balances, will become superfluous. At bottom Gronlund was as much a utopian as Bellamy and, despite his intentions, more of a totalitarian.

Gronlund's book probably influenced Bellamy as well as the Protestant preachers of the Social Gospel. More importantly, it influenced Eugene Debs (1855–1926), who in the first decade of the twentieth century was the principal figure in the Socialist Party. In any case, it was much less influential than Bellamy's work, which had the advantage not only of being a novel but a home-grown product.[32]

The story of American socialism after 1900 is a recital of (1) the struggle between those who advocated political action and those who urged syndicalist direct action, (2) the division after the Russian Revolution of 1917 of the Socialist Party into Communist and Socialists, and (3) the gravitation of many Marxian socialists away from emphases on ideology and strident rhetoric to a pragmatic concentration on specific issues.

At the end of the nineteenth century the German scholar Werner Sombart wrote a book entitled, *Why Is There No Socialism in the United States?* He answered that there was a lack of class consciousness in America because of the open frontiers, the social and economic fluidity which allowed men to rise through individual effort, and the ascending standard of living. He could have added that because of universal suffrage and representative government American wage earners possessed and exploited the opportunity to effect political and social reforms; they could eliminate the impediments to combination into unions and use economic power to better their lot. Hampered by these factors, as the twentieth century moved on, the Socialist Party in America underwent an identity crisis. In the words of a recent historian, it never could finally decide "whether it was a political party, a political pressure group, a revolutionary sect, or a political forum." Nevertheless, as shall be seen, it did ultimately see some of its specific policy proposals enacted into law.[33]

Scholarly Dissent: Lester F. Ward (1841–1913) and "Sociocracy"

A largely self-educated man, Ward began a long career of service in the federal government in 1865, serving as a botanist, geologist, and paleontologist. Deeply learned in natural science, he turned in 1869 as an avocation to the study of man with the intention of writing a book on education and society to be entitled "The Great Panacea." Influenced greatly by Comtean positivism and Spencer's general application of the evolutionary theory, he confessed in 1876: "I had begun to see

that what I was writing was *sociology*, and that I should try to do something original in that science."[34] The result of his efforts was *Dynamic
Sociology* (1883), wherein he propounded a monistic naturalism, contending that "the organic world is a product of the inorganic . . . man
is at best but a highly organized animal" and "society is ruled by the
simple resultant of all the physical and physiological forces which control its members." Without abandoning naturalism, he later qualified his
thesis by emphasizing the centrality of the psychic factor in man. He
maintained that "human society . . . which is the highest product of
evolution, naturally depends upon mind, which is the highest property
of matter." Against Spencer and Sumner he asserted that man alone
can know, control, and direct the laws of evolution. The environment
transforms the animal, man transforms the environment. Likewise, "the
fundamental principle of biology is natural selection, that of sociology
is artificial selection. . . . If nature progresses through the destruction
of the weak, man progresses through the protection of the weak."[35]

Drawing on his knowledge of the natural sciences, Ward convincingly
showed the prodigality and wastefulness of nature, and argued the undesirability of reliance on her laws alone, as well as the need to master
her by artifice. Concerning the Spencerian-Sumnerian notion of survival
of the fittest through unfettered competition, he wrote: "Wherever competition is wholly removed as through the agency of man in the interest
of any one form, great strides are immediately made by the form thus
protected, and it soon outstrips all those that depend upon competition
for their motive to advancement." Regarding society, he further declared: "On the one hand the competition between men resolves itself
into a competition between machines, and instead of the fittest organism it is the fittest mechanism that survives. On the other hand, the
competition between individuals becomes a competition between associations of individuals." He concluded that all that remained valid in
the *laissez-faire* doctrine was the admonition "that it is useless, and
may be dangerous, to attempt to control natural forces until their character is first well understood." Just as it is necessary to understand the
forces of nature in order to master nature, so it is necessary to comprehend "social forces" in order to be able to control society.[36]

Ward identified the basic law of nature, or "natural justice," as the
law of force, a factor under which he included such qualities as wiliness
and sagacity. On this ground he attacked the natural rights philosophy,
declaring that "not until we have succeeded in banishing the metaphysical conception of abstract right . . . shall we be prepared to discuss
intelligently the conditions of man's progress conceived as capable of accomplishments by his own efforts." Consequently analysis must always
be in terms of empirically verifiable forces.[37]

Ward maintained that society is to government as nature is to art.

Whereas society is "spontaneous," government is "a product of genius," requiring "the application of the indirect, or inventive, process." Society is "simply a compound organism whose acts exhibit the resultant of all the individual forces which its members exert," and which acts, whether individual or collective, obey fixed laws. Essential to Ward's exposition of society and government is his concept of mind, which he defined as embracing "all phenomena above those which are simply vital, or relate only to life." Mind comprises (1) the affective faculty, which is the subjective dynamic element of society issuing in social forces, and (2) the thinking faculty which is the objective, directive element of society capable of controlling social forces.[38]

Government, as Ward saw it, did not spring forth originally from "a humane and disinterested sentiment" but from "intelligence." Without government all men were "sufferers and wrong-doers at the same time," a condition which was changed when each individual agreed in "covenants of protection" to rules for his own safety. After propounding this apparently renewed version of the discredited contract theory, Ward, in effect, disavowed it, contending that government always emanates "from the few seeking power, never from the many seeking protection." Insofar as government enforces obedience to laws it prevents gratification of natural impulses and its "whole effect . . . as exerted in this direction, is in this sense opposed to human happiness, and consequently, were there no benefit to offset it, would be opposed to social progress." But government has two other functions besides control—protection and accommodation.[39]

Ward believed that if government were "restricted to its legitimate sphere" the evils it historically had engendered would disappear. In an implicit condemnation of the American founders and existing American government, he charged: "All governments thus far have been devised, and established by, and in the interest of, those desiring to govern." Thus "a true government" would be established by, and in the interest of, those desiring to be governed: "Society would be the source of authority, and the government its agent." What Ward meant is that the common interest must be the ascendant motive in the establishment and conduct of the state, that repression and control for their own sake, or in the interest of either a few or the many divorced from that of the whole, must be eliminated.[40]

Ward's view, despite his disclaimers to the contrary, was ultimately utopian. Proceeding from the assumption that liberty, which he defined as "the power to act in obedience to desire," is the precondition of the realization of happiness, he declared that "as man can never be perfectly happy until he is perfectly free, he can never be so until he can abolish the restrictive and protective attributes of government." Like Rousseau he did not advise a return to the state of "pristine liberty" which man had lost through his wisdom; he promised instead that in the "complex but enlightened state," the "conscious anarchy of intelligence" will recapture on an enhanced level the liberty which obtained originally in "the unconscious anarchy of ignorance."[41]

Ward went on to prescribe the means by which the "ideal government" could be realized. Government, he wrote, might through "increased intelligence" learn to employ "the indirect method" in the form of a system of "attractive legislation" (inducements which will make it the advantage of men to perform socially beneficial acts) under which "a great degree of protective and even restrictive power can doubtless be exerted without reducing the sum total of liberty."* Believing that men are essentially equal and that environmental conditions and the absence of equality of opportunity, especially in regard to education, explained the crucial differences, including vice and crime, Ward put emphasis on scientific education for all as an important vehicle in the ultimate elimination from government of the functions of "control" and "protection." In progressivist fashion he pronounced: "If all the people *knew* what course of action was for their best interests, they would certainly pursue that course."[42]

With "control" and "protection"—those functions that involve constraint—eliminated from government, "accommodation" alone would remain. Ward held that "accommodation" can never be dispensed with because man is imperfect and "needs agents to transact business in localities where he cannot be; to acquire skill and dexterity in subjects with which every one can not afford the time to acquaint himself; and to perform duties by means of organization which individuals, acting independently, would not possess the strength to perform." Finally, in explaining the role of "accommodation" Ward emphasized the need for the use of scientific method. "Government," he stated, "has never recognized the existence of social forces, or made them the object of scientific study, with a view to systematically controlling and directing them." If government could be the province of "social scientists" rather than "social empiricists" (politicians), it might be raised in the form of "attractive legislation" to the level of an applied science.[43]

Society then has the duty to promote its interest by "throwing off the yoke of government" in its "odious sense" and "to establish a truly progressive agency which shall not only be a product of art, but shall itself be an art." In other words, societal intelligence must exercise a directive function by which the natural social forces can be canalized and utilized without being destroyed. The science which treats of these forces is sociology and the government which realizes accommodation

---

* Ward also talked of "attractive labor," a state in which "no one should be obliged to do anything that is in any way distasteful to him; and in which every act should be so agreeable that he will do it from personal preference." (A.S. 368)

and amelioration through the pursuit of "scientific method" is "Sociocracy." Thus "the present empirical, antiprogressive institution, miscalled the art of government, must be transformed into a central academy of social science, which shall stand in the same relation to the control of men in which a polytechnic institute stands to the control of nature."[44]

On this basis Ward declared that "a public assembly governed by parliamentary rules is as inadequate a method as could well be conceived of for anything like scientific legislation." And government by political parties is just as defeating of that purpose. Committee work in legislatures, however, constitutes "the nearest approach we have to the scientific investigation of social questions." On the basis of his close knowledge of American public administration he stated that "the various bureaus of government are in position to feel the popular pulse more sensitively than the legislature." Scientific government can only come forth if the ignorance and bias attendant upon party politics and upon legislation which is the resultant of the forces of conflicting group interests are replaced by the cool objectivity and concern with truth characteristic of the "social scientist" employing "scientific method." Political science, as seen by Ward, has, indeed, roots in a knowledge of history, but even more important to it is the "statistical method." In Baconian fashion he pronounced: "Statistics are simply the facts that underlie the science of government."[45]

Ward looked upon democracy, which he equated with majority rule issuing usually in party government, as a phase through which men must go before realizing "Sociocracy," or scientific government of, by, and for society. In the latter, social scientists will assemble the facts and recommend solutions; legislatures will make the ultimate determination. Politics, in the sense of the conflict of wills and clash of interests, will be replaced by "science."[46]

Ward's social and political theory is replete with the honorific terms of the day; "science," "progress," "forces," "evolution," are emblazoned throughout. Underlying his work as basic premises are the metaphysic of Comte's law of three stages (theological, metaphysical, positivist, or scientific), evolutionary naturalism, the distinction of man from the rest of nature on the basis of his possession of "mind" which allows him to know and direct natural and social forces, and the proposition that politics as the conflict of wills and government in the sense of constraint are phases of human development which can and will be replaced by applied intelligence. The deep chiliastic faith informing his thought is graphically illustrated in the following passage. "Just as reason, even in early man, rendered instinct unnecessary, so further intellectual development and wider knowledge and wisdom will ultimately dispense with both religion and ethics as restraints to unsafe conduct, and we may conceive of the final disappearance of all restrictive laws and of government as a controlling agency."[47]

Ward's utopianism is quite discernible when his thought is measured against the political thought of a James Madison or John Adams. There are passages in his works which sound very much like their statements. For example, he contended that because "the moral progress of the world is more apparent than real. . . . [I]t must be assumed as a basis for all legislation and a postulate for every human transaction that men will pursue the course which secures to them the greatest gain." Similarly he wrote: "The proper way to induce men to desist from unjust action is to make it for their own interest to do so, and teach them in an unmistakable manner that it is so." And he extolled democracy for having turned the egoism of legislators to the service of society. But because he believed that liberty is the power to obey desire, and that it can only be fully realized under the unfettered rule of social science, he rejected the Founding Fathers' emphasis on the rule of law and institutional forms. As he saw it, "liberty regulated and limited by law" means "that the innocent must suffer for the guilty; that because a part of society is depraved, the rest must have onerous and odious laws enacted, which, though made for their protection, take away half their liberties and destroy much of their happiness."[48]

What Madison and Adams would effect principally through forms, the blunting and neutralizing of the clash of individual interests, Ward would effect solely through policy and education. "Sociocracy" cannot be identified with any governmental form: "It recognizes all forms of government as legitimate, and ignoring form, goes to the substance, and denotes that, in whatever manner organized, it is the duty of society to act consciously and intelligently . . . in the direction of guarding its own interests. . . ."[49] In this view a despot who rules in accordance with the dictates of "social science," as expounded by "social scientists," is preferable to a constitutional republic undirected by "applied sociology."

Lacking in understanding of the pressures which affect policy, and of the influence of ideology on "social science" and "social scientists," as well as the abiding character of politics in organizational life, Ward assumed that the control of men by knowledge manifested in policy and education will eventually narrow the irrational aspects of human nature to the point where they are no longer of great significance.

Looked upon as a reaction to the determinism of Spencerian Social Darwinism and the Gospel of Wealth, Ward's thought can be seen as a vindication of man as ultimate master of his destiny and of a common good which can only be properly implemented if "shibboleths" such as the "unfettered law of competition" and "survival of the fittest" are removed. Ward helped give a scholarly basis to what came to be known later as the theory of social sin. "There exists," he wrote, "on a vast scale

a great organized system of wrong unconsciously perpetuated outside
. . . all of the codes. . . ." Against Sumner and Carnegie, he could
also say: "Modern society is suffering from the very opposite of pa-
ternalism—from under-government. . . . The true function of government is not to fetter, but to liberate the forces of society, not to diminish
but to increase their effectiveness."[50] A progenitor of the idea of the
planned society in America, Ward's greatest importance lay not in his
impact on the general public, which was minimal, but in his role as a
critic of competitive individualism and a reviser of Social Darwinism.

At the same time that Ward wrote, significant developments were
taking place in the study of economics in America. Partly under the influence of the German historical school, men like Richard T. Ely and
Simon Patten criticized the tenets of classical economics. In 1885 Ely
led in the formation of the American Economic Association which stated
among its principles the following:

We regard the state as an agency whose positive assistance is one of the indispensable conditions of human progress. . . . We believe that political
economy as a science is still in an early stage of its development. While we
appreciate the work of former economists, we look, not so much to speculation
as to the historical and statistical study of actual conditions of economic life
for the satisfactory accomplishment of that development. . . . We believe in a
progressive development of economic conditions which must be met by a
corresponding development of legislative policy.[51]

In the spirit of Ward's "social scientist," scholars like Ely, John R.
Commons, and Edward A. Ross, following what Merle Curti has called
"the democratic conception of the scholar's role," researched conditions
of employment, regulation and public ownership of utilities, the effects
of immigration on the standard of living, and the phenomenon of "social
sin."[52] Later, under the progressive impulse, local and state governmental
research bodies, sometimes formed in connection with universities, were
founded to supply the "intelligence" which Ward believed must be the
basis of sound legislation.

Satirical Critic: Thorstein Veblen (1857–1929)

Like Ward, Thorstein Veblen accepted Darwinian evolutionary
naturalism while rejecting its Spencerian social formulation. Born of
Norwegian parents in Wisconsin and raised in the milieu of agrarian
protest, he was influenced in his education most particularly by Sumner's
anthropology, William James' psychology, German institutional economics, and his reading of George, Bellamy, and English socialists such
as Ruskin and Morris. An aloof nonconformist who never was able to

keep a university professorship, Veblen became, because of his great learning, detached skepticism, and mastery of satire, perhaps the most pungent critic of the American social system in his day.[53]

Veblen regarded the life of man in society like that of any other species as a struggle for existence and thus a process of selective adaptation. Men are explicable in terms of fundamental interactive "instincts" (natural purposive propensities) and "institutions" (dominant habits of thought concerning relations and activities of the individual within a community). Thought is epiphenomenal, a response to what Veblen called "circumstances" and "situations." Change—the life process—is dependent upon environmental pressure, and is resisted by human inertia, a fact which results in social lag.

Veblen called the three instincts which he saw as basic, the "Instinct of Workmanship," the "Parental Bent" and the "Instinct of Idle Curiosity." The first is characterized by a workmanlike regard for utility and system; the second implies "solicitude for the welfare of the race"; the third is the desire to learn and know irrespective of utility or material gain. These instincts can be thwarted or misdirected by institutions. As Daniel Aaron has put it, "in the Veblenian scheme a constant war is going on between the elemental nature of man and his cultural fabrications."[54]

Social change is caused principally by technological factors which Veblen regarded as fundamental and definitive. Rising upon the technological foundation are the economic institutions. Reflecting both the technological conditions and economic structure is a third level comprised of all other social institutions, including the political. This view is similar to that of Marx (and Morgan) but not identical, in that Veblen laid greater emphasis on the psychological factor, stressing instincts above consciousness. He rejected the Marxian eschatological conception of an inevitable end of history in a socialist paradise, seeing instead only a blind cumulative causation having no final term; and he would not accept without qualification the labor theory of value nor would he canonize any group, including the proletariat.

On this basis Veblen described three general stages in human development which provided the framework within which he criticized the Social Darwinism of Spencer and Sumner, capitalism, and *laissez-faire* economics. In the first stage, savagery, contrary to the formulations of Hobbes and Spencer, and somewhat in accord with those of Rousseau, Marx, and Morgan, men lived peacefully in small communities, indulging their instinct of workmanship in technological innovations such as the domestication of plants and animals, and the invention of tools, which like the land, were shared in common. Aaron comments: "Veblen quite deliberately undercut the prevailing views on primitive society, because he wanted to show that capitalist ethics were not necessarily natural and instinctive . . . and that the traits of primitive men were precisely those unsuited for modern pecuniary culture."[55]

The second stage, barbarism, began when a surplus of goods beyond those needed for subsistence appeared and self-interest replaced the general good as the central purpose. Private property was established and with it came depredation, war, social distinctions, and autocracy. The earlier relative absence of antagonism was thus replaced by emulation,* force, and fraud.

The third stage, that of pecuniary culture, issued first in a "handicraft" phase in which technology and the pecuniary drive were mixed and modern science, democratic Protestantism, and the nation-state appeared. Upon the later development of machines, the craftsman was reduced to an employee and workmanship was replaced by pecuniary competition. The need for matter-of-fact knowledge in operation of machines spurred the development of science and education. But in contemporary society the labor and engineer are opposed by the businessman, who is a throwback to the barbarous age in his motivation by deceit, fraud, profit, and perversion of technology to private purpose. Veblen thought that because human nature, as presently constituted, is, psychologically speaking, barbarian, it is ill adapted to a rational technological order based on the centrality of the machine.

The engineer, or technician, thus represents rationality to Veblen in the free development of the basic instincts and use of technology while the businessman, or capitalist, is an obstructive predatory reversion. Aaron describes them as "the metaphorical archetypes of two warring disciplines in the modern capitalist society."[56]

Veblen saw modern politics as "business politics" geared to pecuniary interests and mired in the residue of patriotic fervor in which the common man, though not benefiting from the chicanery, is captured by the spirit of national prestige and collective honor. The doctrine of natural rights, which antedated the modern business situation, grew up in the common sense of the community and assumed a constructive equality. But it did not contemplate "an abrogation of all conventional prescription." Thus natural liberty meant freedom from restraint on every prescriptive ground but that of ownership. Property rights were included in natural rights and inequality ensued. In America particularly, "the sacredness of pecuniary obligations" has "permeated the common sense of the community" and become almost "the only form of obligation that has the sanction of current common sense." The "conventional principle" of freedom of contract began to grow obsolete when it was established and now stands obstructively athwart the machine process. Consequently law and fact are in great discrepancy.[57]

* Unlike John Adams who saw the emulative propensity as rooted in human nature, Veblen saw it as a cultural phenomenon.

In the same vein, but with the added spur of personal animus, Veblen attacked the university in America as merely another business institution, controlled in part by absentee directors, reflecting in its attitude and many of its products the values and premises of the business community, and thwarting scholarship, true intellectual endeavor, and the instinct of workmanship. Like its business counterpart he indicted it as an anachronism and an institutionalized fraud.

Although Veblen concentrated on criticism, he looked forward to the development of "democratic commonwealths," which he described as "neighborly fellowships of ungraded masterless men given over to 'life, liberty and the pursuit of happiness' under the ancient and altogether human rule of Live and Let Live." Therein "loyal subjection to the national establishment of politicians would have no sacramental value, and patriotic fervor would be no more meritorious than any other display of intolerance."[58] In such societies men would live around the machine, in tune with their basic instincts, uninhibited by past conventions and the pecuniary motive, and directed by the engineers and technicians.

Religious Dissent: The Social Gospel

Except in its early years, American Protestantism was, generally speaking, strongly individualistic, stressing religion as an essentially private relationship of man to his Maker, and emphasizing personal piety and the cultivation of private virtues. The communitarian ideal which periodically manifested itself in separatist perfectionist societies was exceptional. More significant as qualifications of the general case in the early nineteenth century were Unitarianism and Transcendentalism. The former was ethical in its orientation, sanguine in its view of human nature, insistent upon the immanence of God, and consequently humanitarian in its outlook. As has already been seen, Transcendentalism, with its moral idealism and humanitarianism, was sharply critical of materialism. Also important as an influence upon later theological formulations was the thought of Horace Bushnell (1802–1876), who, around midcentury, attempted to humanize Calvinism by emphasizing the centrality and humanity of Christ and the law of love as the essence of religion.[59]

After the Civil War, when the impact of the Industrial Revolution with its dislocations and acquisitive ethic became evident, liberal Protestant theologians in the 1870's defined the following as social problems: unrestricted competition, the conflict between capital and labor, unethical business practices, corrupt urban politics, and urban poverty. In a reformulation of theology in the 1880's, Theodore Munger (1830–1910) stated that the new theology "holds that every man must live a life of his own . . . and give an account of himself to God: but it also . . . turns our attention to the corporate life of man here in the world. . . . Hence its ethical emphasis . . . holding that human society itself is to be redeemed." John Bascom (1827–1911), another progressive theologian and educator of the period, talked of the kingdom of heaven being realized in a "union between scientific research and religious insight; man and God, nature and the supernatural, working together for a perfect individual and social life. . . ." In like vein, Washington Gladden (1836–1918), who has been called "the father of the social gospel," pointed to "the power of Christian love" and stressed that economic problems were moral problems. "What men call 'natural law,'" he said with the Spencerians in mind, "by which they mean the law of greed and strife . . . is unnatural . . . the law of brotherhood is the only natural law." Criticizing socialism and communism as not conducive to individual development, Gladden pointed to cooperative effort, profit sharing, the recognition of labor unions and the right to strike, and public ownership of utilities.[60]

The economist Richart T. Ely (1854–1943) believed that the teachings of Christ appeared "from a purely scientific standpoint to contain just what is needed" to cure social ills, and that the Church could do "far more than political economists toward a reconciliation of social classes." And George Herron, a professor of Applied Christianity, declared flatly that "the Sermon on the Mount is the science of society," and that Cain was "the author of the competitive theory."[61]

The 1890's witnessed a complete acceptance of the Darwinian theory of evolution by progressive theologians. Evolution, the idea of progress, the expectation of the kingdom of God on earth, and the organic, solidaristic conception of society came to constitute the categories of Social Gospel thought.

Against the background of the above developments, the greatest proponent of the Social Gospel, Walter Rauschenbusch (1861–1918), wrote in the first two decades of the twentieth century. A teacher of church history for years, Rauschenbusch never forgot his ministry, as a young man, to the poor of New York's West Side. Spurred on by his conviction that "God is against oppression" and stands "on the side of the weak," he turned in middle age to preach social reform through the application of Christian principles rooted in what he believed to be the heart of Christ's teaching, the kingdom of God. Thus he wrote that "the essential purpose of Christianity was to transform human society into the kingdom of God by regenerating all human relations and reconstituting them in accordance with the will of God." Against the current individualism he declared: "The kingdom of God is . . . a collective conception involving the whole social life of man. It is not a matter of saving human atoms, but of saving the social organism. It is not a matter of getting individuals to heaven but of transforming the life on earth into the harmony of heaven." He related his thesis to the evolutionary hypothesis, stating: "Translate the evolutionary theories into religious faith, and you have the doctrine of the Kingdom of God. This combination with scientific evolutionary thought has freed the kingdom ideal of its catastrophic setting and its background of demonism, and so adapted it to the climate of the modern world."[62]

Rauschenbusch believed that "approximate political equality" was impossible of realization without "approximate economic equality" because politics inevitably is "consciously or unconsciously" dominated by economic interests. Whereas institutions such as the family, the church, the school and, to a degree, politics, are partly Christianized, the economic order is not. Rauschenbusch criticized the capitalist industrial system for being: (1) based on the principle of competition, which is "a denial of fraternity," and which plays to the lower instinct of selfishness rather than good will and solidarity; (2) "the last entrenchment of autocracy," completely lacking in democracy and thus contradicting American ideals as well as Christianity; and (3) the cause, through its profit motive, of unethical practices bringing evil effects, such as adulteration of foods, short weights, spurious advertising, overproduction, etc. In sum, it was "an unregenerate form of the social order, not based on freedom, love, and mutual service . . . but on autocracy, antagonism of interests, and exploitation."[63]

Frankly socialistic in outlook, Rauschenbusch saw the following as requisites of a Christian economic order—social justice, collective property rights, industrial democracy, approximate equality, and cooperation. In its duty to Christianize social life, Rauschenbusch warned, the church "must be content with inspiring the social movement with religious faith and daring, and it must not attempt to control and monopolize it for its own organization." Accordingly, he stated: "To repent of our collective social sins, to have faith in the possibility and reality of a divine life in humanity, to submit the will to the purposes of the kingdom of God, to permit the divine inspiration to emancipate and clarify the moral insight—this is the most intimate duty of the religious man who would help to build the coming Messianic era of mankind." Just as man is Christianized "when he puts God before self; political economy will be Christianized when it puts man before wealth." Although socialist thought is materialistic in its theory of human life and history, Rauschenbusch declared, "it is humane in its aims and to that extent is closer to Christianity" than the existing system.[64]

Rauschenbusch tied his hopes for a Christian socialism issuing in the Kingdom of God to the self-interest of the working class in its struggle for better working conditions and ultimate ownership of the means of production. "Christianity," he advised, "should enter into a working alliance with this rising class, and by its mediation secure the victory of these principles by a gradual equalization of social opportunity and power." He insisted that he was not asking a utopian solution. Because "there is no perfection for man in this life: there is only growth toward perfection," he declared that "at best there is always but an approximation to a perfect social order. The kingdom of God is always but coming."[65]

Social Gospel idealism, moderately and best expressed in Rauschenbusch's thought, was formulated in an atmosphere of optimism. It merged the scientific theory of evolution, the historical conception of progress and ancient Christian millennialism to propound the hope for the ultimate realization of the reign of justice—the replacement of competition with mutual goodwill, help, and love. Like the formulations of George and Bellamy, who also emphasized the importance of religion in the reconstruction of society, the Social Gospel stressed cooperation as a social principle and an organic solidaristic view of society. Like Ward, the Social Gospelers stressed the need for social science, but unlike Ward they made it ancillary to Christian purposes. Because of their preoccupation with remedying the shortcomings of an industrial order, there was a strong tendency in them, as in the work of George, Bellamy, Gronlund, and Ward, to stress environmental (especially economic) conditions and to downgrade original sin as the cause or occasion of social ills. Thus they came to place prime emphasis on "social sin" rather than individual transgressions. They facilely assumed that the biblical preachment of love, when merged with the self-interest of the working class, could approximate an entirely new and regenerated society—the Kingdom of God on earth.

The Individual and the Community: Josiah Royce (1855–1916)

Royce was born, in his own words, "a non-conformist" in California. Imbued with the spirit of the frontier, he believed that it is "the strong individual type of man that in a great Democracy is always necessary," a type which "the conditions of our larger democracy in more eastern regions tend far too much to eliminate." Unlike his individualistic contemporary from the West, Justice Stephen Field, Royce, in the course of his education, drank deeply of German Idealism and came to regard the individual not as an isolated atom but as an integral part of a whole. As a professor of philosophy at Harvard he moved in the course of a long academic career from a basic concern with the Absolute to the articulation of an ethic and a view of community which entailed a critical examination of American life.[66]

"Philosophers," Royce wrote late in life, "have actually devoted themselves in the main, neither to perceiving the world, nor to spinning webs of conceptual theory, but to interpreting the meaning of civilizations which they have represented, and to attempting the interpretation of whatever minds in the universe, human or divine, they believed to be real." As a philosopher in this sense Royce attempted to reinterpret the meaning of American life. Accepting Darwin's thesis, but not Social Darwinism, he wrote in 1881 that in studying evolution, "men have come to neglect other important matters" such as "the true end of life" and "the nature and grounds of human certitude." The result of this one-sidedness, he maintained, is "an unhappy division between the demands of modern thought and the demands of the whole indivisible nature of man." He saw the world as "of importance only because of the conscious life in it," and decried the Evolution theory "because of the subordinate place it gives to consciousness." Evolution is "a great truth, but it is not all truth" and "current thought is, in fact, *naif* and dogmatic, accepting without criticism a whole army of ideas because they happen to be useful as bases for scientific work." He particularly lamented the failure of Transcendentalism, which he called "the distinctly ethical thought-movement of the century." He affirmed his strong belief in the "great idea" of Transcendentalism—"that in the free growth and expression of the highest and strongest emotions of the civilized man might be found the true solution of the problem of life."[67]

Aiming his shafts at the proponents and practitioners of an ethic of individual self-interest, Royce later (1908) declared: "In brief, the people who have more rights than duties have gained a notable and distinguished ethical position in our modern world. The selfish we had always with us. But the divine right to be selfish was never more ingeniously defended, in the name of the loftiest spiritual dignity, than it is sometimes defended and illustrated today." Concerned basically with the phenomenon of human alienation in society, Royce thought that "the fact that, as in our present civilization, [the individual] is formally a free citizen, doesn't remove his character of self-estrangement from the social world in which he moves." Contemporary America, Royce thought, was economically interdependent but socially estranged: "But we are all able to understand our national position better when we see that our nation has entered in these days into the realm of the 'self-estranged spirit,' into the social realm where the distant and irresistible national government, however welcome its authority may be, is at best rather a guarantee of safety, an object for political contest, and a force with which everybody must reckon, than the opportunity for such loyalty, as our distinctly provincial fathers used to feel and express in their early utterances of the national spirit."[68]

More particularly, Royce pointed to three social phenomena bearing evil implications in America. First, the great freedom of social mobility contributed to physical and spiritual rootlessness. Second, the leveling tendency brought about by the modern ease of communication, spread of popular education, and centralization of industrial and social authorities, tended to bring men "to read the same daily news, share the same general ideals, to submit to the same overmastering social forces, to live in the same external fashions, to discourage individuality, and to approach a dead level of harassed mediocrity." Third, "the mob-spirit," which under certain modern conditions has "new form and power," threatened popular government with its hysteria and proneness to demagogy.[69]

Royce, then, came to be preoccupied with the problem of the alienated spirit in a society approaching proportions of giantism. This, he believed, could not be solved unless there emerged a new ethic emphasizing institutions and practices in which the individual can both be, and be recognized as, a person. His book, *The Philosophy of Loyalty* (1908), presented his conception which he equated with the moral law and saw as the vehicle for the full realization of liberty and democracy. Defining loyalty as *"the willing and practical and thoroughgoing devotion of a person to a cause,"* Royce set forth to redefine individualism. He criticized three current individualist conceptions, the concept of personal happiness as the end for man, the acceptance of the existing social order as a plan for life, and the aiming at power as the goal. To the first he replied that happiness defined as the satisfaction of desires is a mere accident "until your desires are harmonized by some definite plan of life." Thus, he declared, "you cannot adopt the pursuit of happiness as your profession." To the second choice Royce rejoined that with it "you find yourself without any determinate way of expressing your individuality." And to the worshipper of power he declared that the attainment of power is a matter of fortune, the lust for power is insatiable, and the power of man is infinitely surpassed by the power of external things.[70]

For an ethic based on a natural inclination Royce substituted the formalism of Kant, seeing as the first principle of a true individualism in ethics the moral autonomy of any rational person, and prescribing as the controlling norm, "loyalty to loyalty." To understand Royce's meaning it must first be noted that he thought that "whoever is loyal whatever be his cause, is devoted, is active, surrenders his private self-will, controls himself, is in love with his cause and believes in it." When loyalties conflict, however, what course is to be followed? Royce answered that "a cause is good, not only for me, but for mankind, in so far as it is essentially a *loyalty to loyalty*," that is, "an aid and a furtherance of loyalty in my fellows. It is an evil cause in so far as, despite the loyalty that it arouses in me, it is destructive of loyalty in the world of my fellows." He concluded by stating: "In so far as it lies in your power, so choose your cause and so serve it, that, by reason of your choice and of your service, there shall be more loyalty in the world rather than less.

And, in fact, so serve your individual cause as to secure thereby the greatest possible increase of loyalty among men." Thus Royce believed that all the principal moral virtues inhered of necessity in the norm of loyalty to loyalty because it requires men *"to respect loyalty in all men, wherever you find it."*[71]

Applying his moral principle in a critical analysis of America, he declared that loyalty is not sufficiently prominent in America as a social end; when it is emphasized, "it is far too seldom conceived as rationally involving loyalty to universal loyalty"; and the self-interested nature of corporations, labor unions, partisan groups and religious sects exemplifies this.[72]

Loyalty to loyalty allows for the development of personhood and leads, Royce thought, to the need to emphasize the development of a new provincialism on the one hand, and a higher organic community on the other. By "provincialism" Royce did not mean sectionalism or a narrow loyalty to local interests. Instead he envisioned a spirit "which makes people want to idealize, to adorn, to ennoble, to educate their own province, to hold sacred its traditions, to honor its worthy dead, to support and to multiply its public possessions." He believed that not the sect, the labor union, or the political party, but only a "widely developed provincial loyalty" could serve best as a mediator between "the narrower interests of the individual and the larger patriotism of our nation," and thus check "the estrangement of our national spirit from its own life."[73]

Regarding the individual as more than a reflection of social qualities and the community as more than an aggregate of individuals, Royce believed that a social organization can be translated into a community on the basis of a common subscription and loyalty to ideals. Drawing heavily in his book, *The Problem of Christianity*, upon St. Paul's concept of a *corpus mysticum* he declared:

Man the individual is essentially insufficient to win the goal of his own existence. Man the community is the source of salvation. And by the community I mean, *not* the collective biological entity called the human race, and not the merely natural community, which gives to us, as social animals, our ordinary moral training. . . . By man the community I mean man in the sense in which Paul conceived Christ's beloved and universal church to be a community,—man viewed as a conscious spiritual whole of life. And I say that this conscious spiritual community is the sole possessor of the means of grace, and is the essential source of the salvation of the individual.[74]

Community, or "the brotherhood of the loyal," is based on a common acceptance as part of the individual life of each member of the same past events and the same expected future events, thus fusing memory and hope. It is produced not by perception or cognition but by what Royce called interpretation. Communities of interpretation based on the principle of loyalty to loyalty would ascend, from the provincial through the national to the universal level on a nonconflicting basis. Specifically Royce thought that the Christian and scientific communities of interpretation were the compatible paradigms. The "beloved community," the highest form of loyalty, would be united in the ideals of freedom, democracy, and cooperation. It would bring together the limited truths contained in individualism and collectivism by developing autonomous persons who freely subscribe to the moral law rendered concrete in the hierarchy of communities, as opposed to organizations, from the provincial to the universal levels, and thus end man's social estrangement.[75]

Royce's ethic of loyalty is subject to the same basic criticism as Kant's ethic of duty. Thus it might be said that the reason that he is able to deduce from his concept of loyalty all of the principal virtues and duties as well as the conception of community is that he reads them into it. More important than technical criticism, however, is the fact that Royce attempted to deal on a philosophical plane with a major problem of modern life—human alienation—within a growing organizational interdependence. Not subscribing as an idealist to the current dogma that economic factors are determinative and ideas are merely epiphenomenal, nor to the naturalism which ultimately construes man in mere material terms, Royce, like Ward, believed that intelligence could change things, but he departed from Ward in believing that intelligence must be guided by the religious motivation of higher purpose. He attempted a task similar to that performed by T. H. Green in England—to reawaken the spirit of community by showing that person and community presuppose each other, that individual rights are not meaningful apart from the community, and that there can be no real common tie established on the basis of calculations of utility or consequences of actions. Nonetheless, because his thought was closer to Kant than to Emerson or even Brownson, it was and remained essentially alien in spirit to the American tradition. Disdaining the pursuit of happiness and accepting a rigoristic concept of loyalty as central, it failed to relate significantly in its concept of the Beloved Community to existing American social and political institutions, habits, and attitudes. As George Herbert Mead once put it, the American "did not think of himself as arising out of society so that by retiring into himself he could seize the nature of that society. On the contrary, the pioneer was creating communities and ceaselessly legislating changes within them. The communities came from him, not he from the community. And it followed that he did not hold the community in reverent respect." On this view Royce's work was less an interpretation of American life than an escape from its crudity.[76] Pragmatism proved to be a more authentic outgrowth of American consciousness than did absolute idealism.

Conclusions

Monistic naturalism and its counterpart, determinism, which underlay Sumnerian Social Darwinism, were adhered to, among dissenters to the Gospel of Wealth examined above, only by the Adams brothers, Gronlund, and, with a shift in emphasis to the pecuniary drive, Veblen. Ward, while thinking in Comtean terms of laws of development, modified his original monism by admitting a qualitative difference between mind and matter. George, Bellamy, and Rauschenbusch distinguished between matter and the immortal soul of man, while Royce, the idealist, thought in terms of the ultimate reality of the Absolute idea. In all of the thinkers who either qualified or spurned monistic naturalism, there was put forth a heavy emphasis on the ability of man with his power of intellect to survey and solve problems through cooperative effort. Each would also agree, contrary to the individualistic Social Darwinists, that the sphere of economics is not autonomous but subject to the strictures of morality. Thus "survival of the fittest" to them meant not survival in an unregulated competitive struggle but survival of the community through applied intelligence and cooperation, supplemented, in the case of all but Ward and Veblen, by Christian love. Likewise they stressed the need for economic equality, if political equality was truly to be realized. The emphasis on community in an organic, solidaristic sense was evidence of the rediscovery of the notion of a common good. In the Social Gospelers, and most particularly, Royce, the effort was in the direction of showing how the individual in the moral community realizes personhood. Equality and community as ideals brought a critique of the natural rights concept and stress upon the irrelevance of rights without the community.

At the same time that all of the thinkers (except Henry Adams) stressed the need for the positive, reform state, most of them denigrated government and politics and exalted administrative, technical, organizational, and scientific competence to solve society's problems. With the ubiquitous question of power apparently resolved by the stress on scientific intelligence and impartial administration, there went along a deemphasis on governmental forms. The anti-institutional bias of the dissenters' thought ran athwart the tradition of the Founding Fathers and bespoke a fundamental optimism which gave a utopian tinge to their thought, with the exception of the Adams brothers. In this light "society" or the "community" replaces "government," which is a transitory phenomenon, as the prime motive factor and vehicle of order. The Kingdom of God on earth, whether professedly Christian or not was as much the *eschaton* in the thought of the secularist Ward and the Marxist Gronlund, as it was in that of George, Bellamy, Rauschenbusch, and Royce.

Similarly, "science," or "administrative competence," replaces "prudence" and "compromise" as the means of social adjustment and progress. The emphasis on "science" was shared with the Spencerian thinkers; the difference lay in the conceptions of man and evolution embraced by the two parties.

NOTES

1. James Bryce, *The American Commonwealth* (New York, 1941, 2 vols.), I, 625, 628–629.

2. Timothy Paul Donovan, *Henry Adams and Brooks Adams* (Norman, Okla., 1961), pp. 3–14.

3. Introduction by Brooks Adams to Henry Adams, *The Degradation of the Democratic Dogma* (New York, 1919, 1947), p. 108; Henry Adams, *The Education of Henry Adams* (Modern Library Edition, New York, 1931), p. 266.

4. Adams, *Education,* p. 474. For Henry Adams' theory of history see: *Education,* pp. 474–498; *Historical Essays* (New York, 1891); *Mont St. Michel and Chartres,* (Garden City, 1959); and "The Rule of Phase Applied to History" in *Degradation,* pp. 261–305.

5. Adams, *Education,* pp. 421–422, 498.

6. Brooks Adams, *The Law of Civilization and Decay* (New York, 1898). Preface to second edition, viii, ix, xi; *Theory of Social Revolutions* (New York, 1913), p. 3.

7. Donovan, *op. cit.,* pp. 126–127.

8. Brooks Adams, *The New Empire* (New York, 1902), p. 41; *Degradation,* p. 109.

9. *Theory of Social Revolutions,* pp. 229, 45, 47, 48, 215.

10. *The New Empire,* p. 42.

11. *The Degradation of the Democratic Dogma,* p. vii.

12. Daniel Aaron, *Men of Good Hope* (New York, 1958), pp. 61, 62; G. R. Geiger, *The Philosophy of Henry George,* (New York, 1933), p. 33; Henry George, *Progress and Poverty,* in *Complete Works of Henry George* (New York, 1904, 10 vols.), I, 476, 477–478. On Utopianism in America see V. L. Parrington, Jr., *American Dreams* (Providence, R.I., 1947).

13. Henry George, *Social Problems* (New York, 1883, 1949), pp. 2, 8. *Progress and Poverty,* p. 504.

14. *Social Problems,* p. 2; *Progress and Poverty,* pp. 504, 505; Geiger, *op. cit.,* p. 340.

15. *Progress and Poverty,* pp. 3–219.

16. *Ibid.,* pp. 336–337, 403–404.

17. Cited in Aaron, *op. cit.,* p. 112; Edward Bellamy, *Looking Backward* (Boston, 1888), pp. 201, 60, 244.

18. *Looking Backward,* p. 328.

19. Cited in Aaron, *op. cit.,* p. 111; *Looking Backward,* pp. 68, 96, 130–131, 63, 90.

20. *Equality* (New York, 1897, 1933), pp. 7, 20, 18–19.

21. *Ibid.,* p. 19.

22. *Ibid.,* pp. 264, 267, 268.

23. On socialism in America see D. D. Egbert and Stow Persons (eds.), *Socialism and American Life* (Princeton, 1952, 2 vols.); Howard H. Quint, *The Forging of American Socialism* (Columbia, S.C., 1953); Charles and Mary Beard, *The Rise of American Civilization* (New York, 1945), II, 249–253, 547–549.

24. Laurence Gronlund, *The Cooperative Commonwealth,* Stow Persons (ed.), (Cambridge, Mass., 1965), pp. 7, 8.

25. *Ibid.,* pp. 67, 70, 71, 72, 73, 74, 77, 83, 94, 95.

26. *Ibid.,* pp. 137, 138, 139, 141–145, 146.

27. *Ibid.,* 146, 148.

28. *Ibid.,* 149, 153, 154, 156.

29. *Ibid.*, 226, 230.

30. *Ibid.*, 6, 231ff., 235, 4.

31. *Ibid.*, 145.

32. On Gronlund's influence, see Person's introduction to the 1965 edition of *The Cooperative Commonwealth*, p. xxii.

33. Werner Sombart, *Why Is There No Socialism in the United States?* (original German edition, Tübingen, 1906); David A. Shannon, *The Socialist Party of America* (New York, 1955), p. 258, quoted in Leonard B. Rosenberg "The 'Failure' of the Socialist Party of America," *The Review of Politics*, XXXI (July, 1969), 329–330. On this point see also Norman Thomas, *A Socialist's Faith* (New York, 1951), pp. 86–95. See also, Daniel Bell, "Marxian Socialism in the United States," in Egbert and Persons, *op. cit.*, I, 215–405.

34. Ward, *Glimpses of the Cosmos* (New York, 1913–1918, 6 vols.), III, 172; for Ward's life, see also Samuel Chugerman, *Lester F. Ward: The American Aristotle* (Durham, N.C., 1939), pp. 22–81.

35. *Dynamic Sociology* (New York, 1920, 2 vols.), I, 37–38; *The Psychic Factors in Civilization* (New York, 1st ed. 1893, 2nd ed. 1906), pp. 3, 135.

36. *Dynamic Sociology*, I, 15–16; *Psychic Factors*, pp. 260, 263–264; "Art is the Antithesis of Nature" (1884), essay reprinted in H. S. Commager, *Lester Ward and the Welfare State* (Indianapolis, 1967), p. 83.

37. *Dynamic Sociology*, I, 503, 32.

38. *Ibid.*, II, 212; I, 35; *Psychic Factors*, p. 3.

39. *Dynamic Sociology*, I, 513, 514, 516; II, 225, 213.

40. *Ibid.*, II, 227, 228.

41. *Ibid.*, II, 233, 234, 235.

42. *Ibid.*, II, pp. 235, 238.

43. *Ibid.*, II, pp. 241, 242, 245, 249.

44. *Ibid.*, II, pp. 251–252.

45. *Psychic Factors*, pp. 309, 310, 311.

46. *Ibid.*, p. 324ff.

47. Ward, *Pure Sociology*, (New York, 1903), p. 135.

48. *Dynamic Sociology*, I, 510, 518; II, 233, 240.

49. Ward, "Theory and Practice Are at War," *Glimpses of the Cosmos*, II, 353.

50. *Dynamic Sociology*, I, 518; quoted in H. S. Commager, (ed.), *Lester Ward and the Welfare State*, introduction by editor, xxxiv.

51. Quoted in Richard T. Ely, *Ground Under Our Feet* (New York, 1938), p. 140.

52. Merle Curti, *The Growth of American Thought* (New York, 1943), p. 593.

53. I am particularly indebted in the following discussion, to the treatment of Veblen by Daniel Aaron in his *Men of Good Hope* (New York, 1951), pp. 207–242, and Stow Persons, *American Minds* (New York, 1958), pp. 298–315.

54. Aaron, *op. cit.*, p. 219.

55. *Ibid.*, p. 220.

56. *Ibid.*, p. 223.

57. Veblen, *The Theory of Business Enterprise* (New York, 1904), pp. 268–275.

58. Cited in Aaron, *op. cit.*, p. 227.

59. See H. R. Niebuhr, *The Kingdom of God in America* (Hamden, Conn., 1956); Charles Howard Hopkins, *The Rise of the Social Gospel in American Protestantism 1865–1915* (New Haven, 1940); Persons, *op. cit.*, pp. 409–421; Ralph Gabriel, *The Course of American Democratic Thought*, pp. 308–330.

60. Hopkins, *op. cit.*, pp. 24, 35, 55, 63, 26, 31; Washington Gladden, *Social Facts and Forces* (New York, 1899), p. 220, quoted in Gabriel, *op. cit.*, p. 314.

61. Quoted in Hopkins, *op. cit.*, p. 77; Quoted in Hofstadter, *Social Darwinism*, p. 110.

62. Walter Rauschenbusch, *A Theology for the Social Gospel* (New York, 1917), p. 276; Rauschenbusch, *Christianity and the Social Crisis* (New York, 1907), pp. xiii, 65; Rauschenbusch, *Christianizing the Social Order* (New York, 1912), p. 90.

63. *Christianity and the Social Crisis*, pp. 263, 254; *Christianizing the Social Order*, Parts III and IV.

64. *Christianizing the Social Order,* pp. 336, 337; *Christianity and the Social Crisis,* pp. 348, 352, 371, 372.

65. *Christianity and the Social Crisis,* pp. 414, 420, 421.

66. Gabriel, *op. cit.,* p. 270; Josiah Royce, *Race Questions, Provincialism and Other American Problems* (Freeport, N.Y., 1908), p. 218.

67. Josiah Royce, *The Problem of Christianity* (New York, 1913, 2 vols.), II, 255; *Fugitive Essays by Josiah Royce* (Cambridge, Mass., 1925), pp. 301–305.

68. Josiah Royce, *The Philosophy of Loyalty* (New York, 1908), reprinted in Stuart Gerry Brown (ed.), *The Social Philosophy of Josiah Royce* (Syracuse, 1950), pp. 94, 159.

69. *Racism, Provincialism and Other American Problems,* pp. 57–108.

70. *The Philosophy of Loyalty,* pp. 75, 100–103.

71. *Ibid.,* 107, 78 114, 115, 128.

72. *Ibid.,* 148, 149, 155ff.

73. *The Philosophy of Loyalty,* pp. 161, 162.

74. *The Problem of Christianity,* I, 405–496.

75. *Ibid.,* I, 72, II, 49–51, 264–269.

76. George Herbert Mead, "The Philosophies of Royce, James, and Dewey in Their American Setting," *International Journal of Ethics,* XL, 222, 223.

PART EIGHT

THE PROGRESSIVE PERIOD AND AMERICAN POLITICAL THOUGHT

Chapter 21

PROGRESSIVISM AND PRAGMATISM

What you want is a philosophy that will not only exercise your powers of intellectual abstraction, but that will make some positive connexion with this actual world of finite human lines.
WILLIAM JAMES

The Populist reform movement of the last two decades of the nineteenth century was in its main features rural, fundamentalist, and sectional, whereas the succeeding Progressive movement (with which it merged after 1900) was principally urban, middle-class and national.* Populism was the first modern political movement of any significance in America to proclaim that the federal government has a prime responsibility to provide for the common good, and the first movement since the Jacksonian period to point up the problems attendant upon industrialization. It accepted unquestioningly the Jeffersonian agrarian myth— harking back to an imagined agrarian paradise existent in America before industrialization and the commercialization of agriculture. Almost as rigidly as the Marxists it preached the notion of society bifurcated into exploited producers (farmers, laborers, etc.), and exploiting parasites (trusts, monopolies, railroad companies, etc.). This view of society was informed by a psychology which saw a conspiracy of the money power against common folk and entertained a suspicion of the numbers, manners, mores, religion, race, and quality of the immigrant hordes flooding to American cities. Decidedly individualistic, the Populist wanted essentially a return to popular government through political and

* The earlier Liberal Republican "mugwump" reform movement of the late 1870's and the 1880's was led by educated professional men who believed that corruption in government might be minimized through civil service reform.

economic reform which would eliminate the advantages afforded in existing policy to the nonproducers.[1]

The development of a middle-class reform concept and its acceptance and propagation by educated professional and academic men gave Progressive thought a note of complexity and moderation which was not present in Populism. Progressivism sought to meet the dangers issuing from the "plutocracy" on the one hand, and from the poverty-stricken on the other. Thus Progressives urged reform of the business order to restore or preserve competition, to restrict and regulate monopoly, to extend credit to farmers, small businessmen, and consumers, and to minimize the exploitation of the worker by effecting standards to better the conditions and rewards of labor. Their principal division on economic lines was between those who sought to return to the old individualism by eliminating monopoly and those who sought to control monopoly by regulation. On the political level, following lines sometimes previously indicated by the Populists, some Progressives urged an extension of democracy through direct primaries, popular election of U.S. Senators, and the initiative, referendum, and recall, while others espoused the replacement of "politics" with "administrative expertise," effected through the short ballot, the commission and manager forms of municipal government, and regulatory commissions. Direct democracy was regarded as a means to purify and invigorate the political process, eliminate the corrupt city "Boss" and his "Machine," and control the expanded governmental regulatory power made necessary by the pursuit of social justice.[2]

On the national scene Progressivism was evidenced in "The New Nationalism" of the Hamiltonian, Theodore Roosevelt, and in "The New Freedom" of the Jeffersonian, Woodrow Wilson. Although the practical programs of the two Presidents were quite similar, there were some divergencies in objectives. Both sought the implementation of equality of opportunity, elimination of special privilege, conservation of the system of private property, establishment of federal graduated income and inheritance taxes, betterment of working conditions and the prohibition of corrupt practices. They also emphasized executive power—Roosevelt using Presidential powers as a steward of the public welfare and Wilson as a strong party and legislative leader. However, whereas Roosevelt conceded the inevitability of corporate combinations and industrial mergers and would meet them with a vigorous national supervision and regulation, Wilson thought in terms of the restoration of free competition. In the end, however, the New Freedom became, in effect, barely distinguishable from the New Nationalism.[3]

The historian of the American reform movement, Richard Hofstadter, has remarked that just as Spencer's philosophy was supreme in the age of enterprise, so pragmatism in the twenty years after 1900 became "the dominant American philosophy and breathed the spirit of the Progressive era." Indeed, pragmatism assumed the idea of progress, the value of democracy and reform through "good government," emphasizing particularly human manipulation and control of the environment against the Spencerian stress on the environmental control of man. And yet the Protestant fervor, readily evident in the thought and actions of Roosevelt and Wilson, which assumed a moral order and law denied by pragmatism, was at least equally a force. As Ralph Gabriel has written: "The pragmatism and the science worship of the Progressive Faith were veneers laid on ethical beliefs which in American history were as old as Puritanism."[4]

American Pragmatism

Pragmatism, as an attitude that tests the solutions to problems by their workability and which emphasizes direct, practical action in meeting the challenges of ever-changing situations, is a general American approach towards life that is probably as old as the first European settlements in the New World. Jonathan Edwards, for example, regarded action as the main index of belief and sincerity; in Jefferson's thought, as has been seen, there existed alongside an ideological commitment to the *a priori* natural rights doctrine, an empirical approach which besides assuming that all our ideas derive from experience, stressed experimentation in confronting specific questions; and the Founding Fathers regarded their institutional creations as experiments the workability of which their descendants were able to verify. Except for issues giving rise to the Civil War, Americans could point out that their disdain for ideology and regard for pragmatic compromise had maintained a national continuity and security within a free society.

As a reasoned philosophy of action, Pragmatism was an outgrowth of the reaction in the late nineteenth and early twentieth centuries to Spencerian determinism, Comtean positivism, British empiricism, and Hegelian absolutism. Accepting fully the Darwinian theory, it emphasized the centrality of evolutionary development, process, change, and the interaction of mind and nature. It manifested itself in two divisions, one of which stressed individualism, the other, society, groups, and the community. It also heavily stressed, particularly in its later phases, the supremacy of "scientific method." Its three main philosophical exponents were Charles Peirce, William James, and John Dewey, who will be examined in turn.[5]

Charles S. Peirce (1839–1914)

Peirce was a mathematical logician brought up in a family atmosphere of scientific inquiry who worked for most of his life as a research scientist employed by the United States Geodetic Survey. He was regarded by James as the author of Pragmatism, which he saw as "a particular application of an older logical rule, 'By their fruits ye shall know them.'" Reacting against the Cartesian notion that the mind can operate intuitively independent of language and signs as well as one's interests, concerns, and plans, Peirce taught that doubt produces inquiry, inquiry produces belief, and belief results in action. On this basis there can be no differences in ideas which do not produce differences in action. Man's reason is then not a faculty which is wholly taken up in contemplation of objects and events, but is a means of transforming them.

Peirce extolled the scientific method as a way of arriving at beliefs and testing hypotheses because it assumes a community of inquirers bound by the method, and its procedure is at once public and self-corrective. Nonetheless, because "every proposition which we can be entitled to make about the real world must be an approximate one; we can never hold any truth to be exact." Believing in the reality of general ideas (abstract predicates, relations, and laws) as conditions of the existential identity of objects in public space and time, he drew a sharp distinction between the true and the merely useful. Applying the pragmatic test to pragmatism itself, he concluded that its acceptance results in general as distinguished from particular ideas or habits of viewing things, or what he called the evolutionary growth of the idea of "law as a reasonableness energizing in the world."[6]

Peirce thought that man's purpose is "to actualize ideas of the immortal, ceaselessly prolific type," a task involving *"countless millions of individuals and extending through an infinite time,"* and embracing a conceived identification of one's interests with those of an unlimited community. Following relentlessly his emphasis on the primary reality of the general in contrast to the particular, and his stress on a community of inquirers, he stated: "The individual man, since his separate existence is manifested only by ignorance and error, so far as he is anything apart from his fellows, and from what he and they are to be, is only a negation." In fact, "personal existence is an illusion and a practical joke." Originally seeing community in an epistemological, nonnormative manner, he came to stress it in a religious and ethical sense with love and duty (the basis to him of cosmic evolution) at its center. Somewhat like Royce he wrote: "The very first command that is laid upon you, your quite highest business and duty, becomes . . . to recognize a higher business . . . a generalized conception of duty, which completes your personality by melting it into the neighboring points of the universal cosmos." Needless to say, this led him to reject Spencerian Social Darwinism outright.[7]

It is evident that while believing "that almost every proposition of ontological metaphysics is either meaningless gibberish . . . or else is downright absurd," and working to rehabilitate philosophy by scientific approaches, Peirce also intended to point philosophy, within the evolutionary framework, toward moral and religious ends. He also felt impelled to dissociate himself from voluntaristic, relativistic, and utilitarian interpretations of his teaching, emphasizing that theoretical investigation rather than utilitarian knowledge is the proper pursuit of science and philosophy. For every question, he maintained, there exists "a true answer" toward which "the opinion of man is constantly gravitating." Such answer "is independent, not indeed of thought in general, but of all that is arbitrary and individual in thought." His work was never brought together in one book and was accessible in his day only to readers of technical journals. Although he foreswore the term "pragmatism" (which he originally used), substituting for it "pragmaticism," a word he called "ugly enough to be safe from kidnappers," certain of the main elements of his thought, with some major qualifications and additions, were amplified and popularized in somewhat different ways by James and Dewey.[8]

William James (1842–1910)

James, a son of the mystical theologian, Henry James I, and a brother of the great novelist, Henry James II, was a physiologist turned psychologist and philosopher. A follower of the Spencerian approach, James in his late twenties became convinced of its grave shortcomings by the work of Peirce. Shortly thereafter he suffered an emotional breakdown from which he emerged to forswear determinism: "My first act of free will shall be to believe in free will." He worked thenceforth to vindicate man and free will against dogmatic, absolutistic, monistic systems in science, philosophy, and religion. Spencer's naturalism, Deism, Transcendentalism, Hegelian idealism, Lewis H. Morgan's law of progressive development, orthodox Christianity, and Newtonian physics all stood condemned as "block universe" approaches opposed to the open "pluralistic universe" which he propounded. James thought that every monistic philosophy was "too buttoned up and white-chokered, too clean-shaven a thing to speak for the vast slow-breeding, unconscious cosmos with its dread abysses and its unknown tides." Regarding Spencer, he declared that it "is not that he makes much of environment, but that he makes nothing of the glaring and patent fact of subjective interests which cooperate with the environment in moulding intelligence."[9]

Thus James believed that "our minds are not here simply to copy a reality that is already complete"; instead, mind "engenders truth upon society." In his book *Pragmatism* (1907), subtitled "A New Name for Some Old Ways of Thinking," he argued that ideas are not copies of objects but instruments developed to help men adequately treat with immediate experience. He was less interested in abstract truth than in what happens when an idea is accepted as true.* Pragmatism, he declared, combines "the scientific loyalty to facts and willingness to take account of them" with "the old confidence in human values and the resultant spontaneity whether of the religious or of the romantic type." It is at once a method (*"The attitude of looking away from first things, principles, 'categories,' supposed necessities; and of looking towards last things, fruits, consequences, facts."*), and a theory of truth (*"Ideas . . . become true just so far as they help us to get into satisfactory relation with other parts of our experience."*). In sum, James taught that a statement has meaning if either it or a belief in it has experimental consequences. Believing that philosophy is a function of temperament, he thought that this formula provided room for both "the tough-minded" (empiricists) and "the tender-minded" (rationalists).[10]

James's experimental theory of knowledge was thus joined to a voluntaristic theory of belief which holds that believing as an act of will is beyond the bounds of verification but within the limits of moral evidence. He talked of the "right to believe at our own risk any hypothesis that is live enough to tempt our own will," by which he meant not that we may act arbitrarily but that "our passional nature not only lawfully may, but must decide an option that . . . cannot by its nature be decided on intellectual grounds." Because James thought that the logic of life renders it imperative to believe more than can be empirically verified, and rejected *a priori* proofs, he concluded that the moral test is requisite. As Ralph Barton Perry has put it: "James's fideism† grows out of his empiricism. It is the sequel to the experimental method, and compensates for the limitation of empirically verifiable knowledge." He aimed at once to humanize science and guard moral responsibility against indifference and scientific skepticism. In Philip Wiener's words, "the will to believe was James's answer to agnostic evolutionism and the dehumanized pseudoscientific quest for metaphysical certainty."[11]

As a consequence James did not agree with the positivistic conclusion that "the question, Is this a moral world? is a meaningless and unverifiable question because it deals with something non-phenomenal." Similarly from a psychological point of view he defended theism, asserting that "God may be called the normal object of the mind's belief."

---

* James admitted, however, in his essay, "The Will to Believe," that "in our dealings with objective nature we obviously are recorders, not makers of the truth; and decisions for the mere sake of deciding and getting on to the next business would be wholly out of place." *Essays on Faith and Morals* (Cleveland and New York, 1967, Meridian Books), p. 51.

† Fideism involves an exclusive or fundamental reliance upon faith as the criterion of final truths and a distrust in the capacity of the intellect to attain certitude.

On the basis of his conception of the mind as triadic in structure, comprising impression, reflection, and reaction, he asserted that "materialism and agnosticism . . . give a solution of things which is irrational to the practical third of our nature," and that "gnosticism," or idealism, erroneously assures that "department Three of the mind, with its doings of right and . . . wrong, must be there only to serve department Two." Sounding a note of warning against skepticism on the one hand and system-building on the other, he stated: "This only is certain, that the theoretic faculty lives between two fires which never give her rest, and make her incessantly revise her formulations."[12]

Contrary to Peirce, whose emphasis was on general concepts, James, a professed nominalist, saw scientific theory as restricted in meaning to the individual perceptions and experiences in which it issues. Thus his thought remained thoroughly individualistic. Although he formulated no political or social theory, the implications of his approach for political thought are nonetheless broad. Besides his warning against the tendency of the rationalist mind to construct systems which defy reality, and of the scientific mind to deny the relevance of all but the experience which is verifiable on purely sensory grounds, his belief in the centrality of the individual as an active moral agent also has great significance.

Illustrative of this is James's early essay "Great Men, Great Thoughts, and the Environment." Concerned with the causes of changes in communities from generation to generation, he argued against Spencerian environmentalism that the difference between historical ages "is due to the accumulated influences of individuals, of their examples, their initiatives, and their decisions." The causes of production of great men "lie in a sphere wholly inaccessible to the social philosopher" who must "accept geniuses as data, just as Darwin accepts spontaneous variations." The only problem is how does the environment affect great men and how do they affect the environment? James answered that the environment "chiefly adopts or rejects, preserves or destroys, in short *selects* him. And whenever it adopts and preserves the great man, it becomes modified by his influence in an original and peculiar way. He acts as a ferment, and changes its constitution. . . ." It follows that "the mutations of society . . . are in the main due directly or indirectly to the acts or the example of individuals whose genius was so adapted to the receptivities of the moment, or whose accidental position of authority was so critical, that they became ferments, initiators of movement, settlers of precedent or fashion, centres of corruption, or destroyers of other persons, whose gifts, had they had free play, would have led society in another direction." Genius is thus "sudden, and, as it were, spontaneous." James concluded that "the reform movement would make more progress in one year with an adequate personal leader than as now in ten without one."[13]

James joined his conception of natural leadership to an advocacy of democracy as an act of faith. Against the criticism that democracy leads to "vulgarity enthroned and institutionalized," he held that "democracy is a kind of religion, and we are bound not to admit its failure." He asserted: "Our better men *shall* show the way and we *shall* follow them."

The notion that a people can run itself and its affairs autonomously is now well known to be the silliest of absurdities. Mankind does nothing save through initiatives on the part of inventors, great or small, and imitation by the rest of us—these are the sole factors active in human progress. Individuals of genius show the way, and set the patterns, which common people then adopt and follow. *The rivalry of the patterns is the history of the world.* Our democratic problem thus is stated in ultra-simple terms: Who are the kind of men from whom our majorities shall take their cue?[14]

James replied that in our democracy, where all else is shifting, college graduates form "the only permanent presence that corresponds to the aristocracy in older countries." He stressed that higher education "should enable us *to know a good man when we see him.*" Intellectuals must, through their critical sense, see that "affections for old habit, currents of self-interest, and gales of passion . . . that keep the human ship moving" are guided by "the ceaseless whisper of the more permanent ideals, the steady tug of truth and justice." Thus he thought that democracy could only succeed if, first of all, it was based upon moral individualism and firm belief, and second, if it recognized three tiers— the people at large, the educated persons who are able to discern a good from a bad man and who influence the people in his direction, and the leaders (great men) who are provided by nature. His strong individualism precluded his acceptance of the explanation of man by Peirce and Dewey in terms of communal relationships.[15]

James's faith in the future of free government was tempered by the advent of America as an imperialist power in 1898. On a pessimistic note recalling that of his great Spencerian contemporary, Sumner, he declared in 1903: "The country has once and for all regurgitated the Declaration of Independence and the Farewell Address, and it won't swallow again immediately what it is so happy to have vomited up. It has come to a hiatus. It has deliberately pushed itself into the circle of international hatreds and joined the common pack of wolves. . . ." The antidote to this unwholesome development, he thought, was for American liberals to join with "the great international and cosmopolitan liberal party, the party of conscience and intelligence the world over" in waging "the long, long campaign for truth and fair dealing which must go on in all the countries of the world until the end of time."[16]

James is most appreciatively understood if it be remembered that in contrast to Peirce his approach to philosophy was not logical but psychological, that his philosophy was a function of his own personal experience, temperament, and artistic concern with the ultimacy of the concrete, particular, unique, vital and colorful, and that his main objective was to vindicate man as a responsible, free moral being against reductionism and the snares of monistic system building. His emphasis on the primacy of action over contemplation, his preoccupation with how men *do* think, in contrast to the logician's concern with how men *should* think, his nominalism and his emphasis on the will to believe, led critics to characterize his thought as antiintellectual and voluntaristic. Like David Hume, whom he much admired, he was concerned with redeeming human nature by showing the limits of reason. Traditional philosophers could justifiably reply that ultimate truth is not made by man but confronts him, and that a will to believe, as such, demonstrates an absence of genuine belief which cannot be acted upon. Similarly, the Pragmatic approach, which has been likened by one of its protagonists to a corridor lined by doors in which personal preference determines which door is to be opened, assumes rather than reveals norms. With James the older individualistic liberal values were basic and his pragmatism was built thereupon; the method can and has been used with equal success by those of opposite inclinations to justify their positions.*

If this is so, James is significant because he aimed at the same goal which John Stuart Mill, when convinced of the value of poetry, sought —the modification of the liberal tendency to view the world in a prosaic way, and the recall of men to a sense of variousness and possibility. This, as the literary critic Lionel Trilling has said, implies the awareness of complexity and difficulty, against the inclination to constrict and render mechanical the conception of the nature of the mind.[17]

John Dewey (1859–1949)

Dewey was born of humble parentage in Vermont and died at the age of ninety after a lifetime of labor spent trying to reconstruct philosophy and education in light of evolutionary theory, scientific method, and the democratic ethos. Attracted early in life to the Hegelian emphasis on process and development, Dewey later rejected the Hegelian dialectic but retained a strong opposition to all dualisms such as subject/object, mind/body, fact/value, theory/practice, and individual/society.[18]

Just as Jefferson is the philosopher of American democracy in its rural

* James is cited favorably by Sorel and Mussolini. To be sure his voluntarism and pragmatic emphases might be seen as congenial to a romantic pragmatism of syndicalism and fascism. But his voluntarism and pragmatism are wedded to liberal values and to democracy as defined above.

phase, so Dewey is the philosopher of its industrial phase. Believing that the task of philosophy is "to clarify men's ideas as to the social and moral strifes of their own day," and to convert "such culture as exists into consciousness," he wrote: "If American civilization does not eventuate in an imaginative formulation of itself, if it merely rearranges the figures already named and placed—in playing an inherited European game— that fact is itself the measure of the culture which we have achieved." As Emerson, generations before, had called for an American intellectual declaration of independence, so Dewey asked for and worked toward American philosophical independence. If philosophy is both reflective of and interactive with a culture, then because America differs from the Greece of Plato and Aristotle, the England of Hume and Mill, and the Germany of Kant and Hegel, it can be true to itself only if it articulates coherently its own experience, conflicts, and aspirations.[19]

Dewey thought that modern philosophical difficulties could in good part be traced to the inability to shake off residues of classical thought which unwarrantedly distinguish between the so-called "real" world of universal ideas and forms, and the "inferior" phenomenal world of everyday experience. Reflecting the stratified socioeconomic situation of ancient Greece, and a cosmology of rest rather than motion, classical thought posited a "closed world" of "fixed forms" and "fixed ends" within a hierarchy of being, and an emphasis, derived principally from its master/slave class society, on the primacy of contemplation over action.[20]

Dewey regarded Sir Francis Bacon's aphorism, "Knowledge is power," as symbolic of the radical and laudatory innovation brought in Western thought by the rise of modern science. Instead of the Aristotelian methods of demonstration and persuasions, which "aim at a conquest of mind rather than of nature," Bacon propounded the "logic of discovery" which "looks to the future" and envisions progress in the consequences of its application. Modern science disdains teleology and fixed ends, discards the concept of a hierarchy of being and aims not at following nature as a regulative principle but at manipulating and controlling it. When nature is no longer seen as "the slave of metaphysical and theological purpose," it is "subdued to human purpose." Experimentalism results in "the substitution of a democracy of individual facts equal in rank for the feudal system of an ordered gradation of general classes of unequal rank."[21]

Dewey regretted that the success of scientific method in controlling nature was not extended to the realm of philosophy. To correct this error is the task of a philosophic reconstruction that "will regard intelligence not as the original shaper and final cause of things, but as the purposeful energetic reshaper of those phases of nature and life that obstruct social well-being." In pursuit of this objective he criticized both British empiricism and German idealism. The modern world had offered to it in philosophy "only an arbitrary choice between two hard and fast opposites: Disintegrating analysis or rigid synthesis; complete radicalism neglecting and attacking the historic past as trivial and harmful, *or* complete conservatism idealizing institutions as embodiments of eternal reason."²²

In his philosophic reconstruction Dewey proceeded from what he called a change in the actual nature of experience brought about not only by scientific method but by the development of a psychology based on biology. In this view, experience is seen as "a matter or an 'affair' of interaction of living creatures with their environment"; it is no longer merely empirical but experimental, involving both "doing" and "under-going," and producing "consequences for life." The passive mind of empiricist thought and the moldlike mind of rationalist thought are re-placed by a conception of knowledge as "not something separate and self-sufficing, but . . . involved in the process by which life is sustained and evolved."²³

Implicit in this view is the rejection of what Dewey called "the spectator conception of knowledge" which sees the mind as copying that which exists outside of it and which, Dewey charged, disregards the dynamic character of life and the interactive influence of organism and environment. The world is not ready-made, ends are not fixed, reality is not static; instead, "the world or any part of it as it presents itself at any given time is accepted or acquiesced in only as *material* for change." Like Marx, who insisted that philosophers must go beyond interpreting the world to changing it, Dewey declared that philosophy "must assume a practical nature; it must become operative and experimental." In other words, philosophy must aim not at understanding but at power.²⁴

Dewey argued that the logic of discovery or inquiry (scientific method) must replace formal logic in philosophy and the study of man. In his view "knowing begins with specific observations that define the problem and ends with specific observations that test a hypothesis for its solution." If hypotheses succeed in this office, "they are reliable, sound, valid, good, true. . . ." Dewey thus substituted a coherence theory of truth for the older correspondence theory. This conclusion followed logically from his insistence that thinking is "instrumental to a control of the environment."²⁵

In his consideration of moral theory Dewey extended his criticism of the classical emphasis on fixed ends and argued that application of experimentalism to morals demands denial of any *summum bonum*. Instead it requires an advance to "a belief in a plurality of changing, moving, individualized goods and ends and . . . a belief that principles, criteria, laws are intellectual instruments for analyzing individual or unique situations." The burden of the moral life is thus shifted from pursuing final ends to detecting and planning remedies for particular ills. Consequently, "the aim of living" is not perfection but "the ever-enduring process of perfecting, maturing, refining"; in short, "growth itself is the only moral end."[26]

In line with his conception of life as developmental change and his disdain of dualism, Dewey rejected the positivistic disjunctions of fact and value and of science and moral preference. He contended that not only statements of what is desired but statements of what ought to be desired are verifiable scientifically. Relying on empirical considerations alone, he argued that just as we cannot say that something is red until we are sure that certain test conditions are satisfied, such as normality of vision, adequacy and correctness of light, etc., so we can conclude that something is desirable only if the conditions of moral normality are shown to exist. In this sense to say that something is desirable is at once a factual and a normative statement which implies moral obligation. Dewey, at this point, was close to asserting a fundamental moral uniformity of human nature which is manifest under ideal conditions, a viewpoint quite similar to the classic natural law thought which he disdained. To the modern logical positivist, following in train of Hume's trifurcation of logic, fact, and value, Dewey must logically reach from these premises the absurd conclusion that all objectively true statements are *ipso facto* normative and entail obligation. Thus the statement that this thing is "objectively red" must also mean that it "ought to appear red."[27] But this objection might conceivably be met by distinguishing, as Dewey does, between "facts which are what they are independent of human desire and endeavor and facts which are to some extent what they are because of human interest and purpose."[28] Be that as it may, the question of the nature of so-called normal conditions is the nub of the problem and is presumably answered by Dewey's conception of the community established on the basis of, and operating in accordance with, scientific method. Joined to the premise that growth is the only norm and that goods and values are inherent in particular situations, Dewey's ethical instrumentalism ultimately presupposes specific norms which are arrived at independent of his method.

Dewey's approach to social and political philosophy was in line with his conception of experience as a matter of interaction between organism and environment, his conception of logic as experimental inquiry concerned not with causes but consequences, and his conception of morality as dealing with particular goods which are not given *a priori* but are discoverable in concrete situations. Thus he rejected on the political plane, as he had on the philosophical, empiricism and idealism; the former for its emphasis on individuality as ready-made; the latter for its propensity to reify society and the state. Both are fundamentally wrong, Dewey asserted, because they are "committed to the logic of general notions under which specific conditions are to be brought." Political philosophy must not be concerned with the arid task of showing relationships between ideas but with the solution of concrete problems by supplying hypotheses to be tested in projects of reform. Heretofore political theories have sprung from the error of "the taking of causal agency instead of consequences as the heart of the problem." Whereas inquirers in politics who confine themselves to "facts" substantially agree, theorists who deal with abstract questions such as the nature and justification of the state greatly disagree. It follows that "it is not the business of political philosophy and science to determine what the state in general should or must be. What they may do is to aid in creation of methods such that experimentation may go on less blindly."[29]

With political philosophy reduced to the role of refining methodology and formulating hypotheses, Dewey, in examining the question of the state, took his point of departure "from the objective fact that human acts have consequences upon others, that some of these consequences are perceived, and that their perception leads to subsequent effort to control action so as to secure some consequences and avoid others." Consequences prove to be of two kinds, those which directly affect parties to a transaction and those which affect others not immediately concerned. When the latter consequences, which Dewey called "indirect," are recognized and an effort ensues to regulate them, "something having the traits of a state comes into existence." In this light he defined the "public" as comprising "all those who are affected by the indirect consequences of transactions to such an extent that it is deemed necessary to have those consequences systematically cared for." A public is organized into a state through its government and the state is "a distinctive and secondary form of association, having a specifiable work to do and specified organs of operation." Just as publics and states vary with spatial and temporal conditions, so do their concrete functions. Since there is "no antecedent universal proposition which can be laid down because of which the functions of a state should be limited or expanded," their extent "is something to be critically and experimentally determined."[30]

Dewey maintained that a community is in existence "wherever there is conjoint activity whose consequences are appreciated as good by all singular persons who take part in it, and where the realization of the good is such as to effect an energetic desire and effort to sustain it in being just because it is a good shared by all." Democracy, whose moral meaning "is found in resolving that the supreme test of all political institutions and industrial arrangements shall be the contributions they make to the all-around growth of every member of society," is "the idea of community life itself." Accordingly, Dewey thought that democracy is "an absurdity where faith in the individual as individual is impossible" and that "this faith is impossible when intelligence is regarded as a cosmic power, not an adjustment and application of individual tendencies."[31]

Individualism is, then, in Dewey's eyes, at the base of democracy, and democracy, when extended to all aspects of association and life within the state, is equivalent to the great desideratum, community. Dewey's individualism, however, differs radically from that of Locke, the Founding Fathers, and the Spencerians, as well as that of James. He rejected outright the doctrine of natural rights, contending that "they exist only in the kingdom of mythological social zoology." He argued: "Men do not obey laws because they think these laws are in accord with a scheme of natural rights. They obey because they believe, rightly or wrongly, that the consequences of obeying are upon the whole better than the consequences of disobeying." Similarly, he declared that "the actual 'laws' of human nature are laws of individuals in association, not of beings in a mythical condition apart from association." The contract theory of the origin of the state is demonstrably false; but historically it had a functional value because "it testified to a growing belief that the state existed to satisfy human needs and could be shaped by human intention and volition." Nevertheless, Lockian individualism "bequeathed to later social thought a rigid doctrine of natural rights inherent in individuals independent of social organization," and thus established a theoretical basis for a strong opposition to collective social action.[32]

Because men can only be understood as interactive with each other and the environment, reconstructed individualism, Dewey maintained, discards the notions of precedent rights and a ready-made individuality and focuses on the end of individual growth or self-realization within community, recognizing that "effective liberty is a function of the social conditions existing at any time." In light of this he restated the end of liberalism as "the liberation of individuals so that realization of their capacities may be the law of their life."[33]

In *Freedom and Culture* (1939), Dewey wrote that "the problem of freedom of cooperative individualities" is one "to be viewed in the context of culture." Seeking on this basis to extract what remained valid in Jeffersonian thought, when excised of its Lockian individualism, he construed "natural rights" to mean "ideal aims and values to be realized—aims which, although ideal, are not located in the clouds but are backed by something deep and undestructible in the needs and demands of humankind." He praised Jefferson's high regard for experiment and change and his stress on "face-to-face associations" in the local wards as the foundation of free government. The latter was completely compatible with Dewey's belief that "democracy must begin at home, and its home is the neighborly community." Finally Jefferson, as

Dewey approvingly read him, held that property rights are created by the social pact and thus subject to regulation, and that the pursuit of happiness demanded equality of rights and freedom from economic as well as political restraint. In his day Jefferson could reasonably see his ideals as best implemented in a *laissez-faire* agrarian political democracy; in the present era the same principles demand positive social and political action which interferes in the economic sphere to effect a realization of full equality and freedom. Thus Dewey believed that action in the essential spirit of Jeffersonian thought in an industrial age implied changes in "the forms and mechanisms through which inherent moral claims are realized."[34]

On these grounds Dewey proclaimed that "as believers in democracy we have not only the right but the duty to question existing mechanisms of, say, suffrage and to inquire whether some functional organization would not serve to formulate and manifest public opinion better than the existing methods." Universal suffrage, he maintained, proceeded from the outmoded idea that "intelligence is an individualistic possession." Concerning political parties and parliamentary government, he added: "The idea that the conflict of parties will, by means of public discussion, bring out necessary public truths is a kind of political watered-down version of the Hegelian dialectic, with its synthesis arrived at by a union of antithetical conceptions."[35]

Dewey prescribed as *the* remedy for the crisis in democracy, "approximation to use of scientific method in investigation and of the engineering mind in the invention and projection of far-reaching plans." It is not stretching the truth to say that he believed that science, defined as cooperative, objective inquiry testing hypotheses and their effectiveness in resolving problems, is democratic, and that democracy, in its developed and extended sense, is scientific. Scientific method is the instrument which in application is not only revelatory of situational ends but has attached to its successful use the highest moral and social virtues, such as "objectivity," "impartiality," "cooperation," "willingness to hold belief in suspense," "ability to doubt until evidence is obtained," "willingness to go where evidence points instead of putting first a personally preferred conclusion," etc. Similarly, scientific method "is the sole guarantee against wholesale misleading by propaganda" and even more important, "it is the only assurance of the possibility of a public opinion intelligent enough to meet present social problems." Finally, "if control of conduct amounts to conflict of desires with no possibility of determination of desire and purpose by scientifically warranted beliefs, then the practical alternative is competition and conflict between unintelligent forces for control of desire." Dewey thus saw democracy, implemented in scientific method, as the answer to the crucial question, "what kind of culture is so free in itself that it conceives and begets political freedom as its accompaniment and consequence?"[36]

To the charge that the common man is not endowed with the degree of intelligence demanded for the successful use of scientific method, Dewey answered: "It is not necessary that the many should have the knowledge and skill to carry on the needed investigations; what is required is that they have the ability to judge of the bearing of the knowledge supplied by others upon common concerns.[37] He thought that "the indictments that are drawn against the intelligence of individuals are in truth indictments of a social order that does not permit the average individual to have access to the rich store of the accumulated wealth of mankind in knowledge, ideas and purposes." On this basis he stressed socialization of the forces of production and social planning by democratic means, as well as a progressive approach to universal public education which discards the fixed curriculum and focuses upon learning by doing, through the cooperative solution of problems and the critical examination of existing social and political institutions.[38]

Democracy, understood as applied social scientific inquiry diffused through the whole of a culture, was regarded by Dewey as having the self-corrective value of the scientific method. Like the latter, however, it cannot be used to justify itself without circular reasoning. Dewey would reply that its justification lies in the consequences it produces in meeting the felt needs of man. But in the end, like James, he is led to regard democracy as a faith. Thus democracy demands "faith in the individual as individual"; it presupposes "believers"; and "in the long run," it "will stand or fall with the possibility of maintaining the faith and justifying it by works."[39]

In commenting upon Dewey's thought it must first be said that although he is professedly disdainful of *a priori* premises, his thought is, like all philosophies, based upon certain ultimate assumptions: reality is process; human intelligence is functional; formal logic has no objective existential references; that which concerns man and his activity is alone significant; man is to be understood in naturalistic terms; growth is the only moral end; scientific method is the organon by which man, society, and the quality of human life will be bettered and the free culture of democracy realized; knowledge and reflection arise only when we are confronted with problematic situations; science grows out of practical needs; and philosophy is reflective of the civilization in which it arises.

Morris Cohen (1880–1943), an American philosopher inclined toward Platonism, and a contemporary of Dewey, has critically analyzed Dewey's thought. Concerning his assumption that all knowledge originates in problematic situations, Cohen answers, "sustained reflection or study may occur more often in our leisure than when we are in practical trouble." To Dewey's notion that ideas are functions of particular historical societies and his specific contention that the doctrine of a single ultimate end is a product of a dead feudal society, Cohen replies: "I should not admit that any doctrine, say, for instance, representative government, is bad because it originated in a system of society which no longer exists." Cohen adds that "reflections on the nature of number, time, space, mind, matter, and knowledge do not vary with political and economic views or changes." In subordinating theoretical knowledge to practical moral ends and seeing philosophy as relevant only if it affords guidance to action, Dewey overlooks the fact that "the special duty of the philosopher is to put the pursuit of truth first whether his fellow citizens are interested or not; and this often requires ethical neutrality or indifference to the issues of the day." Dewey was apparently unappreciative of "the classic values of solitude," seeing rest and play as instrumental to further activity. In a sense, Cohen continues, his is a neo-stoic philosophy which in its insistence "that our thoughts should be directed to the ends of ordinary conduct" works to "dry up the spring of intellectual vision."[40]

Dewey's belief that formal logic has no existential reference is based upon an unwarranted distinction between the existence of objects and the purely procedural character of logical and mathematical relations. Cohen shows that Dewey nonetheless rejects certain doctrines as self-contradictory, a rejection which "is surely not based on the assumption that it is impossible to think or express contradictions, for that is precisely what the holders of these doctrines are accused of actually doing." Because "the principle of contradiction . . . asserts something in regard to existence and not merely in regard to thought or . . . language," Cohen continues, it follows that logic must be viewed "as the simplest chapter in ontology, as a study of the exhaustive possibilities of all being." Admittedly we cannot deduce specific matters of fact from the laws of logic "but, without assuming that the laws of logic are relevant to existence, no inquiry can be launched, much less concluded." Similarly in regard to mathematics, which Dewey sees as liberated "from any kind of ontologic reference," Cohen replies: "But if the marks or sounds, two plus two equals four, had no reference whatsoever to anything beyond themselves, they would have no meaning." Similarly, Dewey's conception of logic as merely descriptive of those methods of discovery that are successful overlooks the fact that while science knows of methods of verification, there are no methods of discovery. If there were, Cohen remarks, "all we need would be discovered, and we would not have to wait for rare men of genius." Cohen admits that the logical consequences of a proposition are essential to its meaning but adds that Dewey's assertion that "the antecedents of a proposition do not 'supply meaning and verity' seems surprising coming from one who places so much emphasis on the . . . origin of our ideas."[41]

Dewey's historical views of the history of science and philosophy are themselves in good part mythical. Cohen writes: "The hope of those who, following Bacon, aim at a reconstruction of philosophy on the model of experimental science is generally supported by a conventional but apocryphal history which is plausible only because ancient and medieval science are for linguistic reasons not popularly accessible." Ancient science was experimental as well as demonstrative while modern science is demonstrative as well as experimental. Just as it is "a myth to suppose that modern science arose when it suddenly occurred to a few men to discard the authority of Aristotle and to examine nature for themselves," and that modern science has abandoned "the basic Hellenic idea of a constant order, law, or relation, in the flux of phenomena," so it is "simply untrue that change rather than fixity is now a measure of 'reality' or energy of being."[42]

Regarding Dewey's ethical views, Cohen contends that his denial of an ultimate substantive good and his advocacy of concentration on removal of specific evils "prevent him from formulating any adequate theoretic guide, any Ariadne thread out of the labyrinthian mazes of experience which philosophy should offer if it is to be of any help in the analysis of diverse social problems." Dewey also apparently ignores "the intensity with which people do divide on specific social issues," while he scores philosophic differences on abstract questions. His teaching that every situation determines its own concrete goods is of no great aid because "the world does not break itself up into a number of distinct atomic situations each with a determinate good." In fact, "that which will remove some economic evil may bring about worse political ones, and vice versa." Left with "no common unit to measure heterogeneous social values," we cannot fulfill the advice "to remove one evil at a time." Similarly we are not helped by the saying "that what is good in any situation cannot be answered *a priori* but depends on actual conditions," if we are afforded "no guide as to nature of the dependence."[43]

Dewey's conviction that democracy is capable of solving particular problems as they arise on the basis of scientific inquiry independent of fixed ends appears to contradict his emphasis on broad social engineering and planning which presuppose not merely prior agreement in the identification of problems but prior agreement concerning goals which illuminate the interrelationship of problems and indicate the direction and sequence of their solution. Since the consequences which one person or group sees as desirable may readily conflict with those which others regard desirable, because of differences in their assumptions regarding the nature and definition of problems and what the desirable consists in, the abiding political problem of reaching adjustment among conflicting claims through compromise remains. In like vein, Dewey's advice that men should substitute "faith in the active tendencies of the day for dread and dislike of them" overlooks the need for a principle of selection which allows men to distinguish between evil and good tendencies.[44]

Because the pragmatic test of truth does not and cannot as such settle philosophic, moral, and political issues, Dewey's thought is strongly humanistic, liberal, and democratic only because (1) somewhat like Royce, who deduced specific substantive principles from the formal principle of loyalty, he tends to read into socially applied "scientific method," the fundamental liberal values; and (2) his instrumentalist thought and approach simply assume these values. Dewey's thought is thus not understandable apart from historical American liberalism, which is so ingrained in him that he feels the need only to extend it to meet modern problems, not to question it. To say otherwise is to assume the validity of that which Dewey was unable to prove—experimentalism as such results in humanistic liberalism.

Dewey differed from James in insisting that social rather than particular consequences be considered relevant. Whereas James focused on the genius or great man as the prime mover in history, Dewey, like Peirce, looked to the group and articulated an individualism which saw men as realizing themselves within human association. Whereas James talked in terms of an open universe and did not preclude consideration of things higher than man, Dewey was completely anthropocentric with a public conception of philosophy which is highly optimistic in its belief that man, through the application of scientific method to the moral and social realms, will add conquest of self to his conquest of nature. There is in his thought no idea of limits; instead he exalts the possibilities of intelligence as power. To quote Cohen again, Dewey's philosophy contains "no sense . . . of the loneliness of the individual human soul, facing the indifferent earth, sea or sky, or the eternal procession of the stars that ever mock man's vain pretension to exalt himself as the master of the universe."[45] Regardful of the past only insofar as it bears on the present in a practical sense, and concerned with the present as the setting in which a better future can be realized, Dewey might be said to have lacked the spiritual depth, humility, and sense of fallibility which James possessed, and which render James more meaningful to man in his contemporary plight.

NOTES

1. On Populism see Richard Hofstadter, *The Age of Reform* (New York, 1955); John D. Hicks, *The Populist Revolt* (Minneapolis, 1931); Norman Pollack, *The Populist Response to Industrial America* (Cambridge, Mass., 1962).

2. Hofstadter, *op. cit.*, pp. 131–212.

3. Roosevelt's pronouncement on "The New Nationalism" is conveniently found

in William H. Harbaugh, *The Writings of Theodore Roosevelt* (Indianapolis and New York, 1967), p. 315ff. See also Woodrow Wilson, *The New Freedom* (New York, 1913), and Arthur S. Link, *Wilson,* II, *The New Freedom* (Princeton, 1947).

4. Hofstadter, *Social Darwinism in American Thought,* p. 123; Gabriel, *op. cit.* p. 338.

5. On Pragmatism as a philosophy, see Herbert Schneider, *A History of American Philosophy,* pp. 515–571; W. H. Werkmeister, *A History of Philosophical Ideas in America* (New York, 1949), pp. 171–237 and 521–561; John E. Smith, *The Spirit of American Philosophy* (New York, 1963); and Philip P. Wiener, *Evolution and the Founders of Pragmatism* (Cambridge, Mass., 1949, paperback edition, 1965).

6. *Collected Papers of Charles S. Peirce,* Chas. Hartshorne and Paul Weiss (eds.) (Cambridge, Mass., 1931–1935, 6 vols.) (References are given to volume and paragraph numbers), V, 465; I, 161; Wiener, *op. cit.,* p. 91. For a short, succinct summation of Peirce's thought, see Smith, *op. cit.,* Chap. 1.

7. *Collected Papers,* II, 763; V, 317; IV, 68; I, 673. See also Joseph P. De Marco, "Peirce's Concept of Community . . . ," *Transactions of the Charles S. Peirce Society,* VII (Winter, 1971), 24–36.

8. *Ibid.,* I, 104; Smith, *op. cit.,* pp. 26–37; cited in Schneider, *op. cit.,* p. 517.

9. Ralph Barton Perry, *The Thought and Character of William James* (Boston, 1935), I, 323; 475ff.; Morris Cohen, *American Thought* (Glencoe, Ill., 1954), p. 288; Gabriel, *op. cit.,* pp. 282ff.; H. S. Commager, *The American Mind* (New Haven, 1950), p. 92. For a short summation and appraisal of James' thought, see Smith, *op. cit.,* pp. 38–79.

10. Perry, *op. cit.,* II, 479; Wm. James, *Pragmatism* (New York, 1907), pp. 54–55.

11. "The Will to Believe," in *Essays on Faith and Morals* (Cleveland and New York, 1967), pp. 60, 42; Perry, *op. cit.,* I, 456; Wiener, *op. cit.,* p. 125.

12. William James, "The Sentiment of Rationality," in *Esays on Faith and Morals,* p. 105; William James, "Reflex Action and Theism," *ibid.,* pp. 116, 123, 126, 128, 138.

13. "Great Men, Great Thoughts and the Environment," *The Atlantic Monthly,* XLVI (October, 1880), 441, 442, 445, 446, 454–455.

14. William James, "The College Bred," in *Memories and Studies* (New York, 1911), pp. 317, 318.

15. *Ibid.,* pp. 319, 315–316, 320.

16. Address by Wm. James, "Report of the Fifth Annual Meeting of the New England Anti-Imperialist League" (Boston, Nov. 28–30, 1903), pp. 21–26; cited in Wiener, *op. cit.,* p. 126.

17. Lionel Trilling, *The Liberal Imagination* (New York, 1953, Doubleday Anchor Paperbacks), pp. 8–10.

18. Dewey wrote more than thirty books in his lifetime, the chief of which are: *The Influence of Darwin on Philosophy* (New York, 1910); *Ethics* (with James Tufts) (New York, 1908); *Reconstruction in Philosophy* (New York, 1920); *Experience and Nature* (Chicago, 1925); *Human Nature and Conduct* (New York, 1922); *The Public and its Problems* (New York, 1927); *Logic: The Theory of Inquiry* (New York, 1938); *Liberalism and Social Action* (New York, 1935); and *Freedom and Culture* (New York, 1939). For secondary works on Dewey, see especially Smith, *op. cit.,* pp. 115–160 and Morton White, *op. cit.,* pp. 47–58, 128–146, 147–160, 203–219.

19. *Reconstruction in Philosophy,* p. 26; *Philosophy and Civilization* (New York, 1931), p. 10.

20. *Reconstruction in Philosophy,* p. 18ff.

21. *Ibid.,* pp. 29, 31, 33, 71, 66.

22. *Ibid.,* pp. 50, 51, 99–100.

23. *Ibid.,* pp. 86, 87.

24. *Ibid.,* pp. 112, 114, 121.

25. *Ibid.,* pp. 148, 156; *Essays in Experimental Logic* (New York, 1953), p. 30.

26. *Ibid.,* pp. 162–163, 165, 177.

27. For a consideration of this phase of Dewey's thought, see White, *op. cit.,* pp. 212–218.

28. *The Public and Its Problems,* p. 7.

29. *Reconstruction in Philosophy,* pp. 188, 192; *The Public and Its Problems,* pp. 20, 34.

30. *The Public and Its Problems,* pp. 12, 15–16, 71, 74.

31. *Ibid.,* pp. 149, 148; *Reconstruction in Philosophy,* p. 186; *The Influence of Darwin on Philosophy,* p. 59.

32. *Liberalism and Social Action,* pp. 17, 41, 4; *Reconstruction in Philosophy,* p. 44.

33. *Liberalism and Social Action,* pp. 34, 56. See also Dewey's work, *Individualism Old and New* (New York, 1930), *passim.*

34. *Freedom and Culture,* pp. 23, 156, 160, 157; *The Public and Its Problems,* p. 213.

35. *Freedom and Culture,* p. 158; *Liberalism and Social Action,* pp. 71, 72.

36. *Liberalism and Social Action,* pp. 73, 80; *Freedom and Culture,* pp. 149, 153, 6.

37. *The Public and Its Problems,* p. 209.

38. *Liberalism and Social Action,* p. 52.

39. *The Influence of Darwin on Philosophy,* p. 59; *Freedom and Culture,* p. 126.

40. Morris R. Cohen, *Studies in Philosophy and Science* (New York, 1949), pp. 158–159, 157, 161, 166, 173; Cohen, *American Thought,* p. 295.

41. Cohen, *Studies,* pp. 150, 151, 147, 149.

42. *Ibid.,* pp. 153, 154, 155.

43. *Ibid.,* pp. 172, 173.

44. The Dewey quote is from *Reconstruction in Philosophy,* p. 212; Cohen, *Studies,* p. 169.

45. Cohen, *American Thought,* p. 299.

Chapter 22

PRAGMATIC JURISPRUDENCE AND POLITICAL SCIENCE

Our Constitution. . . . is an experiment, as all life is an experiment.

OLIVER WENDELL HOLMES

Who likes may snip verbal definitions in his old age when his world has gone crackly and dry.

ARTHUR F. BENTLEY

Like the formulation of public policy, the disciplines of law and political science were heavily influenced in (and beyond) the Progressive era by the dominant pragmatic outlook. Above all they were dedicated to what was called "realism," a turning aside from explanations in terms of origins, abstract ideas and the previous preoccupation with formal institutions to an emphasis upon the discovery and understanding of basic forces, fundamental interests and actual workings or processes. Underlying "realist" scholarship was a growing faith in scientific method, a phenomenon which ultimately was to result in an almost imperceptible transition from Pragmatism to Positivism.

Pragmatism and Jurisprudence

Oliver Wendell Holmes (1841–1935)

Holmes was a son of the famous New England poet, a student of philosophy and law, and a distinguished member of the Massachusetts and United States Supreme Courts. He was most influenced in the formation of his legal theory by the Positivism of Mill, Comte and

Spencer, the evolutionary naturalism of Darwin, and the historical-anthropological approach to the study of human institutions of E. B. Tylor and Sir Henry Maine. A member, with Peirce and James, of the Metaphysical Club which met in philosophic discourse in Cambridge, Massachusetts, from 1870 to 1872 and gave rise to Pragmatism, Holmes differed from his two colleagues in his full acceptance of relativistic skepticism.[1]

Holmes attacked the theory of law generally accepted in nineteenth-century America which, in the words of Roscoe Pound, was "one of eternal legal conceptions involved in the very idea of justice . . . containing potentially an exact rule for every case to be reached by an absolute process of logical deduction." In the course of his critique Holmes swept aside as irrelevant to a scientific study of law all *a priori* normative considerations, including the various natural law theories, Kant's categorical imperative, Bentham's criterion of the greatest happiness of the greatest number, and Mill's and Spencer's principle of freedom.[2]

Holmes once remarked: "When I say that a thing is true, I mean that I cannot help believing it." On this basis he defined truth as "the system of my [intellectual] limitations," which acquires objectivity from "the fact that I find my fellowman to a greater or less extent (never wholly) subject to the same *Can't Helps*." In any case, "certitude is not the test of certainty" and "to have doubted one's own first principles is the mark of a civilized man." What men call "natural law" is the product of "that naive state of mind that accepts what has been familiar and accepted by them and their neighbors as something that must be accepted by all men everywhere." In view of this Holmes advised: "Our business is to commit ourselves to life, to accept at once our functions and our ignorance and to offer our heart to fate." We must become reconciled to the fact "that the ultimates of a little creature upon this earth" are not "the last word of an unimaginable whole." Like his Puritan forebears he concluded that the key to happiness is "to be not merely a necessary but a willing instrument in working out ends which to us are inscrutable."[3]

To Holmes the satisfaction of essential needs is a necessity but not a duty: "I see no *a priori* duty to live with others . . . but simply a statement of what I must do if I wish to remain alive." Like Hume, Holmes believed that after living under common rules with each other men come to accept the rules "with sympathy and emotional affirmation and begin to talk about duties and rights." As with natural law, he could see no cosmic rational basis for natural rights. Believing that men are explicable in terms of the natural evolutionary struggle for survival, he saw force as the *ultima ratio* and thought that "at the bottom of all private relations, however tempered by sympathy and social feelings, is a justifiable self-preference." In the spirit of Hume he believed that reason plays merely the instrumental role of handmaid to the desires and passions which alone constitute motives to action.[4]

In his classic study, *The Common Law* (1881), Holmes approached the law as an anthropological document, using principally the genetic method of exposition. Against the theory of law as a logical instrument he asserted that it was a living organism.

The life of the law has not been logic: it has been experience. The felt necessities of the time, the prevalent moral and political theories, intuitions of public policy, avowed or unconscious, even the prejudices which judges share with their fellow-men, have had a good deal more to do than the syllogism in determining the rules by which men should be governed.[5]

Holmes saw society as composed of men and groups who compete for power in the satisfaction of their desires. His Darwinism led him early in life to conclude that "all that can be expected from modern improvements is that legislation should easily and quickly, yet not too quickly, modify itself in accordance with the will of the *de facto* supreme power in the community, and that the spread of an educated sympathy should reduce the sacrifice of minorities to a minimum. . . . The more powerful interests must be more or less reflected in legislation: which like every other device of man or beast, must tend in the long run to aid the survival of the fittest." Not only does this emphasis on the inevitable primacy of the stronger groups imply a rejection of any superior normative principle and of the Austinian formalistic conception of legal sovereignty* but it goes beyond the Spencerian view which would limit the functions of the state to protection of rights and provision for security, in that it recognizes that the state may and will be used by the dominant group or groups for their own advantage.[6] Thus Holmes wrote concerning government:

What proximate test of excellence can be found except correspondence to the actual equilibrium of force in the community—that is, conformity to the wishes of the dominant power? Of course, such conformity may lead to destruction, and it is desirable that the dominant power should be wise. But wise or not, the proximate test of a good government is that the dominant power has its way.[7]

In his attempt to provide a scientific basis for the understanding of law and a realistic insight into the judicial process Holmes was what Morton White has called a "methodological radical." He began his paper, "The Path of the Law" (1897), by declaring pragmatically that the object of the study of the law is "the prediction of the incidence of the public force through the instrumentality of the courts." If one wants to

* John Austin (1790–1859), an English jurist, argued that law is the expression of the will of the sovereign and is not to be confused with ethics and religion.

know the law as such he must divorce himself from moral and purely formal considerations and "look on it as a bad man, who cares only for the material consequences which such knowledge enables him to predict." This led him to his famous definition: "The prophecies of what the courts do in fact, and nothing more pretentious, are what I mean by the law." Consequently a legal right (as well as a legal duty) "is nothing but a prediction that if a man does or omits certain things he will be made to suffer in this or that way by judgment of the court." Seeing law as a series of predictions, Holmes could regard it as an empirical science with the lawyer possessing knowledge of a group of generalizations concerning the actions of courts under certain conditions.[8]

Particularly did Holmes, like Jefferson and Dewey, reject the worship of the past, believing that continuity with the past is "only a necessity and not a duty." He thought it "revolting to have no better reason for a rule of law than that so it was laid down in the time of Henry IV." His interest in the past was, like Dewey's, "for the light it throws upon the present." He looked forward "to a time when the part played by history in the explanation of dogma shall be very small and . . . we shall spend our energy on a study of the ends sought to be attained and the reasons for desiring them." And again like Dewey he believed that "it is finally for science to determine, so far as it can, the relative worth of our different social ends." This led him to conclude that "the man of the future is the man of statistics and the master of economics," and "every lawyer ought to seek an understanding of economics."[9]

On the one hand Holmes, in the interest of defining law as a science, divorced it from moral considerations; on the other hand he urged judges to be aware of the fact that they "must and do legislate" but "only interstitially," being "confined from molar to molecular motions." He thought that if judges became conscious of their preconceptions they might have a better insight into their worth and a greater humility before the judicial task. He also apparently believed that a judge could decide empirically which of the conflicting desires or values in a case before him more closely expressed public policy. Thus his stress on statistics as an important factor in the jurisprudence of the future. Granting merely for purposes of argument that what is in society's interest can be approximated empirically, it remains possible to maintain that in some situations certain individual moral claims outweigh demands of public policy. To this Holmes gave no answer, being unconcerned as a scientific student of law who denied natural law with questions of moral obligation, including the nature of the "right" and the "just." As Morton White has remarked, Holmes, while denying that ethical statements are empirical, apparently held that although all statements of value are empirical, not all empirical statements are statements of value. Thus he could attack the intrusion of value considerations by judges where they are irrelevant, and advocate where judicial legislation is necessary that a judge decide between conflicting values on a purely empirical basis. Unlike Dewey, Holmes did not attempt to equate the factually desired with the ethically desirable.[10]

Turning from the common law to constitutional law, Holmes, as a member of the Supreme Court of the United States from 1902 to 1931, wrote a number of opinions which later influenced the Court as reconstituted by President Franklin Roosevelt. In general, his attitude toward judicial review is summed up in his statement: "I do not think the United States would come to an end if we [Supreme Court of the United States] lost our power to declare an act of Congress void. I do think the Union would be imperiled if we could not make that declaration as to the laws of the several states."[11] His dissenting opinion in the Lochner case in 1905 is, as previously noted, evidence that he did not reject outright the concept of substantive due process as applied to socioeconomic regulatory legislation. And yet, because he did not believe that judicial legislation is proper in constitutional cases and because he habitually doubted the validity of his own ultimate beliefs ("can't-helps"), he refused to read his own views into the Constitution. Against his brethren in the majority, he declared: "I think that the word 'liberty' in the Fourteenth Amendment is perverted when it is held to prevent the natural outcome of a dominant opinion, unless it can be said that a rational and fair man necessarily would admit that the statute proposed would infringe fundamental principles as they have been understood by the traditions of our people and our law."[12] Holmes' language could not have been objected to by his colleagues in the majority; they believed that any rational and fair man would regard the regulatory legislation involved as violative of traditional principles. The difference lay in Holmes' attitude of skepticism regarding ultimates, his civilized tolerance of difference, and his fundamental belief that in government the stronger force must be accommodated.

While Holmes was quite willing to defer to legislative judgment and experimentation in regulatory cases, he readily intruded a judicial qualification or veto in cases involving legislative restraints on freedom of expression. He wrote in one such case:

Persecution for the expression of opinions seems to me perfectly logical. . . . But when men have realized that time has upset many fighting faiths, they may come to believe even more than they believe the very foundations of their own conduct that the ultimate good desired is better reached by free trade in ideas—that the best test of truth is the power of the thought to get itself accepted in the competition of the market, and that truth is the only ground upon which their wishes can be safely carried out. That at any rate is the theory of our Constitution. It is an experiment, as all life is an experiment.[13]

In this view the Constitution prescribes that majorities must be acceded to but only if, in the absence of a clear and present danger, the channels of communication in the competitive marketplace of ideas are kept open through untrammeled freedom of expression. And just as private "truth" is what the individual "can't help" believing, so acceptance in the free marketplace is the test of public "truth."

To those who in the absence of a clear and present danger would shut off advocates of totalitarian rule Holmes replied: "If in the long run the beliefs expressed in totalitarian dictatorship are destined to be accepted by the dominant forces of the community, the only meaning of free speech is that they should be given their chance and have their way."[14]

In commenting on this point Edward S. Corwin has observed: "In short, the 'ultimate good desired' and the triumph of Destiny are one and the same thing and the function of freedom of speech is to forward this triumph, not to block it, although just why Destiny needs an assist is not clear."[15] If called upon to answer, Holmes would not deny Corwin's assertion but would probably explain in Puritan fashion that individual effort is a principal factor in realizing the inevitable. In fact, it might be said that Holmes was a latter-day Puritan who substituted for the omnipotent God who foreordains man's fate and sets the scene in which good and evil contend against each other, the Darwinian concept of evolutionary development through conflict, with its end of survival in which the rewards are necessarily afforded to the stronger. On this basis he could have no regard for law or rights metaphysically considered. The most that government can do is facilitate the means of conflict through institutions which, hopefully, can be based on explicit rules informed by traditions which provide for individual "rights" and their implementation. Neither a Spencerian who circumscribed the state, nor a Ward who preached progress through state action, Holmes resigned himself to fate while extolling the activistic virtues of heroism. In his thought all that remains of the Founding Fathers' conception of natural rights is that which can be associated with positively ordained constitutional rules understandable in terms of a peculiar history and tradition.

Sociological Jurisprudence

The main exponent of sociological jurisprudence in America was the Nebraska-born Roscoe Pound (1870–1964). Although he never graduated from a law school (he was a Ph.D. in botany who for the most part was self-taught in the law), Pound taught at several university law schools before going to Harvard Law School. There he served for fifty-four years, including twenty years as Dean. Knowledgeable in the classical languages, steeped in the history of Roman and common law as well as the history of legal philosophy, Pound was influenced principally by the European sociological legal scholars Ihering, Ehrlich, and Duguit, the American sociologists Ward and Ross, the Pragmatism of James and Dewey, the antiformalistic approach of Holmes to the law, and Holmes' call to judges to recognize their duty of weighing social considerations.

Principally concerned with the relationship between a legal system and the society which it both reflects and influences, Pound looked more to the function and effect of law than to its logical analysis. He thus defined sociological jurisprudence as "a movement for pragmatism as a philosophy of law; for the adjustment of principles and doctrines to the human conditions they are to govern rather than to assumed first principles; for putting the human factor in the central place and relegating logic to its true position as an instrument." On this basis he thought of law not in the sense "of an abstract harmonizing of human wills but of a concrete securing or realizing of human interests." Similarly he regarded law as merely one means of social control and he considered jurisprudence a social science organically related to the other social sciences.[16]

In order fully to understand Pound's ideas of law, the relation of morals and law, and the judicial function, it is necessary to know his division of legal history into five stages. Against this background he saw legal theories as little more than attempts to give a rational account of the problems of the legal order in different stages of development and of the means by which these problems are met.

The first stage is one of primitive law in a society composed of clans with a weak overall government which aims principally at keeping the peace. Law, morals, and religion are herein largely undifferentiated. It is during this period, however, that a distinction comes to be made between the concept of the just or right by nature and the just by convention. In the second stage, which Pound labeled the period of "strict law," the end aimed at is certainty and formality in the law as characterized by narrow rules, which are regarded as self-sufficient and in no need of infusion from an external factor such as morals. In the third stage emphasis is on mitigation of the formalistic rigors of the "strict law" in the direction of justice through equity. The received body of legal precepts no longer is seen as self-sufficient and the concept of natural law becomes the instrument by which ethical ideas are reinfused into law. The fourth stage, which Pound called the stage of "maturity," is marked by a renewed emphasis on security; the fluidity of the previous stage is corrected and the law is rendered more stable while the equitable advances such as the emphasis on equality are retained. In this period of assimilation and systematization law and morals are again contrasted. The fifth stage is one of renewed growth in which unsecured interests and new ethical perspectives bring about a jurisprudence which seeks to reconcile law and morals. Pound thought that the modern industrial world was in this period, with social interest pressing for recognition in place of the old individualism.[17]

In light of his historical analysis, Pound concluded that the stress by the analytical jurist on law by enactment, by the historical jurist on law by convention, and by the philosophic jurist on law by nature, was, in each case, simplistic. They all touch on the truth but must be seen in light of the fact that "jurisprudence and legislation may not be separated by any hard and fast line, and both presuppose political and social ethics."[18]

Pound viewed society in terms of the interests active therein. A legal order, which presupposes interests, has as its main function the provision of means whereby change is accommodated within a framework of stability. At the foundation of a legal system is a paramount interest in peace and order which leads men to seek fixed means for ordering human action. There are three classes of contending interests—individual, public, and social. Interests are secured chiefly by attributing legal rights to the one who asserts them. Thus "a right is an interest protected by law." Pound distinguished legal from natural rights by declaring that the latter are "claims which human beings may reasonably make," while the former are "means which the state employs in order to give effect to such claims within certain defined limits." He concluded that "when natural rights are put in this form it becomes evident that these individual interests are at most on no higher plane than social interests, and, indeed, for the most part get their significance for jurisprudence from a social interest in giving effect to them."[19]

Pound saw judicial activity as the creative element in law and believed that the judicial process could best make the constant adjustments required in a modern legal system. It might be added that he opposed vehemently, as contrary to government by law, the growth of administrative legislation and adjudication. He called the desired judicial attitude, "social engineering," which he described as follows:

Engineering is thought of as a process, as an activity, not merely as a body of knowledge or as a fixed order of construction. . . . The engineer is judged by what he does. His work is judged by its adequacy to the purposes for which it is done, not by its conformity to some ideal form of traditional plan. We are beginning, in contrast with the last century, to think of jurist and judge and law-maker in the same way. . . . We are thinking of how far we do what is before us to be done, not merely of how we do it; of how the system works, not merely of its systematic perfection.[20]

The judge then must exercise a main function of government by weighing and balancing with the least friction, individual, public, and social interests in the cases before him, aided preferably by social science research.

At the same time that Pound talked of the judge as a "social engineer" with wide discretion, he emphasized the necessity of legal rules in the interest of stability, coherence, and certainty. "If left to act freely in individual cases," he wrote, "without rule or standard, no will, either of king or people, is sufficiently set and constant to insure uniform administration of justice. Law and caprice are incompatible." But although he believed that the social sciences, including jurisprudence, are essentially normative, he did not specifically prescribe norms by which a judge as a social engineer is to decide between competing interests. He urged the satisfaction of as much of "the whole body of human wants" as possible. The judge is simply told to secure all social interests as far as he can and maintain a balance or harmony among them compatible with their security. Ultimately then the judge is burdened with a political problem and left without any definite formula for deciding, unless Pound presumed that a sociologically oriented sense of justice would supply this deficiency.[21]

Most important among other figures emphasizing the primacy of social interests in law was Benjamin Cardozo (1870–1938), a member of the New York Court of Appeals and later the Supreme Court of the United States. In his book *The Nature of the Judicial Process* (1921), Cardozo declared: "I take judge-made law as one of the existing realities of life." He had particular reference to the judicial duty to fill gaps while interpreting the common law, statutes, and constitutions. In the process of judicial development of the law Cardozo held that four methods can be used: the method of philosophy which involves logical progression and analogy; the method of history which looks to evolutionary development of the community; the method of tradition which looks to the existing customs of the community; and the method of sociology which is concerned with "justice, morals and social welfare, the mores of the day."* The sociological method, concerned as it is with "social justice," is the most important; in fact it provides the judge with the norm by which to decide which of the four methods is to be pursued. Because "one of the most fundamental social interests is that law shall be uniform and impartial," there shall in the main be "adherence to precedent" and "symmetrical development, consistently with history or custom" when either has been the motive force, and "with logic or philosophy when the motive power has been theirs." But when uniformity becomes oppressive, "the social interest served by symmetry or certainty must then be balanced against the social interest served by equity and fairness or other elements of social welfare."[22]

* It is obvious that Cardozo's conception of sociology, like that of Pound, is essentially normative and not to be confused with the formal behavioral discipline.

Confronting the question of how a judge can know when one interest outweighs another, Cardozo answered that his knowledge must be gotten just as that of the legislator, "from experience and study and reflection; in brief from life itself." He insisted that judges must have both adequate factual knowledge and an adequate objective standard of measurement. As to the first he stated: "Courts know today that statutes are to be viewed, not in isolation or *in vacuo*, as pronouncements of abstract principles for the guidance of an ideal community, but in the setting and in the framework of present-day conditions, as revealed by the labors of economists and students of the social sciences. . . ." As to the objective standard, Cardozo mentioned: what "some other man of normal intellect and conscience might reasonably look upon as right"; "the customary morality of right-minded men and women"; "accepted standards of the community, the *mores* of the times"; and in some cases (fiduciary relationships, for example) "the highest standards which a man of the most delicate conscience and nicest sense of honor might impose upon himself."[23]

In his task of balancing interests to further social welfare, the judge is limited by "traditions," the "example of other judges," "the collective judgment of the profession," "the duty of adherence to the prevailing spirit of the law," "jural principles," and "the bulk and pressure of rules that hedge him on every side." What matters most is "that the judge is under a duty, within the limits of his power of innovation, to maintain a relation between law and morals, between the precepts of jurisprudence and those of reason and good conscience." The method of sociology is then the method of equity and social justice. Concerned with ends and not with abstract *a priori* principles, it substitutes for the old mechanical a-prioristic natural law, the notion of "right reason and conscience" in the application and development of the common and positive law. In the process the judiciary plays a key creative role fostering change within a framework of stability.[24]

Legal Realism

Legal realism is the name of a movement most prominent between the two world wars (encompassing such names as Karl Lewellyn, Jerome Frank, and Thurman Arnold) which attempted to build upon the insights of Holmes and the sociological school. It had, generally speaking, a twofold aim—to develop a "science of the law" based on observed uniformities of legal behavior and to effect legal reform in the sense of a greater recognition of judicial lawmaking. In the latter task, although there were variations between particular "realists," emphasis was put less upon the judicial formulation of general rules and systematic development of law than upon the satisfactory settlement of individual cases. At best rules were seen as but one of several factors—sociological, psychological, etc.—in a case. Thus there was a broadening recognition of factors which do and which should enter into the decision-making process. With responsibility for legal change placed on the judiciary, and with the elements which go into decision-making recognized, a legal science which is at once predictive of judicial action and productive of social reform was considered possible.[25]

Most legal realists adhered to Holmes' position which aims at a conscious recognition of the reality of judicial lawmaking not so much to increase judicial freedom as to bring about a broader cognizance thereof. Among those realists who believed that what judges and other governmental authorities do is not controlled by law as contained in statutes, rules, etc., but by extraneous factors, the tendency was greater to downgrade rules and disregard logic as relevant and desirable factors, a position at variance with that of Holmes and particularly objected to by Pound. The observations made by Morris Cohen on this point best express the criticism.

Taking a phrase of Justice Holmes out of its contextual limitations, the realistic doctrine becomes: Law is the prediction of what judges will decide. But who is properly a judge, or when is he acting within his legal power, itself depends upon our system of legal ideas. To define the law as what the courts will decide is, as others have pointed out, like defining medicine as what the doctor will prescribe—it misses the question which faces the doctor or the judge, *viz.*, what he *should prescribe* or how he *should* rule.[26]

Legal realism was pragmatic in its antiformalism, its disdain of system and *a priori* principles, its emphasis on extralegal factors, and its focus on problems as they arise. It accentuated even more than the sociological school the assumption that somehow norms of decision are implicit in each situation as it arises.

Summing up developments in American legal thought beginning with Holmes, it might be said that the rejection of the nineteenth-century conception of law as a deductive science led to a frank recognition of a dynamic legal system led by a dynamic judiciary in a dynamic society. Instead of a collection of rules, law was seen as an instrument of social control, which should be primarily regardful of consequences rather than principles. Judges were urged to put aside personal prejudice and give wide acceptance to legislative factors in construing powers of government. Judicial deference to legislative and administrative determinations, particularly in constitutional cases, was stressed as well as the weighing of causes by the judiciary in the light of the social welfare in interstitial instances. Finally, emphasis was not only put on finding uniformities of action but on studying the law in action—evidence of the pragmatic orientation of most of those in the movement.

The new legal theory, as epitomized in legal realism, has been criticized for (1) its failure to clarify the position of the judiciary in our governmental structure at large; (2) its loose definition of ends; (3) its dubious assumption that courts can be efficient legislative bodies; (4) the antidemocratic implications involved in assigning lawmaking powers to the judiciary; and (5) its overlooking the fact that norms must be consciously expressed—an act which involves recognizing some as inherently superior to and more basic than others, which in turn involves the necessity to return to philosophical consideration of fundamentals and ultimates.

Pragmatic Jurisprudence and Constitutional Law

Basic to an understanding of the conception of judicial review embraced by the dissenters to the conservative judicial approach to constitutional law from 1900 to 1937 is the essay written in 1893 by Harvard Law Professor James B. Thayer, "The Origin and Scope of the American Doctrine of Constitutional Law." In Thayer's view a court could legitimately declare a legislative act unconstitutional only "when those who have the right to make laws have not merely made a mistake, but have made a very clear one,—so clear that it is not open to rational question." Thayer's argument was based on the assumption that American government, structured on a separation of powers, presupposes an enlightened electorate and its adequate representation in legislatures, as well as the conviction that a people cannot be saved from its own mistakes by the judiciary. This meant, of course, that presumption of constitutionality must always be afforded by the courts to statutes challenged as unconstitutional.[27]

Thayer's paper had importance because it conveyed an attitude of the judiciary's role that was much more restrained than that then held by the conservative majority on the Supreme Court. Its major drawback lay in the fact that the rational doubt test which it propounded was ambiguous as to whose rational doubt was involved. Thayer had equated it with "that reasonable doubt which lingers in the mind of a competent and duly instructed person who has carefully applied his faculties to the question." While judges like Holmes, Brandeis, and Stone would consider a legislative majority as comprising men of rationality and accept their judgment (at least in cases of socioeconomic regulation), even though their personal conviction was otherwise, men like Sutherland, as we have seen, regarded it a question of private judgment, an inescapable duty of the individual judge.

Recognition of the fact that judges were making independent policy judgments in constitutional cases was, as has been seen, implied in the development of the "Brandeis brief." This statistical presentation of evidence was in accord with the teachings of sociological jurisprudence but, as also has been seen, had only a slight effect upon the theoretical

494   *The Progressive Period and American Political Thought*

premises of judicial conservatives. It might be added that the technique was developed and used not to attack but to establish the validity of social legislation, an objective clearly in accord with the desire of the new jurisprudential theory to limit judicial review.

Opposed then to the meta-constitutional theory of vested rights, which was joined to the mechanical theory of law by the conservative majority on the Court, was the concept of judicial deference to legislative experimentation espoused particularly by Holmes, Brandeis, and Stone. The most succinct formulation of this position was put forth by Stone in 1936 in an opinion dissenting against the Court's declaration of the constitutionality of the Agricultural Adjustment Act:

> The power of courts to declare a statute unconstitutional is subject to two guiding principles of decision which ought never to be absent from judicial consciousness. One is that courts are concerned only with the power to enact statutes, not with their wisdom. The other is that while unconstitutional exercise of power by the executive and legislative branches of the government is subject to judicial restraint, the only check upon our own exercise of power is our own sense of self-restraint. For the removal of unwise laws from the statute books appeal lies not to the courts but to the ballot and to the processes of democratic governments. . . . Courts are not the only agency of government that must be assumed to have capacity to govern.[28]

The switch in position of two judges on the Supreme Court in 1937 and the subsequent changes in personnel on the Court brought about an acceptance of the attitude of judicial deference by the new majority. The commerce and taxing and spending powers granted to Congress by the Constitution were construed broadly in the sense of Hamilton and Marshall. Although the concept of substantive due process as pertaining to socioeconomic legislation was not repudiated as such, what remained was more shadow than substance. Beginning in 1937 the Court rejected the meta-constitutional notion of vested or property rights as primary and vindicated the Constitution as an instrument of power adequate to meet the problems of a national industrial society.

With the field open to pragmatic experimentation by legislators in socioeconomic matters, the Court underwent an institutional identity crisis concerning its proper role in American government and life. By the mid-1940's no Justice remained who wished the Court to return to its pre-1937 role of guardian of property rights. There was also verbal acceptance by all of Holmes' and Stone's conception of self-restraint and recognition of the ballot box as the check upon the political branches. There was disagreement, however, as to whether a natural law approach to the due process clause of the Fourteenth Amendment was valid in cases involving alleged state violations of civil liberties, and as to whether statutes or governmental actions allegedly violative of personal rights should, when challenged in Court, be exempt from the usual presumption of validity. The theoretical views which were developed in answer to these questions will be discussed later.

Pragmatism and Political Science

It will be recalled that American political science from Lieber to Burgess was juristic, formalistic, and metaphysical, focusing on such questions as the nature of the state, government and the nation, the nature and locus of sovereignty, and the description of governmental institutions.

The scholarly work of Woodrow Wilson (1856–1924), who was a professor of politics and President of Princeton University before entering active politics, marks a turn away from the formal and legal approach to a "realistic" study of American institutions. Wilson drew principally upon Edmund Burke's conception of the complexity of politics, and the method used by the English journalist, Walter Bagehot, in exposing the actual functioning of the British Constitution, as well as Bagehot's critique of the American system of government.[29]

Wilson's critical reviews of the work of Burgess and Bryce illuminate his basic conception of political science. He saw Burgess' book, *Political Science and Constitutional Law,* as marred by "a dogmatic spirit, and a lack of insight into institutions as detailed expressions of life, not readily consenting to be broadly and positively analyzed and classified." Charging that Burgess confused the juristic method with the method of political science, Wilson declared: "While it is generally easy enough to determine what the law is, political fact is subtle and elusive, not to be caught up whole in any formula. It is a thing which none but a man who is at once a master of sentences and a seer can bring entire before the mind's eye. . . ." Thus political science "cannot be truthfully constructed, except by the literary method . . . which seeks to reproduce life in speech" and which sees politics as "the vital embodiment of opinion, prejudices, sentiments. . . ."[30]

Wilson regarded Bryce's *The American Commonwealth* as admirable in its realistic treatment of political parties but criticized it for not going "beyond the formal history of measures and of methods to make evident the forces of national development and material circumstances which have lain behind measures." He recommended that democracy be studied from the evolutionary point of view as "a stage of development" which "is not created by aspirations or by new faith," but "is built up by slow habit" in the "process" of "experience."[31]

Wilson's conviction that political science is essentially concerned with life precluded its identification with the method of the natural sciences as well as logic. His literary approach, like that of James, was much closer to that of the insightful artist than that of the positivistic researcher. Thus it is not surprising that Wilson's own contributions were interpretive, impressionistic, and evaluative essays. Rather incongruously, in view of his concern with "life," however, his writing was based on an "experience" which was not direct but derivative.[32]

Wilson's classical critique of Congress, *Congressional Government* (1885), did not draw upon personal observation but on a number of propositions which for the most part he had formulated before he wrote the book. These included the beliefs that (1) the formal Newtonian conception of the Constitution is opposed to its organic evolutionary development, (2) the "literary theory" of checks and balances held by the Founding Fathers is deleterious to effective government, (3) the more power is divided the more irresponsible it becomes, (4) Congressional government is uncontrollable either by the executive or judiciary, and (5) Congressional government with its dispersion and fragmentation of responsibility is inferior to parliamentary government in terms of accountability.[33]

Believing that in politics "the standards of practical common sense" should outweigh the "political witchcraft" embodied in the traditional worship of the formal Constitution, Wilson argued that Congressional government filled the vacuum of power created by the separation of powers. However, because "power and strict accountability for its use are the essential constituents of good government," and because congressional committee government focuses only on legislation, not on administrative oversight or enlightened leadership through debate, the American system of government is deficient. He did not directly propose cabinet government for America in his book; in an earlier essay, however, he had made concrete suggestions as to how to convert to a modified form thereof.[34]

Wilson's treatment of the Presidency in *Congressional Government* is difficult to accept even in its historical context: "The business of the President, occasionally great, is usually not much above routine. Most of the time it is *mere* administration, mere obedience of directions from masters of policy, the Standing Committees. Except in so far as his power of veto constitutes him a part of the legislature, the President might, not inconveniently, be a permanent officer; the first official of a carefully graded and impartially regulated civil service system. . . ." By 1908, when he wrote *Constitutional Government in the United States*, probably owing to the successful assertion and application of Presidential power in the interim, he had changed his mind. He now focused on the chief executive as party and legislative leader and instrument of cohesion, emphasizing that "the President is at liberty, both in law and conscience, to be as big a man as he can."[35]

It is evident that Wilson as political scientist was, as David Easton has written, "reformative rather than purely descriptive in his study."[36] His goal was the realization of responsible exercise of power. Whereas he originally preferred cabinet government, he came to see the possibilities of presidential leadership. In any case, he held throughout to the belief that fragmented power is irresponsible power and inherently undemocratic.

Shortly after Wilson wrote his critique of Congress, the midwestern historian, Frederick Jackson Turner (1861–1932) proposed in his essay, "The Significance of the Frontier in American History," an environmental explanation of American democracy. Turning his back on explanations in terms of Germanic origins and of political ideas and forms, he maintained that "behind institutions, behind constitutional forms and modifications, lie the vital forces that call these organs into life and shape them to meet changing conditions." Thus "the existence of an area of free land, its continual recession, and the advance of American settlement westward, explain American development." The frontier is explanatory of both individualism and liberty, and thus democracy.[37]

This "realistic" interpretation of the American past had great vogue in American academic circles until the 1930's when its internal inconsistencies and the shortcomings of its parochial ignoring of the heritage of European ideas and traditions as influential factors were pointed up, along with the fact that democratic innovations were in good part first made in the well-settled eastern sections of America, and then spread to the West. Nevertheless, the thesis, when sufficiently qualified by speaking of the frontier as one of the important conditioning factors within which ideas, forms, and practices old and new were tested and adapted, has validity. As originally formulated, it bespoke an attempt to arrive at the "real" causative factors underlying American development divorced from mystical, metaphysical, racial, and formalistic explanations.[38]

Whereas Wilson's *Congressional Government* criticized the insufficiency of the American constitutional system and Turner's thesis essayed an environmental explanation of American democracy, J. Allen Smith's *The Spirit of American Government* (1907) reflected a trend to expose "the true character of the Constitution" (historically a subject of general veneration to Americans except for many antebellum abolitionists). Smith described it as a reactionary document formed by the conservative and wealthy who were concerned with the frustration of majority rule and the democratic spirit of the American Revolution, as well as with the preservation and cultivation of economic privileges. In this view Jefferson is arrayed as the hero, Hamilton as the villain. Textual analysis of the Constitution was used to point up its antimajoritarian provisions. Most strongly attacked were: the amendment process, which, contrary to the views of men such as James Wilson and Nathaniel Chipman, was seen as undemocratic because of its difficult operation; the principle of checks and balances; and judicial independence and judicial review.[39]

In his work *Politics* (1908), the historian-political scientist Charles Beard (1874–1948) wrote that it was not "the function of the student of politics to praise or condemn institutions or theories, but to understand and expound them"; thus "for scientific purposes" the study of politics "is separated from theology, ethics and patriotism." Consequently, he thought that "a treatise on causation in politics would be the most welcome contribution which a scholar of scientific training and temper could make."[40] In pursuit of this objective, Beard, in his *An Economic Interpretation of the Constitution* (1913) proceeded from a belief which was shared by many Populists and Progressives—politics must be understood in light of underlying economic realities—to attempt to prove the thesis adumbrated by Smith, that the Constitution was an undemocratic document explicable in terms of the Founding Fathers' economic interests. His work differed from Smith's in being more factual and less polemical. Extended in studies such as *The Economic Origins of Jeffersonian Democracy* (1915), Beard's economic interpretation was widely accepted by publicists and academicians. When challenged with the charge that it was Marxist in essence, he replied with the volume, *The Economic Basis of Politics* (1916), which attempted to show that his approach was squarely within the tradition of Madison, Hamilton, Webster, and Calhoun. Although he was not disrespectful of the Founding Fathers, his work exploded the myth of the Constitution as divinely inspired and the product of a patriotic, disinterested pursuit of "justice" and the "general welfare." Besides being subject to criticisms mentioned earlier,* his scholarship has been sharply attacked in recent years in terms of insufficient evidence, unwarranted conclusions, and narrowness of focus, and as being acceptable only as an "act of faith" and not as "an analysis of historical method."[41]

Whereas the work of Smith and Beard is illustrative of the tendency in Progressivism to explain politics realistically in terms of underlying economic factors, a prime example of Progressivism's impulse to reassert the primacy of politics is the work of Herbert Croly (1869–1930). In *The Promise of American Life* (1909), Croly attacked, in light of the growing collectivization in American society, the uncritical Jeffersonian individualism adhered to by many of his fellow Progressives. Influenced by Comtean positivism, Royce's concept of "community," James' pragmatism, Santayana's ideal of a government by men of merit, and Theodore

* In Chapter 10.

Roosevelt's use of Presidential power, Croly presented "a critical reconstruction of American political ideas . . . by means of an analysis of the meaning of democracy" and a program of reform based upon a new welfare nationalism to be realized through the positive exercise of governmental power and the social ascendancy of men of technical competence.[42]

Croly regarded what he called the Jeffersonian principle of automatic progress and justice through the recognition of "equal rights to all, special privileges to none" erroneous, because "it tends to attribute individual and social ills, for which general moral, economic, and social causes are usually in large measure responsible, to individual wrong doing." If sincere, Jeffersonians are obliged to concede "the superior wisdom of Hamilton's principle of national responsibility," which recognizes the inevitability of governmental concessions of special privileges. Thus the idea that the public interest is affirmed merely by the negative approach of controlling individuals in the exercise of their "equal rights" is replaced by the truth that it must be effected "by positive and aggressive action."[43]

Croly proposed that democratic organization be used for "the joint benefit of individual distinction and social improvement." Such democracy would not be dedicated simply to liberty, which Hamilton had emphasized in his aristocratic approach, or to equality, as stressed by Jeffersonians, but to liberty and equality "insofar as they made for human brotherhood." Thus Croly thought that fraternity, which he regarded as a religion, must serve as the norm in adjusting the conflicts between the claims of liberty and equality. Democracy must be wedded to nationality; Jeffersonian ends must be effected by Hamiltonian means. This alliance of the two principles "will not leave either of them intact; but it will necessarily do more harm to the Jeffersonian group of political ideas than it will to the Hamiltonian," because Hamilton's nationalism "can be adapted to democracy without an essential injury to itself," but Jeffersonian democracy "cannot be nationalized without being transformed." The transformation demands acceptance of national political power broad enough to cope with the problems attendant upon the economic system. In particular, positive national government would rectify inequalities by legislation such as a graduated inheritance tax. Corporate bigness must be recognized as the inexorable result of progressive development in business and industry; therefore, the federal antitrust laws should be repealed and labor unions given national recognition. A national incorporation act can provide a means for governmental control. In all cases, however, the basic principle is that national power be used to effect the general welfare.[44]

Croly did not believe that the shortcomings of democracy could be cured by a greater infusion of democracy; he accepted the devices of the recall and referendum, while rejecting the initiative and direct primary. He thought, perhaps somewhat mystically, that a higher moral attitude of concern for the general good would become strong enough to counteract the conflicting tendencies of special interest groups. He stressed "constructive individualism" defined as "the increase of . . . individuality by competent and disinterested special work," which will influence social amelioration, when men "of high but special technical competence" become leaders. These "exceptional" individuals must undertake to create and educate a public by communicating "their better message in a popularly interesting manner."[45]

Croly's emphasis on the need for "a standard of uncompromising technical excellence" in all arts, including politics, and his statement that "the perfect type of authoritative technical methods are those which prevail among scientific men in respect to scientific work," brings forth the question of what are technical standards in politics. On this Croly was at best vague, although he did, in another work, portray Mark Hanna as a skilled technician in both politics and business. Croly so heavily qualified the notion of technical competence by moral considerations that, as Bernard Crick has written, in the end "his 'technical standards' . . . appear as no more and no less elusive than any maxims for statecraft offered by anyone whose learning, coherence, integrity and experience give him some authority to be heard." In fact, Crick concludes, Croly "is actually upholding a traditional American moralism, but he tries to reinterpret it to fit the sentiments of his own age, by talk of 'authoritative technical standards.'"[46]

Croly's work was not only consonant with, and in aid of, Theodore Roosevelt's "New Nationalism," but it was predictive of a major shift in American government toward an activistic nationalism that promoted the general welfare by granting special privileges to those previously discriminated against; this new nationalism reached fruition in Franklin Roosevelt's "New Deal." Croly aimed at rectifying the perversion of Jeffersonian democratic ideals in their link with fear of a strong national government, by wedding them to the Hamiltonian nationalist ideal which he believed had been perverted in its association with aristocracy.[47]

The principal work of the social theorist Arthur F. Bentley (1870–1955), *The Process of Government* (1908), although relatively uninfluential until after World War II, stands as perhaps the most important and controversial study in political science written during the Progressive period. Opinions of its worth have varied: Beard, although drawing upon it for his own studies and graduate seminars, thought that it was not original but would "help to put politics on a basis of realism"; Morris Cohen, however, reportedly called it the most important contribution in political theory in America in 300 years. For the most part scholarship commenting upon Bentley's work has concentrated on his pragmatic preoccupation with *group pressures* underlying government, ignoring his primary emphasis upon *process* and his attempt relentlessly to pursue the antidualistic and antiformalistic attitude of pragmatism to its furthermost limits.[48]

Bentley's epistemological and methodological presuppositions, which he more fully articulated in later studies, include the following:

1. Social phenomena must not be *explained* in terms of causal factors such as feelings, faculties, ideas, or instincts, but *described* in terms of "activity." Ideas are merely "reflections" of social activity; the raw material of political science is not to be found in documents like the Constitution or legal records but "in the actually performed legislating-administrating-adjudicating activities of the nation and in the streams and currents of activity that gather among the people and rush into these spheres." Individuals must also be described solely in terms of social activity. Rejecting personalistic conceptions as unwarranted intrusions of discrete *a priori* causal forces, Bentley reduced self-knowledge to that which is gained only by external evidence: "I know myself, so far as I have knowledge that is worth while, by observation of my actions, and indeed largely not by my own observations, but by what other people observe and report to me directly or indirectly about my actions."[49]

2. Because "activity" is basic, inquiry must focus on "process" and proceed ultimately not from a self-actional approach ("where things are viewed as acting under their own powers") or an interactional approach ("where thing is balanced against thing in causal inter-connection") but from a transactional approach ("where systems of description and naming are employed to deal with aspects and phases of action, without final attribution to 'elements' or other presumptively detachable or independent 'entities,' 'essences' or 'realities,' and without isolation of presumptively detachable 'relations' from such detachable 'elements'"). In such fashion, Bentley believed dualism and formalism would finally be surmounted. In this view political science seeks neither to understand nor explain, but to describe—the complete science is the complete description. Having ruled out predetermined criteria of selection, Bentley, who spent a number of years as a journalist, proceeded, in his *Process of Government,* to investigate that which is structured as politically relevant in newspaper accounts. He conceded, in effect, a provisional legitimacy to interactional studies but always as pointing toward a completely descriptive transactional overview. Although the *Process of Government* has been ably analyzed in Newtonian terms, its basic thesis is even more compatible to Bentley's later desire to explain what he called "man-society" in terms of Einstein's relativity theory,

postulating a common field of universal interdependent activity and rejecting interactive discrete elements moved by causal forces according to universal laws.[50]

In light of the above, Bentley argued that the phenomena of politics consist in the activities of underlying conflicting groups which must be seen in terms of each other in "one great moving process" giving rise to the differentiated, derivative group adjustment activity called government. Thus "the balance of group pressures *is* the existing state of society." A realistic political science assumes the fictitious character of individuals in its description of the governmental process in terms of underlying group activity. As Bentley put it: "When the groups are adequately stated, everything is stated." Consequently, a legislative act is simply the resultant of conflicting group pressures and never the expression of a common good. In nominalist fashion Bentley denied the existence of a "social whole," such as Ward had expounded, and a "general welfare," such as Croly extolled. Although he talked of a "habit background" and "rules of the game" lying behind the struggle, he would not equate them with a common good. The norm of "common interest" used by Aristotle in classifying governments is termed "an entirely arbitrary test," because "there is nothing which is best literally for the whole people." All that exists is the process of group struggle and the adjustments giving rise to a dynamic balance. As long as there is no unanimity concerning policy (and unanimity never obtains), there can be no common good. Furthermore, to accept the notion on an ethical basis is incompatible with a realistic (descriptive) political science.[51]

Bentley explained constitution-making along with all other governmental operations in this fashion. Concerning Chief Justice John Marshall's decisions, for example, he declared: "We may feel sure that the interests that underlay those decisions, if they could not have gained expression through Marshall, would have gained it in some other way. The power was not in Marshall, but in the interest groups he so adequately recognized and allowed to come so smoothly and speedily to their due dominance in the government." Going beyond Holmes, he regarded law as not what a judge or any governmental official does but "what the mass of the people actually does and tends to some extent to make other people do by means of governmental agencies."[52] Concerning legal logic and judicial review he wrote: "The Supreme Court will effectively use whichever line of reasoning it wishes, to state and explain to the country the decision which it will render on lines which, although passing through reasoning, are reasoning's masters, not its servants."[53] In sum, Bentley saw government not as a primary but as a derivative differentiated group activity and an adjustment process which must be described and thus understood in terms of underlying conflicting group pressures. In effect he reduces political science to a descriptive sociology. He differed from Marx in that he would not accept the notion of rigid classes or groups. His was a functional approach wherein a group is equated with an interest which in turn is equated with activity. Thus a group, like any other fact, is what it does.

After World War II, American political science rediscovered Bentley; it tended, however, in many enlightening and significant studies to put his primary emphasis on process in the background and to focus on groups as basic data. By then he had further pushed his logic to the point where, in deference to the demands of process (now embraced within the field theory), he substituted the term "cross-section" for that of group, and looked toward a new language less tied to common sense and more congruent with the flux which is "reality."[54]

In evaluating Bentley's work it is necessary to distinguish between certain Progressivist assumptions underlying and giving coherence to his political thought and the logical implications of his philosophical premises. Thus on the first count it appears that he believed: (1) if ideas are rejected as causal factors, such fictions as *laissez-faire* and the qualitatively distinct nature of the "political" can be dismissed; (2) if more and more facts are laid bare through realistic description of activity, problems will be exposed to public view; and (3) there exists, despite the clash of interests, a natural social order as evidenced by the dynamic equilibrium of interests which describes society at any time.

On the second count, if all is flux and if man is merely an ever-changing reflex manifestation of social activity known only through external evidence, not only evaluation but any structural criteria or distinctions must be deemed arbitrary. There is no central point of focus; no aspect of the universe in its evolution is qualitatively better than another. As has been recently stated, Bentley's problem is that of Zeno: how to capture the movement of an arrow in flight when existing terminology tends to freeze motion into discrete movements. Of course, beginning with the Greeks, Western philosophy has conceived of order being present in things primarily on the basis of reason and the subsisting personality from whence it emanates. Bentley is at war with this tradition. By rendering man merely another part of the universal flux, he dismisses both Plato's dictum that "God is the measure of all things" and Protagoras' dictum that "man is the measure of all things." In rigorous pursuit of evolutionary naturalism, he thus leaves behind him both theocentric and anthropocentric humanism.*

It will be recalled that among the pragmatic evolutionary naturalists James explained man in terms of a stage of evolutionary organic devel-

---

* Bentley writes in *Relativity in Man and Society,* "Do we make man the standard of values and test progress by him? Man in that sense is an arbitrary construction, a clothing of meanings, the outcome of a bifurcation, based not on knowledge but on a very limited examination."

opment which rendered him not totally distinct from the rest of nature but less subject to its determinism. Dewey, who corresponded with and collaborated in writing articles with Bentley, could not accept Bentley's dismissal of man and his needs as the measure. At best Dewey's approach in terms of the interplay of organism and environment was to Bentley only provisionally permissible on the level of interactional analysis.

Bentley is sometimes compared to Hume, who likewise dismissed the concept of self as logically and scientifically indefensible. It must be remembered, however, that what Hume discarded on the philosophic level be reintruded on the level of "natural belief"—something akin to what Justice Holmes would call a "can't-help." Then, too, it might be said that Bentley's emphasis on "self"-knowledge as purely external resembles the emulative approbativeness so heavily emphasized as a basic human trait by John Adams. Adams, however, never dismissed the notion of self-hood or person-hood, even while believing that men lust for the regard of others. It is because they wish to satisfy their egoism, he believed, that men do seek recognition and take bearings by the opinions of others. Bentley's belief that man knows himself only through the eyes of others leads directly to the notion of the "other-directed personality" which has been recently remarked as a phenomenon of contemporary life.

Finally, Bentley's thesis that all ideas are "a reflection of social activity," along with the notion that law and government are reflective of underlying group pressures and that "the balance of group pressures is the existing state of society," leads logically to what Arthur MacMahon has called a "cynical conservatism," which sees whatever exists as right, and confers what Peter Odegard has called "academic absolution" on the group struggle.[55] One is thus disarmed from sitting in critical judgment upon oppressive regimes and tyrannical forces and ideologies repugnant to human freedom simply because such regimes and ideologies necessarily reflect the existing underlying reality. These ominous implications were plastered over by Bentley's Progressive preferences and remain unnoticed by many even today. Philosophically speaking, Bentley, in his rigorous, logical pursuit of the evolutionary naturalism, scientism,* antidualism and antiformalism of American pragmatism shows the moral vacuum which lies at its center, a vacuum which must be filled by external norms.

Looking back in summary over the Progressive period we find the principal American studies of politics informed by a desire to be "realistic," to demythologize Constitution worship, to describe the "actual"

---

* Scientism indicates an approach which renders the subject matter secondary to "scientific method" or techniques of inquiry.

workings of institutions and the "forces" behind them and to present the "facts" to the judgment of public opinion, in the hope that a reinvigorated democracy might adequately deal with the problems of the day. Charles Beard accurately described the new pragmatic political science as marked by (1) "the decreasing reference to the doctrine of natural rights as a basis for political practice," (2) "increasing hesitation to ascribe political events to Providential causes," (3) rejection of explanations in terms of "the divine and social nature of institutions," and (4) a persistent attempt to get "more precise notions about causation in politics." A. Lawrence Lowell, who contributed significant studies in public opinion and political parties, described the general attitude toward sources, with which Wilson, although not a follower thereof in practice, would have agreed: "The main laboratory for the actual working of political institutions is not a library, but the outside world of public life."[56]

Although Wilson and men like Lowell had a deep appreciation of the complexity of politics and the need ultimately to regard political phenomena through the "mind's eye," as well as seeing politics as irreducible and qualitatively distinct, the desire of the new political science to search for underlying "forces" and "causes" brought men like Smith and Beard to talk of politics as if it were a function of economics, Turner to explain democracy in terms of environment, and Bentley to reduce it to sociology. On the other hand, the journalist Croly helped keep alive a sense of the autonomy of politics as the master practical science in his emphasis on a vigorous Hamiltonian nationalism.

Indeed, the tendency either to veer toward reductionism or to maintain the uniqueness of the political factor was a function of just how much relative deference one accorded the main strands of the new political science in its developed state—pragmatic realism and scientism. Wilson saw the danger that realism would be assimilated in scientism before it happened; Beard reacted after the fact in the 1920's when he declaimed against scientism.[57] Bentley, of course, marks the point when, in the name of realism, scientism begins to submerge the notion of progressive goals to be reached by pragmatic means. American political science thus emerged from the Progressive period with an incipiently split personality.

NOTES

1. For Holmes' life, see the unfinished biography by Mark DeWolfe Howe, *Justice Oliver Wendell Holmes* (Cambridge, 1957, 1963, 2 vols.). For an appraisal of Holmes' role in the pragmatic "revolt against formalism," see White, *op. cit.*, pp. 59–75, 103–106, and Wiener, *op. cit.*, pp. 172–189. For an appraisal of Holmes' jurisprudence, see Fred V. Cahill, *Judicial Legislation* (New York, 1952), pp. 32–45.

2. Roscoe Pound, "Juristic Science and the Law" *Harvard Law Review,* XXXI (June, 1918), 1047, 1048; Howe, *op. cit.,* II, 46, 140, 154–159.

3. "Ideals and Doubts" in *Collected Legal Papers* (New York, 1920, reprinted in 1952), pp. 304, 305, 307, 166; "Natural Law," *ibid.,* pp. 310–311, 312, 315. Howe, *op. cit.,* I, 285–286.

4. *Collected Legal Papers,* p. 313; *The Common Law* (Boston, 1881), p. 44.

5. *The Common Law,* 1.

6. Holmes' comments are in *American Law Review,* VII (April, 1873), 583–584; quoted in Howe, *op. cit.,* II, 44–45.

7. *Collected Legal Papers,* p. 258.

8. *Ibid.,* pp. 167, 171, 173, 169.

9. *Ibid.,* pp. 211, 187, 195, 242.

10. *So. Pac. Co. v. Jensen,* 244 U.S. 205, 221; White, *op. cit.,* pp. 208–213.

11. *Collected Legal Papers,* pp. 295–296.

12. *Lochner v. N.Y.,* 198 U.S. 45, 75–79 (1905).

13. *Abrams v. U.S.,* 250 U.S., 616, 627–628 (1919).

14. *Gitlow v. U.S.,* 268 U.S. 652, 673 (1925).

15. E. S. Corwin, "Bowing Out 'Clear and Present Danger'," *Notre Dame Lawyer,* XXVII (Spring, 1952), 325. Reprinted in A. T. Mason and G. Garvey (eds.), *American Constitutional History: Essays by Edward S. Corwin* (New York, 1964), p. 173.

16. Roscoe Pound, "Mechanical Jurisprudence," *Columbia Law Review,* VIII (Dec., 1908), 609–610; *The Spirit of the Common Law* (Boston, 1921), p. 196. *Law and Morals* (Chapel Hill, 1924), pp. 123, 124. Pound's main works include, in addition to those above: "The Scope and Purpose of Sociological Jurisprudence," *Harvard Law Review,* XXIV, 591, XXV, 140 and 489 (June, 1911, Dec., 1911, and Apr., 1912); *The Formative Era of American Law* (Boston, 1938); *Introduction to the Philosophy of Law* (New Haven, 1922), and *Social Control Through Law* (New Haven, 1942). See Cahill *op. cit.,* pp. 70–83, for a short summation of Pound's views.

17. *Law and Morals,* 115–117.

18. *Ibid.,* p. 117.

19. *Social Control Through Law,* pp. 65–87; "The End of Law as Developed in Legal Rules and Doctrines," *Harvard Law Review,* XXVII (1914), 225–226, cited in Cahill, *op. cit.,* 74n.

20. *Interpretations of Legal History* (London, 1923), p. 152.

21. *Introduction to the Study of Law* (Library of American Law and Practice, 1912), 3, cited in Cahill, *op. cit.,* p. 79.

22. Benjamin N. Cardozo, *The Nature of the Judicial Process* (New Haven, 1921, paperback volume, 1960), pp. 10, 30, 31, 112, 113. For a short summation of Cardozo's thought, see Cahill, *op. cit.,* pp. 83–88.

23. *Ibid.,* pp. 113, 81, 89, 106, 108, 109–110.

24. *Ibid.,* pp. 114, 130, 137, 133–134.

25. The discussion in this section is based on the treatment of "legal realism" in Cahill, *op. cit.,* pp. 97–148, and Morris Cohen, *American Thought,* pp. 169–180.

26. Cohen, *American Thought,* p. 174.

27. James B. Thayer, "The Origin and Scope of the American Doctrine of Constitutional Law," *Harvard Law Review,* VII (1893), 129. Reprinted in Robert McCloskey, *Essays in American Constitutional Law* (New York, 1957), pp. 63–85.

28. *U.S. v. Butler,* 297 U.S. 1, 78–79 (1936).

29. Bagehot's principal work was *The English Constitution* (London, 1867). Wilson's contribution to American political science through 1885 can be better appreciated by consulting Arthur S. Link (ed.), *The Papers of Woodrow Wilson,* vols. 3 and 4 (Princeton, 1967, 1968). See also the one-volume source book edited by E. David Cronon, *The Political Thought of Woodrow Wilson* (Indianapolis, 1965). On the development of American political science in general see Albert Somit and Joseph Tanenhaus, *The Development of Political Science* (Boston, 1967).

30. *The Atlantic Monthly,* 67 (May, 1891), 694–699, reprinted in Ray Stannard Baker and Wm. E. Dodd (eds.), *The Public Papers of Woodrow Wilson 1857–1913*

(New York, 1925, 2 vols.), I, 187–197. The quotations above are found in Baker and Dodd on pages 188, 193, 196.

31. *The Political Science Quarterly,* IV (March, 1889), 153–169, reprinted in Baker and Dodd, *op. cit.,* pp. 159–178. The quotations above are found in the latter at pages 170 and 177.

32. See the appraisal of Wilson in Commager, *op. cit.,* pp. 322–325.

33. See the reprint of *Congressional Government* in Link, *The Papers of Woodrow Wilson,* IV, 13–179. See especially the informative prefatory notes by the editor on pages 6–13. A recent paperback edition of *Congressional Government,* with an introduction by Walter Lippmann, was printed in 1956 by Meridian Books.

34. "Committee or Cabinet Government," *Overland Monthly,* III (January, 1884), 17–33, reprinted in Baker and Dodd, I, 95–129.

35. *Papers of Woodrow Wilson,* IV, 140; *Constitutional Government in the U.S.* (New York, 1908), p. 70.

36. David Easton, *The Political System* (New York, 1953), p. 82.

37. Turner's essay is conveniently reproduced in the group of essays in the Heath New History Series, *Problems in American Civilization,* under the name, *The Turner Thesis* (Boston, 1949), pp. 1–18.

38. See especially the essays by B. F. Wright, Jr., George W. Peirce, and Carlton Hayes, in *ibid.,* 42–50, 65–83, 84–93.

39. J. Allen Smith, *The Spirit of American Government* (Cambridge, Mass., 1965).

40. Charles A. Beard, *Politics* (New York, 1908), pp. 14, 132.

41. See especially, Robert E. Brown, *Charles Beard and the Constitution* (New York, 1965) and Forrest MacDonald, *We the People* (Chicago, 1958).

42. Herbert Croly, *The Promise of American Life* (New York, 1963, paperback), p. 176. See especially the illuminating introduction to this edition by Charles Forcey, and Forcey's treatment of Croly, along with Walter Weyl and Walter Lippmann, in his book *The Crossroads of Liberalism* (New York, 1961).

43. *Ibid.,* pp. 185, 190.

44. *Ibid.,* pp. 207, 214.

45. *Ibid.,* pp. 441, 442, 443.

46. Crick, *op. cit.,* pp. 79, 80.

47. Merrill D. Peterson, *The Jeffersonian Image in the American Mind* (New York, 1962), p. 340.

48. Richard W. Taylor (ed.), *Essays in Honor of Arthur F. Bentley* (Yellow Springs, Ohio, 1957), pp. 32, 33. The best example of the emphasis on groups in later American political science literature is David Truman, *The Governmental Process* (New York, 1951). For recent discussion of Bentley see the articles in *American Political Science Review,* 54 (1960), 944, 971; Norman Jacobson, "Causality and Time in Political Process: A Speculation," *A.P.S.R.,* 58 (March, 1964), 15–23; Peter Odegard, "A Group Basis of Politics: A New Name for an Ancient Myth," *Western Political Quarterly,* XI (Sept., 1958), 689–701; Leo Weinstein, "The Group Approach: Arthur F. Bentley," in Herbert Storing (ed.), *Esays On the Scientific Study of Politics* (New York, 1962), pp. 151–224; Crick, *op. cit.,* pp. 118–130.

49. Arthur F. Bentley, *The Process of Government* (Cambridge, Mass., 1967), pp. 177, 180, 187.

50. Arthur F. Bentley and John Dewey, *Knowing and the Known* (Boston, 1960), p. 108; *Process of Government,* p. 209; Arthur F. Bentley, *Relativity in Man and Society* (New York, 1926). The most recent study of Bentley, which interprets his political thought in terms of the theory of relativity and emphasizes his primary focus on "process," is William L. Buscemi, *Arthur F. Bentley and Behavioral Political Theory,* unpublished doctoral dissertation, University of Notre Dame, 1969. I have been greatly aided in my discussion of Bentley by this study.

51. *Process of Government,* pp. 178, 209, 258–259, 208, 220, 301, 370–371.

52. *Ibid.,* pp. 389–390, 276.

53. *Ibid.,* pp. 389–390, 394.

54. See especially Bentley's, *Relativity in Man and Society;* his *Inquiry into In-*

The Progressive Period and American Political Thought

quiries (Boston, 1954); his work with Dewey, *Knowing and the Known;* and Sidney Ratner *et. al.* (eds.), *John Dewey and Arthur F. Bentley, A Philosophical Correspondence, 1932–1951* (New Brunswick, N.J., 1964).

55. Myron Q. Hale, "The Cosmology of Arthur F. Bentley," A.P.S.R., 54 (Dec., 1960), 958; Floyd W. Matson, *The Broken Image* (New York, 1964), p. 124.

56. Quoted in Crick, *op. cit.,* pp. 102, 104.

57. *Ibid.,* p. 106.

PART NINE

THE CHALLENGE TO CONSTITUTIONAL DEMOCRACY AND CONTEMPORARY AMERICAN POLITICAL THOUGHT

Chapter 23

DISENCHANTMENT AND DEMOCRACY

This philosophy of intelligent control [Pragmatism] just does not measure up to our needs.

RANDOLPH BOURNE

Our problem is to be ruled by the truth about harmonious human relations, and the discovery of the truth is an object of specialized research.

HAROLD LASSWELL

Until the late nineteenth century the expansionist tendencies of the American people were mainly contained in the continental westward movement. It was assumed, as Washington's Farewell Address and the Monroe Doctrine show, that America and the Old World had distinct interests to which each should attend without interference. The original idea of a "City Upon a Hill" had been reshaped into the notion of America as the pacific democratic exemplar unspotted by Old-World politics, militarism, and imperialism. The Spanish-American War of 1898 and the attendant overseas expansion were, as we have seen, justified by men such as Theodore Roosevelt, Brooks Adams and Alfred Mahan, and attacked by men such as William Graham Sumner and William James. Generally speaking, the imperialists, besides arguing in terms of *Realpolitik* and Manifest Destiny, attempted to link expansion with democracy by arguing that American rule over others was tantamount to political tutelage aiming at ultimate self-government. The antiimperialists argued the incompatibility of democracy and imperialism at home as well as in the acquired territories. Imperialism, however, was quite compatible with Progressivism. As a recent historian has put it, they "flourished together because they were both expressions of the same philosophy of government, a tendency to judge any action not by the means employed but by the results achieved, a worship of definitive ac-

511

tion for action's sake . . . and an almost religious faith in the democratic mission of America."[1]

The democratic mission of America, having been extended from the continent to noncontiguous territories and peoples, was further broadened, in the crusade of World War I, to "make the world safe for democracy," a movement which aimed hopefully at the ultimate establishment of a League of Nations. In the pursuit of these objectives the nation was mobilized, opinion was manipulated and controlled, dissent was not merely discouraged, but visited with repressive legislation and public hysteria, and domestic reform was pushed into the background.

Alongside the influence of international politics there was, as the twentieth century moved on, an increasingly close connection between European and American thought. As has been seen, there had always been a decided European influence on America, beginning with the religious and theological traditions and extending through the ages of rationalism, idealism and romanticism, and evolutionary naturalism. The new century witnessed another wave of naturalistic explanations of man and society whose impact on America was greatest in the period between the two world wars. Principal among these were: (1) the theories of the Viennese medical doctor, Sigmund Freud, concerning the nature of mind, the influence of the unconscious upon man, and the method of psychoanalysis; (2) the Marxist materialist interpretation of history, economic determinism, and, after the dissemination of Marx's early works in the post-World War II period, Marxian humanism;* (3) the discovery of the conditioned reflex by the Russian physiologist Ivan Pavlov, and the development of behaviorist psychology; and (4) the explanation of government in terms of the inevitability of elitist rule expounded by the political sociologists Vilfredo Pareto, Roberto Michels, and Gaetano Mosca.

It is interesting to note that in each of the major secular movements of thought historically shared by Europe with America the notion of "nature," although always in a different sense, was basic. However, whereas "nature" seen from the rationalist, idealist and romantic viewpoint was compatible with humanism whether theocentric or anthropocentric, naturalism in either its Darwinian, Marxian and Freudian manifestations, except where qualified as in the case of a Ward, James, and Dewey, appeared antithetical not only to human freedom and the notion of a moral order, but to man himself. As Robert Spiller has expressed it: "Man was being pushed out of the center of the biological world, and his will was being taken from him by such theories as that of natural selection, economic determinism, or subconscious rather than conscious

---

* As previously mentioned, Marxism had no great influence as an organized political force in America. Its greater impact lay in the influence of its ideas upon American intellectuals.

motivation."[2] What validity was then left to the universalistic ideas of the Declaration of Independence, the assumption of a cosmic moral law, human progress and the free individual capable of governing himself rationally? Questions such as this made ready acceptance of the new ideas more difficult for the American, disposed as he was to optimism, than for many Europeans. And yet no matter how strong the urge to return to the womb of innocence there ensued a disenchantment which sometimes went beyond skepticism to cynicism. In the process democratic government and its assumptions were brought under attack.

Critic of War and the State: Randolph Bourne (1886–1918)

Perhaps the most articulate dissenting voice in the war years was that of a young literary critic, Randolph Bourne. A pacifist who would neither aid nor obstruct the military effort, Bourne was discouraged by the support given the war by American intellectuals, particularly John Dewey. He eloquently expressed the aspirations of youth, tending to view politics through the eyes of the artist, and sitting in critical judgment upon those who compromise in the name of "realism." Believing that a person comes into the world with all around him given and serving to mold him, he lamented that this brings one to live "almost entirely . . . as a constituted unit in society rather than a free and personal one." Thus there is a "divorce between social compulsion and personal desire" with the heaviest penalties falling on those who violate "the three sacred taboos of property, sex and the State." Bourne saw life as "an incalculable and importunate stream of desire, which rises in the adult to a will-to-power." Consequently, "the problem of the soul becomes the direction of this desire and energy into creative channels, not its suppression or even control by that reason which is so often a mere disguise of another and more acceptable desire." In such a world, he added approvingly, "personality becomes more desirable than character, creative expressiveness than self-control, cooperation than justice, social freedom than rights."[3]

In his essay, "War and the Intellectuals," Bourne questioned the "realism" appealed to by liberal intellectuals in support of the war: "The pacifist is roundly scolded for refusing to face the facts, and for retiring into his own world of sentimental desire. But is the realist, who refuses to challenge or criticize facts, entitled to any more credit than that which comes from following the line of least resistance? The realist thinks he at least can control events by linking himself to the forces that are moving. Perhaps he can. But if it is a question of controlling war, it is difficult to see how the child on the back of a mad elephant is to be any more effective in stopping the beast than is the child who tries to stop

him from the ground." Bourne saw war itself, not Germany, as the real
enemy and spoke out against "any contemplated 'liberal' world order
founded on military coalitions." The realist, he declared, is doomed to
pay the penalty of seeing disappear one by one the justifications put
forth by accepting the war.[4]

Bourne thought that Dewey's pragmatism had failed its own test—it
no longer worked. It was adequate and even quite desirable for "a society at peace, prosperous and with a fund of good will" and where institutions are malleable, but in its application to politics it tended to slide
over the "crucial question of ends." Thus in critical conditions, he concluded, "this philosophy of intelligent control just does not measure up
to our needs." Pragmatic education had produced a younger generation of liberal public administrators who were attracted by "the technical side of the war . . . not the interpretative or political side," and
who accepted ends "as announced from above," because "they have
never learned not to subordinate idea to technique." The trouble was
not that Dewey ignored values but that "there was always that unhappy ambiguity in his doctrine as to just how values were created, and
it became easier and easier to assume that just any growth was justified
and almost any activity valuable so long as it achieved ends." Besides
technique, Bourne insisted, vision is required. For this reason he chose
James over Dewey, believing that man stood more in need of "the creative desire" than "the creative intelligence."[5]

Bourne turned from a critique of the war intellectuals to a critique
of the state. Hoping for the development of an organic national culture,
he, as Charles Forcey in comparing him to Walt Whitman has said,
"rejected politics in favor of the delights of artistic anarchism." Distinguishing between *government* ("the machinery by which the nation,
organized as a State, carries out its State functions"), *nation* (the cultural organism) and *state* ("a mystical conception"), Bourne derided the
state as "the organization of the herd to act offensively or defensively
against another herd similarly organized." War is "the health of the
state"; it stifles minority opinion and arouses a "tyrannical herd-instinct."
Because it is in the conduct of foreign policy and war that "the State
acts most concentratedly as the organized herd" and because in America
the President is supreme and relatively unchecked in this area, Bourne
criticized the American constitutional system. In fact, he fully accepted
the thesis of Smith and Beard that the Constitution was a reactionary
document; he thought that whereas the Declaration of Independence,
through the principle of the consent of the governed, had reduced the
state "to the homely work of an instrument for carrying out popular
policies," the Constitution reintroduced the powerful "state," and established "an elected king." His basic belief was that states and not peoples
make war on each other, that the state must be minimized, and popular

control as manifested in the nation must be put in the ascendancy. Thus he called for "nations organized for internal administration, nations organized as a federation of free communities, nations organized in any way except that of a political centralization of a dynasty." Such entities, he declared, "could not possibly make war upon each other."[6]

Bourne, who died at the end of the war, expressed the dissent of the artist to the facile regimentation of man in organized political society. Assuming that desire, uninhibited by institutional repression, will lead to a more humane and creative existence, he presaged the youth movement of the 1960's in his idealism, pacifism, and protest against the primacy of technics and organization over human values, as well as in his romanticism, anarchism, and political naiveté.[7]

Cynical Critic of Democracy: Henry L. Mencken (1880–1956)

Bourne had written in sorrow while yet believing in man and in democracy; upon the "return to normalcy" in the 1920's and the years of the Great Depression in the 1930's, criticism of democracy came from men who disagreed with its fundamental assumptions. Perhaps the most vocal and strident was the journalist, satirical essayist, and lexicographer, Henry L. Mencken. An unreconstructed materialist who believed that mind is mainly a function "of purely physical and chemical phenomena," Mencken thought that because the chief emotion in man is fear, man's history is a record of "successive victimizations—by priests, by politicians, by all sorts of quacks." The process of education should be one of ridding man of such fears, but because most men are "congenitally incapable of any such intellectual progress," their thinking is all done "on the level of a few primitive appetites and emotions." It follows that "politics under democracy consists almost wholly of the discovery, chase and scotchings of bugaboos." At his best a scorchingly effective critic of sham, hypocrisy, credulity, and provincialism, Mencken's bitterness brought him to scrape the bottom of his barrel of invective in calling democracy "a form of theology" and associating it with puritanism."[8]

Although he relied on behaviorist psychology, intelligence test results, and Freudian thought when congenial to his position, Mencken's *Notes on Democracy* are based almost wholly upon his low opinion of the common man whom he derisively called "Boobus Americanus." Essentially a believer in cultural minority elitism it is somewhat anomalous that the author of *The American Language*, a great contribution to our knowledge of American life and culture which sees language as a living force and a popular creation, could talk so disparagingly of common intelligence.

Conservative Critics of Democracy

Protesting against the plutocrat in power, the meanness of mass democracy, and the materialism of the age were the so-called "new humanists," Paul Elmer More (1867–1937), Irving Babbitt (1865–1933), and Ralph Adams Cram (1863–1942).

More, a literary essayist and historical scholar, stressed human depravity, inequality, and the consequent need for a natural aristocracy to serve as a *via media* between populism and plutocracy. He described the true aristocrat as one subject to the "inner law of self-restraint" who opposes dispassionate judgment to humanitarian sentimentality.[9]

Babbitt, a Harvard professor and literary critic, in his *Democracy and Leadership* (1924), called for the imposition of the "ethical will" (symbolized by Edmund Burke) over "man's expansive desires" (symbolized by Rousseau), through a frank recognition in government of inequality and the hierarchical and leadership principles. He held "that genuine leaders, good or bad, there will always be, and that democracy becomes a menace when it seeks to evade this truth." Thus modern man must choose between a state led by men of disciplined "moral imagination" and equipped with an institutional restraint upon popular passion such as the Supreme Court of the United States, and a state based on the "idyllic imagination" wherein the "general will" is deified and evil is explained in terms of social institutions. He prescribed the substitution of "the doctrine of the right man for the doctrine of the rights of man." Whereas the aristocratic man is marked by his control over desire, democratic man is reflected in the "spontaneous me" of Walt Whitman. In this view, Washington, Hamilton, and Marshall are favorable symbols, Jefferson and Jackson are invidious symbols. The former proceeded from the spirit of "puritanism," characterized approvingly as "our national spirit of concentration," whereas the latter are associated with democracy, "the expansion of national impulse."[10]

Cram, an architect and social critic, argued in his *The Nemesis of Mediocrity* (1917) and *The End of Democracy* (1937) the moral and political bankruptcy of democracy. Like More and Babbitt, he conceded the need to establish equality of opportunity and to utilize proven ability and condemned the ideas of human equality and majority rule. Believing that the Founding Fathers intended to establish an "Aristocratic Republic" which he associated with his preference, medieval institutions, he considered the original Constitution to have been drawn by "statesmen and gentlemen," in contrast to amendments twelve to nineteen which were the work of "politicians." In place of politics and parties he proposed the substitution of a corporative state based on functional representation within the framework of what would amount to a constitutional elective monarchy and aristocracy.[11]

The most learned of the conservative critics of democracy was George Santayana (1863–1952) a naturalistic philosopher who disagreed sharply with the "new humanism" as well as pragmatism and liberalism. Born in Spain, he came to America as a young boy but remained temperamentally and psychologically a Latin, a factor which probably induced him late in life permanently to leave his adopted country for Rome.

Long before Existentialism became a fad Santayana declared his belief that "this world is contingency and absurdity incarnate, the oddest of possibilities masquerading momentarily as a fact." Seeing "animal faith" as the basis for acceptance of an order of nature and for experiential continuity, he treated reason as built thereupon and exalted the "Life of Reason" as "the progressive organization of irrational impulses." Viewing nature in terms of the aesthetic, moral materialism of the poet Lucretius, he opposed metaphysical approaches which judge reality in terms of an absolute selective principle. In light of this he found wanting the American liberal tradition from Transcendentalism to Pragmatism which holds "that the universe exists and is governed for the sake of man or of the human spirit."[12]

Santayana rejected Pragmatism's "continual substitution of human psychology . . . for the universe, in which man is but one distracted and befuddled animal." He thought that Dewey's philosophy was "calculated to justify all the assumptions of American society" and that it contained "a pervasive quasi-Hegelian tendency to dissolve the individual into his social functions." Dewey, Santayana charged, assumed throughout his system "the dominance of the foreground," and because "in nature there is no foreground or background," his philosophy abandons naturalism and is at bottom metaphysical.[13]

Santayana thought that the liberal at best believes that nations have already institutionalized his utopian ideas. At worst, the liberal imposes on all civilization "a single cheap and dreary pattern," assumes positive institutions which he does not create but inherits, and takes pride in differences and choices even though "it is in the subsoil of uniformity, of tradition, of dire necessity that human welfare is rooted, together with wisdom and unaffected art. . . ."[14]

Santayana saw the "new humanists" not as the descendants of the humanists of the Renaissance but as Calvinists who judge all in terms of a revealed restrictive absolute standard: "The discontent of the American humanists would be unintelligible if they were really humanists in the old sense; if they represented in some measure the soul of that young oak, bursting the limits of Christendom. Can it be that they represent rather the shattered urn, or some one of its fragments? The leaders, indeed, though hardly their followers, might pass for rather censorious minds, designed by nature to be the pillars of some priestly

orthodoxy." While the new humanists lamented the lack of articulate
American ideals, Santayana saw this condition as a sign of national
health, declaring: "The national faith and morality are vague in idea,
but inexorable in spirit." The humanists, in Santayana's eyes, merely
continued the moral absolutism of the genteel tradition. He concluded:
"Call it humanism or not, only a morality frankly relative to man's nature is worthy of man being at once vital and rational, martial and generous; whereas absolutism smells of fustiness as well as of faggots."[15]

A professed "high Tory in his sympathies," Santayana disdained democracy defined not as equality of opportunity, but as egalitarian uniformity, majority rule, and the absence of a natural hierarchy of authority. Against the modern notion of liberty as the right to do as one
wishes, he exalted the Greek idea "that true liberty is bound up with an
institution, a corporate scientific discipline, necessary to set free the perfect man, or the god, within us." Because true freedom results from
knowledge, it only obtains when one "obeys a force which in the best
sense of the word *represents* him." Thus "it is no loss of liberty to subordinate ourselves to a natural leader." A great man, who lives the life of
reason, internally organizing irrational impulses, needs only, upon
mounting the throne, "to read his own soul and follow his only instinctive ambitions" in order to make himself a representative leader. Similarly, "a government is not made representative or just by the mechanical expedient of electing its members by universal suffrage. It becomes
representative only by embodying in its policy, whether by instinct
or high intelligence, the people's conscious and unconscious interests." Democracy is based on the erroneous assumptions "that human
nature in all men is essentially similar," and that consequently mankind
cannot "fully develop its vital liberty without coming to a unanimous
vision of the world and a cooperative exercise of the same virtues." Only
if the lessons of nature and history were ignored and the common citizen
became "something of a saint and something of a hero" could democracy nobly subsist. Santayana's ideal state is a monarchy rooted in the
principle of representative eminence, and structured hierarchically, like
the Catholic Church. The best practicable state to him, however, is a
timocracy, "a government by men of merit," deriving from equality of
opportunity. Finally, in tune with his emphasis on biology, he maintained that the road to moral progress lies not in democracy but in "in-
breeding which allows the potentialities in one incipient variety of human beings to develop."[16]

Concerning the conservative critics as a whole, it can first be said that
they do not demonstrate precisely and convincingly how a government
by the best can be realized in terms of institutions and principles of
selection. They also assume that democracy precludes the best men
from rulership whereas it might be argued that democracy defined as

majority rule does not necessarily preclude, but assumes and better allows for equality of opportunity. As we have seen, Jefferson and Franklin believed that the democracy of a citizenry rooted in public virtue could more readily lead to the selection of "the wise and good" (natural aristocracy) as rulers than any other proposed system.[17]

Santayana disdained the absolutism of the humanists while sharing some of their basic objections to democracy. His individualism brought him to assume unwarrantedly that democracy necessarily implies mediocrity and uniformity. His belief that because "no form of life can be inherently wrong" democracy is an affront to human nature, has no validity if democracy, instead of being equated with uniformity, is equated with that tolerance of all modes of life of which historically it has often been accused. Finally, as a recent student of Santayana's thought has stated: "In the last analysis Santayana's ideals and fears seem more properly relevant to a program of animal breeding, designed to produce superiority in mere size or brute strength, than to the achievement of a political order favorable to excellence in the genuinely moral and intellectual dimensions of man."[18]

Racist Critics of Democracy

Democracy was also attacked in the postwar period by advocates of racial superiority. Earlier arguments by anthropologists on naturalistic evolutionary grounds, and by historians, political scientists, and politicians, such as John Fiske, Herbert Baxter Adams, James K. Hosmer, Woodrow Wilson, Theodore Roosevelt, Henry Cabot Lodge and Albert Beveridge, on cultural grounds, were supplemented by those which maintained biological supremacy of the Nordic over the colored races and the Eastern and Southern European peoples. The results of intelligence tests administered to servicemen during the war were used to justify Nordic superiority on an individual basis, while the analysis of stages of human development by Lewis Morgan into savagery, barbarism, and civilization was sometimes used to justify it on a collective basis. In his works, *The Rising Tide of Color Against White World Supremacy* (1920) and *The Revolt Against Civilization* (1922), Lothrop Stoddard (1883–1950) warned of the threat to white supremacy posed by the growing colored peoples of the world, and maintained that in modern times only the Nordic race has demonstrated a capability of producing and maintaining a civilization. Civilization, however, Stoddard argued, is precarious; whereas in savage and barbarous societies the principle of natural selection serves to eliminate the unfit, in civilized societies natural selection gives way to social selection and a type of humanitarianism which not only preserves the unfit but allows them freely and indiscriminately to procreate and results in racial deterioration. At the same time William McDougall, a Harvard psychology professor, in his *Is America Safe for Democracy?* (1921) maintained that racial intermixture would probably result in a reversion to lower biological types.[19]

Drawing upon the arguments of the Frenchman, Joseph de Gobineau, for Aryan supremacy and the Englishman, Houston Stewart Chamberlain, for Teutonic supremacy, Madison Grant (1865–1937), a corporation lawyer and at one time chairman of the New York Zoological Society, contended that universal suffrage tended toward the preponderance of inferior types. Believing that "moral, intellectual, and spiritual attributes are as persistent as physical character and are transmitted substantially unchanged from generation to generation," Grant declared that American democracy "intrusted the government of this country and the maintenance of . . . ideals to races who have never yet succeeded in governing themselves, much less any one else." The Nordic race, he contended, is one "of rulers, organizers and aristocrats . . . characterized by a great stability and steadiness," which can readily maintain democratic ideals, in contrast to a democracy based on a racially mixed society which will result in national suicide. It followed that the races must be separated by "artificial devices" such as sterilization and segregation.[20]

Analysis of the theory of racial superiority shows that it has two components—the superiority of the white to the colored races and the superiority of Nordics within the white race. The gratuitous assumptions in both cases are that peoples are for the most part homogeneous, that biology determines cultural achievement, and that achievement can be measured by objective standards. Overlooked are the facts that all "races" are hybrid; that "races" can vary in terms of their historical stages of evolution without being necessarily inherently "inferior" or "superior"; that the complexity of a culture does not necessarily indicate "superiority"; that environmental conditions and lack of equal opportunity rather than biology might explain "inferiority"; that standards of cross-cultural evaluation have usually been conceptions relative to a particular culture which are unwarrantedly universalized; that if culture and "race" are not independent of each other they are reciprocally influential; and that even if it could be shown that whites in general are "superior" to colored peoples, it cannot be shown that *all* whites are "superior" to all colored persons. Finally, it is not biology but culture which is the crucial factor for democracy and the relevant question is that which all good democratic political theorists have asked and attempted to answer: What cultural formation is most conducive to free government based on the consent and participation of the governed?[21]

In any case, that the premise of Northwestern European racial superiority and its congeniality to democracy was accepted by a majority of Americans is evident in the fact that the restrictive quota system favoring Northwestern European immigration was enacted into law in 1924 and has only recently been abandoned.

Fascist Criticism of Democracy

The Great Depression, which afflicted the American economy throughout most, if not all, of the 1930's, subjected constitutional representative democracy to its most severe test. Having become associated in the minds of many with capitalism, democracy was consequently associated with its breakdown. The emphasis upon a pragmatic approach to governmental regulation and economic planning within a loose Progressivist framework by President Franklin D. Roosevelt strained logic but preserved the democratic process and the liberal values. Of kindred spirit, yet more convinced of the decadence of capitalism, was the advocate of a socialist economy and forceful leader of the American Socialist Party, Norman Thomas (1884–1969). Denying the Marxist dogmas of economic determinism, inevitable class warfare, and historical materialism, Thomas proposed concrete, pragmatic, and democratic means to the end of a planned economy. Upon the realization of many of these programs in the "New Deal," the Socialist Party declined markedly.

Those who associated liberal democracy with capitalism and advocated their elimination included Marxian Communists and fascists. The Communist critique was, for the most part, a parroting of Marx, and secondary in importance of that of non-Communist Marxian intellectuals. On the other hand, during the period 1921–1941, when many Americans were rediscovering liberal values or flirting with Marxism in reaction to a threatening fascism abroad, there was an incipient growth of fascist tendencies within. A recent historian of the subject has isolated four essential elements of the then budding American fascism which had their roots in the earlier Populist movement and psychology: (1) "An economic program designed to appeal to a middle class composed largely of farmers and small merchants which feels itself being crushed between big business—and especially big finance—on the one hand, and an industrial working class which tends to question the necessity of the wage system and even of private property itself on the other." (2) A conviction that international cooperation is "a device by means of which supranational conspirators are able to destroy the freedom and well-being of the people." (3) "A despair of liberal democratic institutions, resulting from the belief that the press and the other communication media have been captured by the enemy, as have the two major political parties." Along with this "political power is held to belong to the people as a whole and is considered to be best exercised through some form of plebiscitary democracy." (4) "An interpretation of history in which the causal factor is the machinations of international financiers."[22]

The most articulate and learned American proponent of fascism was Lawrence Dennis (1893–), a publicist whose years spent in the American diplomatic service made him miles removed from popular activists of the day such as Huey Long and the Reverend Charles E. Coughlin who have sometimes been called fascists. To Dennis fascism is "an expression of human will which creates its own truths and values from day to day to suit its changing purposes." It follows that "the only conclusive test of the workability of a social system must be that of survival." Any social system "represents a given scheme or hierarchy of ultimate values," but such ultimate values "cannot be validated by the processes of logic or by reason." Like the positivist, the fascist sees reason as merely instrumental to the realization and clarification of values which are an emanation of the will.[23]

Dennis held that the Marxist goal of a classless society without government is unattainable because "social order requires government and administration by a ruling class or power-exercising class which must always be an aristocracy of management, however selected, operating through some set of mechanisms of social control, economic as well as political." Leadership by an elite is inevitable in society. The elite in any society "refers to the influential and powerful, and includes also the outs who are potentially, if not actually, as influential and powerful as the ins at the top."[24]

Joining this notion to his ethical relativism, Dennis concluded: "The right and wrong of any social order . . . is only a matter of how it suits the dominant section of the elite to have the game played. And who the dominant elite shall be can never be permanently determined by law, but must always be determined by force factors." Thus under any regime not only are the masses ruled by an elite but it is might which makes right. In regard to America (and capitalism) the worst that can be said "is that it is not getting the best out of the in-elite, and that it is getting nothing constructive out of the out-elite. . . ." On the other hand, "a wise social philosophy, such as that of fascism, strives to make a place for all members of the elite." In any case, fascism is characterized by the will of the leadership manifested ultimately in force, manipulation and control of opinion, producing a general plan for society which puts aside abstractions, such as the supremacy and equal protection of the law, and is to be measured in terms of "success." Executive judgment and responsibility replace legal norms and judicial interpretation. As such there must be a concentration and integration of power; liberal devices such as separation of powers, federalism, a rigid constitution, judicial review, and all political parties, except the controlling fascist party, must be eliminated. It is the end willed by the elitist leadership which is of prime importance; the means are to be measured pragmatically in relation to their fitness to the willed end.[25]

Although Dennis talked of rule by elites and the definition of purposes in terms of the interest and will of elites as if they were descriptive behavioral laws (a fact which would appear to render his criticism of existing government a futile defiance of the inevitable), he also talked prescriptively of fascism being concerned with "national interest" or "common good," and of fascist elitism as superior to other types. He thought fascism morally superior because it provides "a formula of national solidarity within the spiritual bonds and iron disciplines of which the elite and the masses of any given nation, every one in the measure of his capacity, can cooperate for the common good." But this involves no responsibility of rulers to the governed in the sense of accountability; what responsibility exists is that of the leadership to its ideals which, as we have seen, are not the products of reason but of sheer will.[26]

Like his Communist counterparts, Dennis denies the absolute character of individual rights. Democracy is described as a system allied to a now-decadent capitalism. It is condemned not because it precludes government by an elite (being a form of government it must embody rulership by an elite), but because it allows the masses by majority rule to change elites. Dennis simply denied the competence of the broad body of a people intelligently to sit in judgment of and to distinguish between elites. By broadening the controlling elite and eliminating the democratic institutions permitting dissent, Dennis believed that internal conflict within the state could be eliminated and the nation strengthened.

Dennis' fascism is compounded of the positivist's emphasis on the noncognitive and relative nature of moral norms, the vitalist's emphasis on the primacy of will, the pragmatist's emphasis on workability and success, the cynic's conception of the incompetence of the average man, and the belief that strong leadership must be popularly irresponsible. Dennis is clear that "politics is always essentially a conspiracy of power"; thus he faults both liberals and conservatives because they "think of politics as a game" and "have not awakened to the fact that it is now a war," which always seeks "to destroy the enemy." An open dictatorship by an elite rooted in force can eliminate the need which exists in a democracy for an elite to use "guile and duplicity" in ruling.[27]

In its denial of objective moral principles, its equation of politics with power unconnected to purpose, its conception of power as substantive and nonrelational, its focus on force as the basis of the state to the neglect of such factors as habit, utility, consent, and cooperative desire, its submerging the individual in the corporative state, and its denial of the ability of the people to render "elites" responsible by choosing intelligently between them, Dennis' frank exposition shows the utter incompatibility of fascism with American constitutional democracy.

Elitist Critic of Democracy: James Burnham (1905–)

Whereas Dennis argued the need for government by a fascist elite, James Burnham, a former Marxist of the Trotskyite persuasion, expounded a view based upon the elitist social thought of the Europeans Mosca, Michels, and Pareto, as well as Veblen's emphasis on the importance of "engineers" in society. In *The Managerial Revolution* (1941), he proceeded from the assumption that government is a resultant of organizational dictates beyond the control of the people at large, to conclude that parliamentary control of government like capitalist control of industry was inevitably being replaced by a new ruling class of "managers," i.e., production engineers and administrators. In a later work, *The Machiavellians* (1943), he disavowed ideology and economic determinism and defined politics as a power struggle in which elites use force, fraud, and myth to control society. In this view democracy means merely a condition in which new elements can force their way into the elite from below. While inevitable elitist rule renders "self-government" impossible, Burnham maintained that such rule can be so developed that it permits of liberty and opposition.

Burnham's view was quite dogmatic, elevating a tendency into a universal and inexorable law and assuming the complete passivity of the "masses." It lacked precision in its definition of "manager," and like all approaches which assume an "iron law of oligarchy," paid insufficient attention to the roles played by an intelligent electorate, public opinion, and elected representatives in checking and controlling governmental administrators, as well as the existence within a pluralistic society of a number of elites (labor, business, education, government, etc.), which might effectively limit each other.[28]

Democracy as a "Useful Slogan": Thurman Arnold (1891–1968)

The main works of the Yale legal realist and later trust-buster and federal judge, Thurman Arnold, were representative of a tough-minded approach, compounded of skepticism and pragmatism, and reflected the views of a number of nonideological supporters of the New Deal. The essence of his thesis, presented in *The Symbols of Government* (1936) and *The Folklore of Capitalism* (1937), was: "Social institutions require faith and dreams to give them morale. They need to escape from these faiths and dreams in order to progress. The hierarchy of governing institutions must pretend to symmetry, moral beauty, and logic in order to maintain their prestige and power. To actually govern, they must constantly violate those principles in hidden and covert ways."[29] The "folklore" which is law, economics, and political theory, comprises "hokum" or "theology," which is necessary for society. From the realistic politician's point of view, however, it constitutes something to be used, not believed in or followed. Such creeds are attempts to impose a framework of rationality upon the basically irrational activity of men. The "fact-minded observer" must adopt the psychiatric approach (as the successful politician has always done on a vulgar plane), seeing man as irrational and discarding the outmoded concepts of sin, reason, repentance, and free will. Arnold summed up his recommended "philosophy for humanitarian politicians" as follows:

From a humanitarian point of view the best government is that which we find in an insane asylum. In such a government the physicians in charge do not separate the ideas of the insane into any separate sciences such as law, economics, and sociology; nor then instruct the insane in the intricacies of these three sciences. Nor do they argue with the insane as to the soundness or unsoundness of their ideas. Their aim is to make the inmates of the asylum as comfortable as possible, regardless of their respective moral deserts. In this they are limited only by the facilities of the institution. It is, of course, theoretically possible to treat the various ideas and taboos which affect modern society, just as the alienist treats the delusions of his patients as factors which condition their behavior. This precludes any classification into sound or unsound theories. No psychiatrist, today, attempts to differentiate the *content* of foolish ideas, and of insane ideas. It is equally possible to adopt a point of view toward government where ideas are considered only in light of their effect on conduct. To a certain extent, the government which civilized nations impose on savage tribes does succeed in taking this attitude; and success in dealing with such tribes is largely determined by the ability of the governing group to utilize taboos, instead of trying to stamp them out as unsound.[30]

Such a view Arnold thought might serve as a "practical philosophy for politicians" but not as a general political theory because folklore (which is always necessary) ceases to be folklore when popularly recognized as such.[31]

To Arnold organizations and techniques alone count; principles have only functional value insofar as they are manipulatively used by organizations. Thus he argued that democracy has ceased to be regarded as a set of rational principles but has become a name for an organization controlled by voters. It is then immaterial whether democracy is "morally beautiful" or not, as long as it keeps in touch with the people. The democratic creed of the Founding Fathers is consequently explained as "a useful slogan to stir national pride in a people who had no ruling class."[32]

If Arnold is to be taken seriously, his ideal politician as a wielder of organizational techniques, slogans, and power stands in relation to the

populace as a trained psychiatrist to the insane. He wanted men who
are at once good organizers and humanitarians to rise above principle
and employ the means of power opportunistically and pragmatically.
Whereas a Hegel could proclaim that success in politics consists in one's
ability to identify himself with a principle, Arnold would say that success
in politics consists in one's ability to reduce principles to manipulative
slogans and employ scientific technique to the resolution of the concrete
problems of society. Although he remarked the need of good men, he
presented no theory of the good by which they might be identified.
Similarly, he assumed that such men will remain good even if they use
Machiavellian techniques. Nowhere did he treat of limits upon power;
instead, as one critic has charged, he "gives us a choice between the
insanity of uncontrolled myth and the inhumanity of uncontrolled
power."[33]

Arnold's dismissal of the common man as irrational and bereft of free
will, his disjunction of men into common men and "fact-minded"
leaders, his reduction of principles to slogans, his dismissal of any
concept of fundamental moral law, and his celebration of the primacy
of organization over truth, were indeed part of his tongue-in-cheek
rhetoric of exaggeration; they are also corrosive of the traditional
American liberal faith, leaving no effective means to distinguish between well-organized despotism and constitutional democracy. Organizational success and material comfort elevated into standards justify
whatever means are used to their realization irrespective of attendant
affronts to individual dignity. At best, one can only hope for sensitivity
in the psychiatric manipulators.

Democracy as "Compromise": T. V. Smith (1890–1964)

Disdaining metaphysics and theology, the utilitarian-pragmatic philosopher, teacher, and sometimes legislator, Thomas Vernor Smith,
lauded compromise as a principle of politics, the essence of democracy,
and a way of life. Juxtaposing it to conscience, he maintained that "only
in the utter privacy of a conscience devoted to contemplation or of a
consciousness contentedly otiose would there be no necessity of
compromise." If all men stand implacably upon conscience, conflict
inevitably ensues and meaningful growth in life is impossible. Men
must recognize that conscience is itself "a power drive needing sublimation through politics." Thus "a sense of guilt incident to the practice
of compromise is perhaps the worst enemy of the democratic way of
life."[34]

Smith admitted three limits to compromise: (1) necessity, in the
sense that unless compromises are needed they should not be made;

(2) peace, in the sense that compromise should not be effected when it would lead to war; and (3) progress, in the sense that compromise must be "the major principle of dynamics." Nonetheless, he added, "the limit of compromise is, beyond all doubt, not fixed primarily by appeal to conscience, and any conscience that thinks so becomes by that very fact an apologist for a covert form of dictatorship."[35]

Politicians are "generalized specialists in conciliation," who are absolutely requisite for peace and progress. Smith observed: "Conscience crucifies conscience unless the saints are protected from each other by political sinners who arrange the compromises of consciences and thus constitute the law which private citizens can agree to call 'the public conscience'." He advised conscientious purists: "Let others do the political compromising for you; you stick by your guns so long as they are pointed the other way." This because "to be a claimant and a compromiser at the same time is to injure conscience and to weaken the claim." To be fair we must compare the vices of our practicing politicians "not with the virtues of the secluded individual" but with "the vices of dictators."[36]

Smith's vindication of democracy in the name of compromise was made at the price of denying that democracy does "require or permit, agreement on fundamentals," except those involving procedure. He assumed that (1) the life of "conscience" must be restricted to the private sphere, (2) if it is pursued beyond the private sphere it is equivalent to fanaticism and leads to dictatorship, (3) all men of "conscience" cannot or will not compromise, and (4) the peaceful conciliatory adjustment of disputes and resolution of issues in free government cannot be accepted by the conscientious as a primary principle of conscience.[37]

Similarly, it has been objected that Smith's stipulated limits to compromise in effect do not constitute limits. Thus if peace is regarded as a product of justice it has no place in Smith's formulation. Likewise, on his own terms, one cannot determine finally whether peace or conflict will issue from a compromise until after the event. Then, too, he provides no norm by which to judge necessity except necessity itself, and he tends to equate progress with whatever results from compromise.

In sum it can be stated that Smith's emphasis on the primacy and centrality of compromise, his conception of democracy as simply a process, and his denial of standards to measure conflicting claims, undercut the moral basis of democracy as a system of free government presupposing common standards of truth and justice. His exaltation of politicians as "moral middlemen," although admirable in that it calls attention to their ameliorative role, tends to reduce them to unprincipled trimmers unconcerned with ultimate values.

Behavioral Psychology and Democracy

Developments in the psychological and social sciences between the wars and thereafter also posed grave questions in relation to free government. Social anthropological studies giving rise to cultural and ethical relativism undercut justification of constitutional democracy in terms of fundamental moral law. As the century moved on there was a growing adherence to the assumption that the methods of the natural sciences are equally applicable to man and can produce a predictive and manipulative science of human behavior. Then, too, those who followed Pavlov in psychology, or Marx in social analysis, or Freud in human motivation, tended, like the earlier evolutionists, to limit, if not deny, human freedom and individual moral responsibility.

John B. Watson (1878–1958) assumed the nonrational and involuntary character of human behavior and built a psychology around the stimulus-response reflex arc (which Dewey had earlier refuted), denying any place to consciousness or purpose, focusing wholly on externally observable data, and accepting the environment as the sole causal factor. Seeing man as merely "an assembled organic machine," whose "possibility of shaping in any direction is almost endless," Watson declared it to be the interest of the behaviorist "to control man's reactions as physical scientists want to control and manipulate other natural phenomena." Specifically Watson aimed at manipulation through the conditioned reflex in the direction of individual adjustment to the existing socioeconomic system.[38]

The full implications of Watson's approach and the belief in a "science of man" were brought out in the work of B. F. Skinner (1904–), professor of psychology at Harvard. In his novel *Walden Two* (1948), Skinner turned aside from traditional morality to sketch approvingly a scientifically designed utopian community of benevolent, tolerant, cooperative, and happy individuals formed by "behavioral engineering." The assumptions of the founder and chief "cultural engineer" of the society are: (1) men are "by nature" neither good nor evil; they are simply malleable in terms of control and manipulation of their environment; (2) human freedom is not a legitimate consideration because "if man is free, then a technology of behavior is impossible"; (3) democracy "isn't and can't be the best form of government, because it's based on a scientifically invalid conception of man" which "fails to take account that in the long run *man is determined by the state*"; and (4) competition and emulation breed conflict which is the essence of politics and can be greatly minimized, if not eliminated, by proper conditioning with a consequent withering away of the political state.[39]

The self-effacing psychologist is the "priest" of Walden Two. He recognizes that if man is not controlled by intelligence deriving from the "science of man" he is left to the control of other forces. The general technique is "positive reinforcement," described in relation to man as follows: "When he behaves as we want him to behave, we simply create a situation he likes, or remove one he doesn't like." This involves "a sort of control under which the controlled, though they are following a code more scrupulously than was ever the case under the old system, nevertheless *feel free.*" Force is not involved; in fact, "governments which use force are based upon bad principles of human engineering." Supernatural religion along with the state will wither away in the process. Similarly, history will be studied never for its lessons but only as entertainment, the reasons being that history is completely replaceable by the timeless and universally valid "science of man," and that the "cooperative" man of Walden Two and its counterparts will be essentially different from the "competitive" man of history. American democracy is "a pious fraud" permitting the tyranny of the majority. Control by experts precludes democracy because: "The people are in no position to evaluate experts. And elected experts are never able to act as they think best. They can't experiment."[40]

Walden Two is designed to correct the existing aberration in society wherein control techniques are in the hands of the wrong men. Just as Arnold's political psychiatrist must replace the "politician," so Skinner's behavioral scientist armed with his expertise should replace politics with "the science of man." Similarly because, as the founder of *Walden Two* states, conceptions of moral law are all relative, and even idiosyncratic, the universally valid "science of man" must replace them. With the element of freedom bracketed out for methodological reasons from the beginning, the vital question of political life is swept under the rug. Men are to be made perfect by being rendered incapable of acting antisocially. As a humanistic critic of *Walden Two* has asked: "Is it not meaningful to say that whereas Plato's Republic and More's Utopia are noble absurdities, Walden Two is an ignoble one; that the first two ask men to be more than human, while the second urges them to be less?" Because Skinner assumes that man is the infinitely malleable product of external processes and is bereft of a nature which prescribes limits, man is what is done to him—a task better left to the practitioners of the "science of man" than to priests and politicians. Similarly if, as in Skinner's case, politics is assimilated to an art in the Aristotelian sense of the productive sciences and is removed from the strictures of moral prudence, one can fault the behavioral manipulator not for his crimes but only for his blunders.[41]

In like vein the sociologist George Lundberg (1895–1966) in his book *Can Science Save Us?* (1948) rejected politics and denigrated human freedom and democracy in pleading the case for the behavioral science of man. Social science armed with the results of analyses obtained through value-free techniques of research must replace the resort to "deep-seated, jungle-fed sentiments of justice, virtue, and a general feeling of the fitness of things." As for democracy and freedom we are told: "Scientists must recognize that democracy, for all its virtues, is only one of the possible types of organization under which men have lived and achieved civilization." To the statement that "science can flourish only in freedom," Lundberg replied: "It is a beautiful phrase, but unfortunately it flagrantly begs the question. The question is, under what conditions will the kind of freedom science needs be provided?" The shift in focal and normative emphasis is illuminating and ominous—the professedly value-neutral Lundberg is concerned primarily with the freedom of science and only secondarily with the freedom of man.[42]

Political Science and Democracy: Harold Lasswell (1902–)

There existed in American political science after World War I a similar tendency to move from pragmatism to positivism. Francis G. Wilson has remarked: "It was an atmosphere in which the chastened progressivism and reformism of a previous generation had come to rest in the academic chair." Illustrative of this was the former "Bull-Moose" Progressive and professor of political science at the University of Chicago, Charles Merriam. Seeking to "apply the categories of science to the vastly important forces of political and social control," Merriam urged that politics be studied in relation to biology, psychology, the environment, anthropology, and quantitative analysis.[43]

Most important of Merriam's students and the most well-known and prolific of American political scientists is Harold Lasswell who has taught at Chicago and Yale. Avidly pursuing Merriam's suggestion that a "scientific" political science must not only closely attend to advances in methods and techniques, but substantive developments in cognate fields, Lasswell, in his long career, has pioneered in the formulation of various "analytic concepts," "frames of reference," and "developmental constructs." Possessing neither Merriam's evangelical zeal for democracy nor his hortatory style, Lasswell reacted in the 1920's against the moralistic fervor of Progressivism by assuming, in a manner similar to the literary men of "the lost generation," a debunking approach to political life. In its many manifestations his work over the years has proceeded from the premises that traditional politics is at bottom pathological, that political philosophy has been its handmaid, and that the fully developed political (social) scientist must through his research be essentially a diagnostician of the illness, and hopefully a manipulative therapist. Probing to the source of the epiphenomenon which he regards politics to be, he has drawn, *inter alia,* upon Marx for social analysis, the European elitist school for the analysis of power, quantification for precise formulation, logical positivism for the purgation from the language of politics of empirically nonverifiable and logically indefensible metaphysical residues and for clarified codification of propositions, and, above all, Freud, for the reduction of politics to psychology. As Bernard Crick has observed, Lasswell sees the modern crisis in politics as "not primarily a failure in political prudence, a derangement between ethics and politics, nor yet a shift in geo-political factors," but one deriving from "the way in which we look at politics at all, in what we have hitherto counted as relevant knowledge and proper techniques." In short, Lasswell believes that political problems are largely insoluble by the traditional process of discussion and compromise.[44]

As an answer to what he termed in 1936 the "World Revolutionary situation," he called for "a universal body of symbols and practices sustaining an elite which propagates itself by peaceful methods and wields a monopoly of coercion which it is rarely necessary to apply to the uttermost." At the same time he sought in sociological analysis to gain realistic insight into politics as "the study of influence and the influential," by which it is recognized that the "elite," as opposed to the "mass," principally through manipulation of symbols, is the recipient of the representative values of "deference, income and safety." But most heavily did he emphasize what apparently remains central in his thought, the psychological examination of political actors and the development of a "politics of prevention," which combines personality analysis with behaviorial techniques of inquiry and control. In contrast to his then colleague, T. V. Smith, Lasswell saw the politician as an essentially immature person who, while displacing private motives on public objects, rationalizes in terms of the public interest. Politics is viewed as the sphere of conflict, "the process by which the irrational bases of society are brought out into the open." Politics affords solutions which are not the "rationally best," but "emotionally satisfactory." Democracy proceeds on the premise "that each man is the best judge of his own interest" whereas personality research shows that the individual is a poor judge thereof. Indeed, "the individual who chooses a political policy as a symbol of his wants is usually trying to relieve his own disorders by irrelevant palliatives." We must abandon "the assumption that the problem of politics is the problem of promoting discussion among all interests concerned in a given problem" because discussion "arouses a psychology of conflict which produces obstructive, fictitious and irrelevant values." Instead we must turn to a "politics of prevention," which recognizes that "our problem is to be ruled by the truth about the conditions of harmonious human relations, and the discovery of the truth is an object of specialized research." Very obviously the social scientist-psychologist has on these terms better credentials than the traditional leaders and politicians who historically have contended and even compromised with each other for the right to determine governmental policy. Thus Lasswell states: "If the politics of prevention spreads in society, a different type of education will become necessary for those who administer society or think about it. This education will start from the proposition that it takes longer to train a good social scientist than it takes to train a good physical scientist. The social administrator and social scientist . . . must mix with rich and poor, with savage and civilized, with sick and well, with young and old. . . . He must have an opportunity for prolonged self-scrutiny by the best-developed methods of personality study, and he must laboriously achieve a capacity to deal objectively with himself and with all others in human society." Like Arnold's "fact-minded" leader who uses but disbelieves myth and views society as a madhouse, Lasswell's social administrator-scientist deploys a preventive politics which will be "intimately allied to general medicine, physiological psychology, and related disciplines." Thus "the hope of the professors of social science, if not of the world, lies in the competitive strength of an elite based on vocabulary, footnotes, questionnaires, and conditioned responses, against an elite based on vocabulary, poison gas, property, and family prestige."[45]

Although he formally maintains a positivistic attitude of disregard of absolutes, Lasswell has come to exalt "human dignity" as the essence of democracy. His declaration that "the science of democracy . . . bears much the same relation to general political science that medicine has to biology" clearly implies that the "sciences" of fascism or oligarchy are illegitimate applications of the generic science of man. Lasswell, unlike many of his behaviorally oriented colleagues, is concerned with research not to implement or merely reflect present politics, but to bring about "a free-man's commonwealth" wherein "coercion is neither threatened, applied nor desired." Such democratic community is "one in which human dignity is realized in theory and fact." It is marked by "wide . . . participation in the shaping and sharing of values," and is based on the formation in men of a "democratic character" which maintains "an open as against a closed ego," is "multi-valued, rather than single-valued," possesses "deep confidence in the benevolent potentialities of man," results in "freedom from anxiety" as well as from human destructiveness and prejudice, and an absence of power conflicts, "politicians," and politics. However, since Lasswell also maintains that men do not know their own interests, the question of "goal clarification" becomes all-important. Science alone, it appears, in the form of an elite of sociopsychiatric researchers and administrators, can adequately clarify goals. The "truth," "scientifically" ascertained, apparently will win popular endorsement through propaganda and manipulation. It is interesting to observe in this connection that Lasswell talks of human dignity as something to be realized and not as something which men must now be recognized as possessing because of their common humanity and spiritual destiny. Then, too, he talks at one point of the undesirability of "moral mavericks who do not share the democratic preferences."[46]

Lasswell has been concerned in recent years with the question of the relationship of a "science of man" to human freedom. Unlike Skinner, he does not assume their incompatibility.

It is sufficiently acknowledged that the role of scientific work in human relations is *freedom* rather than prediction. By freedom is meant the bringing into focus of awareness of some feature of the personality which has hitherto operated as a determining factor upon the choices made by the individual, but which has been operating unconsciously. Once educated to the full focus of working consciousness, the factor which has been operating "automatically and compulsively" is no longer in this privileged position. The individual is now free to take the factor into consideration in the making of future choices.[47]

Lasswell believes that "if more individuals can be made aware of the distorting effect of anxiety upon their judgments of personnel and of public and private issues, the continuing reconstruction of civilization toward the most perfect realization of democratic values will be expedited." Scientific method in the study of man, resulting in insight into determining factors concerning personal and community choices, thus brings the condition which Lasswell calls "freedom."[48]

Lasswell's thought has a utopian aspect which derives directly from his assumptions that (1) a complete science of man is possible, (2) such science can aid in bringing about a homogeneous techno-scientific free commonwealth in which anxiety, contention, tension, conflict, and politics are absent, and (3) such science is the vehicle by which freedom is realized.

Concerning the first assumption, there can be few who disagree that much is learned about man through use of disciplined methodology and refined techniques of inquiry. But a truly open inquiry would demand recognition of man's psyche in terms of his spiritual as well as his libidinous and material dimensions. On this basis the possibility of variation and diversity in human experience must be recognized—a fact that would preclude advocacy of or resignation to the inevitability of a "homogenized" culture as well as the consideration of "moral mavericks" as undesirable. Similarly, a "science of man" which does not regard the fact that the soul of man is ultimately a deep mystery to be regarded with reverence is easily led to conclusions that manipulation is permissible and that human rights at best have only a functional or provisional validity.[49]

Concerning the second assumption, one is entitled to ask, even if a frictionless, uniform, tensionless society is possible of attainment, is it desirable? Is man without anxiety yet man or something less? Is it possible and, if so, desirable to eliminate the contingent dimension of human existence which gives rise to the unique and the particular and thus to crucial and beneficial differences in opinion? Should one exchange the Madisonian conception of politics which accepts the inevitability of differences on all levels including those of personality, and seeks, in the interest of freedom, to control their effects, for a "politics of prevention" which is really a prevention of politics? Is it possible to eliminate politics without extinguishing freedom?

Regarding the third assumption, the most that can be said is that bringing inhibitions and determining factors to the level of consciousness can serve at best as an important condition of freedom. Moral and political freedom in the sense of rational choice must follow thereupon. Plato's parable of the puppets is illustrative of the point; man is pulled internally by the many strings of the emotions, desires, instincts. Consciousness of this fact alone does not bring him to follow the gentler pull of the "golden cord of the law." Instead, rational insight into the higher good involved in the moral law brings the realization that one should strain to be free by following that which is divine yet weakest within him. In other words, freedom both involves and follows upon an evaluative judgment and choice concerning the good. It is quite obvious that men can and do differ regarding the good—a fact which gives rise in the community to politics as a civilized mode of discussing and composing conflicts. In other words, Lasswell never gets to the center of the important problem of moral and political freedom and consequently ignores prudence. In fact, as one observer has recently written, to be ruled, as Lasswell wants, "by the truth about the conditions of harmonious human relations" is "to be ruled by those who possess or are presumed to possess that truth." What Lasswell attempts to do is transmute political science as "the science of man" from a practical science (concerned with contingent things) to a theoretical science (concerned with necessary truths). It follows logically that necessary truth is intolerant of difference and that politics, which allows for difference, discussion, and dissent, must be eliminated or at the least, minimized.[50]

Conclusions

In this chapter we have treated of the disenchantment with politics and democracy in American political thought under the impact of two world wars, economic depression, and important European currents of thought. Bourne criticized pragmatism for its ambiguity concerning goals and its growing preoccupation with technics. Sensing the intolerant implications of strong, centralized government which war begets, he attacked the state (political power) as incompatible with freedom. Mencken, the "new humanists," and Santayana all disavowed democracy as mediocrity and asserted the incompetence of the average man. More, Babbitt, Cram, and Santayana, while endorsing equality of opportunity, assailed majority rule, and endorsed in one way or another the notion of a natural leader or natural aristocracy. The racist writers simply asserted, on what they conceived to be scientific grounds, the supremacy of the white man in general and of the Nordic in particular, and the necessity for the dominance of the latter in government. Like his Communist counterparts, the American fascist Dennis sought the total revision of society, as did the social scientists Skinner, Lasswell, and to a degree, Arnold. Whereas the "new humanists" and Santayana thought in terms of the dichotomy, natural aristocracy/people, and trusted to the prudential judgment of the former, and the racists thought in terms of the dichotomy, white-superior/colored-inferior, attributing political wisdom to a putative racial characteristic, Dennis, Brunham, Arnold, Skinner, and Lasswell used the dichotomy, elite/mass, allowing to the former manipulative means of control in light of superiority in power or knowledge of a "science of man." The elitists, with a few exceptions are derisive of the politics of discussion, adjustment, compromise, and conciliation, in contrast to Smith, the great apologist for democracy and compromise, who by reducing democracy to a method alone and thinking of compromise and conscience as incompatible, undercut the moral basis of democracy and politics. More particularly the proponents of "a science of man," Skinner, Arnold, and Lasswell, tended to look on society as composed of experts (social psychologist-administrators) on the one hand, and the ill, on the other. Just as Smith in effect condemned the pursuit of conscience as a power drive seeking sublimation in politics, so Lasswell sees the "politician" as displacing his private motives on public objects. In the view of Arnold, Lasswell, and Skinner, politics is reducible to psychology. They would use myth, propaganda, and probably the conditional reflex to implement the "truth" which is possessed only by the few who have been illuminated by "reality" and the "science of man." Thus whereas Bourne, the "new humanists," and Santayana, all literary men, call for "imaginative vision," with greatly differing notions of the limits of creativity among them, Arnold, Skinner, and Lasswell hearken to "the science of man" as indicative of the road to sanity and, in the case of the latter two, a tension-less, anxiety-free, tractable society. Left out of consideration by these men is the moral law, which they believe, on the basis of cultural and ethical relativism, can never be indicated objectively. Likewise whereas the literary men protest techno-scientific culture, the devotees of the "science of man" either accept it or exalt it. The question of freedom remained a vital note in the thought of Bourne and Smith; to the "new humanists" it was equivalent to adherence to the rule of a natural aristocracy; to Santayana to adherence to the rule of a representative natural leader; to Arnold to rule by the "fact-minded" leader; to Lasswell to rule by social psychiatry; while to Skinner it is irrelevant. Thus the tendency, already manifest in the thought of Lester Ward, to exalt the role of the technical expert in the rule of man and to denigrate politics along with the conception of a fundamental moral law, reached full development in American political thought in the period between the wars.

NOTES

1. William Leuchtenberg, "Progressivism and Imperialism," *Missisippi Valley Historical Review*, XXXIX (Dec., 1952), 500.
2. Robert Spiller, *The Cycle of American Literature* (New York, 1955), p. 144.
3. Randolph Bourne, *Untimely Papers* (New York, 1919), pp. 13, 16–17, 18; Bourne, *War and the Intellectuals* (New York, 1964), p. 168.
4. Bourne, *Untimely Papers*, pp. 42–43, 44, 45–46, 99.
5. *Ibid.*, pp. 119, 124, 127, 129, 130, 131, 139.
6. Charles Forcey, *The Crossroads of Liberalism* (New York, 1961), p. 283; Bourne, *Untimely Papers*, pp. 140, 141, 150, 179, 201–202, 215, 166.
7. See also Randolph Bourne, *History of a Literary Radical and Other Essays*, Van Wyck Brooks, ed. (New York, 1920).
8. H. L. Mencken, *Notes on Democracy* (London, undated), pp. 16, 21, 27, 28, 29.
9. Paul Elmer More, *Aristocracy and Justice* (Boston, 1915), pp. 8, 31, 59, 136.
10. Irving Babbitt, *Democracy and Leadership* (New York, 1924), pp. 5, 6, 7, 16, 75, 147, 233, 240, 260, 267, 268.
11. Ralph Adams Cram, *The End of Democracy* (Boston, 1937), pp. 19, 28, 36, 37, 45, 68, 69, 116, 158, 168, 180, 198, 199, 204.
12. George Santayana, *Soliloquies in England and Later Soliloquies* (New York, 1922), p. 142; Santayana, *The Life of Reason* (New York: 1922–1924, 2nd ed., 2 vols.), I, "Reason in Common Sense," 291; quoted in Richard Colton Lyon, ed., *Santayana on America* (New York, 1968), Introduction, xxii.
13. Quoted in Lyon, *op. cit.*, pp. 14, 111, 115.
14. *Dominations and Powers* (New York, 1951), vii; *The Works of George Santayana* (New York, 1936–1937, 14 vols.), IX, 178, cited in Allen Guttmann, *The Conservative Tradition in America* (New York, 1967), pp. 143–144.
15. "The Genteel Tradition at Bay," reprinted in *Santayana on America*, pp. 136, 158; Santayana, *Character and Opinion in the United States* (New York, 1920), p. 196.
16. Santayana, *Works*, IX, 166; III, 289, cited in Guttmann, p. 144; David Spitz, *Patterns of Anti-Democratic Thought* (New York, 1965), p. 236; Santayana, *The Life of Reason*, II, *Reason in Society*, pp. 75, 121, 128, 136; *Dominations and Powers*, pp. 351, 358.
17. The main critique of the "new humanists" can be found in Spitz, *op. cit.*, pp. 135–163, 271–293.
18. Willard E. Arnett, *George Santayana* (New York, 1968), p. 123.
19. Lothrop Stoddard, *The Rising Tide of Color Against White World Supremacy*, (New York, 1921); Stow Persons, *American Minds*, pp. 281, 284–285, 296.
20. Madison Grant, *The Passing of the Great Race*, p. 26, cited in Spitz, *op. cit.*, p. 176; Grant, introduction to Stoddard, *Rising Tide of Color* (New York, 1921), pp. xi–xxxii, cited in Spitz, *op. cit.*, p. 176; *The Passing of the Great Race*, pp. 228–229, cited in Spitz, p. 177.

21. See the critique of racism in Spitz, *op. cit.*, p. 178ff.

22. Victor C. Ferkiss, "Populist Influences on American Fascism," *Western Political Quarterly*, X (June, 1957), 350, 351. See also Richard Hofstadter, *The Paranoid Style in American Politics* (New York, 1965).

23. Lawrence Dennis, *The Coming American Fascism* (New York, 1936), pp. 105, 14, 107.

24. *Ibid.*, pp. 7, 231.

25. *Ibid.*, pp. 233, 246, 231.

26. *Ibid.*, pp. 239, 252.

27. Dennis, *The Dynamics of War and Revolution* (New York, 1940), p. 186; Dennis, "The Class War Comes to America," *American Mercury*, XLV (1938), 389, cited in Spitz, *op. cit.*, pp. 95–96. For a critique of Dennis' thought, see Spitz, *op. cit.*, pp. 99–123.

28. For a critique of Burnham's thought, see Spitz, *op. cit.*, pp. 52–57.

29. Thurman Arnold, *The Symbols of Government* (New Haven, 1935), p. 229.

30. *Ibid.*, pp. 232–233.

31. *Ibid.*, p. 236.

32. Thurman Arnold, *The Folklore of Capitalism* (New Haven, 1937), pp. 41, 42.

33. Sidney Hook, *Reason, Social Myths, and Democracy* (New York, 1940), p. 61. For other appraisals of Arnold, see John H. Hallowell, *The Moral Foundation of Democracy* (Chicago, 1954), pp. 7–23; Fred V. Cahill, Jr., *Judicial Legislation* (New York, 1952), pp. 130–132; Ralph Gabriel, *The Course of American Democratic Thought*, *op. cit.*, pp. 428–429.

34. T. V. Smith, "Compromise: Its Context and Limits," *Ethics*, LIII (Oct., 1942), pp. 7, 8, 4; *The Compromise Principle in Politics* (Urbana, Ill., 1941), p. 29. Smith's other main works are *The American Philosophy of Equality* (Chicago, 1927); *The Democratic Way of Life* (Chicago, 1926); *The Legislative Way of Life* (Chicago, 1940); *The Promise of American Politics* (Chicago, 1936); and *Discipline for Democracy* (Chapel Hill, 1942).

35. *The Legislative Way of Life*, 26.

36. *The Promise of American Politics*, pp. 249, 248; "Compromise," *Ethics*, pp. 10, 13. See also *The Compromise Principle in Politics*, p. 36.

37. *Discipline for Democracy*, p. 124. I have drawn in good part, in the above and following critique of Smith, upon Hallowell, *op. cit.*, pp. 27–47.

38. John B. Watson, *Behaviorism* (Chicago, 1924, 1958), pp. 269, 11; *The Ways of Behaviorism* (New York, 1926), p. 35. These are cited in Floyd Matson, *The Broken Image* (New York, 1964), p. 56.

39. B. F. Skinner, *Walden Two* (New York, 1948, paperback 1962), pp. 256, 273. Skinner states, in his *Science and Human Behavior* (New York, 1953), at page 447: "The hypothesis that man is not free is essential to the application of scientific method to the study of human behavior."

40. *Ibid.*, pp. 259, 262, 194, 265, 267.

41. Joseph Krutch, *The Measure of Man* (Indianapolis, 1953), p. 59. Critiques of Skinner's thought can be found in Krutch's book at pp. 57–76 and in Matson, *op. cit.*, pp. 69–81, and in Dante Germino, *Beyond Ideology* (New York, 1967), pp. 195–198. Skinner's unrelenting scientism is graphically illustrated in the following statement: "If science does not confirm the assumptions of freedom, initiative, and responsibility in the behavior of the individual, these assumptions will not ultimately be effective either as motivating devices or as goals in the design of Culture." *Science and Human Behavior*, p. 449.

42. George A. Lundberg, *Can Science Save Us?* (New York, 1947), pp. 44, 47. See the commentary on Lundberg in Matson, *op. cit.*, pp. 88–92.

43. Francis G. Wilson, *The American Political Mind* (New York, 1949), p. 414. Merriam's major work of the 1920's, which dealt directly with political science as a branch of the study of man, was *New Aspects of Politics* (Chicago, 1925).

44. Crick, *op. cit.*, p. 181. Lasswell's principal works include *Propaganda Technique in the World War* (New York, 1927); *World Politics and Personal Insecurity* (New York, 1935); *Politics: Who Gets What, When, How* (New York, 1936); *Psy-*

chopathology and Politics (Chicago, 1930). The latter two books are reproduced, along with an essay on "Democratic Character," in *The Political Writings of Harold Lasswell* (Glencoe, Ill., 1951); *Power and Personality* (New York, 1948); *Power and Society* (New Haven, 1950); *The World Revolution of Our Time* (New York, 1951).

45. *World Politics and Personal Insecurity*, p. 237; *Political Writings*, p. 184, 185, 194, 196, 197, 201, 203; *World Politics and Personal Insecurity*, p. 20.

46. *Analysis of Political Behavior* (London, 1948), p. 7, "Democratic Character," *Political Writings*, pp. 473, 474, 495, 497–498, 502, 503, 506; Crick, *op. cit.*, p. 196.

47. "Democratic Character," *Political Writings*, p. 524.

48. *Ibid.*

49. Critical appraisals of Lasswell's thought can be found in Crick, *op. cit.*, pp. 176–209, Matson, *op. cit.*, and Robert Horwitz, "Scientific Propaganda: Harold D. Lasswell," in Herbert Storing (ed.), *Essays on the Scientific Study of Politics* (New York, 1962), pp. 227–304.

50. Horwitz, *op. cit.*, p. 298.

Chapter 24

REALISM AND THE REVIVAL OF HIGHER LAW

In the crisis within the Western society, there is at issue now the mandate of heaven.

WALTER LIPPMANN

Totalitarian rule abroad and World War II brought many Americans to question the ethical and sociological relativism underlying much of scholarship and popular attitudes issuing from pragmatic and positivistic presuppositions. In like vein they began to reconsider beliefs in inevitable progress and the inherent goodness of man. If Hitler was to be combated, they reasoned, was it possible merely to regard him as a threat to the national interest, or was it necessary to go beyond this and judge him in moral terms? If so, how could an ethic which assumed either the complete subjectivity or the culture-bound nature of all human actions suffice? Satisfied with its total inadequacy, some thinkers returned to the ancient conception of an objective moral law rooted in human nature, while others reaffirmed orthodox Christian principles. Their work produced a series of postwar volumes. Among the native American and European émigré authors were Walter Lippmann, Reinhold Niebuhr, Erich Fromm, Heinrich Rommen, Leo Strauss, Jacques Maritain, Yves Simon, and John Courtney Murray.[1] Principal among these because of the impact and influence of their persons and arguments are Lippmann, Niebuhr, and Fromm, who represent three distinct answers to the basic question. Lippmann and Niebuhr are of particular importance because their work, which spans over fifty years of history, is illustrative in each case of an intellectual odyssey quite revealing of changes and developments in American political thought.

Walter Lippmann and the Public Philosophy

Walter Lippmann was born in New York in 1889 of well-to-do parents. Educated in private schools and by extensive travel, he entered Harvard where he was most heavily influenced by William James and George Santayana, as well as the visiting English Socialist, Graham Wallas. He became president of the Socialist Club in 1909, and after leaving the University in 1910 took jobs as a newspaper reporter, an assistant to the editor of a journal, and an aide to a Socialist mayor. After publication of his first two books he joined the staff of the *New Republic*, where he was associated with two other supporters of Theodore Roosevelt—Herbert Croly and Walter Weyl. During the war he acted as an assistant to the Secretary of War and was a member of several governmental committees. In 1917 he served with the group which prepared the memorandum which became the basis of President Wilson's fourteen points, after which he accepted a commission in the army to engage in political propaganda in France. Rejoining the *New Republic* at war's end, he broke with Wilson over the Versailles Treaty, which he denounced "as a breaking of faith with Germany and a violation of moral obligations to the world." In 1920 he resigned from the *New Republic* and, after publishing his book *Public Opinion,* joined the staff of the *New York World,* and soon became editor. Thereafter he continued to publish books and served as the widely read and greatly influential syndicated columnist for the *New York Herald Tribune* until his retirement in 1967.[2]

Lippmann's youthful work, *A Preface to Politics* (1913), was written in the spirit of the reigning intellectual "Revolt Against Formalism." Presenting "a preliminary sketch for a theory of politics," he declared that theory must be judged "only as an effective or ineffective instrument of a desire" and that one must not attempt "to state abstractly in intellectual terms qualities which can be known only by direct experience." Accordingly, he made primary "the deliberate, conscious, willing individual." Whereas, he stated, the old effort was to harness mankind to such abstract principles as liberty, equality and justice, the new effort, following the lead of Wallas, "proposes to fit creeds and institutions to the wants of men, to satisfy their impulses as fully and beneficially as possible."[3]

Underlying this approach is a conception of reason as merely instrumental to the passions and desires. The young Lippmann believed that because "no ethical theory can announce any intrinsic good," one must focus upon human impulses. With Bergson he exalted will; with James he extolled pragmatic creativity; with Nietzsche he advised the subjective evaluation of all things; and with Santayana he maintained that the ideal of rationality is arbitrary and as much dependent as any other ideal on the requirements of a finite organization.[4]

Lippmann's conception of political leadership, which he saw concretized in the person of Theodore Roosevelt, was based on the notions that (1) it is the "power of being aggressively active toward the world which gives man a miraculous assurance that the world is something he can make," and (2) the creative politician "devotes himself to inventing fine expressions for human needs," and "recognizes that the work of statesmanship is in large measure the finding of good substitutes for the bad things we want." Lippmann asked that the exploration of human needs and desires become a deliberate purpose of statecraft. In line with his conception of man he stated: "No genuine politician ever treats his constituents as reasoning animals" but deals instead with "the will, the hopes, the needs and the visions of men." In short, "whoever is bent upon shaping politics to better human uses must accept freely as his starting point the impulses that agitate human beings."[5]

Although Lippmann talked in terms of a three-tier social relationship composed of (1) the people at large, (2) experts, and (3) statesmen who besides embodying the above-mentioned characteristics are expert in choosing experts, he was withal a liberal democrat. He wrote: "To govern a democracy you have to educate it: that contact with great masses of men reciprocates by educating the leader."[6] In light of this, and in the contemporary progressive mood, Lippmann objected to the two-party system but approved the referendum, short ballot, and the separation of municipal, state, and national elections.[7]

For the most part Lippmann's discussion in his first book ignored groups, disdained general ideas except as utilitarian devices, and focused on political leadership and the people at large. Having established man as a bundle of undifferentiated desires and impulses, he prescribed the release and redirection of impulse, but mentioned no specific end. Ultimately the whole analysis was fudged over in the utopian pronouncement that "the more self-governing a people becomes, the less possible is it to prescribe external restrictions. The gap between want and ought, between nature and ideals cannot be maintained. The only practical ideals in a democracy are a fine expression of natural wants." In short, in a democracy led by creative, intuitive leaders implementing human wants, the problem of political morality, and of government itself, is automatically solved.[8]

Because Lippmann thought strongly that the people must be led; that man is essentially irrational; and that there exists no intrinsically valid norm, he believed that a myth, in the sense of Sorel,* was needed.

* The French theorist, Sorel, taught that men are most effectively moved by the evocative imagery of myth.

Theodore Roosevelt's celebrated statement concerning Armageddon was cited as an example; however, Lippmann specifically stated that the "sense of mastery in a winning battle against the conditions of our life is . . . the social myth that will inspire our reconstructions."[9]

In *Drift and Mastery,* which Lippmann published the following year, he still proclaimed the limits of reason, but argued that science is "the discipline of democracy." Without turning away from James, he moved closer to Dewey and no longer mentioned Sorel. Instead of emphasis on intuitive creative leadership, he began to stress expert scientific knowledge, a shift further influenced, as time passed on, by his disillusionment with both Roosevelt and Woodrow Wilson.[10]

Lippmann's wartime education in the manipulation of the minds of men, the inadequacy of men in seeing and judging facts and events, along with his belief that public ignorance constituted the basic problem of democracy, led him to publish, in 1922, one of his most well-known works, *Public Opinion.* Instead of the picture presented by traditional democratic theory of an informed, rational, and intelligent public forming an opinion which constitutes a moral judgment on a group of facts, Lippmann likened the democratic public to the prisoners in Plato's cave, who never directly apprehend reality and subscribe to opinion which is "primarily a moralized and codified version of the facts." Generally speaking, he argued, men have only an indirect knowledge of the environment; in fact there is inserted between man and his environment "a pseudo-environment" due to the distortion of news, the complexity of facts, and the stereotypes or pictures in the minds of men, through which information is filtered.[11]

Lippmann believed that the failure of self-governing people to transcend casual experience and prejudice could only be overcome by creating a machinery of knowledge. Specifically he suggested governmental intelligence bureaus independent of decision-makers, dedicated to objectivity, having access to all information, and covering in their investigations and reports the whole gamut of social science. In other words, Lippmann now put his trust not in creative statesmen employing myth but in the rationality of scientifically oriented experts. As he made clear in a succeeding book, *The Phantom Public* (1924), even if such scientifically oriented intelligence agencies existed, the public still could not gain therefrom the requisite knowledge and comprehension to determine policy. The people are thus left with the task of judging and choosing leaders. Shortly thereafter, in a commentary on the conviction of John Scopes for violating the Tennessee law prohibiting the teaching of the evolutionary theory, Lippmann wrote that the case showed how majority rule resulted in an attack on the belief in the very public education which democracy assumes, thus illustrating "that the dogma of majority rule contains within itself some sort of deep and destructive confusion." On this basis Lippmann abandoned his earlier criticism of the Constitution as a mechanical contrivance, and praised the wisdom of the Founding Fathers in setting up checks and balances to refine the popular will and restrain the impulses of transient majorities.[12]

In his *A Preface to Morals* (1929) Lippmann concerned himself with the problems posed in the dissolution of what he called the "ancestral order," and the values of supernatural religion, by "the acids of modernity." Whereas he had previously assumed ends as naturally evolving out of basic impulses and had concentrated on means, he now turned to the vital question of the choice of ends. Whereas he had earlier identified nature in man with the level of primal impulses, he now distinguished between unrefined desire and mature choice. Whereas he had emphasized the primacy of passion, he now stressed rational, disciplined development.

Surveying wistfully the promises of liberalism, he declared: "We are living in the midst of that vast dissolution of ancient habits which the emancipators believed would restore our birthright of happiness. We know now that they did not see very clearly beyond the evils against which they were rebelling." Thus the liberal premise "that if only external circumstances are favorable the internal life of man will adjust itself successfully," has not been borne out—this, because "the natural man, when he is released from restraints, and has no substitute for them, is at sixes and sevens with himself and the world." Modern man who has "ceased to believe, without ceasing to be credulous, hangs, as it were, between heaven and earth, and is at rest nowhere." There exists "no theory of the meaning and value of events which he is compelled to accept, but he is none the less compelled to accept the events." Similarly, "there is no moral authority to which he must turn now, but there is coercion in opinions, fashions and fads."[13]

As a remedy Lippmann suggested a humanistic "high religion," whose purpose is "to reveal to men the quality of mature experience," and to prophesy and anticipate "what life is like when desire is in perfect harmony with reality." Lippmann's "high religion" was in good part a fusion of the Aristotelian emphasis on the *spoudaios* (wise, mature man) as paradigm, the Stoic stress on imperturbability, the deistic dismissal of divine special providence, and Santayana's delineation of the "life of reason" as aesthetic symmetry.[14]

Evil to Lippmann was no longer seen in terms of the environment or ignorance, but of such personal vices as "greed, uncontrollable sexual desire, arrogance, and imperiousness." In light of this, "the preoccupation of high religion is with the regeneration* of the passions that create

---

* By "regeneration" of the passions Lippmann meant "that growth unto maturity, that outgrowing of naive desire, that cultivation of disinterestedness, which render passion innocent and an authoritative morality unnecessary." *P.M.*, p. 209.

the disorders and the frustrations." Thus "detachment, understanding and disinterestedness in the presence of reality itself" were to Lippmann the basis of liberty and the condition of good order in the individual soul, the statesman, and the state. The disinterested mature man, Lippmann stated in quoting Confucius, can "follow what his heart desires without transgressing what is right. For he has learned to desire what is right."[15]

Lippmann's abiding high regard for science was reflected in his exaltation of the characterological significance of scientific method. Demanding a "spirit of disinterestedness" and strong discipline, scientific method is "high religion incarnate." Whereas in past ages high religion has generally seemed so demanding that it was reserved for a voluntary aristocracy of the spirit, the modern age, based on the diffusion of scientific discipline, can extend its acceptance.[16]

In light of his refurbished conception of human nature, Lippmann distinguished between the *politician* as one who "accepts unregenerate desire at its face value and either fulfills it or perpetrates a fraud," and the *statesman* who "re-educates desire by confronting it with reality, and so makes possible an enduring adjustment of interests within the community." As Lippmann now saw it, statesmanship "consists in giving the people not what they want but what they will learn to want," and it requires the courage of a detached, imperturbable mind proceeding "from an objective and discerning knowledge of the facts." Yet the statesman leads, he does not impose. Lippmann declared that the crucial difference between modern politics and what preceded it is that "the power to act and to compel obedience is almost never sufficiently centralized nowadays to be exercised by one will." Power is distributed and qualified so that it is exerted "not by command but by interaction." Consequently the business of government is "not to direct the affairs of the community, but to harmonize the direction which the community gives to its affairs."[17]

Although in *A Preface to Morals* Lippmann was concerned with establishing an objective norm, he could not finally assert its intrinsic validity. He thought that "if our scientific knowledge of human nature were adequate, we could achieve in the humanistic culture that which all theologies have tried to achieve: we could found our morality on tested truths." But because it is not, he reverted to a modified version of myth, stating that "we have in place of exact knowledge to invent imaginative fictions in the hope that the progress of science will confirm and correct, but will not utterly contradict, our hypotheses." On these grounds it can be fairly inferred that Lippmann's disinterested, mature, tolerant, and yet skeptical, man was an imaginative fiction proposed to serve as a hypothetical norm or ideal of personality, as well as to elicit as far as possible a favorable popular response. In like vein his supposition that scientific discipline in modern technological society works, by a peculiar inner logic, to influence man to bring together his autonomy and rationality, a union which will culminate ultimately in the rational humane community, might be called as much an "imaginative fiction" as a profound hope.[18]

Alarmed by aggressive totalitarian collectivism abroad and the gradual collectivism of the New Deal at home, Lippmann published *The Good Society* in 1937. In the introduction he confessed that he had been writing for more than twenty years with no better guide to the meaning of critical events than "the hastily-improvised generalizations of a rather bewildered man." His personal confusion, he stated, was a reflection in his mind of "a great modern schism: those who seek to improve the lot of mankind believe they must undo the work of their predecessors." It is untrue, he went on, that man must choose between liberty and security. What he had come to realize was that "a directed society must be bellicose and poor" whereas "a prosperous and peaceable society must be free." He agreed with the liberals of old "that progress comes through emancipation from—not the restoration of—privilege, power, coercion, and authority."[19]

Lippmann argued that the principle of division of labor regulated by a free market, and its political corollary, a supreme common law whose principles are equality, certainty, and nonarbitrariness, within the framework of a constitution embodying checks and balances, comprise the bases of a free, progressive, and peaceful society whose logic leads ultimately to its universal extension in a "Good Society."

In this view classical economics, as stated in principle by Adam Smith, and distinguished from the nineteenth-century doctrine of laissez-faire (which merely rationalized the existing legal and property system) and Marxism (which erroneously assumes that the division of labor can be regulated without free markets by an all-powerful officialdom), is not an apology for existing institutions and practices, but a critical norm by which they must be judged. If the norm were fulfilled in practice, Lippmann thought, pressure groups, which "crystallize at those points where the social order is in fact humanly maladjusted to the economy" would not develop. Only if a machine which could produce all things men want and need were invented, or a medicine which would cause men to cease to want diversified products were developed, could the market economy be rendered obsolete.[20]

Lippmann maintained that Western man's principal effort in political thought has been to discover a law superior to arbitrary power. In his first writings he had argued that law must be conformable to man's basic wants and impulses, and had rejected a transcendent principle of morality and justice. In his postwar studies of public opinion he had stressed power as the basis of law. By the time he wrote *A Preface to Morals* he had come to believe in the necessity of procedural guarantees as reflected in the Constitution and in democratic processes. Because he recognized that decision-making is greatly diffused in a pluralistic society, he stated: "The real law in a modern state is the multitude of little decisions made daily by millions of men." Now, in *The Good Society*, he defined democracy as "the government of the people by a common law which defines the reciprocal rights and duties of persons." Impersonal rules rather than authoritative commands, and the principle of equal rights to all and special privileges to none, mark the liberal society. Thus "the denial that men may be arbitrary in human transaction *is* the higher law" to which all other law and political behavior must conform. Constitutional restraints, bills of rights, an independent judiciary, and due process of law are rough approximations of this rational dictate.[21]

The higher law is a progressive, unending discovery of men striving to civilize themselves. Without it there is "no reason by which arbitrary force can be restrained." And yet Lippmann did not justify such higher law except as a necessary presupposition of freedom and order, as well as a corollary of the division of labor and the free market. His emphasis was for the most part not on the material but the formal aspects of the higher law, and its immanent rather than transcendent character in the Great Society. He did, however, approach materiality as well as transcendence when he asserted that because each man has "an inalienable essence" he must be treated as an inviolable person rather than a disposable object. Consequently the excision of arbitrariness from government is a demand not of pragmatic utility but of the sacredness of personality.[22]

By 1938 Lippmann had concluded that there was "a deep disorder in our society which comes not from the machinations of our enemies and from the adversities of the human condition but from within ourselves." Putting aside his manuscript on the subject in the eventful month of December, 1941, he did not finish and publish it until 1955, when it appeared under the title *The Public Philosophy*.[23]

Calling himself a "liberal democrat," Lippmann began by arguing that the Western liberal democracies had witnessed since World War I a devitalization of the governing power. The relationship between governors and governed which is "rooted" in the nature of things, an executive who governs and a popular representative assembly (the consenting, accepting, criticizing, and refusing power) has been dislocated by a "drainage of power . . . away from the governing center and down into the constituencies." The proper relationship of leadership and consent has been in good part reversed through the logic of popular sovereignty based on a conception of the "people" not as a corporate and historic community in the Burkean sense, but as the sum of the voters in the Benthamite sense. Thus the people have acquired power which they are incapable of exercising. As the disorder grows, "executives become highly susceptible to the encroachment and usurpation by elected assemblies; they are pressed and harassed by the higgling of parties, by agents of organized interests, and by spokesmen of sectarians and ideologues."[24]

Lippmann pointed out that historically the enfranchised masses have not most staunchly defended the institutions of freedom; instead the precious Anglo-Saxon heritage of bills of rights, consent of the governed, rule of law, and due process of law, are more than two centuries older than universal suffrage. Friends of liberty, he added, have long understood "the need to protect the executive and judicial powers from the representative assemblies and from mass opinion."[25]

The assemblies and mass electorates have acquired a monopoly of the effective powers because of two facts of twentieth-century life: (1) the enormous expansion of public expenditure, and (2) the "growing incapacity of the large majority of the democratic peoples to believe in intangible realities." The "acids of modernity" have eroded the mystique of authority granted to government by "tradition, immemorial usage, consecration, veneration, prescription, prestige, heredity, hierarchy."[26]

Most pernicious, however, in the Western world are the twentieth-century variants of what Lippmann called the "Jacobin doctrine." The essence of this dogma is that "revolution itself is the creative act" which "will remove the causes of evil in human society." In fact, however, postrevolutionary man has ever turned out to be not the "New Man" but the "old Adam." Specifically mentioning "the mortal sin original" (pride), and "the fallen nature of man," Lippmann declared that the delusion of men that they are gods and can make a heaven of the earth "is not a new and recent infection, but rather the disposition of our first natures, of our natural and uncivilized selves."[27]

The source of the malady in Western man, Lippmann contended, is his turning away from natural law, which forms the basis of "the good society, the liberal, democratic way of life at its best." He added that he personally gradually acquired "a conviction . . . not so much from a theoretical education, but rather from the practical experience of seeing how hard it is for our generation to make democracy work," that there is "a body of positive principles and precepts which a good citizen cannot deny or ignore." Except on the premises of such a public philosophy, "it is impossible to reach intelligible and workable conceptions of popular election, majority rule, representative assemblies, free speech, loyalty, property, corporations and voluntary associations." In fact, the founders of these institutions were all adherents of some school of higher law. Yet today men are no longer being taught the principles of the public philosophy which underlie their institutions. It has become the rule that ideas and principles are private; thus all the first and last things have been removed from the public domain and labeled "subjective." Consequently the liberal democracies, by adopting a policy of "public agnosticism" and "practical neutrality" in ultimate issues, "became the first great society to treat as a private concern the formative beliefs that shape the character of its citizens."[28]

Lippmann propounded the thesis of the natural law tradition that rational man is able to gain a knowledge of what he ought to be and do. This tradition considers such knowledge to be objective and the basis of what Lippmann, following Ernest Barker, called "the traditions of civility." Lippmann explained its precepts as follows:

They are the laws of a rational order of human society—in the sense that all men, when they are sincerely and lucidly rational, will regard them as self-evident. The rational order consists of the terms which must be met in order to fulfill man's capacity for the good life in this world. They are the terms of the widest consensus of rational men in a plural society.[29]

Lippmann was careful to add that the general principles and precepts of natural law must be applied to concrete circumstances through the mediation of prudence. Therefore it is a mistake to conclude that natural law, as such, supplies specific answers to contingent concrete problems as they arise. In this light he showed how property is "the creation of the law for social purposes" and that the right to speak freely is "one of the necessary means of the attainment of truth" and not a right issuing from "the subjective pleasure of utterance." As a necessary means to the discovery of truth, he continued, free speech demands rational rules of evidence and parliamentary procedure as well as codes of fair dealing and comment. Separated from its essential principle, freedom of speech leads to its own destruction. Similarly, the right to free institutions implies the duty to defend and preserve them. And yet the determination of loyalty must be by due process, because "while there can be no right to destroy the liberal democratic state, there is an inalienable right to have the question adjudicated justly. . . ."[30]

Lippmann distinguished between the "realm of existence where objects are materialized to our senses" and "the realm of essence where they are present to the mind." Thus, he declared, "hedonists" withdraw wholly into the realm of existence while "ascetics" completely withdraw from it, and "chiliasts" live for the millenial realization of the realm of essence, while "modern perfectionists" believe in the creative redemptivity and complete regeneration of the self and the community through the revolutionary act. Each of these errors stems from the same disorder: the refusal "to recognize that, on the one hand, the two realms cannot be fused, and that, on the other hand, they cannot be separated and isolated." Although the principles of the public philosophy have their being "in the realm of immaterial entities," they are to be distinguished from "the ideals of a realm of being where men are redeemed and regenerated and the evils of the world have been outgrown." The ideals of freedom, justice, representation, consent, and law are of the earth; "they are concerned with the best that is possible among mortal and finite, diverse and conflicting men." In the natural law tradition the prevailing view has been that the realms of essence and existence are "inseparable but disparate, and that man must work out his destiny in the balance which is never fixed finally between the two." In terms of institutions this means that church and state need to be "separate, autonomous and secure," and yet "they must also meet in all the issues of good and evil." This also explains, Lippmann maintained, "why governing is not engineering but an art," and why power must be checked by power.[31]

Historically, natural law was held to have its source either in God or in the reason of things. Lippmann noted that in both cases it was regarded as objective and transcendent, not the product of whim, prejudice, or rationalization. Because as a proponent of "high religion," he inclines to anthropocentric rather than theocentric humanism, he, while bothered by the "death of God" preachment, is mostly concerned with its implication that there is beyond our private world no public world to which we belong. He did not attempt to prove his natural law thesis, stating instead "that it may be possible to alter the terms of discourse if a convincing demonstration can be made that the principles of the good society are not . . . invented and chosen—that the conditions which must be met if there is to be a good society are there, outside our wishes, where they can be discovered by rational inquiry, and developed and refined by rational discussion." The alternative, he declared, is a continuation of the existing social anomie, progressive barbarization, violence, and tyranny. The public rational principles underlying and informing liberal democracy must be recovered if human dignity is to be preserved. In words borrowed from Aquinas, Lippmann proclaimed that man, in both his private and public lives, must exercise a "royal and politic rule" over his "irascible and conscupiscible powers."[32]

In *The Public Philosophy* Lippmann completed the stages of transformation from his youthful emphasis on the primacy of impulse to a classical stress upon the rational government of the soul, as well as an acceptance of original sin. Initially he denied the existence of an intrinsic good; now he asserted an objective, transcendent natural law. He moved from a position which was critical of checks and balances to their acceptance. His early high regard for majority rule, which was tempered by his ever-insistent emphasis on the need for leadership, was reshaped into the notion of an executive who governs, and a representative assembly which consents, as a dictate of what might be called natural public law.

Criticism of Lippmann's espousal of natural law has been directed principally at the epistemological assumptions involved. Arthur Schlesinger, Jr. dismisses natural law as an "artificial construct" and observes that Lippmann has fled from his early dynamic pluralism to static monism. Criticisms made by Morton White and David Spitz are rooted in a full acceptance of David Hume's critique of natural law. White, who adheres essentially to the position of John Dewey, says that Lippmann's is a "poorly argued version of the doctrine of natural law," an observation with which Lippmann, who had no pretensions of proving the thesis, would probably agree. White goes on to dismiss the concept of self-evident moral principles and the notion of essences, concluding by calling Lippmann's adherence to natural law "a kind of self-encouragement, useful for philosophical whistling in the dark."[33]

Lippmann had admitted in his book the ambiguity of the term "essence" but could find no ample substitute. A recent commentator has written that what Lippmann apparently means by essence is "that in the realm of understanding, man is relatively and distinctly free to seek out and confront the undistorted nature of conceptual absolutes, a confrontation he can never make in the realm of existence." Men live in the world of the senses and the world of the mind, and, as Lippmann argues, "the tension within them is the inexhaustible theme of human discourse." Thus the question arises, on what, except arbitrary grounds, can one count the realm of the senses (existence) more "real" than the realm of the mind (essence)?[34]

David Spitz maintains that the most that natural law theorists can do is show that there is an obvious distinction between the "is" and the "ought" in politics. Lippmann has been defended from this charge by the following reasoning. He does not assert that concrete standards of action deriving from natural law are self-evident to all men, but to men of "right reason." He does not imply that any man or group of men completely possess "right reason." He contends, however, that from Western man's cumulative intellectual endeavor there have emerged basic values which give specific content to the formal "oughtness," which Spitz sees as natural law. Spitz states, as if in answer, that principles put forth by Lippmann, such as the inviolability of the person, are without use or meaning in particular cases. But Spitz himself goes on to reject natural law in the name of majoritarian democracy while smuggling it back in new terminology when he states: "I do not, of course, imply by this that a democrat cannot properly oppose the will of the majority where that will violates democratic, as distinct from natural law standards." Unless, however, Spitz is reliant on purely subjective grounds of opposition, he must establish his preference for democracy in terms of basic values of free government which men can and should grasp and adhere to.[35]

Finally, Archibald MacLeish argues that Lippmann's thesis rejects the basic philosophy of liberalism, "the belief in the liberation of the individual human spirit to find its own way of enlightenment and truth." In rejoinder, Lippmann, quoting directly from MacLeish, shows how MacLeish argues on the one hand for "the boundless liberty of the individual human spirit" while yet speaking of "the modern democratic belief in the greatest possible individual freedom." Lippmann says that there are here, as there are in the nature of things, two ideas of freedom. One is "boundless"; the other is as great only as "possible." He states that he also believes in "the boundless liberty of the *individual human spirit*," but does not believe it possible "in the public actions of everyone." Liberty is "boundless" in the realm of essence, but in the public world of diverse people in a plural society, it "can be only as great as possible." Thus in the public world "it is the business of political philosophy to discern where in the condition of the historical period the bounds have to be, and where they do not have to be—in order that there shall be as much freedom as is possible for all individuals." It follows that "the mortal disease of free societies is to confuse the two realms, and to practice in the public world not a constitutional liberty but that boundless liberty which belongs to the inward country of the human spirit."[36]

The confrontation of MacLeish and Lippmann is illustrative of a great difference within American liberalism, one which brings MacLeish to read Lippmann out of the fraternity, and conservatives to claim Lippmann as one of their own. But if to be a liberal is to deny a natural moral law, then, if Ralph Gabriel's analysis is accepted, liberalism turns its back upon one of the main persisting strands of its American tradition to adopt an approach which denies all "indefectible principles."

Reinhold Niebuhr: Christian Realist

Reinhold Niebuhr (1892–1971) was born the son of a cultured, liberal German immigrant clergyman in Missouri. He attended Elmhurst College in Illinois, a theological seminary in St. Louis, and Yale Divinity School. Ordained minister in the Evangelical Synod in 1915, he became pastor of a small working-class parish in Detroit which he served for the next thirteen years. Observing the workers at the Ford plant, he was affronted by the depersonalizing and dehumanizing influence of a mechanized productive system. This led him to conclude the irrelevance of Christianity, identified as "mild moralistic idealism," to "the power realities of our modern technical society." This appreciation of the power factor in economic life paralleled his earlier judgment that World War I was essentially a contest for power rather than a moral crusade.[37]

Deeply concerned with social injustice, Niebuhr joined the faculty of

Union Theological Seminary in 1928, wrote extensively in and edited religious periodicals, and helped found in 1936 the Fellowship of Socialist Christians in America, a group dedicated to relating Christianity and social reconstruction. During this time he moved from religious preoccupation to political realism, upon his realization that the Gospel injunction of love was in conflict with the commonsense morality of social life. In *Moral Man and Immoral Society* (1932) he rejected the combination in liberal Christianity of pragmatism and the Social Gospel, its reliance upon the politics of reason and love, and its complacent assumption of social progress. Using Marxist socialist analysis, while rejecting Marxist eschatology, he interpreted social morality as a morality of groups motivated by collective egotism, regarded strategy as necessarily based on a calculus of power, unmasked the ideological pretension of *laissez-faire* capitalism, and considered politics as being at best directed toward justice and not love. Thus his early realism was rooted in the notions that political realities are power realities, power must be checked by power, and self-interest is the basic factor in the actions of men, groups, and nations.

The economic depression of the 1930's influenced Niebuhr as greatly as had the war and Detroit. Having joined the Socialist Party in 1928, he supported the Presidential candidacies of Norman Thomas and criticized the New Deal as a piecemeal reform effort. Nevertheless, unlike John Dewey, who also advocated socialism, Niebuhr had little faith in rationality and scientific planning. Instead, he sought a social balance of power in a socialist constitutional democracy.

Having been preoccupied with social analysis. Niebuhr turned, in the late 1930's and the 1940's, to theology to find a deeper biblical explanation of man. Influenced most by St. Augustine, Luther, and Kierkegaard, he expounded a neo-orthodox theology explaining man and life in terms of what he calls the symbols of original sin, grace, atonement and redemption, and resurrection and divine judgment. His greatest work, *The Nature and Destiny of Man*, sums up the shift in his thought from the Social Gospel emphasis on man's relations to his fellow man, to man's relations to God. He now, as a "Christian realist," explained immorality ultimately not in terms of society but of sin. While his fideism precluded him from accepting the ontological theology of his great contemporary, Paul Tillich, it did not lead him, as it did his other great contemporary, Karl Barth, to abandon politics as irrelevant. His objective was not to keep religion and politics from moving away from each other, but to preclude their fusion and to expound the dialectical relationship between love and justice.

In the 1940's Niebuhr finally saw the desirability of a pragmatic approach to politics, a conclusion long implicit in his writings. Now admitting the worth of the New Deal, he helped, after the war, to organize the liberally oriented Americans for Democratic Action.

1. *Man:* Basic to Niebuhr's developed thought is his biblical conception of man created in the image of God. Existing at the juncture of nature and spirit, man is distinguished by his capacity for "self-transcendence," that is, the ability to weigh the importance of his rational faculties and to consider the relation and limits of his reason and natural processes. The self thus paradoxically stands outside both itself and the world, which means that "it cannot understand itself except as it is understood from beyond itself and the world." On this ground Niebuhr dismissed both a consistent naturalism and a consistent idealism as explanations of man. The self "cannot identify meaning with causality in nature; for its freedom is obviously something different from the necessary causal links of nature." Likewise it cannot identify the principle of meaning with rationality because it can question "whether there is a relevance between its rational forms and the recurrences and forms of nature." Man is indeed a *creature* of nature and of history, a fact which indicates finitude and limits, but his freedom allows him to be at the same time a *creator* of history and culture. Niebuhr remarked: "Neither naturalism nor idealism can understand that man is free enough to violate both the necessities of nature and the logical systems of reason." He saw Christianity, with its faith in God as Creator of the world, as transcending "the canons and antimonies of rationality, particularly the antimony between mind and matter, between consciousness and extension."[38]

What Niebuhr essentially meant is that we can best understand man and discover true meaning in life on the basis of the Augustinian fideistic assertion, *"credo ut intellegam"* (I believe in order that I might understand). Thus envisaged, the Christian faith is "the apprehension of a wisdom which makes sense out of life on a different level than the worldly wisdom which either makes sense out of life too simply or which can find no sense in life at all." Rationalism, idealism, scientific humanism, romanticism, positivism, etc., are to him inadequate explanations of the complex phenomena comprising man and life, as well as inadequate means of affording insights, when compared to the symbols of neo-orthodox Christianity.[39]

Niebuhr contended that because modern culture can neither solve "the problem of vitality and form," nor fully understand "the paradox of human creativity and destructiveness," it has been forced to choose between four untenable points of view: "(a) it exalts destructive fury because it is vital, as in fascism; or (b) it imagines a harmony of vital forces in history which the facts belie, as in liberalism; or (c) it admits the dishonest pretensions of rational discipline and the reality of human destructiveness provisionally, but hopes for a complete change in the human situation, as in Marxism; or (d) it despairs of any basic solution for the problem of vitality and discipline and contents itself with palliatives, as in Freudianism."[40]

Niebuhr rejected, as did Lippmann, the modern explanation of human evil in terms of corrupt institutions and/or ignorance to be corrected by social reform and education. Instead, evil is related to man's freedom: "The fact that man can transcend himself in infinite regression and cannot find the end of life except in God is the mark of his creativity and uniqueness; closely related to this capacity in his inclination to transmute his partial and finite self and his partial and finite values into the infinite good. Therein lies his sin." Sin is thus "the unwillingness of man to acknowledge his creatureliness and dependence upon God and his effort to make his own life independent and secure." The evil in man is "a consequence of his inevitable though not necessary unwillingness to acknowledge his dependence, to accept his finiteness and admit his insecurity." Original sin is neither a property of man's essential nature nor a transmission of corruption through social institutions, but an event in each human life. It is characterized by "inordinate self-love," which points to "the prior sin of lack of trust in God." Unlike Rauschenbusch and the Social Gospelers, Niebuhr held that although particular sins have social sources and consequences, "the real essence of sin can be understood only in the vertical dimension of the soul's relation to God because the freedom of the self stands outside all relations, and therefore has no other judge but God."[41]

Because man is involved in both freedom and necessity, he is "anxious." Anxiety is the inevitable attendant of human existence; ideally it can be overcome by faith, but a life completely without anxiety would be lacking in freedom and would not require faith. Man's freedom is thus productive of both his creativity and his destructiveness, and is the condition of his anxiety.[42]

Finally, because of man's prideful pretensions, "all human knowledge is tainted with an 'ideological' taint. . . . It is finite knowledge, gained from a particular perspective; but it pretends to be final and ultimate knowledge." This factor, along with the will to power, which Niebuhr saw as a spiritualized extension of the basic survival impulse, is at the foundation of his consideration of groups and politics.[43]

2. *Natural Law and Scientific Method.* Niebuhr, unlike Lippmann, rejected the traditional conceptions of natural law. He believed that they rest upon a " 'non-existential' description of human reason" and "fail to appreciate the perennial corruptions of interest and passion which are introduced into any historical definition of even the most ideal and abstract moral principles." In fact, he contended, "even if natural law concepts do not contain the ideological taint of a particular class or nation, they are bound to express the limited imagination of a particular epoch. . . ."[44]

Because of his freedom, "one of the facts about man as man is that his vitalities may be elaborated in indeterminate variety." Catholic theory, as Niebuhr saw it, mistakenly speaks of an original righteousness that was lost in the Fall and a natural justice which remains uncorrupted by the Fall. This distinction, he argued, "obscures the complex relation of human freedom to all of man's natural functions and the consequent involvement of all 'natural' or 'rational' standards and norms in sin." Thus there is no uncorrupted natural law, just as there is no completely lost original justice. Both freedom and sin exert a relativizing effect upon all historical norms. The Catholic distinction between a relative and absolute natural law is "too absolute because it is never possible to define the limits of the force of sin or of the ideal possibilities which transcend sin." Because not only the Catholic but the Classic and Enlightenment theories of natural law erroneously assume an order in history conforming to the uniformities of nature, they introduce "some historically contingent norm or social structure into what they regard as God's inflexible norm."[45]

Although Niebuhr talked at times like a complete historical relativist who is saved from denying an abiding structure in human nature by his fideism, he did not deny that man has a verifiable essential nature: "To the essential nature of man belong . . . all his natural endowments, and determinations, his physical and social impulses, his sexual and racial differentiations, in short his character as a creature imbedded in the natural order. On the other hand, his essential nature also includes the freedom of his spirit, his transcendence over natural process and finally his self-transcendence."

Because a part of man's essential nature is his freedom, with its indeterminate possibilities, Niebuhr insisted that love is its only law. He saw the law of love "as a vision of health which even a sick man may envisage, as the original righteousness which man does not possess but which he knows he ought to possess. . . ." In the same vein he remarked: "The self in its freedom is too great to be contained within the self in its contingent existence. It requires an object of devotion beyond itself, and an indeterminate field of fellowship." Thus it might be said that to Niebuhr freedom and love are corresponding nature and norm.[46]

In reference to man as a creature existing within historical and social structures, however, Niebuhr stated that because of "the spiritualized survival impulse" in "the competition between life and life," it is impossible to construct a social ethic out of pure love since the ideal presupposes "the resolution of the conflict of life with life." Consequently, every norm which is apparently expressive of an immutable aspect of man's essence must be held tentatively and in subordination to the law of love.[47]

If Neibuhr was stern in his appraisal of the schools of natural law, he was severe in his critique of "scientific method" conceived as (1) the organon of truth in the study of human behavior, (2) the vehicle of managerial social control, and (3) the instrument of redemption for man. Not being an obscurantist, he admitted that an important though limited role can properly be played by scientific inquiry in some questions of policy formation, in correcting partial and particular points of view, and in questions where the matter examined is amenable to the method. But beyond this he saw it subject to the following shortcomings: (1) Insofar as men are free, "causal sequences in history reach a height and complexity in which the full understanding of the character of an event would require the knowledge of the secret motive of the agent of the action," and in any case, "no scientific investigations of past behavior can become the basis of predictions of future behavior." (2) In the knowledge of historical events, in contrast to the observation of nature, "the *self*, with all its emotions and desires, is at the center of the enterprise; and the mind is at the circumference, serving merely as an instrument of the anxious self." The "ideological taint" touches even "the most scientific observations of social scientists." (3) The need for presuppositions in the form of "conceptual schemes" in behavioral inquiry "reveals the impossibility of observing the 'things themselves.'" Thus John Dewey's belief that the methods of natural science can be transferred to historical and social studies rested upon the "erroneous and, unexamined presupposition" that "the realm of history was essentially identical with the realm of nature," a belief that "obscured the freedom of man and the reality of the drama of history." (4) The basic religious presuppositions of modern culture, the idea of the perfectibility of man and the idea of progress, in reality determine the conclusions of most "scientific" inquiry. (5) The tendency to equate nature with history has not only given rise to a determinism diminishing human creativity, but it has also issued in a contradictory voluntaristic theory "according to which man is called upon to use scientific technics to manage history as he has managed nature." In this category lie the elitist formulations of scholars such as Skinner, Arnold, and Lasswell. Niebuhr commented: "The excessive voluntarism which underlies the theory of an elite is encouraged by the excessive determinism, which assumes that most men are creatures with simple determinate ends of life and that their 'anti-social' tendencies are quasi-biological impulses and inheritances which an astute social and psychological science can overcome or 're-direct' to what are known as 'socially approved goals.'"[48]

Speaking directly to Skinner's *Walden Two*, which he saw as a community lacking "the heroic and noble elements in human nature as completely as destructive animosities," Niebuhr said that man's freedom "transmutes all of nature's necessities into indeterminate ambitions" which "will always prevent that simple harmony which is the utopia of both democratic and communist idealists." He believed that modern psychologists and social scientists persistently misunderstand human nature in the following ways: (1) by not recognizing or obscuring "the full dimension of man's spirit," thus reducing him "to the level of nature's forms of life"; (2) by falsely regarding the spiritual dimension of human existence as virtuous, not recognizing "that the worse forms of human wrong-doing are spiritual"; and (3) by recognizing the spiritual character of evil, but falsely identifying it with religion and promising salvation through "the decay of religion."[49]

3. *Collective Egotism, Power and Government.* Niebuhr argued that the egotism of groups is greater than that of individuals, and that it expands in direct relation to the size of the collectives. This because "in every human group there is less reason to guide and to check impulse, less capacity for self-transcendence, less ability to comprehend the needs of others and therefore more unrestrained egoism." Then, too, the larger the group, the more powerful and able it is to defy social restraints, the less subject is it to internal moral restraints, and the more difficult it is for it to achieve a self-consciousness "except as it comes in conflict with other groups and is unified by perils and passions of war." Collective pride, he declared, pointing particularly to the nation-state, is "man's last, and in some respects most pathetic, effort to deny the determinate and contingent character of his existence." Whereas it may be possible to use "moral and rational suasion and accommodation" to establish justice between individuals, it is practically an impossibility among groups. Therefore, intergroup relations must "always be predominantly political rather than ethical."[50]

Niebuhr asserted, in a manner recalling Madison, that "all political positions are morally ambiguous because, in the realm of politics and economics, self-interest and power must be harnessed and beguiled rather than eliminated." He argued that an "an equilibrium of power" and "an organizing centre" are requisite to communal life. It follows that "political community must be brought into being by considering first how the creation of a power and authority at its center may check the tendency toward distintegration," and second "how a proper equilibrium among the various units may check the tendency toward domination from the center." Whereas the principle of the equilibrium of power furthers justice by preventing domination and enslavement, it must be saved from degeneration into anarchy by government which "must guide, direct, deflect and rechannel conflicting and competing forces in a community in the interest of a higher order." He further held that the primary source of authority and prestige for government is its capacity to maintain order, and that justice, though necessary, is secondary and a later historical development. Most importantly, the task of government has never been achieved in history "without setting force, as the instrument of order, against force as the instrument of anarchy."[51]

Concerning the relation of the law of love to political life, Niebuhr remarked: "An individual may sacrifice his own interests, either with-out hope of reward or in the hope of an ultimate compensation. But how is an individual, who is responsible for the interests of his group, to justify the sacrifice of interests other than his own? . . . The moral obtuseness of human collectives makes a morality of pure disinterested-ness impossible." Thus the achievement of justice "through equilibria of power," and not love, is "the very essence of politics." Because men are sinful, "justice can be achieved only by a certain degree of coercion on the one hand, and by resistance to coercion and tyranny on the other." And yet, the love ethic is relevant to politics. Niebuhr declared: "The problem is to establish tentative harmonies and provisional equities in a world from which sin cannot be eliminated, and yet to hold these provisional and tentative moral achievements under the perspective of the Kingdom of God." In this manner he escapes a Machiavellian con-ception of politics on the one hand, and the unqualified Social Gospel prescription of the law of love as a remedy for politics on the other. Thus he held that "in so far as justice admits the claims of the self, it is something less than love." Nonetheless, "it cannot exist without love and remain justice." Consequently, "laws and systems of justice have a negative as well as a positive relation to mutual love and brotherhood," containing both "approximations of and contradictions to the spirit of love."[52]

Because Niebuhr maintained that equality and justice are principles by which love is applied to historical situations, this dynamic relation-ship of absolute norm and proximate principles apparently served as his surrogate for the natural law formulations to which he objected. In fact, it has been argued by a student of his that, formally con-sidered, the Niebuhrian norm, principles, and applications thereof to historical circumstances, conform to the traditional division of *jus naturale, jus gentium,* and *jus civile.*[53]

4. *Democracy.* On the basis of his theological conception of man's freedom, Niebuhr criticized bourgeois and proletarian idealists for hav-ing a misplaced confidence in the possibility of achieving an easy reso-lution of the tension between self-interest and the general interest. Liberals, or "soft utopians," as he called them, expect perfection to develop out of emerging history, while Marxists, or "hard utopians," claim to embody the perfect community and feel justified morally to use any means of guile or force against opponents. Both erroneously believe in history as a redemptive process. Niebuhr numbered liberals and Marxists among the "children of light," "those who believe that self-interest should be brought under the discipline of a higher law." Opposed to them are the "children of darkness," whom he called "moral cynics who have no law beyond their will and interest." The children of darkness are evil in that they set no value beyond self-

interest, but wise because they understand its power. The children of light are foolish not only because they underestimate the power of self-interest among the children of darkness, but among themselves. They are prone to identify evil with institutions and ignorance, and miss its source in man himself.[54]

Because Niebuhr believed that the conflicts between men are those "in which each man or group seeks to guard its power and prestige against the peril of competing expressions of power and pride," he concluded that "the preservation of a democratic civilization requires the wisdom of the serpent and the harmlessness of the dove." Accordingly, he stated that the biblical faith affords three insights into the human situation which are indispensable to democracy and the children of light: (1) it assumes a source of authority on the basis of which the individual may defy worldly authorities; (2) it appreciates the unique worth of each individual which makes his use as an instrument immoral; and (3) its insistence that the dignity and misery of man have a common source in man's radical freedom is the basis of a viable realism and a defense against "sentimentality."[55]

In light of these points, Niebuhr stated: "Man's capacity for justice makes democracy possible, but man's inclination to injustice makes democracy necessary." The work of democracy is endless; it "is a method of finding proximate solutions for insoluble problems." A free society "is justified by the fact that the indeterminate possibilities of human vitality may be creative." Consequently, "every definition of the restraints which must be placed upon these vitalities must be tentative; because all such definitions, which are themselves the products of specific historical insights, may prematurely arrest or suppress a legitimate vitality, if they are made absolute and fixed." Democratic societies allow for peaceful self-correction, embodying within themselves the principle of resistance.[56]

Niebuhr believed that the Calvinist political anthropology of John Adams and James Madison, with its emphasis on the ideological tainting of reason by passion and interest, is superior to that of Jefferson. In effect, he asks us to return to their biblical realism to reconstruct our theory of democracy. Jeffersonians are criticized for lacking in understanding of "the perennial conflicts of power and pride which may arise on every level of 'abundance' since human desires grow with the means of their gratification." Nevertheless, Niebuhr had great regard for the Jeffersonian emphasis on liberty, and praised Madison for combining his Christian realism with the Jeffersonian passion for liberty. Niebuhr concluded that although great illusion regarding human nature obtains in American culture, "our political institutions contain many of the safeguards which our Calvinist fathers insisted upon." The Christian remembers that "in all political struggles there are no saints but only sinners fighting each other and . . . that history from man's, rather than God's, perspective is constituted of significant distinctions between types and degrees of sin."[57]

Finally, Niebuhr contended that there is no ultimate principle which should be above criticism in a democracy. Not only can truth ride into history on the back of error, but "a society which exempts ultimate principles from criticisms will find difficulty in dealing with the historical forces which have appropriated these truths as their special possession." Similarly, a viable democratic society cannot make democracy or freedom its final end because democracy is itself a form of human society and "man is only partially fulfilled in his social relations." Niebuhr then asked: "What does it profit an individual to be free of social compulsion if he lacks every ultimate point of reference for the freedom of his soul which exceeds the limits of his social institutions?" Thus he began and ended his critique and defense of democracy from the viewpoint of biblical faith, which, he believed, more amply treats and respects the mystery which is man than any other approach.[58]

Criticisms of Niebuhr's Thought

Among the responsible critics of Niebuhr, Morton White objects that Niebuhr's conclusion that man is inordinately selfish is based on his erroneous belief that man is born in sin. As we have seen, however, Niebuhr regarded original sin not as a biological attaint, but as a symbol indicating an inevitable, although not necessary, event in each human life. White also doubts the value for the illumination of the history of political thought or contemporary ideological struggles, of Niebuhr's distinction between "children of light" and "children of darkness." He remarks that "it is almost ridiculous for Niebuhr to present his own version of the Christian view as the only one to navigate between idiotic optimism and equally idiotic pessimism, as if all rationalists and naturalists said that men were gods, while their extreme opponents maintained that they were devils, and only Niebuhr knew the middle way."[59] Niebuhr would probably have admitted the validity of White's stricture but added in explanation that he (Niebuhr) was talking in terms of tendencies in men and that the Christian view best recognizes the radical nature of man's freedom, while noting the radical self-corruption of that freedom. On this basis he believed one can more easily be "realistic" than if one proceeds from a merely naturalistic or merely idealistic conception. Thus it becomes a question of a balanced viewpoint between the naïve tendency of the "children of light" to see naught but goodness, and the cynical tendency of the "children of darkness" to see naught but self-interest. Put in amended form, what Niebuhr says is that most liberals and reformers have tended toward the perspective of the children of light, while Machiavellians and fascists have tended toward that of the children of darkness.

While agreeing with Niebuhr's attack on Dewey's "scientific cheerleading," White rejects Niebuhr's critique of Dewey's attitude toward the use of scientific intelligence in social affairs. He sees no way but scientific method to best achieve social and political ends, a judgment with which Niebuhr, who accepted pragmatic approaches to the realization of ends, would have at least partially agreed. White concludes: "All we have here is the recognition that men are somewhere between the serpent and the dove, and while Niebuhr puts us closer to the serpent, Dewey puts us closer to the dove."[60]

White believes that Niebuhr's skepticism regarding man is separable from his theology, as it logically is. This, however, is to overlook the fact that Niebuhr as a theologian is concerned with ultimates and with man in his relationship to God. Thus his view of man as standing at the juncture of nature and spirit, and prone to self-deception, is at the root of his political criticism. White declares, however, that stripped of its "theological dressing," Niebuhr's theory of human nature is "little more than the doctrine that man is not God." And Niebuhr without theology is "a pale Niebuhr indeed." Once his favorable readers reject his doctrine of original sin, "they have no way of justifying the implications of inevitability and inexorability in that part of his doctrine which they do accept." For these reasons White concludes that despite Niebuhr's pretensions, his thought cannot "sustain a liberal attitude in politics" because "while liberalism in a philosophical sense may be hard to define . . . certain ways of thinking are incompatible with its rejection of dogma and obscurantism."[61]

Thus, just as MacLeish reads Lippmann out of the liberal fraternity so does White with Niebuhr. White apparently thinks that to be a liberal in politics one must not only not be a dogmatist in theology, but also reject first principles. He not only overlooks for the moment his own metaphysical presuppositions, but that Niebuhr was a most active advocate of democracy conceived as a necessary method of getting things done and not as a faith; that Niebuhr advocated not merely tolerance but unbridled questioning of first principles; that Niebuhr was a most vigorous proponent of civil liberties as well as a pragmatic approach in politics. On White's dogmatic terms, the "Christian realist," Madison, and probably even the Jefferson who subscribed to cosmic self-evident first principles rooted in deism, could not in their thought "sustain a liberal attitude in politics."

Nevertheless, it is true that Niebuhr, like Lippmann, tended to reject or greatly qualify the liberalism of the Enlightenment. He felt that historical conservatism has had keener insight into the power factor in human affairs and praised its emphasis on organic processes rather than abstract themes. But Niebuhr rejected the new conservatism of a Russell Kirk, saying that Kirk and men like him, having "discovered the realism of an Edmund Burke, always tend to mix this realism with an uncritical acceptance of inequality, conformity, and the current balance or equilibrium of power in any social scene."[62]

As Niebuhr saw it, the problem is "how to generate the wisdom of true conservatism without losing the humane virtues which the liberal movement developed." In this connection the social critic, Will Herberg, sees no contradictions between Niebuhr's earlier prophetic radicalism and his acceptance of certain conservative insights. Herberg remarks that the " 'prophetic' radicalism implied a radical relativization of all political programs, institutions, and movements, and therefore a thoroughgoing rejection of every form of political rationalism." Add to this "a renewed emphasis on the historic continuities of social life, and Niebuhr's brand of 'conservatism' emerges." From this point of view, Niebuhr's "Christian pragmatism," which sees no political or economic system as an absolute, proceeds. In light of the absolute norm of love and the dictates of justice, all social programs are, in Niebuhr's eyes, relativized. If we accept for purposes of argument White's reduction of Niebuhr's theology to the proposition that man is not God, it is necessary to remark that that is not as commonplace a conception as White implies.[63] To illustrate this point we turn now to the thought of Erich Fromm.

Erich Fromm and the Sane Society

Fromm was born in Germany in 1900 where he received his Ph.D. from Heidelberg in 1922 and trained in psychoanalysis. Coming to America in 1934, he has since engaged in the practice and teaching of psychiatry and has written widely on social-psychological problems.[64]

In *Escape from Freedom* (1941), Fromm argued, with the fascist experience in the background, that though modern man is free *from* medieval ties, he is not psychologically free *to* build a society based on reason and love, and consequently seeks security in submission to a leader, race, or state. In *The Sane Society* (1955), he contended that alienated man in mid-twentieth-century capitalistic, democratic states has fled from freedom to "anonymous authority" and "automaton conformity." Thus Fromm is most concerned with the predicament of modern man and the means by which he might build a "positive freedom" beyond the existing "negative freedom."[65]

While not rejecting Freud, Fromm maintains that the basic passions of man are not rooted in his instinctive needs, but in the specific conditions of human existence and the needs arising therefrom. His anthropology derives in good part from Marx, with particular emphasis on such conceptions as "man for himself," "alienation," and "false consciousness." Likewise he draws upon Aristotelian ethics, particularly in his conception of the mature, productive individual, while rejecting the Aristotelian notions of the prime intellect and the primacy of the contemplative life. Thus he proposes an anthropocentric humanism which sees man as the measure of all, and rejects the idea that there is anything higher and more dignified than human existence. At the same time he stoutly rejects subjectivity and relativism, holding that objective norms are discernible in man's nature. Fromm talks of man's having emerged from an original prehuman harmony with nature through self-awareness, reason, and imagination. Consequently man is an anomaly, "the freak of the universe." He is "part of nature, subject to her physical laws and unable to change them, yet he transcends the rest of nature." This split leads to what Fromm calls "existential dichotomies": such as that of life and death, and that of the need fully to develop potentialities and the brevity of life. On the other hand, "historical dichotomies," which are too often confused with the existential, are man-made and ultimately soluble. Combining Freud and Marx, Fromm writes: "To harmonize, and thus negate, contradictions is the function of rationalizations in individual life and of ideologies (socially patterned rationalizations) in social life." But instead of rationalization, which only masks reality, the solution to existential dichotomies is for man "to face the truth, to acknowledge his fundamental aloneness and solitude in a universe indifferent to his fate, to recognize that there is no power transcending him which can solve his problems for him," and that "there is no meaning to life except the meaning [he] gives his life by the unfolding of his powers."[66]

Fromm says that the abiding existential needs in man are: (1) the need for relatedness; (2) the need for transcendence (which can result in either creativity or destructiveness); (3) the need for rootedness; (4) the need for identity; and (5) the need for a frame of orientation and devotion.[67]

Against this background Fromm criticizes twentieth-century capitalistic, liberal-democratic society as characterized by the "marketing orientation" in which man experiences himself as a commodity to be sold, a thing being manipulated, and in constant quest of the approval of others. Life is thus depersonalized, empty, and meaningless. On the political plane, Fromm declares that "just as work has become alienated, the expression of the will of the voter in modern democracy is an alienated expression." The will of the people is not their own if they are "alienated automatons, whose tastes, opinions and preferences are manipulated by the big conditioning machines."[68]

Fromm's remedy is the mature man who autonomously unfolds his powers in accordance with "the laws of his nature." A full realization of one's potentialities brings at once the highest positive freedom and love of self. From the abundance of self-love there spontaneously issues love of others in terms of care, responsibility, respect, and knowledge. Because productive man gains autonomy by rejecting transcendent authority, he does not satisfy needs by self-denial, obedience, or regard to duty which stem from a moralistic legalism. Speaking to Dostoyevsky's statement, "if God is dead, everything is allowed," Fromm replies, untrue, because if man is alive, "he knows what is allowed, and to be alive means to be productive, to use one's powers not for any purpose transcending man, but for oneself, to make sense of one's existence, to be human." Put another way, man moves ahead to a full consciousness of all aspects of nature by making his unconscious conscious. In this way he will be reunited with nature, his fellow man, and himself, not on the original subhuman level but on a mature level. Thus "the mentally healthy person is the productive and unalienated person; the person who relates himself to the world lovingly, and who uses his reason to grasp reality objectively; who experiences himself as a unique individual entity, and at the same time feels one with his fellow man; who is not subject to irrational authority, and accepts willingly the rational authority of conscience and reason; who is in the process of being born as long as he is alive, and considers the gift of life the most precious chance he has." In him the feeling, "I am," replaces the experience of the self as the sum total of others' expectations.[69]

Just as the productive self-determining individual is the paradigm for individual sanity and happiness, implementation on the ethical, social, economic, political, and cultural planes of the "productive orientation" is the necessary condition for the end of human alienation and the establishment of the "sane society." Essentially Fromm is an optimist; unlike Niebuhr and Lippmann, he denies that a propensity to evil is inherent in man's nature, seeing evil as issuing from institutions. Thus he believes that man can construct a perfect society, stating that "it is quite beyond doubt that the problems of social transformation are not as difficult to solve—theoretically and practically—as the technical problems our chemists and physicists have solved." Society can be designed to provide conditions for the fullest development of human capacities to reason and love.[70]

Fromm's "sane society" is constructed on the principle of communitarian participatory democracy. If man is free only when he lives in accordance with a self-prescribed law, which allows for the complete realization of "the act of living itself," then he must not only directly prescribe his institutions but formulate policy. On the economic plane the worker must not only be well informed about his own work, but of the performance of the whole enterprise, and he must participate in management and decision making. Politically there must be decentralization with emphasis on discussion of issues by small groups of 500 people in terms of local residence or place of work. Such face-to-face groups across the country in their collective decisions on general issues would constitute "the true 'House of Commons,'" which would share power with a house of universally elected representatives and a universally elected executive. Finally, culturally there must be a combination of "work education" for the young, adult education, and a new system of popular art and secular ritual throughout the whole nation.[71]

Although Fromm talks in terms of a "science of man," he ultimately bases his idea of man's potential upon the insights of the "great teachers," such as Buddha, Moses, Socrates, and Christ—the same body of thought which Lippmann calls "high religion." On these grounds, and in the name of fundamental law, he is in opposition to such behavioralists as Skinner, whose manipulative science he believes would violate the "immutable laws inherent in human nature," and thus seriously damage the personality.[72]

Fromm's conception of life as a full development of potentialities has been likened by a recent critic to that of Hobbes. Both emphasize the exercise and extension of powers; Hobbes recognized the antisocial implications; Fromm, because of his denial of evil in man and his assumption of progressive development, rejects their inevitability.[73]

Fromm's indictment of liberalism and of the marketing orientation as leading to "anonymous authority," "automaton conformity," and what David Riesman has called "other-directedness," leads to his prescription of autonomy. In view, however, of the ubiquity of what the Founding Fathers, following many thinkers before them, called the "love of praise" and "the love of fame," and what John Adams called the "passion for distinction," is it entirely true that, as Fromm claims, motivation in terms of the desire to satisfy opinion and gain approval is a cultural phenomenon peculiar only to twentieth-century capitalist society?

Alienation, as Fromm sees it, is a requirement of man's development and consequently can be overcome and eliminated in the "sane society." Discussing this thesis in connection with Fromm's statement that "in the 19th century the problem was that God is dead; in the 20th century the problem is that man is dead," the theologian Paul Tillich has written:

Naturally one will ask: Is there not a connection between the two problems? Is not the self-loss of man in the present society a consequence of the loss of God in the preceding period? Is true humanism possible without a consciousness of something that transcends man? Fromm knows the ethical transcendence as expressed in the laws of love and justice. The theologian must ask: How can man's alienation be overcome except by a power which transcends the law and *gives* what the law demands in vain? How can alienated man over-come alienation by himself? How can the "dead" man of the 20th century revive himself?[74]

In like vein, Niebuhr, while agreeing with Fromm's criticism of moralistic legalism and his recognition of the limitations of a sense of duty, believed that he fails to see that the "real problem of the self is that it seeks to contain itself as free spirit within itself as contingent existence." In this view love of neighbor does not flow from an abun-dance of self-love. Instead, "whatever spiritual wealth the self has within itself is the by-product of its relations, affections and responsibil-ities, of its concern for life beyond itself." To Niebuhr "an insecure and impoverished self" can be made secure neither by the admonition to be concerned with itself nor by the admonition to love others, but only by divine grace.[75]

Following the nineteenth-century German thinker, Ludwig Feuer-bach, Fromm saves the concept "God" by identifying therewith produc-tive man, whose "spontaneous activity is free activity of the self," which implies "the elimination of the split between 'reason' and 'nature.'" In short, man not only creates "the realm of love, reason and justice," but redeems himself, and in so doing, becomes as God.[76]

Looking specifically at Fromm's sociopolitical nostrums, the republican constitutionalist will argue that his institutional recommendations, if unamended, rest ultimately on the assumption of the validity of his naïve pelagianism and faith in progress. Essentially Fromm asserts that by rearranging our social institutions in terms of "communitarian social-ism," we will not only minimize differences between rulers and subjects, but end them, and in the process establish human autonomy. Decentral-ized participatory democracy was, of course, proposed by Jefferson, but Jefferson took cognizance of something Fromm ignores, the possibility of a tyrannous majority and the need for institutional separation of powers, checks and balances, an enforceable bill of rights, and limited govern-mental powers. As Tillich has remarked, Fromm's prescriptions sound utopian. Indeed, though his reliance is heavily on Feuerbach, Marx, and Freud, it is perhaps finally more so on Rousseau. Both Rousseau and Fromm talk in terms of the alienation of perfectible man from nature through reason and self-awareness, and the development of essential and nonessential needs in his acquired nature in the course of his social evolution. Both seek a return on the plane of humanity to the unity and freedom of primal man, Rousseau through the "general will" of the col-lectivity, Fromm through his decentralized communitarian participatory democracy. In each case the political problem is solved by denying or minimizing it. And just as Rousseau exalts above all the simple "feeling of existence," so Fromm exalts "spontaneity" and "living for life." In short, as John Schaar has observed, Fromm sees practically all institutional restraints as unnecessary or harmful to man, and seeks the abolition of the authority of one man over another. Because the fear and hatred of authority suffuses his work, he can build no meaningful political theory.[77]

Unquestionably the problem of participation is a vital one in contemporary life; insofar as Fromm deals with it on a psychoethical basis his work should be read to understand the current human plight. Along with this his major contribution appears to lie, as a recent analyst of his thought has written, in his uniting the Marxian concepts of ideology and false consciousness with the psychoanalytic ideas of rationalization and repression.[78]

Comparison of Lippmann, Niebuhr, and Fromm

Comparing Lippmann, Niebuhr, and Fromm, we find that the first approaches man and government as a philosophical student of practical affairs, the second as a dialectical theologian interested in social ethics, and the third as a Freudian cultural revisionist interested in social psychology. Each is a humanist or personalist; whereas Niebuhr's is a theocentric humanism, Lippmann's and Fromm's humanism is anthropocentric. Lippmann and Niebuhr agree upon original sin as a convenient term to describe man's inevitable propensity to evil; Fromm denies original sin and ascribes evil to the effect of unfavorable institutions upon men. Whereas Lippmann believes in the efficacy of human reason ultimately to discern universally valid principles of individual and political conduct in the form of natural law, Niebuhr thought that the effect of self-interest on the use of reason is so great as to preclude natural law. Fromm asserts the existence of laws of human nature which must be obeyed, but supplies little specific content. In emphasizing "man for himself" Fromm, unlike Niebuhr and Lippmann, claims that man creates the realms of reason and love. Each thinker, however, is insistent upon the existence of a source of objective norms, whether it be nature or revelation. Throughout his works Lippmann has emphasized the importance of political leadership, and in all but his very early works he has stressed the incompetence of public opinion to govern. Niebuhr emphasized the pervasiveness of self-interest in both leaders and the led, with focus on the former. Fromm has paid little attention to this problem, perhaps because he does not think it will exist once the sane society is realized. Although he was originally an advocate of socialism, Niebuhr was later influenced by events and his doctrine of original sin, to the point of abandoning social planning and espousing a pragmatic approach in politics. While Fromm is a socialist, Lippmann, the early pragmatist, became an advocate of an unplanned free market system, a position he later qualified by his acceptance of measures representing prudential means to the realization of the common good. Lippmann sees freedom as involving absence of restraint plus the following of what one ought to do, as indicated by objective moral precepts. Niebuhr saw freedom as involving man's ability to violate the necessities of nature, the dictate of reason and the will of God; living in freedom and necessity man is both creator and creature of history. Fromm sees man's freedom as negative, in the sense of being free from repressive institutional forms, and positive in the sense of self-realization. Lippmann regards democracy as desirable, but within the framework of a natural public law dictate, requiring an executive who leads and a representative popular assembly which criticizes and chooses. Niebuhr saw democracy as possible because of man's capacity for justice, and necessary because of man's inclination to injustice. Fromm argues for society-wide participatory democracy on the assumption of human goodness. He foresees the end of human alienation and anxiety; Niebuhr saw alienation and anxiety as inevitable because man stands at the juncture of nature and spirit; and Lippmann appears to accept them in stoical fashion. Lippmann like Niebuhr emphasizes the realm of politics as, at best, the realm of justice. Niebuhr saw the law of love as imperative but unrealizable in the political world. Fromm believes politics itself can ultimately be replaced by love. Finally, Lippmann and Niebuhr, because of their conception of human nature and knowledge of history, wrote of the utter necessity of constitutional restraints and guarantees; Fromm ignores this vital question, probably because his utopian sane society, in which love ultimately replaces politics, would render them superfluous.

Constitutional Law and Higher Law

After the Supreme Court abandoned the special protection of property rights by 1937, it groped, in the context of increasing assaults on liberty abroad, for a new meaningful role. On the one hand were Justices like Felix Frankfurter and, later, John M. Harlan II who, following Thayer, emphasized judicial self-restraint across the board, along with the test of reasonableness in weighing challenged legislation. Others, beginning tentatively with Chief Justice Harlan F. Stone and continuing more extensively with Hugo Black, William Douglas, Chief Justice Earl Warren, and what at times was a majority of the Court, stressed an activistic implementation of the Bill of Rights and the removal of obstacles to the democratic process.[79]

The course suggested by Stone in a footnote in a 1938 opinion would deny the presumption of constitutionality to legislation restricting the political process or directed at "discrete and insular" minorities. The rationale of the latter is that while the political process, "can ordinarily be expected to bring about repeal of undesirable legislation," minorities, especially the social and religious, are subject to prejudice "which tends seriously to curtail the operation of those political processes ordinarily to be relied upon" for their protection.[80]

Whereas Stone's formulation was based on a meta-constitutional conception of the essentiality of democracy, conceived as majority rule presupposing guaranteed individual liberties, Black attempted to establish a purely positivistic basis for his nationalistic view. Thus liberty in the Fourteenth Amendment is to be explained wholly and solely in terms of the specifics of the Bill of Rights, with emphasis put on the First Amendment freedoms as preferred and absolute. Besides exegetical difficulties which ensue when confronted with vague phrases in the Bill of Rights, and the fact that the Ninth Amendment admits to the possession by individuals of rights other than those specified in the Constitution, the conception of First Amendment freedoms as preferred and absolute is clearly a meta-constitutional judgment beyond Black's proclaimed positivism.[81]

Justice Douglas, following Justice Frank Murphy before him, represents a meta-constitutional point of view which holds with Black that the Bill of Rights is assimilated to the Fourteenth Amendment, but adds, in natural law manner, that such listing is not preclusive of other rights. Thus Douglas could argue for the Court, while Black dissented, that although there is no specific right to privacy mentioned in the Constitution, it is implied in a reading of Amendments 1, 3, 4, 5, 6, 9, and 14.[82]

The position of Frankfurter on the relationship of the Bill of Rights to the Fourteenth Amendment was rooted in what he regarded as the traditional jurisprudence, plus a natural law approach and deference to the pluralism underlying the federal principle. Liberty in the Fourteenth Amendment must be defined not in terms of the Bill of Rights as such, but in terms used by Justice Cardozo, "ordered liberty," or principles of liberty and justice "so rooted in the traditions and conscience of our people as to be ranked as fundamental." Similarly Frankfurter, like Harlan after him, viewed the Constitution as a whole, seeing as equally important to rights the structural principles of federalism and separation of powers. As Harlan has put it: "We are accustomed to speak of the Bill of Rights and the Fourteenth Amendment as the principal guarantees of personal liberty. Yet it would surely be shallow not to recognize that the structure of our political system accounts no less for the free society we have." Nonetheless, Frankfurter's approach has been strongly criticized for its alleged inspecificity, difficulty of principled application, and its consequent tendency toward subjectivity. It should be added that the approach of Frankfurter and Harlan to the question of the relation of the Bill of Rights to actions of the national government is one which turns aside from the reliance on societal consensus evidenced in state cases and toward a strict application.[83]

Building upon the foundations which Stone adumbrated, the Warren Court read the political theory of equalitarian democracy and individual liberty into the Constitution as activistically as the pre-1937 Court read therein an economic theory. Answering the question of how an anti- or counter-majoritarian institution like the Court can best serve democracy, by focusing on the equal and full implementation of civil and political rights and the removal of obstacles to majority rule, the Court has delivered landmark decisions declaring racial segregation unconstitutional, requiring a one-man one-vote approach to the question of the drawing of legislative districts, and exacting a meticulous regard for due process in public administration and, most particularly, the administration of justice. Without specifically adopting Black's total incorporation theory, it has read all of the fundamental guarantees of the federal Bill of Rights into the Fourteenth Amendment as limitations on state action. It attempted to establish peaceful alternatives to violent change, but in the process, in the opinion of such members as Harlan and Black (who became a strict constructionist in cases involving protest), approached the precipice into which the activistic pre-1937 Court tumbled. The one-man, one-vote concept has been particularly criticized for applying an almost unworkable abstract mathematical formula to the complexities of political life and involving federal judges in actual drawing of plans. Justice Harlan (who like every judge on the Court since 1953 agreed wholeheartedly with the desegregation decisions) complained: "I am frankly astonished at the ease with which the Court has proceeded to fasten upon the entire country at its lowest political levels the strong arm of the federal judiciary, let alone a particular political ideology which has been the subject of wide debate and differences from the beginnings of our Nation." In answer it has been stated that the Court's activism is an attempt to apply what we might call Jefferson's meta-constitutional pronouncement that "though the will of the majority is in all cases to prevail, that will to be rightful must be reasonable; that the minority possess their equal rights, which equal law must protect, and to violate would be oppression."[84]

Thus, although its craftsmanship and technical proficiency may have been at times deficient, the Court in the past thirty years has established itself as the conscience and umpire of American democracy. It may now be time, as some aver, to consolidate and conserve the advances while redressing imbalances. In any case, such consolidation will in all likelihood be made in the context of agreement on the Court and in the country, in its sober moments, that, in the words of Justice Jackson, "the very purpose of a Bill of Rights was to withdraw certain subjects from the vicissitudes of political controversy, to place them beyond the reach of majorities and officials and to establish them as legal principles to be applied by Courts."[85]

Realism, National Interest, and Higher Law

World War II and its Cold War aftermath evoked serious reflection on the conduct of foreign policy by Lippmann, Niebuhr, the diplomat-scholar George Kennan and the academician Hans Morgenthau. Each strongly asserted the necessity to recapture the Founding Fathers' sense of the primacy of national self-interest and to move away from the moralistic, legalistic approach. Within this framework there existed significant differences, particularly among Niebuhr, Kennan, and Morgenthau, concerning the relation of self-interest and morality.[86]

Morgenthau believes that "the invocation of moral principles for the support of national policies . . . is always and of necessity a pretense." Kennan notes that the proponent of "the legalistic-moralistic approach to international problems" is dedicated to the ending of war and violence, yet the inflexible fanaticism which ensues "makes violence more enduring, more terrible, and more destructive to political stability." Because the idealist does not understand that "the greatest law of human history is its unpredictability," and that life is "an organic and not a mechanical process," he surrenders to the "colossal deceit" of believing he can reconstruct international society in accordance with his ideals.[87]

Kennan asks us to have "the modesty to admit that our own national interest is all that we are really capable of knowing and understanding." Because right and wrong in concrete international questions are almost undiscoverable, one must consult interest, not principle, but with a desire to adjust to the interest of others. Morgenthau, following Hamilton's injunction, "self-preservation is the first duty of a nation," concludes that realistic thinking is based upon the idea of interest "defined in terms of power." Because the nation is the sole source of order and protector of moral values in a near anarchical international society, both politics and morality require for the nation "one guiding star, one standard for thought, one rule for action: the national interest."[88]

Approaching the question in typical dialectical fashion, Niebuhr both agreed and disagreed with Kennan and Morgenthau. To the latter's charge of "pretense," he answered that "hypocrisy is an inevitable by-product in the life of any nation which has some loyalty to moral principles" and that the alternative is "to sink into consistent cynicism." Then, too, the nation does protect minimal moral values, but its moral legitimacy is ambiguous because the same power underlying national order seems to ensure international disorder. Concerning Kennan, Niebuhr wrote that if his advocacy of modesty is valid his solution is erroneous because "egoism is not the proper cure for an abstract and pretentious idealism." Thus Niebuhr thought in terms of an interplay between interest and principle.[89]

Upon analysis it appears that Kennan and Morgenthau less consciously than Niebuhr intrude norms to adjudge and direct interest. Thus it has been asked, how can Kennan achieve his recommended "moral modesty" unless his perspective is beyond interest? Similarly how can he perceive the difficulty of discerning the just from the unjust position unless he calls on a norm beyond history? Also, how can Kennan condemn totalitarianism, as he does, unless he intrudes a norm? Concerning Morgenthau, his charge of "hypocrisy" is a moral and not a political judgment. He, in effect, also establishes a moderate restrained diplomacy itself as a norm. In short, as a recent commentator, Robert Good, has observed, both Kennan and Morgenthau have "simply insinuated moral principles into their views of national interest." And, Good adds, "what Morgenthau and Kennan only imply, Niebuhr makes perfectly explicit," by holding that "there can be no health in a society of men unless the claims of interest are challenged by a loyalty larger than interest, just as loyalty to principle must be chastened by a sober awareness of the force of interest."[90]

Morgenthau contends that "to know that states are subject to the moral law is one thing; to pretend to know what is morally required of states in a particular situation is quite another." He sees the transcendental norm as critical of every politically expedient act, a realization which, in Good's words, "moderates the temptation to pretense and hypocrisy." Morgenthau, although not consistently, sees moral principles as directive. He writes: "Both individual and the state must judge political action by universal moral principles, such as that of liberty." Good concludes, however, that "Morgenthau's concept of principle is so transcendental that it can play *only* a judgmental role in the life of political, sinful man, saving him from hypocrisy (by demonstrating to him that he is not God), but not necessarily saving him from cynicism (by failing to demonstrate that he is more than a beast)." In connection with this point Morgenthau, as George Lichtheim has pointed out, criticizes Lippmann's recourse to natural law and yet implicitly accepts a natural law doctrine in his own approach. He thinks that the Western world needs a natural law doctrine, but must yet recognize that natural law was historically the ideology of a particular social order. Nonetheless, Morgenthau, an enemy of relativism in private morality, asks how it can be explained "that we can not only understand the moral relevance of the Ten Commandments, originating in a social environment quite different from ours, but also make them the foundation of our moral life," and how can it be explained "that the moral ideas of Plato and Pascal, of Buddha and Thomas Aquinas, are similarly acceptable to our intellectual understanding and moral sense?" He answers: "If the disparate historic systems of morality were not erected upon a common foundation of moral understanding and valuation, impervious to the changing conditions of time and place, we could not understand any other moral system but our own, nor could any other moral system but our own have any moral relevance for us." On these grounds it is likely that Morgenthau's criticism of natural law is more applicable to the politicized modern version, which Strauss calls "modern natural right," than to the classical formulation. In short, though he fully accepts the liberal emphasis on liberty, he cannot accept the strand of liberal thought which assumes man's "essential goodness" and "infinite malleability." Concerned more with "historic precedent" than "abstract principles," and with "the achievement of the lesser evil rather than of the absolute good," Morgenthau sees the world as one of "opposing interests and of conflict between them," in which "moral principles can never be fully realized, but at best approximated through the ever temporary balancing of interests and the ever precarious settlement of conflicts." Insofar as Morgenthau believes that *all* men lust for power, Lichtheim properly answers, "Some don't," and that to realize this does not necessarily render one a utopian. Yet Morgenthau's assumption might be viewed as operational, and thus at one with that of the classical republicans from Machiavelli to Madison, who thought that state-building demanded that one assume every man a knave even if that is not the fact. It is this psychology which brings Morgenthau to declare that "it is exactly the same concept of interest defined in terms of power, that saves us from both moral excess and . . . political folly."[91]

Good tells us that "Kennan presumes that each nation's interest contains its own principles, applicable to itself but irrelevant and even mischievous if applied to others," while Morgenthau's regard for principle is unintegrated with his predominant stress on interest. Niebuhr, however, espoused an idealism that looks beyond the national interest, and a realism that lays bare the pretense in every attempt to transcend national interest. Thus we might conclude, employing terms used in another context by Niebuhr, by saying that to Kennan politics among nations, once such politics are properly severed from a disastrous moralistic orientation, are pathetic in their unavoidable conflict of interest; to Morgenthau they are tragic, in the sense that the choices open are always tainted with evil; while to Niebuhr they are ironic in the sense that they are at bottom rooted in what he called "fortuitous incongruities" which upon "closer examination" are found "to be not merely fortuitous."[92]

A realization of the pathos, tragedy, and irony of political life has been a sobering experience to the American, nurtured as he has been in the hope and expectation of continual progress. Seeking a complete maturity which will save him from both cynicism and utopianism, he gropes toward a realization of an international ethic which prescribes a prudential application of the dictates of liberty and justice, institutionalized in forms which will make it the particular interest of each member nation to work for such ends.

NOTES

1. Cf. Heinrich Rommen, *The Natural Law* (St. Louis, 1947); Jacques Maritain, *The Rights of Man and Natural Law* (New York, 1943); Leo Strauss, *Natural Right and History* (Chicago, 1953); Yves Simon, *The Philosophy of Democratic Government* (Chicago, 1951); and John C. Murray, *We Hold These Truths* (New York, 1960).

2. For sketches of Lippmann's life, see Charles Wellborn, *Twentieth Century Pilgrimage* (Baton Rouge, 1969), pp. 9–44 and, covering his early life, Charles Forcey, *The Crossroads of Liberalism* (New York, 1961), p. 88ff.

3. *A Preface to Politics* (New York, 1913 reprinted in 1933), pp. xii, 225, 199, 9, 84.

4. *Ibid.,* pp. 200, 216.

5. *Ibid.,* pp. 12, 83, 217, 222.

6. *Ibid.,* p. 116.

7. *Ibid.,* pp. 262, 263, 66, 296.

8. *Ibid.,* p. 147.

9. *Ibid.,* pp. 228, 230, 244.

10. *Drift and Mastery* (New York, 1914), p. 276, in Wellborn, *op. cit.,* p. 26.

11. *Public Opinion* (New York, 1922, reprinted 1949), pp. 5, 125, 20.

12. *The Phantom Public* (New York, 1925); Walter Lippmann, "Why Should the Majority Rule?", Harpers, CLII (1926), 400, cited in Wellborn, *op. cit.,* p. 77; Wellborn, *op. cit.,* pp. 78, 79.

13. *A Preface to Morals* (New York, 1929), pp. 208, 6, 152, 19, 9.

14. *Ibid.,* p. 193.

15. *Ibid.,* pp. 206, 208, 220–221, 258.

16. *Ibid.,* p. 239.

17. *Ibid.,* pp. 282, 283, 275.

18. *Ibid.,* pp. 175–176.

19. *The Good Society* (Boston, 1937), pp. x, xii, xiii.

20. *Ibid.,* p. 235.

21. *A Preface to Morals,* p. 275; *The Good Society,* p. 346.

22. *The Good Society,* pp. 347, 334, 361, 377.

23. *The Public Philosophy* (New York, Mentor Paperback, 1955), pp. 12, 13.

24. *Ibid.,* pp. 18, 31, 43, 29.

25. *Ibid.,* pp. 38, 45.

26. *Ibid.,* p. 49.

27. *Ibid.,* pp. 58, 59, 61, 70, 69, 70–71.

28. *Ibid.,* pp. 75, 79, 80, 88, 78.

29. *Ibid.,* p. 95.

30. *Ibid.,* pp. 93, 96, 99, 102.

31. *Ibid.,* pp. 109, 117, 118, 124, 116, 110, 117, 119.

32. *Ibid.,* pp. 137, 106.

33. Schlesinger's comments are cited in Wellborn, *op. cit.,* p. 165; White, *Social Thought in America,* pp. 254, 275.

34. Wellborn, *op. cit.,* p. 166; *The Public Philosophy,* p. 117.

35. David Spitz, *Democracy and the Challenge of Power* (New York, 1958), pp. 150, 124, 204 (note 30); Wellborn, *op. cit.,* pp. 170–172.

36. Archibald MacLeish, "The Alternative," *The Yale Review,* XLIV (June, 1955),

489; Lippmann, "A Rejoinder," *ibid.,* pp. 499, 500.

37. Reinhold Niebuhr, "Intellectual Autobiograhy," in Chas. W. Kegley and Robert W. Bretall, *Reinhold Niebuhr* (New York, 1956), p. 6. I have also used for biographical data, Meyer, *The Protestant Search for Political Realism,* pp. 217–269; D. R. Davies, *Reinhold Niebuhr: Prophet from America* (New York, 1948); and Arthur Schlesinger's article, "Reinhold Niebuhr's Role in American Political Thought and Life," in the Kegley and Bretall volume mentioned above, pp. 125–150.

38. *The Nature and Destiny of Man,* Vol. I, *Human Nature* (New York, 1941, reprinted in 1964), vii, 5, 14, 124, 12.

39. Reinhold Niebuhr, *Faith and History* (New York, 1949), p. 163.

40. *Human Nature,* p. 53.

41. *Human Nature,* pp. 122, 137–138, 150, 252, 257.

42. *Ibid.,* pp. 182–186, 252.

43. *Ibid.,* p. 194.

44. *The Children of Light and the Children of Darkness* (New York, 1944), pp. 70, 74.

45. *Ibid.,* p. 78n.; *Human Nature,* pp. 269, 276, 297; *Christian Realism and Political Problems* (New York, 1953), pp. 133, 157, reprinted in Harry R. Davis and Robert C. Good, *Reinhold Niebuhr on Politics* (New York, 1960), p. 170. See also Niebuhr, *The Nature and Destiny of Man,* Vol. II, *Human Destiny* (New York, 1943, reprinted in 1964), p. 253ff.

46. *Human Nature,* pp. 270, 287; *Christianity and Society* (Spring, 1948), p. 27, cited in Paul Ramsey, "Love and Law," in Kegley and Bretall, *op. cit.,* pp. 85–86.

47. *Faith and History,* pp. 197–198.

48. *Ibid.,* pp. 55–56; *The Self and the Dramas of History* (New York, 1955), pp. 114, 115; *Christian Realism and Political Problems* (New York, 1953), pp. 75, 69, 70; "Christian Faith and Social Action," in J. Hutchison, *Christian Faith and Social Action* (New York, 1953), p. 238. All of the above are reprinted in Davis and Good, *op. cit.,* pp. 43–63.

49. *The Irony of American History* (New York, 1952), pp. 84, 85; "The Blind Leaders," *Christianity and Society* (Spring, 1949), pp. 5, 6, reproduced in Davis and Good, *op. cit.,* p. 62.

50. *Moral Man and Immoral Society* (New York, 1932), pp. xi, xii, xxiii, 48; *Human Nature,* p. 213.

51. "Christian Faith and Political Controversy," *Christianity and Crisis* (July 12, 1952), 97, cited in Davis and Good, *op. cit.,* p. 193; *The Children of Light and the Children of Darkness,* p. 174; *Human Destiny,* p. 266; "The United Nations and World Organization," *Christianity and Crisis* (Jan. 25, 1943), 2, cited in Davis and Good, *op. cit.,* p. 106; "The Idolatry of America," *Christianity and Society* (Spring, 1950), 4, cited in Davis and Good, *op. cit.,* p. 110; "Force and Reason in Politics," *Nation* (Feb. 10, 1940), 216, cited in Davis and Good, *op. cit.,* p. 119.

52. *Moral Man and Immoral Society,* pp. 267, 272; "Christ and Our Political Decisions," *Christianity and Crisis* (Aug. 11, 1941), 1, cited in Davis and Good, *op. cit.,* p. 143; *Christianity and Power Politics* (New York, 1940), p. 14; "Christian Faith and the Common Life," in N. Ehrenstrom, *Christian Faith and the Common Life,* p. 72; cited in Davis and Good, *op. cit.,* p. 153; "Justice and Love," *Christianity and Society* (Autumn, 1950), p. 7, cited in Davis and Good, *op. cit.,* p. 165; *Human Destiny,* p. 251.

53. Ramsay, *op. cit.,* pp. 80–123.

54. Davis and Good, *op. cit.,* pp. 12, 13; *The Children of Light and the Children of Darkness,* pp. 9, 10, 11, 17.

55. *The Children of Light and the Children of Darkness,* pp. 20, 40; *Christian Realism and Political Problems,* pp. 100–102.

56. *The Children of Light and the Children of Darkness,* pp. xiii, 118, 63–64; *Human Destiny,* p. 268.

57. *The Irony of American History,* pp. 21, 30, 96–98, 22; "Leaves from the Notebook of a War-Bound American," *Christian Century* (Nov. 15, 1939), 1405–1406, cited in Davis and Good, *op. cit.,* p. 196.

58. *The Children of Light and the Children of Darkness,* p. 75; "Democracy as a

Religion," *Christianity and Crisis* (Aug. 4, 1947), 1–2, cited in Davis and Good, *op. cit.*, p. 191.

59. White, *op. cit.*, p. 252. For a criticism of Niebuhr's critique of "scientism" see Holton Odegard, *Sin and Society* (Yellow Springs, Ohio, 1956). I agree with the critique of Odegard's work found in Gordon Harland, *The Thought of Reinhold Niebuhr* (New York, 1960), pp. 181–186.

60. *Ibid.*, p. 255.

61. *Ibid.*, pp. 263, 264.

62. "Liberalism and Conservatism," *Christianity and Society* (Winter, 1954–1955), 3, cited in Harland, *op. cit.*, pp. 188–189.

63. Cited in Harland, *op. cit.*, p. 189. For comments on Niebuhr's pragmatism see Harland, p. 190ff.

64. I have been aided in the writing of this section by John Schaar's *Escape from Authority* (New York, 1961), and Guyton B. Hammond, *Man in Estrangement* (Nashville, 1965).

65. *Escape from Freedom* (New York, 1941); *The Sane Society* (New York, 1955), p. 164.

66. *Man for Himself* (New York, 1947), pp. 40, 44, 45.

67. *The Sane Society*, pp. 27–66.

68. *Ibid.*, pp. 68, 99, 184, 185.

69. *Man for Himself*, pp. 20, 248–249, 158; *The Sane Society*, p. 275.

70. *The Sane Society*, p. 282.

71. *Ibid.*, pp. 321ff., 339ff., 343ff.

72. Erich Fromm, *Psychoanalysis and Religion* (New Haven, 1950), pp. 74, 76; cited in Gabriel, *op. cit.*, pp. 469, 470.

73. Schaar, *op. cit.*, p. 153.

74. Paul Tillich, "Erich Fromm's *The Sane Society*," *Pastoral Psychology*, VI (Sept., 1955), 16.

75. *Christianity and Society* (Spring, 1948), 27–28. See also Niebuhr, *The Self and the Dramas of History*, pp. 133–140.

76. *Escape from Freedom*, pp. 258–259, *The Art of Loving* (New York, 1956), p. 72.

77. Schaar, *op. cit.*, p. 302.

78. Hammond, *op. cit.*, p. 180.

79. For the story of the Court in recent years see Alexander Bickel, *Politics and the Warren Court* (New York, 1965).

80. *U.S. v. Carolene Products Co.*, 304 U.S. 152–3, note 4 (1938). For an appraisal of Stone's view see George D. Braden, "The Search for Objectivity in Constitutional Law," *Yale Law Journal*, 57 (1948), 579ff.

81. For Black's view see especially his opinion in *Adamson v. California*, 332, U.S. 46 (1947). For a criticism of Black's view see Braden, *op. cit.*, p. 590ff.

82. *Griswold v. Connecticut*, 381 U.S. 479 (1965).

83. For Frankfurter's views see his opinions in *Adamson v. California, op. cit.*, pp. 59–68, *Malinski v. N.Y.*, 324 U.S. 401 (1945), and *W.Va. Bd. of Educ. v. Barnette*, 319 U.S. 624 (1943). Frankfurter's and Black's views are compared in Wallace Mendelson, *Justices Black and Frankfurter: Conflict in the Court* (Chicago, 1961); Address by John M. Harlan, New York City, Aug. 9, 1964, cited in Alpheus T. Mason, "Judicial Activism: Old and New," *Virginia Law Review*, 55, 395. For a criticism of Frankfurter's position, see Braden, *op. cit.*, p. 583ff.

84. *Avery v. Midland County*, 390 U.S. 474, 490 (1968); Thomas Jefferson, *Notes on Virginia*, cited in Mason, *op. cit.*, p. 402. Concerning the Warren Court, see the Mason article, and Alexander M. Bickel, *Politics and the Warren Court* (New York, 1965).

85. *West Va. Bd. of Educ. v. Barnette*, 638.

86. I am particularly indebted in writing this section to Robert C. Good's article, "The National Interest and Political Realism: Niebuhr's 'Debate' with Morgenthau and Kennan," *Journal of Politics*, XXII (Nov., 1960), 597–619.

87. "National Interest and Moral Principles in Foreign Policy," *American Scholar*, XVIII (Spring, 1949), 207, cited in Good, *op. cit.*, p. 602; *American Diplomacy*

(Chicago, 1951), p. 100, cited in Good, *op. cit.*, p. 603; Morgenthau's principal books are *Scientific Man v. Power Politics* (Chicago, 1946); *Politics Among Nations* (New York, 1948); *In Defense of the National Interest* (New York, 1951); and *Politics in the Twentieth Century* (Chicago, 1963, 2 vols.).

88. *American Diplomacy*, pp. 102–103; *In Defense of the National Interest*, pp. 15–16, 242; *Politics Among Nations* (2nd ed., 1954), 4ff. These are cited in Good, *op. cit.*, pp. 603–605.

89. "The Moral Issue in International Relations" (Unpublished paper for the Rockefeller Foundation); *The Irony of American History*, p. 148. Cited in Good, *op. cit.*, p. 605.

90. Good, *op. cit.*, pp. 608–616.

91. "Another Great Debate," *American Political Science Review* (Dec., 1952), 984, cited in Good, *op. cit.*, p. 612; *Politics Among Nations*, p. 9, cited in Good, *op. cit.*, p. 613; Good, *op. cit.*, p. 613; Lichtheim, *The Concept of Ideology* (New York, 1967), pp. 138–139; *Politics in the Twentieth Century*, I, 372, cited in Lichtheim, *op. cit.*, p. 141.

92. Good, *op. cit.*, p. 616; *The Irony of American History*, Preface, viii.

Chapter 25

POSTWAR CONSERVATISM AND THE NEW LEFT

Society cannot exist unless a controlling power of will and appetite be placed somewhere; and the less of it there is within, the more there must be without.

EDMUND BURKE

We do not nowadays refute our predecessors, we pleasantly bid them goodbye.

GEORGE SANTAYANA

Postwar Conservatism

In 1949 the liberal literary critic Lionel Trilling could write:

In the United States at this time liberalism is not only the dominant but even the sole intellectual tradition. For it is the plain fact that nowadays there are no conservative or reactionary ideas in general circulation. This does not mean, of course, that there is no impulse to conservatism or to reaction. . . . But the conservative impulse and the reactionary impulse do not, with some isolated and some ecclesiastical exceptions, express themselves in ideas but only in action or in irritable mental gestures which seek to resemble ideas.[1]

In the Cold War atmosphere of the late 1940's and 1950's, and in the midst of a society in which affluence was matched by personal anxiety, an intellectual movement called the New Conservatism challenged the traditional liberalism. Foremost among its proponents are the academicians Russell Kirk (1918–) and Peter Viereck (1916–). In his *The Conservative Mind* (1953) Kirk, exalting Burke, stressed: (1) the divine basis of society; (2) affection for the variety of tradition, as distinguished from uniformity and equalitarianism; (3) the need for "orders," classes, and leadership; (4) the inseparability of liberty and property; (5) faith in prescription and recognition of the restricted nature of reason; (6) deliberate and cautious change with Providence as its proper instrument.[2]

Kirk, who admits to having a "Gothic mind, *medieval* in its temper and structure," wants a restoration of aristocracy, but one drawn from the older middle classes rather than the industrial classes. Sounding much like Babbitt and More before him, he proclaimed: "What men really are seeking, or ought to seek, is not the right to govern themselves, but the right to be governed well." His American model is John Adams. He sees the American conservative tradition as embracing natural rights, representative self-government, the constitutional balance of powers, religion, private property, and the family.[3]

While Kirk is enamored of Burke, Viereck admires the Austrian architect of the Concert of Europe, Prince Metternich. In his *Conservatism Revisited* (1949) he focused on Metternich as a symbol of domestic and international order in an analogous period. Concerned with the preservation of "the humane and ethical values of the West," he declared:

The conservative principles *par excellence* are proportion and measure; self-expression through self-restraint; preservation through reform; humanism and classical balance; a fruitful nostalgia for the permanent beneath the flux; and a fruitful obsession for unbroken historic continuity. These principles together create freedom, a freedom built not on the quicksand of adolescent defiance but on the bedrock of ethics and law.[4]

Viereck tries to get beyond stereotypes to explain the real difference between liberal and conservative tempers as consisting in their reactions to such questions as: "Tempo of social change; need for tradition; confidence in modern technics; faith in the masses and in the natural goodness of man; feasibility of changing human nature; importance of utilitarian motives . . . risk of extending full democratic privileges even to those engaged in forcibly destroying democracy; conflict between liberty and a leveling equality; absoluteness or relativeness of existing restraints and standards."[5]

It is hard to see how the New Conservatism as propounded by Kirk and Viereck differs in any significant sense from that of More and Babbitt. It is difficult to understand how the Burkean hierarchical conception of society is any more relevant to contemporary America than it was to the America of the 1920's, or the 1820's for that matter. Regarding Viereck, insofar as he sees the liberal/conservative dichotomy as principally one of attitudes regarding change, and not necessarily involving radical differences in constitutional principles and institutions, he appears accurate in his appraisal. Concerning Kirk, the comment of a conservative historian is appropriate.

He stands as far outside the main body of American conservatives as did Fisher Ames in his last days and Henry Adams in his. . . . He wants desperately to defend the traditions and institutions of his country, yet most of those he cherishes are gone forever. He seeks to cultivate the Conservative mood of reverence and contentment, yet he sounds like a radical in his attacks on what is now, for better or worse, the American way of life. With his great mentor Burke he professes to despise ideology, yet he is himself forced by the loneliness of his intellectual and temperamental position to be an unvarnished ideologue. . . . "he has the sound of 'a man born one hundred fifty years too late and in the wrong country.' "[6]

Among American political scientists, the most vigorous proponent of conservatism has been Willmoore Kendall (1909–1968). No mere trumpeter for Burke, Calhoun, Babbitt, or More, Kendall took his bearings instead from what he called "the institutions and way of life bequeathed to us by the Philadelphia Convention." He began his long attack on liberalism with a scholarly critique of Locke's doctrine of majority rule, but his main target thereafter was John Stuart Mill, whom he interpreted to hold that all questions must be open in society because no man's view has more probable truth value than that of another. Against this he argued that "any viable society has an orthodoxy—a set of fundamental beliefs, implicit in its way of life, that it cannot and should not, and, in any case, will not submit to the vicissitudes of the market place." From this he went on to maintain that America must not allow in principle the unrestricted right to say what one pleases. Instead of the liberal "open society," he suggested upholding American "orthodoxy," that is, the consensus proceeding from "the deliberate sense of the community." Thus Kendall, who once argued the side of the Athenians who decided Socrates' death, and who disapproved of what he called the "forward inertia" of the Supreme Court which is "always in the direction of the Liberal Revolution" (egalitarianism), would approve the banning of books and the proscription of communists, if "the deliberate sense of the community" so determined. More important than legal action to him were modes of social coercion, a position which calls to mind not only Mill's but De Tocqueville's fears of democracy. And yet, Kendall believed that society ought to keep "the door open *as wide as possible* to initiatives and proposals by individual citizens." Nevertheless, if the constitutional order effectively interferes with the domestic war against the evil of Communism, he declared, a change must be sought in the constitutional order.[7]

Kendall distinguished "plebiscitary" democracy, which he pejoratively associated with Presidential politics, from "representative" democracy, which he associated approvingly with Congressional politics. Quite unlike Lippmann, he saw Congress as a principle of stability against the innovative executive. He thought that Congress reflects "the antidemocratic, anti-majority rule bias of the framers," and that its constituency, in contrast to that of the President, is "to a far greater extent a structured community."[8]

Believing that the issue between liberalism and conservatism is the choice between reason and revelation, Kendall vacillated on the question of the exact relation of Christianity to the state. One of his statements is, however, informed by a certitude at which Niebuhr would certainly have shuddered. He asked: How can I accept the liberal order of freedom and toleration "if I believe *my* modicum of truth is not the expression of my finiteness but of the infinity and omniscience of God, so that in insisting upon its truthfulness for you I insist not upon my own infallibility but upon His?"[9]

Kendall's writings focused on a fundamental question which liberalism must confront—can one establish a viable society rooted in a formal conception of freedom which refuses to tolerate only intolerance? How important in the American experience of free government has been the Judaeo-Christian religious ethic? How essential is it for the continuance of the republic? Can it be replaced by a rational ethic which secularizes values? Can a society long exist if a complete moral relativism obtains among its members?

Looking over the varieties of the new conservatism which provide analogues to Jonathan Boucher, Fisher Ames, Orestes Brownson, William Graham Sumner and Babbitt, among others, one finds as common threads a respect for tradition and the past, as well as a regard for the diffusion of power and a longing for community. Perhaps the most effective criticism made of the traditionalist approach is that written recently by Frank Myers, who regards himself a conservative dedicated to the "defense of the freedom of the person." Myers contends that (1) history and tradition can be used to sanction practically any system, (2) the conservative Burkean in effect supports the "subtler, quieter tyranny of 'customarily' imposed community," and (3) freedom does not mean merely to do that which is right but also "the choice between virtue and vice."[10]

The conservative mood of the 1950's which stressed consensus was reflected in historical scholarship and in introspective reinterpretations of the American experience. Louis Hartz's *The Liberal Tradition in America* (1955) maintained that because Americans have accepted the liberal values of Locke from the beginning, fundamental value struggles have not been characteristic of the United States. Americans are thus chronically conservative in their attachment to their abiding liberalism. A liberal himself, Hartz, in the words of a recent commentator, reflected the conservative mood in his search for a timeless American unity.[11]

In a similar temper the historian Daniel Boorstin argued that the essence of America lies in its belief that it has an essence. He interpreted American history in terms of "givenness," which is a "belief in the *continuity* or homogeneity of our history . . . so that our past merges indistinguishably into our present." It consists in the belief that values are in "some way or other automatically defined," that is, "*given* by certain facts of geography or history peculiar to us." Thus there is no need in America for an explicit political theory. Consequently, "we must refuse to become crusaders for liberalism, in order to remain liberals. . . . We must refuse to become crusaders for conservatism, in order to conserve the institutions and the genius which have made America great."[12]

Finally, the sociologist Daniel Bell, in his *The End of Ideology* (1960), recommended the rejection of all absolutes and the acceptance of pragmatism. The age of ideology is at an end, he wrote, because in the Western world "there is today a rough consensus among intellectuals on political issues: the acceptance of a Welfare State; the desirability of decentralized power; a system of mixed economy and political pluralism." Thus the emphasis is put on politics as consensus rather than politics as conflict.[13]

Although conservatives generally disavow behavioralism in the study of man, that approach, which was dominant in American political science during the 1950's and into the 1960's ironically fits in well with the mood which stressed preservation of values. Lacking its own critical principle, unless in the service of otherwise prescribed norms, behavioralism tends to result in a tacit approval of existing institutions.

Criticism of behavioralism during the period came from men like Niebuhr, Lippmann, Leo Strauss and Bernard Crick, all of whom have been called conservative. Crick, an English observer of the American scene, scored "scientism" in the study of politics as "an idealistic attempt to overcome the limitations and uncertainties of politics through an analogy that confuses the genesis, the verification and the application of the theories of the natural sciences." The idea of a science of politics, he stated, is "a caricature of American liberal democracy, a growth upon it, when it loses touch, by scorning history and philosophy, with its roots." Just as Americans have hoped to reduce all apparently great problems of politics to legal terms, "so there has been an academic hope to reduce the study of politics to mere technique."[14] Strauss, a leading scholar in the revival of classical political philosophy, argued that the behavioral premise that only scientific knowledge is genuine knowledge leads to the conclusion that "all awareness of political things that is not scientific is cognitively worthless." In fact, however, political science "stands or falls by the truth of the pre-scientific awareness of political things." While the behavioralist perceives "sense data," the common man perceives "things." But to know sense data as such presupposes the validity of our primary awareness of things as things and people as people. Then, too the actions, passions, and states of the soul can never become sense data. Consequently, "since the political things are given to us in political understanding and political experience, the new political science cannot be helpful for the deeper understanding of political things: it must reduce the political things to non-political data." Lacking orientation regarding political things, the behavioralist who is rooted in logical positivism ends up treating of irrelevancies. The upshot is a political science which (1) reduces itself to sociology—the study of groups, (2) is rooted in "dogmatic atheism," (3) seeks a more precise language which ends up more vague than ordinary language, (4) regards all values as equal, and (5) culminates frequently "in observations made by people who are not intelligent about people who are not intelligent." In the spirit of the Cold War Strauss concluded: "The crisis of liberal democracy has become concealed by a ritual which calls itself methodology or logic. This almost willful blindness to the crisis of liberal democracy is part of that crisis. No wonder then that the new political science has nothing to say against those who unhesitatingly prefer surrender, that is, the abandonment of liberal democracy, to war."[15]

In conclusion a word must be said regarding pluralism, the dominant theory adhered to by American political scientists after World World II. Having roots in Madison's thought but stemming principally from Bentley's group approach and European elitist conceptions, the theory fitted the conservative mood inasmuch as it tended to be held by many as not merely descriptive of American politics but prescriptive of free government itself. Seeing the relevant phenomena as groups led by elites, the pluralist regards American government as a balance of power among interest groups whose memberships overlap. Each group is viewed as having influence in decision making and as limited by necessary mutual group compromises and adjustments. Similarly, each principal group is regarded as sharing a belief in common values including the desirability of working within prescribed modes of adjustment. Government is seen as a sphere wherein group differences are discussed and settled or as an umpire establishing and enforcing rules of settlement of group differences. Conceding the inevitability of rule by elites (and sometimes distrustful of the people at large) pluralists believe democracy exists if the electorate has a choice between competing, changing, and open elites and if the elected elites are formed on the basis of broad support drawn from shifting group coalitions.[16]

The New Left

By the mid-1950's the American radical movement of the two previous decades, which comprehended many organizations mostly of Marxist background, was all but dead. At the end of the decade the surface complacency in American thought and life was challenged by a new radical movement called the "New Left" by one of its fathers, the sociologist C. Wright Mills.[17]

Mills influenced the New Left not only through his book *The Power Elite* (1956) which, in contrast to the dominant pluralist view, pictured American society as controlled and manipulated by interacting business, military, and political elites, but through his "Letter to the New Left," which he wrote in 1960. Therein he asked young radicals to regard themselves as the new vehicle of social change. Decrying the lapse of reasoning into reasonableness, he scored the extant formal and sophisticated liberal rhetoric for having lost the "power to outrage . . . to enlighten in a political way . . . even [the] power to clarify some situation." The liberal formula of a mixed economy, the welfare state and prosperity, Mills proclaimed, is a posture of "false consciousness" which rests "upon a simple provincialism." The phrase, "the end of ideology," as he saw it, pertained only "to self-selected circles of intellectuals in the richer countries," and is a "slogan of complacency, circulating among the prematurely middle-aged," as well as a sign of "the ending of political reflection as a public fact." Academically it stands for, and presumably upon, "a fetishism of empiricism . . . a pretentious methodology used to state trivialities about unimportant social areas." Concerning political and human ideals, the phrase stands for "a denial of their relevance, except as abstract ikons." What needs to be analyzed if there is to be a politics of a new left, Mills wrote, is "the *structure* of institutions, the *foundation* of policies."[18]

In the Port Huron statement, written by Thomas Hayden in 1962 as a manifesto for the most well-known New Left group, Students for a Democratic Society, the contradictions between American ideals and actuality are duly noted, the democratic system is described as "apathetic and manipulated rather than 'of, by, and for the people,'" and "theoretic chaos" is said to have replaced "the idealistic thinking of old." The values affirmed are: (1) man considered as "infinitely precious and possessed of unfulfilled capacities for reason, freedom and love" and not as an object of manipulation; (2) human relations rooted in "fraternity and honesty"; (3) the replacement of power which is "rooted in possession, privilege or circumstance," by "power and uniqueness rooted in love, reflectiveness, reason, and creativity"; (4) the establishment of "a democracy of individual participation"; (5) educative, creative, nonmechanical work in an economy open to "democratic participation and subject to democratic social regulation"; and (6) renunciation of violence "because it requires generally the transformation of the target, be it a human being or a community of people, into a depersonalized object of hate."[19]

This statement of principles appears to have been based in good part upon the writings of Fromm and Mills. It is informed by keen interest in the implementation of justice, the closure of the gap between American ideals and American reality, and a desire to reinstil in the public a sense of the importance of politics, of active and broad participation therein, and of political reflection.

As the decade moved on, the young intellectuals became increasingly dissatisfied with the pace of progress in racial justice, social reform, and with the war in Viet Nam. Concerning the quest for racial justice, it must be mentioned that although significant progress was made in the courts, it was deficient in scope and implementation. Led by Dr. Martin Luther King, Jr., a black Baptist minister guided by biblical and moral law arguments for justice, emphasis was put in the early 1960's upon direct nonviolent action to dramatize the black man's plight, touch the conscience of men, and provoke confrontations with the authorities, which, it was hoped, would lead to fruitful negotiations. King's approach produced important reforms on the local, state, and national levels. When he was murdered, however, in 1968, the fury of many blacks tended to give enhanced credence to those among them and among the white radicals who preached the necessity of violence as the only effective instrument of change.[20]

In the context of domestic strife and a morally ambiguous military exercise abroad, many radical intellectuals and students gradually abandoned the residual faith of the Port Huron statement in liberal democracy and nonviolence. Splitting into various groups and factions, they came more and more to stress the need for "existential politics" to overthrow what they saw as the oppressive and inherently violent socioeconomic, politicocultural system. Underlying their approach was an assumption that if one is right it is necessary to deny liberties to those who are wrong, and a mystical belief in the efficacy and creativity of violence. Thus because the New Left radical apparently believes that means create ends, he stubbornly refuses, except in the most nebulous manner, to declare the ultimate goals and institutions to be realized by the revolution. As Arthur Schlesinger, Jr. has put it, "what distinguishes the New Left is not only its unwillingness to define what it aims for after the revolution but its belief that such mystification is a virtue."[21] In short, it expects Americans to scuttle their admittedly faulty but proven ship in high seas with no alternate vessel available.

All this, of course, is not political theory. Whereas initially, as exemplified in Mills and the Port Huron statement, the reinvigoration of the political process was stressed, the emphasis has shifted and politics has been abandoned by many as yet another snare of the hated system. To better understand New Left ideology, however, it is necessary to examine the thought of Herbert Marcuse and Norman Brown.

Born in Germany in 1898, Marcuse has been associated with the Neo-Marxist Institute of Social Research at Frankfurt. He came to America before World War II and has taught at various universities. Widely read by students and young intellectuals in Europe and America, this septuagenarian has become one of the principal social critics upon whose works the New Left in Europe and America has drawn in attacks on the "Establishment."*[22]

Alongside Freud's pleasure principle (satisfaction of instinctual desires) and his reality principle (civilization restrictions), Marcuse inserts what he calls the performance principle (the current societal manifestation of the reality principle, which implies social domination and alienation). On this basis he argues that Freud's denial of the possibility of a liberation of the pleasure principle is based on a mistaken assumption that scarcity, which gives rise to societal repression, is a permanent factor in life. Freud thus saw the performance principle as the unchanging reality principle; he failed to see that it is historically and not biologically given.[23]

Marcuse believes that Western civilization has reached a level of technology and productivity in which "social demands upon instinctual energy to be spent in alienated labor could be considerably reduced." Thus there looms the possibility of a gradual elimination of "surplus repression" (repression over and beyond that "basic repression" which is demanded by the rational exercise of authority and is quite acceptable to the normal healthy man), and the liberation of the pleasure principle.[24]

Using Freudian insights to advance beyond the Marxian preoccupation with economic man to the realms of myth and poetry, Marcuse replaces Prometheus, the cultural hero of production through repression, with Orpheus and Narcissus, who signify joy, fulfillment, and creative receptivity. Such fulfillment comes not through domination and exploitation but through release of "inherent libidinal forces." The new reality principle symbolized in Orpheus and Narcissus will bring "the erotic reconciliation . . . of man and nature in the aesthetic attitude, where order is beauty and work is play." Looked at in terms of the institutions and psychology of the Performance Principle, such instinctual liberation spells barbarism. Marcuse insists, however, that this will not be the fact if the liberation occurs "as a consequence . . . of victory in the struggle for existence." By this he means that the "reactivation of polymorphous and narcissistic sexuality" can "lead to culture building if the organism

---

* Marcuse's popularity with many extremist students lessened after May, 1967 when he stated that he did not approve disruptions of the universities because there was probably more freedom there than any other place in our society. Walter Kaufmann, "Black and White," *Survey* (Autumn, 1969), 35.

exists not as an instrument of alienated labor but as a subject of self-realization."[25]

Marcuse declares that Plato's *Symposium* shows that "the culture building power of Eros is nonrepressive sublimation." Sexuality is not deflected in attaining its objective and "it transcends it to others, searching for fuller gratification." Where Plato, however, sees Eros culminating its ascent in a preoccupation with beauty as such, Marcuse not only eliminates the distinction between "higher" and "lower" pleasures and holds that each individual must judge his own needs, but contends that the striving for pleasure is without end to the polymorphous self which knows no transcendental norm. In this view society must itself become polymorphous. In such a society coercive authority, whether marital, familial, economic, or political, has no place, because "man is free only where he is free from constraint, external and internal, physical and moral—when he is constrained neither by law nor by need." Politics, which Marcuse equates with the class and power struggle, will then ultimately be replaced by love. Play and display will be interrupted only by the short periods of labor necessary to keep the developed technology functioning.[26]

With this model (which Marcuse asserts is nonutopian but realizable) in mind, Marcuse criticizes the American Establishment. The economy is geared to produce waste and create false needs; its products, along with those of the entertainment industry, "carry with them prescribed attitudes and habits." This produces "repressive desublimation," or the "release of sexuality in modes and forms which reduce and weaken erotic energy." Upon gratification of artificial needs most people become satisfied with the system and consequently are unreceptive to change.[27]

Marcuse believes that tolerance in America is "repressive." He admits that it is afforded to all parties and modes of life, but contends that this renders men unresponsive to arguments for change. The existence of constitutionally protected free speech and open accessibility to the media of communication is insufficient because the very meaning of terms in political debate is determined by the Establishment. The majority considers radical concepts in terms of ordinary language, which is repressive because it is geared to preserve the status quo. In Marcuse's eyes political debate must be open in the sense of popular accessibility to accurate information and the ability to deliberate and choose autonomously. But because the mass media in America are open to all points of view, intelligent and ignorant, informed and misinformed, frivolous and serious, real freedom of self-determination is repressed by tolerance. Marcuse concludes that "the realization of the objective of tolerance would call for intolerance toward prevailing policies, attitudes, opinions, and the extension of tolerance to policies, attitudes, and opinions which are outlawed or suppressed." Thus he desires "withdrawal of toleration of speech and assembly from groups and movements which promote aggressive policies, armament, chauvinism, discrimination on the grounds of race and religion, or which oppose the extension of public services, social security, medical care, etc."[28]

Marcuse is particularly critical of the moral relativism which he sees issuing from academia in America; he regards positivism in its behavioral and linguistic-analytical manifestations, as leading to implicit approval of the status quo. He apparently would politicize academic disciplines to bring about the new man and the society which he believes not merely desirable but historically necessary. He also apparently deviates somewhat from the orthodox Marxist belief that consciousness is socially determined by holding that consciousness of the need for change precedes change itself. Specifically, the new society is not described, except for vague references to socialism and the administration of things replacing coercive government.[29]

Although he would like to see total liberation, Marcuse envisions only the end of "surplus repression." Basic repression (explained above) would remain necessary because "human freedom is not only a private affair." He states that "the renunciations and delays demanded by the general will must not be opaque and inhuman; nor must their reason be authoritarian." He also suggests that a "natural self restraint" may enhance "genuine gratification" by way of "delay, detour, and arrest." Because of this and his retention of "basic repression," a recent commentator concludes that Marcuse hedges on his thesis of liberation.[30]

Nonetheless, it is the promise of "liberation" upon the release of instincts and the end of repression, along with the vision of a new fluid order of shifting forms and hedonistic gratification, with a corresponding widening and ascent of Eros, which Marcuse presents to the young and the disaffected. How particularly his polymorphous paradise of regenerate liberated men is to be realized is somewhat blurred. But the implications of violence are broad enough, as are the overtones that it is autonomous, mature men like Marcuse himself who alone know the truth and have the right to impose it on others.

Philosophically speaking, Marcuse writes against the grain of the broad tradition of Western thought which emphasizes the primacy of reason over passion, distinguishes between higher and lower pleasures, and stresses the centrality of self-restraint in light of transcendent norms. It must be remembered that the ascent of Eros and Logos, as described by Plato, is embodied in the person of Socrates, a man not only of extraordinary intelligence and spirit but of disciplined self-control which is not acquired in a moment but spans the efforts of a long life. Marcuse puts such heavy emphasis on the Dionysian principle of released vitality and sensuous liberation that he all but ignores the Apollonian principle of order.

Marcuse's thesis stands or falls on the question of the validity or invalidity of his assumption that a naturalistic love can replace institutional authority, compromise, and constraint. What the Christian calls *superbia* (pride) and its derivative, the *libido dominandi,* which result in the clash of interests, are to him mere historical traits identified with an era upon which he has pronounced a death sentence. If he is right, Niebuhr, Lippmann, and, to a degree, Fromm, along with practically every eminent thinker in the Western philosophic tradition are wrong. Similarly in error are statesmen-thinkers such as Adams, Jefferson, Hamilton, Madison, and Calhoun.

It is a tempting lure which Marcuse dangles before youth. The vaguely prescribed future administration by the "general will" entails rejection of all the dearly bought institutional guarantees of Anglo-Saxon liberty. In paradise one does not need bills of rights, checks and balances, a common law tradition of liberties, and peaceful institutional adjustment of conflicts. In fact, what Marcuse asks American youth to do is to desert their heritage in exchange for a coarsely presented German romanticism compounded of Hegelian-Marxian, Freudian, and Existentialist elements puffed up in a surrealist pipe dream.

Even more radical in his analysis of man and in his prescriptions is Norman Brown (1913–), a classics scholar who combines Freudian analysis with the insights of mystics and poets. In the preface to his book *Life Against Death* (1959) he states that men like him, who are "temperamentally incapable of embracing the politics of sin, cynicism, and despair have been compelled to re-examine the classic assumptions about the nature of politics and about the political character of human nature." In the process not only should common sense be suspended if answers are to be found, but scientific method is also insufficient. Brown sees scientific method as an attempt "to democratize knowledge" and to "substitute method for insight, mediocrity for genius, by getting a standard operating procedure." Like most members of the New Left, Brown also suspects historical arguments: "There is a hex on us, the specters in books, the authority of the past; and to exorcise these ghosts is the great work of magical self-liberation." In like vein he distrusts formal logic, holding that its principles, along with the notion of time, are hypothetically explicable in terms of categories of repression. Similarly, everyday language is criticized as "the language of work and the reality-principle." With common sense, scientific method, history, formal logic, language and politics faulted, the field is left free "for renewal of civilization by the undemocratic power which makes poets the unacknowledged legislators of mankind."[31]

Like Marcuse, Brown looks to the creation of an "erotic sense of reality" in the establishment of "a Dionysian ego." He differs from Marcuse in regarding repression as not springing from domination in civilization but from the development of the awareness and rejection of death. Brown sees man distinguished from animals "by having separated, ultimately into a state of mutual conflict, aspects of life (instincts) which in animals exist in some condition of undifferentiated unity or harmony." And man will not rest until he "is able to abolish these conflicts and restore harmony, but at the higher level of consciousness." Because the "unity of Life and Death" has been disrupted in man, man has become a historical animal operating in Faustian fashion to escape death through "immortal" works. The difference then between men and animals is that men repress instincts and become neurotic. Animals have an essence united with their existence; man seeks to develop his essence in history. In the process he establishes an "Apollonian ego," the "ego of genital organization" involving limits and repression. The problem for man is to construct instead a "Dionysian ego" which would involve a return on the plane of consciousness to the undifferentiated "body-ego" of infancy, and to the "natural tendency of the human body, which is anarchistic and polymorphously perverse."[32]

Brown believes that "sociability is sickness." Aristotle was in error in stating that society is constituted "for the sake of life and more life"; instead it was constructed "from defect, from death and the flight from death, from fear of separation, and fear of individuality." But the anxiety about death "does not have ontological status, as existentialist theologians claim." Instead, "it has historical status only, and is relative to the repression of the human body; the horror of death is the horror of dying with . . . unlived lines in our bodies." Brown promises that "after man's unconscious search for his proper mode of being has ended— after history has ended—particular members of the human species can lead a life which, like the lives of lower organisms, individually embodies the nature of the species." Each such man will then, like the brutes, be a species animal.[33]

Brown thus preaches "the resurrection of the body," holding that "the death instinct is reconciled with the life instinct only in a life which is not repressed . . . the death instinct then being affirmed in a body which is willing to die." The return to the state of nature which is the undifferentiated bodily "polymorphous perverse" condition of infancy would allow for human perfection as manifested in "joyful play." Men will then be not merely as animals but as gods, time will have ceased, conflict will have been replaced by love, and death will have been overcome by being freely accepted on the grounds stated by Nietzsche that "what has become perfect, all that is ripe—wants to die."[34]

Brown sees the resurrection of the body as "a social project facing mankind as a whole." He believes that it "will become a practical political problem when the statesmen of the world are called upon to deliver happiness instead of power, when political economy becomes a science of use-values instead of exchange-values—a science of enjoyment instead of a science of accumulation." Replying to Marcuse, who will not yet renounce politics, Brown writes: "The next generation needs to be told that the real fight is not the political fight but to put an end to politics." We must move "from politics to poetry," because in "poetry, art, imagination" lies "the real revolutionary power to change the world."[35]

Brown differs from Marcuse not only in regard to the origin of repression and his disavowal of politics, but in denying the need for even "basic repression," once the instincts are reintegrated, and in his concept of reality. If Marcuse's is a surrealist pipedream, it is dreamed by a man who still has his feet, if not his head, on this earth; Brown's flight into fancy (or, if one wishes, visionary imagination) is complete in his book *Love's Body* (1966), a work which one New Left reviewer calls "a witch's caldron of puns, rhymes, etymological prestidigitation, and oracular outpouring."[36]

Brown exalts eros (love) and denigrates logos (reason). Thus he must reject Socrates, who combined both, and accept instead Dionysian frenzy. He supposes, as a recent commentator has observed, that "once the soul made newly active becomes aflame with love . . . there is inextinguishable illumination, and the complex tangles of history and the actual conflicts of interest dissolve forevermore." Brown would reply that at this dangerous moment in man's history it is not a leisure but an utter necessity to think in utopian terms. His critic's answer, however, seems irrefutable: "For many of us who shared—and still share—the agonies of the present century, the very foundations of society and culture are too precarious to allow for the abandonment of logic, learning, experience, method, ingenuity, art, wisdom, and even wit. The melioration of social and political problems requires realism and prudence at least as much as mystical withdrawal. Love must have a mind as well as heart if it is to avail man here below."[37]

The desire to explore avenues of human experience and to overthrow the "system" in favor of the person has brought certain New Left thinkers to attack "the myth of objective consciousness," which they see assumed in scientific inquiry. If man is placed in the position of that which is merely observed, he is then, they reason, equated with all the other stupid things in the world. In a recent work, Theodore Roszak states: "Objective consciousness is alienated life promoted to its most honorific state as scientific method." A culture "which negates or subordinates or degrades visionary experience commits the sin of diminishing our existence." Each man "should become . . . a whole and integrated person in whom there is manifested a sense of the human variety genuinely experienced, a sense of having come to terms with a reality that is awesomely vast."[38]

Concerning the reality which is reached by man's nonrational powers, Roszak adds: "The expansion of the personality is nothing that is achieved by special training, but by a naive openness to experience." Thus the medicine man who resorts to a variety of means, magical, intellectual, nonrational and irrational to discern the ways of the spirits is held as superior in terms of the art of living to the scientific expert.[39] It is widely assumed that mystical insight, imaginative creativity and aesthetic development are instantaneous and not the result of discipline, sacrifice, and even internal torment. The admirable recognition that experience is multidimensional is easily perverted into a blatant anti-intellectualism which exalts the shaman not only above the narrow expert, but above Socrates. There is consequently, in tune with the omnipresent Rousseauistic influence, a desire to return to the compactness of experience found in the primitive mythopoeic community, which instead of viewing nature in the Faustian manner as something to be conquered, regards it on an interpersonal I-Thou pansacramental basis.

Rumbles from the New Left have provoked heavy attacks on behavioralism in the social sciences, the "consensus" approach to the study of American history, and the pluralist and elitist explanations of American politics and society, as adjuncts of the "system" and distortions of reality. This has led to a heightened emphasis by New Left moderates on commitment to ends, on politics as an instrument of change, on broad popular participation in decision making, and on the quest for a value-laden "relevant" political science. Most particularly has the pluralist system been challenged as: (1) hindering significant elements of society from effective access to the balancing process; (2) ignoring problems not represented by organized groups or insufficiently articulated as issues; (3) hindering personality development in the process of adjustment and decision making; and (4) being nondemocratic in the sense of emphasizing elitist control and encouraging or explaining away public apathy.[40]

Just as the behavioralist unconsciously imports an ideology in his approach, so the New Leftist may confuse his prejudices and biases with philosophical principles. In any case the New Left has a sharp division within its ranks—on the one hand are moderates, who while seeking to alter the "system" and reinvigorate science on normative grounds, have not despaired of politics; on the other are those who wish to transcend politics, to eliminate it, and allow for the full, free development of human association in which all human potentialities will be realized. This simplistic conception is so compelling and the "system" is regarded as so rotten that many believe that violence itself is not only necessary but desirable.

Of all the concepts in the lexicon of the New Left perhaps the most used is "liberation." Underlying it is a curious assumption that man can experience such a thing as "total freedom." George Kennan has attempted to answer this by showing that besides the normal needs and frailties of the body and demands of the soul, any freedom from something implies freedom to something. He adds that "because our reality is a complex one, in which conflicts of value are never absent, there can be no advance toward any particular objective, not even the pursuit of pleasure, that does not imply the sacrifice of other possible objectives. Freedom, for this reason, is definable only in terms of the obligations and restraints and sacrifices it accepts. . . . Love . . . is itself an obligation, and as such is incompatible with the quest for a perfect freedom."[41]

Finally, at the heart of much New Left thought is a glaring contradiction: there is heavy stress upon the variety of human experience while at the same time there is, as Walter Kaufmann has recently observed, a Manichean emphasis upon a moral world of white and black, with the former being the unassailable truth possessed by New Left prophets, and the latter the gross falsehood of institutional liberalism.[42] Fanatics must either convulse the world to establish their certain truth or they must leave it. The split among New Left extremists is quite illustrative of this point.

Conclusions

William James counseled against the extremes of agnosticism and gnosticism and reminded us of the rich varieties of human experience. Insofar as liberalism advocates public tolerance of all but intolerance it verges toward what Lippmann calls "public agnosticism." Insofar as New Left thinkers such as Marcuse identify certitude with certainty and seek to impose their revealed truth on all, they propound a gnosticism which Lippmann calls the " Jacobin doctrine."

Between the polar extremes are those on the one hand like Lippmann, who believe that there is a body of fundamental principles underlying free government and civility, which men can know through reason, experience, and the lessons of history. In this general category can also be placed men like Niebuhr, who instead of rational principles stress the importance of recognizing at least the symbolic value of orthodox Christian tenets of faith. Although there is a tendency toward identification of certitude with certainty and the attendant psychology of imposition among a few of the New Conservatives, they generally emphasize support of free government on the basis of tradition, the divine tactic in history, and the moral law. On the other hand, American liberals for the most part assume, as did John Dewey, a higher law conception of democracy embracing the values of personalism, common good, basic liberties, and civility. They differ from Lippmann's natural law approach and Niebuhr's theological approach principally by refusing to accept the notion of original sin, doubts regarding scientific method applied to the study of man, and the denial of the idea of progress.

Concerning man, the polar extremes are defined in terms of those who regard him as inherently corrupt and those who see him as inherently good. It would be an egregious error to place in the former category those who accept original sin, defined as the tendency to inordinate self-assertion. Lippmann, and to an even greater degree, Niebuhr, believe it to be the essence of realism to accept original sin, no matter how it is renamed, as did most of the Founding Fathers. Alongside this they also stress man's capacity for justice, a trait which could not be a property of a corrupted nature. As a consequence they not only accept democracy but emphasize the need for constitutionalism with its emphasis on checks and balances and guarantees of basic liberties. Contemporary liberals who are in the tradition of Jefferson and Dewey and assume the notion of man's goodness, tend to modify this optimism in practice by relying upon constitutional checks on majority rule in the implementation of fundamental civil and political rights. New Left extremists who follow Marcuse in seeing institutions as the instruments of repression of man differ from all of the above in seeking in the name of liberty to obliterate the liberties of those less enlightened than they. Similar in outlook is Fromm who, although he believes that nature posits objective norms for man, fails to provide constitutional guarantees in his proposed "participatory democracy."

Concerning the nature and relation of freedom and authority, the extremes are the assertion of unlimited freedom and the denial of all external authority on the one hand, and the authoritative imposition of a plenary "truth," with the consequent elimination of freedom for the unenlightened on the other. Except for extremists in the New Left who anomalously combine both positions at once, and certain right-wing elements who accept the latter position, the various divisions in contemporary American thought differ in terms of degree between the poles. The New Conservatives generally equate freedom with the possession of virtue but overlook the freedom to choose. Lippmann mentions both. Niebuhr's theological definition of man's nature in terms of freedom makes imperative his acceptance of the elimination of public barriers to a free choice. Liberals like MacLeish rhetorically celebrate "boundless liberty" but in practice accept "constitutional liberty." Concerning authority, Lippmann accepts natural law; Niebuhr, divine revelation; and the followers of Dewey accept, at the very minimum, the authority of truth discovered by "scientific method." Conservatives accept all or some of the above and may add to it the authority of tradition, history, religious institutions, and selected thinkers in the past.

Regarding means of change, extreme right and left abjure peaceful means and advocate violence. Many extreme New Leftists see revolution as a creative invigorating act, the necessary instrument of dialectical negation which will usher in the polymorphous paradise. Most conservatives condemn violence outright while most liberals regard it as a possible last resort in an intolerable situation. Except for the extremists and those who advocate nonviolent resistance, the existing institutional mode for redress of grievances and change is generally accepted.

Many New Leftists approach the question of politics as a purely historical phenomenon, which will disappear upon the imminent full appearance of Aquarius, the age of love and peace. Men like Lippmann and Niebuhr see conflict among men, and thus politics, as inevitable. Neither can envision an Antinomian reign of pure love this side of paradise. Thus they aim at justice, with Niebuhr, for example, holding that love should always be an ultimate even though unrealizable norm. Although many liberals have looked to the replacement of politics by science and administration and have regarded politics as reducible to economics or sociology or explicable as the resultant of conflicting group forces, a growing trend of thought among them is otherwise. In this view politics is irreducible and inevitable and government is not merely the necessary but the desirable positive instrument of regulation, adjustment, and social justice. New Left moderates who have reacted against the consensus psychology and recaptured a sense of the autonomy of politics must also be placed in this category.

Turning to James's admonition that we regard avenues of human experience beyond that of empirical science, it appears that the days of a regnant positivism are numbered. Traditionalists, religionists, metaphysical philosophers, poets, and mystics all oppose the monopoly possessed by "scientific method," with its canon of "intersubjective transmissibility," as the sole vehicle of truth and apprehension of reality. In fact, it might be said that the moment is ripe for the development of a new critical, synoptic political science which will bring the substantial methodological advances of behavioralism under the direction of norms vindicated by philosophy while recognizing the insights of religion, aesthetics, and visionary imagination. In the New Left, however, especially among the followers of Brown, the mystical tendency is so great that common sense, science, logic, and even ordinary language are not merely categorized among diverse approaches to reality, but in effect disdained. The latent antiintellectualism is obvious as are the elitist connotations. If we accept C.E.M. Joad's conception of decadence as "the view that experience is . . . to be valued for its own sake, irrespective of the quality and kind of the experience as well as its object," then much of the New Left "body mysticism" and shamanism can be called "decadent."[43]

Turning to the substance of contemporary thought, we find a strong

nature of prejudice, (3) the relationship between law and justice, and (4) the cultural contributions and inner resources of the American black.

On black American political thought see Herbert J. Storing (ed.), *What Country Have I* (New York, 1970); Howard Bratz, *Negro Social and Political Thought* (New York, 1966); Stokely Carmichael and Chas. V. Hamilton, *Black Power: The Politics of Liberation in America* (New York, 1967); Archie Epps (ed.), *The Speeches of Malcolm X at Harvard* (New York, 1968); Martin Luther King, *Why We Can't Wait* (New York, 1963), *Stride Toward Freedom* (New York, 1958), *Where Do We Go from Here?* (New York, 1967), *Strength to Love* (New York, 1963); Robert Scheer (ed.), *Eldridge Cleaver: Post-Prison Writings and Speeches* (New York, 1969); Whitney Young, *To Be Equal* (New York, 1964); *Beyond Racism* (New York, 1969); Nathan Wright Jr., *Black Power and Urban Unrest.*

21. *The Crisis of Confidence* (Boston, 1969), pp. 30, 31.

22. Marcuse's principal study of Freud is *Eros and Civilization* (Boston, 1955). His principal scholarly work is *Reason and Revolution* (New York, 1941). His most-read recent works of social criticism are, *One Dimensional Man* (Boston, 1964), his essay, "Repressive Tolerance," in *A Critique of Pure Tolerance* (Boston, 1965), and *An Essay on Liberation* (Boston, 1969). I have been aided in my discussion of Marcuse's thought by Theodore Roszak, *The Making of a Counter-Culture* (New York, 1969), pp. 84–123 and Paul Eidelberg, "The Temptation of Herbert Marcuse," *The Review of Politics,* XXXI (Oct., 1969), 442–458.

23. *Eros and Civilization,* pp. 12–16, 35, 132ff.

24. *Ibid.,* pp. 35, 129, 224.

25. *Ibid.,* pp. 161–162, 175, 176, 198, 210.

26. *Ibid.,* pp. 211, 187 (this quotation is Marcuse's approving summation of the German poet Schiller's view).

27. Quoted in Roszak, *op. cit.,* p. 110. Marcuse's critique of American and technocratic culture can be found in his *One Dimensional Man* and his essay "Repressive Tolerance."

28. "Repressive Tolerance," pp. 81, 82, 100.

29. Marcuse's critique of positivism can be found in *One Dimensional Man,* pp. 170–202.

30. Roszak, *op. cit.,* p. 112.

31. *Life Against Death* (Middletown, Conn., 1959), pp. ix, x, 321, 69; "Apocalypse: The Place of Mystery in the Life of the Mind," *Harpers* (May, 1961), 47–49, reprinted in Leo Hamalian and Frederick R. Karl, *The Radical Vision* (New York, 1970), pp. 107–112. The relevant quotations are found in the latter at pages 109 and 111.

32. *Life Against Death,* pp. 175, 83, 86, 91, 92, 102, 176, 110.

33. *Ibid.,* pp. 106, 108.

34. *Ibid.,* pp. 307, 308, 34, 107.

35. *Ibid.,* p. 311; Roszak, *op. cit.,* p. 118.

36. Roszak, *op. cit.,* p. 115.

37. Comment by Benjamin Nelson, in Hamalian and Karl, *op. cit.,* p. 106.

38. Roszak, *op. cit.,* pp. 232, 234–235.

39. *Ibid.,* pp. 236, 242ff.

40. See especially William E. Connolly (ed.), *The Bias of Pluralism* (New York, 1971); Peter Bachrach (ed.), *Political Elites in a Democracy* (New York, 1971); Peter Bachrach, *The Theory of Democratic Elitism* (Boston, 1967); Henry Kariel, *The Decline of American Pluralism* (Stanford, 1961); and E. E. Schattschneider, *The Semi-Sovereign People* (New York, 1960).

41. George Kennan, *Democracy and the Student Left* (New York, 1968, paperback ed.), pp. 10, 11, 12.

42. Kaufmann, "Black and White," *Survey,* 73 (Autumn, 1969), pp. 22–46.

43. C. E. M. Joad, *Decadence* (New York, 1949), p. 95.

Index